Antitrust and Upstream Platform Power Plays

Antitrust and Upstream Platform Power Plays

A Policy in Bed with Procrustes

A. K. VON MOLTKE

OXFORD
UNIVERSITY PRESS

OXFORD
UNIVERSITY PRESS

Great Clarendon Street, Oxford, OX2 6DP,
United Kingdom

Oxford University Press is a department of the University of Oxford.
It furthers the University's objective of excellence in research, scholarship,
and education by publishing worldwide. Oxford is a registered trade mark of
Oxford University Press in the UK and in certain other countries

Published in the United States of America by Oxford University Press
198 Madison Avenue, New York, NY 10016, United States of America

British Library Cataloguing in Publication Data
Data available

Library of Congress Control Number: 2023942358

ISBN 978-0-19-287305-7

DOI: 10.1093/oso/9780192873057.001.0001

Printed and bound by
CPI Group (UK) Ltd, Croydon, CR0 4YY

Preface

Powerful digital platforms have riled up antitrust decision-makers around the world. Intriguingly, one issue has grabbed most of their attention while remaining surprisingly under-rationalized. Over the last few years, decision-makers have indeed mainly been catering to the anxieties of app developers, merchants, content providers, gig workers, and the likes, who all denounce abusive behaviour by the platforms they now depend on to reach us. So, instead of following the usual playbook of 'looking down' along the value chain at the plight of consumers, the recent policy trend has been to 'look *up*' at the ordeal of *suppliers*.

This book is a reaction to the state of affairs. It asks: are such upstream platform power plays really 'competition problems', ones for antitrust, at that? The question, admittedly, is somewhat provocative at first glance; decision-makers have already decided that there is an obvious answer, namely yes. Yet, why, then, is the wider antitrust community so deeply divided on the matter? Plus, why do suppliers in the brick-and-mortar economy remain bottom feeders on the antitrust policy agenda as they have been for decades?—think of farmers victimized by powerful processors and food manufacturers who are themselves squeezed by big grocers like Walmart and Tesco. Besides, wasn't contemporary antitrust (supposed to be) all about *consumer* welfare? At the very least, longstanding consensus still has it that supplier welfare simply cannot be the policy's lodestar. Today, though, when it comes to the platform economy, provider concerns are earmarked as the ultimate priority. It is this paradox that has motivated my research. Given how antitrust has been, is, and will continue to be widely touted as one (if not *the*) appropriate response to the woes of those who supply the Googles of the world, it seems to me that we need a policy introspection to make some sense of what our decision-makers have been, and currently are, up to—precisely what this book offers.

The analysis provided here is altogether normative, theoretical, and practical. *Normative* because it engages in a supplier-mindful soul-searching exercise, which advances our understanding of antitrust's foundations; *theoretical* as it shows how upstream concerns in the platform economy can be rationalized by appealing to economists, but also to business and management scientists, digital ethnographers, as well as political scientists and philosophers; *practical* since it takes a deep dive into the complex antitrust machinery whilst remaining attuned to other policy levers.

With this said, I hope to have piqued the reader's interest enough to move on to the Introduction, which sketches in more detail the book's ambition. The subject matter is polarizing; my modest aim is to offer arguments that might nevertheless prove compelling to anyone with a particular interest for the topic.

To conclude, I would like to both acknowledge several individuals and institutions for their role in making this project possible and emphasize that the views expressed herein are my own and not those of the public institution I currently work for, namely, the Belgian telecommunications regulator (BIPT).

First, I owe thanks to the University of Oxford and the Clarendon Fund for the opportunity, means, and absolute intellectual liberty to conceive the doctorate underlying this book. While many edits were made to account for practical developments that have occurred since November 2020 and to reflect maturing thoughts and new reflections, the essence and structure of my doctoral thesis remain. The support I received from these two institutions was my sole source of external funding for this project (be it financial or in kind). In accordance with the ASCOLA Transparency and Disclosure Declaration, I have nothing else to disclose.

Next, I must recognize the invaluable support of several friends: Nathalie Ska, who always lent me an attentive ear and to whom I also owe the deepest of apologies; Vassilios Copetinas, for our myriad debates and for being the only person in my entourage who could understand certain hardships that have marked my life these past couple of years; Josef Weinzierl, who pushed me intellectually, worried over my well-being, and inspired me more than he could imagine.

Third, my heartfelt gratitude goes to Ariel Ezrachi. He encouraged me after my first stint at Oxford University in 2015–2016 to return and pursue a doctorate; supported me intellectually for the three years it took to complete it; brought me on as a trusted colleague to tutor students and do research by his side; mentored me and, ultimately, befriended me. His brilliance is matched by his kindness and I have been the tremendously fortunate recipient of both.

Finally, this book is above all dedicated to my parents. To my late father, a true erudite with the noblest of hearts, who I hope would have been proud; to my mother, the person I look up to most and to whom I am indebted for everything and more.

Amédée von Moltke
Brussels
November 2022

Summary Contents

Detailed Contents

II. LOOKING UP

Figures and Tables

Figures

Tables

Table of Cases

UNITED STATES

Administrative Decisions (Chronological)

Other (Chronological)

FRANCE

Court Judgements (Chronological)

ADLC Decisions (Chronological)

GERMANY

Court Judgements (Chronological)

Table of Legislation

Abbreviations

ABA	American Bar Association
ACCC	Australian Competition and Consumer Commissionn
ACM	Autoriteit Consument & Markt (NL competition authority)
AdC	Autoridade de Concorrência (PT competition authority)
ADLC	Autorité de la concurrence (FR competition authority)
AG	Advocate General
AI	artificial intelligence
ARCEP	Autorité de Régulation des Communications Électroniques et des Postes (FR Regulatory Authority for Electronic Communications, Postal and Print media distribution)
AU	Australia
B2B	business-to-business
B2C	business-to-consumer
BEUC	Bureau Européens des Unions de Consommateurs (European Bureau of Consumer Unions)
BKA	Bundeskartellamt (DE competition authority)
BMWi	Bundesministerium für Wirtschaft und Energie (DE Federal Ministry for Economic Affairs and Energy)
BMWK (formerly BMWi)	Bundesministerium für Wirtschaft und Klimaschutz (DE Federal Ministry for Economic Affairs and Climate Action)
BRICS Centre	Brazil, Russia, India, China & South Africa Competition Law and Policy Centre
BWB	Bundeswettbewerbsbehörde (AT competition authority)
CADE	Conselho Administrativo de Defesa Econômica (BR competition authority)
CCI	Competition Commission of India
CFREU	Charter of Fundamental Rights of the European Union
CGE	Conseil Général de l'Économie (FR General Council for the Economy)
CMA	Competition and Markets Authority
CNNum	Conseil National du Numérique (FR National Digital Council)
CP	consumer protection
CPS	core platform service
CRA	credit rating agency
DCMSC	Digital, Culture, Media and Sport Committee (UK)
DCT	digital comparison tools
DE	Germany
DMA	Digital Markets Act

DoJ	Department of Justice (US)
DSM	Digital Single Market
EC	European Commission
ECJ	European Court of Justice
ECN	European Competition Network
EOp	equality of opportunity
ESEC	Economic, Social and Environmental Council (FR)
ESMA	European Securities and Market Authority
FAANG	Facebook, Amazon, Apple, Netflix, Google
FCC	Federal Communications Commission (US)
FR	France
FTC	Federal Trade Commission (US)
GAFA(M)	Google, Apple, Facebook, Amazon, (Microsoft)
GWB/ARC	Gesetz gegen Wettbewerbsbeschränkungen / Act against Restraints of Competition
HoL	House of Lords (UK)
HoR	House of Representatives (US)
IA	impact assessment
ICN	International Competition Network
IGF	Inspection Générale des Finances (FR Inspectorate-General for Finances)
IMF	International Monetary Fund
IN	India
IO	industrial organization
IP	intellectual property
JFTC	Japan Fair Trade Commission
KFTC	Korea Fair Trade Commission
MFN	most-favoured nation
MMO	massively multiplayer online
NCA	national competition authority
NL	Netherlands (the)
Ofcom	Office of Communications
OFT	Office of Fair Trading
OMS	online mapping service
OS	operating system
OTA	online travel agent
P2B	platform-to-business
PL	Poland
PT	Portugal
RPG	role-playing game
RSB	Regulatory Scrutiny Board
SBP	superior bargaining power
SCOTUS	Supreme Court of the United States
Study Group	Study Group on Improvement of Trading Environment surrounding Digital Platforms (JP)

TEU	Treaty on the European Union
TFEU	Treaty on the Functioning of the European Union
UC	unfair competition
UK	United Kingdom
UNCTAD	United Nations Conference on Trade and Development
US[A]	United States [of America]

Introduction

Setting the Scene

In the mid-1990s, Bill Gates (the founder of Microsoft) echoed what many others in the know had already prophesized: the commercial internet was going to bring us 'friction-free capitalism'.[1] The expectation at the time was that the 'information superhighway', as they were calling it, would 'extend the electronic marketplace and make it the ultimate go-between, the universal middleman'.[2] Widespread disintermediation was the promise. And another, perhaps more enticing one, doubled it: freedom, especially in the market. After all, the original internet design was biased in favour of decentralized power.[3] The commercial internet, in short, was supposed to herald what *Wired* magazine co-founder, Kevin Kelly, described as disintermediated 'swarm capitalism',[4] which he thought would climax into 'a thousand points of wealth'.[5]

Of course, things did not pan out exactly as planned. Far from killing the middleman, the internet became a breeding ground for a particular species of intermediaries. Prescient minds of the 1990s spoke of 'cybermediaries';[6] today, we refer to them as 'digital platforms' (hereinafter 'platforms'). These middlemen are not only ubiquitous; they are also fundamentally altering the way we produce, consume, work, interact, and even think.

Consider how societies behaved during the first wave of the COVID-19 pandemic that swept across the world in the spring of 2020. How did confined consumers satisfy their need for things like information, basic necessities, ready-made meals, entertainment, and social contact? By trusting Google Search, hoarding on Amazon's marketplace, eating in with Uber and Deliveroo, binge-watching content on Netflix and YouTube, and chatting through Meta (formerly Facebook) -owned services. Platforms, it seems, were the consumer's go-to answer, more so than before the crisis hit. Likewise, where did white-collar employees turn to when they were told to keep working? Videoconferencing platforms like Zoom or Microsoft's

---

[1] Bill Gates, *The Road Ahead* (Viking 1995) ch 8.
[2] ibid.
[3] Yochai Benkler, 'Degrees of Freedom, Dimensions of Power' [2016] Dædalus 18, 18–20.
[4] Kevin Kelly, *New Rules for the New Economy* (Viking 1998) 159.
[5] ibid 156.
[6] Mitra Barun Sarkar, Brian Butler and Charles Steinfield, 'Intermediaries and Cybermediaries: Sarkar, Butler and Steinfield' [1995] Journal of Computer-Mediated Communication <https://bit.ly/2PsVWs6> accessed 18 November 2022.

Antitrust and Upstream Platform Power Plays. A. K. von Moltke, Oxford University Press. © A. K. von Moltke 2023.
DOI: 10.1093/oso/9780192873057.003.0001

Teams. Even governments—those wary of the disease curve—reached out to Apple and Alphabet (the parent company of Google) to help them develop official tracing apps. Why? Because apps must be interoperable with, and widely available on, two sets of key platform infrastructures, which both these firms control: their respective mobile operating systems (OSs) and app stores.

So much for disintermediation. What about decentralized power? Until the mid-2000s, digital markets did live up to the hype. Things were happening fast and furious; swarms of entrepreneurs were tapping into internet-enabled opportunities and the pockets of venture capitalists as if there was no tomorrow. To be sure, some of them did become big, sparking fears of monopolization—remember Yahoo!,[7] AOL,[8] or MySpace?[9] However, none enjoyed what Nobel economist John Hicks called 'the best of all monopoly profits', namely 'a quiet life'.[10] As predicted, digital markets during this period had 'no center, no orbits, no certainty'.[11]

Fast forward to today and the mood has soured. By most accounts, centralizing pathogens have infected our digital markets. The press has collectively labelled them as the 'Big Tech' platforms;[12] business and finance insiders have used acronyms like 'GAFA(M)' or 'FAANG'. These monikers refer to platform firms—Amazon, Apple, Alphabet/Google, Meta/Facebook, (Microsoft), and Netflix—which have all been described as powerful monopolists. Some have added Uber and Airbnb to this mix.[13] Paradoxically, the playbook for online success has not really changed over the years: borrow to fund loss-making ventures now with the promise of 'winner-takes-all-or-most' prosperity tomorrow.[14] The sole difference between the AOLs of the 1990s and the current crop of large platforms is that the former fell into oblivion within five years of ascending to market dominance. Yet, the prevailing sentiment is that today's 'tech giants ... are here to stay and continuing to grow in power and influence'.[15] Truth be told, Eric Schmidt (ex-CEO and executive chairman of Alphabet/Google) believes they are 'even more powerful than most people realize'.[16]

---

[7] Randall Stross, 'How Yahoo! Won the Search Wars' (*Fortune*, 2 March 1998) <https://bityl.co/Fjsl> accessed 19 November 2022.

[8] Joe Salkowski, 'AOL May Also Have Monopoly' *Chicago Tribune* (19 June 2000) <https://bit.ly/2ZZdKl8> accessed 18 November 2022.

[9] Victor Keegan, 'Will MySpace Ever Lose Its Monopoly?' *The Guardian* (8 February 2007) <https://bit.ly/3gFr9Vs> accessed 18 November 2022.

[10] John Hicks, 'Annual Survey of Economic Theory: The Theory of Monopoly' [1935] Econometrica 1, 8.

[11] Kelly (n 4) 9.

[12] See eg The Economist, 'How to Tame the Tech Titans' *The Economist* (18 January 2018) <https://econ.st/2BnIK4c> accessed 18 November 2022.

[13] See eg K Sabeel Rahman, 'The New Utilities: Private Power, Social Infrastructure, and the Revival of the Public Utility Concept' [2018] Cardozo Law Review 1621, 1676.

[14] Martin Kenney and John Zysman 'Unicorns, Cheshire Cats, and the New Dilemmas of Entrepreneurial Finance' [2019] Venture Capital 35.

[15] Harvard Business Review, *Monopolies and Tech Giants: The Insights You Need From Harvard Business Review* (Harvard Business School Publishing 2020) 1.

[16] Eric Schmidt and Jared Cohen, *The New Digital Age: Reshaping the Future of People, Nations and Business* (Knopf 2013) introductory ch.

This book, then, pertains to powerful platforms. More specifically, it probes how they (allegedly) exert their power against a specific group of stakeholders: suppliers. Before going into more details, though, we need to understand how we got here.

1. The New Dynamics

1.1 Platformization

Platforms are everywhere. Policymakers see them as key drivers of the 'digital re-mapping of the world'[17] ushering in the so-called 'Fourth Industrial Revolution'.[18] Some even say platformization of our global societies is 'irreversible'[19] because 'any industry in which information is an important ingredient is a candidate for the platform revolution'.[20] In hindsight, this is maybe not so surprising; the idea that the internet would kill intermediaries—dubbed the 'threatened intermediaries' hypothesis—rested on faulty assumptions. Middlemen do not all perform a single unified service (i.e. coordination) and the internet was not going to affect every conceivable situation of exchange in the same way.[21] The 'network of networks' (as it was also called in its formative years) undeniably did disrupt many analogue-era intermediaries by dramatically lowering costs—ask the music, book, movie, and news publishers. But friction-free capitalism was a pipe dream. Trust issues, search and transaction costs, as well as moral hazard and adverse selection risks were bound to emerge in novel forms and impede seamless interactions between consumers and producers. These are things middlemen have always stepped in to alleviate.[22] This reality coupled with other technological (r)evolutions[23] made the

---

[17] Bundesministerium für Wirtschaft und Energie (BMWi), 'White Paper on Digital Platforms: Digital Regulatory Policy for Growth, Innovation, Competition and Participation' (March 2017) 14 <https://perma.cc/AH32-GHZN> accessed 18 November 2022.

[18] Japan Fair Trade Commission, 'Report Regarding Trade Practices on Digital Platforms (Business-to-Business Transactions on Online Retail Platform and App Store)' (31 October 2019) 5 <https://perma.cc/KLL7-XXZB> accessed 18 November 2022; UNCTAD, 'Digital Economy Report 2019: Value Creation and Capture: Implications for Developing Countries' (2019) ch 2 <https://bityl.co/FjJ6> accessed 18 November 2022.

[19] Study Group on Improvement of Trading Environment surrounding Digital Platforms (here-inafter 'Study Group'), 'Improvement of Trading Environment surrounding Digital Platforms' (12 December 2018) Interim Discussion Paper, 1 <https://perma.cc/9CZ4-6ACX> accessed 18 November 2022; Andrew McAfee and Erik Brynjolfsson, *Machine, Platform, Crowd: Harnessing Our Digital Future* (Norton 2017) 205.

[20] Geoffrey Parker, Marshall Van Alstyne and Sangeet Choudary, *Platform Revolution: How Networked Markets Are Transforming the Economy and How to Make Them Work for You* (Norton 2016) 3.

[21] Stefan Schmitz, 'The Effects of Electronic Commerce on the Structure of Intermediation' [2000] Journal of Computer-Mediated Communication <https://bit.ly/33wXDgD> accessed 18 November 2022.

[22] Daniel Spulber, *Market Microstructure: Intermediaries and the Theory of the Firm* (CUP 1999).

[23] Namely, the World Wide Web, quantum leaps in computer processing and programming languages, as well as the advent of broadband, cloud computing, and modern AI.

internet's transformation into a 'network of platforms'[24] inevitable.[25] That it would morph into what many like Jonathan Kanter (one of the USA's top antitrust officials) would describe as a 'Whac-a-Mole monopolization machine',[26] however, came as a surprise to most observers.

1.2 Platform 'Monopolies'

Media coverage of popular platforms is undoubtedly trigger-happy in its literal and sometimes metaphorical reliance on the monopoly label.[27] None of those targeted by the descriptor are textbook monopolists—firms with absolute control over properly defined markets. Nevertheless, monopoly is a question of degree.[28] And by one metric—concentration[29]—Big Tech platforms do fit the profile, according to detailed work by competition authorities and expert-driven high-level assessments.[30]

Why is this happening, one may ask? Consensus points to a simple explanation: digital markets display multiple features which are coinciding at such an unprecedented scale that very high and durable concentration becomes the likely outcome.

Some of these characteristics boil down to traditional economics: digital products are information products. As such, they can be very cheaply *re*produced and (thanks to the internet) distributed, despite being potentially very expensive to produce. Unit costs can thereby be almost inversely proportional to the number of customers served. This means digital markets will typically exhibit extreme returns to scale, giving an important competitive advantage to incumbents. Furthermore, many digital products—say, online search results—are 'experience goods' (i.e. their quality can only be ascertained upon usage), which increase the value of trusted brands and create switching costs for existing consumers. Economies of scope and learning effects can therefore be generated as well by expanding the product range—think of Alphabet/Google and its myriad branded offers.

---

[24] Shane Greenstein, 'Internet Infrastructure' in Martin Peitz and Joel Waldfogel (eds), *The Oxford Handbook of the Digital Economic* (OUP 2012) 15.

[25] Daniel Spulber, 'The Economics of Markets and Platforms' [2019] Journal of Economics & Management Strategy 159.

[26] Jonathan Kanter, 'Solving the Global Problem of Platform Monopolization' (Speech delivered at the Fordham Competition Law Institute's 49th Annual Conference on International Antitrust Law and Policy, 16 September 2022) <https://bityl.co/Fjsq> accessed 19 November 2022.

[27] See references in Dirk Auer and Nicolas Petit, 'Two Systems of Belief about Monopoly: The Press vs. Antitrust' [2019] Cato Journal 99, 100–102.

[28] AP Lerner, 'The Concept of Monopoly and the Measurement of Monopoly Power' [1934] Review of Economic Studies 157, 161 (n 2).

[29] Concentration tells us whether an industry is populated by many players or is instead dominated by one or a few.

[30] See Appendix A.

A powerful demand-side factor further compounds these supply-side features: network effects. Again, nothing revolutionary per se since economists have known for years that certain products become more valuable to those who use them as the number of consumers grows.[31] These externalities, however, are particularly prevalent and significant in digital markets where they can sometimes arise in all their forms. Take the Facebook social media platform for illustrative purposes. As a consumer, the service becomes a more worthwhile tool for social engagement and connection the more others sign up. Economists speak of a (positive) *direct* network effect. There is also an *indirect* externality at play because as the number of Facebook consumers increases so too does demand for compatible complementary products (think of publisher websites). Finally, the more consumers join Facebook, the more advertisers will be willing to subsidize their usage by buying advertising space on the platform infrastructure. Here, we have a special case of indirect network effects which reflects the fact that Facebook is what economists call a *multi-sided* platform, i.e. a platform which directly connects distinct and interdependent customer groups (in this case, consumers and advertisers).[32] The network effects arising from these interactions are thus more properly denoted as *multi-sided* or *cross-sided*.[33] Beyond terminology, the important thing to remember is that (positive) network effects are key drivers of concentration in digital markets. For there comes a point when it makes little sense for new users not to join the biggest platform that enjoys a 'more-users-equals-more-value' dynamic. Consequently, network effects can create a virtuous cycle for those that benefit from them and may constitute an almost insurmountable obstacle for rivals.

Several other catalysers of monopolistic tendencies in digital markets are likewise worth quickly mentioning. The first two are technological. Nowadays, digital businesses can relentlessly gather on the cheap vast amounts of varied data, which they can exploit by leveraging quantum leaps in artificial intelligence (AI)-driven analytics to continuously improve their products and processes. Together, 'big data' and 'big analytics' potentially exacerbate the impact of demand and supply-side returns to scale and scope.

The remaining factors are more miscellaneous. Think of switching costs, disincentives to multi-home (i.e. the ability to engage with several platforms simultaneously), better access to financing, and superior attractiveness for sought-after workers.

In brief, we have a new conventional wisdom: the internet is no longer the dynamic environment it once was because the arteries of cyberspace are now prone to becoming durably clogged up by entrenched monopolists or oligopolists.

---

[31] Michael Katz and Carl Shapiro, 'Network Externalities, Competition, and Compatibility' [1985] American Economic Review 424.

[32] The literature generally refers to 'two-sided' platforms, although many platforms have more sides.

[33] Inge Graef, *EU Competition Law, Data Protection and Online Platforms: Data as Essential Facility* (Wolters Kluwer 2016) 22.

But how worried should we really be? As concentrated as our digital markets may be, liberal democracies (at least those modelled on the USA and the EU) have not chosen to condemn 'endogenous' monopolies as such.[34] The baseline—reflected in the 'rules of the market order'[35] which govern private economic interactions—is rather that such concentration (even to the point of absolute monopoly) is tolerable, sometimes desirable, so long as it mirrors the type of competition we want to see. This is one of the most central tenets of our antitrust laws.[36] In the extreme scenario where a market just cannot viably support multiple players—what economists call a natural monopoly—we accept it and impose *ex ante restrictions on what the monopolist can do*. Accordingly, the real question is: have the big platforms been misbehaving? Are there, for the purposes of this book, 'competition problems', ones ripe for *antitrust* intervention, to boot?[37] Here, things get messy.

1.3 'Competition' Problems?

To say that platform practices have been and still are dividing the antitrust community severely understates the situation. Reflecting the zeitgeist of our polarized politics, accounts have indeed been, and remain, strikingly antagonistic. One side is damningly critical. Scorn is heaped on the GAFA(M), which are accused of decimating competition or nipping it in the bud. More specifically, fears of excessive hoarding of valuable consumer data,[38] wasteful behavioural and near-perfect price discrimination,[39] and 'killer acquisitions'[40] are routinely conjured nowadays. Ditto for revisited concerns about how rivals of Big Tech may be foreclosed.[41] Together, they underscore the myriad ways in which the consumer's wallet, menu options, privacy, and autonomy could be harmed.[42] Worse, these platforms may

---

[34] That is, monopolies not acquired through merger, which definitely would be caught by merger control laws in many cases.

[35] Geoffrey Brennan and James Buchanan, *The Reason of Rules: Constitutional Political Economy* (CUP 1985) 12.

[36] Auer and Petit (n 27) 102ff (usefully summarizing the statutory and jurisprudential bases for the tenet).

[37] I will use 'antitrust' and 'competition policy' interchangeably to refer to the legal instruments societies have adopted to control *ex post* the business practices of economic entities in the name of competition. This notably excludes economic regulation, merger control, and unfair competition laws.

[38] Maurice Stucke, *Breaking Away: How to Regain Control Over Our Data, Privacy, and Autonomy* (OUP 2021) ch 1.

[39] Ariel Ezrachi and Maurice Stucke, *Virtual Competition: The Promise and Perils of the Algorithm-Driven Economy* (Harvard UP 2016) 83–143.

[40] Sai Krishna Kamepalli, Raghuram Rajan and Luigi Zingales, 'Kill Zone' (15 February 2021) <https://dx.doi.org/10.2139/ssrn.3555915> accessed 18 November 2022.

[41] See eg Fiona Scott Morton and David Dinielli, 'Roadmap for an Antitrust Case Against Facebook' (June 2020) 24ff <https://bityl.co/Fjsw> accessed 19 November 2022; Jonathan Baker, *The Antitrust Paradigm: Restoring a Competitive Economy* (Harvard UP 2019) ch 7.

[42] Orla Lynskey, 'The Power of Providence: The Role of Platforms in Leveraging the Legibility of Users to Accentuate Inequality' in Martin Moore and Damian Tambini (eds), *Digital Dominance: The Power of Google, Amazon, Facebook, and Apple* (OUP 2018).

be hurting us as citizens by compromising the fulcrums of our liberal democracies because of their ability to shape public perceptions and opinions.[43] In sum, a few big platforms have turned 'BAADD' (i.e. 'too big, anti-competitive, addictive and destructive to democracy').[44]

Proponents, by contrast, decry a cabal against what they see as efficiency machines. Platforms are more altruistic consumer attendants than rent-seekers, harvesting and analysing personal data to facilitate new forms of contract and to continuously improve upon the cornucopia of tailor-made and affordable services they offer.[45] Granted, some advocates do acknowledge the concentration which seems to prevail in many platform markets. But they are quick to dismiss the suggestion that this reality reflects the existence of economic power, let alone a winner-takes-all-or-most interplay.[46] The digital economy, they claim, 'is rife with competition and innovation, and consumers are benefitting in meaningful and remarkable ways from dynamic rivalry among companies big and small'.[47]

What emerges from these contrasting canvases is difficult to reconcile. Yet, the optimists are correct about at least one thing: 'there is undoubtedly more research to do'.[48]

Paradoxically, policymakers have been quick to make up their minds. Dozens of reports—produced by competition agencies, commissioned by them, or authored by experts—have been published in recent years. An overwhelming majority of them suggests that antitrust-relevant issues are endemic.[49] Most also conclude that urgent intervention is required.[50] Europe, as is well known, has been at the forefront of these efforts. Antitrust actions at both EU and Member State level have either already been taken or are in the pipelines against Big Tech. The European Commission (EC) actually mooted the need for a new competition tool, which would have tackled structural competition problems beyond the reach of antitrust.[51] Of course, detailed, platform-specific regulation is what the EU now

---

[43] Concerns connecting platforms to fake news are particularly illustrative (see eg Jonathan Kanter and Brandon Kressin, 'Online Platforms and the Commoditization of News Content' (*CPI Antitrust Chronicle*, December 2017) 23 <https://bit.ly/36hEoc3> accessed 18 November 2022).

[44] The Economist (n 12).

[45] See eg Hal Varian, 'Seven Deadly Sins of Tech?' [2021] Information Economics & Policy 100893; Parker, Van Alstyne and Choudary (n 20).

[46] See eg Geoffrey Manne and Dirk Auer, 'Antitrust Dystopia and Antitrust Nostalgia: Alarmist Theories of Harm in Digital Markets and Their Origins' [2021] George Mason Law Review 1279; Jonathan Barnet and others, 'Joint Submission of Antitrust Economists, Legal Scholars, and Practitioners to the House Judiciary Committee on the State of Antitrust Law and Implications for Protecting Competition in Digital Markets' (18 May 2020) <https://ssrn.com/abstract=3604374> accessed 18 November 2022; David Evans, 'Why the Dynamics of Competition for Online Platforms Leads to Sleepless Nights, But Not Sleepy Monopolies' (25 July 2017) <https://ssrn.com/abstract=3009438> accessed 18 November 2022.

[47] Barnet and others (n 46) 4.

[48] ibid.

[49] See Appendix A.

[50] ibid.

[51] EC, 'Inception Impact Assessment—New Competition Tool ("NCT")' Ref.Ares(2020)2877634 <https://bityl.co/FjtB> accessed 19 November 2022.

has in store.[52] Outside Europe, countries like Australia, Japan, South Korea, and India have been similarly proactive; even in the USA, where authorities were slow on the uptake, powerful platforms are now poised to face their day of antitrust reckoning.[53]

Policymakers and antitrust decision-makers have effectively sidestepped academia's internal rifts. More intriguingly, they have been doing so while prioritizing an issue—often without identifying it as such—only a handful of scholars had initially called attention to *explicitly*, namely 'upstream' effects.[54] Therein lies the crux of this book.

2. The Need to 'Look Up'

2.1 Platforms' Discontents

If one were to survey stakeholders about the state of the platform economy, what picture might emerge? Super-platform firms (i.e. Big Tech) would almost certainly be sitting pretty comfortably, comparatively speaking. Amidst the worst economic downturn since the Second World War, they somehow managed to get bigger.[55] And although even these firms aren't immune to systemic shocks, they are definitely better equipped than most to weather a storm.[56]

COVID-19 has obviously been less kind to other powerful platform operators like the online travel agent duopoly[57] and Uber.[58] Despite the runaway inflation experienced by most countries since late 2021, they will probably bounce back.[59] If not, these challenging economic conditions will have likely wiped out their respective industries entirely.

---

[52] Council of the EU, 'DMA: Council Gives Final Approval to New Rules for Fair Competition Online' <https://bityl.co/E3BF> accessed 18 November 2022. See also Chapter 7 of this book.

[53] For regular updates, see Joe Panettieri, 'Big Tech Antitrust Investigations: Amazon, Apple, Facebook and Google Updates' (*ChannelE2E*, 8 November 2022) <https://bit.ly/3cFO4hJ> accessed 18 November 2022.

[54] See eg Maurice Stucke and Ariel Ezrachi, 'Looking Up in the Data-Driven Economy' (*CPI Antitrust Chronicle*, May 2017) 16 <https://perma.cc/BSN3-NH6H> accessed 18 November 2022.

[55] Robin Wigglesworth, 'How Big Tech Got Even Bigger in the Covid-19 Era' *Financial Times* (1 May 2020) <https://on.ft.com/3hvX76T> accessed 18 November 2022.

[56] Tripp Mickle, 'Big Tech is Proving Resilient as the Economy Cools' *New York Times* (28 July 2022) <https://bityl.co/FL1A> accessed 18 November 2022.

[57] See eg Lee Hayhurst, 'Coronavirus: Expedia and Booking among the Big Losers as Billions Wiped off Valuations' (*Travolution*, 27 March 2020) <https://bityl.co/FjtJ> accessed 19 November 2022.

[58] See eg Dave Lee, 'Uber Announces Further 3,000 Job Cuts' *Financial Times* (18 May 2020) <https://on.ft.com/3ftGkQn> accessed 18 November 2022.

[59] See eg Davide Fina and others, 'Market Study on the Distribution of Hotel Accommodation in the EU' (2022) COMP/2020/OP/002, 75–76 <https://perma.cc/RGH9-KDQM> accessed 18 November 2022.

Small(er) rivals—the eBays of the world—will naturally bemoan their misfortunes, perhaps blame the dominant platforms for them, much like they were before crises hit. However, these actors are not our focus here.

What about consumers? Platform practices surely alarm those of us who value privacy and sustainability. Yet, the jury is still out on whether consumers prize the likes of Meta/Facebook and Amazon too much to seriously care.[60]

There remains, then, one category of stakeholders. It regroups the merchants on Amazon's Marketplace; the hoteliers on Booking.com or Expedia; the developers on the Apple App Store or the Google Play Store; the advertisers and content providers on Google Search or Facebook; the music publishers on Spotify or Apple Music; the drivers, couriers, and other labourers on the Ubers, Deliveroos, and Amazon Mechanical Turks of the world; as well as countless others who, paradoxically, are sometimes themselves platform operators like Spotify (on app stores) or Yelp (on general search engines).[61] Business scholars refer to all of them as 'complementors';[62] let us call them (platform) *providers* or (platform) *suppliers*.[63]

From a value chain perspective, they are the ones who sit upstream of the platforms.[64] Without them, the latter would have very little to attract consumers.[65] This is precisely why platform operators regularly refer to them as 'partners',[66] which is what platform capitalism was supposed to be: mutually beneficial trades. Platforms would take the products of suppliers and capture some of their value but only after having enlarged the size of the pie. In exchange for a middleman's cut, they

---

[60] See Roberto Mosquera and others, 'The Economic Effects of Facebook' [2020] Experimental Economics 575 (finding that one week of Facebook was worth $67 to participating consumers); Kiri Masters, '89% of Consumers Are More Likely to Buy Products from Amazon than other E-Commerce Sites: Study' (*Forbes*, 20 March 2019) <https://bit.ly/2Y057p7> accessed 18 November 2022 (reporting findings of a Feedvisor study showing how reliant consumers are on Amazon).

[61] Of course, firms like Spotify and Yelp are attracting increasing attention in antitrust fora because they also compete with the in-house services of Big Tech platforms (like Apple Music or Google Local). But this horizontal aspect deflects attention from the vertical linkage between these businesses, which is how they actually envision their relationship with Big Tech platforms (Competition and Markets Authority (CMA), 'Online Platforms and Digital Advertising: Market Study Final Report' (1 July 2020) [3.47] <https://bit.ly/3Avd1tA> accessed 19 November 2022).

[62] See eg Annabelle Gawer and Michael Cusumano, 'Platforms and Innovation' in Mark Dodgson, David Gann and Nelson Phillips (eds), *The Oxford Handbook of Innovation Management* (OUP 2014) 654.

[63] To be clear, by 'platform provider/supplier', I mean the businesses and people who depend on platforms for intermediation purposes to reach consumers (i.e. merchants on Amazon, Uber drivers, app developers, etc). Those behind the platforms will simply be called platform 'operators'.

[64] James Allen and Nico Flores, 'The Role of Government in the Internet' (18 April 2013) Final report for the Dutch Ministry of Economic Affairs, 11 <https://perma.cc/3YA8-E4G6> accessed 18 November 2022; CMA (n 61) [3.47]; Darryl Biggar and Alberto Heimler, 'Digital Platforms and the Transactions Cost Approach to Competition Law' [2021] Industrial and Corporate Change 1230.

[65] Parker, Van Alstyne and Choudary (n 20) 40 (arguing that a platform's value 'starts with the creation of a *value unit* by the producer').

[66] See eg Nick Denissen, 'Survey Says: Small Businesses Find Success with Amazon' (*Amazon blog*, 16 January 2020) <https://bityl.co/Fjv6> accessed 19 November 2022; Uber, 'We're Committed to Our Driver-Partners' (*Uber Blog*, 3 November 2017) <https://perma.cc/R6RD-7ET7> accessed 18 November 2022; Booking Holding, 'Annual Report (Form 10-K)' (23 February 2022) 2–3 <https://bit.ly/30Gj4KI> accessed 18 November 2022.

promised to foster new opportunities for many individuals and businesses alike. The former would find an escape from the dysfunctions of their local labour markets and earn a living in highly flexible and autonomous work environments; the latter would gain the ability to 'scale without mass' to reach a global audience.[67]

Now, nobody is saying platform capitalism was a sham from the outset. Nor could we: (almost) everyone recognizes the tremendous benefits platforms do generate.[68] In fact, in the early years, the system did seem capable of living up to its positive-sum hype. Uber drivers, for instance, always hark back to the 'good old days'.[69] But over the past decade, providers have been voicing their sense of disillusionment. Powerful platforms—not just Big Tech, mind you—have become predators, they argue, sometimes even parasites; states must intervene, including and especially, by enforcing antitrust.

Provider pleas for help have not fallen on deaf ears. Almost all earlier-mentioned reports display an explicit concern for the plight of platform suppliers.[70] Likewise, many highlight a perceived unfairness in the distribution of value.[71] The EC, for instance, tried to put a number on the identified 'value gap'. It estimated in 2018 that providers who rely on multi-sided business-to-consumer (B2C) platforms could be missing out on as much as €15.85 billion annually due to powerful platform mischiefs,[72] which are now deemed 'systemic and recurrent'.[73] According to the EU Executive, the latter also bear significant responsibility for the €9.47 billion net revenue loss press publishers suffered between 2010 and 2014.[74]

So, platform capitalism promised to create a 'thousand points of wealth'; today, it rather seems to be bringing about brazenly settled platform monopolists, somewhat content consumers, and visibly short-changed suppliers.

Many of us have been and remain alarmed. Who wouldn't feel empathy for the mom-and-pop merchants struggling to attract consumers on Amazon's plethoric marketplace; the small hoteliers trying to salvage their businesses through

---

[67] See eg Liran Einav, Chiara Farronato and Jonathan Levin, 'Peer-to-Peer Markets' [2016] Annual Review of Economics 615; McAfee and Brynjolfsson (n 19) 177–99 and 252–77.

[68] cf Robert Levine, *Free Ride: How Digital Parasites Are Destroying the Culture Business, and How the Culture Business Can Fight Back* (Doubleday 2011).

[69] Michael Sainato, ' "They Treat Us Like Crap": Uber Drivers Feel Poor and Powerless on Eve of IPO' *The Guardian* (7 May 2019) <https://bit.ly/3f52ibU> accessed 18 November 2022.

[70] See Appendix B.

[71] ibid.

[72] EC, 'Impact Assessment Accompanying the Proposal for a Regulation on Promoting Fairness and Transparency for Business Users of Online Intermediation Services' SWD/2018/138 final, 28.

[73] EC, 'Impact Assessment Report Accompanying the Proposal for a Regulation of the European Parliament and of the Council on Contestable and Fair Markets in the Digital Sector (Digital Markets Act)' SWD/2020/363 final, [61].

[74] EC, 'Impact Assessment on the Modernisation of EU Copyright Rules Accompanying the Proposal for a Directive of the European Parliament and of the Council on Copyright in the Digital Single Market and the Proposal for a Regulation of the European Parliament and of the Council Laying Down Rules on the Exercise of Copyright and Related Rights Applicable to Certain Online Transmissions of Broadcasting Organisations and Retransmissions of Television and Radio Programmes' SWD/2016/301 final, 156, 160.

Booking.com; or the Uber 'partners' driving themselves to exhaustion for below-minimum-wage-level 'fees' to make ends meet; all of whom allege platform abuses.

There are countless stories of how powerful platform firms apparently mistreat the providers who enabled them to become so valuable in the first place. That policymakers have taken notice surely ought to be applauded. As John Maynard Keynes warned in 1933, this kind of capitalism 'is not intelligent, it is not beautiful, it is not just, it is not virtuous'.[75]

Still, what many (including antitrust decision-makers) have been finding as of late—that these are *competition* problems and that *antitrust* has a key role in redressing them—is striking. For these types of worries had been on the back burner for years, and in some respects, for decades. As symptomatic of an undefined policy problem as they may be, then, are upstream platform power plays really 'competition problems', ones for antitrust, at that?

This is the question I intend to address along with some of the key queries nested within it. Indeed, if antitrust enforcement truly is warranted, what are the reasons, can they be rigorously articulated, and when would they make sense? Furthermore, assuming intervention is justifiable, can the policy be usefully deployed? If so, should it? If not, why not?

The list is fairly ambitious. Even so, the central issue these questions all trace back to—the 'upstream'—is fundamentally familiar; powerful platforms merely cast it in a new light and force us to stop tiptoeing around it. Let me briefly elaborate on this and outline where we are going with the book.

2.2 Antitrust as a Relevant Policy Response?

In 2019, Elizabeth Warren (the former US presidential hopeful) chastised Amazon for behaving in a way that erodes the profits of small businesses who rely on the firm's marketplace platform to reach consumers. Why the scorn, especially since her preferred remedy would be an antitrust-mandated breakup of Amazon? '[I]t's not fair',[76] was her tweeted reply.

Powerful platforms assuredly have made antitrust 'sexy again'.[77] But there is nothing new about this sort of rhetoric. The Sherman Act of 1890—America's original competition statute—was actually enacted on such producerist inclinations.[78] The lone difference is that suppliers calling for protection at the time

---

[75] John Maynard Keynes, 'National Self-Sufficiency' [1933] Studies: An Irish Quarterly Review 177, 183.

[76] Elizabeth Warren, 'Warren on Amazon' (*Twitter*, 24 April 2019) <https://bit.ly/2SayDoC> accessed 18 November 2022.

[77] Carl Shapiro, 'Antitrust in a Time of Populism' [2018] International Journal of Industrial Organization 714, 714.

[78] Rudolph Peritz, *Competition Policy in America: History, Rhetoric, Law* (rev edn, OUP 2000) ch 1.

were small dealers victimized by the powerful railroad trusts. What has since changed is that antitrust in the USA (and around the world) has taken a technocratic turn which has left supplier-side issues essentially purged from the purview of decision-makers.

Farmers, for instance, are still being exploited; just no longer by the industrial 'robber barons', but by powerful processors and food manufacturers who are themselves squeezed by big grocers like Walmart and Tesco. Yet, as a small contingent of competition lawyers has noted, upstream concerns in the brick-and-mortar economy have rarely been heeded under contemporary antitrust theory and practice.[79] Furthermore, firms like McDonald's are still charting their way to 'bigness' by minutely controlling businesses and labour suppliers in ways which skirt both the labour and antitrust laws ... as they were in the 1950s when the organizational innovation known as franchising came into prominence. Back then, though, antitrust decision-makers would have had something to say on what is simply an alternative path to centralized vertical control.[80]

The fact that, today, policymakers and antitrust decision-makers are 'looking up' speaks volumes about the importance of platforms in our socio-economy and the political saliency surrounding anything they do. For there can be no denying that for many years—roughly four and two decades in the USA and the EU respectively—the antitrust community has tended to 'look down' to cater to *consumers*, rather than up at the plight of those who sit upstream in any given value chain.

At the same time, even most centrist and progressive scholars reject the idea of making supplier interests the touchstone of antitrust.[81] So, what does this reveal of the attitude our decision-makers are now adopting? Inasmuch as antitrust has been, is, and will continue to be, an envisaged response, we need a policy introspection to make some sense of what is going on, precisely what this book offers.

---

[79] Peter Carstensen, *Competition Policy and the Control of Buyer Power: A Global Issue* (Edward Elgar 2017) (taking a mainly US perspective); Ignacio Herrera Anchustegui, *Buyer Power in EU Competition Law* (Concurrences 2017) (taking an EU perspective).

[80] Brian Callaci, 'The Historical and Legal Creation of a Fissured Workplace: The Case of Franchising' (PhD thesis, University of Massachusetts Amherst 2019) ch 1.

[81] See eg Stefan Thomas, '*Ex Ante* and *Ex Post* Control of Buyer Power' in Fabiana Di Porto and Rupprecht Podszun (eds), *Abusive Practices in Competition Law* (Edward Elgar 2018) ('[w]hile the prevention of consumer harm can legitimately be considered as at least one of the goals of antitrust law, it would not be convincing to say the same about "supplier harm"'); John Kirkwood, 'Reforming the Robinson–Patman Act to Serve Consumers and Control Powerful Buyers' [2015] Antitrust Bulletin 358, 361 ('the overarching goal should be consumer welfare, not supplier welfare'). See also Carstensen (n 79) 24 ('no scholar seems to advocate that producer welfare should be a primary goal of competition policy'). Even those most adamant on antitrust reform state that their argument 'is not that antitrust should embrace redistribution as an explicit goal, or that enforcers should harness antitrust in order to promote progressive redistribution'. (Lina Khan and Sandeep Vaheesan, 'Market Power and Inequality: The Antitrust Counterrevolution and Its Discontents' [2017] Harvard Law & Policy Review 235, 237).

One aspect of the exercise follows from an argument made by some platform critics who say antitrust must shift lodestars to correct its contemporary disregard for the suffering of (platform) providers. Put differently, the claim affirms (or at least suggests) that antitrust's prevailing goal is inherently insensitive to upstream effects.[82] This call for soul-searching is met in Part I. There, two chapters explore the two available options if the policy is to remain connected to the one thing everyone agrees it has to relate to, namely 'competition'.

Another element of the introspection pertains to how and when upstream platform power plays can be rationalized as antitrust-relevant competition problems. Some commentators have criticized decision-makers, accusing them of skirting the issues.[83] Similarly, important voices in the antitrust community have lambasted academics championing the cause of platform suppliers for being sketchy.[84] The three chapters that make up Part II take these charges seriously by attempting to rationalize specific concerns voiced by (allegedly) victimized providers.

Finally, there is the question of whether antitrust is a befitting answer to our upstream worries. The two chapters comprising Part III address this matter through two angles: first, by seizing up the key cogs of the antitrust machinery, i.e. its enforcement standards, power radar, and remedial apparatus; second, by reflecting on other ways provider interests can be safeguarded.

In so doing, this book makes three broad arguments, which ultimately point to a Procrustean dilemma.

One: changing antitrust's lodestar may be desirable, but it is not a prerequisite for looking upstream. We will see that there is nothing inherent to antitrust's contemporary objective which would render provider fears invisible to decision-makers. The real problem with the contemporary set-up is that it is deceptive and, more importantly, supported by questionable normative foundations which should be (re)discussed. All the more so since the only credible alternative—one that respects the idea that antitrust is about competition but not providers per se—does have worthy normative credentials, which are more directly connected to the upstream.

Two: upstream platform power plays can be formally made out as potential competition problems under either approach to antitrust, but there are important caveats that create a conundrum for enforcers. As will be explained, the technocratic route has pitfalls making erroneous conclusions more likely. Yet, while shifting lodestars would enable decision-makers to rationalize intervention in a wider array of cases, doing so means recognizing that antitrust is a moral enterprise just as much as it is an economic one. This is not something to be taken lightly.

---

[82] See eg Marshall Steinbaum and Maurice Stucke, 'The Effective Competition Standard: A New Standard for Antitrust' [2019] University of Chicago Law Review 595, 600.

[83] See eg Barnet and others (n 46) 1–2.

[84] See D Daniel Sokol, 'Antitrust's "Curse of Bigness" Problem' [2020] Michigan Law Review 1259, 1261–62; Manne and Auer (n 46) 1288ff; Joshua Wright and Aurelien Portuese, 'Antitrust Populism: Towards a Taxonomy' [2020] Stanford Journal of Law, Business & Finance 131.

Paradoxically, we will further see how certain situations can be made out as potential competition problems even when they stir anxieties pertaining primarily to things that, by reasonable measure, ought to be beyond antitrust's normative remit.

Three: antitrust can redress (some of) our upstream worries. However, it will be argued that the interventions required often come with a price, which enforcers in liberal democracies have to think twice about paying, especially given the other available policy levers at our disposal, including the option of new, innovative, regulation.

2.3 Caveats

The scene is now set, save for several refinements on terminology, scope, and methodology.

Regarding terminology, a few words on the notions of 'platforms' and 'upstream' effects are in order. References to Netflix and (to a certain extent) Spotify as platforms will have surprised some. For they would point to industrial organization (IO) economists who define platforms as intermediaries that match distinct, but interdependent user groups whose mutually benefiting direct interactions generate cross-sided network externalities, which the 'platform' has to internalize to sustain its value proposition. From this perspective, Netflix is admittedly not a platform because it is not *multi-sided* in the technical IO sense.[85] Resultingly, merchants on Amazon Marketplace are not really 'suppliers' sitting 'upstream'. This is because, for the IO economist, Amazon Marketplace would qualify as a platform and merchants would therefore merely be viewed as one of two user groups (the other being us, consumers) *purchasing* an intermediation service from Amazon. Simply put, merchants are *customers* under this view.

Multi-sided market economics has important implications, which we cannot ignore. Four reasons nevertheless lead me to reject, for present purposes, its definition of platforms and the implications this has on how the topic explored here is framed.

First, economists frequently butt heads over whether a firm is 'multi-sided'.[86]

Second, multi-sidedness (however conceived) is not necessarily immutable as businesses can strategically shift to a one-sided model and vice versa.[87]

---

[85] Content providers and consumers do not interact *directly* like they do on YouTube—interactions via Netflix are indirect since consumers do not actually deal with content providers who instead license their content to Netflix.

[86] Dirk Auer and Nicolas Petit, 'Two-Sided Markets and the Challenge of Turning Economic Theory into Antitrust Policy' [2015] Antitrust Bulletin 426, 432–36.

[87] See, similarly, Paul Belleflamme and Martin Peitz, 'Platforms and Network Effects' in Luis Corchón and Marco Marini (eds), *Handbook of Game Theory and Industrial Organization, Volume II: Applications* (Edward Elgar 2018) 287–89.

Third, this book is really about antitrust and its treatment of 'upstream' effects, i.e. effects of business practices that, in the first instance, are borne by those without whom platforms (however defined) would have little to no value proposition. Functionally, these economic agents *provide/supply* products to consumers, albeit through middlemen (namely, platforms). They are 'upstream' because this is their position when one adopts a value chain perspective.[88] As noted earlier, it is also how these businesses perceive themselves.[89] To my mind, it would thus be odd to foreclose them from the discussion merely because they rely on intermediaries generally viewed as platforms (such as Uber or Amazon's retailing arm) except by (some) IO economists. As we will see shortly (in Chapter 1), this is a matter of coherence as well: the antitrust analysis of harm to such merchants should not depend on whether they distribute their wares via Amazon's (single-sided) retailing arm or through its (multi-sided) marketplace.

Fourth, multi-sided market economics ignores insights from other potentially relevant disciplines that display a more technological understanding of the concept of 'platform', conjuring ideas of an infrastructure which users can build upon.[90]

Accordingly, platforms—digital unless otherwise specified—are to be taken as intermediaries that operate a digital product (hereinafter the platform 'infrastructure', 'system', 'architecture', or 'product') through which they facilitate and organize interactions between consumers and providers/suppliers (together, the 'users') which generate network effects they actively manage.[91] Figure I.1 below provides an illustrative typology.

Turning to scope, the focus will be on B2C platforms and a limited array of their (alleged) upstream mischiefs. Space management is but one reason. Recall that what drives my interest lies in antitrust's consideration of supplier harm in the platform economy. The scoping choice is hence justified because upstream worries either do not arise in other platform contexts (think of non-profit platforms like Wikipedia), or might, and probably do, surface elsewhere but not with the same acuteness (such as with pure B2B platforms like Amazon Web Services). Plus, given the centrality of, not just consumer welfare reasoning in antitrust, but of consumer welfare rhetoric, which (almost) always has the real (i.e. end-) consumer in mind, the monograph's inquiry and its conclusions resonate louder when the focus is kept on the platforms consumers actually use.

---

[88] Recall the references in n 64. See, similarly, Oliver Budzinski and Juliane Mendelsohn, 'Regulating Big Tech: From Competition Policy to Sector Regulation?' [2023] ORDO (forthcoming); Marshall Steinbaum, 'Establishing Market and Monopoly Power in Tech Platform Antitrust Cases' [2022] Antitrust Bulletin 130, 137.

[89] CMA (n 61).

[90] See eg Mark de Reuver, Carsten Sørensen and Rahul Basole, 'The Digital Platform: A Research Agenda' [2017] Journal of Information Technology 124, 126.

[91] See, similarly, Paul Belleflamme and Martin Peitz, *The Economics of Platforms: Concepts and Strategy* (CUP 2021) 29.

Figure I.1 Typology of platforms

Source: United Nations Conference on Trade and Development, *Digital Economy Report 2019: Value Creation and Capture: Implications for Developing Countries* (UNCTAD 2019) https://bityl.co/FjJ6.

So, this book does concern the so-called Big Tech platforms. Yet, it does *not* pertain *solely* to them. For whereas these firms certainly are the source of many upstream anxieties, they are not alone. Platform providers like hoteliers, ride-hailing drivers, and musicians, for example, would rather have the like of, respectively, Booking.com, Uber, and Spotify marked as targets for antitrust intervention.[92]

Finally, two remarks on methodology. First, despite the ambition to cast a light on the global nature of the issues at hand, there will be a tendency to draw primarily from European and, to a lesser degree, North American experiences, sources, and materials. This bias is not overly crippling, though. Europe has been at the vanguard when it comes to the matters examined herein. In addition, both the EU and the USA have established antitrust frameworks the rest of the world look towards for inspiration.

Second, the book is resolutely multidisciplinary, drawing insights from lawyers, economists, business scholars, digital ethnographers, and, perhaps most significantly, from political scientists and philosophers. This ambition comes with inevitable risks of oversimplification. The straitjacket created by word constraints further exacerbates them. I am aware of these challenges and have made every effort to mitigate their impact and caveat my analysis and claims where necessary.

With the foregoing in mind, let us now begin.

---

[92] See eg Natasha Lomas, 'Online Travel Giant Booking.com Faces Antitrust Probe in Spain' (*TechCrunch*, 17 October 2022) <https://bityl.co/FCyA> accessed 18 November 2022.

PART I
SOUL-SEARCHING

Antitrust, in many jurisdictions, is a policy which has come to be wedded to a singular aim. Margrethe Vestager—antitrust's most renowned contemporary enforcer-in-chief—aptly captured its ethos when she stated in 2016 that her 'job is—as it always has been—to make sure consumers are treated fairly'[1] '[b]ecause competition policy isn't there to ... help one company, and hold back another. It's there to defend consumers'.[2]

The argument that 'consumer welfare' not only is, but should be, antitrust's primary guide, was relatively uncontroversial until recently. Powerful platforms have been game changers. Their rise is partly what reignited a fierce debate over 'antitrust's soul'.[3] Initially confined to the US, the issue rapidly caught fire across the Atlantic,[4] made its way to global fora,[5] and boiled over beyond academic circles into politics and the popular agenda.[6] This has left enforcers like Commissioner Vestager openly asking: 'what are the goals and limits of competition policy?'.[7]

Why the controversy, one may ask? The short answer is that, for many observers, antitrust 'lost its mojo'[8] and the consumer welfare lodestar is to blame.

---

[1] Margrethe Vestager, 'Competition and the Digital Single Market' (Speech delivered at the Forum for EU–US Legal–Economic Affairs, 15 September 2016) <https://bit.ly/3axnJRd> accessed 18 November 2022.

[2] Margrethe Vestager, 'Competition is a Consumer Issue' (Speech delivered at the BEUC General Assembly, 13 May 2016) <https://bit.ly/2w3uVpi> accessed 18 November 2022. See also D Daniel Sokol, 'Antitrust, Industrial Policy, and Economic Populism' in Damien Gerard and Ioannis Lianos (eds), *Reconciling Efficiency and Equity: A Global Challenge for Competition Policy* (CUP 2019) 285 (rejoicing at the singular focus on consumer welfare 'most jurisdictions have adopted').

[3] Ariel Ezrachi and Maurice Stucke, 'The Fight over Antitrust's Soul' [2018] Journal of European Competition Law & Practice 1.

[4] Ariel Ezrachi, 'EU Competition Law Goals and the Digital Economy' (6 June 2018) Oxford Legal Studies Research Paper No 17/2018 <https://ssrn.com/abstract=3191766> accessed 18 November 2022; Anna Gerbrandy, 'Rethinking Competition Law within the European Economic Constitution' [2019] Journal of Common Market Studies 127.

[5] See eg 'OECD Global Forum on Competition Discusses Competition Under Fire' (2019) <https://bit.ly/3GpGfxM> accessed 19 November 2022 (discussing the alleged 'inadequacy of the consumer welfare standard').

[6] See eg Gilad Edelman, 'The Big Tech Hearing Proved Congress Isn't Messing Around' (*Wired*, 29 July 2020) <https://bit.ly/3id6LuT> accessed 18 November 2022.

[7] Margrethe Vestager, 'Merger Control: The Goals and Limits of Competition Policy in a Changing World' (Speech delivered at the International Bar Association 26th Annual Competition Conference, 9 September 2022) <https://bityl.co/EIrG> accessed 18 November 2022.

[8] Cristoforo Osti, 'Antitrust: A Heimlich Manoeuvre' [2015] European Competition Journal 221, 222.

Now, it is widely accepted that contemporary antitrust has been (overly) short-termist and price-centric in its focus. Some have claimed (or suggested) that this shows consumer welfare-minded antitrust simply *cannot* 'look up'.[9] Their solution? Be radical: address the problem like a neuro-ophthalmologist would treat a patient with tumour-induced Parinaud syndrome,[10] i.e. *remove* the underlying condition.

Others, by contrast, have argued that the remedy overshoots. Reconstructive (as opposed to ablational) surgery is enough (if at all needed) because the consumer welfare lodestar is not *inherently* conducive to upgaze paresis.[11]

This is the backdrop for Chapter 1. As will be explained, there is much more to 'consumer welfare' than meets the eye. Focusing on its myopic application obscures what may ultimately prove to be a deeper problem: potentially questionable *foundations*, which our concern for platform providers only exacerbates. The conclusion, therefore, is an invitation to openly (re)discuss the lodestar's normativity.

But assuming consumer welfare is indeed normatively irreparable, what is the alternative? Remember, we want the policy to be sensitive to upstream worries; yet consensus has it that supplier interests cannot themselves be the touchstone. Plus, competition policy must remain connected to *competition*. Given these imperatives, there is only one other lodestar antitrust can justifiably further: competition, *as such*.

Granted, the claim has nothing revolutionary in it. Some American scholars—the so-called neo-Brandeisians (after the Progressive-era champion of US antitrust enforcement, Justice Louis Brandeis)—argue that this lodestar already steered decision-makers during earlier years.[12] Likewise in the EU, where protecting the competitive process has, until recently at least, always been considered paramount by the judicature.[13] Supposedly, this alternative paradigm entails a 'more normative'[14] approach to antitrust.

The problem one might flag, though, is that since we are discussing goals, axiomatic accounts—what is currently on offer—surely cannot suffice because there is nothing self-evident about 'competition'. This is our task in Chapter 2, which articulates a normative theory of the competitive process lodestar that also explains why provider anxieties can be *directly* catered to.

---

[9] See, notably, Marshall Steinbaum and Maurice Stucke 'The Effective Competition Standard: A New Standard for Antitrust' [2019] University of Chicago Law Review 600.

[10] A condition whose main symptom is 'upgaze paresis'—the inability to look up.

[11] See, notably, Kevin Caves and Hal Singer, 'When the Econometrician Shrugged: Identifying and Plugging Gaps in the Consumer-Welfare Standard' [2018] George Mason Law Review 395.

[12] Tim Wu, *The Curse of Bigness: Antitrust in the New Gilded Age* (Columbia Global Reports 2018) concluding ch. See also Steinbaum and Stucke (n 9); Lina Khan, 'Amazon's Antitrust Paradox' [2017] Yale Law Journal 712, 743ff.

[13] cf Cases C-6/72 *Continental Can* ECLI:EU:C:1973:22 [1973] ECR 215, [22]–[26]; C-450/19 *Kilpailu- ja kuluttajavirasto* ECLI:EU:C:2021:10 [2021] not yet published, [34]; with Case C-377/20 *Servizio Elettrico Nazionale* ECLI:EU:C:2022:379 [2022] not yet published, [46].

[14] Andreas Mundt quoted in Rupprecht Podszun, 'Conference Debriefing (21/22): Sustainability, Platforms' (*D'Kart*, 3 October 2020) <https://bit.ly/3oOA2Qm> accessed 18 August 2022.

Tangentially, one comes to appreciate how the 'goal(s)' debate, which our upstream concerns have further fuelled, is but an ethical battle over the value of competition—over whether it is to be desired for its outcomes or because it is a process in itself worthy of protection.

1

'Consumer Welfare'

Antitrust's Consequentialist Turn

1. Introduction

The history of antitrust so far has a 'Kuhnian' feel to it, developing in stages, much like Thomas Kuhn understood the process of scientific evolution. That is, a ruling framework (or 'paradigm') dominates the way the discipline is theorized and practised; inevitable shortcomings creep up over the years; and when these flaws become untenable, a crisis emerges, sometimes sparking an exceptional 'paradigm shift'.[1]

Take the USA and the EU: conventional historical narratives tie turning points in decisional attitudes with revolutions in the marketplace of (economic) ideas where, in our modern times, the (post-) Chicago School views have come to prevail.[2] Naturally, whether based on price theory or contemporary game theory, these ideas are all about consumer welfare.

The consumer welfare paradigm assuredly never did receive unanimous approval.[3] Its dominance has also never been so seriously challenged as today. Powerful platforms and their upstream exertions are a big reason. As suggested previously, though, critics advocating a paradigm *shift* have not made a decisive pitch. Proponents of the status quo, or of a less radical fix, have been quick to counter that (part of) the argument for change simply emphasizes a *practical* defect in the consumer welfare lodestar which does not fundamentally enfeeble it.[4] Their retort is not unfounded. As Parts II and III of this book will respectively show, our upstream anxieties *can* be rationalized as competition problems under the current approach; shifting to the alternative only makes it potentially *easier* for decision-makers to

---

[1] Thomas Kuhn, *The Structure of Scientific Revolutions* (University of Chicago Press 1962).

[2] Counter-historical accounts are worth keeping in mind, though. See eg Nicola Giocoli, 'Competition Versus Property Rights: American Antitrust Law, the Freiburg School, and the Early Years of European Competition Policy' [2009] Journal of Competition Law & Economics 747; Heike Schweitzer and Kiran Klaus Patel, 'EU Competition Law in Historical Context' in Kiran Klaus Patel and Heike Schweitzer (eds), *The Historical Foundations of EU Competition Law* (OUP 2013).

[3] See eg Richard Bernhard, 'Competition in Law and in Economics' [1967] Antitrust Bulletin 1099, 1129–63.

[4] A Douglas Melamed and Nicolas Petit, 'The Misguided Assault on the Consumer Welfare Standard in the Age of Platform Markets' [2019] Review of Industrial Organization 741, 750 (arguing that 'the problems that critics have identified are practical, not legal or conceptual; and abandoning the CW standard will not solve them').

Antitrust and Upstream Platform Power Plays. A. K. von Moltke, Oxford University Press. © A. K. von Moltke 2023. DOI: 10.1093/oso/9780192873057.003.0002

intervene. In other words, 'looking up' in the platform economy does not necessarily require forsaking consumer welfare as a lodestar. If a paradigm change truly is needed due to the incumbent's feebleness, one has to accordingly show that the weakness is *normative*. What follows thus examines whether ammunition for such an argument exists and how our upstream concerns fit in the equation, if at all.

To this end, Section 2 starts with some conceptual clarifications. Over half a century's worth of scholarly accounts on the consumer welfare paradigm have failed to produce terminological consistency. Even the latest, platform-infused ones suggest confusion over the substance of what is really a polymorphic ideal. Having clarified the different forms 'consumer welfare' may take and what each variation substantively entails, Section 3 then looks at the paradigm's foundations for potential weaknesses. Moreover, it examines whether, and if so how, our interest in the plight of platform providers might drive or compound them.

2. 'Consumer Welfare': A Polymorphic Ideal

Consumer welfare, as a concept, entered the lexicon of competition lawyers through the early writings of the late Robert Bork and became a mainstay following the 1978 publication of his magnum opus, *The Antitrust Paradox*.[5] Bork's works have had an enduring impact on generations of scholars, practitioners, and judges alike within and beyond the USA. But the consumer welfare notion he originally depicted has morphed. So much so that several proxies now coexist, each encapsulating somewhat distinct and potentially conflicting policy implications that have little resemblance to what Bork himself envisioned. To avoid confusion, the following briefly clarifies the Borkian understanding of consumer welfare (Section 2.1), before identifying its various offshoots (Section 2.2), which will be put under the normative microscope in Section 3.

2.1 Borkian Consumer Welfare

Few have appreciated (or explicitly acknowledged) the true intention behind Bork's expounding of the US antitrust laws as enshrining a consumer welfare prescription whereby '[c]onsumer welfare ... is merely another term for the wealth of the nation'.[6] This is because he was appealing to the mainstream (i.e. neoclassical)

---

[5] Robert Bork, *The Antitrust Paradox: A Policy at War with Itself* (Basic Books 1978) .
[6] ibid 90. Those who do include, among others, Gregory Werden, 'Antitrust's Rule of Reason: Only Competition Matters' [2014] Antitrust Law Journal 713, 718–23; Barak Orbach, 'The Antitrust Consumer Welfare Paradox' [2010] Journal of Competition Law & Economics 133, 138–41 together with 148–49; Heike Schweitzer, 'The Role of Consumer Welfare in EU Competition Law' in Josef Drexl and others (eds), *Technology and Competition: Contributions in Honour of Hanns Ullrich* (Larcier 2010) 515–16.

economist's understanding of the concept. Here, the reader will hopefully forgive a slight digression, which shall prove useful later.

Economists have always wanted to decipher how to allocate scarce resources so that maximum welfare for individuals in society may be achieved.[7] For policy-advising purposes, it is important to understand the methodological steps ortho-doxy has them make.

- 'Welfare' as 'wealth'

First, the mainstream economist adopts an understanding of 'welfare' which does not mesh well with the layperson's. Most philosophers would denounce it. More on this shortly; for now, suffice it to note that welfare effectively means 'wealth', re-flected by monetary surplus.[8]

- Economy-wide or within-market welfare

Second, there are two distinct analytical frameworks for appraising the welfare effects of actions. One is *general* equilibrium analysis. This is essentially a multi-market approach which considers the economy in its entirety.[9] The other is *partial* equilibrium analysis whereby the economist focuses on an isolated part of the economy known as the 'market'.[10] The antitrust lawyer will perhaps be partial to the latter given the entrenchment of market definition in the practice of competition law. It is important, though, to see that the two methods entail different impli-cations. Indeed, an action's welfare effects in a specific market do not necessarily correspond to changes across markets and throughout the economy. Theoretically, therefore, we might say that proper economic *welfare* analysis is conducted under *general* equilibrium whereas *partial* equilibrium is but a limited *surplus* ana-lysis which, under certain conditions, will reflect welfare predictions in general equilibrium.[11]

---

[7] For detailed accounts on what follows, see eg Richard Just, Darrell Hueth and Andrew Schmitz, *The Welfare Economics of Public Policy: A Practical Approach to Project and Policy Evaluation* (Edward Elgar 2004); Allan Feldman, 'Welfare Economics' in Steven Durlauf and Lawrence Blume (eds), *The New Palgrave Dictionary of Economics* (rev edn, Palgrave Macmillan 2008).

[8] A consumer's surplus is the difference between what (s)he is willing to pay for a product and the price (s)he actually pays. Similarly, producer surplus is the difference between the price (s)he actually receives for the relevant product and the minimum amount (s)he is willing to accept in order to main-tain the same level of supply. By adding up their respective surpluses one obtains total (social or aggre-gate) surplus.

[9] For a useful historical description of early general equilibrium theory, see Donald Walker, 'Early General Equilibrium Economics: Walras, Pareto, and Cassel' in Warren Samuels, Jeff Biddle and John Davis (eds), *A Companion to the History of Economic Thought* (Blackwell 2003).

[10] Economists do not ignore other market variables but simply take them as constant.

[11] For a useful synthesis of the literature explaining these conditions, see Gregory Werden, 'Consumer Welfare and Competition Policy' in Josef Drexl, Wolfgang Kerber and Rupprecht Podszun (eds), *Competition Policy and the Economic Approach: Foundations and Limitations* (Edward Elgar 2011) 12.

- Benchmarks for evaluation

Third, there are two alternative benchmarks orthodox economists rely on for policy-advising purposes. The first is called Pareto-optimality. This is an ideal end state where economic welfare is mathematically found to be maximized because no further changes to the state of affairs would be capable of improving anyone's welfare without simultaneously decreasing that of someone else.[12] Of course, it says nothing about how policymakers should do policy. For this, economists accordingly refer to the (strong) Pareto principle (or Pareto-superior criterion), which enables the ranking or comparison of alternative states of affairs. By this standard, state B is superior (or more allocatively efficient or welfare-enhancing) when compared to state A if moving to the former improves the welfare of at least one individual without adversely affecting the welfare of anyone else.[13]

The second benchmark is a weaker form of allocative efficiency known as Kaldor–Hicks efficiency.[14] The differing policy implications between the two standards are easily explained. The first rejects any change where someone would lose out; the second, by contrast, accepts such an outcome, provided that winners can *hypothetically* compensate the losers.[15]

- The 'consumer' in consumer welfare

Finally, neoclassical economists profess neutrality in policy-advising. Effectively, they reject the idea of making value judgements between members of society— between consumers and producers, for instance, or between consumers in different markets. Their concern usually pertains to the welfare consequences of actions on *society as a whole*. The term 'consumer' is hence really a proxy for 'buyer'. And this notion embodies any member of society engaged in consumptive activities. Consequently, 'consumer welfare' is a misnomer seldom used in economics because it depicts the welfare of *society*.[16]

To summarize, for the mainstream (i.e. neoclassical) economist, 'consumer welfare' theoretically means *general* equilibrium *social* (i.e. total or aggregate) *welfare* where Pareto-efficiency is achieved. Because multi-market analysis is difficult and the Pareto benchmark is so restrictive, consumer welfare, in practice, is *partial* equilibrium *social* (total or aggregate) *surplus* where Kaldor–Hicks efficiency is realized.

---

[12] Feldman (n 7) 3. For a discussion, see Mark Blaug, 'The Fundamental Theorems of Modern Welfare Economics, Historically Contemplated' [2007] History of Political Economy 185.

[13] Just, Hueth and Schmitz (n 7) 15.

[14] Jonathan Wight, 'The Ethics Behind Efficiency' [2017] Journal of Economic Education 15, 15ff.

[15] See Just, Hueth and Schmitz (n 7) 32–38.

[16] Werden (n 11) 13.

With this in mind, one can now appreciate why many have misconstrued Bork's *normative* claim. Most contemporary commentators interpret Bork's association of consumer welfare with 'the wealth of a nation' as an endorsement of *partial* equilibrium total surplus[17] or consumer surplus,[18] and are, ergo, critical of his seemingly misleading labelling.[19] However, it is precisely this reference—combined with his understanding of 'consumers as a collectivity'[20] and of competition as an end state in which Pareto-optimality is achieved[21]—that reveal Bork's normative affinity for *general* equilibrium total *welfare*.[22] Much of the confusion presumably stems from his vernacular choices. Yet, consumer welfare rhetoric has mushroomed as a result, embracing several semantic variations with differing substantive content.

2.2 The Offshoots of Borkian Consumer Welfare

2.2.1 Total surplus

One widely supported alternative to (general equilibrium) total welfare as a goal for antitrust is (partial equilibrium) total surplus, which is normatively connected to Kaldor–Hicks efficiency. Under this approach, the anticompetitive character of a business practice only becomes apparent if overall efficiency declines or is likely to decrease in a properly defined market. Briefly,[23] its proponents (i.e. most economists[24] and many lawyers[25]) defend it on the conviction of its economic and philosophical superiority,[26] assumed objectivity,[27] and on the belief that non-efficiency considerations are either irrelevant or better dealt with through different policy

---

[17] See eg Rex Ahdar, 'Consumers, Redistribution of Income and the Purpose of Competition Law' [2002] European Competition Law Review 341, 348–49.

[18] See eg Tim Wu, *The Curse of Bigness: Antitrust in the New Gilded Age* (Columbia Global Reports 2018) ch 4.

[19] Some commentators have also mistakenly understood Bork as referring to the 'welfare of individual consumers' (eg Paul Brietzke, 'Robert Bork, the Antitrust Paradox: A Policy at War with Itself' [1979] Valparaiso University Law Review 403, 410).

[20] Bork (n 5) 110.

[21] ibid 51 (giving his preferred definition of competition as 'any state of affairs in which consumer welfare cannot be increased by moving to an alternate state of affairs through judicial decree').

[22] As Werden (n 6) 718–23 explains, this interpretation is also consistent with Bork's earlier writings.

[23] Some arguments are deliberately simplified here. Section 3 addresses them more thoroughly.

[24] See, inter alia, Massimo Motta, *Competition Policy: Theory and Practice* (CUP 2004) 22; Joseph Farrell and Michael Katz, 'The Economics of Welfare Standards in Antitrust' [2006] Competition Policy International Journal 33.

[25] Louis Kaplow, 'On the Choice of Welfare Standard in Competition Law' in Daniel Zimmer (ed), *The Goals of Competition Law* (Edward Elgar 2012) 3–26; Richard Posner, *Antitrust Law* (2nd edn, University of Chicago Press 2001) 9–32.

[26] Richard Posner, *The Economics of Justice* (Harvard UP 1981) 88–115; Charles Rule and David Meyer, 'An Antitrust Enforcement Policy to Maximize the Economic Wealth of All Consumers' [1988] Antitrust Bulletin 677.

[27] Thomas Nachbar, 'The Antitrust Constitution' [2013] Iowa Law Review 57, 64 (suggesting that one of the major benefits of a total surplus standard lies in the alleged commensurability of economic effects).

levers.[28] Any other approach, so the argument goes, would not only entail significant 'welfare' sacrifices,[29] but would likewise be impracticable,[30] generate considerable costs, and ultimately compromise legal certainty.[31] In a nutshell, antitrust
ought to be 'completely technocratic'[32] and rely on static partial equilibrium models
to target only those practices for which there are no redeeming efficiencies.[33]

2.2.2 (*Strong*) consumer surplus

A somewhat related variation of the consumer welfare paradigm is consumer surplus. This one seems to have cemented its place as the dominant proxy for consumer
welfare in antitrust discourse.[34] Colloquially translated as the 'direct and explicit economic benefits received by the consumers of a particular product as measured by its
price and quality',[35] consumer surplus can be grounded in neoclassical price theory.[36]
For, following price theoretic models, both consumer surplus and total surplus will be
equally maximized in the competitive equilibrium.

Under this approach, antitrust focuses primarily on consumers by relying on
static models to target market power exertions that are likely to increase consumer prices or reduce output in a relevant market.[37] Here is where the earlier-
mentioned gripe over short-termism and price-centricity kicks in. Obviously, it
reveals little on why the consumer welfare paradigm might be normatively defective; nor does it explain why (platform) providers warrant antitrust protection. Besides, a stronger version of the consumer surplus aim, which (supposedly)
moves beyond price and output effects to include things like choice, variety, and
innovation, exists anyway.[38]

[28] Timothy Brennan, 'Should Antitrust Go Beyond "Antitrust"?' [2018] Antitrust Bulletin 49, 54–64.
[29] Louis Kaplow and Steven Shavell, 'Fairness versus Welfare' [2001] Harvard Law Review 961, 971;
D Daniel Sokol, 'Tensions between Antitrust and Industrial Policy' [2015] George Mason Law Review
1247, 1249.
[30] Renato Nazzini, *The Foundations of European Union Competition Law: The Objective and Principles
of Article 102* (OUP 2011) 15–47.
[31] Roger Blair and D Daniel Sokol, 'Welfare Standards in U.S. and E.U. Antitrust Enforcement' [2013]
Fordham Law Review 2497, 2505.
[32] Sokol (n 29) 1265.
[33] Posner (n 25) 23 (positing that Kaldor–Hicks efficiency is probably the only component of social
welfare that antitrust laws can do much to promote).
[34] Werden (n 11) 14.
[35] Joseph Brodley, 'The Economic Goals of Antitrust: Efficiency, Consumer Welfare, and
Technological Progress' [1987] New York University Law Review 1020, 1033.
[36] Roger Van den Bergh, *Comparative Competition Law and Economics* (Edward Elgar 2017) 95–97;
Josef Drexl, 'On the (A)political Character of the Economic Approach to Competition Law' in Drexl,
Kerber and Podszun (n 11) 317.
[37] Van den Bergh (n 36) 95–96; Ben Van Rompuy, *Economic Efficiency: The Sole Concern of Modern
Antitrust Policy? Non-Efficiency Considerations within Article 101 TFEU* (Kluwer Law International
2012) 48.
[38] 'Supposedly', since price has generally been used as a proxy in economic scholarship and antitrust
analysis (Van den Bergh (n 36) 98; Louis Kaplow and Carl Shapiro, 'Antitrust' in A Mitchell Polinsky
and Steven Shavell (eds), *Handbook of Law and Economics*, vol 2 (Elsevier 2007) 1080).

Interestingly, advocates of (*strong*) consumer surplus are not a united group. Some argue these lodestars are about efficiency (or administrative simplicity);[39] others invoke fairness grounds, distributive[40] or corrective.[41] There are even a few who justify their support on political economy considerations.[42]

2.2.3 Consumer choice/sovereignty

The final consumer welfare offshoot is framed in terms of 'consumer choice'. Proponents describe it as 'the state of affairs where the consumer has the power to define his or her own wants and the ability to satisfy these wants at competitive prices'.[43] This approach purports to go beyond the alleged narrowness inherent to neoclassical economic models. How? By bolstering the analysis with the ultimate aim of ensuring an optimal degree of options for consumers.[44] Still, much like its siblings, consumer choice is not to be confused with a ' "social and political values" paradigm ... which [would arguably be] standardless and unduly hostile to business'.[45] In practice, antitrust intervention would thereby be warranted whenever an activity (i) 'unreasonably restricts the totality of price and nonprice choices that would otherwise have been available',[46] or (ii) 'harmfully and significantly limits the range of choices that the free market, absent the restraints being challenged, would have provided'.[47]

---

[39] Phillip Areeda and Herbert Hovenkamp, *Antitrust Law: An Analysis of Antitrust Principles and Their Application* (Supplement 8/2019, rev edn, Wolters Kluwer 1978) [111], [114a]–[114c].

[40] Russell Pittman, 'Consumer Surplus as the Appropriate Standard for Enforcement' [2007] Competition Policy International Journal 205, 207–15; Ahdar (n 17) 344–51.

[41] John Kirkwood and Robert Lande, 'The Chicago School's Foundation Is Flawed: Antitrust Protects Consumers, Not Efficiency' in Robert Pitofsky (ed), *How the Chicago School Overshot the Mark: The Effect of Conservative Economic Analysis on U.S. Antitrust* (OUP 2008) 90–104; John Kirkwood, 'The Fundamental Goal of Antitrust: Protecting Consumers, Not Increasing Efficiency' [2008] Notre Dame Law Review 191, 197–201; Steven Salop, 'Question: What Is the Real and Proper Antitrust Welfare Standard? Answer: The True Consumer Welfare Standard' [2010] Loyola Consumer Law Review 336, 350–51.

[42] It has been suggested that the consumer surplus standard would be politically more palatable (Barbara Baarsma, 'Rewriting European Competition Law from an Economics Perspective' [2011] European Competition Journal 559, 571). Moreover, some economists who express their normative preference for total surplus suggest using a consumer surplus approach because the latter may, in practice, be more successful at achieving the real desired end (see references mentioned in Section 3.3.1.4, later in this chapter).

[43] Robert Lande, 'Consumer Choice as the Ultimate Goal of Antitrust' [2001] University of Pittsburgh Law Review 503. Lande also advances—without distinguishing it from the notion of 'consumer choice'—the concept of 'consumer sovereignty'. The latter is defined as 'the set of societal arrangements that causes that economy to act primarily in response to the aggregate signals of consumer demand, rather than in response to government directives or the preferences of individual businesses' (Neil Averitt and Robert Lande, 'Consumer Sovereignty: A Unified Theory of Antitrust and Consumer Protection Law' [1997] Antitrust Law Journal 713, 715).

[44] Neil Averitt and Robert Lande, 'Using the Consumer Choice Approach to Antitrust Law' [2007] Antitrust Law Journal 175. Though the distinction between consumer choice and *strong* consumer surplus is hard to make out, it seems to lie in the former's willingness to take non-price parameters (like innovation) (even) more seriously.

[45] ibid 177.

[46] ibid 182.

[47] ibid 184.

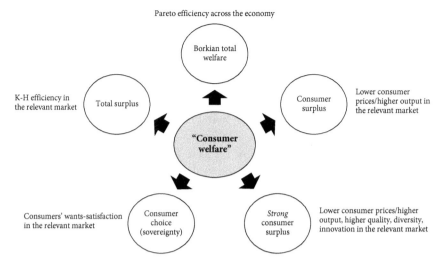

Figure 1.1 Antitrust's 'consumer welfare' paradigm
Source: author's own creation.

According to its proponents,[48] consumer choice must be the objective 'because it asks the right question':[49] 'what do consumers want from the market?', to which the answer (they say) is not merely competitive prices, but options.

2.3 Summation

In sum and as captured by Figure 1.1, 'consumer welfare' means different things to different people. Nonetheless, most would agree that it *can* accommodate our up-stream worries, albeit *indirectly*: only when harming providers is also inefficient or compromises other consumer interests.

3. Appraising the Normativity of 'Consumer Welfare'

Having clarified what consumer welfare can entail, a more critical look at each of its avatars is in order. Remember, though, that the ambition is not to conclusively demonstrate that the consumer welfare paradigm *is* normatively defective. It is ra-ther to show that there is ammunition for such an argument and to explain how

---

[48] Beyond Averitt and Lande, these would include, among others, Paul Nihoul, ' "Freedom of Choice": The Emergence of a Powerful Concept in European Competition Law' [2012] Concurrences 55.
[49] Averitt and Lande (n 44) 178.

our platform provider anxieties may contribute to it. That being recalled, total welfare is up first.

3.1 Total Welfare

From the outset, the question of whether total welfare (i.e. Paretian efficiency) ought to guide antitrust appears to be a moot one so it will not be dwelled on for very long. Pushed to its logical conclusion, antitrust steered by this approach would implode because there will seldom be a Pareto-efficient business practice (i.e. one that does not adversely affect the welfare of anyone).[50] Meta/Facebook, for instance, could implement changes to the Facebook newsfeed that might objectively benefit every stakeholder involved—say advertisers, publishers, and consumers—except Twitter, whose attractiveness might suffer. Yet, assuming Meta/Facebook is a monopolist, intervention might be warranted, although by most accounts, this is competition *at its best*. And if it is antitrust enforcement itself which should be Pareto-efficient, then the goal is just synonymous with radical laissez-faire.

Incidentally, proper *welfare* analysis, we just saw, requires the general equilibrium framework. As Bork himself recognized at the time—another reason why many misinterpret his *normative* claim—economists still struggle to model welfare effects of business practices across (all) markets.[51] Notwithstanding further objections to Pareto efficiency,[52] advocating any standard of economic welfare as an antitrust objective therefore seems rather problematic: the policy cannot aim to maximize (or protect) welfare because its current methodology simply cannot account for welfare analysis.[53]

3.2 Total Surplus

Unlike (general equilibrium) total welfare, (partial equilibrium) total surplus (or Kaldor–Hicks efficiency) is consistent with the tools of contemporary antitrust. What's more, this avatar can, indirectly, accommodate the claims of those worried about the plight of platform providers. For example, a change in the way Uber's

---

[50] Lawrence Sullivan, 'Trade Regulation, Cases and Materials' [1974] Columbia Law Review 1214, 1219–20. See also Richard Posner, *Economic Analysis of Law* (9th edn, Wolter Kluwer Law & Business 2014) 14–15.

[51] Bork (n 5) 115; Peter Hammer, 'Antitrust Beyond Competition: Market Failures, Total Welfare, and the Challenge of Intramarket Second-Best Tradeoffs' [2000] Michigan Law Review 849, 853–59.

[52] Such as those voiced by liberal rights proponents like Amartya Sen, 'The Impossibility of a Paretian Liberal' [1970] Journal of Political Economy 152. See also the discussion on total surplus in Section 3.2.

[53] Orbach (n 6) 160 ('using goals [such as consumer welfare] that suggest that antitrust somehow engages in direct welfare optimization is confusing and misleading'); Sullivan (n 50) 1219–22 ('allocative efficiency is useless as a guide to antitrust policy').

algorithm matches drivers and consumers might reduce drivers' surplus more than it increases the wealth of consumers (in the relevant market). This aggregate efficiency narrative, however, diverts the attention from the fact that efficiency is a normative construction. Its foundation is a utilitarian—thus consequentialist (or outcome-based)—ethical defence of a particular understanding of economic competition.[54] Here, there are, at a minimum, three potential weaknesses to be examined.[55]

The first pertains to the vexed matter of redistribution (Section 3.2.1). The second relates to a problematic conflation of concepts (Section 3.2.2). The third—shared by all consumer welfare avatars—plainly rejects a consequentialist outlook of competition. Following this last objection, competition is valuable *as such*, which entails *direct* consideration for the plight of platform providers (instead of indirect attention under any understanding of consumer welfare). Since it is effectively an argument for the alternative paradigm, the last demurral is bracketed until the next chapter.

3.2.1 Wealth redistribution

The total welfare objective (i.e. Pareto efficiency) would not tolerate any balancing of positive and negative impacts of firm behaviour. The total surplus lodestar, by contrast, is agnostic to redistributive effects between economic agents.[56] This could be problematic. Whereas many may deem the ethical premise of Pareto efficiency broadly acceptable—recall, nobody should lose—one cannot say the same for the Kaldor–Hicks variation. My guess is few democratic majorities would countenance, even implicitly, a competition policy which allows for *hypothetically* compensated[57] reductions in their wealth merely because the gains of others outweigh their losses.[58] The mere fact that societal distaste for monopolistic behaviour has

---

[54] Utilitarianism falls in the broader category of teleological ethics known as *consequentialism*, which expresses the normative view that the rightness of actions must be evaluated exclusively in light of their consequences. This contrasts with *deontology*, which says that some choices cannot be justified by their effects (Walter Sinnott-Armstrong, 'Consequentialism' in Edward Zalta (ed), *The Stanford Encyclopedia of Philosophy* (rev edn, Stanford University 2021) 8 <https://goo.gl/sp4sbP> accessed 19 August 2022). As observed by Wight, the normative dimension of efficiency is something microeconomic textbooks rarely discuss openly ((n 14) 15ff).

[55] For a list of other objections, see Ioannis Lianos, 'Some Reflections on the Question of the Goals of EU Competition Law' in Ioannis Lianos and Damien Geradin (eds), *Handbook on European Competition Law: Substantive Aspects* (Edward Elgar 2013) 9–16.

[56] Though some have argued that Kaldor–Hicks efficiency is actually biased in favour of those with income and market power (eg Cento Veljanovski, 'Wealth Maximization, Law and Ethics—On the Limits of Economic Efficiency' [1981] International Review of Law & Economics 5, 12).

[57] Even the most illustrious welfare economists recognize that compensation rarely occurs in practice (see John Hicks, 'The Foundations of Welfare Economics' [1939] Economic Journal 696).

[58] Similarly, see Daniel Zimmer, 'Consumer Welfare, Economic Freedom and the Moral Quality of Competition Law—Comments on Gregory Werden and Victor Vanberg' in Drexl, Kerber and Podszun (n 11) 77; Drexl (n 36) 316. cf Posner (n 26) 96–98 (arguing that Kaldor–Hicks efficiency—which he initially distinguished from wealth maximization before acknowledging their synonymy—is ethically defendable because uncompensated losers assumedly consent *implicitly* to such an outcome by entering the market).

been reflected in constitutional documents and criminalized in certain parts of the world, suggests that antitrust never has been completely oblivious to social justice and that something more than (Kaldor–Hicks) efficiency must be at work.[59]

But, naturally, if the social justice concern at hand is fairness in the distribution of wealth, one has to still coherently explain why antitrust enforcement in its pursuit would be *normatively* justified. Both the consensus view—that other policy levers with better discriminating capacities (like taxation and subsidy schemes) are better equipped for the job[60]—and its counterpoint—that such a position 'can only conceal, firstly, that markets always have an effect on distribution; secondly, that the distributive effects depend on the initial distribution of wealth in society ... and, thirdly, that the efficiency criterion cannot offer a conclusive measurement for social value of market results in a given situation'[61]—somewhat skirt this foundational question.

In other words, questioning the normativity of Kaldor–Hicks efficiency-minded antitrust on the informed intuition that societies would likely not condone its possibly unfair distributive effects, amounts to offering a half-baked argument, one which doesn't cut the mustard even when properly proofed, as we will see after Kaldor–Hicks efficiency's second, more potent, potential weakness is entertained.

3.2.2 Welfare as 'monetary surplus'

The second possible flaw of the Kaldor–Hicks efficiency lodestar is its association with the idea of 'welfare', understood in its technocratic, rather than demotic sense.[62] As alluded to in Section 2, mainstream economists have a particular conception of the notion. While some may criticize its impoverished content, it is the underlying explanation that is somewhat debatable. Let me briefly unpack it.

Welfare, as laypeople perceive it, can probably be synonymized with 'well-being'.[63] Welfare as well-being, regrettably, is amorphous, which is a problem for policymaking purposes. At this point, the neoclassical economist borrows from the utilitarian philosopher the concept of 'utility', a term generally used as a proxy for satisfaction and happiness.[64] For those adamant on associating welfare with other dimensions, the total surplus lodestar is perhaps already crippled beyond repair.[65] Let us nevertheless dig deeper since mainstream economists take another

---

[59] See, similarly, Adi Ayal, *Fairness in Antitrust: Protecting the Strong From the Weak* (Hart 2016) 99.

[60] Kaplow (n 25) 8–16; Farrell and Katz (n 24) 11–12; Nazzini (n 30). See also Alan Devlin and Bruno Peixoto, 'Reformulating Antitrust Rules to Safeguard Societal Wealth' [2008] Stanford Journal of Law, Business & Finance 225, 272–78 (supporting redistribution through private mechanisms (eg profit-sharing plans and stock markets) rather than public ones).

[61] Drexl (n 36) 315.

[62] What follows also applies to Pareto efficiency.

[63] Similarly, see Herbert Hovenkamp, 'Legislation, Well-Being, and Public Choice' [1990] University of Chicago Law Review 63, 69.

[64] Just, Hueth and Schmitz (n 7) 3–4.

[65] See eg Stavros Makris, 'Applying Normative Theories in EU Competition Law: Exploring Article 102 TFEU' [2014] University College London Journal of Law & Jurisprudence 30, 35.

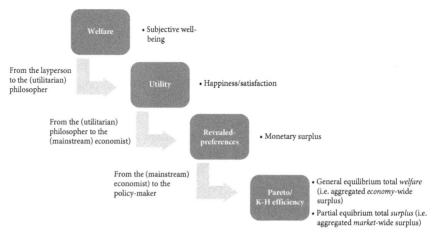

Figure 1.2 Understanding welfare and welfare-oriented policymaking
Source: author's own creation.

step to ground this variation of the consumer welfare paradigm. More specifically, they further reduce the idea of welfare by equating utility with a rational person's expressed preferences. Why? For scientific reasons. Unlike happiness and satisfaction, which are subjective, difficult to measure objectively, and probably impossible to compare across individuals, someone's choices can be numerically represented and ordered within a mathematical function enabling such comparisons. Once this second conceptual reduction is achieved, the neoclassical economist is able to advise the antitrust decision-maker. But it is important to note how the advice is formed. Due to methodological limitations, the models used to rationalize competition problems will often be based, or premised, on a conception of competition called 'perfect competition'.[66] As is well known, the only thing perfect about this depiction is that it makes the math stick—how many markets actually fit the description of a polypoly of anonymous, rational, wealth-maximizing price-takers, where there is no uncertainty nor innovation?

To summarize (also in Figure 1.2): for mainstream economists, welfare means utility minus its eudaemonistic content, which is replaced by a revealed-preference metric, usually money (i.e. surplus). This thinned-down conception of welfare is deployed thereafter to model static effects of practices against the Kaldor–Hicks

---

[66] Models either use perfect competition as the baseline or as a premise from which some assumptions are then relaxed to build a setting of 'imperfect' competition to deal with monopoly, duopoly, oligopoly, information asymmetries, product differentiation, etc. See eg Paul Belleflamme and Martin Peitz, *Industrial Organization: Markets and Strategies* (2nd edn, CUP 2015) 41–104. Efforts to upend this approach have used game-theoretic rationales to build imperfect competition endogenously. In these models, perfect competition becomes a degenerate form of competition (see further Nathalie Berta, Ludovic Julien and Fabrice Tricou, 'On Perfect Competition: Definitions, Usages and Foundations' [2012] Papers in Political Economy 7, 13–15).

efficiency benchmark in a controlled context where an unrealistic understanding of competition is used either as the baseline or as a first-step premise. Hence, accepting total surplus-centric antitrust entails endorsing the idea that the policy should be grounded in what can only be described as a constrained utilitarian defence of a peculiar vision of competition;[67] it means antitrust aimed at protecting wealth using mathematically precise tools in more or less realistic settings.

To be sure, some may have no problems with this. However, my point is that here is a potential normative shortcoming which needs to be (re)discussed, not ignored because the goal's apparent scientificity is assumed to be a marker of normative superiority.

3.3 (*Strong*) Consumer Surplus

Advertising antitrust as a means to serve the consumer's interest in low(er) prices and high(er) output (quality, diversity, and/or innovation) is one way of mustering popular support for the policy. Yet, referring to a slogan without giving deeper thought to its significance can distract from foundational matters. Consumer welfare, taken to mean total welfare or total surplus, are cases in point. The same is true for the consumer surplus goal.[68] Here, two broad sets of issues arise. The first relates to normative foundations, as such (Section 3.3.1); the second pertains to the question of whose surplus 'consumer surplus' is really at stake, and the ensuing normative implications (Section 3.3.2).

3.3.1 Theoretical foundations
As Section 2 explained, several distinct fulcrums seem to be at work, namely efficiency, justice to consumers, and political economy considerations. Most critical appraisals fail to fully appreciate this eclecticism. What follows offers a succinct corrective.

3.3.1.1 *Efficiency*
The efficiency rationale is the most prominently advanced justification. It has two possible weaknesses. The first is rather paradoxical since consumer surplus is advertised as 'purely economic'. Economists (we noted earlier) are primarily interested in *social* welfare with redistribution being 'treated as a wash'.[69] Consumer surplus, as a policy goal, therefore has no basis in modern welfare economics precisely because it arbitrarily discriminates against producers.[70] To return to our

---

[67] Veljanovski (n 56) 5, 8.
[68] The following equally applies to *strong* consumer surplus.
[69] Oliver Williamson, 'Economies as an Antitrust Defense Revisited' [1977] University of Pennsylvania Law Review 699, 711.
[70] Van den Bergh (n 36) 97; Marc Duhamel and Peter Townley, 'An Effective and Enforceable Alternative to the Consumer Surplus Standard' [2003] World Competition 3, 18–19.

Uber example: under such a competition policy, drivers could (theoretically) be inefficiently driven into poverty insofar as their squeezed surplus is shared with consumers, say, through low hire prices.

Why, then, is it both endorsed and associated with the efficiency rationale? The answer was alluded to previously: consumer surplus is consistent with neoclassical price theory inasmuch as it provides a useful benchmark for approximately measuring Kaldor–Hicks efficiency. More prosaically, '[t]he consumer is not protected on her or his own behalf but only from a methodological standpoint'.[71] Many of its proponents thus only tolerate this offshoot of the consumer welfare paradigm on administrative simplicity grounds and on the assumption that total surplus and consumer surplus usually move in tandem in practice,[72] rather than for its normative superiority.[73]

Does the justification convince? Either it brings us back to the welfare-as-efficiency problem mentioned previously; or it reveals the elephant in the room, which is that 'the consumer [surplus] goal is intrinsically intertwined with wealth distribution'[74] and is not as objective as 'purists' would have us believe.[75] Accordingly, justice to consumers is another fulcrum in need of examination.

3.3.1.2 Distributive justice

The leading philosophical claim underlying the consumer surplus objective appears to be based on the belief that consumers, assumed to form a distinct class of persons, deserve a minimum level of economic welfare. This entitlement would itself follow from a moral commitment binding a society.[76] The concern thereby is one of distributive justice—'dealing with deserved endowments and relative position in society'[77]—with its purveyors presumably appealing to political philosopher John Rawls for a theory.[78]

Rawls will be central to our analysis in Part II. His ideas enable us to rationalize certain upstream platform power plays as competition problems, albeit under the *competitive process* paradigm. For the moment, just note that, for Rawls, a society's fairness principles only track fairness when they follow from impartial

---

[71] Drexl (n 36) 317.

[72] Motta (n 24); Blair and Sokol (n 31) 2499. See also Pinar Akman, *The Concept of Abuse in EU Competition Law: Law and Economic Approaches* (Hart 2015) 32–34 (discussing five situations in which the application of the two standards would yield different conclusions).

[73] Herbert Hovenkamp, 'Progressive Antitrust' [2018] University of Illinois Law Review 71, 124.

[74] Drexl (n 36) 320.

[75] i.e. economic efficiency proponents. For the analogy to 'purity', see Ariel Ezrachi, 'Sponge' [2017] Journal of Antitrust Enforcement 49, 49–50.

[76] See eg Pittman (n 40) 207–15; Ahdar (n 17) 344–51.

[77] Ayal (n 59) 109.

[78] The assumption is based on the observation that '[w]hile many theories of justice could be employed to defend redistribution as an aim, John Rawls' theory is the most widespread and accepted by the legal academy' (Geoffrey Rapp, 'Monopoly's Hidden Justice: How Lax Antitrust Enforcement May Stimulate Charitable Giving and Overcome the Political Economy Barriers to Redistributive Taxation' [2001] University of Missouri-Kansas City Law Review 303, 308).

deliberations.[79] Fortunately, he explained how decision-makers might achieve this. In a nutshell: use a thought experiment and imagine what principles society would select if placed in a so-called original position where everyone ignores how contingent inequalities (in things like wealth or abilities) are to be distributed in the real world.[80]

So, for argument's sake, assume that liberal societies behind Rawls's hypothetical veil of ignorance would choose to direct antitrust towards consumer surplus. The problem with such a claim is that it is normatively 'both too broad and too narrow'.[81]

It *overshoots* because it fails to distinguish between consumers (most notably, the rich and the poor), as well as between products (luxurious and staple ones, in particular), with the morally questionable fallout that antitrust would regularly be servicing the rich at the expense of the poor[82]—like when the latter's taxes are used to fund probes against big luxury shopping platforms to quell the anger of their (presumably) wealthy clients.[83]

Concurrently, the claim *undershoots* since its application could lead to outcomes inconsistent with what any plausible theory of social justice would require. Cloud workers, for instance, ought to be prosecuted if they somehow managed to coalesce against powerful platforms like Amazon Mechanical Turk and Upwork in a conspiracy bent on raising their earnings, which typically do not exceed US$6/hour.[84]

3.3.1.3 Corrective justice

Remaining within the realm of rights, a third alternative foundation can be couched in terms of *corrective* justice. The reason is that some authors have claimed (US) antitrust is, and must be, about protecting consumers from the unfair 'theft' of their surplus.[85] To wit, consumers enjoy a *right*—not just an interest—to surplus.[86]

---

[79] John Rawls, *A Theory of Justice* (Harvard UP 1971).

[80] ibid 12, 136–38.

[81] Ayal (n 59) 109–11.

[82] The distributive impact of antitrust enforcement is a tricky empirical question, one I have explored with colleagues elsewhere. Looking at interventions in the UK between 2006 and 2020—which, by most (or at least many) accounts, has been devoted to some understanding of consumer welfare—we find that the poorest households actually have benefited proportionately more than their wealthiest counterparts. However, the type of enforcement tool, which body is enforcing antitrust, and the sectors under scrutiny, all impact relative household savings (see Christopher Decker and others, 'Competition Law Enforcement and Household Inequality in the United Kingdom' [2022] Journal of Competition Law & Economics 905).

[83] In 2022, the Korea Fair Trade Commission did just that, reacting to a boom in consumer complaints against the likes of Mustit, Trenbe, and Balaan (see 'Major Luxury Shopping Platforms Scrutinized by South Korean Regulator for Possible Unfair Terms' *mlex* (31 August 2022) <https://content.mlex.com/#/content/1405322> accessed 18 November 2022).

[84] Lars Hornuf and Daniel Vrankar, 'Hourly Wages in Crowdworking: A Meta-Analysis' [2022] Business & Information Systems Engineering 553.

[85] See (n 41).

[86] Ayal (n 59) 90ff.

Is the proposition convincing? Adi Ayal, a theorist who has given the question rigorous intellection, says it isn't. And his exposition is, at minimum, compelling (not to say convincing).[87] As he writes, to craft the corrective justice claim for consumer surplus, one has to first make the heroic assumption that the consumer's right to surplus originates from the competitive process itself, mediated by antitrust. That is, assume that 'antitrust … involves giving a property right in the competitive outcome'.[88] Were this premise accepted, its underwriters would still have to explain why a just—say, Rawlsian—society would have condoned it to begin with.[89] As our inquiry just a few paragraphs above suggests, such an endeavour is not for the faint-hearted.

3.3.1.4 Political economy

A final line of reasoning seeks to justify the consumer surplus goal on political economy considerations. These supporters assume that social welfare is the superior consumer welfare avatar. They nonetheless vouch for an ostensible appeal to consumer surplus because it will, in practice, prove more successful at achieving their preferred end.[90]

What is the reasoning? Well, antitrust decision-makers can be prone to biases due to information asymmetries, whereas firms may self-select their conduct and engage in lobbying tactics. Differently stated, competition agencies are fallible and firms have selfish motivations they can hide when interacting with them. So, if the desired goal is social welfare, decision-makers would be wise to ostensibly commit to the consumer surplus lodestar instead.

There probably are merits to this logic. Disappointingly, the latter adds little to our inquiry on normative desirability; it simply assumes total welfare/surplus and/ or consumer surplus have solid foundations. Furthermore, it is equally dishonest inasmuch as the everyday consumer's interests will usually not be the proximate worry. This bridges neatly to the second potential weakness of the consumer surplus lodestar.

---

[87] ibid 90–101. Mark White, 'On the Justification of Antitrust: A Matter of Rights and Wrongs' [2016] Antitrust Bulletin 323, makes a similar, but less sophisticated argument. Consumers, he writes, have no right to surplus because, as a matter of positive law, firms are free to set prices.

[88] Salop (n 41) 350. As Ayal (n 59) 91–92 explains, the alternative—that producers would have a forced duty to enable consumers to enjoy their surplus—cannot be justified. The only plausible argument is that 'no party has a right to any *specific* price … [b]ut, the prices offered must [be] the result of an external process limiting the discretion of both seller and buyer', i.e. competition, protected only insofar as it delivers consumers with their rightful share of the surplus.

[89] Ayal (n 59) 100.

[90] David Besanko and Daniel Spulber, 'Contested Mergers and Equilibrium Antitrust Policy' [1993] Journal of Law, Economics & Organization 1; Bruce Lyons, 'Could Politicians Be More Right Than Economists? A Theory of Merger Standards' (2003) EUI Working Papers <https://bit.ly/3EBXqcP> accessed 25 November 2022); Damien Neven and Lars-Hendrik Röller, 'Consumer Surplus vs. Welfare Standard in a Political Economy Model of Merger Control' [2005] International Journal of Industrial Organization 829.

3.3.2 The consumer's many faces

Up to this point, whenever the consumer was evoked, reference was being made to the end/final consumer, unless otherwise stated. But what do we make of the idea (widely approved, especially in Europe) whereby the addressee of the consumer surplus goal is in reality (also) the immediate buyer—the *customer*? To me, endorsing it just makes 'consumer welfare's' beguiling nature glaring and its normativity that much more questionable, seeing that customers will routinely (if not typically) be *providers*. Cases involving platforms aptly illustrate the conundrum.

Consider two scenarios, sketched in Figure 1.3, with Amazon as the main protagonist.

In the first, the platform victimizes merchants—say, cushion manufacturers—using its *multi-sided* marketplace infrastructure to ultimately reach end consumers. To keep things simple, suppose further that, in so doing, Amazon harms (i.e. diminishes the surplus of) merchants but unquestionably benefits final consumers without saddling them with any negative trade-offs whatsoever.[91] Here, merchants are in fact customers of the platform (which takes a commission on every completed merchant-to-consumer transaction) although they are effectively (cushion) *producers* from a functional perspective. If one argues that antitrust should intervene because Amazon has harmed consumer welfare (by decreasing 'customer' surplus), then the argument is really pushing, against consensus, for *producer* surplus.

Were the claim coupled with a convincing justification, this would be fine. To my knowledge, it never has been, owing, in all likelihood, to the major hurdles such a venture would have to pass. For one, there is definitely no (Pareto or Kaldor–Hicks) efficiency basis. For another, the corrective justice foundation already flounders when the final consumer is taken as the addressee.[92] Finally, if Rawlsian distributive justice is invoked, one has to keep in mind that its beneficiaries, following Rawls, are meant to be society's least advantaged members.[93] Put differently, it would have to be shown that our merchants—and for coherence's sake, any other category of customers/producers—actually are worse off than final consumers, not merely because of the impugned behaviour but generally since we are debating over antitrust's soul. Developing countries aside,[94] this is unlikely.[95]

---

[91] With this assumption, we obviate the need to make a further value judgement between present-day consumers and those who might be affected in the future.

[92] Ayal (n 59) 118 (arguing that a right to profits endowed to producers is hard to justify).

[93] In Rawls's theory of justice, this is the 'difference principle'. See further, and for reference, Chapter 4, Section 4.2.2.2 of this book. Incidentally, Lianos (n 55) 28, argues that Rawlsian consumer surplus would favour *end consumers*. The International Competition Network (ICN) seems to make a similar argument (ICN, 'Unilateral Conduct Workbook—Chapter 1: The Objectives and Principles of Unilateral Conduct Laws' 11th Annual ICN Conference (April 2012) [16] <https://bit.ly/3u24M4J> accessed 19 November 2022).

[94] Josef Drexl, 'Consumer Welfare and Consumer Harm: Adjusting Competition Law and Policies to the Needs of Developing Jurisdictions' in Michal Gal and others (eds), *The Economic Characteristics of Developing Jurisdictions: Their Implications for Competition Law* (Edward Elgar 2015) 289.

[95] See eg ICN (n 93) [16(i)].

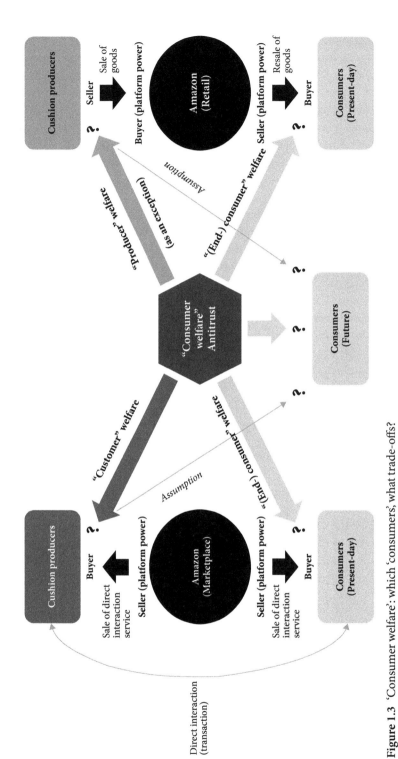

Figure 1.3 'Consumer welfare': which 'consumers', what trade-offs?
Source: author's own creation.

Now, what if the assumption insuring end consumers against long-term harm was relaxed? It could thereafter be claimed that by protecting customers—our cushion providers purchasing Amazon's marketplace services—one is in truth safeguarding the interests of *future* final consumers. But the argument has teeth only if it is true that customer harm usually does somehow trickle down to end consumers, which is a debatable proposition.[96] Otherwise, advertising antitrust enforcement in such cases as a commitment to *strong* consumer surplus is just to bait-and-switch to producer surplus, a lodestar sitting on even shakier foundations than consumer surplus. Besides, hardwiring this claim into antitrust's fabric makes the policy incoherent, as our second scenario reveals.

Here, Amazon is still victimizing the same cushion manufacturers. However, instead of having them buy the platform's multi-sided marketplace services to reach end consumers, the assumption is that they are selling their cushions to Amazon which, in turn, *retails* them to final consumers through its single-sided platform arm. Whereas this situation is more like traditional *buyer* power cases, 'customer' surplus can, *ipso facto*, no longer be invoked as an argument. To stay within a consumer welfare narrative, one must thereby resort to pleading a producer surplus claim, couched as an *exception* to the consumer surplus rule on the empirically debatable grounds that enforcement will ultimately benefit consumers.[97]

In sum, efficiency and fairness are far from bulletproof normative grounds to support (*strong*) consumer surplus variants of the consumer welfare paradigm. Even if one assumes away the highlighted issues, these lodestars make antitrust incoherent and force it to make incommensurable trade-offs, especially in situations involving platforms. The cushion manufacturers from our illustration might have a leg to stand on when their strategy to reach present-day end consumers means that their tormentor, Amazon, is supplying them direct access to such consumers; this makes them protectable 'customers' in the eyes of antitrust decision-makers who genuinely place the interests of future final consumers above those who buy today. Yet, if the same cushion manufacturers chose to deal only with Amazon, their enforcement case against perhaps the same power plays—a whimsical delisting of their wares, for instance—would have to be normatively framed as an exception to the rule. Why? Because they would not be customers and, ergo, could not be viewed as 'consumers' worthy of protection.

---

[96] Pinar Akman, ' "Consumer" versus "Customer": The Devil in the Detail' [2010] Journal of Law and Society 315.

[97] This seems to be the argument made by John Kirkwood, 'Collusion to Control a Powerful Customer: Amazon, E-Books, and Antitrust Policy' [2014] University of Miami Law Review 1, 30ff.

Mind you, these are difficulties that similarly bedevil the last consumer welfare avatar on our list—consumer choice—towards which we now transition to.

3.4 Consumer Choice/Sovereignty

Theoretically, consumer choice is fundamentally distinct from the other consumer welfare offshoots examined above. As articulated by its proponents, it unmistakeably conjures ideas of corrective justice.[98] The rights discourse is summoned anew, this time to lay claim to an optimal degree of choice among products.

Like the (*strong*) consumer surplus variants, expounding a consumer entitlement to optimal choice involves convoluted and ultimately shaky intellectual gymnastics. It requires explaining how the competitive process itself endows consumers with such a *right*.[99] Plus, assuming one could convincingly do so, the entitlement's justification would still need to defeat objections beyond those which, we saw a moment ago, can be levelled against (*strong*) consumer surplus. For aiming antitrust at the defence of consumer choice, as such, would routinely entail sacrificing competition on the altar of increased product variety and/or innovation, detrimental as doing so may be.[100] It demands, for example, that a powerful web browser operator be damned for planning to disable third-party cookies—these are the data records stored on our devices, which enable publishers to track us on the web—as the implementation of such a policy would, according to some enforcers, 'unfairly' 'den[y] … web users substantial choice in terms of whether and how their personal data is used for the purpose of targeting and delivering advertising to them'.[101]

In addition, bringing behavioural economists into the fold could further debilitate the consumer choice paradigm. Given that consumers are prone to biases, heuristics, and imperfect willpower that frequently conduce poor decisions,[102] one might ask why consumer choice per se should be of such a concern.[103]

---

[98] Averitt and Lande (n 44) 187 (n 35) (positing that the consumer choice approach considers price-fixing cartels as 'undesirable in themselves' because '[p]rices fixed at an artificial level *rob consumers* of the competing price options to which they are *entitled*') (emphasis added). The authors clearly deny 'efficiency' any normative relevance for consumer choice, which 'represents nothing less than a new paradigm' (ibid 178).

[99] Much like consumer surplus, the consumers' claim to such a right must be grounded in the competitive process itself since the alternative—a forced duty imposed on suppliers to enable such a state of affairs—cannot seriously be considered. For a more sophisticated argumentation, see Ayal (n 59) 112–16.

[100] Similarly, see Van den Bergh (n 36) 99; Lianos (n 55) 23; Nazzini (n 30) 31.

[101] *Google—Privacy Sandbox Proposals* (Case 50972) CMA Decision 11 February 2022, [3.81]. Note that the CMA also expressed other concerns unrelated to consumer choice.

[102] Maurice Stucke, 'Behavioral Economists at the Gate: Antitrust in the Twenty-First Century' [2007] Loyola University Chicago Law Journal 513, 518–36 (summarizing the contribution of behavioural economics).

[103] Nicolas Petit, 'Intel, Leveraging Rebates and the Goals of Article 102 TFEU' [2015] European Competition Journal 26, 64–65.

Finally, if this lodestar is not (only) about end consumers,[104] it certainly runs into the same problems exposed earlier in the context of (*strong*) consumer surplus.

4. Concluding Reflections

Consumer welfare has been the dominant intellectual paradigm behind contemporary competition policy. Its emergence and subsequent crystallization in the legal lexicon mirrored the patterns followed by any scientific paradigm. Like the latter, though, consumer welfare's dominance does not necessarily reflect its normative superiority, something only a 'rational reconstruction of [its] history'[105] uncovers. Having just carried out the exercise, we can definitely attest to this.

Over time, consumer welfare has taken on a life of its own. Supported by consequentialist bedrocks bound to positive outcomes competition is mathematically proven, or morally assumed, to generate—efficiency or various other consumer interests—the paradigm has very little to do with the layperson's perception of welfare, nor is it necessarily concerned with actual consumers.

Of course, the mainstream economist might retort that surplus is the best proxy we currently have and that a supplier's lost surplus is a form of consumer welfare because everyone is eventually a consumer. Some would therefore argue that 'consumer' welfare ought to mean 'counterparty' or 'trading partner' welfare.[106] Even so, such a reply will only ever bite once a convincing normative foundation for this new lodestar is offered and the rhetoric of consumer welfare is abandoned altogether.

That said, when these issues are ignored, the consumer welfare paradigm, correctly construed as either total surplus, (*strong*) end-consumer surplus, or final-consumer choice, *can* be sensitive to upstream worries; decision-makers just have to 'look down' first. This (we will see come the end of Part II) does make the antitrust enterprise more challenging. Nevertheless, the fact is that, over the years, competition agencies and courts occasionally have shielded providers from the exactions of powerful buyers *without* thoroughly investigating whether consumers were harmed. Surely, those suppliers must have been themselves entitled to protection.[107] The question, then, is: how can our decision-makers 'look up' directly and not be rightly chastised for displaying 'uncritical sentimentality'[108] towards suppliers?

[104] Averitt and Lande (n 44) 183, argue that their consumer choice model 'protects all entities engaged in purchase transactions'.
[105] Imre Lakatos, 'History of Science and Its Rational Reconstructions' in John Worrall and Gregory Currie (eds), *The Methodology of Scientific Research Programmes* (CUP 1978) 102.
[106] See eg Jonathan Baker, *The Antitrust Paradigm: Restoring a Competitive Economy* (Harvard UP 2019) 179.
[107] Similarly, see Daniel Zimmer, 'The Basic Goal of Competition Law: To Protect the Opposite Side of the Market' in Zimmer (n 25) 491–93.
[108] Bork (n 5) 54.

Clearly, antitrust cannot be the custodian of concerns alien to *competition*. Calling for provider fairness likewise does run the risk of creating a 'vagrant claim applied to any value that one happens to favour'.[109] Can we nonetheless truly affirm that antitrust is normatively devoid of 'any moral content'?[110] These are difficult but essential matters. Luckily, there is an alternative paradigm to consumer welfare that properly wrestles with them. Let us turn to it.

[109] Areeda and Hovenkamp (n 39) [111d].

[110] Herbert Hovenkamp, *The Antitrust Enterprise: Principle and Execution* (Harvard UP 2005) 47.

2

'Competition, as Such'

Antitrust's Deontological Side

1. Introduction

Throughout the 1990s and early 2000s, everything about digital markets was fast and chaotic. Platform power, let it be recalled, seemed nothing like the market clout which would swiftly prompt our trustbusters into action during the industrial age. Big Tech platforms were akin to Big Pharma minus the complacency: competition *for* the market was similarly intense but the Schumpeterian gales of creative destruction appeared to be never-ending. So, when Google, Amazon, Facebook, and, later, Uber or Airbnb took off, many expected them to rapidly reach orbit before probably just as quickly flaming out into oblivion.

This story has not (yet) unfolded. As noted in the introductory chapter, digital markets today are not merely concentrated; they are also marshalled by incumbents that did not collapse after hitting the fateful five-year obsolescence mark. Furthermore, evidence of their (upstream) mischiefs has been piling up for over a decade.

For critics, blameworthy targets are obvious: consumer welfare-centric antitrust (especially in the USA) alongside symmetrically oriented merger control.[1] Still, some antitrust scholars argue that the critique is misplaced. Consumer welfare, they say, merely needs a practical tweak, particularly when the problems are upstream. Instead of focusing on prices (i.e. consumer surplus), we ought to put more emphasis on quality and innovation (i.e. *strong* consumer surplus or consumer sovereignty), if necessary by substituting consumers with 'customers/counterparties' for policy-targeting purposes.[2] This naturally implies either turning antitrust into a potentially groundless producerist policy (as was explained in Chapter 1) or (as we shall see in Chapter 6) asking decision-makers to achieve what they cannot reasonably do for the moment.

There is, however, another, more radical, approach: shifting paradigms. And if antitrust has to pertain to competition and cannot be guided primarily by supplier

---

[1] See, notably, Tim Wu, *The Curse of Bigness: Antitrust in the New Gilded Age* (Columbia Global Reports 2018) ch 7.
[2] See eg Jonathan Baker, *The Antitrust Paradigm: Restoring a Competitive Economy* (Harvard UP 2019) ch 9.

Antitrust and Upstream Platform Power Plays. A. K. von Moltke, Oxford University Press. © A. K. von Moltke 2023.
DOI: 10.1093/oso/9780192873057.003.0003

interests, the alternative seems pretty clear: redirect the policy towards the 'protection of competition'.

Neo-Brandeisians have championed the move in the USA. For this lodestar apparently has two advantages: its focus 'on [the] protection of a *process*, as opposed to the maximization of a *value*',[3] and its 'better legal pedigree'.[4]

What is missing, though, as has always been, are clear and coherent normative foundations.[5] Advocating a paradigm shift by relying—like neo-Brandeiseans do[6]—on an interpretative theory of either (or both) legislative intent and/or early jurisprudence only works if those decision-makers had themselves articulated a convincing normative account. Yet, legal historians tell us that US antitrust lawmakers and judges of the late-nineteenth and early-twentieth centuries were guided by the axiomatic idea of 'a natural, harmonious, rights-based economic order simultaneously tending to maximise opportunity, efficiency, wealth, fairness, and political freedom'.[7] Sadly, we know today that all things supposedly good about competition are not self-evidently 'central, largely consistent, and capable of vigorous implementation through "nondiscretionary" ... decisionmaking'.[8]

Looking to the younger legal order that is the EU for normative underpinnings does not yield a satisfactory answer either. There, a (shaky) consensus has it that German Ordoliberal ideas undergird the judicature's historical endorsement of the competitive process lodestar.[9] But Ordoliberalism—often incorrectly depicted as if it were a monolithic thought current—would probably not condone enforcing antitrust with moral overtones.[10] Plus, a core tenet of its most recognizable spearhead, Walter Eucken, is impossible to reconcile with EU antitrust's legally enshrined tolerance of market dominance.[11]

What this chapter accordingly sets out to offer is a compelling sketch of a normative account of this alternative paradigm. To this end, a two-part discussion is

---

[3] Wu (n 1) concluding chapter.

[4] ibid. See also Marshall Steinbaum and Maurice Stucke 'The Effective Competition Standard: A New Standard for Antitrust' [2019] University of Chicago Law Review 595; Lina Khan, 'Amazon's Antitrust Paradox' [2017] Yale Law Journal 712, 743ff.

[5] See eg John Newman, 'Procompetitive Justifications in Antitrust Law' [2019] Indiana Law Journal 501, 514 ('the actual content of the competitive-process approach remains mercurial, a cipher. The scholarly arguments in favor of it never seem to identify what, exactly, constitutes the "competitive process"').

[6] See n 4.

[7] James May, 'Antitrust in the Formative Era: Political and Economic Theory in Constitutional and Antitrust Analysis, 1880–1918' [1989] Ohio State Law Journal 257, 394.

[8] ibid 299.

[9] For a good discussion, see Peter Behrens, 'The Ordoliberal Concept of "Abuse" of a Dominant Position and Its Impact on Article 102 TFEU' in Fabiana Di Porto and Rupprecht Podszun (eds), *Abusive Practices in Competition Law* (Edward Elgar 2018) 5–25.

[10] ibid 24–25.

[11] As Irene Oswalt-Eucken notes, her father Walter would have pilloried article 102 Treaty on the Functioning of the European Union (TFEU) (consolidated version) [2016] OJ C202/47. For he believed that 'it is not the abuse of economic power which should be prevented but economic power itself' (Irene Oswalt-Eucken, 'Freedom and Economic Power: Neglected Aspects of Walter Eucken's Work' [1994] Journal of Economic Studies 38, 41).

proposed. The first (re)clarifies what is at stake (Section 2). For contrary to what (at least some) paradigm-shifters (still) seem to believe, protecting the competitive process does mean safeguarding a value: competition, *as such*.[12] The second part then fully engages with this *deontic* assertion,[13] expounding why we can appeal to ideals of democracy, freedom, and fairness to rationalize upstream platform power plays as potential antitrust-relevant problems (Section 3). What becomes apparent is that, under such an approach, the policy does take a 'polycentric'[14] turn because the voice of every affected market stakeholder is equally accounted for. On the other hand, contrary to what is regularly suggested, it does not, nor can it, morph into a sword bent on dispersing, let alone eradicating, economic power per se, or on correcting unwanted outcomes.

2. Competition as a Value

Contemporary antitrust has been guided by a paradigm—consumer welfare—which ostensibly prioritizes efficiency or furtively supports some idea of justice to the exclusive benefit of consumers or customers.[15] Either way, competition is treated as a proxy for an outcome deemed desirable, come what may. Directing the policy towards the protection of the competitive process, in contrast, partly distances it from such a purely consequentialist outlook. Here, competition is deemed, in itself, worthy of consideration, regardless of its actual consequences which may be unpalatable.[16] Although 'toxic' at times,[17] this complex, multidimensional, phenomenon 'is something very human';[18] it has become an 'institutionalized imaginary'[19] and will remain an 'inescapable fate'.[20] The argument for valuing competition, as such, accordingly has to lie in two things: its inherent connection

---

[12] cf Wu (n 1) concluding chapter ('The "protection of competition" test is focused on protection of a *process*, as opposed to the maximization of a *value*').

[13] Remember, deontology is a category of teleological ethics that says that some choices cannot be justified by their effects.

[14] Ioannis Lianos, 'Polycentric Competition Law' [2018] CLP 161.

[15] Recall Chapter 1 in this volume.

[16] Similarly, see Oles Andriychuk, 'Rediscovering the Spirit of Competition: On the Normative Value of the Competitive Process' [2010] European Competition Journal 575, 581–83.

[17] Maurice Stucke and Ariel Ezrachi, *Competition Overdose: How Free Market Mythology Transformed Us from Citizen Kings to Market Servants* (HarperCollins 2020) chs 1–4.

[18] Margrethe Vestager, 'EVP Vestager Remarks at the Schwarzkopf Foundation Virtual Event: "Competition: the Rules of the Game"' (13 October 2022) <https://bit.ly/3tOeyXW> accessed 21 November 2022.

[19] Tobias Werron, 'Why Do We Believe in Competition? A Historical–Sociological View of Competition as an Institutionalized Modern Imaginary' [2015] Journal of Social Theory 186, 197. Similarly, see Oles Andriychuk, 'Thinking Inside the Box: Why Competition as a Process is a Sui Generis Right—A Methodological Observation' in Daniel Zimmer (ed), *The Goals of Competition Law* (Edward Elgar 2012) 104–06.

[20] Viktor Vanberg, 'Consumer Welfare, Total Welfare and Economic Freedom—On the Normative Foundations of Competition Policy' in Josef Drexl, Wolfgang Kerber and Rupprecht Podszun (eds), *Competition Policy and the Economic Approach* (Edward Elgar 2011) 50.

with a society's culture[21] and the belief that antitrust cannot be normatively sundered from the latter.

In this regard, we need to appreciate that competition does not arise out of thin air; it always requires an institutional background to support its birth and development.[22] The existence of economic competition, as a lynchpin of a liberal market economy, is hence the product of some form of political deliberation, ultimately reflecting a collective faith in the benefits of the process and a commitment to its virtues. This pledge is, first, anchored by experience and economic knowledge. Both suggest that a well-functioning competitive system can be expected to promote a set of instrumentally desirable results, such as economic efficiency and the consumer's other interests in the market. Undistorted and unrestricted competition will indeed (usually) spur firms to offer customers the best possible deals to win their favours and to displace rivals.[23]

Evidently, these are all merely potential outcomes of a process which, when working properly, is by definition *uncertain*, as antitrust decision-makers have long emphasized.[24] Committing to the competitive process paradigm thus means taking a leap of faith. But there is more to it than a promise of appealing consequences.

Economic competition, in most liberal democracies, is probably not just a mere by-product of politics. Instead, it is likely framed by rules of the game enshrined in a polity's economic constitution, which is actively and deliberately designed to reflect idiosyncratic beliefs a society holds regarding how market interactions should be structured.[25] To put things differently, the competitive system in such polities is 'ordered'. It therefore does not develop 'spontaneously' (i.e. through human action but not design) within a barebones institutional framework (initially limited to protecting life and property, and to enforcing

---

[21] By culture, I mean the 'set of beliefs, values, and preferences, capable of affecting behaviour, that are socially (not genetically) transmitted and that are shared by some subset of society' (Joel Mokyr, *A Culture of Growth: The Origins of the Modern Economy* (Princeton UP 2016) 8).

[22] See, similarly, Christoph Lütge, *The Ethics of Competition: How a Competitive Society Is Good for All* (Edward Elgar 2019) chs 6–7.

[23] See, similarly, Gregory Werden, 'Consumer Welfare and Competition Policy' in Drexl, Kerber and Podszun (n 20) 36. See also Luc Peeperkorn, 'Conditional Pricing: Why the General Court Is Wrong in *Intel* and What the Court of Justice Can Do to Rebalance the Assessment of Rebates' [2015] Concurrences 43, 48. Note, though, that the nexus between competition and innovation remains unclear (see, recently, Richard Gilbert, *Innovation Matters: Competition Policy for the High-Technology Economy* (MIT Press 2020) chs 3–4, 6).

[24] See eg Case C-8/08 *T-Mobile* ECLI:EU:C:2009:343 [2009] ECR I-4529, [35] (conduct is unlawful 'if it reduces or removes the degree of uncertainty as to the operation of the market in question with the result that competition between undertakings is restricted'); *Great Atlantic & Pacific Tea Co vs FTC* 440 US 69, 80, 83 (1979) ('in a competitive market, uncertainty among sellers will cause them to compete').

[25] Contrary to what may be assumed, this is not an exclusively Ordoliberal idea. In economics, it is central to many discussions in the wider institutional movement (see the various contributions in Agnès Labrousse and Jean-Daniel Weisz (eds), *Institutional Economics in France and Germany: German Ordoliberalism versus the French Regulation School* (Springer 2001); David Gerber, 'Constitutionalizing the Economy: German Neo-Liberalism, Competition Law and the "New" Europe' [1994] American Journal of Comparative Law 25, 44–45, and the references listed there in fn 88 (emphasis added).

the laws of contract and tort) that evolves without a specific goal.[26] In the EU and USA, for instance, apex courts seem to have endorsed this assertion by confirming the constitutional nature of the antitrust laws as key fulcrums of the open market economies the people(s) they respectively serve aim to nurture by means of a legal order.[27]

Ordered economic competition is actually analogical to democracy but in the economic realm. For competition requires that *all* market actors be equally free to exercise their economic rights—to be considered as equal members of a market society—unimpeded by illegitimate private restrictions.[28] In so doing, the competitive process is linked to (one idea of) freedom. Competition's democratic essence is likewise tied to (a specific understanding of) fairness because, like political democracy, it cannot develop without the implementation of (some vision of) a level playing field.[29] By accounting for the ideals of democracy, freedom, and fairness, antitrust guided by the competitive process imperative hence recognizes and commits to protecting what is expunged under the consumer welfare paradigm, to wit: the ' "liberal spirit" of economic competition'.[30]

Reformulating what has just been written, then: antitrust's competitive process paradigm envisions economic competition as a coordinating device whose existence owes to political societal choices, which in (most) liberal democracies will have been purposely made. Such an ordered process can promote outcomes that contribute to our well-being through increased efficiency and/or the realization of (other) consumer interests. Yet, for the latter to ensue, the rules of the economic game must be devised and enforced to preserve what really makes competition

---

[26] cf FA Hayek, *Law, Legislation and Liberty: A New Statement of the Liberal Principles of Justice and Political Economy* (Routledge 2013) 269.

[27] For the EU, see Cases C-294/83 *Les Verts* ECLI:EU:C:1986:166 [1986] ECR 1339, [23]; and C-52/09 *TeliaSonera* ECLI:EU:C:2011:83 [2011] ECR I-527, [20]–[22] (respectively (1) expounding the EU treaties as the 'basic constitutional charter' of the EU; and (2) observing that the EU treaty rules on antitrust 'function ... precisely to prevent competition from being distorted'). See also Case T-43/02 *Jungbunzlauer* ECLI:EU:T:2006:270 [2006] ECR II-3435, [83] (observing that the system of undistorted competition, which the antitrust rules aim to ensure, 'is necessary for the adoption, within the Community, of an economic policy conducted in accordance with the principle of an open market economy with free competition'). Similarly for the USA, see *United States v Topco Associates Inc* 405 US 596, 610 (1972); *Northern Pacific Railway Co v United States* 356 US 1, 4 (1958); *City of Columbia v Omni Outdoor Advert Inc* 499 US 365, 388 (1991) (respectively describing the antitrust laws as (1) akin to a 'Magna Carta of free enterprise ... as important ... as the Bill of Rights'; (2) 'aimed at preserving free and unfettered competition as the rule of trade'; and (3) 'reflect[ing] a basic national policy favoring free markets over regulated markets'). On the constitutionalization of EU and US antitrust, see, respectively, Wolf Sauter, *Coherence in EU Competition Law* (OUP 2016) 30–33; Paul Brietzke, 'The Constitutionalization of Antitrust: Jefferson, Madison, Hamilton, and Thomas C. Arthur' [1988] Valparaiso University Law Review 275.

[28] See further Section 3.1 of this chapter.

[29] See further Section 3.2.2 of this chapter.

[30] William Davies, *The Limits of Neoliberalism: Authority, Sovereignty and the Logic of Competition* (rev edn, SAGE 2017) 81.

intrinsically valuable—what gives it a democratic character—which is to say, its two *constitutive* values: (one view of) freedom and (a particular vision of) fairness.[31]

Advocating the protection of competition, as such, accordingly means directing antitrust towards these constitutive values on the historically and economically informed assumption that doing so will probably entrain beneficial results, which are not themselves decisive in the first instance.[32] In such a legal order, 'looking up' becomes instinctive for two reasons.

One is that finding restrictions or distortions of competition cannot be made contingent on proof of immediate harm to the consumer's many interests in the market;[33] nor can the determination be negated by a business practice's positive effects, which may nonetheless *justify* its ultimate acceptance.[34]

The second reason is that the competition to be safeguarded under this approach is seen as a *multidimensional* phenomenon; not the purely horizontal game of mainstream economics where players are basically indistinguishable from each other, owing to the postulate known to every antitrust lawyer whereby competition simply cannot exist beyond well-defined markets made up of substitutable products (or labourers). Following the insights of unorthodox economists like J. K. Galbraith[35] and business scholars such as Michael Porter,[36] competition is taken here to *also* have a *vertical* dimension since suppliers and intermediaries are not merely partners under this view;[37] they withal strive to 'take market shares, percentage margins and dollar sales or share-of-category dollar sales from each other'.[38] In other words,

---

[31] I am inspired by Ian Carter, *A Measure of Freedom* (OUP 1999) 54–55 (arguing that freedom is neither intrinsically nor instrumentally valuable but has potential 'constitutive value' because it is a 'constitutive part of some intrinsically valuable complex phenomena').

[32] Similarly, see David Gerber, 'The Future of Article 82: Dissecting the Conflict' in Claus-Dieter Ehlermann and Mel Marquis (eds), *European Competition Law Annual: 2007* (Hart 2008) 42–44.

[33] See Joined cases C-501/06, C-513/06 P, C-515/06 P and C-519/06 P *GlaxoSmithKline Services* ECLI:EU:C:2009:610 [2009] ECR I-9291, [62]–[64] (holding that when antitrust 'aims to protect … competition as such … it is not necessary that final consumers be deprived of the advantages of effective competition in terms of supply or price'). Similarly, see *National Society of Professional Engineers v United States* 435 US 679, 695 (1978) (holding that when antitrust is guided by a 'faith in the value of competition', this 'precludes inquiry into the question of whether competition is good or bad').

[34] See Case C-307/18 *Generics* ECLI:EU:C:2020:52 [2020] electronic Reports of Cases, [104], [165]–[167] (recalling that (1) a 'restriction of competition' does *not* lose this characterization by virtue of procompetitive effects; and that (2) conduct that impairs competition can nonetheless be *justified* owing to its favourable effects). Similarly, see *National Society of Professional Engineers* (n 33) 695 (ruling that US antitrust 'prohibits unreasonable restraints on competition.... It is this restraint that must be *justified*') (emphasis added).

[35] See JK Galbraith, *American Capitalism: The Concept of Countervailing Power* (Hamish Hamilton 1952).

[36] See Michael Porter, 'The Five Competitive Forces That Shape Strategy' [2008] Harvard Business Review 78.

[37] One that has also become a mainstay in marketing theory and practice. See eg Barton Weitz and Qiong Wang, 'Vertical Relationships in Distribution Channels: A Marketing Perspective' [2004] Antitrust Bulletin 859.

[38] Robert Steiner, 'Vertical Competition, Horizontal Competition, and Market Power' [2008] Antitrust Bulletin 251, 254.

they 'compete' over a common objective: capturing more of the available surplus value.[39]

So articulated, consequentialist and deontic ethics undergird the competitive process paradigm. It is consequentialist as it recognizes that distorting or restricting competition can sometimes be defended when necessary to realize a particularly desirable result. Still, the paradigm remains fundamentally deontic insofar as it appreciates that making any outcome the touchstone of antitrust would normatively impoverish the policy. Competition is a means to achieve appealing ends. But, under this vision, it is 'a political and social *desideratum* no less than an economic one'.[40]

The foregoing discussion was meant to clarify an important preliminary about antitrust's 'competitive process' paradigm, i.e. that (1) it is fundamentally supported by a deontic claim, tied to ideas of democracy, freedom, and fairness, following which competition has intrinsic value worthy of legal protection; and that accordingly (2) it requires *direct* consideration for the upstream. Can one articulate this in a compelling theory that accords with well-established antitrust principles?[41] The answer, I argue below, is yes.

3. Expounding the Normativity of 'Competition, as Such'

Efficiency and other consumer interests may have instrumental value insofar as they contribute to a society's well-being. This is what consumer welfare-centric antitrust is all about. Its shaky normative foundations, however, were outlined in Chapter 1.

Societal well-being, of course, is an *ultimate* objective of *any* public policy.[42] Sadly, it probably cannot itself serve as an *immediate* touchstone.[43] So, insofar as provider welfare is equally not an option, the lone, coherent, way forward is to say: rather than fixating on competition's results, let's focus on the preceding process instead.

---

[39] Ioannis Lianos, 'The Vertical/Horizontal Dichotomy in Competition Law: Some Reflections with Regard to Dual Distribution and Private Labels' in Ariel Ezrachi and Ulf Bernitz (eds), *Private Labels, Brands and Competition Policy: The Changing Landscape of Retail Competition* (OUP 2009) 167.

[40] Paul McNulty, 'Economic Theory and the Meaning of Competition' [1968] Quarterly Journal of Economics 639, 639.

[41] An insightful, albeit abstract, attempt is that of Oles Andriychuk, *The Normative Foundations of European Competition Law* (Edward Elgar 2017) ch 4. To my mind, however, his theory flounders somewhat because it makes the concept of freedom carry too much of the argumentative workload and fails to properly articulate the relationship between competition, freedom, and democracy. Competition under the competitive process paradigm, I argue below, cannot merely be a 'feature of liberal democracy', nor must it be identified with freedom, something Andriychuk explicitly warns against but nonetheless seems to fall prey to.

[42] See eg Treaty on European Union (TEU) (consolidated version) [2016] OJ C202/13, art 3; US Const, preamble.

[43] Maurice Stucke, 'Should Competition Policy Promote Happiness?' [2013] Fordham Law Review 2576, 2596–2602 (raising without defeating 'reasonable objections' to such an enterprise).

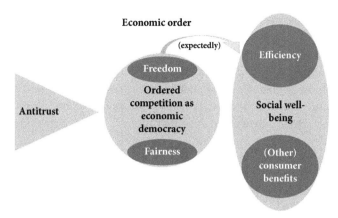

Figure 2.1 Antitrust's 'competitive process' paradigm
Source: author's own creation.

Two related imperatives, claimed in the previous section and tentatively captured in Figure 2.1, follow from the proposition.

The first is to appreciate that, under this alternative vision, effective competition is necessarily dynamic and uncertain. In turn, this means any ambition to predict its outcomes with Euclidean precision has to be set aside.[44] Economic evaluations of 'welfare' effects, therefore, only become appropriate at a latter (justificatory) level of analysis.

The second imperative is to recognize how competition is inherently valuable because it reflects a societal commitment to democracy and thus to freedom and fairness. To be clear: competition in this model is analogous to (one vision of) political democracy grounded in (specific conceptions of) freedom and fairness. The latter two values are constitutive in the sense that without them economic competition would not be able to unfold, nor (incidentally) generate the positive results society expects it to. Antitrust, under this paradigm, accordingly protects the competitive process as economic democracy by targeting business practices that threaten its conditions of operation, while accepting that certain distortions and restrictions might be justified when the benefits are credibly overwhelming.

With this in mind, let us turn to expounding competition as economic democracy and thereby lay the groundwork for our discussion in Parts II and III.

---

[44] See, similarly, Ernst-Joachim Mestmäcker, 'The Development of German and European Competition Law with Special Reference to the EU Commission's Article 82 Guidance of 2008' in Lorenzo Federico Pace (ed), *European Competition Law: The Impact of the Commission's Guidance on Article 102* (Edward Elgar 2011) 47–48.

3.1 Competition as Economic Democracy

In the political order, democracy can very generally be defined as 'a method of group decision making that is characterised by a kind of equality among the participants at an essential stage'.[45] Envisioning its economic equivalent presents an admittedly challenging conundrum for societies that choose to deal with the problem of allocating scarce resources by establishing a market economy. After all, the somewhat reductionist but widespread ideal of political democracy—popular sovereignty, 'enshrined in the doctrine of "one person one vote"'[46]—does seem at odds with the 'one dollar one vote' logic apparently prevailing in the marketplace of products and labour.[47]

Now, a way out of this quandary might be to follow what (some) antitrust paradigm-shifters do (usually unwittingly, indirectly, and/or uncritically) to tie the goal of protecting competition, as such, with democracy, and, resultingly, the idea of defending suppliers.[48] That is, appeal to contemporary republican political theory of the 'neo-Roman' current.[49] Doing this puts us in a bind, though. Not, mind you, because a compelling conceptual connection between democracy and neo-Roman republicanism cannot be made (it can);[50] but because the latter is difficult to reconcile with economic competition, or at least any realistic and normatively plausible rendition of it that *antitrust* could be called upon to safeguard directly.[51] Indeed, neo-Roman republicanism postulates freedom as 'nondomination', i.e. complete emancipation from subordination and dependency[52] or 'the absence of *capacities* for arbitrary interference'.[53] Its leading theorist, however, himself recognizes that this is compatible with a competitive market system only under 'extremely idealistic assumptions',[54] some of which antitrust could never

---

[45] Thomas Christiano, 'Democracy' in Catriona McKinnon, Robert Jubb and Patrick Tomlin (eds), *Issues in Political Theory* (4th edn, OUP 2019) 71.

[46] Robin Hahnel, 'Why the Market Subverts Democracy' [2009] American Behavioral Scientist 1006, 1010.

[47] ibid 1015.

[48] See eg Elias Deutscher and Stavros Makris, 'Exploring the Ordoliberal Paradigm: The Competition–Democracy Nexus' [2016] Competition Law Review 181, fn 54; Lina Khan, 'The Separation of Platforms and Commerce' [2019] Columbia Law Review 973, fn 544.

[49] The other current is dubbed 'neo-Athenian'. A succinct overview of their differences can be found in Charles Larmore, 'Liberal and Republican Conceptions of Freedom' [2003] Critical Review of International Social and Political Philosophy 96, 102–03. For a more comprehensive discussion, see Hidetomi Omori, 'Liberty and the Rule of Law in Two Strands of Republicanism' [2019] Okayama Law Journal 926.

[50] See eg Christian Rostbøll, 'Non-Domination and Democratic Legitimacy' [2015] Critical Review of International Social and Political Philosophy 424.

[51] *En passant*, note that the other, 'neo-Athenian', current is even less amenable to markets and competition (see, most notably, Michael Sandel, *What Money Can't Buy: The Moral Limits of the Market* (Allen Lane 2012)). Some neo-Brandeisians share this particular brand of ideology (see eg K Sabeel Rahman, 'Domination, Democracy, and Constitutional Political Economy in the New Gilded Age: Towards a Fourth Wave of Legal Realism' [2016] Texas Law Review 1329).

[52] Philip Pettit, *Republicanism: A Theory of Freedom and Government* (OUP 1997) 5.

[53] ibid 276 (emphasis added).

[54] Philip Pettit, 'Freedom in the Market' [2006] Politics, Philosophy & Economics 131, 142.

mediate under well-established principles of positive law.[55] And although other neo-Roman republican thinkers would have us convinced of their 'celebratory' attitude towards economic competition,[56] one must realize that what they para-doxically have in mind 'has little claim to be called "competition" at all',[57] since it is 'perfect competition'—yes, the end state of affairs (not a *process*) mentioned in Chapter 1, which rarely arises outside textbooks and whose sole virtue lies in its causal correlation with static (Pareto) efficiency. To be sure, perfect competition does lift the spectre of domination by completely 'purging power from economic relations'.[58] But the perspective of such a 'competitive' market economy where everyone is thereby 'free' to play and end up with no more nor less than their ori-ginal stake, hardly seems like anything to get excited about.[59]

How, then, can one say that competition is economic democracy? The way, to my mind, is to return to equality accounts of political democracy and start from the widely acclaimed theory articulated by political philosopher, Thomas Christiano.[60] Democracy, under this vision, means 'equal consideration of interests'.[61] It refers, more specifically, to a collectively binding procedure for serving a special category of deeply interdependent interests held by citizens—the so-called interests in the 'collective properties' of a society—under conditions whereby 'everyone has an equal right to play a role'.[62]

Of course, drawing an analogy with competition from this highly simplified sketch would border on intellectual dishonesty. For one, political democracy,

---

[55] The antitrust laws, for instance, currently cannot prevent power asymmetries from (in Pettit's words) 'allowing domination within market exchange' (142) (see eg Joined cases T-191/98 and T-212/98 to T-214/98 *Atlantic Container* ECLI:EU:T:2003:245 [2003] ECR II-3275, [939] ('the mere holding of a dominant position is not in itself prohibited by the competition rules laid down in the Treaty'); *Verizon Communications Inc v Law Offices of Curtis V Trinko LLP* 540 US 398, 407 (2004) ('The mere possession of monopoly power, and the concomitant charging of monopoly prices, is not only not un-lawful; it is an important element of the free-market system'). Where there is (a whiff of) neo-republican domination, antitrust defers to labour laws (see eg Case C-413/13 *FNV Kunsten* ECLI:EU:C:2014:2411 [2014] electronic Reports of Cases, [21]–[42] (any provider who is 'entirely dependent on his principal' is not an 'undertaking' whose activities would otherwise fall within the scope of EU competition law, but is rather an 'employee' or a 'false self-employed' person); *Taylor v Local No 7, International Union of Journeymen Horseshoers of the United States and Canada* 353 F2d 593, 605 (4th Cir 1965) ('[anti-competitive] activities ... would be exempt from operation of the antitrust laws (1) if the parties to a dis-pute stand in the relationship of employer and employee and dispute some aspect of that relationship, or (2) if the employer-employee relationship of others is the crux of the dispute between the parties').
[56] Robert Taylor, 'Market Freedom as Antipower' [2013] American Political Science Review 593, 594.
[57] FA Hayek, *Individualism and Economic Order* (University of Chicago Press 1980) 92.
[58] Taylor (n 56) 594.
[59] See, similarly, Preston King, 'Liberty as Power' [1999] Critical Review of International Social and Political Philosophy 1, 13.
[60] I will draw almost exclusively from Thomas Christiano, *The Rule of the Many: Fundamental Issues in Democratic Theory* (Routledge 2018), which should be taken as the reference alluded to in subse-quent cross-references to this note. An abridged version of Christiano's theory and a more comprehen-sive one can, respectively, be found in 'An Argument for Democratic Equality' in Thomas Christiano (ed), *Philosophy and Democracy* (OUP 2003) and *The Constitution of Equality* (OUP 2008).
[61] Christiano (n 60) 53.
[62] ibid 56.

according to Christiano, involves not just any equality; it demands 'some equality in political power',[63] which seems to bring us back to our initial observation that, unlike citizens, players in the economic game do not have equal 'voting' power. For another, it is difficult to picture what 'collective property' competition might serve when the former is defined as something whose alteration invariably affects (almost) everyone.[64]

Challenging as they are, these are not insuperable rejoinders. To see this, letting go of the market organization apprehended as a purely apolitical and anonymous construct is a prerequisite. We have to instead reinterpret it as a *communitas*, i.e. a good, collectively owned by all participants who derive their entitlement from their very involvement in its operation, which does more than merely amalgamate indistinctive inter-individual relations formalized through contracts.[65] So understood, the market is political as well because it only makes sense against a backdrop of institutions— property, contract, and tort laws, especially—through which collective relations are knitted between functional groups of persons, for instance consumers/producers and employees/employers. The *communitas* model, in other words, does not envision the market solely as a vacuous sum of contracts concluded by independent persons at a particular moment in time; it likewise integrates the idea that each of these atomistic interactions can always be subsumed within permanent, global, and intergroup collective relations enabled by political institutions.

Ergo, the first step to conceiving economic democracy involves conceptualizing the market, the surplus it generates, as a 'collective property'. Why? Precisely because, under such a view, this output—the result of a collective effort—is 'a social patrimony, the social patrimony of a market society'.[66] It so follows that, since economic actors, as members of historical categories of participants,[67] all contribute to the collective surplus generated by the market organization,[68] they each enjoy a status akin to that of citizenship in the political order.[69] This is what endows them individually with an 'equal right to play a role' in the economic game. Competition, like political democracy, is therefore the mechanism liberal societies purposely design to enable every person to exercise this entitlement.[70]

Crucially, economic democracy so construed does not, need not, nor can it mean *absolute* equality in economic power.[71] The reason? Well, first, power is an

---

[63] ibid.
[64] ibid 60.
[65] Christian Barrère, 'Defining Economic Democracy: A Challenge. An Institutionalist Framework' in Alain Marciano and Jean-Michel Josselin (eds), *Democracy, Freedom and Coercion: A Law and Economics Approach* (Edward Elgar 2007) 88–91.
[66] ibid 93.
[67] To wit, as consumers, producers, employees, employers, investors, etc.
[68] Either through the exchange of goods and information or through productive activities that are only possible because of social institutions.
[69] Barrère (n 65) 94.
[70] Similarly, see Adi Ayal, *Fairness in Antitrust: Protecting the Strong From the Weak* (Hart 2016) 117.
[71] Barrère (n 65) 95.

inescapable reality even in a liberal society.[72] For liberty necessarily involves 'the initial building block of power'[73]—unless, of course, a neo-Roman republican conception of the value is embraced, with the aforementioned paradox this would entail for any competition policy that purports to protect competition as a dynamic *process* from which a society expects *desirable* outcomes.

Second, some philosophers argue, compellingly, that unequal (political) power cannot plausibly be described as objectionable as such.[74] So to rejoin that economic relationships are a special source of unadulterated egalitarian demands would mean 'giving up on [an] independent argumentative support for our democratic intuitions, rather than simply restating them'.[75]

Third, even the norm of political equality under democracy cannot really be conceived as an unqualified principle of equal power. Countries that embrace first-past-the-post or winner-takes-all electoral systems (like the UK and the USA, respectively) would otherwise have little claim to be called democracies. Moreover, democratic decision-making covers, not just the collective selection by citizens of societal goals, but also an assessment of how best to achieve those objectives, as well as the subsequent enactment of laws and policies to fulfil the ones that are feasible.[76] Yet, 'it is clear that political officials have more power than others to undermine the pursuit of the aims of a democratic assembly'.[77]

Finally, as Christiano himself concedes, 'there ought to be flexibility and room in a democracy for discussion about the exact principles of democratic equality'.[78] In fact, democracy, according to him, requires 'equality in *certain kinds of instruments or resources* for achieving one's ends'.[79] This, we shall shortly see, is perfectly compatible with competition and antitrust because what Christiano seems to be alluding to is a specific dimension of *fairness* called *equality of opportunity*. Given how 'fairness' discourse has haunted the antitrust community for years,[80] I will devote an entire section to it shortly.

At this point, though, one can already grasp the gist of a properly grounded competitive process paradigm. It envisions competition as the economic pendant of political democracy conceived as equal liberty, a procedure which implies the

---

[72] See Margrethe Vestager, 'Dealing with Power in a Brave New World: Economy, Technology and Human Rights' (speech delivered at the Anna Lindh Lecture, 18 March 2019) <https://bit.ly/2XjSLbx> accessed 18 November 2022 ('The truth is, power is an unavoidable part of human life').

[73] King (n 59) 4. Like King, I use the terms 'liberty' and 'freedom' 'perhaps recklessly, as substantively interchangeable'.

[74] See eg Daniel Viehoff, 'Power and Equality' in David Sobel, Peter Vallentyne and Steven Wall (eds), *Oxford Studies in Political Philosophy*, vol 5 (OUP 2019).

[75] ibid 36.

[76] Thomas Christiano, 'The Uneasy Relationship between Democracy and Capital' [2010] Social Philosophy & Policy 195, 200–01.

[77] ibid 207.

[78] Christiano (n 60) 77.

[79] ibid 63 (emphasis added).

[80] See Niamh Dunne, 'Fairness and the Challenge of Making Markets Work Better' [2021] Modern Law Review 230.

equal right to participate (in politics and, by analogy, the economy) under 'fair' conditions.[81] Economic liberty (or freedom), here, is not (nor can it be) neo-Roman republican non-domination, as certain antitrust paradigm-shifters would have it. Instead, it is both the absence of power abuses and equal admission to the public economic realm.[82]

Like political democracy, then, competition stimulates, directs, and coordinates the exercise of these individual freedoms that are, by definition, not absolute.[83] In so doing, it can be said to place *limits* on economic power liberal market societies could never conceivably extinguish. Like political democracy, competition thereby frustrates abusive power plays,[84] which could, if left unchecked, revive the spectre of economic planning. Not through government, but by the hand of powerful private actors, a threat many might argue is particularly acute in our platform economy, which does have a tendency for 'self-created economic law'.[85] It is in this sense that effective competition can rightfully be depicted as 'the most remarkable and ingenious instrument for reducing economic power known in history'.[86]

To summarize: following this alternative approach to antitrust, undistorted and unrestricted competition is economic democracy for two reasons. One: it guarantees all market players, including providers, as 'citizens' of the economic order, the equally protected freedom to 'voice an opinion' regarding the distribution of the social patrimony of the market over which no one group can lay an exclusive claim to. And two: it does so by ensuring that inevitable inequalities of results flow, not from arbitrary exertions of economic power, but from differences (in economic performances, for example) condoned by societies themselves, which they will have embedded (perhaps implicitly) within the rules supporting the competitive order.[87] This is why, under the competitive process paradigm, antitrust can justifiably rationalize a problem to be corrected when suppliers are harmed without

---

[81] Maria Paula Saffon and Nadia Urbinati, 'Procedural Democracy, the Bulwark of Equal Liberty' [2013] Political Theory 441. See, similarly, European Commission for Democracy through Law (Venice Commission), 'Report on the Timeline and Inventory of Political Criteria for Assessing an Election' (21 October 2010) Study No 558/2009, [26]–[32] <https://bit.ly/3UR6fXf> accessed 19 August 2022 ('A democratic election is a free and fair election').

[82] See Hannah Arendt, *On Revolution* (Penguin 1990) ch 1.

[83] Similarly, see Josef Drexl, 'On the (A)political Character of the Economic Approach to Competition Law' in Drexl, Kerber and Podszun (n 20) 328.

[84] Saffon and Urbinati (n 81) 461 ('people should participate in democracy not because they are capable of making correct decisions, but because their participation minimizes the risk of power abuses').

[85] Hans Großmann-Doerth, 'Selbstgeschaffenes Recht der Wirtschaft und Staatliches Recht' in Nils Goldschmidt and Michael Wohlgemuth (eds), *Grundtexte zur Freiburger Tradition der Ordnungsökonomik* (Mohr Siebeck 2008) 77 (free translation).

[86] Mestmäcker (n 44) 44, citing and explaining this 'most quoted but rarely analysed dictum' of Franz Böhm, 'Democracy and Economic Power' in Institut für ausländisches und internationales Wirtschaftsrecht an der Johann-Wolfgang-Goethe Universität (ed), *Cartel and Monopoly in Modern Law*, vol 1 (CF Müller 1961) 42.

[87] See further Section 3.2.2 of this chapter. Similarly see Wolfgang Fikentscher, Philipp Hacker and Rupprecht Podszun, *Fair Economy: Crises, Culture, Competition and the Role of Law* (Springer 2013) 58. By analogy, see also Christiano (n 60) 81–82.

consumer welfare being (immediately) at risk. For such a policy must guarantee each member of the market society 'the chance to enhance their understanding of their interests as well as justice on a publicly available equal basis'.[88]

Naturally, allusions to 'justice' will upset many in the antitrust community who take it to mean or entail the pursuit of 'fairness'. The substantive role of this value torments antitrust. Earlier, I promised a few words on it; let me now oblige.

3.2 Competition and Fairness

3.2.1 Competition's moral content

Consensus has generally been that antitrust is devoid of any moral content and that fairness should be unabashedly purged from the policy's discourse.[89] While harsh, this sounds fair (bad pun intended). The concept certainly does seem indeterminate and impracticable; relying on it might put antitrust's decisional consistency at risk.[90] More fundamentally, competition, *by definition*, generates unequal results.[91] So for those who abhor these inequalities on fairness grounds, competition is inherently unfair. There will always be winners and losers; losers will get less, if any, of the available surplus, whereas winners will sometimes obtain rewards disproportionate to their contributions and/or to what losers receive. Competition's consequences will hence forever be open to claims of unfairness; antitrust can do little about that.[92]

This notwithstanding, the policy's decision-makers cannot—not under the competitive process paradigm—dismiss outright intuitive suggestions that fairness is an emotion viscerally ingrained in the human psyche.[93] Why not? The answer is simple. Recall that we are discussing *ordered* economic competition, i.e. a process moulded by rules which are themselves the fruit of a society's intentional political choices. To my mind, there is an argument to be made that such a society (at least if it subscribes to liberal democracy) will have appreciated and accordingly

---

[88] Christiano (n 60) 69.

[89] See, notably, Herbert Hovenkamp, *The Antitrust Enterprise: Principle and Execution* (Harvard UP 2005) 47.

[90] See eg Phillip Areeda and Herbert Hovenkamp, *Antitrust Law: An Analysis of Antitrust Principles and Their Application* (Supplement 8/2019, rev edn, Wolters Kluwer 1978) [111d]; Renato Nazzini, *The Foundations of European Union Competition Law: The Objective and Principles of Article 102* (OUP 2011) 22–24.

[91] See Davies (n 30) 41 ('to argue in favour of competition ... is necessarily to argue in favour of inequality, given that competitive activity is defined partly by the fact that it pursues an unequal outcome').

[92] Proponents of a 'more normative' approach to antitrust recognize this too. See Stucke and Ezrachi (n 17) ch 9 ('in any competition, there will be winners and losers. The latter may indeed be injured or unhappy. As antitrust professors, we do not take issue with this').

[93] Michael Shermer, 'The Mind of the Market: Evolutionary Economics Explains Why Irrational Financial Choices Were Once Rational' (*Scientific American*, 2008) <https://bit.ly/2LvUNg0> accessed 18 November 2022 (claiming that '[t]he moral sense of fairness is hardwired into our brains and is an emotion shared by all people and primates tested for it').

embedded in (the spirit of) its economic constitution the following idea: for competition to arise and persist, market players need 'mutual trust and confidence in the behavioural ethics of each other'.[94] The explanation for this is twofold. First, fairness demonstrably matters to people.[95] Second, competition completely sundered from fairness and conducted as if it were '[w]arfare'[96] is not only costly for society;[97] it no longer has anything to do with *competition* because such a process will have degenerated into a self-destructive Hobbesian *contest*.[98]

The reader, however, would be right to call me out here. Isn't fairness, by consensus, both impractical and conceptually indeterminate? The first objection relates to how antitrust is enforced—how to structure and design suitable legal tests and remedies?—which is an issue addressed in Chapter 6. The second goes to the policy's 'soul' and is attended to below.

3.2.2 Competition and the two sides of 'fairness'

As some have argued, '[b]are calls to fairness are unilluminating: there are too many different understandings of what the concept might mean to direct the substantive task of enforcement'.[99] Luckily, when normatively anchored by the competitive process paradigm, we can actually spare ourselves the chore of parsing out every single theory of fairness thinkers of all backgrounds alike may have expounded. Remember: with this lodestar, competition is economic democracy, and its constitutive values are antitrust's touchstones in recognition of the fact that, if the process is working well, its outcomes cannot be predicted with absolute precision. In effect, to protect the competitive process entails safeguarding the fundamentals without which it would probably not be able to generate the benefits societies expect it to. Under this approach, antitrust cannot in the first instance fret over market *results*, wrenchingly unfair as they can be. Why? Because, like political democracy, competition's normative value 'is not grounded on its capacity to produce correct decisions'.[100]

---

[94] Amartya Sen, 'Moral Codes and Economic Success' in Samuel Brittan and Alan Hamlin (eds), *Market Capitalism and Moral Values* (Edward Elgar 1995) 26. See eg TFEU, preamble (recognizing the need for 'fair competition').

[95] See EC (Joint Research Center), 'What Makes a Fair Society? Insights and Evidence' (2017) <https://data.europa.eu/doi/10.2760/861535> accessed 18 November 2022); Ricardo Barros and others, *Measuring Inequality of Opportunities in Latin America and the Caribbean* (World Bank 2009) 46.

[96] *Schachar v American Academy of Ophthalmology Inc* 870 F2d 397, 399 (7th Cir 1989).

[97] For this argument, see Stucke and Ezrachi (n 17) ch 9.

[98] First-generation Ordoliberals seemed intuitively attuned to this. See Fanz Böhm, Walter Eucken and Hans Großmann-Doerth, 'The Ordo Manifesto of 1936' in Alan Peacock and Michael Willgerodt (eds), *Germany's Social Market Economy: Origins and Evolution* (Palgrave Macmillan 1989) 24 ('Free competition must not be stopped on the erroneous grounds of alleged unfair practice. On the other hand, it must not be allowed to degenerate into truly unfair competition either'). On the distinction between 'competition' and 'contest', see, similarly, Lütge (n 22) 7.

[99] Dunne (n 80) 237.

[100] Saffon and Urbinati (n 81) 461.

That today many observers are troubled by powerful platforms capturing too much of the available surplus at the expense of others may be laudable. Yet, for antitrust decision-makers guided by the competitive process imperative, arguably unfair outcomes simply cannot stand as proximate worries.[101] The fairness they must be attuned to is different. It is that which *precedes* competition's results: *ex ante* fairness (or equality of opportunity (EOp)).[102] This contrasts with substantive (or outcome or *ex post*) fairness, which relates to things like the 'stakes' of the game or the actual identity of its winners. Insofar as substantive fairness is tied to a player's behaviour, it is a matter for unfair competition law.[103] And where no clear nexus with a particular business practice exists, societies have to take their responsibilities. That is, collectively decide whether to protect some players—say, news publishers—as a group, or to exclude certain sources of rents from a powerful platform's reward.[104]

The reasoning is as follows: similarly to political democracy, competition is 'only a part of a completely just [market] society'.[105] While its normative virtue lies in its capacity to prevent Hobbesian destruction through equal liberty, competition (like political democracy) 'does not command the production of specific substantive outcomes'.[106] So when the latter are abhorrently unfair, it is *justice* which demands that the competitive process be restricted, as it would in a democratic polity.[107] *Coherence*, though, blocks us from mediating such abridgments through the very policy that, under this approach, protects competition; other levers of public action are there for that.

Setting theory aside, my point is that antitrust has to sanction unfair conduct when guided by the competitive process lodestar *inasmuch* as the EOp

---

[101] Naturally, outcome fairness may indirectly—as a by-product of enforcement—be relevant (see my work with Christopher Decker and others, 'Competition Law Enforcement and Household Inequality in the United Kingdom' [2022] Journal of Competition Law & Economics 905).

[102] By analogy, see Saffon and Urbinati (n 81) 442ff. See also Venice Commission (n 81) [30]–[32].

[103] See, similarly, Rudolf Callmann, 'What Is Unfair Competition' [1940] Georgetown Law Journal 585, 604–07 (antitrust is about preventing 'a violation of the competitive order as such by contravening or disavowing its *very fundamentals*'; whereas unfair competition law protects 'the interest of the *competitors*' by redressing 'a tort *sui generis*' ultimately grounded in 'the law of *equity*') (emphasis added).

[104] See Stigler Center, 'Stigler Committee on Digital Platforms: Final Report' (September 2019) 36 <https://bityl.co/Fjqi> accessed 19 November 2022. See also Stephen Weatherill, 'The Challenge of Better Regulation' in Stephen Weatherill (ed), *Better Regulation* (Hart 2007) 5.

[105] Christiano (n 60) 81–82.

[106] Saffon and Urbinati (n 81) 459.

[107] Christiano (n 60) 81–82. To clarify: by 'justice', I mean the adherence to rules (which deal with both the distribution of outcomes and the procedures which precede them) that reflect appropriateness in decision contexts. 'Fairness', understood as a 'global perception of appropriateness', is therefore '"downstream" from justice' (Jason Colquitt and Jessica Rodell, 'Measuring Justice and Fairness' in Russell Cropanzano and Maureen Ambrose (eds), *The Oxford Handbook of Justice in the Workplace* (OUP 2015) 188). This distinction, which I borrow from contemporary organizational justice researchers, is similar to that made by those legal philosophers who see 'justice' as the basis for societal and organizational legitimacy and 'fairness' as a perception about the moral integrity of a given situation (see Barry Goldman and Russel Cropanzano, '"Justice" and "Fairness" Are Not the Same Thing' [2015] Journal of Organizational Behavior 313, 315–16).

without which sustainable competition would be imperilled.[108] In practice, this means targeted interventions aimed at counteracting the effects of (certain) (dis)advantages players bring to the economic game.[109] And, as will be further detailed in Chapter 4, there are several reasons we may want our antitrust decision-makers to do so beyond facile appeals to 'the people's will' and the plainly vacuous idea of *ex ante* fairness on its own. Impartiality, respect for persons, legitimate expectation, merit, desert, efficiency, even self-realization: all these values lurk behind EOp; each of them, we shall see, can be used to formalize harm to the 'competitive process', much like different economic models will say different things on the consumer welfare implications of a particular behaviour.

Granted, more is needed here first; the critical reader would otherwise rightly berate me for assuming there is anything pellucid in distinguishing *ex ante* from *ex post* fairness.

Truth be told, any theory of EOp correlates with an idea of what outcomes (broadly understood) should look like—of what kinds of inequalities in results are to be deemed morally acceptable. To reformulate: the boundaries between fairness as EOp and fairness in consequences are not completely impermeable.[110] However, EOp theories of interest to antitrust decision-makers guided by the competitive process imperative, for reasoning and enforcement purposes, only encroach upon substantive fairness indirectly (and at varying levels of intensity). For they merely affect the *structure* (or *pattern*) of outcomes, not their *content*.

Put prosaically: recall that competition necessarily produces winners and losers. What competitive process (and thus EOp) -minded antitrust decision-makers have to heed is not what, or how much, each player receives (i.e. the stakes), nor who wins and loses per se (i.e. identity-based outcome fairness). They must rather have an eye to how the ordering (i.e. the structure or pattern) comes about—the process. Stated differently (and, again, this will be further explored in Chapter 4), the relevant question is not whether, for example, Alphabet/Google's behaviour squeezes news publishers dry of their 'fair share' of surplus in the (online) advertising value chain, or whether the cut Apple takes for distributing apps on its App

---

[108] Of course, some argue that antitrust should pursue outcome fairness. But their accounts are, at a minimum, incomplete since no normative relation to *competition* is properly established. See, notably, Ioannis Lianos, 'The Poverty of Competition Law' in Damien Gerard and Ioannis Lianos (eds), *Reconciling Efficiency and Equity: A Global Challenge for Competition Policy* (CUP 2019) 76–87. See also Anna Gerbrandy, 'Rethinking Competition Law within the European Economic Constitution' [2019] Journal of Common Market Studies 127, 129; Thomas Horton, 'Fairness and Antitrust Reconsidered: An Evolutionary Perspective' [2013] McGeorge Law Review 823.

[109] See, similarly, Case C-525/16 *MEO* ECLI:EU:C:2018:270 [2018] electronic Reports of Cases, [26] ('the mere presence of an immediate disadvantage affecting [some players over others] does not ... mean that competition is distorted or is capable of being distorted').

[110] James Buchanan, 'Fairness, Hope, and Justice' in Roger Skurski (ed), *New Directions in Economic Justice* (University of Notre Dame Press 1983) 65–66.

Store is 'highway robbery'.[111] As Epic Games (famous for developing the *Fortnite* video game) found out, when '[a]ntitrust law protects competition … extraordinarily high profit margins [and] success [are] not illegal'[112] in themselves. What is (or at least, ought to be) decisive is whether the platform won (or is winning) the market game based on practices that endow it with, or leverage, unfair advantages, which skew the competitive process.

This may not be the case where societies value a restricted understanding of EOp, such as one which posits that there is no unfairness whenever competition is 'open to all'. Nonetheless, it would be short-sighted to assume that theories articulating such a narrow vision of EOp are all our decision-makers have to play with. As suggested above, EOp-attentive antitrust seeks to counteract the effects of (certain) (dis)advantages which structure market results.[113] Such (dis)advantages can flow from *procedural* defects, as well as from *background* conditions, i.e. some competitors are unacceptably better equipped than others. The question is whether decision-makers can appeal to these more far-reaching visions of EOp, which is a matter of coherence with the polity they are institutions of. Antitrust is more than 'a set of economic prescriptions … it is also an expression of a social philosophy'.[114] Decision-makers, therefore, are not free to intervene as they please—at least, they shouldn't be, a point we will return to throughout this book.

In sum, competitive process-centric antitrust is more inclusive than when guided by consumer welfare because, beyond individual freedom, it has to preserve the EOp without which competition would lose its democratic credentials and ultimately disintegrate. EOp is *ex ante* fairness, which (Chapter 4 will explain), itself, has ideologically more or less progressive (or conservative) variations. Here, antitrust does not—cannot—redress unfair *outcomes* per se, which pertain to any other conceivable element of fairness.[115] One is stakes fairness, the dimension related to 'regulating what is at stake in the competition, ensuring a broader distribution of the prizes, and limiting how much competitors can gain or lose'.[116] Another

---

[111] Congressman David Cicilline quoted in Nilay Patel, 'Apple's App Store Fees Are "Highway Robbery", Says House Antitrust Committee Chair' (*The Verge*, 18 June 2020) <https://bit.ly/3cLv6bo> accessed 18 November 2022.

[112] *Epic Games Inc v Apple Inc* 559 FSupp 3d 898, 921–22 (NDCal 2021).

[113] See, similarly, Paul Gomberg, *How to Make Opportunity Equal: Race and Contributive Justice* (Blackwell 2007) 1 (stating that EOp, ideally, means 'no one should have unfair advantages in the competition').

[114] Robert Bork and Ward Bowman Jr, 'The Crisis in Antitrust' [1965] Columbia Law Review 363, 364.

[115] This is probably why the EU courts (which, as mentioned earlier, historically underscored the paramount importance of the competitive process for EU antitrust) have struggled when wrestling with the interpretation of TFEU, art 102(a)—a competition law provision that explicitly seems to target unfair *outcomes* (see Case C-372/19 *SABAM* ECLI:EU:C:2020:598 [2020] not yet published, Opinion of AG Pitruzzella, [21]–[22], [26]). As others have explained in detail, the very existence of such an ostensibly redistributive provision owes to a political compromise that was actually animated by deregulatory intentions (see, notably, Heike Schweitzer, 'The History, Interpretation and Underlying Principles of Section 2 Sherman Act and Article 82 EC' in Ehlermann and Marquis (n 32) 128ff).

[116] Lesley Jacobs, *Pursuing Equal Opportunities: The Theory and Practice of Egalitarian Justice* (CUP 2004) 46.

is identity-based fairness (such as that potentially owed to producers or consumers or any other (sub)groups, say vulnerable consumers or producers).[117] And there certainly are more, inchoate, facets. Yet, none of them can be of immediate concern if it is still true that antitrust is and must be about 'competition', a process akin, under this alternative approach, to political democracy whose normative value resides in its 'unbeatable capacity to protect and promote equal liberty'.[118]

4. Concluding Reflections

In our increasingly platform-driven age, the argument for placing a premium on efficiency and consumer interests has never been so compelling.[119] But antitrust—a policy that, for many years now, has been anchored by a paradigm which caters to these ideals—is once again in search of a new equilibrium. Back in 1979 when the tide decisively shifted towards the consumer welfare lodestar in the USA, Robert Pitofsky famously warned that sundering antitrust from the political values inherent to competition was 'bad history, bad policy, and bad law'.[120] Never have his musings seemed more felicitous than today as liberal capitalist societies do appear to be at a crossroad. Many of our digital markets are not only marshalled by a few powerful platforms; they are likewise effectively controlled by individuals who believe that 'competition is for losers'.[121] In so doing, the latter are short-sighted in one fundamental respect. A monopolist's efficiencies have little value if achieving them means behaving in ways which potentially compromise the sustainability of the entire economic system. As we gaze into antitrust's soul, we need to keep this in mind and 'remember that markets are there to serve people, not the other way round'.[122] And if a large enough fraction of the widespread allegations of upstream platform misconduct are true, we may have a serious problem on our hands. Indeed, victimized platform providers cannot reasonably be expected to maintain their faith in

---

[117] John Rawls's famed 'difference principle' (mentioned in Chapter 1), which gives priority to the least well-off in society, is one theoretical foundation for this.

[118] Saffon and Urbinati (n 81) 442.

[119] See comments made by (then-) US and EU antitrust enforcers-in-chief, Makan Delrahim and Margrethe Vestager, regarding the efficiencies of acquisitions made by large technology groups (see Kadhim Shubber, 'US Antitrust Chief Signals Comfort with Tech Deals' *Financial Times* (12 July 2018) <https://on.ft.com/2JhF8Pr> accessed 18 November 2022), and the importance of protecting consumers in digital markets (see Margrethe Vestager, 'Competition and a Fair Deal for Consumers Online' (speech delivered at the Netherlands Authority for Consumers and Markets Fifth Anniversary Conference, 26 April 2018) <https://bit.ly/2VjYwn2> accessed 18 November 2022).

[120] Robert Pitofsky, 'The Political Content of Antitrust' [1979] University of Pennsylvania Law Review 1051, 1051.

[121] Pieter Thiel, 'Competition Is for Losers' *Wall Street Journal* (12 September 2014) <https://on.wsj.com/2JRRGQm> accessed 18 November 2022.

[122] Margrethe Vestager, 'Competition and Sustainability' (speech delivered at the GCLC Conference on Sustainability and Competition Policy, 24 October 2019) <https://bit.ly/2QIUUJB> accessed 18 November 2022.

what was billed to them as a form of double thank-you capitalism.[123] After all, 'our economic system can't work if there is no trust'.[124]

The conundrum is ultimately political. Market competition is not spontaneous, not in most liberal democracies.[125] The rules of the economic game reflect intentional societal decisions. So when it comes to antitrust, the policy most directly assigned to supervising economic competition, societies have a choice to make. Are they better served by a paradigm that prioritizes competition's potential outcomes, namely improved efficiency or (when correctly construed) satisfied consumer interests? Or should they instead (re-)embrace competition, *as such*, a lodestar that requires protecting the constitutive values without which the process would ultimately degenerate into a Hobbesian contest?

Whatever one's position on this dilemma, those resistant to change have been right to criticize advocates of the lone credible alternative antitrust paradigm for supporting their advocacy with neither robust normative legs nor practical prescriptions. This chapter has attended to the first of these two shortcomings. At a minimum, it quells fears that antitrust becomes guided by a hotchpotch of sociopolitical goals betraying a bias against corporate size;[126] or that it turns the policy into a tool for arbitrary wealth redistribution,[127] which, ironically, is a risk inherent to the consumer welfare paradigm (as we saw in Chapter 1). Properly conceived, safeguarding competition means preserving what enables the process to develop sustainably, namely the freedom (both *from* abuses of economic power and *to* partake in the economic game) and fairness (or, more accurately, the dimension of fairness called EOp) owed to every member of the market society, including suppliers whose stake in the economic game is no less, but also no more important than that of consumers. Like political democracy, this paradigm 'does not demand from [antitrust] anything *other* than the protection of equal freedom—which is, of course, a lot already'.[128]

The simple upshot for now is that if one believes the plight of platform suppliers ought to make our antitrust decision-makers tick, then we have to look deep into the policy's soul because provider interests per se have never been, and cannot be, seriously touted as a proper antitrust paradigm. The exercise has foundational

---

[123] See *Google-Snippets* (Case 92 O 5/14 Kart) Berlin Regional Court Judgment 19 February 2016 ECLI:DE:LGBE:2016:0219.92O5.14KART.0A, [64] (describing the relationship between Alphabet/ Google's search platform, publishers, advertisers and consumers as 'win–win').

[124] Joseph Stiglitz, *People, Power, and Profits: Progressive Capitalism for an Age of Discontent* (Norton 2019) ch 5.

[125] Mid-1980s to late-1990s New Zealand may be one noteworthy exception. During this period, the country embraced widespread laissez-faire combined with light touch, efficiency-focused, antitrust (see Niamh Dunne, *Competition Law and Economic Regulation: Making and Managing Markets* (CUP 2015) 77).

[126] See eg Nicolas Petit, *Big Tech and the Digital Economy: The Moligopoly Scenario* (OUP 2020) ch 2; Timothy Brennan, 'Should Antitrust Go Beyond "Antitrust"?' [2018] Antitrust Bulletin 49.

[127] See eg D Daniel Sokol, 'Antitrust's "Curse of Bigness" Problem' [2020] Michigan Law Review 1259.

[128] Saffon and Urbinati (n 81) 445.

importance and reveals what a society truly expects from antitrust and for what reasons.

At the end of his near-fifteen-year crusade to rewrite the history of US antitrust, Bork marketed the consumer welfare lodestar using a powerful message: the policy, he wrote in 1978, was 'at war with itself'.[129] By most contemporary (bipartisan) accounts, Bork was probably right.[130] But given the discontent it has since sown, consumer welfare was no panacea. Pivoting towards the competitive process touchstone, as articulated herein, might bring normative peace to the policy by giving it an arguably sounder and more inclusive normative fulcrum.

So sketched, though, the canvas is incomplete. How does the paradigm work when applied to our platform provider anxieties and contrast with consumer welfare-centric antitrust *in practice*?[131] This is what will occupy us hereafter. Over the next three chapters, we will come to appreciate that the paradigm choice is not decisive for the purposes of *rationalizing* upstream platform power plays as potential 'antitrust injuries'. However, as explained in Part III, it does have an impact on how decision-makers will *intervene*, i.e. how competition law will be enforced and interfaced with other available policy levers.

---

[129] Robert Bork, *The Antitrust Paradox: A Policy at War with Itself* (Basic Books 1978).

[130] See eg D Daniel Sokol 'Antitrust, Industrial Policy, and Economic Populism' in Damien Gerard and Ioannis Lianos (eds), *Reconciling Efficiency and Equity: A Global Challenge for Competition Policy* (CUP 2019) 285 (describing 1950–1960s US antitrust as an 'embarrassment'); Robert Pitofsky 'Introduction: Setting the Stage' in Robert Pitofsky (ed), *How the Chicago School Overshot the Mark: The Effect of Conservative Economic Analysis on U.S. Antitrust* (OUP 2008) 4 (describing this period as 'almost impossible to defend today').

[131] Neo-Brandeisian accounts are often criticized on both fronts (see eg Sokol (n 127) 1262; A Douglas Melamed and Nicolas Petit, 'The Misguided Assault on the Consumer Welfare Standard in the Age of Platform Markets' [2019] Review of Industrial Organization 741, 764).

PART II

LOOKING UP

Antitrust decision-makers are increasingly, and with a rare sense of urgency, investigating and adjudicating claims of allegedly abusive upstream platform power plays. But what does it actually mean to 'look up'? That is, can we rationalize upstream effects as potential antitrust-relevant 'competition problems'? If so, can these concerns be rigorously formalized or must we rely on informal, perhaps even intuitive, theories? Therein lies the crux of our inquiry here.

Now, Part I just laid down building blocks for the upcoming discussion. We explored there the tenets underlying the two normative approaches that may guide antitrust, i.e. the outcome-based consumer welfare paradigm, which has dominated contemporary antitrust, as well as the alternative, more deontic, competitive process one. Henceforth, both lodestars are taken as is and put to the test. For the values underpinning them—be they (real) consumers' interest or some measure of economic efficiency, on the one hand, or freedom and *ex ante* fairness on the other—can usefully serve our investigation of the ills apparently afflicting the platform economy's upstream environments. Identifying issues that should strike a chord with decision-makers will hereby be achieved by conceptualizing 'competition problems' as the symptoms caused by business practices, which may imperil the value(s) antitrust is taken to pursue.

Having said this, recall from the introductory chapter that my ultimate aim with this book is to make a compelling case for the following proposition: upstream platform power plays create a Procrustean dilemma for antitrust decision-makers. To this end, Chapter 1 revealed how normatively enfeebled the consumer welfare paradigm might be, something our upstream worries further magnify. So why not shift paradigms, especially since an alternative—one which more directly caters to (platform) provider anxieties without falling into uncritical and incoherent sentimentality—does exist?

A hypothesis is path dependence.[1] As the next three chapters purport to demonstrate, we can theorize mistreatments of platform suppliers as potential

---

[1] Political scientists have long argued that path dependence—the 'institutional conditions which either block or weaken deliberate attempts to change the status quo'—is relevant in the context of public policy (Jacob Torfing, 'Rethinking Path Dependence in Public Policy Research' [2009] Critical Policy Studies 70).

competition problems under either approach. However, decision-makers contemplating the move to the competitive process lodestar may baulk—maybe rightfully so—when push comes to shove even though shifting would enable them to rationalize harm more directly and in a wider array of cases. The reason? A consensus demand for rigour in theory-building.[2] As Commissioner Vestager says:

> [T]hese days you hear some voices arguing that authorities should do even more, by enforcing our rules even more strongly [against powerful platforms which threaten the survival of the businesses that rely on them]. But we need to be careful. Competition enforcement works because it's firmly based on evidence and the law, and on sound economic analysis of how markets work. And no matter how important it may be to tackle the dark side of digitisation, we can only do our bit if we stick firmly to those principles.[3]

This obviously makes the antitrust enterprise harder than if one could simply rely on informal reasoning. When the goal is to protect competition, as such, though, the challenge is exacerbated by the fact that antitrust is a field where, lawyers aside, only the economist's opinion matters. Given that the competitive process paradigm is about political values, rigour would have decision-makers appeal to people like political philosophers whose insights have never (or marginally) made it into antitrust discourse.[4] Hence, even if it is ultimately found to be normatively unsound and/or error-prone, striving for consumer welfare does enable decision-makers to stay within their comfort zone.

To make this argument, we will explore three categories of practices, practices contemporary antitrust would, by conventional taxonomies, have viewed (primarily) as 'exploitative' in nature and, resultingly, dismissed almost outright.

Chapter 3 deals with what is denoted as 'despotism'. Certain platforms can usefully be analogized to (quasi-)autocratic states whose benevolence we cannot take for granted. For there is a fine line between self-created platform rules that effectively create a positive-sum game and those that are really no different from despotism.

Chapter 4 then looks at 'game-mastering'. Upstream platform dynamics can often be framed as a game-master–players relationship where providers are players

[2] BEUC, 'The Role of Competition Policy in Protecting Consumers' Well-being in the Digital Era' (October 2019) 18 <https://bit.ly/3USSvv9> accessed 19 November 2022 ('there is a consensus that agencies should base their actions on ... analytical rigour').
[3] Margrethe Vestager, 'Defending Competition in a Digital Age' (Speech delivered at the Florence Competition Summer Conference, 24 June 2021) <https://bityl.co/EpAz> accessed 18 November 2022.
[4] See eg then FTC Commissioner Leary who assumed that 'it is unlikely that any view of core values can be proven in a rigorous way' (Thomas Leary, 'Freedom as the Core Value of Antitrust in the New Millennium' (Speech delivered at the ABA Antitrust Section 48th Annual Spring Meeting, Chair's Showcase Program, Antitrust at the Millennium: Looking Back and Moving Forward, 6 April 2000) <https://perma.cc/T7BU-2A59> accessed 18 November 2022).

and platforms are game-masters who organize the games and, sometimes, also actively partake in them.[5] As will be explained, the crux here is not the ostensible rules game-masters may devise to ensure maximum profits or (less cynically) proper game development. It pertains instead to how game-masters may covertly fiddle with them.

Finally, Chapter 5 examines how decision-makers might make sense of allegations that powerful platforms 'scrape' the fruits of suppliers' labour or 'Sherlock' them out of their valuable ideas. Stripped of their rhetorical enhancers, these claims are about turning the free-riding defence so successfully invoked to escape antitrust liability into a self-standing antitrust offence.

---

[5] In the latter scenario, while platform provider anxieties also acquire a horizontal dimension, they remain 'close to exploitative in nature' (Marc van der Woude, quoted by Nicolas Hirst, 'Intel, Google Shopping Rulings Don't Conflict, Top EU Judge Says' *mlex* (31 March 2022) <https://bityl.co/EpC0> accessed 18 November).

3
Despotism

1. Introduction

In 1996, digital activist John Perry Barlow published a cringeworthy but no less influential manifesto entitled *A Declaration of the Independence of Cyberspace*. It reflected the original ethos of the internet as a network organically meshed with the idea of decentralized power.[1] For in cyberspace, he prophesized, '[g]overnments of the Industrial World ... have no sovereignty'.[2] A little over a decade later, however, the World Wide Web had become populated by the likes of Facebook, which, by the admission of its CEO, Mark Zuckerberg, is '[i]n a lot of ways ... more like a government than a traditional company'.[3]

Fast forward to today, many platforms do bear eerie resemblances to states within the Westphalian paradigm.[4] Yes, the analogy is flawed—one might rather speak of *quasi*-states. It is nonetheless striking to observe that the largest platforms have user bases and revenues to match, or even outstrip, that of most states. Their 'territories', although not made of discrete land bounded by physical borders, are similarly vast, clearly demarcated, experienced spaces with virtual boundaries; these often do foster (much like nations) a sense of shared identity and community.[5] Moreover, some of them seemingly behave like sovereign actors in the international legal order. Haven't super-platforms engaged in diplomacy,[6] weighed in on issues of international governance,[7] waded into housing

[1] Yochai Benkler, 'Degrees of Freedom, Dimensions of Power' [2016] Dædalus 18, 19–20.
[2] John Perry Barlow, 'A Declaration of the Independence of Cyberspace' (1996) <https://bit.ly/3gok ALB> accessed 19 November 2022.
[3] David Kirkpatrick, *The Facebook Effect: The Inside Story of the Company That Is Connecting the World* (Simon & Schuster 2010) 254.
[4] On the Westphalian paradigm whereby modern state sovereignty is marked by external and internal dimensions, see Dieter Grimm, *Sovereignty: The Origin and Future of a Political and Legal Concept* (Columbia University Press 2015) 77–98.
[5] See, similarly, Julie Cohen, 'Law for the Platform Economy' [2017] University of California Davis Law Review 133, 200; Julie Cohen, 'Cyberspace as/and Space' [2007] Columbia Law Review 210 (arguing that cyberspace is most usefully understood as 'connected to and subsumed within an emerging, networked space that is inhabited by real, embodied users and that is apprehended through experience').
[6] The EU opened a Silicon Valley office on 1 September 2022 (European External Action Service, 'US/Digital: EU opens new Office in San Francisco to Reinforce Its Digital Diplomacy' (1 September 2022) <https://bityl.co/EBkQ> accessed 18 November 2022). Denmark and France had sent 'digital ambassadors' to Silicon Valley several years before (Felix Maschewski and Anna-Verena Nosthoff, 'Res Publica ex Machina: On Neocybernetic Governance and the End of Politics' (*Institute of Network Cultures*, 18 October 2018) <https://bit.ly/2VtsqDb> accessed 18 November 2022).
[7] For instance, Microsoft and Facebook have signed with other high-tech companies a 'Digital Geneva Accord' to fight government-sponsored cyberattacks (David Sanger, 'Tech Firms Sign "Digital

Antitrust and Upstream Platform Power Plays. A. K. von Moltke, Oxford University Press. © A. K. von Moltke 2023.
DOI: 10.1093/oso/9780192873057.003.0004

policy,[8] and ignited wooing games for their headquarters as governments do for pledges of foreign investment?[9]

Crucially, it is not just external sovereignty that is on display. Platforms also regulate their respective domains, wielding a degree of authority to make autocrats green with envy. As explored in this chapter, centralized governance is a key component of many platforms (Section 2). The ensuing rules and institutions shape our experiences and actions within the infrastructures these firms design and operate. Such a model of private planning is thankfully by and large socially beneficial. But what if the platforms take a despotic turn? Can we rationalize this as a competition problem? The answer is a qualified yes.

First, although the consumer welfare paradigm may be amenable to certain claims of despotism, its reactivity will likely depend on several factors, including (i) the chosen consumer welfare avatar; (ii) the strand of economic reasoning decision-makers rely upon, as well as (iii) the degree of speculation societies will allow them to engage in (Section 3).

Second, despite the alternative, competitive process, lodestar's more intuitive fit for capturing these fears, fashioning a sound antitrust algorithm is not a straightforward exercise (Section 4).

2. Autocratic Platforms

Platforms are a species of online intermediaries whose value proposition embeds a paradoxical tension between two logics: generative and distributed innovation, on the one hand, control of the digital infrastructures they operate, on the other.[10] However, for multi-sided platforms in particular, designing an appealing architecture conducive to sticky (cross-sided) network effects does not, on its own, guarantee sustainability. Similarly to traditional markets, platform infrastructures can 'fail', corroded by things like negative externalities and information asymmetries generated by misbehaving users.[11] Hence the need for what business, economics, and information systems scholars denote as platform 'governance' (or 'regulation').

Geneva Accord" Not to Aid Governments in Cyberwar' *New York Times* (17 April 2018) <https://nyti.ms/2ETvMqU> accessed 18 November 2022).

[8] Thomas Hale, 'Tech Companies Become the State, Phase One' *Financial Times* (5 November 2019) <https://on.ft.com/2VFOsFd> accessed 18 November 2022).

[9] See eg Nellie Bowles, 'For Cities Wooing Amazon's New Headquarters, Nothing Is Too Strange' *New York Times* (25 September 2017) <https://nyti.ms/2xDgKFD> accessed 18 November 2022.

[10] Ben Eaton and others, 'Distributed Tuning of Boundary Resources: The Case of Apple's iOS Service System' [2015] Management Information Systems Quarterly 217.

[11] Kevin Boudreau and Andrei Hagiu, 'Platform Rules: Multi-Sided Platforms as Regulators' in Annabelle Gawer (ed), *Platforms, Markets and Innovation* (Edward Elgar 2009) 165; Geoffrey Parker, Marshall Van Alstyne and Sangeet Choudary, *Platform Revolution: How Networked Markets Are Transforming the Economy and How to Make Them Work for You* (Norton 2016) 162–63.

This moniker encapsulates the various (in)formal norms and institutions implemented by many platforms to drive value creation, and which effectively mould
competition within the digital environments the latter build and oversee.[12]

The normative significance of these rule-making and policing functions cannot
be understated. For while platform governance may be necessary to conduce socially desirable outcomes, it is generally the by-product of a 'regime of autocratic
control'.[13]

2.1 Private Autocratic Governance

Platforms are usually not democratically controlled businesses; they are rather
more privately owned, hierarchically managed corporations. Plus, whereas appetite for public oversight is increasing around the world, the governance mechanisms they devise remain largely discretionary and devoid of public accountability.
Many platforms are thus akin to private autocrats governing their domains in state-
like facture and exercising 'irrevocable and absolute sovereignty'.[14]

To start with, they prescribe and restrict behaviours, thereby conditioning access to their respective platform infrastructures and shaping how users interact
together and with the platform itself. Apple requires app developers to adhere to
certain format, content, and marketing rules before approving their distribution
on its App Store; social media platforms like Meta/Facebook moderate the types of
authorized speech; and so forth.

Platform governance likewise includes incentive and nudging mechanisms that
influence user behaviour. Default options, filters, and rankings embedded in most
platform systems are the most obvious examples.[15] Others can be more discrete,
such as Amazon's 'one-click buy' button, which prods consumers onto the path of
least resistance to completing purchases.[16]

Equally ubiquitous are trust-building institutions. Review, rating, and recommendation devices inevitably come to mind in this regard, but there are many
other functionally similar instruments, such as the use of certification and warran-
ties by Uber and Airbnb.[17]

---

[12] See eg Panos Constantinides, Ola Henfridsson and Geoffrey Parker, 'Platforms and Infrastructures
in the Digital Age' [2018] Information Systems Research 381, 383; Boudreau and Hagiu (n 11) 169.

[13] Eaton and others (n 10) 238.

[14] Jonas Schwarz, 'Platform Logic: An Interdisciplinary Approach to the Platform-Based Economy'
[2017] Policy & Internet 374, 382.

[15] EC (DG GROW), 'Business-to-Business Relations in the Online Platform Environment: Final
Report' (2017) 8–9 <https://data.europa.eu/doi/10.2873/713211> accessed 18 November 2022.

[16] Vinoth Kumar, 'How Does Amazon Put a Customer on the "Path of Least Resistance"?'
(*Hackernoon*, 20 November 2018) <https://bit.ly/2VDZqgd> accessed 18 November 2022.

[17] See, generally, Paul Belleflamme and Martin Peitz, 'Inside the Engine Room of Digital
Platforms: Reviews, Ratings, and Recommendations' (22 February 2018) Aix-Marseille School of
Economics WP 2018 No 06 <http://dx.doi.org/10.2139/ssrn.3128141> accessed 18 November 2022.

Finally, numerous platforms institutionalize mechanisms to resolve disputes between their users.[18] Consider labour platforms like Upwork that adjudicate claims by freelancers contesting negative reviews; or Meta/Facebook's 'Oversight Board', which rules on content moderation spats relating to its social media infrastructure.[19]

In sum, platform regulation is altogether variegated, versatile, panoptic, and pervasive. It comprises prescriptive, restrictive, incentivizing, nudging, trust-building, and adjudicative norms, and institutional devices that private corporations unilaterally design, amend, implement, and enforce through the laws of contract and code.[20]

Non-state governance, to be sure, is neither novel nor specific to platforms; sports associations and leagues, for instance, have always organized sports competition according to self-determined rules, which regulate things like access, conditions of play, and revenue-sharing.[21] Nor is platform regulation necessarily problematic, *as such*—not for antitrust at least.[22] Self-arrogated rule-setting powers are indeed needed for optimal friction reduction, which, at heart, is what platforms do. Given their largely for-profit nature, one might expect them to formulate norms that serve all stakeholders involved.[23] In addition, few other options exist since public alternatives may be inefficient, unrealistic, and/or prone to capture.[24]

Yet, little systematic analysis has been conducted on what purposes platform governance serves and on how it helps achieve various organizational goals.[25] Furthermore, claims by providers regularly contradict the somewhat optimistic narrative advanced by early theorists who suggested that platform governance 'is as much about "pleasing all sides" [as] it is about platform profit seeking'.[26]

---

[18] See, generally, Rory Van Loo, 'The Corporation as Courthouse' [2016] Yale Journal on Regulation 547.

[19] Kate Klonick, 'Inside the Making of Facebook's Supreme Court' *New Yorker* (12 February 2021) <https://bityl.co/FEWG> accessed 18 November 2022.

[20] For more detailed illustrations, see eg David Evans and Richard Schmalensee, *Matchmakers: The New Economics of Multisided Platforms* (Harvard Business Review Press 2016) 135–48; Eaton and others (n 10) 217; Boudreau and Hagiu (n 11) 171–76. See also the insightful theoretical discussion in BRICS Competition Law and Policy Centre, 'Digital Era Competition: A BRICS View' (2019) ch 3 <https://bit.ly/3EIglnE> accessed 19 November 2022.

[21] Ken Foster, 'Is There a Global Sports Law?' in Robert Siekmann and Janwillem Soek (eds), *Lex Sportiva: What Is Sports Law?* (TMC Asser Press 2012).

[22] See, similarly, *Epic Games Inc v Apple Inc* 559 FSupp 3d 898, 948–49 (NDCal 2021) (regarding app store governance); *E-Kanopi* (Case 10/0081F) ADLC Decision 13-D-07 28 February 2013, [46] (regarding search advertising governance).

[23] Boudreau and Hagiu (n 11) 170.

[24] Rory Van Loo, 'Rise of the Digital Regulator' [2017] Duke Law Journal 1267, 1296–1310 (arguing that public platforms are likely to be inferior, in need of considerable financial and legislative support, and prone to capture); Boudreau and Hagiu (n 11) 169–176 (noting the shortcomings of public governance and arguing that private platform governance is theoretically and empirically more efficient).

[25] Liang Chen and others, 'Governance and Design of Digital Platforms: A Review and Future Research Directions on a Meta-Organization' [2022] Journal of Management 147, 173.

[26] Boudreau and Hagiu (n 11) 186.

2.2 The Claims

Rule-setting consumer-facing platforms inevitably come to possess superior bargaining power over their providers once they achieve critical mass and are able to sustain positive network effects.[27] This is because the platform-to-supplier relationship departs significantly from the classical intermediary/upstream set-up where reciprocal relation-specific investments introduce a degree of mutual dependence.[28] When platforms—especially multi-sided ones—are involved, the dynamic changes; it is mainly upstream providers who make relation-specific investments, which means the baseline becomes one where the balance of economic power is tilted towards platforms. What is generally the exception in the brick-and-mortar economy—think of grocery retailing—is hence the default in the platform age.[29]

Platform power is something Chapter 6 explores in more detail. Note here, however, that in a monopoly scenario, the platform can obtain complete control over the market access of providers, effectively becoming a bottleneck.[30] When the business is multi-sided, this situation can predictably lead it to appropriate most of the value created within the network it oversees.[31] Even in less extreme cases, such platforms will frequently have the ability and incentives to milk their dependent suppliers.[32]

Of course, neither skewed value capture by autocratic platforms, nor their superior bargaining power are in themselves competition problems. Remember: power imbalances are inevitable and, by consensus, provider-oriented substantive fairness to suppliers cannot be a guiding lodestar for antitrust purposes. But how must antitrust decision-makers handle claims of what can only be denoted as 'despotic' behaviour?

---

[27] Kevin Boudreau, 'Platform Boundary Choices & Governance: Opening-Up While Still Coordinating and Orchestrating' [2017] Entrepreneurship, Innovation, and Platforms 227, 235.

[28] ibid fn 5.

[29] The qualifier 'generally' is needed because power asymmetries favouring intermediaries are perhaps more widespread than is usually acknowledged (Peter Carstensen, *Competition Policy and the Control of Buyer Power: A Global Issue* (Edward Elgar 2017) ch 1).

[30] Heike Schweitzer and others, 'Modernisierung der Missbrauchsaufsicht für Marktmächtige Unternehmen' (29 August 2018) Report No 66/17, 67 <https://bityl.co/FjGH> accessed 18 November 2022.

[31] Jungsuk Oh, Byungwan Koh and Srinivasan Raghunathan, 'Value Appropriation Between the Platform Provider and App Developers in Mobile Platform Mediated Networks' [2015] Journal of Information Technology 245 (assuming perfectly substitutable apps and a monopolist app store that is the sole available distribution channel; predicting a 75 per cent appropriation rate; and further supporting the prediction with an empirical discussion of the Apple and Google app stores).

[32] Schweitzer and others (n 30) 67 (noting that this is particularly the case where consumers are only interested in a sufficiently large number of suppliers and where positive indirect network effects are significant). See also Paul Belleflamme and Martin Peitz, 'Platforms and Network Effects' in Luis Corchón and Marco Marini (eds), *Handbook of Game Theory and Industrial Organization: Volume II, Applications* (Edward Elgar 2018) 304 (modelling a scenario of competing platforms with multi-homing suppliers and single-homing consumers; and finding this creates a bottleneck effect enabling the platforms to squeeze providers).

Consider the Australian Competition and Consumer Commission (ACCC)'s broader inquiry into platforms and its decision to examine complaints levelled by publishers against Alphabet/Google's former 'First-Click-Free' policy. The latter required media businesses—under the threat of reprisals—to provide some of their paywalled content to consumers *free of charge*.[33] Luckily for us, the authority's final report sheds little light on the practice beyond finding that it dented publisher revenues.[34] This leaves the relevant question unanswered: can we rationalize the platform's take-it-or-leave-it 'offers' as potential competition problems?

In a different context, was the US Department of Justice (DoJ) wrong to dismiss booksellers and authors when they called for an investigation into Amazon's alleged bullying tactics back in late 2014?[35] For in the months prior, the platform had very publicly flaunted its power by exerting unprecedented pressure on Hachette—one of the big five publishers—in a dispute over e-book distribution revenues.

And beyond the super-platforms, what is antitrust to make of calls made by a few free-spirited (labour and competition) lawyers and economists for greater scrutiny of labour platform practices?[36] Sobering evidence of entrenched bargaining power asymmetries leading to below-minimum wages with platforms like Uber or Amazon's Mechanical Turk may well strike left-leaning minds as 'the smoking gun of exploitation';[37] inequality probably is 'a feature rather than a bug'[38] in the world of platform labour. Still, this reality says nothing on why *antitrust* decision-makers like the US Federal Trade Commission (FTC) should feel emboldened to '[c]rack [d]own on [c]ompanies [t]aking [a]dvantage of [g]ig [w]orkers',[39] even if doing so might 'serve the goals of competition and labour policy in a single stroke, and thereby afford added societal value in an era when both policies are badly in need of a boost'.[40]

[33] ACCC, 'Digital Platforms Inquiry: Final Report' (June 2019) 233–35 <http://bit.ly/3TKrNmY> accessed 19 November 2022.

[34] ibid 235.

[35] Jeffrey Trachtenberg, 'Authors Guild Met with DoJ to Seek Investigation into Amazon's Practices' *Wall Street Journal* (1 October 2014) <https://on.wsj.com/2yzk87h> accessed 18 November 2022.

[36] See eg Sanjukta Paul, 'Uber as For-Profit Hiring Hall: A Price-Fixing Paradox and Its Implications' [2017] Berkeley Journal of Employment and Labor Law 233; Victoria Daskalova, 'Regulating the New Self-Employed in the Uber Economy: What Role for EU Competition Law?' [2018] German Law Journal 461; Eric Posner, Glen Weyl and Suresh Naidu, 'Antitrust Remedies for Labor Market Power' [2018] Harvard Law Review 536; Marshall Steinbaum, 'Antitrust, the Gig Economy, and Labor Market Power' [2019] Law and Contemporary Problems 45.

[37] Trebor Scholz, *Uberworked and Underpaid: How Workers Are Disrupting the Digital Economy* (Polity Press 2017).

[38] Niels Van Doorn, 'Platform Labor: On the Gendered and Racialized Exploitation of Low-Income Service Work in the "On-Demand" Economy' [2017] Information, Communication & Society 898, 907.

[39] FTC, 'FTC to Crack Down on Companies Taking Advantage of Gig Workers: Agency Policy Statement Outlines Areas Where FTC Will Act to Protect Gig Workers from Unfair, Deceptive, and Anticompetitive Practices' (15 September 2022) <https://bit.ly/3tUV1VG> accessed 23 November 2022.

[40] Randy Stutz, 'The Evolving Antitrust Treatment of Labor-Market Restraints: From Theory to Practice' (31 July 2018) <https://ssrn.com/abstract=3332642> accessed 18 November 2022.

As the remainder of this chapter explains, theory-building around these types of claims is possible, regardless of the endorsed antitrust paradigm. Nevertheless, the venture is by no means straightforward if rigour is required. Let us use consumer welfare lenses first.

3. Despotism and 'Consumer Welfare'

Consumer welfare is a polymorphic paradigm. This approach to antitrust, we understand from Chapter 1, really reveals a commitment to a specific avatar, namely, total surplus, (*strong*) consumer surplus, or consumer choice.[41] Here, we will see that despotic behaviour by autocratic platforms can potentially be caught depending on the chosen proxy. Rigorous consumer welfare-minded decision-makers, though, will need to pick their models carefully.

3.1 Marketer Platforms

In their relationship with providers, platforms that choose the single life are, essentially, marketers, purchasing inputs they resell downstream.[42] Ergo, as a supermarket would in the brick-and-mortar world, single-sided platforms like Netflix can enjoy buyer power vis-à-vis suppliers. Our Amazon claim is a case in point.

The platform has a documented history of neglecting publisher interests. As industry observers know, terms for the distribution of e-books were up for renegotiation in 2014. And Amazon, they would recall, was ruthless with Hachette, itself a powerful conglomerate, when it came to control rights over retail pricing. Threats of reduced inventory, delayed deliveries, and increased print book prices eventually all morphed into real reprisals that allegedly injured the publisher, but also its authors.[43] According to some commentators, this was evidence of a *monopsony* power play.[44]

3.1.1 The monopsony theory
In economics, the presence of a monopsonist is a potential problem that is equally serious as that of a monopolist. According to the standard model, such a firm will squeeze its suppliers by withholding purchases to a point where the latter effectively

---

[41] Remember: total *welfare* is not used in practice, nor does anyone pretend it can be (today).

[42] Andrei Hagiu and Julian Wright, 'Marketplace or Reseller' [2015] Management Science 184; Daniel Spulber, *Market Microstructure: Intermediaries and the Theory of the Firm* (CUP 1999) (distinguishing 'marketers'—which include retailers, wholesalers, and dealers—from 'brokers').

[43] David Streitfeld, 'Writers Feel an Amazon–Hachette Spat' *New York Times* (9 May 2014) <https://nyti.ms/35bNo24> accessed 18 November 2022.

[44] See eg Paul Krugman, 'Amazon's Monopsony Is Not OK' *New York Times* (19 October 2014) <https://nyti.ms/2Cs48pR> accessed 18 November 2022.

end up pricing inefficiently (i.e. below their marginal costs of production). This misallocation of resources always translates into deadweight loss for society.[45] Worse, higher (or at minimum, never decreasing) consumer prices will tend to further compound these total surplus reductions.[46] So too will potentially harmful long-run effects on product diversity, quality, and innovation.[47] Consumer welfare (however understood) is thus clearly at stake.[48]

All the same, Amazon (to return to our example) was no textbook monopsonist in the early 2010s, nor is it probably today for that matter. Why? Because the specifications underlying conventional economic models are so stringent that the phenomenon has been profiled as an anomaly unlikely to arise beyond employment and agricultural commodities.[49] Formal economics aside, monopsony is intuitively improbable as well. Assuming it is rationally run, a firm like Amazon gains little by squeezing the life out of publishers; this would cripple its ability to serve consumers and make profits.[50]

In brief, marketer platform despotism as a reflection of monopsony is a possible theory of harm to consumer welfare. But it is a rather implausible one.

3.1.2 Bargaining theories

For economists, monopsony abuses are a grave yet highly unlikely scenario. Even so, owing to the development of more sophisticated tools, some game theorists have taken a keen interest in modelling the effects of bargaining power asymmetries between vertically related firms beyond the monopsony context. What do they find?

Generally, their conclusions are positive: the exercise of superior bargaining power is usually found to reflect what is known as Galbraithian *countervailing power*—a situation where a strong buyer disciplines powerful upstream suppliers into bringing their prices closer to the allocatively efficient level (i.e. marginal costs).[51] And because the ensuing cost savings will often be passed on downstream,

---

[45] Ignacio Herrera Anchustegui, *Buyer Power in EU Competition Law* (Concurrences 2017) 33–34, 52–53; Carstensen (n 29) 42.

[46] For instance, where the monopsonist also has considerable seller market power it will reduce its sales downstream, pushing consumer prices up (Anchustegui (n 45) 52–57).

[47] ibid.

[48] ibid 52–59.

[49] More specifically, monopsony is said to only ever occur where the sole buyer (or a coordinated oligopsony) benefits from: an upward slopping supply curve (which reflects increasing marginal costs of supply); an inelastic supply curve (implying suppliers have little to no outside options to sell their output); the existence of economic rents ripe for extraction; and the existence of high entry barriers on the buyer side (ibid 37–40; Carstensen (n 29) 42)). For a detailed analysis of Amazon's lack of monopsony power, see John Kirkwood, 'Collusion to Control a Powerful Customer: Amazon, E-Books, and Antitrust Policy' [2014] University of Miami Law Review 1.

[50] Anchustegui (n 45) 41.

[51] JK Galbraith, *American Capitalism: The Concept of Countervailing Power* (2nd edn, Blackwell 1980) 108–34.

consumer surplus will predictably trend higher too.[52] A far cry from monopsony, superior bargaining power is therefore typically seen as socially benign, beneficial to consumers, and sometimes actually favourable to suppliers.[53] Accordingly, many economists might still feel that 'concerns about buyer power in the digital world may be ... premature and ill-placed'.[54]

That said, some would caution consumer welfare-minded antitrust decision-makers against magnanimity. Germain Gaudin, for instance, notes that papers associating superior bargaining power with positive effects are overly case-specific and ultimately unhelpful for antitrust purposes.[55] His theoretical model, by contrast, has broader applicability. Most notably, it suggests that the conditions under which rough bargaining by a powerful retailer improves consumer welfare (through lower retail prices) are in reality quite restrictive.[56]

One caveat: bargaining models and their predictions are both complex and very sensitive to departures from the defined parameters.[57] Several models for any given conduct may, moreover, exist, each differing from the others in terms of finely grained assumptions. So much so, in fact, that decision-makers may understandably become confused.[58] Going back to our Amazon conundrum illustrates this nicely.

As previously mentioned, the platform's feud with Hachette (and with all the other major publishers) pertained to who should have the right to set retail prices for e-books distributed through Amazon's digital infrastructure. Antitrust lawyers will no doubt be aware that this was something publishers had the temerity to collude over with Apple in a conspiracy (in)famously outlawed in 2012 for two years.[59] Paradoxically, the majors *did* get their way once the ban expired as Amazon eventually caved. E-books would no longer be first sold at a wholesale price to the platform which, in turn, would set the retail price (i.e. wholesale pricing); the large

---

[52] See the literature reviews in Germain Gaudin, 'Vertical Bargaining and Retail Competition: What Drives Countervailing Power?' [2017] Economic Journal 2380, 2383–84; Anchustegui (n 45) 59–60.

[53] See eg Pierre Mérel and Richard Sexton, 'Buyer Power with Atomistic Upstream Entry: Can Downstream Consolidation Increase Production and Welfare?' [2017] International Journal of Industrial Organization 259 (finding that, where powerful buyers internalize the fact that exercising their power over suppliers might attenuate upstream innovation and entry, increasing buyer concentration can actually benefit suppliers).

[54] Antonio Buttà and Andrea Pezzoli, 'Buyer Power and Competition Policy: From Brick-and-Mortar Retailers to Digital Platforms' [2014] Economia e Politica Industriale 159, 169. cf Monopolkommission, 'Competition policy: The Challenge of Digital Markets' (2015) Special Report No 68, [387] <https://perma.cc/6B3V-55QT> accessed 18 November 2022 (stating that 'it is not obvious that buyer power should be judged in any other way in e-commerce than in classical trade').

[55] Gaudin (n 52) 2381, 2384–85.

[56] ibid 2391ff (in particular, market demand must be very convex).

[57] For an overview of the economics of bargaining models, see Joshua Wright and John Yun, 'Use and Abuse of Bargaining Models in Antitrust' [2020] University of Kansas Law Review 1055, 1057–64.

[58] More generally, Wright and Yun find that complexity largely explains the uneven adoption of bargaining models in US antitrust practice. The authors accordingly argue that 'their use should be limited by fact-specific evidence' (ibid 1095).

[59] *United States v Apple Inc* 791 F3d 290 (2d Cir 2015). Technically, publishers had already agreed to cease (attempts aimed at) setting retail prices of e-books in a settlement with the DoJ.

publishers would, instead, now pay the platform sales royalties to distribute their products at a price they themselves would determine (i.e. agency pricing).

Naturally, this raises the following question: can the DoJ really be faulted for giving publishers like Hachette the cold shoulder when they appealed for its assistance to deal with Amazon's brutal bargaining tactics? Putting this query to the game theorist begets a reply that is equally loquacious and equivocal.

For example, one model, which assumes a bilateral duopoly, would absolve Amazon.[60] Why? Because it suggests wholesale pricing is always better for consumers unless horizontal competition between platforms (say, Amazon and Barnes & Nobles) is less intense than that between publishers.

Another study, on the other hand, contradicts this prediction entirely under slightly different specifications.[61] Yet, in a subsequent analysis, its author finds that when one considers both the platform's incentive to lock in consumers and a longer time frame, results are more nuanced. The wholesale system, it turns out, is better for consumers at first, but worse long term. Still, the researcher predicts as well that agency pricing, while preferable if one values lower retail prices, may inhibit vigorous competition between suppliers on the platform (i.e. *within*-platform competition) and erode consumer choice.[62]

To complicate things further, another model would always vindicate the cause of publishers ... provided a monopoly publisher is assumed and effects on the market for Kindle readers are ignored.[63] Otherwise, the conclusion is that Amazon's behaviour would likely lower e-book prices in order to stimulate sales of its e-reader. The authors, though, themselves overlook a similar, earlier, study whose results are far more ambiguous.[64] And there is more!

Other economists have faulted all their colleagues for abstracting away the bargaining element.[65] Unlike the latter (who examine situations like our Amazon–Hachette dispute but wrongly assume contracts are *always* negotiated under take-it-or-leave-it conditions), these economists integrate bargaining. Strikingly, they find that the consumer's wallet is heavier when control over retail pricing is in

[60] Øystein Foros, Hans Jarle Kind and Greg Shaffer, 'Apple's Agency Model and the Role of Most-Favored-Nation Clauses' [2017] RAND Journal of Economics 673.

[61] Justin Johnson, 'The Agency Model and MFN Clauses' [2017] Review of Economic Studies 1151 (here, contractual terms are determined endogenously).

[62] Justin Johnson, 'The Agency and Wholesale Models in Electronic Content Markets' [2020] International Journal of Industrial Organization 1.

[63] Vibhanshu Abhishek, Kinshuk Jerath and Z John Zhang, 'Agency Selling or Reselling? Channel Structures in Electronic Retailing' [2016] Management Science 2259.

[64] Germain Gaudin and Alexander White, 'On the Antitrust Economics of the Electronic Books Industry' (24 September 2014) <https://ssrn.com/abstract=2352495> accessed 18 November 2022. See also, for a more general model, German Gaudin and Alexander White, 'Vertical Agreements and User Access' [2021] American Economic Journal: Microeconomics 328.

[65] Babur De los Santos, Daniel O'Brien and Matthijs Wildenbeest, 'Agency Pricing and Bargaining: Evidence from the E-Book Market' (October 2021) <https://bityl.co/Fjtk> accessed 19 November 2022.

the platform's hands. That is, insofar as publishers do not have considerably more bargaining power.

So, was the DoJ overly dismissive? As the foregoing suggests, there is no clear answer. In hindsight, maybe the authority did get it right. A recent empirical study indeed shows that e-book prices would be *lower* than they are today had Amazon's despotic behaviour *succeeded*.[66] Its authors further estimate that the fight actually was evenly matched. This gives weight to their theoretical model, which emphasizes the importance of how bargaining power is distributed for prediction purposes.[67]

In short: despotism by marketer platforms is nothing to excessively fret over, at least inasmuch as Amazon and consumer welfare-minded antitrust are concerned ... right? Not so fast. For what do we make of consumer anxieties not captured by any of the above-mentioned works, which focus almost exclusively on (short-run) price and output effects? Had Amazon prevailed in its tussle with book publishers, maybe the latter would have reduced the quality and/or variety of their output; perhaps their incentives to innovate in production and design would have diminished; and in the (possibly not-so-distant) future, some may have failed, resulting in a loss of diversity.[68]

These are all worthy 'consumer welfare' concerns. *But*—and this will become a recurring theme throughout the next three chapters—one can *always* conjecture harm caught by the *strong* consumer surplus and consumer choice variations of the consumer welfare paradigm, be it through reduced choice/diversity, lowered quality, and/or dampened innovation (incentives). The problem is that these are worries which, in general, will come from the gut, 'educated' as it may be, rather than from a formal model. Besides, when they can be rigorously formalized, such theories of harm will frequently be based on ambiguous foundations.

The takeaway from the discussion, then, is as follows: powerful marketer platforms that take a despotic turn certainly should prompt our consumer welfare-minded antitrust decision-makers into action, even when monopsony is not at play. However, there are two caveats.

First, only those focused on either total surplus or consumer surplus will usually be able to rely on rigorously formalized theories. Enforcers who profess a commitment to things like quality and innovation will undeniably bolster their approval ratings with consumers who put a premium on these parameters. At the same time, regarding the practices we have been exploring here, (informed) intuition will tend to be their lone guide.

---

[66] ibid (finding that retail prices for e-books published by the majors and distributed by Amazon increased by approximately 14 per cent once the transition to agency pricing was completed).

[67] ibid.

[68] Christopher Sagers, *United States v. Apple: Competition in America* (Harvard UP 2019) 236ff; John Kirkwood, 'Reforming the Robinson–Patman Act to Serve Consumers and Control Powerful Buyers' [2015] Antitrust Bulletin 358, 364ff.

Second, caution is warranted because platform despotism's negative effects on 'consumer welfare' are far from unequivocal. Our aside on Amazon illustrates this for marketer platforms. The following subsections show that the same is true in other contexts.

3.2 Broker Platforms

'Platforming' is an endogenous business model decision. Some may choose the single life; others will open up their digital infrastructure to enable direct inter-actions between distinct customer groups, i.e. become *multi*-sided.[69] Whereas the former are effectively marketers, the latter are more akin to brokers.[70] This has po-tentially important ramifications.

3.2.1 Prolegomenon

As noted in the introductory chapter, a relatively young, but now mainstream strand of the industrial organization (IO) scholarship deals specifically with these types of platforms. In fact, these multi-sided market economists have been prolific over the past decade. Significantly for present purposes, apex courts on both sides of the Atlantic have added hype to their models in landmark antitrust rulings.[71]

Fortunately (for me), experts have already done the job of extricating key in-sights from this literature, saving us from another digression that wouldn't do justice to it anyway.[72] Nonetheless, one lesson is apparently so fundamental I would be remiss for not recounting it. It is that adopting a single-sided logic—relying on models involving marketer platforms—would be a mistake.[73] Policymakers, we are told, have to always remember that multi-sided platforms require the right mix of users to ignite and sustain their businesses. Why? Because these firms cater to distinct customer groups—providers and consumers—whose demand curves and economic welfare are interdependent. This means the effects of their practices ought to be analysed on all sides mediated through the platform infrastructure and balanced accordingly.[74]

---

[69] See, generally on this question, Paul Belleflamme and Martin Peitz, *The Economics of Platforms: Concepts and Strategy* (CUP 2021) ch 4.

[70] Hagiu and Wright (n 42) 184, 185.

[71] *Ohio v American Express Co* 138 SCt 2274, 2280ff (2018); Case C-67/13 P *Cartes Bancaires* ECLI:EU:C:2014:2204 [2014] electronic Reports of Cases, [72]–[87].

[72] Bruno Jullien and Wilfried Sand-Zantman, 'The Economics of Platforms: A Theory Guide for Competition Policy' [2021] Information Economics and Policy 100880.

[73] This is now 'conventional wisdom', according to Francesco Ducci, 'Procedural Implications of Market Definition in Platform Cases' [2019] Journal of Antitrust Enforcement 419, 424.

[74] See also, notably, David Evans and Richard Schmalensee, 'Ignoring Two-Sided Business Reality Can Also Hurt Plaintiffs' (*CPI Antitrust Chronicle*, April 2018) 47 <https://bit.ly/3kmyc7c> accessed 18 November 2022.

Simply stated, the thrust of multi-sided market economics appears to be that what may seem problematic under a one-sided approach can be misleading. The most often-cited example is that of price predation: below-cost pricing on the consumer side might not be predatory if it is actually a subsidy borne by providers to stimulate adoption of the platform infrastructure.[75]

With this brief excursus in the rear-view mirror, let us return to our allegedly despotic platforms.

3.2.2 Application

Formalizing the consumer welfare harm potentially flowing from despotic broker platforms is a difficult task since there is a conspicuous gap in the IO literature. To date, researchers have focused on these firms' pricing practices and on conducts that could affect horizontal competition between platforms (such as cartels or foreclosure tactics like tying or exclusive dealings).[76] The study of infrastructure design and governance, by contrast, has been somewhat neglected.[77] Put differently, there is a paucity of useful economic research regarding what has been denoted here as platform despotism.[78] Until theory catches up, harm will regularly have to be rationalized by relying partly on intuition and partly by extrapolating insights from more general multi-sided platform models whose assumptions may not necessarily fit the situations we are interested in. In so doing, however, competition problems can often become harder to see.

Consider Alphabet/Google, an information broker, and its now-abandoned First-Click-Free policy. Media organizations have long argued that the practice crippled their ability to monetize their content through subscription paywalls, while reinforcing the platform's grip on consumers and advertisers.[79] Crucially, publisher dependence on referral traffic, generally, and from Google Search, especially, is well documented.[80] Between a forced giveaway and online suicide, the 'choice' was probably obvious for many.[81] This might explain how the platform

---

[75] See, in particular, Julian Wright, 'One-sided Logic in Two-sided Markets' [2004] Review of Network Economics 44, 48.

[76] Much of this literature underscores the need to consider platforms' price structure (i.e. the distribution of prices charged to each side), as opposed to the price level (i.e. the net price). For references and discussion of seminal works, see Jullien and Sand-Zantman (n 72).

[77] See the literature review in Tat-How Teh, 'Platform Governance' [2022] American Economic Journal: Microeconomics 213. See also Chen and others (n 25) 167.

[78] See also EC (DG GROW) (n 15) 17 (underscoring this reality); Jean Tirole, *Economics for the Common Good* (Steven Rendall tr, Princeton UP 2017) 396 (noting that '[t]he economic analysis of these issues ... is in its infancy').

[79] See eg European Publishers Council, 'Public Comments of the European Publishers Council Submitted in the Context of the FTC "Hearings on Competition and Consumer Protection in the 21st Century"' (20 August 2018) 6 <https://perma.cc/AG2M-2UBA> accessed 18 November 2022.

[80] See eg CMA, 'Online Platforms and Digital Advertising: Market Study Final Report' (1 July 2020) [5.362]–[5.368] <https://bit.ly/3Avd1tA> accessed 19 November 2022; ACCC (n 33) 218.

[81] For instance, when the *Wall Street Journal* chose to opt out of First Click Free, its traffic from Google Search plunged by 44 per cent (Danny Sullivan, 'Wall Street Journal's Google Traffic Drops 44% After Pulling Out of First Click Free' (*Search Engine Land*, 5 June 2017) <https://bit.ly/2xU1VkU> accessed 18 November 2022).

could enforce a policy which was potentially detrimental to its 'partners' for nearly a decade, despite economic theory postulating that multi-sided platforms *must* cater to all their user groups.[82]

Now, the ACCC did find that First Click Free had negative fallouts on the subscription numbers of publishers that paywall their content.[83] Yet, as the authority pointed out, the practice made perfect economic sense for a broker platform like Alphabet/Google.[84] Free access to otherwise paywalled content for consumers made Google Search more attractive to them, but likewise in turn to advertisers who effectively subsidize the operation of the infrastructure. Consequently, the overall wealth pie more likely expanded and consumers certainly did benefit in the short term. If consumer welfare means total surplus or consumer surplus, one can easily sympathize with the antitrust decision-maker who fails to see a competition problem.

By contrast, when the focus is on *strong* consumer surplus or consumer choice, harm can always be theorized. Lower publisher revenues might result in reduced incentives to invest into producing quality and diverse content, all of which benefit consumers. Again, though, this is the sort of speculation one can rarely back with a formal model or by evidence causally tying the despotic behaviour at hand to the alleged effects.

In sum, when IO theorists who counsel against using more traditional models enter the fray, formalizing a theory of consumer welfare harm becomes more challenging, regardless of how the paradigm is construed. The potentially perverse consequences of such a multi-sided logic are maybe better appreciated in the context of labour platforms.

3.3 Labour Platforms

The compensation most labour platform providers obtain for their services is notoriously low. Some scholars say this reflects the monopsony power wielded by platforms and/or their consumers.[85] Implicitly, theirs is a call to shift the focus of analysis. The labour platform-to-provider relationship, they would argue, really unfolds within a labour market where platforms are monopsonist employers (or monopsony facilitators).

---

[82] Evans and Schmalensee (n 74) 48.
[83] ACCC (n 33) 235.
[84] ibid.
[85] See eg Suresh Naidu and Eric Posner, 'Labor Monopsony and the Limits of the Law' [2022] Journal of Human Resources 284, 296 (arguing that '[t]hese platforms ... tend to be natural monopsonies'); Posner, Weyl and Naidu (n 36) 536.

While these allegations occasionally betray somewhat loose handling of the concept, there are reasons to believe that platform providers do face 'monopsony-like' conditions in certain industries.

Consider ride-hailing and food delivery. At first glance, the latter seem quite dynamic and competitive, despite their increasingly high levels of concentration; Uber, Deliveroo, and the likes have long dangled bonus payments to entice drivers to sign up, while maintaining attractive prices for consumers.[86] Nevertheless, if perfect and complete data were publicly available, one might find proof of an upward-slopping labour supply curve—the bellwether test for monopsony in labour markets.[87]

One reason may be conjectural as platforms like Uber owe much of their success to broader macroeconomic shifts. Fissured labour markets, marked by a growing reliance on contingent, flexible, and (bogus) self-employed work, have become pervasive over the past two decades.[88] This—combined with a deep pool of economically vulnerable and 'commodifiable' unemployed, under-employed, and mis-employed workers—could partly explain how these platforms managed to thrive, notwithstanding considerable levels of provider churn.[89] For if these markets were truly competitive, rational platforms would not be able to sustain their businesses, as per both standard and multi-sided market theory. Not while simultaneously depressing wages (or 'fees') to the point where many suppliers just exit the market. Uber and Amazon Mechanical Turk, for instance, reportedly face respective turnarounds among drivers and 'Turkers' of roughly 150 per cent and 140 per cent each year.[90] Besides, some economists have empirically examined and confirmed the existence of monopsony power on the consumer side of Amazon's labour platform.[91] Importantly, these broader macroeconomic trends are here to stay if early COVID-19-era data are anything to go by.[92]

---

[86] Shannon Bond, 'Uber and Lyft to Offer Shares to Drivers as Part of IPOs' *Financial Times* (28 February 2019) <https://on.ft.com/2H5AaYu> accessed 18 November 2022.

[87] An accurate measurement would require access to information relating to standard metrics like the marginal product of labour, total revenue, marginal revenue product, and marginal labour costs.

[88] David Weil, *The Fissured Workplace: Why Work Became So Bad for So Many and What Can Be Done to Improve It* (Harvard UP 2014). See also Lawrence Katz and Alan Krueger, 'The Rise and Nature of Alternative Work Arrangements in the United States, 1995–2015' [2019] Industrial & Labor Relations Review 382.

[89] Gemma Newlands, Christoph Lutze and Christian Fieseler, 'Power in the Sharing Economy' (30 April 2017) 6 <https://ssrn.com/abstract=2960938> accessed 18 November 2022.

[90] Michael Cusumano, Annabelle Gawer and David Yoffie, *The Business of Platforms: Strategy in the Age of Digital Competition, Innovation, and Power* (HarperBusiness 2019) ch 3, s 3 (for Uber); Scholz (n 37) 29 (for Amazon Mechanical Turk).

[91] Arindrajit Dube and others, 'Monopsony in Online Labor Markets' [2020] American Economic Review: Insights 33.

[92] Fabian Stephany and others, 'Distancing Bonus or Downscaling Loss? The Changing Livelihood of Us Online Workers in Times of COVID-19' [2020] Tijdschrift voor Economische en Sociale Geografie 561 (focusing on the USA and finding that workers are increasingly resorting to labour platforms and that demand quickly recovered, even surpassing pre-pandemic levels in some occupational areas).

A second reason for the potential presence of monopsony conditions may be that the latter are, to some extent, artificially manufactured by the platforms themselves through various governance mechanisms. Ethnographic studies of Uber and Lyft drivers are insightful in this regard. They point to the intensive use of data-driven, algorithmically implemented behavioural nudges and scheduling prompts. What for? To prod drivers into working longer hours in order to ensure constant (over)supply on the provider side of the platform.[93] The 'surge pricing' algorithm is a well-known example.[94] Other mechanisms blend technology with gamification and involve sending predictive messages to drivers about future occurrences of high demand, or prompts to exploit their tendency to set earning goals.[95] Plus, a cross-national survey of labour platform users in the EU further suggests that artificially driving up supply of providers is the basic purpose of these discrete governance mechanisms[96]—a finding not confined to ride-hailing platforms.[97]

The ostensible organizational efficiencies these platforms do entrain are important.[98] But the fact remains that, in theory, monopsony is not conducive to consumer welfare (however understood). Well, not until the empirical literature and a multi-sided logic are accounted for. To see this, focusing on Uber, which has been the preferred test subject of economists, is useful.

One study finds that, during the first twenty-four weeks of 2015, Uber generated roughly US$1.60 of consumer surplus for every dollar spent by consumers in the

[93] Alex Rosenblat and Luke Stark, 'Algorithmic Labor and Information Asymmetries: A Case Study of Uber's Drivers' [2016] International Journal of Communication 3759.

[94] M Keith Chen, 'Dynamic Pricing in a Labor Market: Surge Pricing and Flexible Work on the Uber Platform' in *Proceedings of the 2016 ACM Conference on Economics and Computation* (Association for Computing Machinery 2016) <https://doi.org/10.1145/2940716.2940798> accessed 18 November 2022 (using proprietary Uber data and finding that '[o]verall, it appears that the dynamic pricing mechanism is very effective in encouraging short-term supply growth on the Uber platform by encouraging partners already on the system to contribute more time than they otherwise would have'). See also Rosenblat and Stark (n 93) 3759, 3765–71 (finding that many drivers continue to absorb the costs of being available, accessible, and responsive to the platform, despite the absence of any guarantee they will effectively be compensated for their time).

[95] Rosenblat and Stark (n 93) 3765–71. See also Jamie Woodcock and Mark Jonson, 'Gamification: What It Is, and How to Fight It' [2018] Sociological Review 542 (explaining that this is associated with management practices, which seek to extract maximum effort or output from workers through the introduction of gamic elements to make an activity more pleasant, enjoyable, or bearable).

[96] Gemma Newlands, Christoph Lutze and Christian Fieseler, 'European Perspective on Power in the Sharing Economy' (3 January 2018) 47–48 <https://ssrn.com/abstract=3046473> accessed 18 November 2022. Admittedly, one should interpret survey results cautiously. Beyond the method's intrinsic limitations, only 9.1 per cent of the 6,000 respondents were platform providers. Moreover, the proportion of ride-hailing platform providers was not disclosed. Nevertheless, the study usefully corroborates more discrete ethnographic research.

[97] See eg Frank Field and Andrew Forsey, 'Delivering Justice? A Report on the Pay and Working Conditions of Deliveroo Riders' (July 2018) 9 <https://perma.cc/V2PJ-MQUL> accessed 18 November (finding that Deliveroo also artificially manufactures an oversupply of couriers by, for instance, not limiting the number of couriers that can access the order zones it creates).

[98] World Bank, *World Development Report 2019: The Changing Nature of Work* (World Bank 2019) 40 <https://bit.ly/3EMOdQr> accessed 19 November 2022 (stating that the rise of these platforms 'marks a shift in the potential nature of firms more generally').

platform's four largest US markets.[99] On a yearly basis, this translates into an esti-mated US$2.88 billion in consumer surplus, or US$6.76 billion when extrapolated to the entire nation.

Another, more recent, analysis reinforces these findings.[100] It shows that from March to April 2017, Uber's algorithmic management increased total and con-sumer surpluses in the city of Houston by respectively 1.91 per cent and 3.55 per cent of gross revenue.

Additionally, effects are not solely monetary. Some researchers find that quality and choice have improved as a result of how Uber runs its business: consumers gain significantly through shorter waiting time and more comfortable travelling when compared to taxis and subways.[101] Moreover, they benefit because tech-aided matching nudges drivers into providing their services in areas underserved by other transportation modes.[102]

And drivers in all this? It seems that their wealth is being shifted to consumers.[103]

Therefore, monopsony-inducing algorithmic control of drivers looks like a win-ning proposition for consumers and the economic welfare of society as a whole. A potential competition problem we could formally rationalize under a one-sided economic approach accordingly becomes nearly impossible to visualize under a multi-sided lens.

The dilemma probably extends beyond Uber to labour platforms more gen-erally. As some scholars have theorized, if these firms value efficiency, they *must* govern the infrastructure in a way that 'negatively affects (i.e. reduces) the cost of labour and the time it takes for workers to complete a work task'.[104] This means det-rimental effects upstream are in fact necessary to conduce efficient outcomes in the short run, even if it 'can also lead to unfair treatment of workers and threaten the long-term sustainability of platform work'.[105]

---

[99] Peter Cohen and others, 'Using Big Data to Estimate Consumer Surplus: The Case of Uber' (2016) NBER Working Paper No 22627 <https://www.nber.org/papers/w22627> accessed 18 November 2022 (using proprietary Uber data).

[100] Juan Camilo Castillo, 'Who Benefits from Surge Pricing?' (8 August 2022) <https://ssrn.com/abstract=3245533> accessed 18 November 2022.

[101] Chungsang Tom Lam and Meng Liu, 'Demand and Consumer Surplus in the On-demand Economy: The Case of Ride Sharing' (11 October 2017) <https://bityl.co/FjuA> accessed 19 November 2022 (using publicly available New York City (NYC) transportation data and granular data on surge pricing and wait time on Uber and Lyft in 2016).

[102] Chungsang Tom Lam and Meng Liu, 'The Geography of Ridesharing: A Case Study of New York City' [2021] Information Economics and Policy 100941 (using NYC taxi, Uber, and Lyft records with data on Uber and Lyft dynamic pricing and wait time). Reaching a similar con-clusion through a different perspective, see Kibum Kim, Chulwoo Baek and Jeong-Dong Lee, 'Creative Destruction of the Sharing Economy in Action: The Case of Uber' [2018] Transportation Research 118.

[103] Castillo (n 100) (finding that drivers' surplus decreased by 1.01 per cent of gross revenue).

[104] Elham Shafiei Gol, Mari-Klara Stein and Michel Avital, 'Crowdwork Platform Governance Toward Organizational Value Creation' [2019] Journal of Strategic Information Systems 175, 185.

[105] ibid.

3.4 Summation

Despotic practices of autocratic platforms can be rationalized as potential competition problems under the consumer welfare paradigm. However, theory-building around these matters is not straightforward.

For one, formalizing the potential harm will frequently be possible only if consumer welfare means consumer or total surplus. The reason is that, beyond static surplus effects, there will rarely be (today at least) models providing a rigorously constructed narrative explaining why and when these types of practices might lessen diversity, degrade quality, and/or dampen innovation (incentives). In other words, the additional harms decision-makers committed to *strong* consumer surplus or consumer choice would be attuned to will usually have to be rationalized through (informed) speculation.

For another, even when economists can usefully lend a helping hand, the complexity of their work can confuse antitrust authorities and courts. The latter may, at the very least, need to expend considerable resources into parsing out what is relevant from what is not. The point should not be understated, especially when broker platforms are concerned, and the issue of multi-sidedness becomes salient. Remember, economists themselves will regularly disagree on when multi-sidedness is to be accounted for.[106] They may occasionally even butt heads over whether a multi-sided platform is at stake,[107] and, if so, on what ground(s).[108]

With this in mind, it is time to examine how the competitive process paradigm fares in comparison.

4. Despotism and 'Freedom'

4.1 Prolegomenon

For many of us, the intuitive reaction to charges of platform despotism would probably be that such behaviours offend our sense of what 'free' competition is about. Naturally, this has little to do with consumer welfare. Freedom, as explained in Chapter 2, is a constitutive part of the economic democracy antitrust has to safeguard under the competitive process paradigm.

That said, recall the overall claim I am attempting to make a compelling case for with this book: our upstream worries place antitrust in bed with Procrustes. One

---

[106] See eg Andre Boik, 'Prediction and Identification in Two-Sided Markets' (March 2018) <https://dx.doi.org/10.2139/ssrn.3104846> accessed 18 November 2022.

[107] Dirk Auer and Nicolas Petit, 'Two-Sided Markets and the Challenge of Turning Economic Theory into Antitrust Policy' [2015] Antitrust Bulletin 426, 432–36.

[108] cf ibid 455, with Richard Gilbert, 'E-books: A Tale of Digital Disruption' [2015] Journal of Economic Perspectives 165, 170–71, regarding e-books.

aspect of the argument (foreshadowed in the introduction to this part) goes as follows: whereas shifting paradigms might leave the policy standing on sounder normative foundations when directed upstream, change is not a simple proposition. Consumer welfare, we just saw, clearly can do the job, albeit a laboured one, when autocratic platforms take a despotic turn. Furthermore, if the consensus demand for analytical rigour still holds, competitive process-minded decision-makers would have to roam beyond the chartered territory of (neoclassical) economics to vindicate their fears.[109] This is a venture many will likely be loath to undertake. Why? Because formalizing a freedom-based theory of harm means appealing to political philosophers who, unlike modern economists, are not 'trained to take an interesting question and squeeze it as quickly as possible into a formal model'.[110] If decision-makers in jurisdictions like the USA and the EU were not inclined to do so during times when such claims were routinely made but rejected for their lack of rigour,[111] they will probably remain reluctant today.

Not without reason, mind you. For we should have no illusions that the harm to competition flowing from despotic platforms can actually be formalized under a *self-standing* concept of freedom. Reviewing the political philosophy scholarship reveals that attempting to do so would plunge antitrust into a discursive sinkhole.

Indeed, freedom as neo-republican 'non-domination', we already know, is difficult to reconcile with a dynamic market economy and well-established antitrust principles.[112] Besides, to have the policy aim at its protection would, in practice, probably sometimes (maybe typically) entail enforcement covertly guided by a particular vision of *outcome* fairness,[113] which the competitive process paradigm cannot coherently register directly.[114]

Freedom is also often defined as the absence of interference, a view espoused by the classical liberal and libertarian political traditions.[115] Yet, endorsing this conception simply leads to a freedom paradox, which decision-makers have long found creates an insoluble dilemma since any exertion of power would then be problematic from an antitrust perspective.[116]

---

[109] See, similarly, Lawrence Sullivan, 'Economics and More Humanistic Disciplines: What Are the Sources of Wisdom for Antitrust?' [1977] University of Pennsylvania Law Review 1214.

[110] John Roemer, *Theories of Distributive Justice* (Harvard UP 1996) 2.

[111] See eg *Continental Television Inc v GTE Sylvania Inc* 433 US 36, 54 (1977) (agreeing with critics describing older jurisprudence—which relied on freedom to rationalize the harm flowing from vertical restraints—as 'a perversion of antitrust analysis').

[112] See Chapter 2, Section 3.1, p 53 in this book.

[113] Indeed, US Progressive-era thinkers like Robert Hale seemed to use 'freedom' 'as a rhetorical stand-in for material wealth' to ultimately argue for a more equal distribution of it (Barbara Fried, *The Progressive Assault on Laissez-Faire: Robert Hale and the First Law and Economics Movement* (Harvard UP 2001) 70 (expounding Hale's work)).

[114] See Chapter 2, Section 3.2.2 in this book.

[115] See Ian Carter, 'Positive and Negative Liberty' in Edward Zalta (ed), *The Stanford Encyclopedia of Philosophy* (rev edn, Stanford University 2022) <https://stanford.io/2LExXnc> accessed 18 November 2022.

[116] See eg Case T-168/01 *GlaxoSmithKline Services* ECLI:EU:T:2006:265 [2006] ECR II-2969, [171] ('any contract concluded between economic agents operating at different stages of the ... chain has the

Finally, one could suggest borrowing from views on freedom pegged to self-mastery or autonomy enabled by one's ability to achieve valued ends, which in turn requires the widest range of choices and capacities.[117] This understanding, though, seems inapposite for antitrust purposes as it does not involve *constraints*, but rather the presence of something indeterminate, identifiable in the works of visionaries like Jean-Jacques Rousseau and Immanuel Kant.[118] Even if it were relevant, how would decision-makers determine when it has been impinged? For example, do Uber and Amazon Mechanical Turk deprive labourers of their autonomy by algorithmically manipulating them? Or do they instead empower them by enabling individuals who would otherwise be marginalized from traditional labour markets to generate an income?

Freedom, in sum, is an inherently pluralistic ideal.[119] Notionally, it cannot, on its own, further inform our understanding of what may constitute an antitrust injury. The question is whether there are more heuristically helpful concepts that enable us to say antitrust is protecting the freedom of providers all the same while remaining rigorous. This is the endeavour the remainder of this chapter devotes itself to.

4.2   Coercion

4.2.1   Prolegomenon

Famed economist/political scientist Charles Lindblom once wrote that 'liberty in market systems exists only if everyone is able to escape coercion at the hands of any one buyer or seller by turning to another'.[120] And beyond its obvious causal correlation with unfreedom,[121] doesn't 'coercion' hit home for (some of) the fears entertained in this chapter? A few of our antitrust enforcers would certainly agree.[122] What's more, coercion is not conceptually obscure to antitrust. For one, it was

---

consequence of … restricting them … in their freedom of action'); *GTE Sylvania* (n 111) 54 ('As Mr. Justice Brandeis reminded us: "Every agreement concerning trade, every regulation of trade, restrains. To bind, to restrain, is of their very essence"').

[117] Renee Prendergast, 'The Concept of Freedom and Its Relation to Economic Development—A Critical Appreciation of the Work of Amartya Sen' [2005] Cambridge Journal of Economics 1145, 1147–48.

[118] ibid.

[119] For an insightful overview of the three main families of views and a collection of essays written by some of their respective paragons, see David Miller, 'Introduction' in David Miller (ed), *The Liberty Reader* (first published 2006, Routledge 2016).

[120] Charles Lindblom, *Politics and Markets: The World's Political-Economic Systems* (Basic Books 1977) 49.

[121] See also Warren Samuels, 'The Concept of "Coercion" in Economics' in Warren Samuels, Steven Medema and A Alan Schmid (eds), *The Economy as a Process of Valuation* (Edward Elgar 1997) 134.

[122] See eg State of California DoJ, 'Attorney General Bonta Announces Lawsuit Against Amazon for Blocking Price Competition' (14 September 2022) <https://bityl.co/FjyB> accessed 19 November 2022 (alleging that 'Amazon coerces merchants into agreements that keep prices artificially high, knowing full well that they can't afford to say no').

probably the basis of vertical restraints jurisprudence in the USA before the paradigm shift towards consumer welfare reasoning.[123] It remains, for another, central in some jurisdictions, especially those whose competition laws corset powerful firms below levels of market dominance.[124] Plus, if Nobel economist F. A. Hayek is right when he claimed that '[t]he task of a policy of freedom must ... be to minimize coercion or its harmful effects, even if it cannot eliminate it completely',[125] can we not say competitive process-minded antitrust surely needs to oblige?[126]

Granted, many dismiss coercion as one of those 'metaphysical entities'[127] with 'no operative economic meaning'.[128] As Hayek himself wrote, it 'is nearly as troublesome a concept as liberty itself, and for much the same reason'.[129] But the ambition here is not to settle the meaning of this recondite concept. It is merely to ascertain whether coercion can provide a more heuristically useful device for formalizing a freedom-based theory of harm to competition that might capture despotic practices of autocratic platforms. Moving forward, let us nevertheless be wary of semantic constructions in which deception is finessed.

4.2.2 Theorizing coercion

Coercion has riveted thinkers across the social sciences and within different areas of the law alike.[130] By parsing out this rich literature, one thing becomes clear: ways to formalize the coerciveness of cases similar to those examined in this chapter—instances of highly 'constrained volition'[131] in private settings[132]—do exist. Theorists agree that coercion involves a threat (as opposed to an offer) to bring the coercee below a certain baseline.[133] Where consensus splinters is over what kind of

---

[123] See Jean Burns, 'The New Role of Coercion in Antitrust' [1991] Fordham Law Review 379; William Page, 'Legal Realism and the Shaping of Modern Antitrust' [1995] Emory Law Journal 1.

[124] See eg the guidelines on superior bargaining power rules enshrined in Japanese and South Korean antitrust laws (referenced and discussed by Thomas Cheng and Michal Gal, 'Superior Bargaining Power: Dealing with Aggregate Concentration Concerns' in Fabiana Di Porto and Rupprecht Podszun (eds), *Abusive Practices in Competition Law* (Edward Elgar 2018)).

[125] FA Hayek, *The Constitution of Liberty: The Definitive Edition* (Ronald Hamowy ed, University of Chicago Press 2011) 59.

[126] See *Associated General Contractors of California Inc v California State Council of Carpenters* 459 US 519, 528 (1983) ('Coercive activity that prevents its victims from making free choices between market alternatives is inherently destructive of competitive conditions').

[127] Richard Posner, *The Problems of Jurisprudence* (Harvard UP 1990) 185.

[128] Wesley Liebeler, 'Resale Price Maintenance and Consumer Welfare: Business Electronics Corp. v. Sharp Electronics Corp' [1989] University of California Los Angeles Law Review 909, fn 93.

[129] Hayek (n 125) 199.

[130] For a useful review of its historical development in a variety of settings, see Hiba Hafiz, 'Beyond Liberty: Toward a History and Theory of Economic Coercion' [2016] Tennessee Law Review 1071.

[131] Alan Wertheimer, *Coercion* (Princeton UP 1987) 9 (arguing that cases of 'constrained volition'—a situation where an agent is confronted with unwanted alternatives but is capable of making rational decisions—are the '*standard* cases of coercion').

[132] There is an abundant scholarship on coercion by the state, which does not appear relevant here (see Hafiz (n 130) for a review). Indeed, despite the analogy of platforms with states, platforms are (for the most part) still private law entities.

[133] This consensus follows from Nozick's seminal exposition (Robert Nozick, 'Coercion' in Sidney Morgenbesser, Patrick Suppes and Morton White (eds), *Philosophy, Science, and Method: Essays in Honor of Ernest Nagel* (St Martin's Press 1969)).

baseline should be used—an empirical/statistical/descriptive one or a normative/moral one?—and under what specifications.[134]

4.2.2.1 Empirical

Taking the empirical route is appealing because the analysis supposedly becomes purely factual. The problem, though, is that neutrality apparently eludes those who profess it.

Consider libertarian paragon Robert Nozick's seminal discussion. A proposal, he argued, is a coercive threat if, among other things, 'it makes the consequences of [the coercee]'s action worse than they would have been in the normal and expected course of events'.[135] To me, the difficulties inherent in Nozick's descriptive framework for antitrust purposes are manifest. What is the 'normal or natural expected course of events'? Who determines it? And against what benchmark? These issues are likely to prove intractable for decision-makers and pave the way for arbitrary rulings riddled by value judgements.

For instance, when Amazon threatened to artificially increase delivery times on Hachette books to bully the publisher into submission, what was the objectively 'normal' alternative situation? On the one hand, although the platform already had a reputation for being an aggressive negotiator, maybe this was taking things an unexpected step further.[136] On the other hand, unless Amazon was clearly dominant at the time, it would have undoubtedly been entitled to go so far as to delist Hachette's books.[137] And were the platform dominant in 2014, the argument would then be that Amazon coerced the publisher by threatening to commit a potential antitrust offence and getting its way as a result. To be sure, there may well be coercion in such a scenario. But the example shows how the empirical baseline is not necessarily free of value judgements.[138]

Covert reliance on normative baselines appears to be a common issue with many ostensibly empirical theories of coercion. There would be no qualms if it were 'freedom' being funnelled through the backdoor. Evidently, it rarely (if ever) is.

Reflect on David Zimmerman's account, which could be relevant for our labour platform worries.[139] He argues that wage proposals are coercive where the

---

[134] Wertheimer (n 131) 7 and 204–07; Hafiz (n 130) 1086; Grant Lamond, 'Coercion' in Hugh LaFollette (ed), *International Encyclopedia of Ethics* (Blackwell 2013) 5; Hamish Stewart, 'A Formal Approach to Contractual Duress' [1997] University of Toronto Law Journal 175, 214.

[135] Nozick (n 133) 447.

[136] Apparently, Amazon employed 'some of the most aggressive tactics in industry history during negotiations ... with Hachette' (Shannon Bond and Henry Mance, 'Book Wars: Amazon's Page Turner' *Financial Times* (15 August 2014) <https://on.ft.com/2xMEjhS> accessed 18 November 2022).

[137] See, similarly, Oliver Budzinski and Karoline Köhler, 'Is Amazon the Next Google?' [2015] ORDO 265, 279.

[138] In fact, Nozick (n 133) 447, seemed to recognize this: '[t]he term "expected"', he wrote, 'is meant to shift between or straddle *predicted* and *morally required*'.

[139] David Zimmerman, 'Coercive Wage Offers' [1981] Philosophy & Public Affairs 121. Another is that of Michael Trebilcock, *The Limits of Freedom of Contract* (Harvard UP 1993) 93–96 and 101.

worker 'would prefer to move from the normally expected pre-proposal situation to the proposal situation, but *he would strongly prefer even more to move from the actual pre-proposal situation to some alternative pre-proposal situation*.'[140] The alternative 'pre-proposal situation', he adds, has to be 'historically, economically and technologically feasible'.[141] Even so caveated, this theory is 'vulnerable to a *reductio ad absurdum*'.[142] Or else it is moralized, with coercion hitched to some potentially limitless ideal of substantive fairness.[143] To make it more empirical, one would have to substitute the subjective preferences of the putative coercees—say, Uber drivers—with assessments made by some fictional, reasonable, arbiter. The downside of doing so? Benign paternalism, at best, or complete arbitrariness, at worst.[144]

Of course, we could avoid some of these pitfalls by endorsing the old, institutional economics, algorithm for thinking about coercion, i.e. assume it rests within the scarcity assumption itself.[145] The concept would become redundant, however. Worse, it might bridge to excesses of past antitrust jurisprudence where coercion was believed to inhere power asymmetries and did not even require evidence of pressure.[146]

4.2.2.2 Normative

Considering the foregoing, it may be true that 'any useful conception of coercion is irreducibly normative',[147] for us at least.[148] Despite the bevy of baselines one could conjure,[149] this approach seems rather straightforward given our aspirations: liberty 'is liberty not equality or fairness or justice or culture, or happiness or a quiet conscience'.[150] Still, the better view is probably to be prudent and start from a point of consensus before expanding the theory's reach.

The welfarist (as opposed to freedom-based) nature of his theory is eloquently explained by Stewart (n 134) 229–30.

[140] Zimmerman (n 139) 132.

[141] ibid.

[142] Lawrence Alexander, 'Zimmerman on Coercive Wage Offers' [1983] Philosophy & Public Affairs 160, 161. Indeed, taken at face value, every proposal would be coercive because there will always be a preferred pre-proposal situation that the offeror prevents the offeree from obtaining.

[143] ibid.

[144] Hafiz (n 130) 1091.

[145] Samuels (n 121) 143–44.

[146] Page (n 123) 24–27.

[147] Kathleen Sullivan, 'Unconstitutional Conditions' [1989] Harvard Law Review 1413, 1428.

[148] Wertheimer (n 131) 212 (arguing that 'coercion claims are contextual'; there need not be '*a* best answer to the choice *between* the various tests').

[149] See eg Harry Frankfurt, 'Coercion and Moral Responsibility' in Ted Honderich (ed), *Essays on Freedom of Action* (Routledge 2015) 71–72 (using substantive unfairness as a baseline); or Kaushik Basu, 'Coercion, Contract and the Limits of the Market' [2007] Social Choice and Welfare 559 (relying on Pareto efficiency).

[150] Isaiah Berlin, *Freedom and Its Betrayal: Six Enemies of Human Liberty* (Henry Hardy (ed), 2nd edn, Princeton UP 2014) 186.

At a minimum, then, can we not say a freedom-based antitrust coercion claim might succeed where the contentious proposal involves the successful threat to commit what is unlawful?[151] That is, successfully threatening to breach (any) *legal* rights, such as those flowing from contracts or even antitrust itself.[152]

Had it been invoked, this primitive theory might have convinced one US antitrust judge in a 2009 case factually similar to our Amazon story.[153] There, a small print-on-demand book publisher called BookLocker had sued after the platform threatened to remove BookLocker's 'Add-to-Shopping-Cart' button unless the publisher agreed to print them using Amazon's printing service. The allegation was admittedly framed as an unlawful tie, an offence usually reasoned by the conduct's exclusionary (as opposed to its exploitative) effects. Furthermore, the dispute was settled soon after the platform's motion to dismiss was rejected. But there is something noteworthy for present purposes. The judge, while recognizing the unusual nature of the tying claim—there was no actual tie, nor was this claimed— opined that evidence of such threats was enough to 'permit the plausible inference that Amazon [was] unlawfully forcing purchase of its P[rint-]O[n-]D[emand] printing'.[154] His intuition—that tying would be illegal so successfully threatening it must be unlawful too—seems better explained by a legal theory of coercion.

Importantly, to my mind, coercion as the threat of unlawful behaviour extends to take-it-or-leave-it 'offers' which enable the firms making them to circumvent the legal rights of their 'beneficiaries'. This is how one can properly rationalize some of the most controversial antitrust rulings against platforms.

Take the Autorité de la concurrence (ADLC)'s controversial interim decision against Alphabet/Google in April 2020.[155] The agency argued there that the platform had prima facie sinned by bullying press publishers into licensing their content for free. How exactly? By threatening the removal from its online search infrastructure of 'press snippets'—these are the short extracts, photographs, infographics, and videos of press publications the search engine displays alongside the hyperlinks that refer to the source website. Notably, the ruling explicitly states that one of the grounds for qualified illegality was the apparent circumvention of a purportedly redistributive French copyright legislation.[156]

Now, Chapter 5 will return to what lurks behind the behaviour. As will be explained, when Alphabet/Google displays press snippets that are *not* legally

---

[151] See, notably, Stewart (n 134) 175 (whose theory is mainly centred on this principle). See also Robert Nozick, *Anarchy, State, and Utopia* (first published 1974, Basic Books 2013) 194; Wertheimer (n 131) 39, 215ff, 308.

[152] See Pinar Akman, 'The Relationship between Economic Duress and Abuse of a Dominant Position' [2014] Lloyd's Maritime and Commercial Law Quarterly 99, 109.

[153] *BookLocker.com Inc v Amazon.com Inc* 650 FSupp 2d 89 (DMe 2009).

[154] ibid 102.

[155] *Syndicat des éditeurs de la presse magazine* (Case 19/0075M) ADLC Decision 20-MC-01 19 April 2020.

[156] ibid [242]–[254].

protected, the issue is not coercion. It rather pertains to whether the platform is 'scraping' or, more forthrightly, *free-riding* on publishers' efforts. Hence, in the ADLC's case, the practice could be deemed coercive *insofar as* the contentious content was entitled to legal protection. For in such a situation, 'victims' are cowed into foregoing the legitimate exercise of their rights, which is the basic ethical commitment of any freedom-based theory.[157]

Coercion, so understood, formalizes what the authority only intuitively got right. After all, relying on an EU precedent, which itself does not explain why circumventing non-antitrust laws might be a competition problem, leaves it open to criticism.[158] A fortiori, since the cited ruling could be construed as refuting what the ADLC alleged.[159]

Having said this, how much further can we stretch the concept of coercion if the competitive process paradigm precludes us from pandering to providers for their own sake?

Perhaps one could include situations where the proposal fundamentally impairs victims' 'autonomy'.[160] This is what the Bundeskartellamt (BKA) (in)famously did in its controversial, downstream-looking, *Facebook* decision, which condemned the eponymous platform's take-it-or-leave-it, privacy law-impinging terms of service.[161] Fortunately, the ruling can likewise be read as an implementation of the narrower theory just outlined above.[162] Why 'fortunately'? Well, if autonomy means the ability to make rational choices, coercion loses its notional potency; nearly all trading relations are voluntary by this measure. The theory would, moreover, become potentially boundless. As philosopher Gerald Dworkin writes, '[a]utonomy is a term of art introduced by a theorist in an attempt to make sense of a tangled net of intuitions, conceptual and empirical issues, and normative claims'.[163]

Do other options exist? Possibly. Nevertheless, objections can already be levelled at what is a purely legal theory of coercion. The most crippling one, to me, exposes its circularity. The criticism has an implacable logic to it; hiding behind

---

[157] See references supra (n 151). Note that Wertheimer (n 131) 217–18 is more ambitious: his theory extends beyond legal rights to cover *moral* rights. The problem, though, is that he minimizes the difference between moral and legal rights (see ibid 308). Epistemologically, he could be correct. Yet, insofar as we are concerned with 'freedom', Wertheimer's account is problematic since moral rights may derive from fairness concerns.

[158] *Syndicat des éditeurs de la presse magazine* (n 155) [242].

[159] Case C-457/10 P *AstraZeneca* ECLI:EU:C:2012:770 [2012] electronic Report of Cases, [132] ('the illegality of abusive conduct under Article [102 TFEU] is unrelated to its compliance or non-compliance with other legal rules'). More recently, see also Case C-377/20 *Servizio Elettrico Nazionale* ECLI:EU:C:2022:379 [2022] not yet published, [67].

[160] See Stewart (n 134) 189–97 (discussing—in the context of contract law—'improper proposals').

[161] *Facebook* (Case B6-22/16) BKA Decision 6 February 2019, [527].

[162] ibid [525ff], esp [541] together with [899] ('The substantive application of data protection law through competition law … promotes consistency. … The [data protection] benchmark is therefore also meaningful for an assessment under antitrust law, taking the objective of promoting free competition into account').

[163] Gerald Dworkin, *The Theory and Practice of Autonomy* (CUP 1988) 7.

consensus approval or directing such critics[164] to the defects of their own alternatives would merely skirt the matter. Yet, any antitrust system that values freedom
has to be troubled by the behaviour of those whose economic power effectively acts
as a moat against the legal order itself. To come back to the ADLC's dilemma: if, on
the one hand, the French copyright legislator did in fact intend to reduce power
asymmetries so that publishers could, at their request, (more) effectively bargain
for compensation with platform operators like Alphabet/Google, but, on the other
hand, the economic context is such that unremunerated licences de facto become
the general rule when it comes to Alphabet/Google, would it not be absurd to say
that 'competitive process-minded' antitrust must remain oblivious?[165]

Those magnanimous enough to indulge the riposte may naturally raise questions pertaining to practicability and policy interfacing. These points are treated in
Chapters 6 and 7, respectively.

Paradoxically, even by the standards of my modest ambitions, others may rather
chastise me for conceptually impoverishing coercion. Labour platform practices,
they might say, are routinely implemented 'without giving off a whiff of coercion'.[166]
This raises the following question: given that we are walking a tightrope with our
legal theory of coercion, is there another compelling way to formally frame such
concerns as competition problems without normatively de-anchoring the theory
of harm from the value of freedom? Let's have a look.

4.3 Oppression

While he 'did not present a "theory" of liberty ... for our times',[167] Isaiah Berlin—
one of the premier thinkers of freedom—did suggest unfreedom could result from
'oppression'.[168] Interestingly, economic oppression has been portrayed by experts as
an evil *antitrust* was historically meant to root out.[169] Some of our lawmakers have

---

[164] See, notably, Robert Hale, 'Coercion and Distribution in a Supposedly Non-Coercive State' [1923]
Political Science Quarterly 470, 476; Anthony Kronman, 'Contract Law and Distributive Justice' [1980]
Yale Law Journal 472, 482.

[165] For a similar but also opposing intuition, see Case C-252/21 *Meta Platforms* ECLI:EU:C:2022:704
[2022] not yet published, Opinion of AG Rantos, [23] ('compliance or non-compliance of [a] conduct
with ... the [non-antitrust rules at hand], not taken in isolation but considering all the circumstances
of the case, may be a vital clue as to whether that conduct entails resorting to methods prevailing under
merit-based competition, it being stated that the lawful or unlawful nature of conduct under [EU antitrust law] is not apparent from its compliance or lack of compliance with ... other legal rules'). AG
Rantos' intuition here appears to have been followed by the Court (Case C-252/21 *Meta Platforms*
ECLI:EU:C:2023:537 [2023] not yet published, [47]).

[166] Noam Scheiber, 'How Uber Uses Psychological Tricks to Push Its Drivers' Buttons' *New York
Times* (4 April 2017) <https://nyti.ms/2VWm3xi> accessed 18 November 2022.

[167] Steven Lukes, 'The Singular and the Plural: On the Distinctive Liberalism of Isaiah Berlin' [1994]
Social Research 687, 693.

[168] Berlin (n 150) 183.

[169] See eg Warren Grimes, 'Antitrust Law as a Response to Economic Oppression: The United States'
Experience' [1997] Nihon University Comparative Law 113.

also picked up on this rhetoric in debates over powerful platforms.[170] Tellingly, Uber and Lyft drivers have as well.[171] Might 'oppression' then serve as an additional fulcrum for enforcers to prosecute 'non-coercive' acts of an allegedly despotic nature, especially those of labour platforms? What follows shows that an affirmative answer is possible. But there is a catch.

4.3.1 Theorizing oppression

Oppression is one of those timeless concepts which will forever inspire thinkers. Modern liberals like Thomas Hobbes and John Locke (to name a couple) seemingly deployed it to frame the tyrannous rule of an unconstrained autocrat resulting in the negation of liberal political rights, economic deprivations, and physical brutality.[172] More so than coercion, however, oppression is almost always taken as something unmistakeable, be it in the few antitrust renditions of it, or in the philosophical literature. To my knowledge, Ann Cudd's account is alone in offering more in terms of careful conceptual analysis. Hers is one erudite philosophers have praised for its scope and precision;[173] so borrowing from it for our inquiry seems like a rather safe bet.

According to Cudd, 'oppression is an institutionally structured harm inflicted on groups by other groups using direct and indirect material and psychological forces that violate justice'.[174] More specifically, she argues, it obtains when there are (i) social institutions or practices that (ii) create direct or indirect material and psychological forces, which ultimately (iii) harm unjustly one particular social group whose identity exists apart from the oppressive harm.

Oppressive harm, it appears, is something fundamentally unequal and unjust, i.e. it befalls unequally on different groups of individuals who are *unjustifiably* unequal[175] because the harm is arbitrary, 'undeserved and unavoidable'.[176] Direct forces of oppression include unjust rules of behaviour,[177] whereas indirect ones 'work through the affective and cognitive psychological processes that form beliefs, desires, and ultimately, actions of the individuals'.[178] But 'the two kinds of

---

[170] See eg House of Representatives (Judiciary Subcommittee on Antitrust, Commercial and Administrative Law), 'Investigation of Competition in Digital Markets: Majority Staff Report and Recommendations' (2 October 2020) 6, 390 <https://bit.ly/3EMRD5m> accessed 19 November 2022.

[171] See eg complaint by Taje Gill, Esterphanie St Juste and Benjamin Valdez, [182], [189] in *Gill et al v Uber Technologies, Inc et al*, No 3:22-cv-04379 (NDCal 2022).

[172] See Ann Cudd, *Analyzing Oppression* (OUP 2006) 6.

[173] See Paul Benson, 'Analyzing Oppression by Ann E. Cudd' [2009] Hypatia 178.

[174] Cudd (n 172) 26.

[175] ibid 51.

[176] ibid 53, 131.

[177] 'Social institutions', as per Cudd, are rules or other institutions that 'specify behaviours in specific situations for persons who fit particular roles regardless of their individual characteristics, and the specified behaviours are in some sense required under threat of some penalty for noncompliance' (ibid 50).

[178] ibid 52.

oppressive forces often work in concert and reinforce each other', which means that they are inimical to freedom, regardless of how one understands the value.[179]

Oppression thus:

> runs a typical sequence: it begins when members of one group violently attack individuals of another social group and proceeds as the dominant group wields economic force on the subordinates. The oppressed respond rationally by choosing within the constraints that they are offered by the oppressors, and they gradually accommodate their beliefs and desires to the oppressive conditions that they find through both rational and nonrational psychological processes.[180]

Returning to our platform providers, is Cudd's framework helpful? Consider labour platforms for reflective purposes.

As noted in Section 2 of this chapter, most (non-labour-law-oriented) accounts tend to emphasize the arguably blatant unfairness of the compensation providers secure for their services. Be that as it may, they miss what is relevant here—what 'one cannot *and often does not want to see*'.[181] To wit, the hardwiring of institutional constraints on suppliers within the platform infrastructure's design that systematically place the interests of consumers/employers as sovereign. Empirical studies by digital ethnographers, digital media researchers, and some labour lawyers have evidenced this, although all underscore the complexity which makes it hard to uncover and explains why it is 'scarcely reflected in the legal academic literature'.[182]

The most obvious restrictions are embedded in these platforms' terms of service. Those of Amazon's Mechanical Turk are especially enlightening since they exacerbate bargaining power asymmetries in favour of consumers (called 'Requesters'). How? Most notably, by endowing Requesters with two things: (i) absolute discretion on the conditions of the bargain to be struck with suppliers,[183] and (ii) the ability to engage in compensation-theft.[184] In the same vein, gig labour platforms like Uber enforce tightly drafted and unilaterally amendable take-it-or-leave-it terms that, in particular, deprive providers of any control over fares.[185]

---

[179] ibid 225–26.

[180] ibid 227–28.

[181] Van Doorn (n 38) 899.

[182] Ryan Calo and Alex Rosenblat, 'The Taking Economy: Uber, Information, and Power' [2017] Columbia Law Review 1623, 1649.

[183] This includes matters such as compensation, providers' approval ratings, and self-reported country. See eg Lilly Irani, 'Difference and Dependence among Digital Workers: The Case of Amazon Mechanical Turk' [2015] South Atlantic Quarterly 225, 227; Antonio Aloisi, 'Commoditized Workers: Case Study Research on Labor Law Issues Arising from a Set of On-Demand/Gig Economy Platforms' [2016] Comparative Labor Law & Policy Journal 653, 667.

[184] ibid. Amazon's rules enable Requesters to keep work product *they* deem unsatisfactory without, however, having to compensate providers.

[185] See, generally, Newlands, Lutz and Fieseler (n 89) 8–9; Rosenblat and Stark (n 93) 3763; Aloisi (n 183) 673 (regarding Uber); Field and Forsey (n 97) 13 (concerning Deliveroo).

Other constraints are far subtler; they are buried in code, generating 'few discrete unavoidable demands and involv[ing] little direction by *any* human being'.[186] Ride-hailing and food-delivery platforms, for example, algorithmically impede effective choice-making of their drivers and couriers in a myriad of ways. Manufacturing information asymmetries (which magnifies bargaining power imbalances) is one.[187] Gamifying the platform infrastructure (which, as previously noted, maintains a constant flow of supply on the provider side) is another.[188]

Rating mechanisms, while usually portrayed as efficient means to reduce information asymmetries and search costs,[189] are, for suppliers, restrictive institutional devices as well. The modus operandi is insidious: by affecting eligibility and rankings within the platform infrastructure, these systems effectively put consumers 'in the driving seat' (bad pun intended) and conduce what sociologists denote as 'emotional labour'. This means service providers (like Uber drivers) 'suppress or contain their emergent emotions to present a placating or welcoming demeanour to customers, regardless of that customer's reciprocal emotional state'.[190] Why? Because by contrast to online marketplaces for goods (like Amazon.com), reputation mechanisms on labour platforms do not operate as signals of supplier quality;[191] they instead serve as a means for consumers to punish providers.[192]

Platform-adjudicated consumer/provider dispute resolution institutions are instruments that may likewise qualify as 'oppressive forces' if allegations of systematic bias in favour of consumers are true.[193]

What's more, the fact that these harms are to some degree self-inflicted would not invalidate a finding of oppression. Recall: oppression, as Cudd explains, can arise and endure indirectly.[194] This is the case where the oppressed 'choose' the conditions under which they suffer. For structural constraints (such as poverty or

---

[186] Deepa Das Acevedo, 'Unbundling Freedom in the Sharing Economy' [2018] Southern California Law Review 793, 814.

[187] Calo and Rosenblat (n 182) 1661 (finding that Uber implements, inter alia, a policy of blind ride acceptance, whereby the driver is unaware of the consumer's destination (and thus the remunerative value of the trip)); Alex Veen, Tom Barratt and Caleb Goods, 'Platform-Capital's "App-etite" for Control: A Labour Process Analysis for Food-Delivery Work in Australia' [2020] Work, Employment and Society 388, 397–398 (finding that Deliveroo and UberEats withhold critical information from couriers, such as the complete details of deliveries and how the different factors (like proximity to restaurants) affect their ability to receive orders).

[188] See Section 3.3, p 86 of this chapter.

[189] Belleflamme and Peitz (n 17).

[190] Rosenblat and Stark (n 93) 3775. See also Newlands, Lutz and Fieseler (n 89) 21–22.

[191] Apostolos Filippas, John Horton and Joseph Golden, 'Reputation Inflation' [2022] Marketing Science 305 (finding that, with labour platforms, consumers/employers tend to inflate their ratings because they are aware of the costs negative public feedback may impose on providers).

[192] Alex Wood, 'The UK Government's Consultation on Employment Classification and Control: A Response' (*Digital Inequality Group*, 15 May 2018) <https://bit.ly/2W3qKEJ> accessed 18 November 2022.

[193] See eg Rosenblat and Stark (n 93) 3765.

[194] Cudd (n 172) 146, 152–53.

unemployment) may cause them to organize their preferences and make decisions which come to perpetuate their oppression.

In short, powerful labour platforms (such as Uber and Amazon's Mechanical Turk) arguably do engage in what has been termed as provider 'oppression'. Oppression would follow from the combination of subtle, multifaceted, and frequently invisible institutional devices infused with a logic of consumer supremacy and cloaked in the language of technological solutionism to mask cumulatively significant restraints on providers that are, or at least could be said to be, (largely) arbitrary, undeserved, and unavoidable.

Hence, assuming labour platform 'partners' are independent contractors in the legal sense—they regularly aren't, but this is what the platforms keep peddling—can we not say these non-coercive incursions on their freedom are potential competition problems, which competitive process-minded antitrust decision-makers should be wary of? A well-known tenet of antitrust indeed has it that competition requires every undertaking to 'determine independently the policy he intends to adopt on the ... market'.[195] This principle precludes the embedding within vertical dealings of subordination, which ought to only ever exist in employment relations.[196]

4.3.2 Caveats

There are reasonable objections to what has just been written. Some may demur at the suggestion that providers—even those of labour platforms—can form a 'social group' as Cudd understands the notion, i.e. '*a collection of persons who share (or would share under similar circumstances) a set of social constraints on action*'.[197] This critique is not undefeatable. The soundness of having a 'social group' requirement is debatable[198] and some platform suppliers—more specifically, gig labour platform suppliers like Uber drivers—may actually fit Cudd's definition of it anyway, seeing that they have been shown to have a 'far greater perception ... among themselves, as a collective group'.[199]

---

[195] See eg Joined cases C-40 to 48, 50, 54 to 56, 111, 113 and 114/73 *Suiker Unie* ECLI:EU:C:1975:174 [1975] ECR 1663, [173].

[196] See, notably, *United States v Richfield Oil Corp* 99 FSupp 280, 291 (SDCal 1951) (finding that an oil company which structures its dealings with gas stations so as to evade labour laws cannot also escape antitrust scrutiny by then claiming that the significant control it exerts over them is akin to ownership). See also Case C-161/84 *Pronuptia* ECLI:EU:C:1986:41 [1984] ECR 353, [23] (finding that 'provisions which impair [a] franchisee's freedom to determine his own prices are restrictive of competition').

[197] Cudd (n 172) 44. For example, it has been suggested that cloud-based labour platforms, because of their cloud-based nature, inhibit the development of 'class-consciousness' among labour suppliers (Mark Graham, Isis Hjorth and Vili Lehdonvirta, 'Digital Labour and Development: Impacts of Global Digital Labour Platforms and the Gig Economy on Worker Livelihoods' [2017] Transfer 135, 155).

[198] Benson (n 173) 180 (arguing that 'Cudd does not do enough to establish that the identities of the social groups targeted in oppression exist independently of the harms at issue').

[199] Newlands, Lutz and Fieseler (n 96) 52.

More challenging, though, is the fact that the theory of oppression described above is moralized. That is, it requires some sort of background moral theory. Oppressive harm, to repeat, is something *unjust*, i.e. it befalls (in Cudd's words) 'unequally', in an 'arbitrary', 'undeserved', and 'unavoidable' manner. But what counts as an injustice fundamentally has to depend on a background theory, which explains why, as a matter of justice, the providers of our discussion are morally entitled to (not) be treated in a certain way. Here, Cudd unfortunately leaves us a bit in the lurch.[200] So, while relying on her theory may be (somewhat) helpful for rationalization, endorsing it for antitrust enforcement is likely to pave the way for ad hoc, potentially paternalistic, decision-making.

Apple's travails in the Netherlands may turn out to be a fitting cautionary tale. As the informed observer knows, the firm challenged an intervention by the Autoriteit Consument & Markt (ACM), which struck, not (directly) at the platform's infamous 30 per cent App Store distribution fee, but at the anti-steering and exclusive in-app payment obligations it imposes on (dating) app suppliers (such as Match Group, owner of Tinder, among others).[201] Noteworthy for present purposes are the agency's (disclosed) reasons: they seem to be centred precisely around the idea that Apple's behaviour was unjustly encroaching on dating app providers' freedom of choice.[202] And this conclusion was apparently reached by applying the proportionality principle.

Without speculating on what ACM really stated in its decision, Cudd's account of oppression could quite easily be formatted to fit this case, particularly the 'injustice' element. Proportionality analysis, after all, is simply a doctrinal tool for rights adjudication. Importantly, 'proportionality analysis is moral analysis',[203] one which inevitably must rely (at least partly) on the adjudicator's intuition of what justice requires in a particular case, given that an accepted general substantive moral theory of balancing that provides guidance about how to correctly balance competing rights or interests does not currently exist.[204]

---

[200] Cudd (n 172) 231. Note that she seems to envision a liberal contractarian view of the sort developed by John Rawls in *A Theory of Justice*, or the more libertarian version of David Gauthier in his *Morals by Agreement*.

[201] *Apple* (Case ACM/19/035630) ACM Decision 24 August 2021.

[202] At the time of writing, the full reasoning of ACM is not available. It can partly be reconstructed by relying on the summary published by the authority (<https://bityl.co/E3qB> accessed 18 November 2022) and by relying on what the Rotterdam District Court made of the decision when it upheld its findings following interim proceedings (in *Apple v ACM* (Case ROT 21/4781 and ROT 21/4782) Rotterdam District Court Judgement 24 December 2021 ECLI:NL:RBROT:2021:12851). For useful analyses, see Inge Graef, 'What the Dutch Apple Case Can Teach Us About Future Challenges for Competition Enforcement' [2022] Journal of Antitrust Enforcement 570; Friso Bostoen, 'The ACM's Apple Decision: To Boldly Go Where No Enforcer Has Gone Before' [2022] Journal of Antitrust Enforcement 583.

[203] Kai Möller, 'Proportionality: Challenging the Critics' [2012] International Journal of Constitutional Law 709, 726.

[204] One ambitious attempt can be found in Kai Möller, *The Global Model of Constitutional Rights* (OUP 2012).

Ad hocism thereby almost inevitably ensues. In our *Apple* case: why (beyond the fact that they complained to the ACM) *dating* app providers? What made *them* the victims of (oppressive) injustice and not other, equally dependent, suppliers who likewise don't compete horizontally against Apple, bearing in mind that the enforcer is empowered to act *ex officio* and had already amassed significant expertise following a market study in 2019?

Of course, ad hocism, *as such*, is not necessarily a debilitating flaw: decision-makers might well offer very detailed and precise accounts of both the interests at stake and the intuitions that steer them to favour one over the other(s) in the name of justice. This notwithstanding, what if their moral intuitions (i) are plainly wrong, (ii) clash with those held by the (majority of) people they are meant to serve, and/or (iii) are perverted by inapposite considerations, such as outcome fairness, which, we saw in Chapter 2, cannot coherently guide antitrust under the competitive process imperative? Labour platforms are an obvious example of this more troubling risk.

Remember, I claimed that the likes of Uber could arguably be viewed as engaged in provider oppression because of how their entire business model seemingly depends on pleasing consumers by exerting panoptic control over suppliers.[205] Yet, what is it exactly in these restraints (or how they operate) that is unjust and, crucially, would the advanced reasons still hold if suppliers' compensation was (a lot) higher?

These are tricky questions for antitrust enforcers, such as the FTC, who, today, would openly forsake the consumer welfare paradigm[206] and pledge to '[p]olic[e] unfair methods of competition that harm gig workers [through] reduced compensation or poorer working conditions.'[207] For one, given the empirical evidence (which suggests many providers are actually satisfied with the status quo),[208] platform labour is clearly not a black or white experience; nor are its effects

---

[205] Work by Uber-affiliated economists seems to actually confirm this reading of the business model. See Meng Liu, Erik Brynjolfsson and Jason Dowlatabadi, 'Do Digital Platforms Reduce Moral Hazard? The Case of Uber and Taxis' [2021] Management Science 4665 (finding that devices such as monitoring, rating, and conflict resolution, probably explain why (in their empirical setting) Uber drivers took fewer detours than taxi drivers, resulting in passenger time-savings).

[206] FTC, 'FTC Rescinds 2015 Policy that Limited Its Enforcement Ability under the FTC Act' (1 July 2021) <https://bityl.co/ERqw> accessed 18 November 2022.

[207] FTC (n 39).

[208] Field and Forsey (n 97) 12 (finding that some UK Deliveroo couriers value flexibility and income the platform provides). For similar findings regarding Uber/Lyft drivers in several jurisdictions, see Amanda Peticca-Harris, Nadia de Gama and MN Ravishankar, 'Postcapitalist Precarious Work and Those in the "Drivers" Seat: Exploring the Motivations and Lived Experiences of Uber Drivers in Canada' [2018] Organization 36, 42–52; Marcia Vacklavik and Liana Pithan, 'The Agency Search: The Meaning of Work for App Drivers [2018] Revista de Administração Mackenzie 1, 13; Breton Malin and Curry Chandler, 'Free to Work Anxiously: Splintering Precarity among Drivers for Uber and Lyft' [2017] Communication, Culture & Critique 382, 389–390; Calo and Rosenblatt (n 182) 1641. Likewise, for cloud work platforms such as Amazon Mechanical Turk, see Alex Wood and others, 'Good Gig, Bad Gig: Autonomy and Algorithmic Control in the Global Gig Economy' [2019] Work, Employment and Society 56, 64–66; Graham, Hjorth and Lehdonvirta (n 197) 153.

generalizable. For another, my guess is that a rigorously formulated answer, genuinely agnostic to substantive fairness worries, would likely anchor the intuitive 'injustice' potentially at play here in some formulation of the neo-republican ideal of 'non-domination' explored earlier in this book. Indeed, several political scientists argue that non-domination is not (solely) about freedom but that it is (also) 'the bedrock of justice'.[209] Plus, compelling renditions of 'algorithmic domination' in the labour platform economy have been made as well.[210] All the same, going down this route lands us right back into the quagmire of contradictions outlined in Chapter 2 and recalled at the outset of this section: non-domination is not something antitrust can be made to protect if it truly means to coherently nurture a dynamic 'competitive process'.

Accordingly, rather than invoking a theory of oppression (such as Cudd's) to underpin a case for active intervention, which will invariably attract cries of undue paternalism and/or allegations of power misuse, antitrust decision-makers would be wiser using it as a ground for 'bold deference', at least in some cases, like those involving labour platforms. More on this in Chapter 7.

4.4 Summation

What is called 'freedom', to borrow from Nobel economist Paul Samuelson, 'is really a vector of almost infinite components rather than a one-dimensional thing that can be given a simple ordering'.[211] As a stand-alone concept, it provides little to antitrust decision-makers wary of potentially despotic exertions of autocratic platforms. Formalizing these anxieties as plausible, freedom-based, competition problems therefore requires more heuristically pregnant concepts.

'Coercion' is one such notion which may offer a way forward, albeit a perhaps narrow one. 'Oppression' might be another. At minimum, it does put some legs to a rather startling idea, floated in a highly influential report, whereby antitrust enforcement is said to be potentially warranted when 'a platform whose main strategic objective is to attract more individual users could provide attractive conditions on the consumer side by *sharing with them part of the benefits of its monopsony power on the business side*'.[212] Still, the moralized nature of a carefully thought out theory

---

[209] See Ian Shapiro, 'On Non-Domination' [2012] University of Toronto Law Journal 293, 332. See also Frank Lovett, *A General Theory of Domination and Justice* (OUP 2010) (widely cited as the premiere theorist of non-domination as social justice).

[210] See eg James Muldoon and Paul Raekstad, 'Algorithmic Domination in the Gig Economy' [2022] European Journal of Political Theory <https://doi.org/10.1177/14748851221082078> accessed 18 November 2022.

[211] Paul Samuelson, *The Collected Scientific Papers of Paul A. Samuelson*, vol 2 (Joseph Stiglitz (ed), Oxford & IBH Publishing 1966) 1414.

[212] Jacques Crémer, Yves-Alexandre de Montjoye and Heike Schweitzer, 'Competition Policy for the Digital Era' (2019) 62 <https://bit.ly/3hQynLn> accessed 19 November 2022 (emphasis added).

of oppression and the ad hocism it invites, render it, at best, difficult to manage for antitrust aspirations, and, at worst, open to dangerously self-righteous impulses.

5. Concluding Reflections

Analogizing platforms to quasi-states is insightful. It enables policymakers to see what is otherwise largely invisible and imbued with techno-progressive ideology: many platforms are akin to digital sovereigns, devising and enforcing institutions that shape our behaviours, interactions with others, and, ultimately, the distribution of value within their respective 'territories'.

Platform governance is evidently not a competition problem in itself. More paradoxically, nor is its autocratic nature. When a powerful platform turns despotic, though, vigilant antitrust decision-makers may need to spring into action.

Truth be told, fears of platform despotism can be articulated within a consumer welfare rationale. Nevertheless, the multi-sided nature of some of these platforms, combined with an endorsement of those IO economists who specialize in them, can make potential competition problems more difficult to formalize.

Theories of harm more consonant with the value of freedom can be crafted under the competitive process paradigm too. No doubt, this requires the 'more interdisciplinary', 'more rigorous and empiricism-driven approach to understanding market behaviors and business practices' that some would have our antitrust decision-makers adopt.[213] But the prescription is a recipe for disaster if no safeguards are in place to prevent its implementation from 'slip[ping] into ideologically self-serving tautology'.[214] The plight of labour platform providers is a delicate case in point. Enforcers intent on having antitrust stamp out practices which 'unfairly harm workers' in the name of 'free' competition in labour markets[215] should be cautioned that '[l]iberty does not mean all good things or the absence of all evils',[216] lest it become a Trojan horse for interests antitrust cannot coherently be made to protect.

---

[213] Lina Khan, 'Memo from Chair Lina M. Khan to Commission Staff and Commissioners Regarding the Vision and Priorities for the FTC' (22 September 2021) 2 <https://perma.cc/X2QR-XT7M> accessed 18 November 2022.

[214] Philipe Tetlock and Erika Henik, 'Theory- versus Imagination-Driven Thinking about Historical Counterfactuals: Are We Prisoners of Our Preconceptions?' in David Mandel, Denis Hilton and Patrizia Catellani (eds), *The Psychology of Counterfactual Thinking* (Routledge 2005) 199.

[215] See eg FTC, 'FTC Policy Statement on Enforcement Related to Gig Work' (15 September 2022) <https://perma.cc/ZPR3-XN3R> accessed 18 November 2022), together with Executive Order 14036 ('Promoting Competition in the American Economy').

[216] Hayek (n 125) 68.

4

Game-Mastering

1. Introduction

Powerful platforms, we just saw, are very much akin to (quasi-)autocratic states that may veer towards despotism. When brought to their attention, our antitrust decision-makers should be able to spot the competition problem in this. But 'looking up' is by no means straightforward. Through consumer welfare lenses, the exercise is counter-intuitive, indirect, and error-prone; switching to the competitive process perspective creates new challenges decision-makers may—possibly rightly—be reluctant to embrace, even if doing so does eliminate the discomfort of having to look down first.

This chapter turns to a separate matter: the possibility that powerful platforms engage in what is denoted here as 'game-mastering'. The vernacular choice is not a gimmick; the concerns fundamentally are distinct. To appreciate the difference in optics, let us begin by (i) briefly explaining in what sense analogizing platforms to game-masters can be meaningful for present purposes and by (ii) describing the types of claims that, *ipso facto*, may be of interest (Section 2). As we shall see, game-mastering acts as an umbrella notion, encapsulating a variety of strategies. Unsurprisingly (depending on where one stands), consumer welfare-minded decision-makers can make them out as potential competition problems as well. Once again, the real issue pertains to the demand for rigour, which will regularly place them between a rock and a hard place when they attempt to formalize their theories of harm (Section 3). However, this is not to say reorienting antitrust towards protecting competition, as such, necessarily provides a simple panacea. Similarly to what Chapter 3 uncovered for despotic platforms, this alternative policy lens does make looking up a more direct and probably more intellectually honest exercise. At the same time, rendering the affected value—*ex ante* fairness—intelligible faces significant challenges (Section 4).

2. Game-Mastering Platforms

2.1 Platforms as Game-Masters

Those familiar with role-playing games (RPGs) will have surely come across the figure of the game-master. From traditional pen-and-paper (or tabletop) RPGs

Antitrust and Upstream Platform Power Plays. A. K. von Moltke, Oxford University Press. © A. K. von Moltke 2023.
DOI: 10.1093/oso/9780192873057.003.0005

(like *Dungeons & Dragons*) to massively multiplayer online (MMO) ones (say, *World of Warcraft*), they tend to be unavoidable. Game-masters have also become synonymous with many functions.[1] Dictating the narrative flow (by giving dynamic feedback to the actions of players) is one. Enforcing the rules of the game established by the creator (who may incidentally be the same person) is another. Game-masters likewise develop the environment within which the game unfolds and ensure constant player engagement.[2]

These responsibilities assuredly evoke those assumed by platforms. Like game-masters, the latter provide an environment—the digital infrastructure—which they must nurture through incremental (or, sometimes, radical) design changes to attract users and keep them on board. They too are in charge of policing user behaviour.

That said, leaving it at this would be deeply unsatisfying; the analogy would add little to our discussion in Chapter 3 where platforms' regulatory tendencies were likened to private autocratic governance. To shed light on the novel optic introduced here, it is therefore useful to turn to the gaming ethnographers who find that RPG game-masters occasionally ' "fudge" the rules without the players being aware'.[3] Admittedly, 'fudging' often aims to protect the spirit of the game.[4] Sometimes, it is more accidental than malicious.[5] Now and again, though, game-masters purposely set out to covertly endow a particular (group of) player(s), maybe even their own, with a potentially significant advantage. As explained below, similar dynamics unfold in the context of powerful platforms.

2.2 The Claims

Right off the bat, note that our discussion pertains to conduct which may be difficult to detect. Game-mastering, as understood here, is not about the ostensible rules platforms may devise, an issue examined in Chapter 3. It rather relates to practices that covertly undermine those rules or deviate from their spirit. So, what kind of game-mastering claims might land on the antitrust decision-maker's docket? To my mind, three subcategories, summarized in Figure 4.1, can be usefully conceptualized.

---

[1] Anders Tychsen and others, 'The Game Master' in Yusuf Pisan (ed), *Proceedings of the Second Australasian Conference on Interactive Entertainment* (Creativity & Cognition Studios Press 2005).
[2] ibid 215–16.
[3] Mike Denny, 'Star Wars Galaxies: Control and Resistance in Online Gaming' (MA thesis, Carleton University 2010) 10.
[4] René Glas, *Battlefields of Negotiation: Control, Agency, and Ownership in World of Warcraft* (Amsterdam UP 2012) 161–63.
[5] For a 'notorious' example which even caught the eye of top legal blogs, see Andres Guadamuz, 'Avatars Behaving Badly' (*TechnoLlama*, 3 June 2009) <https://perma.cc/RS7W-G2L5> accessed 18 November 2022.

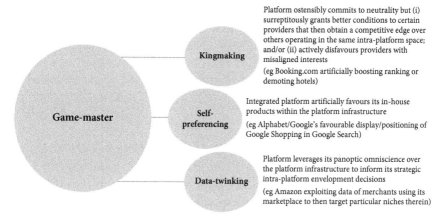

Figure 4.1 Game-mastering claims
Source: author's own creation.

The first arises when an ostensibly neutral powerful platform stealthily engages in what is denoted as 'king-making'.[6] To me, this moniker captures best what many decision-makers and commentators seemingly have in mind when they fret over platforms furtively:

○ granting better conditions in terms of visibility and/or sale optimization to providers willing and able to offer due consideration for the benefit; or
○ demoting suppliers loath to loosen their purse strings or whose interests are simply misaligned with those of the platform.[7]

Firms like Amazon and Meta/Facebook unsurprisingly appear as prime suspects.[8] Others less in the limelight—say, the powerful online travel agents (OTAs), Booking Holdings and Expedia—might be equally, if not more, worthy bogeymen.[9]

---

[6] Others have used the more cumbersome descriptor of 'selling monopoly power' (Jacques Crémer, Yves-Alexandre de Montjoye and Heike Schweitzer, 'Competition Policy for the Digital Era' (2019) 64 <https://bit.ly/3hQynLn> accessed 19 November 2022).

[7] See eg Stigler Center, 'Stigler Committee on Digital Platforms: Final Report' (September 2019) 73 <https://bityl.co/Fjqi> accessed 19 November 2022 (expressing concern about how 'the platform's whims can determine [the vendors] future').

[8] Amazon was fined in Italy for precisely this (Pietro Lombardi and Giorgio Leali, 'Italy Fines Amazon €1.13B for Abusing Market Dominance' *Politico* (9 December 2021) <https://bityl.co/Dw6Y> accessed 18 November 2022). In the UK, the Digital, Culture, Media and Sport Committee (DCMSC) invited the CMA to investigate Meta/Facebook to determine whether the platform is 'unfairly using its dominant market position in social media to decide which businesses should succeed or fail' (DCMSC, 'Disinformation and "Fake News": Final Report' (18 February 2019) 42 <http://bit.ly/31jVgc5> accessed 18 November 2022).

[9] Hereinafter I shall refer to 'OTA bias'. See European Competition Network (ECN), 'Report on the Monitoring Exercise Carried Out in the Online Hotel Booking Sector by EU Competition Authorities in 2016' (2017) [50] <https://bityl.co/FjrD> accessed 19 November 2022 (reporting such complaints

The second type of potentially unnerving game-mastering examined here is labelled 'self-preferencing'.[10] It pertains to situations where a powerful, integrated, platform is accused of anticompetitively favouring its in-house products within the platform infrastructure where it thereby acts as both a game-master and a player. Ubiquitous and benign prima facie, antitrust agencies and courts are nonetheless increasingly swamped with such allegations levelled against the 'Big Four'— Alphabet/Google,[11] Meta/Facebook,[12] Amazon,[13] and Apple[14]—as well as other locally powerful platforms.[15]

Finally, game-mastering claims may relate to *how* platforms *enter* (or, in the argot of business academics, 'envelop')[16] the spaces occupied by some of their providers. In a nod to the gaming culture, let this be christened as 'data-twinking'. A slight digression into media studies explains why.

In the context of MMORPGs, generic twinks are characters who begin the adventure with gear and/or abilities they would normally not have been able to amass on their own.[17] Twinking, in its most basic form, thus 'involves using accumulated wealth and/or power of a high-level character to boost the performance of a low-level character'.[18] A variation of the practice is deployed in dedicated competitive settings where the twink gains an upper hand over rivals as a result.[19] Suppose, then, that the player is a game-master as well, a status associated with a godlike view of the game. Based on such knowledge, (s)he could easily create a player-character

---

by hoteliers in the EU). See also Davide Fina and others, 'Market Study on the Distribution of Hotel Accommodation in the EU' (2022) COMP/2020/OP/002 <https://perma.cc/RGH9-KDQM> accessed 18 November 2022 (confirming that the ECN findings are still relevant in 2022).

[10] To my knowledge, the label was coined by Adam Raff and Shivaun Raff, 'Penalties, Self-Preferencing, and Panda: Why Google's Behavior Makes Antitrust Sanctions Inevitable' (31 August 2011) *Foundem* <https://bityl.co/Fjqu> accessed 19 November 2022.

[11] See eg CMA, 'Online Platforms and Digital Advertising: Market Study Final Report' (1 July 2020) Appendix P [52ff] <https://bit.ly/3Avd1tA> accessed 19 November 2022.

[12] See eg ACCC, 'Digital Platforms Inquiry: Final Report' (June 2019) 134–36 <http://bit.ly/3TKr NmY> accessed 19 November 2022 (providing multiple illustrations).

[13] See eg Bundeswettbewerbsbehörde (BWB), 'Austrian Federal Competition Authority Initiates Investigation Proceedings Against Amazon' (14 February 2019) <https://bityl.co/Fjvn> accessed 19 November 2022 (investigating Amazon for allegedly trying to 'inordinately favour its own products' by, for instance, covertly demoting merchants in its marketplace rankings or by adding incorrect delivery details to their accounts).

[14] See eg CMA, 'Mobile Ecosystems: Market Study Final Report' (10 June 2022) [6.6ff] <https://bityl. co/Exy1> accessed 18 November 2022 (discussing allegations made by app providers).

[15] In South Korea, for example, the local e-commerce giant, Coupang, has been the target of such allegations (Jenny Lee, 'South Korea's Coupang Target of Fresh Antitrust Probe for Allegedly Manipulating Search Algorithms' *mlex* (6 July 2021) <https://bityl.co/F7O8> accessed 18 November 2022).

[16] See Thomas Eisenmann, Geoffrey Parker and Marshall Van Alstyne 'Platform Envelopment' [2011] Strategic Management Journal 1270 (theorizing 'platform envelopment'). See also Sai Lan, Kun Liu and Yidi Dong, 'Dancing with Wolves: How Value Creation and Value Capture Dynamics Affect Complementor Participation in Industry Platforms' [2019] Industry and Innovation 943 (extending the envelopment theory to *within*-platform situations).

[17] Glas (n 4) 103.

[18] ibid.

[19] ibid.

enhanced by inception with insights unavailable to others and without them even being aware of this. To wit, leverage panoptic omniscience over the games (s)he alone oversees to make strategic decisions as players, i.e. to 'data-twink'.

Returning to platforms, the label's fit ought to be more apparent. Does it not capture the worries expressed by certain critics and competition authorities regarding, for example, Amazon's (alleged) exploitation of the data it (purportedly) extracts from sellers using its marketplace platform to drive its private-label activities at their expense?[20]

Given these considerations, one should have a better sense of the distinct dynamics this chapter explores. The question is: can we rationalize them as potential competition problems? Mirroring Chapter 3, our journey to an answer starts from a consumer welfare perspective.

3. Game-Mastering and 'Consumer Welfare'

Chapter 3 introduced the reader to the strands of economics antitrust decision-makers might appeal to when confronted with claims of platform despotism, in particular that of multi-sided markets. Occasional paucity of theoretical and empirical work meant that part of our inquiry there had to be guided by general insights and, to a certain extent, more intuitive consumer welfare reasoning. With game-mastering tactics, economists have more to say. Depending on where one stands, we shall see that this can be either a boon or a bane. King-making, self-preferencing, and data-twinking practices, it will be explained, *can* tick off consumer-welfare-minded decision-makers. Yet, their upgaze will, again, regularly be coloured by:

- the endorsed consumer welfare avatar,[21] i.e. total surplus,[22] consumer surplus,[23] *strong* consumer surplus,[24] or consumer choice/sovereignty;[25]
- the type of (economic) insights considered; and
- the (value) judgements one needs to make when confronted with sometimes contradictory models that generate ambiguous predictions.

With this in mind, king-making is a good place to start.

---

[20] EC, 'Antitrust: Commission Opens Investigation into Possible Anti-Competitive Conduct of Amazon' (17 July 2019) <https://bit.ly/2JC4JWU> accessed 18 November 2022); Lina Khan, 'Amazon's Antitrust Paradox' [2017] Yale Law Journal 712, 785–86.

[21] Again, recall that total *welfare* is not used in practice, nor does anyone pretend it can be (today).

[22] Or Kaldor–Hicks efficiency measured through short-run price/output effects.

[23] Measured through short-run price/output effects and infused by considerations of distributive justice.

[24] Which also accounts for quality, choice, diversity, and innovation considerations.

[25] Which is similar to *strong* consumer surplus but reflects concerns for corrective justice.

3.1 King-making

That a powerful platform not only can, but also might have the incentive to, covertly skew the way it ranks and/or presents its suppliers to consumers seems instinctively troubling. Allegations of OTA bias serve as a handy backdrop for the discussion.

3.1.1 Incentives?

Booking platforms infrastructures operated by the likes of Booking Holdings and Expedia are generally viewed as brokers facilitating deals between consumers and hoteliers.[26] As noted in Chapter 3, standard multi-sided market economics suggests that these firms must cater to all sides. One could therefore argue that king-making is a spurious problem because it just does not make for rational business.[27] Differently put, powerful OTAs would have no incentives to fiddle with their search algorithms to either favour hotels willing to pay higher commissions or demote those insisting on lower agency fees. Hotel suppliers may well be notoriously dependent on these platforms to access consumers;[28] but, to borrow from one competition agency, 'consumers would quickly notice if [say, Booking.com] is not providing an unbiased picture of the offerings it compares and its usage by consumers would decline as they could switch to using other alternative websites'.[29]

How does this argument fare? Not so well, it seems. Indeed, economists have empirically demonstrated that, for a given hotel price offered on either Booking.com or Expedia, a more competitive price at the other OTA or on the hotel's own website led to a lower ranking.[30] In their words, 'OTAs make the ranking of their recommended search results dependent on factors that are relevant for the OTA to maximize its profit, but arguably not to maximize the match value of customers'.[31]

3.1.2 Harm?

Powerful OTAs can have a profit-maximizing incentive to selectively make or break hoteliers. Being the masters of their online booking infrastructures, they

---

[26] See eg Thomas Larrieu, 'Topics in Industrial Organization Applied to Competition Policy' (PhD thesis, University of Paris-Saclay 2019) 18–19; *Booking.com* (Case 13/0045F) ADLC Decision 15-D-06 21 April 2015, [98].

[27] As per Bruno Jullien and Wilfried Sand-Zantman, 'The Economics of Platforms: A Theory Guide for Competition Policy' [2021] Information Economics and Policy 100880, 'while platform activities create new opportunities for abusive conduct, the main question is often not so much whether a powerful platform has the ability to do so, but rather whether it has the incentives to do so'.

[28] For a study, see Brigitte Stangl, Alessandro Inversini and Roland Schegg, 'Hotels' Dependency on Online Intermediaries and Their Chosen Distribution Channel Portfolios: Three Country Insights' [2016] International Journal of Hospitality Management 87.

[29] *Priceline.Com/Kayak* (Case ME/5882-12) OFT Decision 14 May 2013, [91].

[30] Matthias Hunold, Reinhold Kesler and Ulrich Laitenberger, 'Rankings of Online Travel Agents, Channel Pricing, and Consumer Protection' [2020] Marketing Science 92, 100ff.

[31] ibid 111.

likewise possess the ability to do so. Be that as it may, what is the potential con-sumer welfare harm? For, can we not say 'king-making' is no different to what the (in)famous Robinson–Patman Act forbids in the USA, namely, second-line price discrimination? As antitrust lawyers know well, this piece of legislation has long been disfavoured.[32] Not merely because it bans practices which are generally found to be allocatively efficient and pro-consumer,[33] but because it demonstrably has negative effects on competition and consumers as well.[34]

The informed observer has a retort, though. OTA bias might:[35]

- ∘ push hoteliers to pass on inflated agency fees down to consumers through hiked-up room rates;
- ∘ perpetuate market norms whereby consumers book through OTAs despite the availability of cheaper alternatives, such as the hotelier's own website;
- ∘ impair consumers' ability to effectively exercise their freedom of choice; and/or
- ∘ diminish hoteliers' incentives to improve their existing offerings (for instance, through property upgrades) or to expand their business in ways that would increase consumer choice and drive down room prices.

Despite fitting a consumer welfare narrative to a tee, rigorous antitrust decision-makers have reasons to be sceptical. For these intuitive theories might not stack up to the contradictory body of economic evidence accumulated over decades, albeit in a context of analogue competition.[36] Such decision-makers would accordingly ask: can we formally rationalize the anxieties generated by our king-making OTAs? The answer is yes.

Marketing economists have taken a keen interest to the issue. Following one recent, formal, study, a monopolistic OTA will likely rank (or more prominently display) hotels with the highest room prices, intermediation fees, and conversion rates (i.e. booking likelihood). The reason? Doing so enables the platform to in-directly mimic the effects of price parity clauses.[37] This matters given that parity clauses have attracted considerable antitrust and legislative scrutiny over the past

---

[32] Daniel Crane, 'Antitrust Antitextualism' [2020] Notre Dame Law Review 1205, 1240.

[33] See Antitrust Modernization Commission, 'Report and Recommendation' (2007) 317ff <https://bit.ly/3USu6FT> accessed 19 November 2022.

[34] See Hagit Bulmash, 'An Empirical Analysis of Secondary Line Price Discrimination Motivations' [2012] Journal of Competition Law & Economics 361 (empirically finding that the legislation 'helps to maintain coordinated competition between suppliers, increases the free-rider problem, keeps monopoly prices high, and harms horizontal as well as vertical competition').

[35] See Benjamin Edelman, 'Impact of OTA Bias and Consolidation on Consumers' (12 July 2017) 5–6 <https://perma.cc/4K47-QFT2> accessed 18 November 2022.

[36] See, usefully, Robert O'Donoghue and Jorge Padilla, *The Law and Economics of Article 102 TFEU* (3rd edn, Hart 2020) 960–67.

[37] Hunold, Kesler and Laitenberger (n 30) 92, 95ff. The authors conjecture that a richer model involving competing OTAs would lead to similar outcomes.

decade, especially in the EU.[38] And while the jury is still out on the full consumer welfare implications of these types of vertical restraints,[39] there is enough to substantiate significant concern, even where they are of the supposedly less harmful genre. Parity clauses, wide *and* narrow, sometimes soften competition between OTAs.[40] When they do, hoteliers pay higher commissions, which they probably pass on to consumers.[41]

Interestingly, a recent empirical study, which analysed the short- and medium-run impact of absolute legislative bans on these contractual devices in France and Italy, supports the theory. These interventions, its authors find, resulted in significant price reductions for consumers.[42]

Returning to king-making, what can we infer from this? By surreptitiously fiddling with their search algorithms, powerful OTAs can fly under the radar, especially where parity clauses have been banned (either outright or through voluntary commitments). Doing so enables them to induce hotels into inflating room rates on competing channels (such as their own website), which is something any consumer welfare-minded antitrust decision-maker would frown upon.

Worryingly, the same economists further argue that behaving this way could, theoretically, be in the long-term interest of powerful OTAs, even if it means sacrificing short-run profits.[43]

Hence, despite the absence of any likely exclusionary effects—the gold standard under contemporary antitrust—at the hotel level, consumer welfare *is* potentially at stake. Consumer surplus might be harmed through inflated room prices; total surplus may well take a hit if overall output dips (should higher room rates push consumers towards alternative short-let accommodation providers or deter them from travelling altogether); and there will definitely be losses in both *strong* consumer surplus and (effective) consumer choice as king-making entails consumers will not be served with their best-matching search results, something which is akin to a decrease in quality.

To be sure, some may say the latter effects—consumer deception—are better dealt with through consumer protection law since they really reflect an information

---

[38] For a brief overview, see ibid 95.

[39] See eg Thibaud Vergé, 'Are Price Parity Clauses Necessarily Anticompetitive?' (*CPI Antitrust Chronicle*, January 2018) 51–53 <https://bit.ly/31oCYsh> accessed 18 November 2022.

[40] 'Narrow' parity clauses are often portrayed as less harmful because they only prevent hotels from offering better terms on their own website(s). By contrast, 'wide' parity clauses also forbid hoteliers from undercutting the OTA on any alternative distribution channel. The former can be just as pernicious though (Matthias Hunold and others, 'Evaluation of Best Price Clauses in Online Hotel Bookings' [2018] International Journal of Industrial Organization 542 and the references therein at 545–46).

[41] ibid.

[42] See Andrea Mantovani, Claudio Piga and Carlo Reggiani, 'Online Platform Price Parity Clauses: Evidence from the EU Booking.com Case' [2021] European Economic Review 103625.

[43] See Hunold, Kesler and Laitenberger (n 30) 111.

asymmetry problem.[44] But this relates to an issue—policy interfacing—examined later in Chapter 7.

The preceding notwithstanding, there is another model which usefully serves our rationalization ambitions here.[45] It shows that when an OTA ranks hotel listings under a utility-based ranking—one which sorts results according to consumer's idiosyncratic preferences or 'match value'—consumer surplus *rises* sharply when compared to *Expedia*'s ranking.[46] Ergo, whenever a powerful OTA does not deliver consumers with their best-match hotels, there is potentially lost consumer surplus flowing from unrealized utility gains generated by better matches and from increased consumer search costs.[47] These results can be explained by a demonstrable 'position effect'. That is, consumers are less willing to click on lower ranked hotels (although this does not affect their final purchasing decision).[48]

In addition, the study clarifies how Expedia would itself benefit by adopting a utility-based ranking: the number of transactions occurring within its booking infrastructure would increase, further stoking the virtuous cycle of cross-sided network effects.[49] King-making OTAs are, hence, not efficiency-maximizing businesses either.[50]

3.1.3 Endemic?

Consumer welfare, it appears, truly is at risk and our anxieties over king-making need not be tied to 'super-platform' status. However, can the foregoing insights be generalized? What if, say, musicians (or, more realistically, their record labels) complained about skewed playlists on Spotify, the current leader in music streaming?[51] To rephrase: what if the 'Payola' issue, which has long plagued the radio industry, was morphing into something more insidious in the digital age?[52]

---

[44] In the UK, the CMA tackled king-making OTAs for exactly this reason and relied on consumer protection law to do so (see CMA, 'Hotel Booking Sites to Make Major Changes after CMA Probe' (6 February 2019) <http://bit.ly/31xnznw> accessed 18 November 2022). See also Mark Patterson, *Antitrust Law in the New Economy: Google, Yelp, LIBOR, and the Control of Information* (Harvard UP 2017) 123 (seemingly recognizing this point).

[45] Raluca Ursu, 'The Power of Rankings: Quantifying the Effect of Rankings on Online Consumer Search and Purchase Decisions' [2018] Marketing Science 530.

[46] ibid 548–49.

[47] ibid.

[48] ibid 538ff.

[49] ibid 548ff (finding an increase of at least 2.4 per cent).

[50] For similar findings, see Jae Hyen Chung, 'Estimation of Sequential Search Models' (PhD thesis, University of Chicago Booth School of Business 2019) 47–49 (finding a 25 per cent increase in consumer surplus under a utility-based ranking when compared to an Expedia ranking; and arguing that '[o]ne possible explanation for this difference is that Expedia places hotels with higher commission rate for itself on the upper part of the results page, leading consumers to make clicks on those hotels due to the position effect').

[51] See eg CMA, 'Music and Streaming: Final Report' (29 November 2022) [2.87] <https://bityl.co/JsZ6> accessed 29 November 2022.

[52] Payola is jargon for manufacturing popular hits by paying for radio play. See, generally, Kim Kelly, 'A Brief History of American Payola' (*Vice*, 14 February 2016) <https://bit.ly/35Itl9R> accessed 18 November 2022.

The suggestion is not mere fearmongering, despite the firm's playlist neu-trality pledge.[53] Some cultural economists, who have examined the effects of the platform's playlists on both the promotion of songs and their discovery, caution that growing concentration in music streaming is placing an increasingly large degree of power in the hands of a few businesses which may have king-making incentives.[54]

The reason? Playlists are progressively replacing DJs as the 'new musical starmakers'.[55] Being listed, preferably highly, on the most popular ones boosts, sometimes substantially, the number of times an artist's work is streamed.[56] Recommendation systems, in other words, affect what consumers listen to and, ergo, the success of artists. Spotify, though, operates and curates nearly all the hit playlists on its streaming infrastructure. And since its revenue-generating business relies on a one-sided retailing model,[57] the firm could choose to favour cheaper content to induce content providers into trimming licensing fees. That is, promote music for which it pays lower royalties to gain an upper hand over (major) record labels like Universal, Sony, and Warner. Again, this is not science fiction; econo-mists have modelled the theory.[58]

But what about the consumer welfare harm? Economic models, as Chapter 3 il-lustrated, are often sensitive to departures from the defined parameters. Given their underlying assumptions, we evidently cannot seamlessly apply to music streaming the narratives discussed in the OTA context. Unlike Booking.com, Spotify is in-deed more retailer than broker; and, contrary to hotels, music providers compete within the platform exclusively on quality, not prices.

Granted, formal studies examining king-making under slightly more compat-ible assumptions do exist.[59] Bracketing the questionable ones which remain,[60] these models still tend to suggest that consumer welfare, however understood, will

---

[53] The firm has stated that it is 'absolutely against any kind of "pay to playlist", or sale of playlists'. (Robert Cookson, 'Spotify Bans "Payola" on Playlists' *Financial Times* (20 August 2015) <https://on.ft.com/2KTk1qG> accessed 18 November 2022).

[54] See Luis Aguiar and Joel Waldfogel, 'Platforms, Power, and Promotion: Evidence from Spotify Playlists' [2021] Journal of Industrial Economics 653.

[55] Nosheen Iqbal, 'Forget the DJs: Spotify Playlists Are the New Musical Starmakers' *The Guardian* (28 April 2019) <http://bit.ly/2PfBu0E> accessed 18 November 2022.

[56] Aguiar and Waldfogel (n 54).

[57] Spotify's money-making venture is the one-sided streaming platform, which involves acquiring licences over content that is then distributed to subscribers who pay a rate set by Spotify. The firm also runs a freemium version of its service, which is effectively a multi-sided platform subsidized by advertisers.

[58] See Marc Bourreau and Germain Gaudin, 'Streaming Platform and Strategic Recommendation Bias' [2022] Journal of Economics & Management Strategy 25.

[59] For a detailed survey, see Jan Krämer and Daniel Schnurr, 'Is There a Need for Platform Neutrality Regulation in the EU?' [2018] Telecommunications Policy 514, 518–23 (positing that insights from this literature can be applied beyond general search engines because all platforms organize provider offerings).

[60] For instance, monopoly at the platform level is assumed and content quality is often treated as ex-ogenous (i.e. causally independent from other variables in the model).

improve, rather than decline. At worst, effects become ambiguous if one accounts for informed intuitions on investment incentives.[61]

Of course, in line with what Chapter 3 claimed, speculating over how Spotify's (allegedly) biased playlists might harm consumer welfare in other ways is always possible. Favouring cheaper content in a bid to drive royalty prices down surely might, for example, be chastised for its potentially quality-decreasing and/or innovation-depressing consequences. Yet, even these stories sound flimsy.

First, pegging music quality to its acquisition price seems somewhat incongruous. Consumers have idiosyncratic tastes when it comes to music,[62] and content quality is notoriously unpredictable.[63] If king-making favours the discovery of artists whose talents were overlooked by the majors, the practice might just as well be portrayed as pro-quality, pro-choice, and pro-diversity.

Second, assuming the 'expensive-is-better' premise is accepted, one must then clarify whose interests are to be protected under broader variations of antitrust's consumer welfare lodestar. For the upstream providers, our powerful streaming platforms like Spotify are bargaining with are the (major) record labels, not the artists. These *intermediaries* are (in general) not exactly minnows. More importantly, they are the ones controlling the livelihood of real creators. We therefore need to be mindful of uncritically assuming that musicians' incentives to 'innovate' are vicariously tied to those who market their work, a point Chapter 5 unpacks more thoroughly.

So, what is the takeaway at this juncture? The key message is that consumer welfare-centric antitrust does not have to be visually impaired when confronted with claims of platform king-making. Harmful effects can be theorized, sometimes formally. Nevertheless, not all king-makers are invariably bad from this perspective: quite the reverse. Caution may thus be justified when it comes to enforcement. This is something we return to later, in Part III, as more pressing matters await. Among them, 'self-preferencing', which is up next on our journey in the upstream.

3.2 Self-preferencing

To many policymakers and their expert advisers, self-preferencing tactics are the poster children for abusive conduct in the platform economy. Insofar as consumer welfare remains the paradigm, is the stigma really warranted? Might it not even be

---

[61] See Krämer and Schnurr (n 59) 522 (observing that these models predict increases in consumer and total surpluses).

[62] See Hannes Datta, George Knox and Bart Bronnenberg, 'Changing Their Tune: How Consumers' Adoption of Online Streaming Affects Music Consumption and Discovery' [2017] Marketing Science 5, 6.

[63] See Joel Waldfogel, *Digital Renaissance: What Data and Economics Tell Us about the Future of Popular Culture* (Princeton UP 2018) 11ff; 168ff.

argued again that, if these platforms truly are guided by their lust for profits, self-preferencing would be irrational?

3.2.1 Incentives?

Economists are regularly at loggerheads when it comes to explaining the profit-maximizing logic behind platform practices. Despite compelling (anecdotal) evidence suggesting self-preferencing frequently does occur,[64] some would effectively deny this, relying on (their own interpretation of) multi-sided market theory and leveraging economics.[65] Self-preferencing, by their account, is (generally) irrational as it would prompt consumers to switch away to rivals and thereby disrupt the virtuous cycle of network effects that make or break any platform.[66] Businesses like Alphabet/Google should, moreover, have no such incentives because of the so-called single monopoly profit theorem. Either the platform infrastructure (a general search engine, for instance) and the products it supports (say, vertical search services) belong to vertically related markets in which case only one monopoly rent is available for extraction (upstream or downstream); or the products are complements making leveraging irrational since the platform would be renouncing profits from its core product (here, general search).[67]

Now, several formal economic models do put the incentives issue to rest. Some are specific to self-preferencing by a monopolistic general search platform like Google Search and defeat both objections (i.e. multi-sidedness and single monopoly profit theorem).[68] Others prove that self-preferencing is actually rational in many different contexts, including those where the platform acts as a (single-sided) marketer. Yes, provided consumers are sufficiently insensitive to bias, Netflix does have a profit-maximizing incentive to skew the personalized recommendations

---

[64] See eg Dana Mattioli, 'Amazon Changed Search Algorithm in Ways That Boost Its Own Products' *Wall Street Journal* (16 September 2019) <https://on.wsj.com/2J8QyYq> accessed 18 November 2022 (reporting how Amazon engineers were pressured into skewing Amazon's search algorithms in favour of in-house products).

[65] See Robert Bork and J Gregory Sidak, 'What Does the Chicago School Teach about Internet Search and the Antitrust Treatment of Google?' [2012] Journal of Competition Law & Economics 663, 674 ('The economics of two-sided markets cannot be over-emphasized in this case.')

[66] ibid 674–75.

[67] ibid 675–77.

[68] To keep things brief, such a platform might well bias its organic search results to favour its in-house verticals when the upsides outweigh the risk of consumers switching to a rival (say, Bing) (Emanuele Tarantino, 'A Simple Model of Vertical Search Engines Foreclosure' [2013] Telecommunications Policy 1). Vertical search services, furthermore, are themselves multi-sided platforms. This creates the conditions for defeating the single monopoly profit theorem as it expands the set of customers from which new rents can be extracted (Jay Pil Choi and Doh-Shin Jeon, 'A Leverage Theory of Tying in Two-Sided Markets with Nonnegative Price Constraints' [2021] American Economic Journal: Microeconomics 283; Edward Iacobucci and Francesco Ducci, 'The Google Search Case in Europe: Tying and the Single Monopoly Profit Theorem in Two-Sided Markets' [2019] European Journal of Law and Economics 15, 34–39). See also Eisenmann, Paker and Van Alstyne (n 16) 1280 (applying the seminal model of Michael Whinston, 'Tying, Foreclosure and Exclusion' [1990] American Economic Review 837, to argue that platform markets routinely violate the narrow conditions under which the single monopoly profit theorem holds true).

it makes to them in order to favour its in-house productions[69] (such as *House of Cards*).[70]

In sum, self-preferencing can be rational for powerful integrated platforms in a variety of settings. The broader point, though, is that the inextricably complex economics of such practices, combined with conflicting insights from those whose job it is to untangle them, put antitrust decision-makers (ostensibly) committed to protecting consumer welfare in a tough spot. This in turn can lead even the more resourceful and technically competent ones into making oddly reasoned conclusions. Factually (very) similar situations involving Alphabet/Google on three different continents are cases in point, as our next topic illustrates.

3.2.2 Harm?

The incentives and ability to self-preference are there. Regardless, where is the consumer welfare harm? Let us focus for discursive purposes on Alphabet/Google, which, pursuant to an EU decision in 2017,[71] became the first platform condemned for behaving this way.

3.2.2.1 *(Informed) informal theories?*

The facts behind the landmark intervention are well known: Alphabet/Google was found to have infringed EU antitrust law by favouring its comparison-shopping service (Google Shopping) in the organic results of its general search engine (Google Search). How? By fidgeting with its ranking algorithms and by displaying its in-house comparator in a more attention-grabbing way than those of third parties.[72]

Having recalled this, note that, while publicized with consumer welfare rhetoric, the decision's actual content suggests the EC was actually focused on protecting competition, as such.[73] Incidentally, there was little ambiguity back when then Commissioner Joaquín Almunia was at the helm; consumer welfare concerns were conspicuously absent at the time.[74] This notwithstanding, assume, for argument's

---

[69] Bourreau and Gaudin (n 58) (sensitivity to bias depends on the magnitude of consumers' utility loss resulting from biased recommendations. The lower the magnitude, the less consumers are sensitive to bias).

[70] See David Carr, 'Giving Viewers What They Want' *New York Times* (25 February 2013) <https://nyti.ms/3fdbkVd> accessed 18 November 2022.

[71] See *Google Search (Shopping)* (Case AT.39,740) EC Decision 27 June 2017.

[72] Liability was confirmed in Case T-612/17 *Google and Alphabet (Google Shopping)* ECLI:EU:T:2021:763 [2021] not yet published. This ruling is currently under appeal in Case C-48/22 P.

[73] cf EC, 'Report on Competition Policy 2017' COM(2018) 482 final, 4 <https://bit.ly/3OjUOVo> accessed 19 November 2022 (describing the case as one of 'widening choice for consumers') with *Google Search (Shopping)* (n 71) [331]–[332], [667] (tying it to equality of opportunity and the protection of competition, as such).

[74] Joaquín Almunia, 'Statement on the Google Investigation' (5 February 2014) <https://bit.ly/3TLEcqF> accessed 19 November 2022 ('*Our concern* was that [verticals] could be significantly less visible or not directly visible, leading to an *undue* diversion of internet traffic') (emphasis added).

sake, that the authority was in fact committed to some understanding of consumer welfare, and ask: how would the story of harm have played out?

In a peer-reviewed paper published almost a year after the decision became publicly available, the EC's own economists shared some interesting insights worth mentioning here. According to them:

> The Google Shopping decision is a leveraging abuse case. Google used its dominance in the market for general search services to give its comparison shopping service an artificial advantage and *exclude* competing comparison shopping services, which leads to *anticompetitive foreclosure* ... The anticompetitive foreclosure *is established* in the Decision by the *likelihood* of having negative consequences on competition.[75]

The quoted passage makes sense to antitrust cognoscenti; *anticompetitive* foreclosure certainly has been the bread-and-butter narrative of the policy's contemporary enforcement agenda against single-firm abuses.[76] But there is a hitch in claiming that the EC *established* it, at least in the way conventionally thought of as meaningful to a rigorous consumer welfare advocate.

What *is* demonstrated, as the first instance judges confirmed on appeal,[77] is that (i) web traffic—be it generally or referred from Google Search—is important to compete in the shopping-comparison industry;[78] (ii) actual and lasting traffic diversion ensuing from Alphabet/Google's self-preferencing did occur;[79] which means (iii) third-party shopping comparators could *potentially* be excluded.[80]

What is *not* evidenced is the *likely* (i.e. not the self-defeating standard of actual) *exclusion* of firms *as efficient* as Google Shopping, demonstrably *caused* by the impugned conduct, without which consumer welfare harm in the form of higher prices and reduced innovation can only be inferred through (informed) *intuition*.[81]

Undeniably, the rigorous consumer welfare advocate will have to concede that the narrative is airtight if what is at stake is consumer choice—if the relevant standard of foreclosure is satisfied whenever *any* player affected by the impugned

---

[75] Andrea Amelio and others, 'Recent Developments at DG Competition: 2017/2018' [2018] Review of Industrial Organization 653, 661 (emphasis added).

[76] See, eg EC, 'Guidance on the Commission's Enforcement Priorities in Applying Article 82 of the EC Treaty to Abusive Exclusionary Conduct by Dominant Undertakings' [2009] OJ C45/7.

[77] *Google and Alphabet (Google Shopping)* (n 72) [445]–[454].

[78] *Google Search (Shopping)* (n 71) [445]–[451], [542]–[588].

[79] ibid [452]–[541].

[80] ibid [593].

[81] See *Google Search (Shopping)* (n 71) [593]–[594] ('the Conduct has the *potential* to foreclose competing comparison shopping services, which *may* lead to higher fees for merchants, higher prices for consumers, and less innovation'; potential 'higher costs for merchants are *capable* of leading to higher product prices for consumers') (emphasis added). In terms of dynamic efficiency harms, the decision falls short of what formal reasoning requires (see eg Pablo Ibáñez Colomo, 'On the Application of Competition Law as Regulation: Elements for a Theory' [2012] Yearbook of European Law 201, 215–16).

behaviour is (potentially) precluded from entering, or is eliminated from, the market, or when life simply becomes harder as a result.[82] Likewise, there is a robust quality-based story to be spun as well. Keep in mind that Google Shopping was deemed inferior to existing alternatives,[83] and the EC did invoke an *effective* consumer choice rationale.[84] Both accounts would indeed fit within the *strong* consumer surplus and consumer choice variations of the consumer welfare paradigm.

All the same, if the case genuinely was about safeguarding market diversity/consumer choice per se, its apparent contradiction with binding contemporaneous judicial authority would have been glaring.[85] And if the intervention had been more about correcting consumer deception, one would have expected some explanations on two fronts. First: why was EU consumer protection legislation considered inadequate or irrelevant? Second: why was a transparency-oriented remedy deemed insufficient?[86]

In brief, if 'anticompetitive foreclosure' truly was the theory of harm supporting the *Google Shopping* decision, it definitely was not rigorously formalized, nor was it tested against a meaningful consumer welfare standard.

Admittedly, our aim is merely to check whether we can really rationalize self-preferencing as a potential competition problem. By this measure, the preceding discussion maybe just highlights an issue of rigour, not a defect in the consumer welfare paradigm. Plus, if (informed) intuition is the best we have, this should perhaps be reflected in how our competition laws are *enforced*.

Enforcement, though, is a separate matter, one addressed later in Part III. Besides, reliance on informal theories can generate inconsistencies that may ultimately undermine them altogether. Look at the one targeting Alphabet/Google: the same narrative—traffic importance, combined with the idea whereby traffic diversion equals anticompetitive foreclosure, which in turn leads to consumer welfare harm—was deployed in the early 2010s by the US FTC in nearly identical factual circumstances. As is well known, no liability was incurred.[87] According to the

---

[82] *Google Search (Shopping)* (n 71) [641]–[642] ('The Commission concludes that the Conduct is also capable of having, or likely to have, anti-competitive effects. . . . The Conduct *may* therefore make it *more difficult* . . . to compete against Google') (emphasis added). See also *Google and Alphabet (Google Shopping)* (n 72) [445] (concluding that the EC had 'established actual effects'), [382] (holding that causality can be established through correlation).

[83] *Google Search (Shopping)* (n 71) [490]–[491].

[84] ibid [599] (underscoring the deceptive nature of the behaviour on consumers).

[85] See Case C-209/10 *Post Danmark* ECLI:EU:C:2012:172 [2012] electronic Report of Cases, [21] ('It is in no way the purpose of [EU antitrust law] to ensure that competitors less efficient than the undertaking with the dominant position should remain on the market').

[86] Transparency remedies were actually considered when the case was being pursued under the consensual commitment procedure. But the way the EC addresses their insufficiency is either missing (see *Google Search (Shopping)* (n 71) [129]) or shows that the concern was unrelated to effective consumer choice (see [127]–[128], highlighting fairness-related worries).

[87] FTC, 'Statement of the Federal Trade Commission Regarding Google's Search Practices *In the Matter of Google Inc.* FTC File Number 111-0163' (3 January 2013) <https://bityl.co/Fjvs> accessed 19 November 2022.

authority, evidence supported the conclusion that the contentious conduct likely *benefited* consumers through the improvements of their search experience. These gains, it stated, outweighed the negative impact the practice surely did bear on rival vertical (i.e. specialized) search providers (such as Yelp).[88]

Hence, intuitive foreclosure reasoning can breed confusion. Not that other theories of harm to 'consumer welfare' are inconceivable; they simply raise major questions. Take the Competition Commission of India (CCI)'s finding that Alphabet/Google's self-preferencing of its Google Flights service in Google Search 'unfairly' deprived consumers of additional choices.[89] What is the underlying logic, one may ask, as the order is quite perplexing.

For one, its operative analysis reveals a potpourri of (at best mildly substantiated) narratives. None explains how *consumers* were unfairly treated because of the behaviour.[90] And whereas the disclaimer remedy imposed by the CCI provides a hint,[91] this cannot distract from the fact that what is then a consumer deception (i.e. *effective* consumer choice) case is not reasoned as one.

For another, the lone part of the decision which does address the substantive conclusion of unfair potential losses in consumer choice (through the foreclosure of competing flight comparators) confoundingly conflates two issues: fairness to consumers and that which might be owed to rivals under antitrust.[92]

---

[88]   ibid 2–4. An insightful confidential report drafted by the FTC's legal staff (which was released under the Freedom of Information Act to the *Wall Street Journal*) seemingly dovetails with the stance adopted by the Commissioners (FTC Bureau of Competition, 'Internal Memorandum re Google Inc. File No 111-0163' (8 August 2012) 78ff <https://bityl.co/Fjy0> accessed 19 November 2022). However, caution is warranted. Indeed, only the report's even pages were published. Some of the missing odd pages contained information relating specifically to self-preferencing and may have thus qualified the staffers' conclusions.

[89]   *Matrimony.com Limited vs Google LLC & Others and Consumer Unity & Trust Society (CUTS) vs Google LLC & Others* (Joined cases 07 and 12/2012) CCI Decision of 8 February 2018, [420] . The CCI ruled on a plethora of claims (which the decision makes difficult to number accurately). Ultimately, the agency rejected all but three: self-preferencing of Google Flights, prefixing the ranking of Universal Results, and exclusivity requirements imposed on publishers using its AdSense service—the latter two pertaining to practices that had (long) been discontinued.

[90]   See ibid [231]–[253]. There are two *defensive* leveraging narratives: diversion of indispensable traffic might (i) lead rival flight comparators to purchase (additional) Google keyword ads whose costs might then increase ([248]); and (ii) enable Alphabet/Google to 'collect more user data to reinforce its advantage in search advertising' ([249]). One also finds an *innovation* theory: rivals, deprived of consumer data they might otherwise have harvested, may no longer be able to innovate on their products ([249]). Finally, the CCI advances an *offensive* leveraging story: traffic diversion could lead to the foreclosure of (equally efficient) rival flight comparators thereby enabling Alphabet/Google to displace them ([248] together with [253]). Only the latter is explicitly tied to the substantive conclusion whereby consumers are potentially deprived of additional choices.

[91]   At [422], the CCI orders Alphabet/Google to cease misleading consumers by displaying an appropriate disclaimer.

[92]   At [253], the CCI states that its 'comprehensive examination' revealed that third-party flight comparators might be foreclosed due to the 'unfair diversion of traffic' caused by the behaviour. But how can it be inferred from this finding that *consumers* might have been *unfairly* treated? There may be unfairness in the fact that unsuspecting consumers might be misled into clicking on the platform's prominently positioned/ranked in-house verticals. But this is not what the CCI argues.

The takeaway here is accordingly simple: although one can frame self-preferencing as a potential competition problem under a consumer welfare approach, (informed) intuitive theories can be poor guides. The latter may, moreover, be deployed to mask fears which have little to do with any understanding of consumer welfare.

3.2.2.2 Formal theories?

To date, decision-makers have rationalized the harm from self-preferencing without relying on formal economic analyses. What if we queried economists today? My sense is that their quick answer would be: 'it depends'. Like our other upstream power plays explored earlier, several game-theoretic studies dissect self-preferencing tactics. Each model comes with distinct assumptions that will sometimes alter the diagnosis even when the defined parameters are not (or at least do not seem) drastically different. Again, our *Google Shopping* case serves as a good illustration.

Inspired by the EC's decision, some economists have attempted to formalize the foreclosure theory by analogizing self-preferencing to bundling. A pair of them tells us exclusion of as efficient vertical search providers is a credible outcome.[93] Yet, these economists' consumer welfare predictions are ambiguous. In the baseline model, providers' profits are dented, but consumers *benefit* through lower prices. Still, this gain could conceivably be trumped by a quality-based harm because self-preferencing artificially nudges consumers into using the game-master's in-house product which is *assumed* to be an inferior option. To complicate things further, this latter prediction changes once the model is expanded to factor things like consumers with different preferences and intergroup network effects.[94]

Unfortunately, other studies are scarcely less ambiguous. One of them, for instance, extends the above-mentioned model.[95] What does it show? Self-preferencing can have opposite consequences on total and consumer surpluses depending on the strength of advertiser network effects, which, in turn, are affected by consumers' aversion to ads and by the likelihood of ad viewership converting into sales.[96]

---

[93] Choi and Jeon (n 68).

[94] And even here, predicted effects are ambiguous.

[95] See Gaurav Jakhu, 'Bundling in Platform Markets in the Presence of Data Advantage' (18 September 2018) <https://bit.ly/3tYGF6E> accessed 19 November 2022.

[96] Compare also the conflicting predictions on self-preferencing in more recent models proposed by Yusuke Zennyo, 'Platform Encroachment and Own-Content Bias' [2022] Journal of Industrial Economics 684 (positive effects on consumer and total surpluses); and by Andrei Hagiu, Tat-How The, and Julian Wright, 'Should Platforms Be Allowed to Sell on Their Own Marketplaces?' [2022] RAND Journal of Economics 297 (negative effects). See also Alexandre de Cornière and Greg Taylor, 'A Model of Biased Intermediation' [2019] RAND Journal of Economics 854 (finding equivocal effects on consumers); Krämer and Schnurr (n 59) 523–24 (reviewing other models and finding that welfare predictions are ambiguous).

Mind you, the foregoing is not to criticize economists; multiplicity of models is certainly their profession's most valuable contribution. The point is instead to stress how formally rationalizing self-preferencing as a potential competition problem under the consumer welfare paradigm does not yield a straightforward answer, nor will all antitrust decision-makers be equipped to carry out the work required to make such a story of harm stick.

3.3 Data-twinking

King-making and self-preferencing generate intuitively troubling effects on consumer welfare which can be formalized in some circumstances. But what of data-twinking? From the get-go, this practice seems to exacerbate the theorization dilemma.

3.3.1 'Consumer welfare' as a smokescreen?

The crux of the issue relates to how a game-master's panoptic omniscience over its platform infrastructure distorts within-platform competition when the game-master can also be a player. Therefore, more so than king-making and self-preferencing, data-twinking intuitively appears to arouse anxieties alien to consumer welfare.

Consider Amazon, a platform with a godlike view of the actions of consumers and suppliers who use its marketplace infrastructure. Plying the jargon of 'information asymmetries' downplays the significance of this position. For what is truly notable is not the game-master's ability to harvest an outsized data trove. It is rather the fact that optimized information held by Amazon bestows upon its retail activities a potentially *unfair advantage*. The point is better made by borrowing from some of the platform's former employees. They have explained how pervasive access and use of data on things like consumer searches and price sensitivity drives the firm's retail strategy, enabling it to ' "target ... private label products with perfect precision" '.[97]

Unfairness in competition, however, does not (nor is it supposed to) make consumer welfare-centric antitrust tick. Regrettably, economic theory has little to offer on the dynamics and effects of data-twinking, per se, i.e. the behaviour viewed in isolation from the more general matter of organic business integration, which is something that will interest us in the next chapter. So, can harm be convincingly rationalized?

---

[97] Capital Forum, 'Amazon: EC Investigation to Focus on Whether Amazon Uses Data to Develop and Favor Private Label Products; Former Employees Say Data Key to Private Label Strategy' (5 November 2018) <https://perma.cc/4XRW-TGTC> accessed 18 November 2022.

3.3.2 Incentives?

The multi-sided platform's advocate, we have seen, will regularly attempt to nip our worries in the bud by questioning the very rationality of the impugned upstream power play. Economic theory, they would recall, tells us that for broker platforms like Amazon Marketplace to thrive, the interests of both consumers and suppliers matter. As Amazon put it itself in sworn testimony to the US Congress in July 2019, 'we don't use individual seller data to directly compete with them'[98] since '[o]ur incentive is to help the seller succeed because we rely on them'.[99] What's more, the jury is still out on whether and, if so, in what circumstances (big) data harvested by firms to engage in product improvement or diversification can even constitute a competitive advantage.[100]

Anecdotal evidence presents a compelling counterpoint to this somewhat Panglossian view of things.[101] An internal report reviewed by the *Wall Street Journal*, for instance, sheds light on how Amazon data-twinked the bestselling car-trunk organizer manufactured by a merchant called Fortem.[102] The document contains twenty-five columns of information on the latter's sales and expenses, which the platform's own employees confirmed were used to guide Amazon's private-label strategy. In their words: '[b]y knowing Amazon's profit-per-unit on the third-party item, they could ensure that prospective manufacturers could deliver a higher margin on an Amazon-branded competitor product before committing to it'.[103] With the hindsight of a healthy US$4-per-unit profit on Fortem's US$25 product, the platform would have agreeably been remiss for not launching its own copycat, which it eventually did in October 2019.[104] After all, 'your margin is my opportunity', is probably what Amazon's founder, Jeff Bezos, would have said.[105]

Beyond trivia and anecdotes, note that recent economic research does appear to back them up. One particularly interesting model zeroes in on the growing significance of data-driven (cross-sided) network effects in product innovation and

---

[98] Ben Rubin and Corinne Reichert, 'Google, Facebook and Amazon Face Tough Questioning over Potential Monopolies' (*CNET*, 16 July 2019) <https://bityl.co/Fjve> accessed 19 November 2022 (quoting Amazon's associate general counsel).

[99] Ryan Tracy, 'Tech Giants Draw Fire in Congress; Lawmakers Suggest Internet Companies Need More Oversight to Ensure Competition' *Wall Street Journal* (16 July 2019) <https://on.wsj.com/2Whz yFg> accessed 18 November 2022 (quoting Amazon's associate general counsel).

[100] Emilio Calvano and Michele Polo, 'Market Power, Competition and Innovation in Digital Markets: A Survey' [2021] Information Economics and Policy 100853; Gary Biglaiser, Emilio Calvano and Jacques Crémer, 'Incumbency Advantage and Its Value' [2019] Journal of Economic & Management Strategy 41, 44, and the literature cited in both papers.

[101] Capital Forum (n 97).

[102] Dana Mattioli, 'Amazon Changed Search Algorithm in Ways That Boost Its Own Products' *Wall Street Journal* (16 September 2019) <https://on.wsj.com/2J8QyYq> accessed 18 November 2022.

[103] ibid.

[104] ibid.

[105] Quoteresearch, 'Your Margin Is My Opportunity: Jeff Bezos? Adam Lashinsky? Om Malik? Apocryphal?' (*Quote Investigator*, 13 January 2019) <https://perma.cc/Y69Q-F23P> accessed 19 November 2022.

conglomerate strategies.[106] In particular, it shows that a dominant platform theoretically does have an incentive to leverage data-driven network effects—these are data-induced reductions in the marginal cost of innovation—generated through the provision of a 'core' data-based product to successfully enter other markets. Why? Because data acquired in the dominated core market decrease the innovation costs of creating other products.[107] Diversifying thus becomes an economically rational business decision insofar as the economic burden of serving consumers with an acceptable substitute is low enough.[108] Prosaically: a powerful platform obtains data through the digital infrastructure it oversees; this trims its innovation costs and incentivizes it to secure new data by diversifying when entry costs are not excessively high.

Furthermore, two empirical studies by marketing economists are particularly worthy of note. The first is rather modest, looking at Amazon's behaviour during April 2010. It finds that, although Amazon's private-label offerings were small when compared to the total number of products up for grabs across multiple (sub) categories of its marketplace platform, the firm sold a disproportionately large number of high-demand products.[109] To illustrate, Amazon only offered 5.8 per cent of the 2,460,108 products marketed in the 'Tool & Home improvement' category of the platform. But it also sold 88 of the top 100 bestsellers.

According to the authors, Amazon's omniscience over its marketplace infrastructure does not simply enable impeccable targeting of obvious bestselling segments therein; by the same token, it helps the platform cherry-pick those mid-tail niches where expected demand is, *ex ante*, not sufficiently high for the platform to readily sell directly, while not low enough for it to ignore completely.[110]

The second study is more recent and comprehensive.[111] It investigates Amazon's entry pattern across a wide range of its marketplace segments between 2013 and 2014. The finding? Amazon's behaviour was 'motivated primarily by the desire to capture more value'.[112] More specifically, the platform used its data to target goods with higher prices, lower shipping costs, and greater demand.

Truth be told, the paper's authors acknowledge that one cannot exclude the possibility that data had little to no role in Amazon's entry strategy.[113] They find this to be rather implausible, though, and such reservations do seem warranted. Indeed,

---

[106] Jens Prüfer and Christoph Schottmuller, 'Competing with Big Data' [2021] Journal of Industrial Economics 967.

[107] ibid 984.

[108] ibid.

[109] Baojun Jiang, Kinshuk Jerath and Kannan Srinivasan, 'Firm Strategies in the "Mid Tail" of Platform-Based Retailing' [2011] Marketing Science 757.

[110] ibid 758.

[111] Feng Zhu and Qihong Liu, 'Competing with Complementors: An Empirical Look at Amazon.com' [2018] Strategic Management Journal 2618.

[112] ibid 2631.

[113] ibid 2636.

if data, especially those gleaned from merchants, were worthless, why would the platform investigate suspected data leaks and bribes of its employees,[114] or run the risk of perjuring itself over allegations of data-twinking?[115]

3.3.3 Harm?

So much for incentives.[116] Where is the consumer welfare harm from data-twinking?

Upstream foreclosure and its ensuing negative effects are definitely conceivable. This notwithstanding, recall that we are not dealing with the merits of organic business integration, not directly. Data-twinking, to repeat, is about the distortive impact a powerful platform's panoptic omniscience over its digital infrastructure can have on competition. And as previously noted, economists are just starting to grapple with this.

With this in mind, recent work does show that the practice can be detrimental to the consumer's wallet in certain circumstances. If one focuses on Amazon, for example, the outcome depends on the interaction of a variety of parameters like the degree of competition between merchants before Amazon decides to data-twink, the platform's fee structure (i.e. per unit vs proportional) and fee level, as well as the amount of data the firm decides to leverage.[117]

Taking a more dynamic perspective, there is definitely an intuitive worry over innovation: incentives to invest of data-twinked suppliers may take a hit, something the *strong* consumer surplus and consumer choice variations of the consumer welfare paradigm assuredly do capture. In this regard, one study is worth going back to here—the one showing how a powerful platform may have an incentive to leverage the data-driven network effects generated through the provision of a core digital infrastructure to successfully penetrate other markets when the risk–reward calculus is sufficiently favourable.[118] Compellingly, the modellers flag a two-folded problem. One: positive cross-sided network effects foster

---

[114] See Jon Emont, Laura Stevens and Robert McMillan, 'Amazon Investigates Employees Leaking Data for Bribes' *Wall Street Journal* (16 September 2018) <https://on.wsj.com/2MBY511> accessed 18 November 2022.

[115] See Tony Romm and Jay Greene, 'House Lawmakers Demand Amazon CEO Jeff Bezos Testify in Antitrust Probe, Threatening Potential Subpoena' *Washington Post* (1 May 2020) <https://wapo.st/2Wnc2a0> accessed 18 November 2022.

[116] On incentives, see also Yiting Deng and others, 'Can Third-Party Sellers Benefit from a Platform's Entry to the Market?' (11 October 2022) <https://ssrn.com/abstract=4254034> accessed 18 November 2022 (finding that a platform will avoid entering niches in its infrastructure with low market potential, but that it will also intentionally avoid markets that can hurt its commission revenue despite their high market potential); Nada Belhadj, Didier Laussel and Joana Resende, 'Marketplace or Reselling? A Signalling Model' [2020] Information Economics and Policy 100834 (predicting that data-twinking is rational when (i) selling via a platform and selling via one's own website are not strong substitute distribution channels and/or when (ii) a high-value good is substantially more valued than a low-value one).

[117] Wing Man Wynne Lam and Xingyi Liu, 'Data Usage and Strategic Pricing: Does Platform Entry Benefit Independent Traders?' (2021) Toulouse School of Economics <https://bityl.co/FjuG> accessed 19 November 2022.

[118] Prüfer and Schottmuller (n 106).

winner-takes-all-or-most dynamics in the core market. Two: these results are predicted to arise in the enveloped market as well.[119] Harm to consumer welfare can consequently be made out because, once tipped, markets are predicted to yield lower steady-state rates of innovation.[120] The mechanism? Relatively lower innovation costs flowing from data-driven, cross-sided, network effects inhibit the innovation incentives of both the incumbent and its rivals as the former is induced to rest on its laurels whereas the latter become discouraged by the incumbent's data-driven cost advantage.[121]

Interestingly, more recent theoretical models that stylize Amazon's data-twinking of its merchants further confirm that the practice can be predicted to negatively impact the latter's incentives to innovate.[122]

Besides, there is at least one empirical study to support the supplier incentive-to-innovate narrative of data-twinking in the context of Amazon.[123]

On the flip side—yes, data-twinking disappointingly doesn't lend itself to an easy answer either—things may not be as dire as suggested. The above-mentioned Amazon finding, it could be argued, should not overshadow the fact that the behaviour may be driven by efficiency motivations: data-twink to lure new consumers into the enveloped niche and thereby expand the overall pie.[124] The practice might, moreover, be fuelled by a desire to signal product quality to consumers, especially those who would not return subpar products (due to costs).[125] The economic welfare of consumers, society and, surprisingly, suppliers will therefore not necessarily take a hit. Providers (say, Amazon Marketplace merchants) may continue to thrive because of the quality-signalling effect data-twinking can generate.[126] Overall demand could expand and enable them to achieve greater profits despite the increased pricing pressure caused by the platform's entry.[127] In addition, although banning data-twinking can be predictably beneficial across the board (i.e. enhance innovation, consumer surplus, and total welfare), this outcome has been shown to only obtain when the policy either shields highly innovative suppliers who the

---

[119] ibid 984ff.

[120] ibid.

[121] The model is tailored to Alphabet/Google's expansion from general search to online cartography. But its authors claim their predictions would hold in any data-driven market where user data reveal some information about users' preferences or features and where these data can easily be logged.

[122] Hagiu, The, and Wright (n 96) 309–12; Federico Etro, 'Product Selection in Online Marketplaces' [2021] Journal of Economics Management and Strategy 614, 630.

[123] Zhu and Liu (n 111) 2618.

[124] Nicolai van Gorp and Paul de Bijl, 'Digital Gatekeepers: Addressing Exclusionary Conduct' (7 October 2019) 32 <http://dx.doi.org/10.13140/RG.2.2.10666.95689> accessed 18 November 2022.

[125] Ye Qiu, 'Strategizing for E-Commerce: Science and Art in Communication and Pricing' (PhD thesis, University of Texas 2018) 37ff.

[126] ibid 54ff.

[127] ibid. See also Deng and others (n 116) (confirming this empirically and showing that the outcome will obtain when the platform's market potential is moderate and when the demand–expansion effect is sufficiently high). Note that Lam and Liu (n 117) also show that suppliers may benefit through a different mechanism.

platform wouldn't have an incentive to data-twink anyway or when it is combined with a ban on self-preferencing.[128]

The upshot, then, is that data-twinking is a form of game-mastering which creates a similarly complex challenge for consumer welfare-minded antitrust. A potential competition problem can be made out; yet, the most immediate harm to consumers—higher prices—will very regularly not obtain, whereas potentially serious longer term consequences in terms of innovation will only raise red flags with decision-makers who are both (i) guided by the consumer choice or *strong* consumer surplus lodestars, and (ii) willing to indulge in a(n) (un)healthy dose of speculation.

3.4 Summation

As Nobel economist Jean Tirole writes:

> [T]here is a *feeling* that the new digital platforms have an unprecedented ability to a) favour their own brands when making a recommendation to consumers, and b) cheaply gather substantial information about third-party products and selectively create copycats for the most successful one.[129]

To this we can add the means to (c) furtively and arbitrarily skew the way suppliers are proposed to consumers.

Importantly, we have seen that the prevailing sentiment is not completely off the mark. These platforms do not merely have the ability to engage in what has been denoted here as 'game-mastering'; they will sometimes have the added incentive to do so. Likewise, it was further demonstrated that, assuming away debates on normative foundations, consumer welfare is not a conceptually defective paradigm. Rationalizing our king-making, self-preferencing, and data-twinking fears as potential competition problems is possible from this perspective.

Even so, building on these claims is by no means simple. Maybe more so than for despotic platforms, care is required as intuition will often deceive. Plus, rigorous decision-makers will once again find themselves confronted with the sobering reality that formal research in this area remains relatively scarce, difficult to navigate, and equivocal.

Accordingly, one key challenge is complexity. Another lies in the fact that consumer welfare harm will sometimes only be cognizable by decision-makers guided by broader understandings of the paradigm, i.e. *strong* consumer surplus

---

[128] Hagiu, The, and Wright (n 96) 314–16.
[129] Jean Tirole, 'Competition and the Industrial Challenge for the Digital Age' (3 April 2020) 10 <https://perma.cc/Y6VK-ZCZA> accessed 18 November 2022 (emphasis added).

or consumer choice, the difficulty being in such instances that formal models will generally be in short supply.

With this said, we can now switch lenses and explore how game-mastering fares under the alternative competitive process paradigm.

4. Game-Mastering and 'ex ante Fairness'

4.1 Prolegomenon

In the early stages of her administration's probe into Amazon data-twinking allegations, Commissioner Vestager had this to say:

> We have concerns. People are coming to us and saying, 'What is this? How to understand it—is this a level playing field when [platforms like Amazon] both can access all our data, but they can also sell all the products that we sell ourselves?'[130]

This is interesting coming from an antitrust enforcer who, just two years earlier, was emphasizing how her job was, and had always been, about defending *consumers*.[131] For, like the potentially despotic practices examined in Chapter 3, the intuitive worry behind game-master mischiefs, such as data-twinking, has little to do with 'consumer welfare'. Levelling the playing field is about ensuring *fairness* to *rivals*, be they horizontal or vertical. It relates, more specifically, to a dimension of fairness frequently called *equality of opportunity* (EOp).[132] And EOp, as argued in Chapter 2, is something for antitrust decision-makers guided by the *competitive process* paradigm.

Now, history shows that competition agencies and courts have sometimes explicitly sought to safeguard the value.[133] The EC invoked it in its aforementioned *Google Shopping* decision;[134] ditto for the first instance judges upon review by the way.[135] Academics too, of diverse horizons to boot, have defended the idea that the policy ought to be mindful of EOp.[136] Regrettably, most (to not say all) of

---

[130] Margrethe Vestager quoted by Ben Remaly, 'Vestager Hints at Amazon Concerns' (*Global Competition Review*, 28 September 2018) <https://bit.ly/2LMHbjA> accessed 18 November 2022.

[131] See Part I overview (nn 1–2).

[132] See, similarly, Ricardo Paes de Barros and others, *Measuring Inequality of Opportunities in Latin America and the Caribbean* (World Bank and Palgrave Macmillan 2009) 45 (stating that EOp is 'at the heart of the concern about the ability of society to … provide a level playing field').

[133] See eg Case C-280/08 P *Deutsche Telekom* ECLI:EU:C:2010:603 [2010] ECR I-9555, [230]; Case T-336/07 *Telefónica and Telefónica España* ECLI:EU:T:2012:172 [2012] electronic Reports of Cases, [204]. See also *United States v American Linseed Oil Co* 262 US 371, 388 (1923); *Brown Shoe Co v United States* 370 US 294, 324 (1962); *Ford Motor Co v United States*, 405 US 562, 570 (1972).

[134] *Google Search (Shopping)* (n 71), [331]–[332], [343].

[135] *Google and Alphabet (Google Shopping)* (n 72), [180] together with [432]–[433].

[136] See, among others, Eleanor Fox, 'Modernization of Antitrust: A New Equilibrium' [1981] Cornell Law Review 1140; Alfonso Lamadrid de Pablo, 'Competition Law as Fairness' [2017] Journal of

these sources merely pay lip service to the concept. This has unsurprisingly led some commentators to portray EOp as if it were a coherent ideal which could self-evidently explain every antitrust decision pertaining to allegedly unfair practices.[137]

The gripe is not purely semantic; it brings us back to the first aspect of the general claim this book is attempting to make a compelling case for. Prosaically: looking up in the platform economy becomes a more natural exercise and rests on potentially sounder normative foundations when mediated by the competitive process approach; but switching paradigms is not so obvious a proposition if the consensus demand for rigour still holds. As explained below, our game-mastering worries can be rigorously theorized when one appeals to the political philosopher's ideas on EOp. The task, however, is intricate as incompatible renditions of the value abound, each rivalling the others in terms of abstraction and apparent irrelevance for the antitrust enterprise.[138]

To be clear, though: the purpose is not to critically muse on the political philosophy of EOp. It is to ask whether the concept behind this ideal is heuristically useful for formalizing our game-mastering anxieties under the competitive process paradigm.

In attempting to answer this question, recall the analytical skeleton sketched in Chapter 2. There, a distinction between outcome and *ex ante* fairness/EOp was expounded. Protecting the latter, it was further argued, is the sole aspect of fairness competitive process-minded antitrust can justifiably attend to. It entails targeted interventions to correct (certain) (dis)advantages players may bear in the economic game flowing from unfair procedural defects and/or background conditions.

What follows builds on these insights and connects them to our game-mastering matters. At the risk of irking the political philosopher, anthropomorphisms, analogies, and other simplifications will be made in the process. Such intellectual shortcuts are necessary and need not overly trouble us given the boundaries of the inquiry. The antitrust community, after all, has not repudiated economists, despite

---

European Competition Law & Practice 147, 148; Josef Drexl, 'Déséquilibres Économiques et Droit de la Concurrence' in Laurence Boy (ed), *Les Déséquilibres Économiques et le Droit Économique* (Larcier 2014) 43–44; Roger Zäch and Adrian Künzler, 'Efficiency or Freedom to Compete? Towards an Axiomatic Theory of Competition Law' [2009] Zeitschrift für Wettbewerbsrecht 269; Shuya Hayashi, 'The Goals of Japanese Competition Law' in Josef Drexl, Laurence Idot and Joël Monéger (eds), *Economic Theory and Competition Law* (Edward Elgar 2009) 45–46; Kotaro Suzumura, 'Competition, Welfare, and Competition Policy' in Ulrich Schmidt and Stefan Traub (eds), *Advances in Public Economics: Utility, Choice and Welfare* (Springer 2005) 8–10.

[137] See, eg Sara Abdollah Dehdashti, 'B2B Unfair Trade Practices and EU Competition Law' [2018] European Competition Journal 305.

[138] Every EOp theory I have come across is either highly abstract, part of a broader theory of justice, or developed to address shortcomings in social policy (for instance, in access to education and jobs, or healthcare).

the liberties they routinely take with reality. Against this backdrop, let us now explore how antitrust decision-makers can look up by taking EOp seriously.

4.2 The Ideal(s) of EOp

EOp has a brief, but rich history.[139] Despite the lack of consensus around a singular formulation, philosophical reflections on it can be usefully clustered into
two broad categories that essentially track the distinction (suggested in Chapter 2)
between procedural and background (un)fairness. There are thus formal theories
(Section 4.2.1) and substantive ones (Section 4.2.2).[140]

4.2.1 Formal
Formal EOp seems relatively straightforward prima facie. Clearly, one might say,
this conception merely fleshes out the well-known slogan popularized during the
French Revolution that positions should be open to talents and people judged on
their abilities in competitive settings.[141] As explained below, there is more than a
little truth to this. A subtle distinction, which cannot be dismissed as hair-splitting,
must nonetheless be made between two species of formal EOp.

4.2.1.1 Neutral
The first may be named 'neutral' EOp and is the simplest formulation of the ideal.
Even some libertarians would countenance it.[142] More intelligibly for the antitrust
community, it reflects the idea whereby powerful game-masters would have a duty
to make available the games they operate to all players on equal terms. Following
this view, EOp-mindful antitrust decision-makers have to be wary of whimsical or
prejudiced market decisions which (dis)advantage some over others.

King-making fears fit neatly here. For example, (within-platform) competition
between hoteliers becomes arbitrarily distorted when powerful OTAs skew their
search results to favour hoteliers able and willing to loosen their purse strings.
Ditto where Meta/Facebook's treatment of app developers rests on whether their
business models are aligned with the platform's own interests.[143]

---

[139] See Paul Gomberg, *How to Make Opportunity Equal: Race and Contributive Justice* (Blackwell
2007) 2 (tracing its first literal formulation to a late-nineteenth-century economics journal).

[140] Theorists name their theories (and those of others) in various ways and infuse them with different
content. However, distinguishing *formal* from *substantive* conceptions seems to me the best starting
point for present purposes.

[141] Richard Arneson, 'Equality of Opportunity' in Edward Zalta (ed), *The Stanford Encyclopedia
of Philosophy* (rev edn, Stanford University 2015) 2 <https://stanford.io/2XBJ3SB> accessed 18
November 2022.

[142] See, eg FA Hayek, *The Constitution of Liberty: The Definitive Edition* (Ronald Hamowy ed,
University of Chicago Press 2011) 148–55; Antony Flew, *The Politics of Procrustes: Contradictions of
Enforced Equality* (Prometheus 1981) 45–46 and 112–14.

[143] DCMSC (n 8) 41–42.

But why is this so? Most philosophers would probably identify the idea of *impartiality* as the moral fulcrum of what I call 'neutral' EOp[144] (although some may argue that it is more about *respect* owed by the game-master to the players).[145] If this is correct, the problematic nature of a particular game-mastering tactic lies in how the platform implements its rules—the Meta/Facebook developer guidelines and Booking.com's ranking policy in our above-mentioned examples. Without them, we would have little to assess partiality.[146]

To my mind, such a theory enables us to formalize what the ADLC implicitly perceived when it condemned Alphabet/Google for having suspended Navx—a supplier of online databases for GPS navigation devices and smartphones—from its AdWords service (since rebranded as 'Google Ads') used to reach Google Search consumers.[147] Foreclosure was indeed not the issue here.[148] Nor were Alphabet/Google's advertiser rules, despite the extensive bouncer's rights they reserved to the platform.[149] Instead, what the agency took exception to was the whimsical nature of Alphabet/Google's decision, given that some of Navx's direct competitors, similarly reliant on AdWords, had been treated more leniently for no objectively justified reason.[150] The negative effects on consumers were speculative; hence, only a sensitivity to neutral EOp could properly rationalize antitrust intervention.[151]

Similarly, this theory gives legs to what the ACCC instinctively described as 'likely to be inconsistent with what might reasonably be expected of a competitive market',[152] when it highlighted Alphabet/Google's and Meta/Facebook's ability to arbitrarily block small businesses from using their services.

Note that self-preferencing moves could be made out to be inimical to neutral EOp as well. Upon reflection, though, there is something intellectually dishonest about the proposition. For what seems to have irked plaintiffs and some decision-makers in those situations is not so much the partiality (or disrespect) which may transpire. It is rather the fact that those platforms are (allegedly) not competing on the *merits*.[153] This observation leads us to the second species of formal EOp: meritocratic EOp.

---

[144] See, eg Janet Richards, 'Equality of Opportunity' [1997] Ratio 253, 258–60.

[145] See eg David Miller, *Principles of Social Justice* (Harvard UP 1999) 102 ('[i]t is disrespectful of people not to give equal attention to their claims, not to attempt to gain an accurate picture of their circumstances, not to explain the reasons for decisions, and to use methods that violate their dignity').

[146] As per Thomas Scanlon, *Why Does Inequality Matter?* (OUP 2018) 44, neutral EOp is an 'institution-dependent notion'. Similarly, see Richards (n 144) 260. cf Miller (n 145) 102.

[147] *Navx* (Case 10/0011M) ADLC Decision 10-MC-01 30 June 2010.

[148] ibid [175], [185]–[186], [193].

[149] ibid [173], [176]–[178].

[150] ibid [184].

[151] ibid [222]–[238], [243] (explaining the distortion), [244] (speculating on long-term consumer harm flowing from potentially higher prices, reduced innovation, and lower quality).

[152] ACCC (n 12) 164–65.

[153] See, notably, Commissioner Vestager's statement regarding the *Google Search (Shopping)* case in EC, 'Antitrust: Commission Fines Google €2.42 Billion for Abusing Dominance as Search Engine by Giving Illegal Advantage to Own Comparison Shopping Service' (27 June 2017) <https://bit.ly/2shvEeB> accessed 18 November 2022.

4.2.1.2 Meritocratic

The slogan 'competition on the merits' has tormented antitrust for decades. As the OECD once observed, '[l]awyers, judges and competition law enforcement officials have been using this phrase for many years to explain and justify their arguments and decisions, but there is no consensus on what the term means'.[154] Philosophers, by contrast, have thought long and hard about 'merit' and how it relates to EOp. So, how can their reflections inform us?

In a nutshell, meritocratic EOp means ensuring that the pattern of competitive outcomes is determined solely by the performances and abilities of rival undertakings pursuant to predetermined criteria.[155] Under this formulation of the value, then, antitrust must, as Commissioner Vestager would put it, 'make sure that what determines the winners and losers is how well they play the game, and *nothing else*'.[156] This entails sanctioning those who place obstacles in the paths of others which prevent the best among them from emerging.[157]

Of course, the idea of being 'the best' in market competition is somewhat opaque as it fails to specify the benchmark for making the assessment. While attending to this issue might beget insoluble controversies,[158] some would say discord can be avoided. William Galston, for example, writes that 'societies do not just declare the existence of certain tasks to be performed; they also make known, at least in general terms, the kinds of abilities which will count as qualifications to perform these tasks'.[159] This claim does seem plausible enough as it concerns market competition. Don't antitrust decision-makers assume that businesses vie for the consumer's patronage on metrics revealed by the latter's choices, such as prices, quality, diversity, and innovation?[160]

So understood, neutral and meritocratic EOp are similar since they are both institution-dependent theories.[161] Applying them means examining how the platform implements its rules, rather than the rules themselves.

---

[154] OECD, 'Competition on the Merits' (2005) DAF/COMP(2005)27, 9 <https://bit.ly/3ghZ4Z7> accessed 19 November 2022.

[155] John Roemer, *Equality of Opportunity* (Harvard UP 1998) 16 (distinguishing 'merit' from 'desert', which is sensitive only to effort). See also Shlomi Segall, *Equality and Opportunity* (OUP 2013) 87; Matt Cavanagh, *Against Equality of Opportunity* (OUP 2002) 35 (implicitly making the same distinction).

[156] Margrethe Vestager, 'EVP Vestager Remarks at the Schwarzkopf Foundation Virtual Event: "Competition: the Rules of the Game" ' (13 October 2022) <https://bit.ly/3tOeyXW> accessed 21 November 2022 (emphasis added).

[157] Richards (n 144) 261.

[158] Arneson (n 141) 5.

[159] William Galston, 'A Liberal Defense of Equality of Opportunity' in Louis Pojman and Robert Westmoreland (eds), *Equality: Selected Readings* (OUP 1997) 174.

[160] See, eg Makan Delrahim, ' "... And Justice for All": Antitrust Enforcement and Digital Gatekeepers' (Remarks for the Antitrust New Frontiers Conference, 11 June 2019) <https://bit.ly/3gr4XD8> accessed 19 November 2022 (stating—in his capacity as top-ranking DoJ official for antitrust issues—that '[a]s we think about antitrust enforcement in the digital economy, the key issues that antitrust enforcers must untangle are whether a company is growing due to superior price, quality, and innovation').

[161] Scanlon (n 146) 44–52.

To illustrate, consider the Alphabet/Google self-preferencing allegations. The argument whereby Google Shopping's positioning/display in Google Search distorted meritocratic competition, rests on an idea of merit whose content is tied to the competition organized by Alphabet/Google through the general search engine. What counts as merit here—the abilities/performances that are relevant for obtaining a prominent ranking—is determined by the rules which structure this competition. Following Alphabet/Google's stated policy, these rules aim to ensure 'high standards of relevance and quality'[162] in organic search results. *From this perspective*, there accordingly is a potential competition problem if Alphabet/Google search verticals (like Google Shopping or Google Local) actually are inferior to third-party rivals who all compete within Google Search.[163]

Granted, 'meritocratic' EOp might be the wrong label. Some philosophers would say a vision of EOp which reflects a best-player-wins imperative is underpinned by *legitimate expectations*, not merit.[164] That is, suppliers may have a claim against game-mastering platforms because, having played by the game-master's rules and objectively outperformed the latter's in-house competitor, they could legitimately expect to win. Moreover, other thinkers would argue that meritocratic EOp cannot plausibly be tied to fairness at all. For them, it is, at bottom, an efficiency principle in disguise,[165] a view often (unwittingly) embedded in contemporary antitrust jurisprudence.[166]

Whatever the case may be, the upshot remains the same: antitrust decision-makers *can* appeal to EOp with more than mere lip service.

Taking stock of our discussion so far: we *can* formally rationalize our game-mastering concerns by resorting to EOp, but there is clearly nothing self-evident about the notion. From my understanding, it is possible to conceptualize the value as a purely formal principle which embodies (or is associated with) procedural fairness (deceptively so if meritocratic EOp is indeed an efficiency humbug). Importantly, two distinct species of formal EOp, neutral and meritocratic, arguably coexist. They should not be misleadingly conflated to give the impression that they each dovetail towards a single ideal.[167]

---

[162] Google, 'Information Quality and Content Moderation' (2020) 20 <https://perma.cc/HCX7-Y7H2> accessed 18 November 2022.

[163] For such empirical claims, see *Google Search (Shopping)* (n 71) [490]–[491]; Hyunjin Kim and Michael Luca, 'Product Quality and Entering through Tying: Experimental Evidence' [2019] Management Science 596.

[164] See, eg Galston (n 159) 174. cf Cavanagh (n 155) 72–76.

[165] See Norman Daniels, 'Merit and Meritocracy' [1978] Philosophy & Public Affairs 206. For a sophisticated account of why meritocratic EOp is arguably about efficiency rather than fairness, see Cavanagh (n 155) 44–80.

[166] See eg Case C-413/14 P *Intel* ECLI:EU:C:2017:632 [2017] not yet published, [134].

[167] See Richards (n 144) 262–63 (explaining that to conflate them either (i) overlooks the fact that one is then creating a composite ideal underlain by multiple, distinct, ethical bases; or (ii) entails making an assumption (i.e. ground-level impartiality is inherent to, and inseparable from meritocratic EOp) which is (a) false (because it is actually possible to run a merit-based competition which condones arbitrary discrimination); and (b) potentially unhelpful (since the assumption would also further presuppose

To be sure, a particular system of antitrust may compel its courts and competition agencies to pursue a policy that is sensitive to both, in which case
formal EOp may be a fitting label to describe it. Nevertheless, the point here is
that decision-makers purporting to take EOp seriously need to be clear on two
things. One: what are the tenets and assumptions undergirding their actions?
And two: are the latter compatible with the ordered competition desired by the
societies they serve?

That said, a competition policy which only safeguards formal EOp has limited
reach for addressing our upstream worries. As explained, when attentive to this
value, antitrust might be able to rationalize as potential competition problems
certain types of game-mastering practices.[168] Yet, such a policy surely cannot extend to (all) the allegedly unfair situations involved, for instance, in Amazon's
data-twinking or in the App Store 'tax' Apple levies on third-party developers, in
particular those who face the platform's in-house productions.[169] In these cases,
formal EOp 'fades at the edges when it is pushed'.[170] The question, then, is: are there
other ways for antitrust to capture them while remaining faithful to EOp? The answer, as suggested earlier, is 'yes'. What follows explains why.

4.2.2 Substantive

Formal EOp has been described as morally 'stilted, narrow, and coldly artificial'.[171]
Following Bernard Williams's seminal exposition of how the principle can end up
crystallizing systems of privilege,[172] many philosophers have sought to substantively bolster it. EOp, they all argue, must more faithfully reflect the 'level playing
field' metaphor, which procedural fairness fails to achieve on its own. Competitors
come armed (or saddled) with varying types of (dis)advantages that ultimately
weigh on the structure of results. Some of these are borne from factors within their
individual control,[173] a reality only the most radical egalitarian would fret over.

---

that ground-level impartiality can be taken for granted, which then begs the question as to why it would
have anything to do with merit)).

[168] Recall our developers on Facebook, the surreptitious sale of competitive advantages by powerful
OTAs, or the self-preferencing some platforms (reportedly) indulge in.
[169] Rochelle Toplensky and Anna Nicolaou, 'Spotify Files EU Antitrust Complaint against Apple'
Financial Times (13 March 2019) <https://on.ft.com/2ktVJJF> accessed 18 November 2022.
[170] Charles Frankel, 'Equality of Opportunity' [1971] Ethics 191, 203.
[171] ibid 204.
[172] Williams illustrated this through the example of a hypothetical warrior society where the recruit-
ment process of warriors—a class historically foreclosed to all but the wealthiest families—becomes
subjected to formal EOp. Despite the reform, the rich continue to be recruited over virtually everyone
else. Why? Because wealth-derived competitive advantages make them better warriors. So, although
everyone is considered and judged on merit, formal EOp is insensitive to certain competitive (dis)ad-
vantages; it merely perpetuates the pre-existing situation (see Bernard Williams, 'The Idea of Equality'
in Pojman and Westmoreland (n 159) 98–100).
[173] These include things like choices, effort, preferences, ambition, and motivation.

Other (dis)advantages, however, flow from morally arbitrary variables, making them (potentially) unfair and ripe for counteraction.[174]

Roughly sketched, this is what substantive political philosophical theories of EOp are about. They are attempts to render EOp sensitive to the effects of (dis) advantages in competitions resulting from background conditions in addition to those emanating from procedural defects. To wit, substantive EOp theories try to justify measures that would further reduce disparities in players' prospects of success arising from competitive (dis)advantages which can be deemed unfair.

Still, a more granular look at the literature impels us to make finer distinctions. To me, three broad types of substantive EOp theories are worth distinguishing for the antitrust enterprise: 'Starting-gate'; 'Rawlsian'; 'Radical'.

4.2.2.1 Starting-gate

Starting-gate EOp theories relate to the meritocratic account detailed above. Their proponents, while denouncing the latter for its conservative bias, contend that it does get one thing right: the competitive process has to be carried out in ways enabling the 'best' to emerge as winners. What the starting-gate theorists abhor is the obliviousness their formalist counterparts display at the counterfactual. The question we ought to be asking, they argue, is: who would come out on top if each competitor had had fair access to what is needed to win in the first place?[175] For the rules of the economic game would be fundamentally 'unfair' if players merely had the chance to play by the same rules without having entered the game—come to the 'starting-gate'—on proximately equal or similar terms.[176]

Starting-gate philosophers, though, are not always forthcoming on their specifications of fair (dis)advantages. Take John Shaar's account; it tells us little more than 'all competitors should have the *same* advantages'.[177] Our antitrust decision-makers, needless to say, cannot do much with this.[178]

Other theorists, fortunately, do bite the bullet. David Miller's EOp theory, for instance, argues that true merit in competition tracks talents, choices and *effort*,[179] where effort matters 'only because it counts, along with talent and choice, as a factor in determining what a person achieves'.[180] Miller further indicates that, for

---

[174] These are what Rawls would denote as natural and social 'contingencies' (John Rawls, *A Theory of Justice: Revised Edition* (Harvard UP 1999) 14). Others simply speak of 'circumstances'.

[175] See eg Andrew Mason, *Levelling the Playing Field: The Idea of Equal Opportunity and Its Place in Egalitarian Thought* (OUP 2006) 38.

[176] James Buchanan, 'Fairness, Hope, and Justice' in Roger Skurski (ed), *New Directions in Economic Justice* (University of Notre Dame Press 1983) 66.

[177] John Schaar, 'Equality of Opportunity, and Beyond' in Pojman and Westmoreland (n 159) 144 (emphasis added).

[178] To be fair, Schaar did note that his account was more a critique of formal EOp than an attempt at a fully fleshed alternative.

[179] Miller (n 145) 177, 248.

[180] ibid 184. Miller, though, confusingly writes that he is theorizing 'desert'. But with desert, the *only* relevant consideration is 'effort'.

him, unacceptable competitive advantages include as well those which flow from 'integral' luck.[181] More specifically, he would require institutions to 'reduce the effects of luck by *not allowing gains to be carried forward from one venture to the next*'.[182] This suggests that background fairness might likewise be compromised when winners leverage the edges they derive from their success in one competition to another.

Let us briefly pause here. Despite initial scepticism regarding intelligibility, Miller's theory actually can help us in our attempt to rationalize certain game-mastering scenarios, especially those which would elude formal EOp.

Consider Amazon's data-twinking. Rewarded with, inter alia, data for its tremendous achievements as a marketplace operator, Amazon obtains an advantage. But when leveraged to inform its retail business, the platform breaches Millerian EOp since the advantage originates from the outcome of a different competition: the one pitting, under a (contentiously) narrow market definition, goods e-commerce marketplace platforms against each other. If antitrust were receptive to such an argument, curtailing the use of competition-sensitive data powerful platforms collect as game-masters might thus be viewed as a justified levelling measure. Such an intervention would reflect a particular vision of how to structure competition wherein a specific type of luck is singled out to prevent it from magnifying many times over. Why? Because its reverberations affect one's ability to succeed in another market and thereby reduces the commercial uncertainty normally prevailing in a competitive environment.

With this in mind, one might also consider the theory formalized by Nobel economist James Buchanan. According to him, economic competition operates under a 'finders are keepers' principle.[183] And the fairness inherent to it, he writes, depends on the factual matrix at hand. If many games exist, starting-gate equality is not really an issue provided people can join them voluntarily while retaining the option to exit.[184] Where fairness of competitive advantages does become a critical concern is when there is simply one, inescapable, game. Here, Buchanan argues that:

> If there are demonstrable and acknowledged differences in endowments, talents, and capacities, differences that are discernible at or before the effective starting point, there would seem to be persuasive arguments for discriminatory handicapping, *even at a reckoned cost in lost social value*.[185]

---

[181] That is, luck which affects the performance itself, such as a runner being tripped during a race (ibid 143ff).

[182] ibid 201 (emphasis added).

[183] Buchanan (n 176) 59.

[184] ibid 60.

[185] ibid 60–61 (emphasis added).

Buchanan's EOp requires that competitors have fair chances of winning. This, it seems, in turn means success is to be determined by elements which every player can control and by chance factors which affect them all equally.[186] Societies, then, have to mitigate the effects of (dis)advantages flowing from social circumstances with which competitors enter the game.[187]

What the above might signify for *antitrust* is rather murky. Buchanan himself proposes to implement handicaps through 'constitutionalized' intergenerational transfers of assets and publicly financed education.[188] More importantly, interventions (he writes) must *not* interfere with the market process as such. They should instead directly target 'the sources of the undesired consequences, which is the distribution of premarket power to create economic values'.[189] In the context of our analysis, these reflections would rather support *ex ante* regulatory measures, not antitrust. For example, forcing platforms to share their competition-sensitive data in certain circumstances;[190] or preventing them from enveloping the spaces of their suppliers, as India did a few years ago already.[191] We shall return to these questions that relate to intervention (as opposed to theory-building) in Part III.

At this juncture, what is the takeaway from the preceding exposition? It is that, unlike narrower formulations, starting-gate EOp is sensitive to some elements of background (un)fairness, such as advantages borne from success in other competitions and from social contingencies. More game-mastering situations could be caught as a result because, under these accounts of EOp, being the 'best' performer, narrowly construed, is not all that counts. Furthermore, this EOp ideal has little to do with legitimate expectations, and even less so with efficiency considerations. Rather, it is about *enhanced* merit[192] (although some say *respect for persons* is the real underlying value).[193]

That being said, starting-gate EOp is not to be confused with a second type of substantive EOp theory, which can be described as 'Rawlsian'.[194]

---

[186] ibid 69.

[187] Buchanan writes of the unfairness of advantages flowing from 'birth', which include natural and social contingencies. However, he concedes that the edge players have owing to their luck in the genetic lottery is something one must simply accept (ibid 59, 69–70).

[188] ibid 63–64 and 68–69.

[189] ibid 68.

[190] See references in Appendix E.

[191] Simon Mundy, 'India's Ecommerce Crackdown Upends Big Foreign Players' *Financial Times* (14 January 2019) <https://on.ft.com/2Hi6pFK> accessed 18 November 2022. This policy prescription is particularly *en vogue* (see, eg OECD, 'Lines of Business Restrictions—Background note' (2020) DAF/COMP/WP2(2020)1 <https://bit.ly/3Grnb2d> accessed 19 November 2022).

[192] Miller (n 145) chs 7–9.

[193] Mason (n 175) ch 2 (arguing that Miller is misguided and that what really lies beneath starting-gate EOp is respect for persons).

[194] Joseph Fishkin, *Bottlenecks: A New Theory of Equal Opportunity* (OUP 2014) 31ff, makes a similar distinction. Segall (n 155) 6, groups them together under the label 'substantive EOp' but we will see that dwelling on Rawlsian EOp separately is insightful for our purposes.

4.2.2.2 *Rawlsian*

Rawlsian EOp theories unsurprisingly track the insights of their namesake. John Rawls, of course, is (one of) the most recognized contemporary political philosophers whose contributions to the liberal tradition often inspire legal scholarship. For the uninitiated, suffice it to note that our indebtedness to him stems from (but is by no means limited to) the theory of justice he expounded in his 1971 magnum opus, *A Theory of Justice*. In short, Rawls articulated there the idea whereby a just society, comprised of rational and self-interested members, would be organized following principles these individuals would agree upon if a state of impartiality could be secured beforehand.[195] Assuming this 'original position', Rawls argued that societies would choose two main principles. The first would endow everyone with an equal right to the most extensive basic liberties compatible with similar freedoms for all.[196] The second would come in two parts—the first being lexically prior to the second in case of conflict—prescribing the conditions under which social and economic inequalities would have to be deemed morally acceptable. More specifically, Rawls wrote that such inequalities should be arranged so that they are:

- open to all (this is what he called the 'fair equality of opportunity principle' (FEO)); and
- to the greatest benefit of the least advantaged (viz. the 'difference principle').[197]

The difference principle (mentioned in Chapter 1) articulates a form of identity-based *outcome* fairness. FEO, by contrast, bears some striking similarities to our starting-gate EOp conceptions. Rawls, sympathetic as he was to the idea of tying EOp to the liberal principle of careers open to talent,[198] was indeed greatly disturbed by the fact that leaving it at this would allow contingencies to strongly influence the structure of competitive outcomes. To correct the 'obvious injustice'[199] these morally arbitrary factors could foster, he argued that EOp ought to counteract some of their effects.[200]

How is this different from starting-gate variations? Rawls's vision of EOp, for example, would likewise not remedy unfairness wrought by the 'natural lottery'.[201] In addition, those with the same level of talent and effort, he similarly wrote, need to have 'roughly equal prospects'[202] of success. To me, there are essentially two potentially relevant differences.

---

[195] See Chapter 1, Section 3.3.1.2.
[196] Rawls (n 174) 53.
[197] John Rawls, *A Theory of Justice* (Harvard UP 1971) 60ff.
[198] ibid 70.
[199] ibid 72.
[200] ibid.
[201] ibid 74. Rawls did argue that advantages derived from the 'natural distribution of abilities and talents' were unfair. However, his solution for this was the 'difference principle'.
[202] ibid 73.

First, Buchanan and Miller explicitly opposed interfering after a certain point in time. More prosaically, if one pictures a starting-gate, their EOp principles would bite *before* the competitors take their cue.[203] A Rawlsian egalitarian, on the other hand, would, if necessary, support meddling with the competitive process itself.[204] This could broaden the horizon of upgazing *antitrust* decision-makers. Drawing from Rawls, they might be able to rationalize enforcement in cases where a game-master's own player has an edge because of the circumstances in which it comes into existence.

To illustrate, reflect on Spotify's claim that Apple's App Store rules are abusively unfair and ripe for antitrust enforcement. Apple levies a 30 per cent 'tax' on Spotify whenever consumers acquire a subscription via the App Store. Daniel Ek (Spotify's CEO) says this is unfair because Apple Music (the game-master's own player) is treated differently.[205] Rawlsian EOp formalizes his intuition by tying unfairness to the advantage derived from the 'kinship' between Apple's App Store and the firm's own in-house music streaming service.[206]

Naturally, one may ask: how so? This question ties into the second potential divergence between starting-gate and Rawlsian theories of EOp, i.e. the underlying value which makes them responsive to background unfairness. Although we could read the (enhanced) merit principle into Rawlsian EOp,[207] good authority suggests that Rawls was more guided by considerations of *self-realization*,[208] or *self-respect*,[209] not (enhanced) merit (or respect for persons).

At this point, many will undoubtedly be disgruntled. Some platform detractors and upstream stakeholders might argue that even Rawlsian EOp does not go far enough.[210] Or maybe the portrayal of substantive EOp theories sketched here is a fundamentally flawed one, perverted by my desire to reify them for the antitrust

---

[203] Buchanan (n 176) 59, writes that '[u]nfairness in the economic game ... tends to be attributed to the distribution of endowments with which persons *enter* the game in the first place, *before* choices *are* made, *before* luck rolls the economic dice, *before* effort is exerted'. Similarly, Miller emphasized that his vision of EOp means '*initial* opportunity sets should be equal, not necessarily opportunity sets at some later time when choices have already been made' (David Miller, 'Liberalism, Equal Opportunities and Cultural Commitments' in Paul Kelly (ed), *Multiculturalism Reconsidered Culture and Equality and Its Critics* (Polity Press 2002) 47).

[204] See Fishkin (n 194) 32; Clare Chambers, 'Each Outcome Is Another Opportunity: Problems with the Moment of Equal Opportunity' [2009] Politics, Philosophy & Economics 374, 385–89 (further noting that under an opposite interpretation, Rawlsian and Millerian EOp 'would be very similar').

[205] Daniel Ek, 'Consumers and Innovators Win on a Level Playing Field' (*Spotify*, 13 March 2019) <https://bityl.co/FjvH> accessed 19 November 2022.

[206] For an implicit application, see *GDF Suez* (Case 14/0038M) ADLC Decision 17-D-06 9 September 2014 (condemning GDF for having leveraged significant data advantages 'inherited' from its former monopoly status).

[207] Scanlon (n 146) 60; Mason (n 175) ch 3, both acknowledge this possibility while ultimately rejecting it. Merit 'appears to play at best a derivative role' (Mason (n 175) 78).

[208] Richard Arneson, 'Equality of Opportunity: Derivative Not Fundamental' [2013] Journal of Social Philosophy 316, 320.

[209] ibid 324. See also Flew (n 142) 103.

[210] See eg Stigler Center (n 7) 90 (lamenting the unlikelihood that their proposed amendments to antitrust would 'entirely eliminate the competitive advantage inherent in large [platforms]').

community. If verified, this would render numerous claims of abusive game-mastering groundless from an *ex ante* fairness perspective. Luckily, there is (at minimum) one more alternative worth exploring. Let the reader be warned: it has far-reaching implications befitting only the most ideologically 'left'-leaning anti-trust systems.

4.2.2.3 Radical

Despite disagreements on how to formalize EOp, both starting-gate and Rawlsian theories converge on one idea: competitive tussles *should* be determined by the choices competitors make, their ambitions, and skills, as well as by the efforts they display; competition *shouldn't* be skewed by unfair advantages players derive from other circumstances whose effects, accordingly, ought to be counteracted. One reason to do this, as noted earlier, is that the latter are morally arbitrary. Another motivation which lurks, at least inchoately within Rawls's FEO, is the belief that there is something unfair about holding people responsible for factors which affect their prospects of success while being beyond their control.

Still, some may lambast the starting-gate and Rawlsian egalitarians for failing by their own logic. For if competitive edges derived from contingencies are unfair because they are morally arbitrary and beyond individual control, can we not say the same thing for those borne through contingencies like the lottery of nature? Rawlsian egalitarians would rejoin that, although their EOp conception is undeniably wrenched by this incoherence, the injustice it entails can be corrected with appropriate principles of *outcome* fairness.[211] This, however, would not satisfy those sympathetic to the current of EOp theorists labelled here as 'radicals'.[212] The sphere of *ex ante* fairness, the latter would argue, extends to *all* advantages which originate in contingencies/circumstances. Otherwise, a playing field could never be fittingly described as being 'levelled'.[213]

Closer examination of radical EOp reveals a problem, though. Beyond the normative difficulties they might entail, most of them will be of little help to antitrust decision-makers troubled by game-mastering platforms; these theories are either for the taxman[214] or would leave any policymaker

---

[211] Rawls (n 174) 64ff (arguing that the injustice caused by these types of advantages are to be corrected by the difference principle (mentioned in Chapter 1 (n 93) of this book).

[212] I follow Segall (n 155) 1, in referring to these EOp theories as being 'radical'. Others speak of 'luck egalitarianism' (Elizabeth Anderson, 'What Is the Point of Equality?' [1999] Ethics 287, 289); 'responsibility-sensitive' EOp (Mason (n 175) 90); 'level-playing-field' EOp (Roemer (n 155) 4); 'factor-selective' EOp (Marc Fleurbaey, 'Equal Opportunity or Equal Social Outcome?' [1995] Economics and Philosophy 25); and—perhaps tellingly—'socialist' EOp (GA Cohen, *Why Not Socialism?* (Princeton UP 2009) 11).

[213] For an accessible book-length treatment of this philosophical current, see Kasper Lippert-Rasmussen, *Luck Egalitarianism* (Bloomsbury 2016).

[214] Ronald Dworkin, 'What Is Equality? Part 2: Equality of Resources' [1981] Philosophy & Public Affairs 283; Ronald Dworkin, *Sovereign Virtue: The Theory and Practice of Equality* (Harvard UP 2000). Dworkin's EOp theory is too sophisticated and nuanced to be summarized in a footnote but it effectively

Table 4.1 Roemerian EOp

type	circumstance	Tranche T_1		T_2		...	T_{100}	
	effort (degree in quantiles)	e_1		e_2		...	e_{100}	
t_a	c_1	r_1	O_1	r_1	O_2	...	r_1	O_{100}
	c_2	r_2		r_2			r_2	
t_b	c_3	r_3	O_1	r_3	O_2	...	r_3	O_{100}
	c_4	r_4		r_4			r_4	
...	...	...	...	...	...	...	...	...
t_z	c_x	r_x	O_1	r_x	O_2	...	r_x	O_{100}
	c_x	r_x		r_x			r_x	

O = outcome r = resulting impact of c and O

Source: author's own creation.

bewildered.[215] Not that useful formulations of radical EOp don't exist; to my knowledge, they are simply in short supply.

A prime candidate, in this regard, is the algorithm devised by economist John Roemer. Beyond its technical precision, his is particularly noteworthy because decision-makers have endorsed it, albeit not (yet) for antitrust purposes.[216] What's more, the Roemerian algorithm for EOp policymaking and the assumptions it relies upon are easy enough to understand. Table 4.1 summarizes them, and a stylized example is provided later for good measure.

Essentially, one begins by specifying an outcome individual agents strive for. The latter are then divided along two lines. The first, named 'types', regroups agents based on their respective circumstances. 'Circumstances' are all the biological and social elements of the agents' environment that are (i) beyond their control, yet

asks the *social* policymaker to compensate those with whom nature was not so generous by using a thought experiment (like Rawls).

[215] See eg GA Cohen, 'On the Currency of Egalitarian Justice' [1989] Ethics 906, and Richard Arneson, 'Equality and Equal Opportunity for Welfare' [1989] Philosophical Studies 77. The latter acknowledges that his proposal would be practically impossible even for the distributive authorities he is addressing.

[216] eg Paes de Barros and others (n 132) 29ff. See also Giuseppe Pignataro, 'Equality of Opportunity: Policy and Measurement Paradigms' [2012] Journal of Economic Surveys 800, 802 (noting that 'Roemer's algorithm [is] considered in the literature as the staple policy on this issue').

affect their ability to achieve the outcome, and (ii) judged by society to be worthy of compensation. The ensuing situation is thus one where all agents in any given type share (almost) the same circumstances.

The second line, which can be called 'tranches',[217] partitions agents by the degree of effort they expend. 'Effort' is taken as a shorthand for all 'applications of autonomous volition'.[218]

With Roemer, the structure of outcomes is sensitive to nothing else but effort.[219] Circumstantial (dis)advantages are hence problematic from this EOp perspective because they prevent the most 'industrious' from winning.

Now, how does one determine between agents of different types who has exerted more effort? The answer, per Roemer, lies in a distinction drawn between *levels* (or absolute amounts) of effort and *degrees* (or ranks expressed in quantiles or centiles) of effort.[220] By definition, every agent expends a certain level of effort. But the fact that two agents belonging to two different types expend the same *amount* of effort does not mean they sit at the same *rank* within their respective type distribution of effort.[221] It is this rank, Roemer writes, which is decisive. Two reasons are offered. One: it reflects 'how hard a person tries'[222] to succeed; and two: how effort *levels* are distributed within one's type is beyond individual control as it depends on the amount of effort expended by others of the same type.[223] Therefore, those who have expended the same *degree* of effort (i.e. who sit at the same rank of their respective type distribution of effort) must be roughly similar in their achievements.[224]

These technicalities aside, Roemerian EOp has, at minimum, two fundamentally sweeping ramifications for present purposes.

First, given that Roemer leaves the determination of what counts as circumstances to political debate,[225] antitrust decision-makers would be able to justify

---

[217] Francisco Ferreira and Vitorocco Peragine, 'Individual Responsibility and Equality of Opportunity' in Matthew Adler and Marc Fleurbaey (eds), *The Oxford Handbook of Well-Being and Public Policy* (OUP 2016) 756; John Roemer, 'Defending Equality of Opportunity' [2003] The Monist 261, 270.

[218] Roemer (n 155) 6.

[219] See also John Roemer and Alain Trannoy, 'Equality of Opportunity' in Anthony Atkinson and François Bourguignon (eds), *Handbook of Income Distribution*, vol 2A (Elsevier 2015) 233–34.

[220] Roemer (n 217) 265–66.

[221] Suppose agents A and B, respectively placed in types t_a and t_b. Their effort *levels* are 90 and 50 respectively. A has thus expended more effort than B in absolute *amounts*. However, B may have expended more effort than A in terms of *degrees* if, for example, B ranks at the 80th centile of t_b's specific distribution of effort, while A sits at the 40th centile of t_a's specific distribution of effort.

[222] Roemer (n 155) 15.

[223] Roemer (n 217) 265–66.

[224] Using the example from (n 221), if B was more successful than A under the same configuration, there would be no inequality of opportunity. However, if A also ranked at the 80th centile of t_a's distribution of effort, the resulting inequality would be entirely attributable to circumstances and should thus be compensated.

[225] This is how he can argue that his proposal is ' "political" rather than "metaphysical" ' (John Roemer, *Theories of Distributive Justice* (Harvard UP 1996) 278).

defining 'types' in ways which might otherwise be difficult to sustain. This in turn opens the door to conceiving all the situations we have been exploring here as potential competition problems.

To give a germane example, assume a UK market for online mapping services (OMSs), such as Google Maps, Streetmap, and Digimap. The latter compete both horizontally against each other and vertically with general search platforms for value appropriation. Type t_a regroups those owned by operators of a general search engine (most notably, Alphabet/Google). The remaining OMSs are allocated to type t_b. Suppose now that (a) one OMS from t_a—Google Maps—consistently achieves high rankings owing to the favourable placement it receives in the organic search results of the dominant general search engine, which happens to be its affiliate (i.e. Google Search); and that (b), as a result, Google Maps sits at the 30th centile of t_a OMSs' distribution of effort. Following Roemer's algorithm, all those t_b OMSs sitting at the same or higher rank of t_b's distribution of effort end up compensated. Why? Because Google Maps, *although it may be the 'best'*,[226] has expended fewer (degrees of) effort than, say, Streetmap (a t_b OMS) to rank highly on Google Search.

Obviously, it is no stretch to extend such reasoning to other situations of vertically integrated platforms whose in-house offerings are similarly 'boosted' in their prospects of success. For instance, a 2018 report alleged that Amazon unfairly favours its private labels by advertising them right before consumers add rival products to their shopping carts.[227] The argument advanced therein was not that the platform's own products were inferior—quite the contrary. Instead, it flagged the unfairness in Amazon private labels being advertised '"at exactly the moment the customer is ready to buy"'.[228] Where is the unfairness? Well, apparently, '[a]bout 90% of shoppers who make a purchase on Amazon select the option on the page to "Add to cart" or "Buy now", rather than scrolling below that to choose an offer from other sellers'.[229] In other words, Amazon's private labels can win by being 'lazier' than merchants whose niches it invades, something Roemerian EOp cannot tolerate.

The second sweeping implication of resorting to Roemer's algorithm for antitrust purposes is normative. Doing so means subscribing to the view that economic competition is to be won through 'effort' so that justice in markets tracks *desert*, not *merit*.[230] This is an issue we shall return to shortly in Chapter 5 after recapping everything that was just discussed.

---

[226] See *Streetmap.EU Ltd v Google Inc & ors* [2016] EWHC 253 (Ch) [119].

[227] Jay Greene, 'Aggressive Amazon Tactic Pushes You to Consider Its Own Brand before You Click "Buy"' *Washington Post* (28 August 2019) <https://wapo.st/349hj85> accessed 18 November 2022.

[228] ibid.

[229] ibid.

[230] Roemer is clear about the fact that his EOp theory is normatively anchored by 'desert' (see Roemer (n 155) 15–16 and (n 217) 279–80). Note, however, that not all radical EOp theories are about desert.

4.3 Summation

EOp is a value antitrust cannot discard if it seriously wants to protect the competitive process. However, similarly to what we uncovered with freedom, paying lip service to EOp obscures the fact that the concept does not embody a singular ideal. As Chapter 6 further explains, this is important if societies value the rule of law.

To summarize (also in Figure 4.2): early on, *ex ante* fairness and *ex post* fairness were distinguished, and it was argued that competitive process-minded antitrust could not be sundered from the former to which EOp is intrinsically connected.[231] The reason is simple: under this approach, economic competition is to be operated under antitrust rules which ensure fairness in the structure/pattern of outcomes (as opposed to its content). Business practices that harm stakeholders may *ipso facto* become problematic when they are the result of powerful undertakings exploiting competitive advantages which can be deemed unfair.

This chapter shows that one can flesh out intuitions on EOp in multiple, intellectually rigorous ways. Each entails both an appeal to different underlying values and distinct policy prescriptions. Formal EOp, on the one hand, reflects (or is potentially associated with) *procedural* fairness and has two specific formulations: neutral and meritocratic. By conflating them, antitrust decision-makers would be demonstrating their commitment to ensuring open, unbiased, competition on the merits (i.e. on the talents, abilities, and performances of economic undertakings). On the other hand, EOp can be substantively enriched to gratify sensitivities of *background* fairness. Like formal theories, different values undergird each substantive variant. These include (among others) enhanced merit, self-realization (or respect for persons), and desert. Decision-makers—at least, in liberal democracies—need to be conscious of this and transparent about which value underlies their actions.

What the preceding analysis hopefully shows, then, is that some of our upstream concerns, denoted as game-mastering, can be formally rationalized as potential competition problems under the competitive process paradigm. The latter, though, does require a new, moralizing, mindset. Moreover, remember that our discussion here centres on theory-building. Part III will deal with the practical issues of intervention.

5. Concluding Reflections

In many ways, platforms evoke the game-masters those of us familiar with RPGs will have inevitably encountered. Like the latter, the former enjoy panoptic omniscience over the competitive environments suppliers are now increasingly impelled

---

[231] See Chapter 2, Section 3.2.

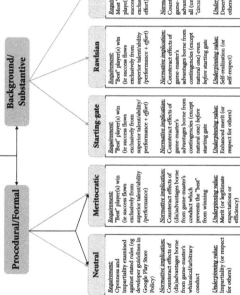

Figure 4.2 Antitrust and fairness.
Source: author's own creation.

to partake in. And platforms too will often play the games they are supposed to nurture. Naturally, this reality is not a problem in itself, let alone a market competition problem. Rogue game-mastering, however, is another matter altogether.

Powerful platforms, like game-masters, have the ability and incentives to exploit their godlike view of the games they oversee to twink their own players at the stage of inception and/or self-preference them later in time. Furthermore, even when they forsake participation, game-mastering platforms may well distort the value capture process by engaging in covert and potentially harmful king-making.

Against this backdrop, a key challenge for antitrust decision-makers is diagnostic in nature. Certainly, intuitive consumer welfare theories will regularly identify such behaviours as conceivably suspect. But as one learned competition judge opined in befitting circumstances, 'issue[s] [are] to be determined on the basis of the evidence ... not on instinct or personal experience'.[232] Once gut rationalizations are disavowed, explaining competition problems becomes challenging and often contingent on what consumer welfare is taken to mean, as well as on the decision-maker's ability and willingness to navigate complex and frequently ambiguous economics.

This notwithstanding, our game-mastering worries seem more related to what most of us would describe as (un)fairness in competition anyway. To me, deploying consumer welfare rhetoric is intellectually dishonest when done to square anxieties that really have little to do with the values the paradigm conceals. So, while '[n]ot every case of unfairness is a matter for competition law',[233] the point is precisely that some of them are.[234] When these cases come around, they ought to be articulated and reasoned as such.

In my mind, any legal system committed to the competitive process paradigm should strive to safeguard some measure of *ex ante* fairness. At the same time, merely pandering to EOp is no less disingenuous than a backhanded pledge to consumer welfare. Like the latter, the former is not a singular ideal. Decision-makers, accordingly, need to tread carefully. In particular, occasionally obscure philosophical verbiage cannot distract them from the fact that many formulations of the value make little sense for the antitrust enterprise. Some accounts may even be inconsistent with the systems of ordered competition their respective societies have envisioned for themselves.

The dangers of moralizing antitrust should not be understated since high-ranking officials at leading competition agencies have increasingly been resorting

---

[232] *Streetmap* (n 226) [99].

[233] Margrethe Vestager, 'Setting Priorities in Antitrust' (Speech delivered at the GCLC, 1 February 2016) <https://bit.ly/3gx4Bpw> accessed 18 November 2022.

[234] cf Lewis Crofts, 'Pursuit of "Fairness" Alone Can't Underpin Antitrust Probes, UK's Marsden Says' *mlex* (25 October 2017) <https://bityl.co/EDEA> accessed 18 November 2022 (reporting comments expressed by then Inquiry Chair of the CMA, Philip Marsden, stating that '[f]airness isn't a theory of harm. Promotion isn't a theory of harm').

to inchoate fairness rhetoric in recent years.[235] To be clear, the policy cannot, as some would seemingly have it, *'entirely* eliminate the competitive advantages inherent in large [platforms]'.[236] For a contest involving players who have absolutely equal prospects of success is not a competition but a lottery.

Ultimately, the mandate of antitrust authorities and courts is to ensure that in the interpretation and application of their respective economic constitutions the law is observed.[237] Where societies have chosen to establish a system of ordered competition that requires 'the greatest degree of equality concerning starting positions',[238] decision-makers should spare no theories to this end. Elsewhere, EOp cannot be allowed to become an open sesame for the discontented. As Alexis de Tocqueville once cautioned:

> There is in fact a manly and legitimate passion for equality that incites men to want to be strong and esteemed. This passion tends to elevate the small to the rank of the great. But in the human heart a depraved taste for equality is also found that leads the weak to want to bring the strong down to their level and that reduces men to preferring equality in servitude to inequality in liberty.[239]

These words ring especially true today regarding the upstream platform power plays central to our next chapter: free-riding.

---

[235] See references in Thibault Schrepel, 'Antitrust without Romance' [2020] New York University Journal of Law & Liberty 326, 358–83.

[236] Stigler Center (n 7) 90 (emphasis added).

[237] In some jurisdictions, this is made explicit (see, eg TEU, art 19).

[238] Sylvain Boyer, 'German Contemporary Analyses of Economic Order: Standard Ordnungstheorie, Ordoliberalism and Ordnungsökonomik in Perspective' in Agnès Labrousse and Jean-Daniel Weisz (eds), *Institutional Economics in France and Germany: German Ordoliberalism Versus the French Regulation School* (Springer 2001) 110 (describing the Ordoliberal conception of ordered competition that may have influenced the German legal order).

[239] Alexis de Tocqueville, *Democracy in America: Historical–Critical Edition of* De la Démocratie en Amérique (Eduardo Nolla ed, James Schleifer tr, Liberty Fund 2010) 89.

5
Free-Riding

1. Introduction

'Information wants to be free.' Anyone with a remote affinity to digital culture will recognize this iconic aphorism which epitomized the zeitgeist of the 1990s. Those familiar with it may also know that the phrase is generally attributed to Stewart Brand (the editor of the *Whole Earth Catalog*). Less well known is that his words were taken out of context. Actually, the quote itself is inaccurate. What Brand told Steve Wozniak (co-founder of Apple) in an exchange at the first Hackers' conference in 1984 was that:

> [I]nformation sort of wants to be expensive because it is so valuable—the right information in the right place just changes your life. On the other hand, information almost wants to be free because the costs of getting it out is getting lower and lower all of the time.[1]

The tension Brand and Wozniak were debating over three decades ago is worth recounting precisely because it animates the upstream fears underlying our discussion here. Indeed, scores of providers put considerable effort into creating content and developing new ideas embodied in a variety of useful, sometimes highly innovative, products. This benefits us and understandably comes with the expectation of a return on investment. Prospects of rewards, however, are somewhat dented in our increasingly internet-enabled world. For, online, we seemingly assume that everything must be available for free or at a discounted rate.

Powerful platforms, it seems, do bear a (large) part of the responsibility for the development of this entitlement philosophy. Alphabet/Google, for instance, has never been shy about its ambition 'to organize the world's information and make it universally accessible'.[2] As a result, (many) consumers are no longer

---

[1] Joshua Gans, ' "Information Wants to be Free": The History of That Quote' (*Digitopoly*, 25 October 2015) <https://perma.cc/DB5K-HNYY> accessed 18 November 2022 (linking to original footage of the exchange).

[2] Alphabet, Annual Report (Form 10-K) (2 February 2022) 4 <https://bityl.co/Dx24> accessed 18 November 2022; Google, 'Annual Report (Form 10-K)' (28 March 2005) 1 <https://bit.ly/3fHz4jD> accessed 18 November 2022.

Antitrust and Upstream Platform Power Plays. A. K. von Moltke, Oxford University Press. © A. K. von Moltke 2023.
DOI: 10.1093/oso/9780192873057.003.0006

in the habit of paying for things like journalism.[3] Similarly, Amazon's pricing strategy for its private-label goods often seems irrational at first glance. Jeff Bezos has candidly admitted that '[w]e do price elasticity studies. And every time the math tells us to raise prices.'[4] But, as Bezos added, keeping prices low ensures consumer loyalty.[5] By taking the content and ideas of others and then democratizing access to all this information, these platforms have therefore enlisted consumers as vital political allies in their competition with providers for value capture.[6]

Be that as it may, should our *antitrust* decision-makers be troubled? Using what is in the *public domain*, after all, is not something most would describe as inimical to the competitive process even when done at the costly expense of those whose work infills it. Plus, to the extent consumers benefit (which clearly appears to be what many of them believe),[7] there is no apparent consumer welfare problem either.

A paradox hence emerges. If an issue arises from powerful platforms taking and democratizing access to (the substance of) freely available information to the detriment of those who may have put considerable sweat of the brow into producing it, said issue instinctively sounds more related to unfair reward–distribution than to consumer welfare or competition as such. More prosaically, the intuitive concern with what are effectively cases of platforms *free-riding* on the efforts of suppliers most likely follows from one's perceptions on provider-oriented outcome fairness. As this chapter shows, it nonetheless is possible to see potential competition problems here as well, regardless of the endorsed anti-trust paradigm (Sections 3 and 4). To rephrase: we can rationalize enforcement to quell worries that pertain primarily to things (which ought to be) beyond antitrust's purview.

To make sense of the argument, though, one needs to first examine the type of claims this introduction has been tiptoeing around and explain why they are para-doxical for antitrust (Section 2).

---

[3] Nic Newman and others, 'Reuters Institute Digital News Report 2022' (2022) 19–20 <https://bit.ly/3TPB6SH> accessed 19 November 2022. See also Tim Groot Kormelink, 'Why People Don't Pay for News: A Qualitative Study' [2022] Journalism <https://doi.org/10.1177/14648849221099325> accessed 18 November 2022.

[4] Charlie Rose, 'Amazon's Jeff Bezos Looks to the Future' *CBS News* (1 December 2013) <https://cbsn.ws/2WkjF1X> accessed 18 November 2022 (interviewing Bezos).

[5] ibid.

[6] K Sabeel Rahman and Kathleen Thelen, 'The Rise of the Platform Business Model and the Transformation of Twenty-First-Century Capitalism' [2019] Politics & Society 177, 186–87.

[7] By some estimates, for instance, consumers' average valuation of 'free' Google Search results reaches €121.56/week (Bodo Herzog, 'Valuation of Digital Platforms: Experimental Evidence for Google and Facebook' [2018] International Journal of Financial Studies 87).

2. Free-Riding Platforms

2.1 The Claims

Tirole has written that '[p]latforms must create value, and not be parasites'.[8] Implicit in this truism is the hint that parasitic behaviour is in fact occurring, an empirical question many platform providers have been vocal about over the past decade, especially in the last few years. So, what exactly are they bemoaning? Their grievances, as suggested above, effectively point to value 'misappropriation' under the banner of consumer interests. More specifically, economic power is said to be abused upstream in two ways.

First, there is content 'scraping' with Alphabet/Google as the usual (would-be) culprit. Scraping is jargon. In the language of data and computer scientists, it refers to a form of data mining that involves using automated software applications (i.e. 'scrapers' or 'bots') to harvest data (say, pictures or text) from web pages.[9] Importantly, scraping is both ubiquitous and intrinsically neutral. Some retailers like Walmart reportedly have internal teams dedicated to lifting pricing data from rivals' websites.[10] Others externalize this task by resorting to specialized firms such as Competera.[11] Academics, too, are among the most avid users of scrapers.[12] In short, the practice 'might sound sinister, but it's part of how the web works'.[13]

Even so, large platforms are not akin to everyone else. When they scrape, trust-busters must intervene. This is what many providers have claimed when accusing Alphabet/Google of propping up some of its vertical search services with their content, which they allege has been effortlessly scraped without authorization or compensation. Consider:

o news publishers like News Corp and Axel Springer (respectively owners of publications such as the *Wall Street Journal* and *Business Insider*) that have long railed against Alphabet/Google's unsanctioned provision of increasingly

---

[8] Jean Tirole, *Economics for the Common Good* (Steven Rendall tr, Princeton UP 2017) 395.

[9] John Zabriskie, 'Bots, Scrapers, and Other Unwanted Visitors to Your Web Site: Can You Keep Them Out?' [2009] Computer & Internet Lawyer 5, 5. See also Jeffrey Hirschey, 'Symbiotic Relationships: Pragmatic Acceptance of Data Scraping' [2014] Berkeley Technology Law Journal 897, 903–06. Note that, although 'scraping' is technically distinct from 'hyperlinking', the two are inextricably linked (Thomas Höppner, 'Google: Friend or Foe of Ad-Financed Content Providers?' [2013] Journal of Media Law 607, 617).

[10] Klint Finley, '"Scraper" Bots and the Secret Internet Arms Race' (*Wired*, 23 July 2018) <https://perma.cc/X8R5-TXLQ> accessed 18 November 22.

[11] ibid.

[12] See eg Benjamin Edelman, 'Using Internet Data for Economic Research' [2012] Journal of Economic Perspectives 189.

[13] Finley (n 10).

lengthy press snippets in the search results of its Google Search and Google News infrastructures;[14]

o stock photography agencies, such as Getty Images and Dreamstime, which have repeatedly voiced their fears over the firm's unauthorized display of their imagery in its Google Images service;[15]

o review sites like Yelp and E-Commerce that denounce Alphabet/Google's unapproved harvesting of their user-generated reviews and photographs of local businesses, which the firm allegedly incorporates into its Google Local and Google Shopping verticals;[16] and

o other companies such as Genius, which joined in on the claim by accusing Alphabet/Google of lifting the sometimes hard-to-decipher lyrics of songs published on its website to feed Google Search.[17]

Incidentally, while these providers depict their enterprise as a struggle to preserve the lifeblood of the internet,[18] their demands from antitrust have been quite different. As investigations in the EU, Italy, and Germany reveal, press publishers and stock photography agencies have not been utterly objecting to Alphabet/Google's unabashed scraping of their publications and imagery. What they want is for scraping to continue but on their terms.[19] By contrast, firms like Yelp and Genius object to the very implementation of the practice.

The second claim of value misappropriation pertains to a practice known as 'Sherlocking', a moniker picked up by the Dutch competition agency[20] and

---

[14] See eg News Corp Australia, 'Submission to the ACCC's Digital Platform Inquiry' (20 April 2018) <https://perma.cc/6MQL-DRCS> accessed 18 November 2022). At the time of writing, snippets seem to only be displayed in Google Search.

[15] See Dreamstime's complaint [9], in *Dreamstime.com v Google* No C 18-01910 WHA (NDCal 2019); Getty Images, 'Letter to Commissioner Vestager' (2016) <https://perma.cc/6LGW-KCAE> accessed 18 November 2022 (note that following a 2018 settlement, Getty Images withdrew its EU antitrust complaint).

[16] See *E-Commerce/Google* (Case No 08012.010483/2011-94) CADE General Superintendence Technical note No 15/2018; Yelp, 'Letter to FTC Chairman Maureen Ohlhausen' (11 September 2017) <https://perma.cc/FW8C-E5QP> accessed 18 November 2022.

[17] Robert McMillan, 'Lyrics Site Accuses Google of Lifting Its Content' *Wall Street Journal* (16 June 2019) <https://on.wsj.com/35Of23q> accessed 18 November 2022.

[18] See eg Christian Oliver, 'FT Explainer: What Is Getty's Complaint against Google?' *Financial Times* (27 April 2016) <https://on.ft.com/2Sho4Cr> accessed 18 November 2022; FairSearch, 'Google's Transformation From Gateway to Gatekeeper: How Google's Exclusionary and Anticompetitive Conduct Restricts Innovation and Deceives Consumers' (2011) <https://perma.cc/S9HM-DZW9> accessed 18 November 2022.

[19] See *Google/VG Media* (Case B6-126/14) BKA Decision 8 September 2015, [168ff] (finding that publishers were not endowed with compensation rights under copyright law and that antitrust enforcement would effectively mean imposing on Alphabet/Google a duty to scrape on their terms). See also BDZV and VDZ, 'Press Publishers' Response to Google's Third Commitments Proposal. European Commission's Competition Investigation of Google—AT.39.740' (4 September 2014) 10–13 <https://perma.cc/Y59C-6ZXJ> accessed 18 November 2022 (responding to Alphabet/Google's final commitment proposal to date in the EU probe).

[20] ACM, 'Market Study into Mobile App Stores' (11 April 2019) 99 <https://bityl.co/Fjys> accessed 19 November 2022.

US lawmakers.[21] The dynamics of this behaviour are as old as commerce itself. Sherlocking is jargon to describe a powerful platform taking over concepts or ideas from its providers to supply in-house versions of the products in which these pieces of information are embodied.

The history behind the label serves as a nice illustration.[22] Sherlock was the name of the search feature (now known as Spotlight) built into the Macintosh OS (macOS). At first, it was a relatively simple file-searching tool with some very basic web functionality (such as translation). Consumers were obviously left wanting for more. This created opportunities for clever entrepreneurs to carve out niches for themselves within Apple's OS infrastructure. In 2001, one developer named Dan Wood did just that. He published Watson, a US$30 app specifically designed to complement Sherlock by expanding its range of internet functionalities. Looking up movie schedules and calculating exchange rates were two of the many new features Mac consumers could now experience. Unsurprisingly, Watson turned into an instant hit. Yet, by 2002, the app had become redundant because Apple had quickly released a revamped version of Sherlock which could do everything Watson had to offer (and more)—for free.

Truth be told, many have been Sherlocked and not solely by Apple. For example, Apple, but also Alphabet/Google, Microsoft, and Amazon have all replicated the personal cloud storage concept pioneered by Dropbox. And once within-platform integration is uncovered as the real anxiety, data-twinking—say, Meta/Facebook's use of its now-discontinued Onavo software to detect and imitate popular apps on its social media platform[23]—can likewise be viewed as a form of Sherlocking.

So, to reformulate, providers have been relying on jargon to advance two antitrust claims that are effectively about value *mis*appropriation:

- 'scraping', or the extraction of data and their subsequent reuse in a (vertically and/or horizontally) competing specialized service; and
- 'Sherlocking', or the replication of information expressed in the products of dependent platform suppliers to enter into direct (intra-platform) competition with them.

Can these practices genuinely generate potential competition concerns? Before attending to this question, it is important to briefly reflect on the doctrinal

---

[21] House of Representatives (Judiciary Subcommittee on Antitrust, Commercial and Administrative Law), 'Investigation of Competition in Digital Markets: Majority Staff Report and Recommendations' (2 October 2020) 364 <https://bit.ly/3EMRD5m> accessed 19 November 2022.

[22] The following draws from Justin Pot, 'What Does It Mean When Apple "Sherlocks" an App?' (*How-To Geek*, 14 March 2017) <https://bityl.co/Fjvj> accessed 19 November 2022.

[23] Elizabeth Dwoskin, 'Facebook's Imitation Not Quite Flattery' *Washington Post* (11 August 2017) <https://bit.ly/2zrpl1d> accessed 18 November 2022.

implications of what the providers behind these allegations are actually seeking from antitrust, i.e. the recognition of free-riding as an antitrust offence in and of itself.[24]

2.2 Beyond the Rhetoric

Whenever they are accused of victimizing upstream providers, platforms tend to invoke the rhetoric of consumer empowerment. Here, the tables are turned: powerful rhetoric is used to coax enforcement against the platforms. Indeed, critics usually liken scraping and Sherlocking to 'free-riding' and 'theft'.[25] While doing so creates a stigma, such sweeping analogies can similarly deceive.

2.2.1 Free-riding

Consider the free-rider analogy. Throughout its history as a studied phenomenon in the social sciences, free-riding has almost always been described in the most pejorative of terms.[26] This line of thinking permeates antitrust today as well. In some countries, the free-rider narrative has buttressed some truly radical shifts in the law. Take the USA: free-rider 'problems' have been so successfully invoked over the past four decades that most vertical restraints, which were once illegal per se, are now treated as if they are incapable of anticompetitive effects.[27] Even in jurisdictions like the EU (which adopts a notoriously more stringent approach to the same issues), free-riding pleas are regularly heeded nowadays.[28]

That said, one must note a couple of paradoxes. First, with scraping and Sherlocking, the free-riding story is not, as it usually is, advanced to justify the *relaxation* of antitrust rules. It is instead invoked to ground an argument for *enforcement*. Although not unprecedented,[29] this remains striking.

---

[24] See, explicitly, Dow Jones, 'Comment of Dow Jones & Company to the Federal Trade Commission' (Hearings on Competition and Consumer Protection in the 21st Century, 20 August 2018) 2–5 <https://perma.cc/82HK-L4YY> accessed 18 November 2022.

[25] See, notably, House of Representatives (Judiciary Subcommittee on Antitrust, Commercial and Administrative Law) (n 21) 187. See also FairSearch (n 18); references in Iris Hsiang Chyi, Seth Lews and Nan Zheng, 'Parasite or Partner? Coverage of Google News in an Era of News Aggregation' [2016] Journalism & Mass Communications Quarterly 789, 790.

[26] For a historical account, see Philippe Fontaine, 'Free Riding' [2014] Journal of the History of Economic Thought 359.

[27] Robert Pitofsky, 'Has the Free Rider Explanation for Vertical Arrangements Been Unrealistically Expanded?' in Robert Pitofsky (ed), *How the Chicago School Overshot the Mark: The Effect of Conservative Economic Analysis on U.S. Antitrust* (OUP 2008) 179–80.

[28] See eg Case C-230/16 *Coty Germany* ECLI:EU:C:2017:941 [2017] electronic Reports of Cases.

[29] For example, in the EU, firms have traditionally been able to invoke capacity constraints to justify certain practices. However, in some cases, lack of capacity is actually what triggered enforcement (Pablo Ibáñez Colomo, 'Restrictions on Innovation in EU Competition Law' [2016] European Law Review 17).

Second, many commentators have rightly chided decision-makers for their almost evangelical acceptance of the free-rider get-out-of-jail-free card.[30] Some of these critics, however, would probably just as readily endorse the argument to depict scraping or Sherlocking platforms as 'clearly anticompetitive'.[31] This double standard is curious because there is nothing *obviously* wrong with these practices from a *consumer welfare* or *competitive process* perspective. Why else would LinkedIn (the social media platform) have been found by two US courts to have potentially '*violate[d]* the policy or spirit' of the Sherman Act by *preventing* a small data analytics firm called hiQ from scraping the public profiles of its users?[32]

2.2.2 'Stealing'

One justification advanced by LinkedIn was to protect itself from theft, which, as noted earlier, is the second analogy routinely used to frame scraping and Sherlocking claims. Tellingly perhaps, Steve Jobs himself famously stated in 1996 that Apple has 'always been shameless about stealing great ideas'.[33] Now, if the analogy were accurate, both practices would elicit fears already explored in Chapter 3. The reason? 'Theft' presupposes ownership by those who claim it. So, by the same token, scraping and Sherlocking would pertain to powerful platforms bullying providers into foregoing the exercise of their property rights.[34]

Of course, suppliers who push the scraping claim will generally (the EU being a potential exception in certain instances) *not* be entitled to intellectual property (IP) protection, either for lack of exclusive rights to stake their case on, or because scraping is covered by a defence that limits their property.[35] Ditto for those who

---

[30] See Warren Grimes, 'The Sylvania Free Rider Justification for Downstream-Power Vertical Restraints: Truth or Invitation for Pretext?' in Pitofsky (n 27); Marina Lao, 'Free Riding: An Overstated, and Unconvincing, Explanation for Resale Price Maintenance' ibid.

[31] Ben Thompson, 'Ends, Means, and Antitrust' (*Stratechery*, 28 June 2017) <https://perma.cc/D6P4-G9WN> accessed 18 November 2022.

[32] *hiQ Labs Inc v LinkedIn Corp* 273 FSupp 3d 1099, 1118 (NDCal 2017), affirmed and remanded, 938 F3d 985 (9th Cir 2019) (emphasis added). Note that the case revolved around a once-obscure cybersecurity statute (called the Computer Fraud and Abuse Act). It made its way to the Supreme Court, which (in 2021) instructed the Ninth Circuit to reconsider in light of one of its more recent rulings on this statute. On remand, the judges confirmed their initial findings (*hiQ Labs Inc v LinkedIn Corp*, Case No 17-16783 (9th Cir 2022)).

[33] Dan Farber, 'What Steve Jobs Really Meant When He Said "Good Artists Copy; Great Artists Steal"' (*CNET*, 28 January 2014) <https://bityl.co/FjvM> accessed 19 November 2022 (quoting Jobs).

[34] As argued in Chapter 3, the same could be said if victims were bullied into foregoing other legal rights to successfully defeat scraping and Sherlocking platforms, such as those flowing from contract, cybersecurity, or tort laws. I assume here that the latter are unavailable to victims (either because they do not enjoy such rights or because the law would prevent them from successfully invoking them).

[35] See eg Michael Carrier, 'Only "Scraping" the Surface: The Copyright Hold in the FTC's Google Settlement' [2013] University of British Columbia Law Review 759. Stock photography agencies have themselves conceded that copyright is not a viable route for them (Conor Risch, 'Too Big to Sue: Why Getty Images Isn't Pursuing a Copyright Case against Google in the US.' (*Photo District News*, 17 May 2016) <https://perma.cc/D2LN-HQ8C> accessed 18 November 2022 (reporting comments by Getty Images)). By contrast, lyrics are protected by copyright. But, as Genius found out, property is vested with the actual authors of the songs, not those (like Genius) who curate and annotate them (Kim Lyons, 'Google Wins Court Battle with Genius over Song Lyrics' (*The Verge*, 11 March 2022) <https://bityl.co/EJrr> accessed 18 November 2022).

rage over Sherlocking as there simply cannot be any property in ideas.[36] This is the most basic tenet of IP law.[37] As Thomas Jefferson famously wrote, '[i]f nature has made any one thing less susceptible than all others of exclusive property, it is the action of the thinking power called an idea.'[38]

Why is the observation important? It matters because turning free-riding into an antitrust offence has a truly paradoxical implication. The policy would effectively be deployed to *create* mangled *property* entitlements to prevent powerful platforms from using parts of the public domain.[39] One antitrust official has actually been candid on this when he says of scraping that 'some firms should not be able to get data.'[40] Yet, antitrust has only ever been allowed to interfere with the *exercise* of legal exclusivity, not its *existence*.[41]

To be clear, the foregoing observations are not an indictment against 'propertarian' antitrust. There is, glaringly, an interfacing issue at play between antitrust and property law. But this is a different matter to be discussed later.[42] The point here is merely to stress what is doctrinally at stake, namely, the paradoxical use of competition policy to circumscribe the public domain.

With this in mind, let us now examine how the paradox might be rationalized, beginning with a consumer welfare perspective.

3. Free-Riding and 'Consumer Welfare'

Over the last two chapters, we have seen that our upstream worries can be squared within a consumer welfare narrative. In fact, harm can quite easily be rationalized

---

[36] cf Stigler Center, 'Stigler Committee on Digital Platforms: Final Report' (September 2019) 116 <https://bityl.co/Fjqi> accessed 19 November 2022 (arguing that antitrust may be warranted when powerful platforms 'expropriate the ideas and strategies of [suppliers]').

[37] See eg Claudy Op Den Kamp and Dan Hunter, 'Introduction: Of People, Places, and Parlance' in Claudy Op Den Kamp and Dan Hunter (eds), *A History of Intellectual Property in 50 Objects* (CUP 2019) 2. To be clear, *expressions* of ideas can be protected. For instance, technical features of a gaming app that optimizes, say, the user identification process through the camera interface might be patentable. Similarly, copyright will protect the source code. But the idea of a gaming app that revolves around the concept of, say, a battle royale, cannot be protected as such (see, usefully, Brendan Guildea, 'App Stores: A Digital No Man's Land or Innovation's Bane?' [2016] Journal of Intellectual Property Law & Practice 445).

[38] James Boyle, *The Public Domain: Enclosing the Commons of the Mind* (Yale UP 2008) 20 (quoting and offering a close reading of Jefferson's letter to Isaac McPherson).

[39] Some will take offence at this characterization because genuine property rights have *erga omnes* effects. However, property has also been described as a 'broad and roomy concept' (Robert Merges, *Justifying Intellectual Property* (Harvard UP 2011) 4). I use it here only to make the point that with free-riding claims, antitrust is called upon to justify some form of exclusion, which is the core feature of any property entitlement.

[40] Simon Van Dorpe, 'EC Official Flags Theory of Harm to Innovation through Scraping' *PaRR* (8 September 2017) <https://perma.cc/T6EB-UFJB> accessed 18 November 2022 (reporting comments made by Cyril Ritter, an official of the EC's competition directorate).

[41] Hedvig Schmidt, 'Competition Law and IP Rights: Not So Complementary: Time for Realignment of the Goals?' [2019] World Competition 451, 455–60.

[42] See Chapter 7.

when the paradigm is taken to mean *strong* consumer surplus or consumer choice. For it can always be intuitively argued that when they victimize dependent providers, platforms will (eventually) decrease choice, variety, quality, and/or innovation in the long run. Consumer welfare—while it might rest on normatively questionable foundations—has so far not proved to be impotent. The real difficulty is formalizing upstream power plays in a way that passes the consensus rigour test.

This section shows that something similar can be written of scraping and Sherlocking. There will be a slight twist, though, as 'free rider concerns do not become decisive simply because they can be articulated'.[43]

3.1 Scraping

3.1.1 Prolegomenon

(Anticompetitive) foreclosure, as mentioned in Chapter 4, is the go-to theory of harm for single-firm abuses. When players are excluded from the market, choice and diversity take a hit; if they were efficient, prices might creep up and output may nosedive as well. Interestingly, this is not the story claimants and competition agencies have been spinning when it comes to scraping.

For instance, in the USA, the FTC's early-2010s probe into Alphabet/Google 'considered whether this conduct could have diminished the incentive of Google's rivals to invest in bringing new and innovative content and services to the [i]nternet in the future or reduced Google's own incentive to innovate in the relevant markets'.[44] Likewise, in the EU, the EC made it clear that its own investigation into the platform's unauthorized use of third-party content is about protecting 'incentives to invest in the creation of original content for the benefit of internet users'.[45] And, in Brazil, had the complainant adequately established that Alphabet/Google was lifting product reviews from its price comparators, incentives to innovate would have captured the Conselho Administrativo de Defesa Econômica (CADE)'s attention.[46]

Innovation, then, is the common thread behind the consumer welfare anxiety over scraping. Alleged victims and antitrust authorities are not alone in voicing

---

[43] Herbert Hovenkamp, 'Exclusive Joint Ventures and Antitrust Policy' [1995] Columbia Business Law Review 1, 96.

[44] FTC, 'Statement of the Federal Trade Commission Regarding Google's Search Practices *In the Matter of Google Inc.*' FTC File Number 111-0163 (3 January 2013) 3 <https://bityl.co/Fjvs> accessed 19 November 2022.

[45] EC, 'Commission Seeks Feedback on Commitments Offered by Google to Address Competition Concerns—Questions and Answers' (25 April 2013) <https://bit.ly/3Gvw5M8> accessed 19 November 2022. Note that the status of the EC's scraping probe is not clear.

[46] *E-Commerce/Google* (n 16) [144].

3. FREE-RIDING AND 'CONSUMER WELFARE'   157

them; a few academics have done the same.[47] In addition, antitrust discourse of late has been prominently featuring theories of harm focusing directly on innovation.[48] Some have warned decision-makers to stay clear of them. For one, the harm would be impossible to prove unless the requisite legal test(s) were set at a ridiculously low bar.[49] For another, accepting such theories would effectively turn property systems on their heads.[50] Both objections are reasonable. Even so, they relate to how antitrust is to be respectively enforced and interfaced, two issues addressed in the final two chapters of this book. Again, at this stage, our inquiry centres solely on theory-building: can we make a potential innovation argument out of scraping?

3.1.2 Innovation theories

A useful way to answer the question above is to return to the three most publicized antitrust scraping allegations, i.e. those of review sites' content, stock imagery, and news publications. To be sure, every situation involves distinct legal and economic contexts that need to be accounted for. Nevertheless, the structure of the incentives-to-innovate tale buttressing each claim is identical. Prosaically: scraping generates a substitution (i.e. business-stealing or traffic-diverting) impact that overrides any potential complementary (i.e. traffic-boosting) and market-expansion effects it might incidentally conduce. This, in turn, leads to lower revenues for providers, which dampens their incentives to innovate.

Take the case of news articles, which, unlike the other two, has attracted scholarly attention from economists.[51] Theoretically, scraping can be a boon for media organizations. Press snippets displayed by, say, Google Search, might pique the interest of consumers enough to generate a click-through to the publisher's website. The influx of traffic could thereafter be converted into two potential revenue sources: advertising—from the landing page and, when consumers so navigate their way, from other pages, such as the prized homepage[52]—and/or subscription sales. Moreover, if this positive traffic effect accrues to smaller, more specialized, or obscure publishers (i.e. the long tail), scraping would further expand the market, increasing media diversity and consumer choice.

---

[47] See, notably, Howard Shelanski, 'Information, Innovation, and Competition Policy for the Internet' [2013] University of Pennsylvania Law Review 1663, 1700.
[48] See eg the collection of essays in Paul Nihoul and Pieter Van Cleynenbreugel (eds), *The Roles of Innovation in Competition Law Analysis* (Edward Elgar 2018).
[49] Colomo (n 29) 215.
[50] ibid 217–18.
[51] The models consider news aggregators like Google News. They are nonetheless relevant because general search engines like Google Search display the same kind of snippets (see, similarly, ACCC, 'Digital Platforms Inquiry: Final Report' (June 2019) 230 <http://bit.ly/3TKrNmY> accessed 19 November 2022).
[52] Susan Athey, Markus Mobius and Jeno Pal, 'The Impact of Aggregators on Internet News Consumption' (April 2021) NBER Working paper No 28746, 14 <https://bityl.co/FjtY> accessed 19 November 2022.

According to economists, however, such a win–win outcome is contingent on consumer click-throughs, something the design and relevance of snippets may considerably influence.[53] Therefore, and although this is not modelled, publishers' incentives to invest in high-quality content could diminish if consumers generally end their reading experience on the search engine because they get the gist of an article's substance from the displayed extracts. Worse, scraping might be problematic despite consumers clicking through to publishers' websites since referral traffic to single articles may insufficiently compensate lost homepage traffic and its potentially associated revenues.[54] Adding insult to injury, the practice might even dilute the brands of certain news organizations. Commoditization could thereby compound this double substitution effect and further erode publisher incentives to invest.[55]

A similar narrative can be deployed for stock imagery. If consumers can use image search platforms like Google Images to not simply discover, but to easily copy imagery as well, it is no stretch to theorize how content providers may become discouraged.[56] Scraping might negate the need to navigate to the original website, depriving its owner of traffic, data, and potentially associated revenues. Likewise, 'framing'—a linking technique which makes third-party content an integral part of one's own website—is liable to rob providers of their recognition.[57]

And more of the same for review sites, which may be further harmed if scraped content is repurposed in an inaccurate and/or misleading way, or worse, passed off as if they were original.[58]

In short, it is possible to make a competition problem out of scraping by relying on innovation concerns—as we have seen, it always is. This notwithstanding, there are things to say about the partly formal, partly intuitive theories of harm, which ground them.

Consider the case of review sites content first. There is no publicly available independent study quantifying the traffic effects of scraping by, say, Alphabet/Google, of Yelp reviews, let alone one that directly correlates the behaviour to reduced revenues and investments. Naturally, some may object to this assertion. Did the FTC legal staffers not confidentially opine that the 'natural and probable effect of Google's [scraping] is to diminish the incentives of vertical websites to invest in, and to develop, new and innovative content'?[59] Undeniably, the staffers did. Yet, their conclusion does

[53] Chrysanthos Dellarocas, Zsolt Katona and William Rand, 'Media, Aggregators, and the Link Economy: Strategic Hyperlink Formation in Content Networks' [2013] Management Science 2360.

[54] Doh-Shin Jeon and Nikrooz Nasr, 'News Aggregators and Competition among Newspapers on the Internet' [2016] American Economic Journal: Microeconomics 91.

[55] See Athey, Mobius and Pal (n 52) 15.

[56] Getty Images, 'Submission to the ACCC Digital Platforms Inquiry Issues Paper' (10 April 2018) 7 <https://perma.cc/U9AJ-YGLS> accessed 18 November 2022.

[57] ibid.

[58] FairSearch (n 18) 30.

[59] FTC Bureau of Competition, 'Internal Memorandum re Google Inc. File No 111-0163' (8 August 2012) 40 <https://bityl.co/Fjy0> accessed 19 November 2022.

not seem based on anything other than (informed) intuition. It also sits uneasily with the confounding statements made by then Commissioners Rosch and Ohlhausen. Both affirmed that the FTC's investigation had revealed two things. One: 'overall traffic to the alleged victims increased substantially while the alleged scraping was occurring and traffic to these websites from Google grew at an even faster rate'.[60] And two: harm to innovation was 'likewise lacking in factual support'.[61] Victims had actually 'continued to thrive and expand ... since this conduct occurred'.[62]

At the other end of the spectrum, evidence appears to substantiate the existence of a traffic-diverting effect in the context of image search. A report by the audience development firm, Define Media Group, examined the impact on eighty-seven websites of Alphabet/Google's 2013 decision to frame high-resolution pictures directly within the user interface of its image search platform infrastructure. The results? A collective drop in referral traffic of 63 per cent in the first full week of the update, with no signs of a rebound after a further eleven weeks.[63] The report concludes that '[i]t's difficult not to consider Google's Image UI change a shameless content grab—one which blatantly hijacks material that has been legitimately licensed by publishers so that Google Image users remain on their site, and are de-incentivized from visiting others'.[64]

Finally, what of news? Here the canvas is murky. On the one hand, field experiments by some economists suggest that the amount of information news aggregators offer regarding articles does affect the probability consumers will navigate to publishers' websites.[65] More specifically, lengthier snippets and those coupled with images are found to increase the likelihood that consumers will devote their limited attention exclusively to scraped content.[66] Furthermore, in 2016, the EC already found that '47% of consumers browse and read news extracts on these websites without clicking on links to access the whole article in the newspaper page, which erodes advertising revenues from the newspaper webpages'.[67]

---

[60] FTC, 'Concurring and Dissenting Statement of Commissioner J. Thomas Rosch Regarding Google's Search Practices *In the Matter of Google Inc*.' FTC File no 111-0163' (3 January 2013) 4 <https://bityl.co/Fjvu> accessed 19 November 2022. See also FTC, 'Separate Statement of Commissioner Maureen Ohlhausen *In the Matter of Google Inc*.' (3 January 2013) 1–2 <https://bityl.co/Fjvv> accessed 19 November 2022.

[61] ibid.

[62] ibid.

[63] Shahzad Abbas, 'How Google's Image Search Update Killed Image SEO' (15 April 2013) Define Media Group report <https://perma.cc/E78C-YYDN> accessed 18 November 2022.

[64] ibid.

[65] Chrysanthos Dellarocas and others, 'Attention Allocation in Information-Rich Environments: The Case of News Aggregators' [2016] Management Science 2457.

[66] ibid (noting, however, that when several articles compete with each other (because they cover the same story), consumers are more likely to click on the link which provides a longer snippet and includes an image).

[67] EC, 'Impact Assessment on the Modernisation of EU Copyright Rules Accompanying the Proposal for a Directive of the European Parliament and of the Council on Copyright in the Digital Single Market and the Proposal for a Regulation of the European Parliament and of the Council Laying Down Rules on the Exercise of Copyright and Related Rights Applicable to Certain Online Transmissions of

On the other hand, these results must be taken with a grain of salt because they suffer from notable limitations.[68] Plus, they are contradicted by a string of other empirical studies[69] and by confusing allegations made by certain press publishers themselves,[70] which all evidence scraping's complementary (as opposed to substitutive) impact.[71] As the ACCC summarizes, '[t]he presence of snippets *does* affect click-through rates [but one can] *not agree* that longer snippet lengths necessarily have a negative effect on referral traffic.'[72] Why else would the majority of publishers in France, when faced with Alphabet/Google's decision to axe snippets unless they consented to free licences, authorize the platform to display the *maximum* number of words, the *highest* quality of photos, and the *longest* length of video previews?[73]

'Where does all this leave us?', one may ask. Well, scraping evidently can damage platform providers' ability to monetize their content. Any magnanimous antitrust decision-maker guided by *strong* consumer surplus or consumer choice should be able to see a competition problem in this since innovation is potentially at risk. The incentives-to-innovate theory of harm will not play out in all circumstances, though. Moreover, the theory is not a particularly robust one given the empirical data. Besides, it relies on assumptions that, while intuitively sensible, are in fact questionable. Let us briefly unpack this last assertion.

3.1.3 Creators, intermediaries, and incentives

Whenever the scraping claim is invoked, it tends to be paired with a rhetorically powerful idea. Antitrust enforcement, the story goes, would be about safeguarding

---

Broadcasting Organisations and Retransmissions of Television and Radio Programmes' SWD/2016/301 final, 185.

[68] For instance, Dellarocas and others (n 65) do not capture the positive complementary effect scraping does bring about. And the EC's assertion is inconclusive and somewhat misleading because it considers EU consumers' behaviours irrespective of the type of platform used to access news content.

[69] See eg Athey, Mobius and Pal (n 52) (finding, in particular, that (i) *overall*, news publishers experienced drops in referral traffic, which suggests Google News complements, rather than substitutes publishers; and that (ii) despite the existence of a substitution effect with regards to publishers' homepages, referrals to article pages more than compensate this effect); Joan Calzada and Ricar Gil, 'What Do News Aggregators Do? Evidence from Google News in Spain and Germany' [2020] Marketing Science 134 (confirming the complementary (as opposed to a substitution) effect under a similar setup). See also Lesley Chiou and Catherine Tucker, 'Content Aggregation by Platforms: The Case of the News Media' [2017] Journal of Economics & Management Strategy 782 (using a different setup but also finding a traffic-boosting effect).

[70] See eg *Google-Snippets* (Case 92 O 5/14 Kart) Berlin Regional Court Judgement 19 February 2016 ECLI:DE:LGBE:2016:0219.92O5.14KART.0A, [18]–[19] (publishers submitted evidence to show that snippets were essential for driving referral traffic from Google platforms).

[71] However, caution is warranted here. Athey, Mobius and Pal (n 52) also find that scraping does negatively impact larger publishers because it reduces traffic to their respective website's homepage and undermines their curation role. This could be problematic if part of the long-term incentives for these publishers to invest in their brands comes from the way they curate news.

[72] ACCC (n 51) 231 (emphasis added).

[73] *Syndicat des éditeurs de la presse magazine* (Case 19/0075M) ADLC Decision 20-MC-01 19 April 2020, [90]–[93] together with [103]–[110].

the incentives to innovate and livelihood of individual creators (such as journalists and photographers) above those of the organizations that publish and commercialize their content.[74] This proposition—which, as noted in Chapter 4, record labels too could advance in the name of musicians to prompt antitrust enforcement against king-making streaming platforms—is problematic as it rests on several assumptions regarding the dynamics of intellectual production and distribution many too readily accept as self-evident.

- Creator incentives and money

The first difficulty reflects a disconnect between the incentives-to-innovate rationale and the realities of creative practice. Indeed, whereas neoclassical economic theory presupposes that monetary inducements are indispensable for stoking creativity and innovation, the soundness of this empirical claim is often debatable.

Take photographers and the microstock industry, for example.[75] The sad truth is that many professionals and amateurs willingly supply agencies like iStockphoto (which is owned by Getty Images), Shutterstock, and Dreamstime for pennies on the dollar.[76] Given the production costs–royalties ratio, money is probably more a token of social and psychic validations than a (primary) motivation.[77] Even beyond microstock, significant anecdotal evidence suggests that what animates many professional photographers is less economic incentives than a burning obsession to capture and convey a story they are passionate about.[78]

Interestingly, a similar canvas can be painted for journalists who navigate the equally treacherous waters of a profession marked by very skewed supply and demand curves. Multiple studies indicate that 'few aspiring journalists in most Western countries choose a career in journalism because of its financial rewards'[79] and that 'non-material incentives are of relatively high value to most journalists'.[80]

---

[74] See eg Maurice Stucke and Ariel Ezrachi 'Looking up in the Data-Driven Economy' (*CPI Antitrust Chronicle*, May 2017) 20–21 <https://perma.cc/BSN3-NH6H> accessed 18 November 2022; Getty Images (n 15).

[75] Microstock photography is a segment of the broader stock photography industry where agencies like Getty Images license pre-produced (still or video) imagery for use in general publishing (by advertisers, book publishers, etc.).

[76] Eric Johnson, 'The Economics and Sociality of Sharing Intellectual Property Rights' [2014] Boston University Law Review 1935, 1969–70 (estimating that the average microstock contributor made about US$3.11/image in 2014, which—when computed into wages—amounts to US$4.65/hour).

[77] ibid 1971–73.

[78] See the various testimonies garnered by Olivier Laurent, 'Why We Do It: Photographers and Photo Editors on the Passion That Drives Their Work' (30 June 2017) *Time Magazine* <https://perma.cc/86N2-Z8YC> accessed 18 November 2022.

[79] Susanne Fengler and Stephan Russ-Mohl, 'The Crumbling Hidden Wall: Towards an Economic Theory of Journalism' [2008] Kyklos 520, 528.

[80] ibid 529. See also Jim Willis, *The Mind of a Journalist: How Reporters View Themselves, Their World, and Their Craft* (SAGE 2010) 1–11 (describing the lure of journalism as a combination of immaterial incentives, including 'the love of reading and writing', 'intense curiosity', and a 'desire to contribute to society').

Finally, while some consumers have claimed compensation from firms like Yelp for their reviews,[81] these allegations have been dismissed for lacking good faith foundations.[82] As sociologists have shown, out of all the motivations individuals may have for spending time and energy into reviewing products, money is not one of them.[83]

For the record, I am *not* saying this is all fair—far from it—nor that rewarding these individuals is invariably a bad move. Echoing the sentiment of many IP lawyers, my point is instead to stress that the connection between monetary inducements and creativity is too easily assumed, not investigated.[84] We cannot simply take it as given that antitrust enforcement over scraping on *innovation* grounds has (overriding) positive effects on the incentives of creators.

Granted, a retort would be to highlight the need for first-order intermediaries to recoup their investments without which passionate creators would arguably be unable to disseminate their works to the public. Stock photography agencies, some may for instance argue, do not merely enhance the discovery of photographers; they expend greatly to provide valuable resources and technical service support to contributors, helping them develop their imagery and satisfy emerging trends in specific market niches.[85] The rejoinder brings us to a second set of problematic assumptions.

- Creators and first-order intermediaries

The incentives-to-innovate theory seemingly assumes that the interests of first-order intermediaries and those of initial creators are inevitably aligned. Again, this is something which ought to be examined. Remember, middlemen who profess their solicitude for creatorship are not creators. They are entrenched interests that will routinely and unabashedly claim for themselves the status of creators-by-proxy.[86]

Consider the case of Getty Images. Before settling its antitrust dispute with Alphabet/Google, the stock photography agency regularly spoke on behalf of photographers whose livelihoods it accused the platform of endangering.[87] Ironically,

---

[81] See eg *Jeung v Yelp Inc* No 15-CV-02228-RS, 2015 WL 4776424 (NDCal 2015).

[82] ibid 3.

[83] Edward McQuarrie, *The New Consumer Online: A Sociology of Taste, Audience, and Publics* (Edward Elgar 2015).

[84] Julie Cohen, 'Property as Institutions for Resources: Lessons from and for IP' [2015] Texas Law Review 1, 34.

[85] Robert DeFillippi and others, 'Crowd-Sourcing and the Evolution of the Microstock Photography Industry: The Case of iStockphoto and Getty Images' in Robert DeFillippi and Patrick Wikström (eds), *International Perspectives on Business Innovation and Disruption in the Creative Industries: Film, Video and Photography* (Edward Elgar 2014) 235–38 (examining the practices of Getty Images).

[86] Julie Cohen, 'Between Truth and Power' in Mireille Hildebrandt and Bibi van den Berg (eds), *Information, Freedom and Property: The Philosophy of Law Meets the Philosophy of Technology* (Routledge 2016) 68.

[87] See Getty Images (n 15).

Getty Images has itself contributed immensely to the chronic decline of professional photography by leveraging digitization to its advantage.[88]

Caution is thus warranted when it is suggested that supporting marketers through innovation-minded antitrust enforcement safeguards incentives to creative work as it might do if creator motivations were directly attended to.

Now, suppose it was acknowledged that the innovation theory against scraping is focused strictly (or mainly) on first-order intermediaries. Shouldn't antitrust be there to protect their incentives to take risks? Policymakers have certainly vindicated this argument on numerous occasions, albeit usually with the backing of a democratic vote.[89] But they have done so while ignoring a generic feature common to all industries involving intellectual products: 'Goldman's law', i.e. the impossibility of predicting the success of intangibles and what goes into making them successful to begin with.[90] The incentives-to-innovate narrative obscures this reality. So, although the importance of first-order middlemen for the production and distribution of intellectual products ought to be acknowledged, innovation-minded antitrust must not make the mistake legislators occasionally do when they endow them with property rights (i.e. overstate their role).

Consider database producers. Back in 1992, the EC reasoned that the growth of a European market for information would require considerable investments in producing and marketing databases.[91] As a result, the EU voted legislation specifically aimed at incentivizing investors—which include our scraping victims by the way—through the grant of sui generis property designed to ward off misappropriation by free-riders.[92] Sadly, things have not panned out exactly as planned.

In 2005 (almost a decade after the legislation was adopted), the EC found that the protection (i) had 'had no proven impact on the production of databases';[93] (ii) 'comes precariously close to protecting basic information';[94] and that (iii) repeal was to be seriously envisaged.[95] Why the report remains unheeded is a mystery to me seeing that a review conducted in 2018 was no more upbeat.[96] Worse, it concluded that '[t]he Commission may want to consider abolition. There is no evidence that the sui generis right has had a positive effect. There is evidence that it causes problems. There is evidence that it is not needed in the US.'[97] Furthermore,

---

[88] See DeFillippi and others (n 85); Joel Waldfogel, *Digital Renaissance: What Data and Economics Tell Us about the Future of Popular Culture* (Princeton UP 2018) 154–59.

[89] Mark Lemley, 'Property, Intellectual Property and Free Riding' [2005] Texas Law Review 1031.

[90] See Waldfogel (n 88) 3. See also Cohen (n 84) 37–39.

[91] See EC, 'First Evaluation of Directive 96/9/EC on the Legal Protection of Databases' (12 December 2005) <https://bit.ly/3tHniyO> accessed 19 November 2022.

[92] See Directive 96/9/EC of the European Parliament and of the Council of 11 March 1996 on the Legal Protection of Databases [1996] OJ L77/20, recital 39.

[93] EC (n 91) 20.

[94] ibid 24.

[95] ibid 25–26.

[96] Kristina Karanikolova and others, 'Study in Support of the Evaluation of the Database Directive' (2018) <https://data.europa.eu/doi/10.2759/04895> accessed 19 November 2022.

[97] ibid 126.

the study expressed genuine concern over how these entitlements may negatively impact the investment incentives of other market players.[98] This brings us to the final set of difficulties flowing from the idea that antitrust enforcement against scraping would truly be to protect the consumer's interest in innovation.

- Platform incentives

Conventional formulations of the incentives-to-innovate theory of harm seem to assume that only those of the alleged victims are worthy of protection. If consumer welfare-minded antitrust is serious about innovation, one fails to see why the incentives of powerful scraping platforms would be ignored or handicapped in the analysis.

The conduct will definitely sometimes generate considerable dynamic efficiencies. For example, the ACCC found that 'Google's practice of [scraping news content] in organic search results enhances consumer welfare by providing context of the results to the user's query, and assisting the user in assessing the relevance of the results.'[99] Had it known its behaviour would be sanctioned, maybe the platform would not have innovated in the first place or will cease doing so in the future.

What should, accordingly, matter is whether overall innovation is negatively affected. If this is wrong and the incentives to innovate of (certain) providers alone ought to be protected, it bears on those who would push for such a policy to submit a convincingly reasoned defence of it.

The emerging picture is ultimately somewhat hazy. Insofar as 'consumer welfare' is taken to mean *strong* consumer surplus or consumer choice, it certainly is possible to frame scraping as an issue ripe for antitrust enforcement. Innovation might well be at stake here. But one ought to be wary of incentives-to-innovate theories increasingly invoked nowadays generally without evidence.

Scraping, we have seen, does not necessarily generate the traffic diversion effect that is presumed to starve allegedly victimized providers of their expected revenues, quite the reverse. Nor does the behaviour invariably dampen the creative drive of individuals whose support is enlisted by immediate 'victims'—first-order intermediaries—under the pretence that both their interests always dovetail or that enforcing antitrust to protect them will spark creation by those whom they themselves depend on. And scraping does not inevitably harm the innovation incentives of first-order intermediaries in ways that should inexorably trump those of powerful scraping platforms.

Just to clarify, these observations are not to defend platform (mis)conduct; they are merely to stress the care one ought to proceed with in making a *competition* problem out of scraping on *innovation* grounds.

---

[98] ibid 46–47.
[99] ACCC (n 51) 226.

This brings us back to the assertion made in the introduction of this chapter. Scraping can be rationalized as a competition problem. Consumer welfare, though, is probably not primarily at stake. Rather, as the then president of the Italian competition authority stated in the aftermath of his agency's investigation into news scraping by Alphabet/Google, '[t]he main issue has to do with *fair reward* for online publishing providers and the economic exploitation of this work by other subjects'.[100] Whether or not the worry merits intervention, he rightly added, is for societies themselves to decide, possibly by reforming their respective property systems.[101] The French, we mentioned in Chapter 3, have made such a choice with regards to press publishers as part of a collective decision made by the peoples of Europe.[102]

3.2   Sherlocking

3.2.1   Prolegomenon

So much for scraping. What of Sherlocking? As stated in Section 2, the issue here does not relate to taking actual works of others to prop up one's own offering. The fear pertains instead to powerful platforms organically integrating their businesses by lifting the ideas and concepts of dependent providers to effectively enter into horizontal competition with them. Of all the behaviours examined so far, it is probably the most challenging one to rationalize as a potential competition problem if it remains true that '[t]he antitrust laws do not protect [suppliers] from competition'.[103]

Indeed, for many economists, 'if a dominant platform is vertically integrated but does not apply discriminatory practices, there is no harm to consumers or competition'.[104] This is because (organic) integration is usually viewed favourably as it tends to be driven by efficiency motivations[105] and entrepreneurial ambitions.[106]

In the platform context, the positive narrative has a special spin. To illustrate, take Apple. In 2014, the firm simultaneously entered several niches of its app store

---

[100] Antonio Catricalà, 'Google in Italy ... ' [2011] Journal of European Competition Law & Practice 293, 293 (emphasis added).

[101] ibid.

[102] See further Chapter 7.

[103] House of Representatives (Judiciary Subcommittee on Antitrust, Commercial and Administrative Law) (n 21) 364.

[104] Nicolai van Gorp and Paul de Bijl, 'Digital Gatekeepers: Addressing Exclusionary Conduct' (7 October 2019) 18 <http://dx.doi.org/10.13140/RG.2.2.10666.95689> accessed 18 November 2022. See also Nicholas Economides, 'Competition, Compatibility, and Vertical Integration in the Computing Industry' in Jeffrey Eisenach and Thomas Lenard (eds), *Competition, Innovation and the Microsoft Monopoly: Antitrust in the Digital Marketplace.* (Springer Science+Business Media 1999) 211ff.

[105] Like developing synergies, reducing transaction costs, improving coordination, eliminating double margins, and so forth.

[106] Van Gorp and de Bijl (n 104) 17–18.

when it introduced the Health app. This was a disruptive move at the time because, whereas existing third-party solutions did enable consumers to track their health and fitness, none of them offered a complete picture. By pulling data from suppliers like Nike or Mayo Clinic, Health provided a complementary hub to consolidate everything into a single comprehensive interface.[107] Five years later, Apple added a free, accurate, and privacy-friendly period tracker feature to its own offer. Effectively, it Sherlocked a concept pioneered by a firm called Glow, which companies like Flo, Ovia, and hundreds of other menstrual cycle-tracking app developers had further tweaked.[108] Was the act guided by predatory instincts or by efficiency motives? Most likely the latter or, less charitably, both. Why? Because Glow was known to be vulnerable to hackers;[109] Flo had been exposed for its unsavoury data-sharing partnerships;[110] Ovia was suspected of being in cahoots with US employers tempted by 'menstrual surveillance' to alter the health coverage of their female staff;[111] and the overwhelming majority of existing alternatives were notoriously inaccurate.[112]

This is standard multi-sided market theory: Apple has to protect its OS and app store platform products from fragmentation.[113] How? By ensuring that the right kind of suppliers are on board to match consumers who expect a 'base level of safety, security, privacy, quality, low costs, an intuitive user interface, and innovative, new features'.[114] For economists, Sherlocking is hence often probably more (or equally) about quality control of the platform infrastructure than monopolizing the space of providers;[115] it complements (poorly enforced) platform self-regulation and papers over what some might argue are government oversights.[116] This is similar to what some studies find when Amazon data-twinks merchants who rely on its marketplace infrastructure.[117]

---

[107] Chris Welch, 'Apple HealthKit Announced: A Hub for All Your iOS Fitness Tracking Needs' (*The Verge*, 2 June 2014) <https://bit.ly/3bUYF6r> accessed 18 November 2022.

[108] Amber Neely, 'Hands on with Cycle, Apple's New Menstrual Cycle Tracker in iOS 13' (*appleinsider*, 19 June 2019) <https://bit.ly/2xXWHEw> accessed 18 November 2022.

[109] Jerry Beilinson, 'Glow Pregnancy App Exposed Women to Privacy Threats, Consumer Reports Finds' (*Consumer Reports*, 28 July 2016) <https://bit.ly/3cv47OK> accessed 18 November 2022.

[110] Sam Schechner, 'You Give Apps Sensitive Personal Information. Then They Tell Facebook' *Wall Street Journal* (22 February 2019) <https://on.wsj.com/2WRhlyL> accessed 18 November 2022.

[111] Drew Harwell, 'Is Your Pregnancy App Sharing Your Intimate Data With Your Boss?' *Washington Post* (10 April 2019) <https://wapo.st/2EZCD83> accessed 18 November 2022.

[112] Michelle Moglia and others, 'Evaluation of Smartphone Menstrual Cycle Tracking Applications Using an Adapted APPLICATIONS Scoring System' [2016] Obstetrics & Gynecology 1153.

[113] See, similarly, *Epic Games Inc v Apple Inc* 559 FSupp 3d 898, (n 608) (NDCal 2021).

[114] ACM (n 20) 22.

[115] David Evans, 'Governing Bad Behavior by Users of Multi-Sided Platforms' [2012] Berkeley Technology Law Journal 102. See also Wen Wen and Feng Zhu, 'Threat of Platform-Owner Entry and Complementor Responses: Evidence from the Mobile App Market' [2019] Strategic Management Journal 1336, 1363 (noting that Alphabet/Google's introduction of its own flashlight app might have been motivated by concerns over the privacy practices of existing providers).

[116] Celia Rosas, 'The Future Is Femtech: Privacy and Data Security Issues Surrounding Femtech Applications' [2019] Hastings Business Law Journal 319 (arguing that such femtech apps should be more tightly regulated).

[117] See Chapter 4, Section 3.3.3.

The upshot, then, is that for antitrust decision-makers guided by the consumer surplus or total surplus variations of the consumer welfare paradigm, Sherlocking cannot seriously be seen as a potential problem. Yes, it almost always raises the costs of victimized platform providers; copycats of Apple, Amazon, Alphabet/Google, and Meta/Facebook (to name a few) will in all likelihood be cheaper and/or display some kind of quality improvement, pushing providers to do more to convince consumers. Nonetheless, such effects generate particular concerns of foreclosure and innovation only the *strong* consumer surplus and consumer choice lodestars can capture. Let us examine these potential harms in turn.

3.2.2 Foreclosure theories

If a premium is placed on consumer choice and diversity per se, Sherlocking by a powerful platform is always intuitively troubling. Returning to our Apple illustration: although having their ideas lifted by the platform will not necessarily put incumbent fertility app providers out of business, many of them probably will fail. And those who do survive will certainly have had to work harder to attract consumers even if Apple is assumed to not self-preference its in-house productions within the App Store; brand recognition and superior advertising presumably are powerful pull factors in their own right.[118] Formal research in the context of mobile apps allows us to push this intuition further.

App providers compete in a crowded 'superstar' app economy where a small minority reaps the majority of rewards.[119] To get the attention of iPhone users, these suppliers need to go through Apple's App Store and advertise their offers as much as they can afford to.[120] Given such market dynamics, reports of ubiquitous 'copycatting' are not really surprising.[121] Copycats, by definition, borrow heavily from what is already on the marketplace. Still, unlike those of third parties, Apple's in-house productions will assumedly (i) not be deceptive (be it by their appearance or functionality) and (ii) meet decent quality standards. This is important because researchers have empirically demonstrated that copycat apps can have a (more or less) business-stealing *or* sales-boosting effect depending on their quality and imitation type.[122] More specifically, low-quality imitations and those that are deceptive—even when of a high build—tend to *increase* the sales of originals.[123]

---

[118] Christine Moorman, 'Why Apple Is Still a Great Marketer and What You Can Learn' (*Forbes*, 12 January 2018) <https://bit.ly/3cA1ivT> accessed 18 November 2022.
[119] See ACM (n 20) 24.
[120] ibid.
[121] See eg Stuart Dredge, 'Should Apple Take More Action against March of the iOS Clones?' *The Guardian* (3 February 2012) <https://bit.ly/2FtFUNd> accessed 18 November 2022.
[122] Quan Wang, Beibei Li and Param Vir Singh, 'Copycats vs. Original Mobile Apps: A Machine Learning Copycat-Detection Method and Empirical Analysis' [2018] Information Systems Research 273.
[123] ibid 285–86.

Only copycats that combine high-quality *and* low levels of deception cannibalize the revenues of innovators.[124]

In short, Apple's ability to Sherlock the apps of providers who depend on its app store has conceivable exclusionary effects, regardless of whether its motivations are predatory or socially benevolent. But the foreclosure theory does not bear out unless the platform's copycat satisfies the consumer's short-run preference for superior products. To rationalize a consumer welfare problem with Sherlocking, one must therefore be guided by a desire to preserve consumer choice and diversity for their own sake. For either there is an incredibly speculative worry that, by offering superior copycats within its own infrastructure, the platform will eventually lock-in consumers to the point of driving out (potentially superior) competing *platforms* (say, Alphabet/Google's Android OS and Play Store products).[125] Or else the focus is solely on preserving atomistic market structures *within* the platform infrastructure itself.

These are not the foreclosure effects economists and contemporary consumer welfare-minded antitrust decision-makers usually fret over. In the USA, the FTC made this abundantly clear in its (in)famous 2010 *Intel* consent decree.[126] Intel—whose microprocessors frequently are non-digital, multi-sided platform infrastructures[127]—was, in fact, explicitly permitted to Sherlock the concepts of other firms provided its copycats could be shown to have redeeming qualities.[128]

Intel, incidentally, had a rich history of Sherlocking many of its dependent providers even before its discount practices attracted antitrust scrutiny in the aforementioned case.[129] Intriguingly, empirical studies examining the firm's entry patterns between 1990 and 2004 show that it was particularly wary of antagonizing its base of complementing suppliers. During this period, Intel mostly Sherlocked those whom it thought were underperforming.[130] Yes, the firm occasionally did invade the turf of providers whose products were hardware platforms, such as motherboards or chipsets.[131] Yet, when it did, Intel made sure not to put the squeeze on them; instead, it actively relinquished its IP and subsidized competitive entry.[132]

---

[124]   ibid.

[125]   See eg ACM (n 20) 58.

[126]   *Intel Corporation* 150 FTC 473 (2010).

[127]   Contrary to what may be assumed, Intel chips are often not just inputs for PC suppliers (Andrei Hagiu and Daniel Spulber, 'First-Party Content and Coordination in Two-Sided Markets [2013] Management Science 933, 935). This is because app developers *do* make investments or design choices specific to the microprocessors embedded in computers like smartphones, tablets, video game consoles (Ryan Cohen and Tao Wang, *Android Application Development for Intel® Platform* (Apress 2014) 19).

[128]   *Intel Corp* (n 126) pt V, A.

[129]   For a detailed list, see Annabelle Gawer and Rebecca Henderson, 'Platform Owner Entry and Innovation in Complementary Markets: Evidence from Intel' [2007] Journal of Economics & Management Strategy 1, 27–28.

[130]   Annabelle Gawer and Michael Cusumano, *Platform Leadership: How Intel, Microsoft, and Cisco Drive Industry Innovation* (Harvard Business School Press 2002) ch 4.

[131]   See Gawer and Henderson (n 129) 1.

[132]   ibid.

These findings are compelling for two reasons. First, they suggest that, much like other multi-sided platform practices, Sherlocking is probably best accounted for by a narrative of mixed motives. Second, the results offer actual support for the theory one can always intuitively, but rarely rigorously, formulate when it comes to upstream platform power plays, i.e. lowered platform provider incentives to innovate.

3.2.3 Innovation theories

Unlike most other platform practices explored so far, a theory of harm to innovation can be formalized with regards to Sherlocking; we do have a number of economic models that rigorously identify specific conditions under which lowered provider incentives to invest is a credible outcome.[133] And while platform advocates would probably question their relevance,[134] there fortunately is a burgeoning stream of research that is quickly closing the gap. Some academics, we just saw, have examined Intel's Sherlocking patterns. Their findings support the harm-to-innovation narrative with the caveat that the firm did take steps which successfully mitigated the potential problem. More recent works enable us to bolster these insights; they may be even more relevant because they test the theory on the platforms currently in the limelight.

One of them examines Alphabet/Google's entry into the 'Flashlights', 'Guided Access', and 'Podcasts' segments of its app store infrastructure.[135] The authors find that entry and the threat of entry had ambiguous consequences. On the one hand, both led to decreased innovation efforts in affected niches and inflated prices;[136] on the other hand, they encouraged affected developers to (i) shift their innovation efforts to other, currently under-served or inexistent segments, and to (ii) reduce wasteful efforts in developing redundant products.[137] Moreover, Sherlocking and

---

[133] See eg Joseph Farrell and Michael Katz, 'Innovation, Rent Extraction, and Integration in Systems Markets' [2000] Journal of Industrial Economics 413, 418, 424 (where a key condition is that the monopolist in market A must Sherlock its way into market B with a copycat that is inferior from a quality perspective); Jay Pil Choi, Gwanghoon Lee and Christodoulos Stefanadis, 'The Effects of Integration on R&D Incentives in Systems Markets' [2003] Netnomics 21 (whose findings depend on the cost of R&D (which is presumed to be fixed) and on the assumption that the monopolist is less efficient than the providers it Sherlocks); David Miller, 'Invention Under Uncertainty and the Threat of Ex Post Entry' [2008] European Economic Review 387 (where the key forces that drive lower innovation predictions are the uncertainty inherent in the innovation process and differences in the firms' entry costs); Xingyi Liu, 'Vertical Integration and Innovation' [2016] International Journal of Industrial Organization 88 (whose prediction of lowered investments is predicated on the assumption that innovation is only important in the upstream market).

[134] Notwithstanding the lack of consensus on what constitutes a multi-sided platform, economists would generally agree that Amazon's Marketplace, Apple's iOS and App Store, the Facebook social network, and Alphabet/Google's Google Search are all multi-sided infrastructures. But the models mentioned in (n 133) take a single-sided approach and ignore issues of cross-sided network effects central to multi-sided market economics.

[135] Wen and Zhu (n 115) 1336.

[136] ibid 1349ff. Innovation efforts were measured by looking at the frequency of app updates released by providers (such as adding new features, redesigning the interface, and fixing bugs).

[137] ibid.

its threat were found to induce potential short-run benefits for consumers: impacted developers who had strong products actually increased their innovation efforts in the affected market without hiking prices.[138]

Another study looks at the same platform's Sherlocking of photography app providers.[139] It shows that the behaviour expanded the market by drawing more consumer attention and growing demand.[140] In turn, this stimulated cross-sided network effects, which positively impacted innovation (measured by the introduction of a major update), albeit mostly by larger and more diversified developers.[141] Significantly, the authors note that their paper complements and supports the work of two colleagues who had found that Meta/Facebook's integration of Instagram— that is, entry through corporate merging rather than Sherlocking—had similar consequences: more innovation from large third-party providers of photo- and video-sharing social apps, less from smaller ones.[142]

These results can be further nuanced by considering those of a fourth study, which compares the impact of Apple and Alphabet/Google's Sherlocking of health app providers.[143] It finds that, while affected suppliers tend to suffer from the behaviour overall, negative innovation effects vary from one app store to another and depend on developer-specific features. For example, Sherlocking by the more open and flexible app store operator (i.e. Alphabet/Google) had positive consequences for incumbents who experienced a significant uptick in downloads.[144]

All of this, it bears emphasizing, is consistent with predictions generated by the latest theoretical literature, which shows that platforms operating in such a 'dual mode' will have ambiguous effects on innovation.[145]

With this in mind, what conclusions should we draw? To me, there are three.

One: Sherlocking conceivably—perhaps plausibly—dampens app providers' incentives to innovate. This intuition can be both rigorously formalized and probably extended to other segments of the platform economy, such as online marketplaces for tangible goods. Recall from Chapter 4, there is at least one empirical study finding that Amazon's data-twinking (which is Sherlocking plus the

---

[138]   ibid 1358.

[139]   Jens Foerderer and others, 'Does Platform Owner's Entry Crowd Out Innovation? Evidence from Google Photos' [2018] Information Systems Research 444.

[140]   ibid 453, 457.

[141]   ibid 453–54, 457. Note that unlike Wen and Zhu (n 115) 1336, whose study covers a three-year period, this model only examines innovation effects over six months.

[142]   Zhuoxin Li and Ashish Agarwal, 'Platform Integration and Demand Spillovers in Complementary Markets: Evidence from Facebook's Integration of Instagram' [2017] Management Science 3438.

[143]   Hye Young Kang, 'Intra-Platform Envelopment: The Coopetitive Dynamics Between the Platform Owner and Complementors' [2017] Academy of Management Proceedings 11205.

[144]   ibid 11216 (finding that Alphabet/Google's entry increased downloads of affected apps by 32 per cent).

[145]   See, notably, Andrei Hagiu, Tat-How The and Julian Wright, 'Should Platforms Be Allowed to Sell on Their Own Marketplaces?' [2022] RAND Journal of Economics 297, 305–09; Federico Etro, 'Product Selection in Online Marketplaces' [2021] Journal of Economics Management and Strategy 614, 628–29.

data-advantage component) 'discourages third-party sellers from continuing to offer the products'.[146]

However, two: we cannot say these negative effects are likely.

By contrast, three: Sherlocking's overall impact on innovation is in all likelihood equivocal. Providers are not all affected in the same way, context matters, and platform incentives must (or at least should) be accounted for by consumer welfare-minded antitrust decision-makers seriously committed to innovation.

To summarize on Sherlocking: one can definitely rationalize rigorously the practice as a potential competition problem consumer welfare-centric antitrust ought to be sensitive to. Again, once debatable normative foundations are assumed away, the paradigm cannot be vilified for being conceptually blind to the upstream. Nevertheless, we need to be clear on which version of the lodestar is at play and the implications thereof. For Sherlocking is not really worrying unless 'consumer welfare' means *strong* consumer surplus or consumer choice. This is because platforms that vertically integrate by 'free-riding' on the ideas of independent providers will almost certainly generate static efficiency gains benefiting consumers in the short run. Exclusionary effects are admittedly likely and lowered producer incentives to innovate are plausible. But the foreclosure of inferior firms and speculative anxieties on innovation are not things decision-makers guided by the consumer surplus or total surplus offshoots of the paradigm would lose sleep over.

Despite the foregoing, reservations to pegging Sherlocking to consumer welfare harm are warranted. Granted, issues of consumer choice and diversity certainly do fit the bill. Even so, both can just as easily serve to push a narrative genuinely grounded in fairness-to-consumer considerations—*strong* consumer surplus or consumer sovereignty—as they might be deployed as Trojan horses to funnel a fairness-to-provider lodestar through the backdoor. To say that leveraging the public domain to organically integrate a business is not problematic until done by a powerful (platform) firm because this is when marketplace diversity is truly threatened, is indeed no different from suggesting that incumbent suppliers deserve protection for their own sake. Since evidence on the behaviour's innovation implications are ambiguous, it is likewise difficult to ward off suspicion that the real (or at least primary) issue at stake is *provider* welfare.

3.3 Summation

Taking stock of our discussion so far: many platform providers (and their advocates) have claimed that scraping and Sherlocking are platform mischiefs ripe for intervention. Stripped of their rhetorical enhancers, these allegations entail

---

[146] Feng Zhu and Qihong Liu, 'Competing with Complementors: An Empirical Look at Amazon. com' [2018] Strategic Management Journal 2618, 2632.

turning free-riding, as such, into an antitrust offence. This can be formally rationalized from a consumer welfare perspective with the following caveats. First, a competition problem is hard to conceive unless the paradigm means *strong* consumer surplus or consumer choice. Second, on the evidence, there is a considerable risk these alternative lodestars will be used to cover concerns that do not honestly cater to the consumer's interest in having access to a more abundant and/or vibrant marketplace.

Mind you, we saw earlier how theory-building around fears of despotic and game-mastering platforms runs into similar, albeit less acute, difficulties. What the analysis here further confirms is that 'looking up' with consumer welfare lenses in place always makes the inquiry awkward, befitting the fact that upstream platform power plays do not instinctively stand out as potential consumer welfare problems. That said, things are slightly trickier with scraping and Sherlocking: unlike despotism and game-mastering, it would be somewhat disingenuous to describe these forms of free-riding as inimical to the constitutive values of the competitive process. Let me explain.

4. Free-Riding and 'Fairness'

4.1 Prolegomenon

In a landmark 1918 ruling, the US Supreme Court (SCOTUS) condemned what, in those days, effectively amounted to news scraping.[147] There, the Court held that, although society had deemed it unworthy of property, the organized collection of news had required investments by the plaintiff that were presumably such as to warrant a time-limited, non-statutory 'quasi property' right barring the defendant—and the defendant alone—from free-riding on its competitor's efforts without authorization.[148]

IP and tort law experts know all about the *INS* decision. After all, it was 'almost single-handedly responsible for launching the common law misappropriation doctrine into the world'.[149] And whenever these lawyers touch on the case, the name of one of the sitting justices nearly always comes up. Tellingly for our purposes, it is that of Justice Brandeis. Why is this noteworthy? It matters because Brandeis— the champion of those advocating the competitive process approach to antitrust in the USA—was the sole dissenting voice to the majority ruling. His dissent, it bears

[147] *International News Service v Associated Press* 248 US 215 (1918) (hereinafter *INS*).
[148] ibid 236.
[149] Christopher Wadlow, 'Unfair Competition by Misappropriation: The Reception of *International News* in the Common Law World' in Catherine Wai-Man Ng, Lionel Bently and Giuseppina D'Agostino (eds), *The Common Law of Intellectual Property: Essays in Honour of Professor David Waver* (Hart 2010) 308.

emphasizing, was not merely to quibble. When it comes to competition, he wrote, '[t]he law sanctions, indeed encourages, the pursuit [of] profits due largely to the labor and expense of the first adventurer'.[150]

To be clear, Brandeis was not calling for unbridled free-riding. His view was rather that whether practices like scraping and Sherlocking are meaningfully unfair for 'victims' is for a society to decide itself,[151] an argument which relates to what will be addressed in Chapter 7, i.e. interfacing different policy levers. On the other hand, Brandeis's first point is fundamental here because it seems to infirm the very idea that scraping and Sherlocking platforms can ever be chastised by a policy genuinely aimed at safeguarding the 'competitive process'. The sentiment finds further echo in a unanimous 1989 SCOTUS decision outlawing state anti-plug moulding statutes on the grounds that 'imitation and refinement through imitation are both necessary to invention itself and the very lifeblood of a competitive economy'.[152] Plus, US decision-makers are not rogue in upholding such a view. For instance, in Australia, the apex court until 1986 once held that:

[C]ompetition must remain free: and competition is safeguarded by the necessity for the plaintiff to prove that he has built up an 'intangible property right' .... A defendant, however, does no wrong by entering a market created by another and there competing with its creator. The line may be difficult to draw: but unless it is drawn, competition will be stifled.[153]

Scraping and Sherlocking are thus difficult to square as potential competition problems under the competitive process paradigm at first glance. This notwithstanding, they *can* be upon closer scrutiny. Jogging our memory helps to understand why.

As expounded in Chapter 2, with these antitrust lenses fitted on, economic competition cannot be completely sundered from fairness considerations, lest it lose the right to be called competition at all, having degenerated into a self-destructive Hobbesian contest. At the same time, when antitrust aims to (coherently) safeguard the competitive process, it can directly attend to just one of fairness' two dimensions: *ex ante* (as opposed to *ex post*) fairness. This means unfair outcomes of competitive interactions cannot underpin a case for enforcement—they cannot

---

[150] *INS* (n 147) 259 (Brandeis dissenting).

[151] ibid 257, 264 ('To appropriate and use for profit, knowledge and ideas produced by other men, without making compensation or even acknowledgment, may be inconsistent with a finer sense of propriety .... A Legislature, urged to enact a law ... may prevent appropriation of the fruits of its labors by another').

[152] *Bonito Boats Inc v Thunder Craft Boats Inc* 489 US 141, 146 (1989). These laws prohibited businesses from Sherlocking, or, more technically, from reverse-engineering—direct-moulding—existing products to market their own versions. See further David Carstens, 'Preemption of Direct Molding Statutes: Bonito Boats v. Thunder Craft Boats' [1990] Harvard Journal of Law & Technology 167.

[153] *Cadbury Schweppes Pty Ltd v Pub Squash Co Pty Ltd* (1981) 55 ALJR 333, 339.

buttress a 'theory of harm'. The policy's job would instead be to prevent such situations from arising to begin with by ensuring that the playing field is as levelled as the societies they ultimately serve would have envisioned it to be.

Furthermore, recall that *ex ante* fairness—EOp—can be usefully formalized to rationalize our upstream concerns.[154] As detailed below, one of the EOp theories outlined there can be deployed here. Its normative implications need to be fully appreciated, though, because doing so confirms what has been argued all along: scraping and Sherlocking can be made out as antitrust-relevant problems; but, for most people, fretting over these practices really reveals a sympathy for the plight of platform providers that is overwhelmingly (if not solely) anchored by individual beliefs on *substantive* fairness.

4.2 Free-Riding and *ex ante* Fairness

4.2.1 EOp-sensitive antitrust recalled

EOp-mindful antitrust, as Chapter 4 explained, zeroes in on certain (dis)advantages players bring to the economic game, and tries to restore fairness in the structure (or pattern) of outcomes (as opposed to their content). When construed narrowly, the policy's reach is unsurprisingly quite limited; criticism cannot be levelled against powerful platforms that do more than arbitrarily discriminate between their dependent providers or against them to favour their in-house productions. Even under a slightly broader formulation, EOp-sensitive antitrust would only be able to target powerful platforms whose digital infrastructures are effectively rigged in ways that prevent the 'best' offers from succeeding within them. Put differently, this understanding of *ex ante* fairness is offended when within-platform competition is uncoupled from merit due to the platform operator's behaviour.

These recollections should make one thing clear: neither scraping nor Sherlocking can easily be fitted in such formal EOp theories. As claimed throughout this chapter, when a powerful platform scrapes content from providers or Sherlocks ideas the latter embodied in their products, the issue is not that within-platform is no longer open to all, structured on merits, and/or conducted so that economic agents deal with each other impartially to capture value. To wit, assuming consumers consciously plebiscite (for example) Alphabet/Google's scraping-enhanced lyrics service or Apple's copycat apps, the concern cannot be that within-platform competition was arbitrarily skewed or not based on merit. The worry is rather that these in-house platform productions will have benefited from the platform's behaviour in a way that enables them to succeed without having to expend the same amount of *effort* as competing providers. From an EOp perspective, therefore, the

---

[154] See Chapter 4, Section 4.2.

lone issue with free-riding platforms is that it disconnects the pattern of within-platform competition from considerations of *desert*.

Of course, there are substantive EOp theories that (to varying degrees) do integrate the idea that the structure of competition ought to track effort: starting-gate, Rawlsian, and radical formulations of the value.[155] However, it is difficult to see how scraping and Sherlocking could be described as potentially problematic under the first two. Rawls, for instance, would probably not have let considerations pertaining to effort prevail over things like performance in the final *EOp* analysis.[156] And the usefulness of starting-gate EOp seems to be restricted to *ex ante* regulation.[157] This leaves us with radical EOp of which Roemer's account is the sole plausible, antitrust-intelligible, and rigorously outlined option I have encountered.

4.2.2 Free-riding and Roemerian EOp

The idea that powerful free-riding platforms scourge the competitive process by compromising *ex ante* fairness is easy enough to understand if Roemer's specification of the ideal is espoused.[158] Recall that (under this view) the guiding moral premise is a desert-based belief: competition should be structured so that winners will be those who will have earned their position by 'out-exerting' their rivals. Following the Roemerian algorithm, one could thereby depict Alphabet/Google's scraping of Yelp reviews as being unfair because some of the success its Google Local service achieves is undeserved. More accurately, the playing field in the local search space is arguably distorted since Alphabet/Google is riding on the coat-tails of Yelp's successful efforts to prop up its own local search offer.

Be that as it may, resorting to such a formulation of EOp has major ramifications.

The first relates to how the theory is implemented. Roemer's algorithm, Chapter 4 noted, abstracts from the issue of determining what counts as a relevant exertion; this is for our (political) institutions to settle, according to him. In my modest view, there are, at minimum, three important ensuing challenges for antitrust. One concerns legitimacy since antitrust decision-makers are routinely derided (rightly or wrongly) for their seemingly meagre democratic credentials.[159] Another relates to the risk of capture, given that, without clear guidelines, pressure groups can unduly influence our institutions. Finally, there is the second-best

---

[155] ibid.

[156] Andrew Mason, *Levelling the Playing Field: The Idea of Equal Opportunity and Its Place in Egalitarian Thought* (OUP 2006) 79. See also Thomas Scanlon, *Why Does Inequality Matter?* (OUP 2018) 54ff.

[157] See Chapter 4, Section 4.2.2.2.

[158] Marc Fleurbaey, 'The Facets of Exploitation' [2014] Journal of Theoretical Politics 653, 672 (noting that the analysis of free-riding 'comes nicely close to recent development of theories of justice as equality of opportunity' to which Roemer is prominently associated).

[159] See eg Christopher Townley, *A Framework for European Competition Law: Co-ordinated Diversity* (Hart 2018) ch 3.

problem: assuming the first two difficulties could be alleviated, decisions may in the final analysis no longer faithfully track desert.[160]

The second implication follows precisely from the last point: Roemerian EOp aims to ensure that the pattern of competition is sensitive *exclusively* to effort. This is not something to be taken willy-nilly. Obviously, viewed from an antitrust perspective, Roemer's vision is equally (if not more) divorced from reality than the assumption of 'perfect competition' used in mainstream economic textbooks; real-world economic competition is as much a game of effort as it is one of talent, ambition, and chance.[161]

Does this mean it makes no sense, as a matter of public policy, to implement decisions geared towards fostering competitive outcomes structured by desert? Not necessarily. As claimed in Chapter 2, most antitrust systems around the globe are probably grounded in a foundational political decision, which mirrors a given society's vision of how competition is to be ordered. In such systems, the competitive process is framed by rules actively designed by the polity, reflecting the latter's idiosyncratic beliefs on the structuring of its economy. *Insofar as doing so would be consistent with the type of competition envisioned by the peoples they serve*, antitrust decision-makers would, accordingly, be justified in formalizing their anxieties regarding powerful free-riding platforms by resorting to Roemerian EOp. Evidently, only social-minded jurisdictions could be amenable to such a move.

Consider, for instance, the USA and the EU. In the former, a tenet of antitrust law, which has survived the passage of time, prescribes that competition is to be won through 'superior skill, foresight and industry'.[162] To me, we can interpret this as reflecting the US citizenry's political decision to establish a system of ordered competition striving, as a matter of principle, to structure outcomes in a (perhaps enhanced) *meritocratic* way. If this is (still) plausibly true,[163] as the flak meritocracy (still) gets suggests,[164] US decision-makers cannot appeal to Roemerian EOp (or any other chiefly desert-based EOp theory) to combat scraping and Sherlocking (or any other practice for that matter). Why? Because the ideal supporting the theory is fundamentally inconsistent with the one envisioned by the American

---

[160] Marc Fleurbaey, 'Equal Opportunity or Equal Social Outcome?' [1995] Economics and Philosophy 25, 39.

[161] FA Hayek, *Law, Legislation and Liberty: A New Statement of the Liberal Principles of Justice and Political Economy* (Routledge 2013) 234; James Buchanan, 'Fairness, Hope, and Justice' in Roger Skurski (ed), *New Directions in Economic Justice* (University of Notre Dame Press 1983) 58; Michael Walzer, *Spheres of Justice: A Defense of Pluralism and Equality* (Basic Books 1983) 109.

[162] *United States v Aluminum Co of America* 148 F2d 416, 430 (2d Cir 1945). For an illustration of the present-day relevance of this tenet, see eg Andrew Finch, 'Principal Deputy Assistant Attorney General Andrew Finch Delivers Introductory Remarks at the 2018 Antitrust Writing Award Ceremony' (12 April 2018) <https://bit.ly/3OjlvcS> accessed 19 November 2022.

[163] As Thomas Piketty, *Capital et Idéologie* (Seuil 2019), explains, ideologies structure societies and their understandings of fairness. However, they are not immutable, so US decision-makers may well be out of touch with ideological shifts of the American demos.

[164] See eg Michael Sandel, *The Tyranny of Merit: What's Become of the Common Good?* (Allen Lane 2020).

demos—*desert* is not *merit!* The EU, by contrast, is a polity constitutionally bound to providing its constituents a 'highly competitive *social* market economy'.[165] What this means in practice is somewhat unclear, but it realistically would legitimate appeals by decision-makers to substantive formulations of EOp. Didn't then EC president Jean-Claude Juncker state that ensuring a 'fair playing field ... is the social side of competition law'?[166]

Regardless, several final words of caution are in order. First, despite its potentially intuitive allure, the idea whereby winners in the economic game are those who (in Roemerian parlance) 'try the hardest' is not one for consensus. For it demands that the inefficient, untalented, underperforming, haphazard, and/or unlucky undertakings have similar prospects of success as the efficient, talented, overperforming, well-organized, and/or lucky ones with the same motivation and drive to win.[167]

Prolonging this thought, effort may sometimes deserve attitudes of praise and admiration. Even so, to say desert justifies differences in economic success, or—to clear the path to the last difficulty—in rewards, is another matter altogether.[168]

Finally, Roemerian EOp should not be invoked to dodge thorny questions of *outcome* fairness, particularly those relating to *stakes*, which are beyond antitrust's remit.[169] Many will surely concur with the truism that effort is often unfairly *rewarded*. Platforms maybe do capture too much value at the expense of their hardworking, upstream, vertical (and sometimes simultaneously horizontal) competitors (i.e. suppliers).[170] Since this matter of stakes fairness is both controversial and sensitive, it is understandably tempting to just avoid it by conflating it with the issue of how patterns of outcomes are formed. For it is easier to assume that winners of a desert-based competition also deserve whatever rewards accompany their success than to deal with the harsh, but probable reality that the stakes of the market game are determined by the economics of supply and demand.

The takeaway from the preceding discussion is simple then. As asserted earlier, we *can* rigorously rationalize our free-riding platforms fears as potential competition problems under the competitive process paradigm. To do so, though, decision-makers must invoke an EOp theory which is so 'left'-leaning ideologically that

---

[165] TEU, art 3(3) (emphasis added).

[166] Jean-Claude Juncker, 'State of the Union 2016' (14 September 2016) 11 <https://data.europa.eu/doi/10.2775/968989> accessed 19 November 2022.

[167] Making a similar point, see Richard Arneson, 'Equality of Opportunity' in Edward Zalta (ed), *The Stanford Encyclopedia of Philosophy* (rev edn, Stanford University 2015) 29–30 <https://stanford.io/2XBJ3SB> accessed 18 November 2022.

[168] See Scanlon (n 156) 125; Fleurbaey (n 160) 40.

[169] See, similarly, Stigler Center (n 36) 36 ('there are sources of platform rents that *society* may determine through appropriate *regulation* should not be part of the winner's reward') (emphasis added).

[170] For this view, see eg EC, 'Impact Assessment Report Accompanying the Proposal for a Regulation of the European Parliament and of the Council on Contestable and Fair Markets in the Digital Sector (Digital Markets Act)' SWD/2020/363 final, [65], [355].

allegations of power misuse will never be far behind in most present-day antitrust systems. The truth is probably that anxieties over scraping and Sherlocking will generally pertain more to *substantive* fairness than competition anyway. Returning briefly to *INS* confirms this intuition.

4.3 Free-Riding and Outcome Fairness

INS's underlying rationale has always bewildered commentators.[171] Some have argued that the Court was guided by an incentives-to-innovate theory similar to those explored in Section 3.[172] Yet, most experts agree that the justices were more steered by their convictions over *ex post* fairness with consensus splintering thereupon.

Some claim that the ruling was grounded in Locke's labour theory of value,[173] which (incidentally) is one of the most prominent outcome fairness-based justifications for private property rights.[174] The plaintiff in *INS*—by analogy, our victimized platform providers as well—are entitled to relief under this account because free-riding rivals deprive them of the full fruits of their investments over which they enjoy a natural right by virtue of having infused the commons with their labour.[175] On a side note, such reasoning may have seduced the FTC legal staffers tasked with investigating Alphabet/Google's scraping of Yelp content in the early 2010s. They indeed concluded that the behaviour 'sent a message to the broader marketplace that Google could, and would … extract the fruits of its rivals' innovations'.[176]

Pressing forward, *INS*, according to others, was rather underpinned by a logic inherent in the law of restitution for unjust enrichment.[177] The majority opinion's author, Justice Pitney, assuredly did admonish the scraping defendant for 'endeavoring to reap where it has not sown [and] appropriating to itself the harvest of those who have sown'.[178]

---

[171] Christopher Wadlow, 'A Riddle Whose Answer Is "Tort": A Reassessment of International News Service v Associated Press' [2013] Modern Law Review 649, 654.

[172] See eg Richard Posner, 'Misappropriation: A Dirge' [2003] Houston Law Review 621, 627–28.

[173] See eg Douglas Baird, 'Common Law Intellectual Property and the Legacy of International News Service v. Associated Press' [1983] University of Chicago Law Review 411.

[174] See, usefully, Daniel Attas, 'Lockean Justification of Intellectual Property' in Alex Grosseries, Alain Marciano and Alain Strowel (eds), *Intellectual Property and Theories of Justice* (Palgrave Macmillan 2008).

[175] John Locke, *Two Treatises of Government* (McMaster University Archive of the History of Economic Thought 1999) 115–26, esp [26], [40], [42]. cf Attas (n 174).

[176] FTC Bureau of Competition (n 59) 90.

[177] See eg Shyamkrishna Balganesh, ' "Hot News": The Enduring Myth of Property in News' [2011] Columbia Law Review 419; Rudolf Callmann, 'He Who Reaps Where He Has Not Sown: Unjust Enrichment in the Law of Unfair Competition' [1942] Harvard Law Review 595.

[178] *INS* (n 147) 239–40.

Finally, maybe *INS* was simply based on an inchoate understanding of substantive fairness.[179]

Either way, it is beyond the scope of this work to go into more details. The point here is merely to buttress the argument made throughout this chapter. Whether impelled by the gut or by formal reasoning, worries surrounding scraping and Sherlocking have, in the first instance, little (if anything) to do with consumer welfare or competition, as such. They are predominantly about *provider*-oriented *outcome* fairness.

4.4 Summation

In sum, scraping and Sherlocking can potentially harm the competitive process just as they may decrease consumer welfare. To formally reason the competition problem, one has to nevertheless do one of two things: go against intuition and formal theory, which both primarily point to issues of substantive fairness beyond antitrust's reach; or endorse a vision of EOp that is (i) compatible with only the most social-minded antitrust systems, and (ii) ethically controversial, at best— Brandeis, for example, would have certainly rejected it.[180]

5. Concluding Reflections

Dependent providers who fall prey to powerful scraping and Sherlocking platforms come across as the most sympathetic of victims. By so behaving, aren't these platforms obviously akin to parasites, stealing information they did not themselves labour to produce and reaping rewards they do not deserve? Relatedly, attention is frequently drawn to how surplus value is currently diffused throughout the platform economy. For isn't something seriously amiss if, during the peak weeks of the first COVID-19 wave, some of the largest platform firms were going on hiring sprees and adding more market value whereas almost every other business was haemorrhaging cash and staff?[181]

The platform economy, unquestionably, is rife with unfairness. Despite this sobering state of affairs, to portray scraping and Sherlocking as if they are cardinal antitrust sins is to overindulge in platform bashing.

---

[179] Wadlow (n 171); Rudolf Callmann, 'What Is Unfair Competition' [1940] Georgetown Law Journal 585.

[180] *INS* (n 147) 259 (Brandeis dissenting) ('competition is not unfair in a legal sence [sic], merely because the profits gained are unearned, even if made at the expense of a rival').

[181] Elizabeth Dwoskin, 'Tech Giants are Profiting—And Getting More Powerful—Even as the Global Economy Tanks' *Washington Post* (29 April 2020) <https://wapo.st/2DA8pYt> accessed 18 November 2022.

If the premise that competition policy must pertain to 'competition' is accepted, these practices cannot be depicted as patently problematic. Likening them to theft may carry rhetorical sway, but 'analogy without theory is blind'.[182] Once examined for what they are—instances of free-riding—the lone thing conspicuous with scraping and Sherlocking is that they are in fact what competition regularly *requires*.[183] Admittedly, rigorously making them out as competition problems is possible. The question, however, is whether decision-makers should be conjuring the available theories of harm to this end, knowing that the latter will either be supported by ambiguous economics or be grounded in, at best, contentious ethics.

Interestingly, antitrust talk on these matters is somewhat reminiscent of several (in)famous 1970s cases, which pitted IBM against manufacturers of products that complemented its non-digital platform infrastructures.[184] These lawsuits, as seasoned antitrust observers will recall, targeted (in part) 'Big Blue's' integration of concepts developed by producers of plug-compatible devices (like tape and disk drives) into its own mainframes.[185] Veterans will no doubt likewise remember that liability was never incurred.[186] The cases are noteworthy nonetheless because they were litigated in the cusp of two eras of US antitrust. One was hell-bent on preserving atomistic market structures; the other sometimes embraces industry concentration on the promise of high(er) efficiency and low(er) retail prices. IBM's fortune was that the ideological tide had shifted towards the latter by the time the last gavel was struck.

Now, some may say '[m]any people would rather see a system that was less productive overall but forced others to do their "fair" share'.[187] True as this may be, a market economy where winning is pegged primarily to effort (as opposed to, say, performance) is not one many *majorities* in liberal democracies will have probably envisioned for themselves. And if the latter assertion is wildly inaccurate, we ought to ask why some of the free-riding 'victims' of today aren't by the same token subjected to more antitrust scrutiny.

Consider Axel Springer, a vocal critic of Alphabet/Google's scraping of its content. As academics know well, a few publishers (including Springer) have long

---

[182] Ronald Dworkin, 'In Praise of Theory' [1997] Arizona State Law Journal 353, 371.

[183] Kal Raustiala and Christopher Sprigman, *The Knockoff Economy: How Imitation Sparks Innovation* (OUP 2012).

[184] See eg *Telex Corp v International Business Machines Corp* 510 F2d 894 (10th Cir 1975); *ILC Peripherals Leasing Corp v International Business Machines Corp* 458 FSupp 423 (NDCal 1978).

[185] For a detailed account, see James Cortada, *IBM: The Rise and Fall and Reinvention of a Global Icon* (MIT Press 2019) ch 12.

[186] See eg *Telex* (n 184) 928; *ILC Peripherals* (n 184) (both reasoning that IBM should not be prevented from doing what was common practice in the industry, especially when its integrated product constituted an innovation). For a critique, arguing that these cases should have been judged against the 'concentration-is-bad' standard which prevailed between the 1940s and the 1960s, see Lawrence Sullivan, 'Monopolization: Corporate Strategy, the IBM Cases, and the Transformation of the Law' [1982] Texas Law Review 587.

[187] Jenny Stewart, *Public Policy Values* (Palgrave Macmillan 2009) 49.

cornered the market for academic publishing. Ironically, their online journals are effectively multi-sided platform products like the Google Searches of the world.[188] Here is what progressive Nobel economist Joseph Stiglitz has to say on this highly profitable oligopoly to which we have entrusted the dissemination of some of our most important ideas:

> The irony is that the publishers get the articles for free (in some cases, they even get paid to publish them), the research reported is typically funded by the government, the publishers get academics to do most of the editorial work (the review of the articles) for free, and educational institutions and libraries (largely government-funded) then pay the publishers. Their high prices and excess profits, of course, mean that there is less money to fund research.[189]

If Alphabet/Google is free-riding on Springer, therefore, so too is the latter 'reaping where it has not sown'.

For the record, the point is not to say none of the foregoing is troubling. It is rather to stress that being able to make competition problems out of powerful Big Tech platforms scraping and Sherlocking their way to success does not necessarily give licence for antitrust enforcement. Theories of harm have to be applied, not because they can be, but because they make sense in a specific factual, political, economic, and legal matrix. Moreover, if the real issues relate mainly to wealth redistribution and/or economic power as such, there is something to say about whether enforcing the policy is worth envisioning at all. These last two observations bridge nicely to the final part of this book: how should we intervene to address the upstream concerns that have entertained us over the past three chapters?

---

[188] Doh-Shin Jeon and Jean-Charles Rochet, 'The Pricing of Academic Journals: A Two-Sided Market Perspective' [2010] American Economic Journal: Microeconomics 222, 224–25.

[189] Joseph Stiglitz People, Power, and Profits: Progressive Capitalism for an Age of Discontent (Norton 2019) ch 3.

PART III

INTERVENTION

Upstream platform power plays are potential competition problems. Recapping briefly what our discussion of platform despotism, game-mastering, and free-riding has shown: antitrust enforcement against these practices can be rationalized, rigorously to boot. This can be done even when some of them generate fears that overwhelmingly pertain to things which are, or at least ought to be, beyond the policy's purview. More importantly, diagnosing antitrust-relevant harm is not contingent on a paradigm shift. To be sure, 'looking up' with consumer welfare goggles on will never be a natural exercise. Lenses generally left unused—*strong* consumer surplus or consumer choice—will have to be more routinely fitted; greater resources will need to be put into getting the economics right; and rigour will sometimes have to be sacrificed when formal analysis is either unavailable or ambiguous. But none of this makes the consumer welfare ideal conceptually defective for diagnostic purposes. On the other hand, the alternative competitive process lodestar, which possibly has the advantage of sounder normative foundations, enables decision-makers to more solidly reason their upstream worries in a wider array of cases. This paradigm also turns antitrust into an overtly moralizing enterprise, which is no trivial matter.

The foregoing caveats notwithstanding, the reality remains that our platform providers do have an antitrust leg to stand on, regardless of the policy lodestar one may fancy. Hence, what are judges and competition agencies—including those who have already vindicated their cause or are in the process of doing so—to make of the situation? Is the antitrust toolkit flexible enough to redress our upstream concerns—as several blockbuster interventions might arguably suggest—and if so, why? Should enforcement really be contemplated when push comes to shove and, either way, for what reasons? These questions frame the following discussion that spreads over two chapters.

Chapter 6 looks 'under the hood' of the antitrust machinery, which is where our interest mainly lies. It shows how looking up in the platform economy exacerbates key difficulties that have long been the source of occasional seize ups. The way forward, for decision-makers, is a matter of enforcement philosophy—of choosing between optimal, reasonable, and resolute enforcement. That choice, though, is coloured by beliefs on both the nature of antitrust as a tool—is it more policy (*sensu stricto*)[1] than law?—and the goal(s) it is aimed at.

Chapter 7 addresses the higher-level issue of intervention, as such. When it comes to dealing with the plight of platform providers, we must keep in mind the pool of policy options. *Antitrust* decision-makers, it will accordingly be argued, have to be wary of their solipsistic tendencies while remaining attuned to the strategic potential of their instrument. In other words, antitrust is not the sole available lever of action, nor is it necessarily a befitting one, which does not mean it should be altogether foreclosed from the discussion.

---

[1] I borrow here from Anthony Michael Kreis and Robert Christensen, 'Law and Public Policy' [2013] Policy Studies Journal 38, 40, who narrow down the concept of 'policy'—broadly defined as 'instruments through which societies regulate and control themselves'—to capture 'the discretionary instruments of regulation that operate within ... confines of the law'.

6

Antitrust's Internal Quandaries

1. Introduction

Competition laws around the world tend to be rubbery in their textual formulation and sector agnostic in their scope.[1] This makes them particularly resilient to technological evolutions that periodically upend existing market dynamics. Nuances aside, of course, they remain essentially proscriptive in nature, irrespective of the normative end(s) that may be ascribed to them. To rephrase: antitrust is not in the business of actively promoting (let alone maximizing) consumer welfare[2] or competition as such.[3] It is, *in principle*, a 'regulative (not regulatory)'[4] policy that targets bad behaviour rather than undesirable market structures.

Still, as observed in the introductory chapter, a new consensus has emerged: digital markets have (or will) become durably colonized by powerful platforms whose harmful exertions, especially those directed at providers, need to be urgently reined in. Antitrust, in this regard, is often seen as a go-to option even where regulation has been enacted.[5] In fact, calls for its unthrottled activation have rarely been this loud.[6] And yet, the instrument's apparatus is notoriously complex and costly to operate.[7] Enforcement standards have to be set and respected (Section 2); a power radar must first register problematic forms and levels of economic power before intervention is considered (Section 3); and remedies are to be

---

[1] See eg TFEU, arts 101, 102; Sherman Act, ss 1–2.

[2] See eg A Douglas Melamed and Nicolas Petit, 'The Misguided Assault on the Consumer Welfare Standard in the Age of Platform Markets' [2019] Review of Industrial Organization 741, 745–47; Eleanor Fox, 'Against Goals' [2013] Fordham Law Review 2157, 2159.

[3] See eg Ernst-Joachim Mestmäcker, 'The Development of German and European Competition Law with Special Reference to the EU Commission's Article 82 Guidance of 2008' in Lorenzo Federico Pace (ed), *European Competition Law: The Impact of the Commission's Guidance on Article 102* (Edward Elgar 2011) 42–44.

[4] ibid 46.

[5] As in Europe, for instance (see eg Margrethe Vestager, 'Keynote of EVP Vestager at the European Competition Law Tuesdays: A Principles Based Approach to Competition Policy' (25 October 2022) <https://bit.ly/3EqcJFw> accessed 21 November 2022).

[6] For regular updates, see Joe Panettieri, 'Big Tech Antitrust Investigations: Amazon, Apple, Facebook and Google Updates' (*ChannelE2E*, 8 November 2022) <https://bit.ly/3cFO4hJ> accessed 18 November 2022.

[7] See *New York v Deutsche Telekom AG*, 439 FSupp 3d 179, 186–87 (SDNY 2020) (bemoaning how antitrust adjudication often turns the decision-maker 'into a fortuneteller' whose 'murky function demands a massive enterprise' that generally (i) 'consumes years at costs running into millions', (ii) involves 'battalions of the most skilled and highest-paid attorneys' who in turn 'enlist the services of other professionals ... all brought ... to render expert opinions', and (iii) creates a record 'that can occupy entire storage rooms to capacity').

Antitrust and Upstream Platform Power Plays. A. K. von Moltke, Oxford University Press. © A. K. von Moltke 2023.
DOI: 10.1093/oso/9780192873057.003.0007

properly devised and implemented before enforcement can be deemed successful (Section 4). Therefore, what can, and should, our decision-makers do?

As this chapter argues, they have three enforcement options. One is to be 'scientific' and strive for *optimality*. When followed to the letter, decision-makers' remedial discretion is considerably enhanced, but, paradoxically, their ability to find liability may be quite limited. Another avenue is to take a more *reasonable* approach that can enable potentially far-reaching interventions depending on the jurisdiction at hand and the specifics of its antitrust system. By placing a premium on systemic coherence, however, this route will sometimes markedly impede enforcement. Lastly, there is *resolute* enforcement. Sweeping redress can actually be quite swiftly achieved by following this path, making it well suited to decision-makers animated by precautionary instincts and wary of the erosion of public confidence. For this final approach is laser-focused on upending the status quo.

Which of the three options is preferable? Much like the goal(s) debate explored in Part I, we will see that the answer turns on beliefs. My own view is simple and dovetails again with the idea of a Procrustean dilemma. Optimal enforcement is both illusive and not necessarily desirable; but being reasonable underwhelms when urgency strikes; at the same time, outcome-driven resolute enforcement has a price liberal democracies ought to be wary of paying.

With this in mind, let us now begin our deep dive into the antitrust apparatus.

2. What (Kind of) Enforcement Standards?

The principle that saddles powerful businesses with a special responsibility less significant players escape is a mainstay in many antitrust systems.[8] All the same, when it comes to platforms, as the ACCC noted, it is difficult to determine precisely what standard of behaviour they are, or should be, meeting.[9] This observation plunges us into the thick of the antitrust machinery.

2.1 The (Range of) Options

Legal tests complemented by evidence precepts are what render our notoriously open-textured competition laws operational.[10] The former delineate the

---

[8] See eg Case C-307/18 *Generics (UK)* ECLI:EU:C:2020:52 [2020] electronic Reports of Cases, [153]; ACCC, 'Digital Platforms Inquiry: Final Report' (June 2019) 230 <http://bit.ly/3TKrNmY> accessed 19 November 2022; *E-Commerce/Google* (Case No 08012.010483/2011-94) CADE General Superintendence Technical note No 15/2018, [108]–[109]. A noteworthy exception is contemporary US antitrust.

[9] ACCC (n 8) 1.

[10] Both are sometimes respectively denoted as 'legal standards' and 'evidence standards'.

boundaries of lawful conduct and are a matter of substantive antitrust. They take one of two forms. Either a (categorical or qualified) *rule* (that ascribes in advance a legal consequence to the commission of a particular practice based on a premise about its probable effects);[11] or a *standard* (which conditions the (un)lawfulness of a given behaviour on an analysis of its probable effects).[12] As is well known, however, a hermetic distinction between the two categories is somewhat artificial;[13] both rules and standards can be simple or complex.[14] Plus, their respective triggers may be defined through operational factors (making them structured tests), or with vague terms that might change from one case to another (rendering them unstructured).[15] These triggers relate to both the goal(s) antitrust is understood to pursue (as they determine what the relevant effects are for liability purposes) and the threshold to be reached regarding the probability of relevant effects materializing.

For example, if, on the one hand, the policy is directed towards the protection of competition, as such, a relevant effect for triggering liability could (inter alia) be framed in terms of the mere exploitation of an advantage; or instead one that the victim(s) (who might also be required to meet some level of efficiency) cannot overcome. Likewise, the level of market coverage of the impugned conduct may serve as an additional trigger. The same could be said of the degree of economic power held by the putative infringer. On the other hand, the relevant probability threshold of effects may be set anywhere between theoretical possibility and absolute certainty.[16]

Naturally, from an enforcer's perspective, a legal test formatted as an unstructured rule is highly appealing because it amounts to a mental shortcut that can be wielded with a certain amount of discretion.

Evidence principles, on the flip side, are creatures of procedure. They provide decision-makers with devices enabling them to deal with the uncertainties and potential deadlocks of the adjudicatory process entails.[17] These devices include the burden and standard of proof, as well as the principles governing the production of evidence and the appraisal of its probative weight. Given space constraints, just

---

[11] A categorical rule would be called 'per se'. A qualified rule can be denoted as 'by-object', following EU terminology where it is more common.

[12] In the jargon of EU competition lawyers, one would speak of an 'effects-based' legal test. In the USA, 'rule of reason' is the employed terminology.

[13] See eg Yannis Katsoulacos, 'On the Concepts of Legal Standards and Substantive Standards (and How the Latter Influences the Choices of the Former)' [2019] Journal of Antitrust Enforcement 365, 371.

[14] Louis Kaplow, 'Rules Versus Standards: An Economic Analysis' [1992] Duke Law Journal 557, 589–90.

[15] Pablo Ibáñez Colomo, *The Shaping of EU Competition Law* (CUP 2018) 67–68.

[16] In between the thresholds of possible/potential/theoretical effects, on the one hand, and actual effects, on the other, one could imagine setting the bar at a level of *plausibility, likelihood*, or *very high likelihood* (i.e. an 'in all likelihood' threshold).

[17] As Andriani Kalintiri, *Evidence Standards in EU Competition Enforcement: The EU Approach* (Hart 2019) 7 explains, 'evidence standards and substantive legal tests are not completely airtight'.

the first two—burden and standard of proof—will be discussed here, marginally at that.

Rules on the burden of proof relate to its allocation. A distinction is generally made between the burden of persuasion (or legal burden), which is allocated to one specific party throughout the proceedings, and the evidential burden (or burden of production), which may shift between litigants.

Regulation of the standard of proof (which pertains to the degree of evidence required for a claim to be deemed proven) is regularly framed in probabilistic terms, at least in common law jurisdictions.[18] Civil law systems, which are mostly unfamiliar with the concept, leave the issue of evidence sufficiency to the personal conviction of the decision-maker.[19]

With these refreshers in mind, one should have a clearer picture of the available options. In the abstract, it is possible to conjure a variety of configurations tailored to the different kinds of practices explored in Part II. Some will doubtless argue that 'per se rules and presumptions of illegality must become the default in antitrust law'.[20] Others will advocate the exact opposite.[21] Decision-makers (and their advisers), for their part, have been more nuanced, although a preference for 'by-object' legal tests—qualified rules—is conspicuous with some defending lower standards of proof, to boot.[22]

This trend is noteworthy as it veers away from the general direction antitrust has taken in major jurisdictions where the bar for intervention has been (significantly) reinforced over the years. Take the USA: it is common knowledge that rule-based legal tests have been 'in disrepute'.[23] What's more, commentators frequently argue that '[s]ometimes the burdens of proof imposed on plaintiffs at the behest of defendants are irrationally demanding'.[24] And whereas enforcement standards in the EU have undeniably been more conducive to intervention, the picture is significantly more nuanced than many make it out to be. The judicature has indeed grown increasingly suspicious of rule-based legal tests.[25] In addition,

---

[18] Yannis Katsoulacos, 'On the Choice of Legal Standards: A Positive Theory for Comparative Analysis' [2019] European Journal of Law and Economics 125, 129. Common benchmarks (associated with a progressively higher probability) include: 'substantial evidence', 'preponderance of evidence' (or 'balance of probabilities'), 'clear and convincing evidence' and 'beyond reasonable doubt'.

[19] ibid.

[20] Sandeep Vaheesan, 'Accommodating Capital and Policing Labor: Antitrust in the Two Gilded Ages' [2019] Maryland Law Review 766, 823.

[21] See eg Thibault Schrepel, 'New Structured Rule of Reason Approach for High-Tech Markets' [2017] Suffolk University Law Review 103.

[22] See Appendix C. See also Cecilio Madero Villarejo, 'Antitrust in Times of Upheaval' (Speech delivered at the 2019 CRA Conference, 10 December 2019) 5 <https://bityl.co/FjJq> accessed 18 November 2022.

[23] Herbert Hovenkamp, *The Antitrust Enterprise: Principle and Execution* (Harvard UP 2005) 116.

[24] Andrew Gavil, 'Moving Beyond Caricature and Characterization: The Modern Rule of Reason in Practice' [2012] Southern California Law Review 733, 739.

[25] Jose Luis da Cruz Vilaça, 'The Intensity of Judicial Review in Complex Economic Matters—Recent Competition Law Judgments of the Court of Justice of the EU' [2018] Journal of Antitrust Enforcement

the standard of proof is arguably close to what we would expect in criminal proceedings.[26]

Given the new market dynamics, then, are the contemporary enforcement standards fit for purpose? As suggested previously and explained below, the answer depends on how one approaches the question.

2.2 Optimal, Reasonable, or Resolute Standards?

2.2.1 Optimal standards

The optimal approach is one many economists would support. Based on decision theory (i.e. error–cost analysis), they would have our decision-makers determine the kind and content of enforcement standards according to their respective, predicted, social costs. In a nutshell, the optimal standards (of liability and proof) for assessing a particular practice would thus be those that, overall, minimize two sets of costs. First, those flowing from the decision errors they will inevitably generate: wrongful convictions (i.e. false positives or type-I errors) and mistaken acquittals (i.e. false negatives or type-II errors). Second, the administrative costs associated with establishing and operating these standards.[27]

Insofar as antitrust remains anchored by the consumer welfare paradigm, this approach would largely favour effects-based legal tests.[28] Not necessarily because of a belief that 'rules represent a bias, and only the rule of reason can adequately enable courts to make an appropriate decision in every case ... to achieve this goal.'[29] Instead, the logic would more probably rest on the idea that '[t]he error–cost framework calls for a more interventionist antitrust rule only when Type II error costs are substantial, there is a long-standing precedent indicating that the given practice is anticompetitive, and theory and evidence suggest a strong likelihood that the practice is anticompetitive.'[30] To my knowledge, those questing for optimal legal tests would not change their recommendation when it comes to platforms

---

173, 183. See also Colomo (n 15); Nicolas Petit, 'Analysis and Reflections: Intel and the Rule of Reason in Abuse of Dominance Cases' [2018] European Law Review 728.

[26] See Kalintiri (n 17) 83ff.

[27] The literature on this topic is vast and need not be reviewed here. See, usefully, Jonathan Baker, *The Antitrust Paradigm: Restoring a Competitive Economy* (Harvard UP 2019) 73.

[28] See eg Yannis Katsoulacos, Svetlana Avdashevab and Svetlana Golovan, 'Legal Standards and the Role of Economics in Competition Law Enforcement' [2016] European Competition Journal 277, 283–84; Robert O'Donoghue and Jorge Padilla, *The Law and Economics of Article 102 TFEU* (3rd edn, Hart 2020) 276.

[29] Schrepel (n 21) 114.

[30] Geoffrey Manne and Joshua Wright, 'Google and the Limits of Antitrust: The Case Against the Case Against Google' [2011] Harvard Journal of Law & Public Policy 171, 180.

and their upstream exertions.[31] Moreover, as it relates to evidence principles, some would likely endorse more pro-*defendant* standards of proof.[32]

That said, two brief remarks will suffice. The first is that it is difficult to fault these recommendations. They may simply reflect the 'natural way for economists to function'.[33] Plus, the economics of upstream platform power plays, as we saw in Part II, are both relatively novel and quite ambiguous: there are potential, maybe even plausible, negative effects, but they are not necessarily likely; and while the harm may be substantial, assessing magnitude is something for which analytical tools remain deficient.[34]

This brings us to the second observation. Regardless of the chosen antitrust paradigm, are optimal standards really desirable? The approach is widely recognized to 'only rarely yield better than crude approximations'[35] because the relevant cost variables are 'difficult or impossible to measure'.[36] Hence, its entire operation rests on assumptions about markets and institutions.[37] This means 'optimal' standards are mediated, not through science, but ideology[38]—ideology of a presumably conservative nature.[39] To my mind, therefore, the approach's desirability cannot seriously be defended unless the antitrust decision-maker consistently mirrors the popular will, at least on average.[40] So, what would *reasonable* and *resolute* standards look like?

2.2.2 Reasonable standards

2.2.2.1 Prolegomenon
The reasonable approach is one that would presumably be counselled by those obsessed neither by decision-makers' inevitable fallibility nor their conviction rates. Its methodology is quintessentially legal, which is not to say economics-illiterate. As it concerns the standard of proof, it entails finding a balance between 'the minimum threshold of evidence sufficiency that can be tolerated from a fairness

---

[31]   See eg Melamed and Petit (n 2) 741, 767; Jorge Padilla, 'Neoclassical Competition Policy without Apology' (2 November 2022) 13–15 <https://bit.ly/3VhQJDI> accessed 21 November 2022.

[32]   Murat Mungan and Joshua Wright, 'Optimal Standards of Proof in Antitrust' [2022] International Review of Law and Economics 106083.

[33]   FTC, 'Hearings on Competition and Consumer Protection in the 21st Century' (15 October 2018) 67 <https://bit.ly/3Em90J4> accessed 19 November 2022 (intervention by Joseph Farrell).

[34]   Ronald Cass, 'Antitrust for High-Tech and Low: Regulation, Innovation, and Risk' [2013] Journal of Law, Economics and Policy 169, 197.

[35]   Richard Posner, 'An Economic Approach to Legal Procedure and Judicial Administration' [1973] Journal of Legal Studies 399, 402.

[36]   Hovenkamp (n 23) 55.

[37]   Baker (n 27) 74.

[38]   Marina Lao, 'Ideology Matters in the Antitrust Debate' [2014] Antitrust Law Journal 649, 666.

[39]   David Lawrence, 'Antitrust Division Policy Director David Lawrence Delivers Keynote at Brigham Young University Law Conference "Tech Platforms in a New Age of Competition Law"' (21 October 2022) <https://bit.ly/3EjWeL7> accessed 19 November 2022 (pointing to an 'emerging consensus' among enforcers that 'error–cost analysis' amounts to 'trying to get it wrong on purpose').

[40]   Similarly, Baker (n 27) 65. Verifying this empirically would, admittedly, be challenging.

perspective against the maximum threshold respectively, beyond which the sustainability of the enforcement becomes threatened'.[41]

Regarding legal tests, the reasonable approach would account for the following factors:

- Error costs

Given the inherent limitations of decision theory, reason counsels an even-handed concern on false positives and false negatives, regardless of the goal antitrust is understood to pursue.[42]

- Rationalization tools

A key factor in the choice between rules and standards revolves around how one rationalizes the competition problem arising from a particular behaviour. From this flows the premise (about the conduct's nature and effects) that will support the decision. Relevant harm can be explained informally, for example, by relying on intuition. Another informal analytical tool—a popular one with antitrust decision-makers—is 'experience'.[43] However, the reasonable approach would complement informal analysis with formal devices applied in a rigorous, non-selective, fashion.[44] Why? Because formal reasoning serves as a bulwark against arbitrariness. For enforcement would be arbitrary if legal tests were based on premises known to be incorrect and/or insufficiently nuanced.[45]

Obviously, advocates of this approach might disagree on whether (neoclassical) economics should be the exclusive purveyor of wisdom. To the extent competition, as such—an overtly moralizing paradigm—is endorsed as the policy's lodestar, I see little reason to foreclose any other possibly useful discipline for rationalization purposes.[46] As our inquiry in Part II shows, political philosophy can meaningfully inform our understanding of how business practices can harm ideals such as freedom and equality of opportunity (EOp). Besides, antitrust is routinely depicted

---

[41] Kalintiri (n 17) 74.

[42] See, similarly, Philip Lowe, 'Consumer Welfare and Efficiency—New Guiding Principles of Competition Policy?' (Speech delivered at the 13th International Conference on Competition and 14th European Competition Day, 27 March 2007) 9 <https://bityl.co/Fk2h> accessed 19 November 2022. See also Lawrence (n 39).

[43] See eg Case C-67/13 P *Cartes Bancaires* ECLI:EU:C:2014:2204 [2014] electronic Reports of Cases, [51]; *Broadcast Music Inc v Columbia Broadcasting System Inc* 441 US 1, 2 (1979).

[44] Similarly, see BEUC, 'The Role of Competition Policy in Protecting Consumers' Well-being in the Digital Era' (October 2019) 18 <https://bit.ly/3USSvv9> accessed 19 November 2022.

[45] Similarly, see Colomo (n 15) 323.

[46] Similarly, see Lawrence Sullivan, 'Economics and More Humanistic Disciplines: What are the Sources of Wisdom for Antitrust?' [1977] University of Pennsylvania Law Review 1214; Albert Foer, 'Civil Liberties and Competition Policy: A Personal Essay Dedicated to John J. Flynn' [2011] Antitrust Bulletin 731, 732.

as a multidisciplinary field, even by economists.[47] For sure, taking values seriously means appealing to rigorously formulated theories to explain what may seem intuitively troubling; but so too must these theories be intelligible and compatible with what societies envisaged their respective competitive orders to look like. This brings us to the next point.

- Coherence

A reasonable legal test is not just informed by formal analysis; it is also coherent. In other words, it has to 'make sense' when viewed against the broader antitrust system of which it forms a part. How so? By being rationally related, instrumentally or intrinsically, to the values and principles that undergird it.[48] This rule-of-law imperative, admittedly, places significant constraints on the decision-maker's discretion, as illustrated in a moment. Nonetheless, it is coherence which ensures that our competition laws will evolve in a reasonably predictable and non-arbitrary way.[49] Reason cannot compromise on this.[50]

Importantly, the requirement arms the decision-maker with a limited justification for adopting a potentially inconsistent test.[51] As Neil MacCormick writes, '[c]omplete consistency is not a necessary condition of coherence, since unlike consistency, coherence can be a matter of degree'.[52]

With these considerations in mind, what would this approach entail in practice when applied to our upstream platform power plays?

2.2.2.2 Application

- Standards of proof

Regarding, briefly, standards of proof, the institutional landscape will weigh considerably on what may be deemed reasonable. Take antitrust systems (like those in

---

[47] See eg Oliver Budzinski, 'Modern Industrial Economics: Open Problems and Possible Limits' in Josef Drexl, Wolfgang Kerber and Rupprecht Podszun (eds), *Competition Policy and the Economic Approach: Foundations and Limitations* (Edward Elgar 2011) 111.

[48] Neil MacCormick, *Rhetoric and the Rule of Law: A Theory of Legal Reasoning* (OUP 2005) 48, 189ff.

[49] See MacCormick (n 48) 12, 16, 131–32.

[50] See, similarly, Case C-413/14 P *Intel* ECLI:EU:C:2016:788 [2016] not yet published, Opinion of AG Wahl, [103]–[105] ('Sound and coherent legal categorisation benefits not only undertakings in terms of increased legal certainty, but also assists competition authorities in the enforcement of competition law. Arbitrary categorisation does not. The Court seems to agree.... Assuredly it did so in order to ensure a coherent jurisprudential approach').

[51] In the EU, the judicature has stressed that EU institutions must 'avoid, *as a matter of principle*, inconsistencies that might arise in the implementation of the various provisions of EU law'. (Case T-612/17 *Google and Alphabet (Google Shopping)* ECLI:EU:T:2021:763 [2021] not yet published, [194] and the case law cited therein) (emphasis added).

[52] MacCormick (n 48) 190.

Europe) where enforcement relies primarily on administrative authorities carrying out quasi-criminal proceedings. There, the public interest imperative of effective enforcement needs reconciling with the fundamental rights bestowed upon undertakings whose enjoyment may be at risk.[53] It accordingly makes sense to maintain high standards that, if not identical to those applied in criminal cases, may be flexible enough to be stretched close to them, which is what we currently find in the EU.[54] As one learned antitrust judge once opined, in such a model, 'it is hard to conceive, at least in free democratic societies, that citizens and firms can be condemned on the basis of estimates, approximations or guesses, even if they are informed ones'.[55]

Some will no doubt argue that opaque and complex digital markets with platforms operating as 'black boxes' are game changers justifying a more relaxed attitude. The issues examined in Part II definitely are sometimes challenging to detect;[56] few businesses will go to the length Genius did to make its case, for instance,[57] possibly out of fear.[58] Nevertheless, improved whistle-blowing schemes and information-gathering powers for enforcers appear to be more becoming solutions to this specific issue.[59]

- Legal tests

Regarding legal tests, several remarks are in order.

➢ The limits of the consumer welfare paradigm

The first is that, insofar as consumer welfare remains antitrust's paradigm, standards (as opposed to rules) are probably the reasonable way to go given *current* knowledge. A reasonable rule-based test (qualified or not) would indeed imply that harm can be rationalized through formal analysis and predicted to be likely in most circumstances. This is surely what the European Court of Justice (ECJ) has in mind when it insists that to justify a practice:

---

[53] In the EU, these would include their economic freedom and right to property, as well as their presumption of innocence (see Charter of Fundamental Rights of the European Union (CFREU) [2016] OJ C202/389, arts 16, 17, and 48).

[54] See Kalintiri (n 17) 85.

[55] Marc van der Woude, 'Judicial Control in Complex Economic Matters' [2019] Journal of European Competition Law & Practice 415, 418.

[56] ACCC (n 8) 13, 139.

[57] Genius had watermarked its song transcriptions with a Morse-code message to substantiate its claim that Alphabet/Google had scraped its content.

[58] EC, 'Impact Assessment Accompanying the Proposal for a Regulation on Promoting Fairness and Transparency for Business Users of Online Intermediation Services' SWD/2018/138 final, 9, 26.

[59] See, similarly, CMA, 'Letter to the Secretary of State for Business, Energy and Industry Strategy' (21 February 2019) 26, 32 <https://bit.ly/3USe9zp> accessed 19 November 2022.

[B]eing classified as a restriction of competition 'by object', without an analysis of its effects being required, there must be sufficiently reliable and robust experience for the view to be taken that that [conduct] is, by its very nature, harmful.[60]

Yet, we saw in Part II that the motives and consumer welfare effects of upstream platform power plays are ambiguous. The issue of self-preferencing is illuminating in this regard.

Recall from Chapter 4 that the conduct's negative impact on consumers (through the foreclosure of efficient third-party providers) is possible, not likely. Similarly, impingements on effective choice may ensue in some cases, but not in others.[61] And while innovation can always be used as a trump card, empirical evidence is scant and no general framework to support the theory exists. We simply do not have the means to consistently conduct rigorous innovation assessments, a shortcoming economists readily recognize.[62] Worse, some say '[t]here is very little that is actually done in this',[63] which is precisely why contemporary consumer welfare-driven antitrust has navel-gazed on short-run consequences and cannot realistically do much more than that if rigour is required.

Given this state of affairs, should decision-makers give in to precautionary instincts, which would have them lower the probability threshold of effects because the resulting harm might be substantial? Appealing as it is, this argument cannot pass muster with reason. For a legal test that merely requires relevant effects to be theoretically possible is nothing more than a liability rule in disguise.[64] Furthermore, measuring the magnitude of dynamic economic effects is not something we have a good handle on either. The CADE, for instance, recognized as much in a decision on scraping allegations against Alphabet/Google.[65] This difficulty equally harrows top-rated agencies like the EC.[66] Consider the latter's impact assessment accompanying its proposal for a now-adopted regulation aiming to ensure 'fair' platform-to-business relations.[67] Initially, the document had been

---

[60] Case C-228/18 *Budapest Bank* ECLI:EU:C:2020:265 [2020] not yet published, [76] (approvingly citing AG Bobek's opinion, which argued that a consensus among economists on the inherently anticompetitive nature of a practice is of utmost importance to determining whether a rule-based test is justified).

[61] For instance, cf *Google Search (Shopping)* (Case AT.39,740) EC Decision 27 June 2017, [490]–[491]; with *Streetmap.EU Ltd v Google Inc & ors* [2016] EWHC 253 (Ch), [119].

[62] See eg Stigler Center, 'Stigler Committee on Digital Platforms: Final Report' (September 2019) 92 <https://bityl.co/Fjqi> accessed 19 November 2022; Wolfgang Kerber, 'Competition, Innovation, and Competition Law: Dissecting the Interplay' in Damien Gerard, Bernd Meyring and Eric Morgan de Rivery (eds), *Dynamic Markets, Dynamic Competition and Dynamic Enforcement* (Bruylant 2018) 35ff.

[63] FTC, 'Hearings on Competition and Consumer Protection in the 21st Century' (16 October 2018) 293 <https://bit.ly/3tK6Mhz> accessed 19 November 2022 (intervention by Cristina Caffara).

[64] See eg *Intel* Opinion of AG Wahl (n 50) [118].

[65] *E-Commerce/Google* (n 8) [144] ('it is difficult to assess how much has been lost due to a lack of incentives for innovation') (free translation).

[66] For an annual ranking of competition authorities, see GCR, 'Rating Enforcement 2022' (7 September 2022) <https://bityl.co/EwHe> accessed 18 November 2022.

[67] EC, 'Impact Assessment Accompanying the Proposal for a Regulation on Promoting Fairness and Transparency for Business Users of Online Intermediation Services' SWD/2018/138 final.

faulted by the EC's own independent quality control unit, the Regulatory Scrutiny Board (RSB). The reason? Evidence supporting the magnitude of innovation problems were insufficient and biased.[68] Although a subsequent version was ultimately green-lighted, the RSB remained mum on innovation effects.[69] Tellingly, the EC conceded that there were 'no robust quantitative estimates for these innovation dynamics'.[70]

Pushing the point further, one might seriously question whether innovation ought to play a prominent role in antitrust given current methodological deficiencies.[71]

➢ The scope of the competitive process paradigm

The second observation pertains to the kind of tests reasonableness recommends under the competitive process lodestar. As Part II showed, we can rigorously rationalize various upstream platform exertions as potentially inimical to the values inherent to this alternative antitrust paradigm. The issue, then, is one of coherence. Does it make sense to adopt more rule-based tests for these types of behaviour? The answer is likely to be jurisdiction- and conduct-specific.

Take our game-mastering tactics. These practices do generate legitimate antitrust anxieties under this approach because they can compromise EOp. As we saw in Chapter 4, the value has several formulations. Each is undergirded by distinct ideals, which may not all 'fit' within a particular legal order committed to competition, as such. Coherence, however, requires the chosen EOp theory to 'hang together purposively'[72] with the roadmap a society will have (maybe implicitly) stipulated, much like an economic theory has to be based on realistic assumptions. This is why social-minded polities alone could justifiably appeal to substantive EOp theories to subject, say, self-preferencing platforms, to a liability rule that bites even when the favoured in-house product is a superior option.

The EU is a potential case in point. Remember, here is a polity with a 'leftward-tilted' constitutional commitment to the market economy.[73] To me, this slant is perceptible in *Google Shopping*—the General Court's judgement to be precise. There, the first instance judges arguably subjected Alphabet/Google's self-preferencing to

---

[68] RSB, 'Opinion—Impact Assessment/Fairness in Online Intermediated Trade' Ref.Ares(2017) 5899542, 2, annexed to RSB, 'Opinion—Impact Assessment/Fairness in Online Intermediated Trade' SEC(2018)209 <https://perma.cc/TA83-TMCB> accessed 18 November 2022.

[69] RSB, 'Opinion—Impact Assessment/Fairness in Online Intermediated Trade' SEC(2018)209, 1–3 <https://perma.cc/TA83-TMCB> accessed 18 November 2022.

[70] EC (n 67) 29.

[71] Pablo Ibáñez Colomo, 'On the Application of Competition Law as Regulation: Elements for a Theory' [2012] Yearbook of European Law 261, 263.

[72] MacCormick (n 48) 230.

[73] See Chapter 5, Section 4.2.2 p 176.

what looks like a (qualified) rule (albeit, an unstructured one),[74] crafted to apply regardless of the impugned firm's performance.[75] The choice of such a legal test is decidedly controversial. On the one hand, the Court's economic reasoning—that self-preferencing by a search engine like Google Search 'cannot but involve a certain form of abnormality'[76]—appears to be at odds with empirical studies attesting to the contrary, irrespective of economic power levels.[77] On the other hand, haphazard appeals to public law principles (of equal treatment),[78] inapplicable (net neutrality) legislation,[79] and the nebulous idea of 'ultra/superdominance',[80] leave an uneasy impression: that the judges (i) (un)wittingly contradicted themselves by adding to the EC's own motives,[81] and (ii) purposely went out of their way to paper over the fact that higher judicial authority was being sidestepped in the process,[82] so as to (iii) extend to Alphabet/Google a logic originally intended for state-owned monopolists who, because of their endowments, were always a finger away from imperilling competition and were, resultingly, subjected to a praetorian 'ultra/super special responsibility' of sorts.[83] In short, the Court treads on thin ice here. But despite these kinks, the ruling is not fundamentally unsound. For one, the skirted ECJ judgement, which dealt with king-making in a context of analogue competition, was likely premised on knowledge that could be deemed inapposite in *Google Shopping*.[84] For another, EOp was the unmistakeable lynchpin of the judges' rationale, although the value was not given the proper developments it deserved.[85]

Be that as it may, several caveats to what has just been argued are in order.

---

[74] *Google and Alphabet (Google Shopping)* (n 51) [155]–[197]. For a similar reading of the legal test, see Justin Lindeboom, 'Rules, Discretion, and Reasoning According to Law: A Dynamic-Positivist Perspective on *Google Shopping*' [2022] Journal of European Competition Law & Practice 63, 68–71.

[75] *Google and Alphabet (Google Shopping)* (n 51) [151] (EU antitrust condemns 'in particular'—so not exclusively—conduct that departs from performance-based competition), [188] together with [266], [414]–[416], and [541] (prima facie liability can be found irrespective of performance).

[76] ibid [179].

[77] See the literature discussed in Patrick Maillé and Bruno Tuffin, *Telecommunication Network Economics: From Theory to Applications* (CUP 2014) 263.

[78] *Google and Alphabet (Google Shopping)* (n 51) [155].

[79] ibid [180].

[80] ibid [180], [182].

[81] At ibid [135], the judges stress that they 'cannot under any circumstances ... substitute their own reasoning ... for that of the [EC]'. But none of the preceding points were advanced by the EC. Moreover, the affirmation at [415]—that the EC did not focus on 'the intrinsic performance of Google's comparison shopping service'—seems at odds with the agency's reasoning, which very much insisted on the product's inferiority (see *Google Search (Shopping)* (Case AT.39,740) EC Decision 27 June 2017, [343], [490]–[491]).

[82] See Case C-525/16 *MEO* ECLI:EU:C:2018:270 [2018] electronic Reports of Cases, [28], [31].

[83] See, similarly, Pablo Ibáñez Colomo, 'Will Article 106 TFEU Case Law Transform EU Competition Law?' [2022] Journal of European Competition Law & Practice 385.

[84] In *MEO*, the ECJ approvingly cites the AG's opinion. The latter, though, was deeply sceptical of the behaviour's rationality (see Case C-525/16 *MEO* ECLI:EU:C:2017:1020 [2017] electronic Reports of Cases, Opinion of AG Wahl, [54]–[55], [79]). But we saw in Chapter 4 that *platforms* often do have such king-making, as well as self-preferencing, incentives.

[85] See *Google and Alphabet (Google Shopping)* (n 51) [180], where the Court pays lip service to EOp 'for the sake of completeness'.

First, given that upstream platform power plays are likely to generate positive short-run effects, a qualified, rather than per se, liability rule would seem appropriate.

Second, coherence requires attention to the presumption of innocence. The latter is relevant as liability rules shift the *legal* burden onto the defendant to justify its behaviour.[86] Due process reasons would hence demand that the *standard of proof* for *justifications* be the balance of probabilities (or its equivalent subjective conviction threshold).[87]

Finally, a rule does not necessarily have to be *simple*, which brings us to a final observation.

> ➤ The value of complex, but structured legal tests

As stated earlier, legal tests can be complex in that they can have multiple triggers. To ensure coherence while minimizing inconsistencies, reasonableness counsels that we rely on them and that we do so in a structured manner. Neither the kind of test (rule or standard) nor the policy goal ('consumer welfare' or 'competition as such') ought to influence this. As Lon Fuller would say, the contrary—generalized ad hocism—would be 'the first and most obvious way ... to fail to make law'.[88]

Consider, for example, the issue of despotic platforms explored in Chapter 3. As explained there, one can rationalize some of these worries under the competitive process paradigm. How? Through a theory of coercion that sees a competition problem in powerful platforms bullying providers into abstaining from effectively exercising their legal rights. A simple liability rule would nevertheless prove contentious, even in jurisdictions like the EU where the threat to systemic coherence would be less acute.[89] Such a legal test, critics would say, stretches the special responsibility saddling powerful firms too far.[90] Ergo, additional triggers are needed.[91]

---

[86] This is explicitly recognized, for instance, by the draft bill underpinning a reform to German antitrust law that has since introduced a qualified liability rule for, inter alia, self-preferencing and data-twinking by powerful platforms (see BMWi, 'Bundesministeriums für Wirtschaft und Energie, 'Entwurf eines Zehnten Gesetzes zur Änderung des Gesetzes gegen Wettbewerbsbeschränkungen für ein fokussiertes, proaktives und digitales Wettbewerbsrecht 4.0 (GWB-Digitalisierungsgesetz)' (7 October 2019) 77 <https://bit.ly/3EmF67p> accessed 19 November 2022).

[87] See Kalintiri (n 17) 55–56 and the literature referenced therein.

[88] Lon Fuller, *The Morality of Law* (2nd edn, Yale UP 1969) 33, 39.

[89] See Cases C-179/16 *Hoffmann-La Roche* ECLI:EU:C:2018:25 [2018] electronic Reports of Cases, [92]–[95] (holding that an agreement between pharmaceutical manufacturers to disseminate misleading information in contravention of pharmaceutical legislation can constitute an antitrust infringement 'by-object'); C-32/11 *Allianz Hungaria* ECLI:EU:C:2013:160 [2013] electronic Reports of Cases, [47] (holding that agreements between car insurers and dealers could constitute antitrust infringements 'by object' when those agreements are contrary to national insurance laws).

[90] See eg *Facebook* (Case VI-Kart 1/19 (V)) Düsseldorf Higher Regional Court Judgement 8 August 2019 ECLI:DE:OLGD:2019:0826.KART1.19V.00, [44] ('the dominant company has a special responsibility only for competition, not beyond that for the observance of the legal system by avoiding any violation of the law') (free translation).

[91] cf Monopolkommission, 'Competition policy: The Challenge of Digital Markets' (2015) Special Report No 68, [523]–[528] <https://perma.cc/6B3V-55QT>18 November 2022 (supporting per se illegality).

One of them could relate to the range of rights whose violation might be deemed relevant for antitrust purposes.[92] Another might involve curtailing the enforcer's discretion in interpreting the scope of such rights.[93] Likewise, a causality requirement between power and conduct (or potentially reinforcing such a proviso where it already exists) may be envisioned.[94] This is what the ADLC appears to have implicitly done when it took action against Alphabet/Google's for threatening the removal of press snippets in response to the previously mentioned French copyright law reform.[95] The move evidently does open the door to a bevy of further questions[96] whose answers are likely to be jurisdiction-specific.[97] The point, however, is precisely that these debates are salutary, especially when the upstream power play at hand is particularly difficult to square within either antitrust paradigm—think of free-riding practices.[98]

More generally, a reasonable legal test would have an eye on remedies.[99] As will be explored in more detail shortly, a tricky challenge with enforcing antitrust to address upstream platform power plays is that (moderately) effective redress will usually have a proactive outlook to it. The ensuing incoherence can fortunately be mitigated with a well-designed liability trigger. An interesting option in this regard would be to introduce an 'indispensability' screen when intervention would

---

[92] See eg Tobias Lettl, 'Missbräuchliche Ausnutzung einer Marktbeherrschenden Stellung nach Art. 102 AEUV, § 19 GWB und Rechtsbruch' [2016] Wirtschaft und Wettbewerb 214, 217 (arguing that only rules on market structure and/or market conduct should be relevant).

[93] In this sense, see Case C-252/21 *Meta Platforms* ECLI:EU:C:2023:537 [2023] not yet published, [44]–[59] (expounding a duty for the antitrust enforcer to both (i) interpret non-antitrust rules consistently with that of the authority primarily entrusted with their supervision, and (ii) inform and cooperate with said authority).

[94] For instance, in the EU, while the issue is not completely unambiguous, it is generally accepted that there is no such requirement. It does, however, exist in German antitrust (which has long explicitly recognized the idea that breaches of non-antitrust laws can constitute antitrust infringements). See Lettl (n 92) 214.

[95] *Syndicat des éditeurs de la presse magazine* (Case 19/0075M) ADLC Decision 20-MC-01 19 April 2020, [254].

[96] For instance, a choice would need to be made between normative and strict causality, a distinction known to German antitrust lawyers. Strict causality means power is what enables the conduct (i.e. the conduct was available only to the powerful platform). Conduct is in a normative causal relationship with power when power is what causes the conduct to produce its anticompetitive effects.

[97] It is well known, for example, that the USA displays a judicial reluctance to penalize powerful firms for engaging in conduct lawfully available to others (William Holmes and Melissa Mangiaracina, *Antitrust Law Handbook: 2018–2019 Edition* (Thomson Reuters 2018) 489–98). This attitude is not shared by the EU (see eg Case C-457/10 P *AstraZeneca* ECLI:EU:C:2012:770 [2012] electronic Report of Cases, [23] ('in the majority of cases, abuses of dominant positions consist of behaviour which is otherwise lawful under branches of law other than competition law')).

[98] Similarly, see Renato Nazzini, 'Google and the (Ever-Stretching) Boundaries of Article 102 TFUE' [2015] Journal of European Competition Law & Practice 301, 310.

[99] Similarly, see Phillip Areeda and Herbert Hovenkamp, *Antitrust Law: An Analysis of Antitrust Principles and Their Application* (Supplement 8/2019, rev edn, Wolters Kluwer 1978) [303c2].

be proactive.[100] In other words, require proof that the contentious platform infrastructure is an 'essential facility' where remediation would be structural or entail regular positive duties for the impugned platform. Nothing revolutionary here, just a generalization of what is already implicit in EU and (albeit less perceptibly) US antitrust.[101] The rationale is both normative and practical. Normative, as the filter accounts for two sets of competing interests: fundamental rights versus competition and short-term versus long-term impact of proactive enforcement.[102] Practical, because proactive remedies are more costly to administer than most reactive, cease-and-desist, obligations.[103]

2.2.3 Resolute standards

Reasonable enforcement standards, obviously, can greatly impede intervention. Consequently, decision-makers may want to adopt a more resolute approach, one that is more bent on shaking up the status quo.[104]

Recall, for instance, the *Navx* decision discussed in Chapter 4. There, the ADLC correctly, albeit implicitly, identified the real crux of the problem behind Alphabet/ Google's king-making, namely, neutral EOp. The agency's choice of a qualified rule was an arguably reasonable one. But the legal test was crafted in an unstructured way, i.e. it shifted the legal burden onto the defendant to justify its conduct without providing clearly operational triggers for qualified liability.[105] While understandably desirable from the enforcer's perspective, the discretion this entails carries a considerable risk of ad hocism. Subsequent cases dealing with the same practice have shown how battered legal certainty becomes.[106]

The EU *Google Shopping* saga offers another good illustration of this approach. As suggested a few pages ago, while confirming that the issue at stake was EOp

---

[100] Similarly, see Pablo Ibáñez Colomo, 'Indispensability and Abuse of Dominance: From Commercial Solvents to Slovak Telekom and Google Shopping' [2019] Journal of European Competition Law & Practice 532, 536.

[101] ibid 532ff (analysing EU jurisprudence and finding that proactive remedies are available only when 'indispensability' is part of the liability test). In the USA, 'indispensability' is implicit in the 'essential facilities' doctrine. See Case C-165/19 P *Slovak Telekom* ECLI:EU:C:2020:678 [2020] not yet published, Opinion of AG Øe, [68]–[69] (confirming both points).

[102] See Case C-7/97 *Bronner* ECLI:EU:C:1998:264 [1998] ECR I-7794, Opinion of AG Jacobs, [56]–[57].

[103] Similarly, see Colomo (n 100) 532, 536. See further Section 4 of this chapter.

[104] Writing of '"policy-driven" enforcement', see Pablo Ibáñez Colomo and Andriani Kalintiri, 'The Evolution of EU Antitrust Policy: 1966–2017' [2020] Modern Law Review 321, 364.

[105] The decision fault's Alphabet/Google's differential treatment of competing advertisers but does not provide guidance on how to determine which advertisers are relevant for assessment purposes (see *Navx* (Case 10/0011M) ADLC Decision 10-MC-01 30 June 2010, [222]–[238]).

[106] *E-Kanopi* (Case 10/0081F) ADLC Decision 13-D-07 28 February 2013, [62]–[76] (no liability); *Gibmedia* (Case 15/0020M) ADLC Decision 15-D-13 9 September 2015, [169]–[173] (interim relief rejected but liability confirmed on the merits in *Gibmedia (merits)* (Case 15/0019F) Decision 19-D-26 19 December 2019, [343]–[513]); *Amadeus* (Case 18/0048M) ADLC Decision 19-MC-01 31 January 2019, [155]–[163] (interim measures granted and confirmed on appeal in *Google v Amadeus* (Case No 1903274) Paris Court of Appeal Judgement 4 April 2019).

200 ANTITRUST'S INTERNAL QUANDARIES

all along, the first instance judges failed to articulate a legal test with clearly defined boundaries.[107] Instead, they green-lighted the enforcer's approach of, first,
identifying a practice that offended its intuitive understanding of a value (in this
case, EOp) it believed warranted protection under its interpretation of the law;
then building around this intuition by demonstrating the existence of certain factors,[108] which were relevant only because the enforcer deemed them to be so;[109] before finally thinking about the remedy.[110] Since judicial review in this case basically
boiled down to an active inconsistency check (i.e. verifying whether the case law
had been actively contradicted), the EC came out of it with bolstered discretion to
shape the law and the outcomes of its application.[111]

European authorities, mind you, are not alone in sometimes prioritizing resolute over reasonable but constrained enforcement. Nor are game-mastering tactics the sole upstream platform power play singled out for such treatment. Take
Brazil, where the CADE hinted that content scraping should similarly be subjected
to an unstructured 'by-object' test by stating that potential negative effects on incentives to innovate would be sufficient to trigger prima facie liability.[112] And, in
the USA, the FTC has attempted to generalize this approach through a policy statement adopted in late 2022.[113] Intended as a guide on how the agency 'will police
the boundary between fair and unfair competition through both enforcement and
rulemaking,'[114] the document outlines two key criteria in this regard. One: 'conduct *may* be coercive, exploitative, collusive, abusive, deceptive, predatory, or involve the use of economic power of a similar nature [or] be otherwise restrictive or
exclusionary, *depending on the circumstances*'.[115] Two: 'conduct must *tend* to negatively affect competitive conditions'.[116] Yet, save for the notice that both principles
are to be weighed using a sliding scale and the explicit abjuration of liability standards in favour of (quasi per se) rules,[117] little is actually offered by way of substantive guidance. As dissenting Commissioner Christine Wilson notes:

---

[107] See body text after (n 73) of this chapter.
[108] i.e. the dynamics of network effects in search, consumer search patterns, and the importance, for
price comparators, of referral traffic from Google Search.
[109] As the Court approvingly states, the EC's analysis was based, first, on '*suspect elements* ... in particular an unjustified difference in treatment ... and, secondly, of *specific circumstances* ... relating to the
nature of the infrastructure from which that difference in treatment arises' (see *Google and Alphabet
(Google Shopping)* (n 51) [197]) (emphasis added).
[110] ibid [244] ('There can be no automatic link between the criteria for the legal classification of the
abuse and the corrective measures enabling it to be remedied').
[111] See, similarly, Yasmine Bouzoraa, 'Between Substance and Autonomy: Finding Legal Certainty in
Google Shopping' [2022] Journal of European Competition Law & Practice 144.
[112] *E-Commerce/Google* (n 8), [144].
[113] FTC, 'Policy Statement Regarding the Scope of Unfair Methods of Competition Under Section 5 of the
Federal Trade Commission Act' (10 November 2022) <https://bityl.co/FjEq> accessed 18 November 2022.
[114] FTC, 'FTC Restores Rigorous Enforcement of Law Banning Unfair Methods of Competition' (10
November 2022) <https://bityl.co/FjEY> accessed 18 November 2022.
[115] FTC (n 113) 9 (emphasis added).
[116] ibid (emphasis added).
[117] ibid 9–12. I write 'quasi per se' because, although the document does not exclude the possibility of
overriding justifications, it all but closes the door on them.

3. WHAT (FORM(S) OF) POWER?   201

[T]he Policy Statement provides that merely labeling conduct with an appropriate adjective can establish liability.... These labels require subjective interpretation, and frequently lack established antitrust or economic meanings. But the Policy Statement does not provide content to the adjectives. Consequently, identifying whether conduct falls under one of the labels depends on the whims and political worldviews of ... sitting Commissioners.[118]

There is certainly nothing inherently shocking about these incidents. In some jurisdictions (like the EU and the USA of yesteryear), public enforcers might simply have a tendency to shape enforcement standards so as to expand the law's reach.[119] This may be especially true where negotiated procedures (which both obviate the need for a fully-fledged legal analysis and are less exposed to judicial review) are available.[120] In Japan, for example, the JFTC has clearly stated that it will double down on commitment proceedings in digital markets precisely because they 'can contribute to quick problem solving ... without establishing facts'.[121]

So, what is the upshot of our discussion? It is that, if status quo-busting enforcement is the endgame, resolute standards are the way to go. Indeed, whereas the reasonable approach can make for swift intervention when the competitive process paradigm is endorsed, rule-of-law considerations do hamper it. Whether and when resoluteness ought to trump reasonableness, though, are questions whose answers are driven primarily by policy (*sensu stricto*), not law.

3. What (Form(s) of) Power?

Enforcement standards are vital cogs in the antitrust apparatus. But greasing them will prove somewhat futile without a clear understanding of what the instrument is meant to target in the first place. The 'goal(s)' issue is fundamental in this respect. As we now appreciate, it doesn't merely reflect a particular outlook on why competition is to be valued and on why upstream harm might be rationalized as a relevant problem; it can likewise impact the kind of enforcement standards our

---

[118] FTC, 'Dissenting Statement of Commissioner Christine S. Wilson Regarding the "Policy Statement Regarding the Scope of Unfair Methods of Competition Under Section 5 of the Federal Trade Commission Act"' (10 November 2022) 6, 13 <https://bityl.co/FjF2> accessed 18 November 2022.

[119] See Colomo (n 15) chs 3–4, 6 (analysing over 600 formal EC antitrust decisions and finding that the authority has consistently sought to define the scope of its power expansively by resorting to 'by-object' legal tests). As for the USA, the FTC's expansive interpretation of its powers under section 5 FTC Act during the 1970s is notorious (see, usefully, J Howard Beales III, 'The Federal Trade Commission's Use of Unfairness Authority: Its Rise, Fall, and Resurrection' [2003] Journal of Public Policy & Marketing 192).

[120] Colomo (n 15) 288–99.

[121] JFTC, 'Report Regarding Trade Practices on Digital Platforms (Business-to-Business Transactions on Online Retail Platform and App Store)' (31 October 2019) 9 <https://perma.cc/KLL7-XXZB> accessed 18 November 2022.

decision-makers may adopt. There is another, transcendental, matter in this complex equation. For whatever one's view on the appropriate antitrust paradigm, we must not forget that the policy 'is a response to the universal pursuit of economic power'.[122]

Its pervasive concentration in the platform economy, we saw in the introductory chapter, has been widely reported. The problem, as Commissioner Vestager puts it, is that '[t]ackling power in the digital world can sometimes feel a bit like grappling with Proteus. Everything about it is constantly changing—not just the technology, but also how businesses work.'[123] Let us push this observation further.

3.1 The Forms of (Platform) Power

Power 'is one of the most palpable facts of human existence',[124] one sociologists and political theorists have long been riveted by. Contemporary antitrust lawyers, by contrast, have rarely lost sleep over the notion's meaning. For them, it is nothing more than the ability to raise prices above marginal costs (or to lower output below the competitive equilibrium).[125] This is the technical definition of *market* power, which is how mainstream economists conceive power.[126] What our upstream anxieties reveal, however, is a strain in our conceptual toolkit.[127] Yet, not everything about platform power is novel and mysterious. Its relevant forms are, in fact, generally known and/or have been encountered by antitrust decision-makers in the past. Digitization has simply provided them with new breeding grounds, as explained below.

3.1.1 Market power
To begin, there is the traditional 'market prices/output control' species mentioned above. Because of historical path dependence, aided by the rise of the consumer welfare paradigm, antitrust's attention has overwhelmingly been on the market power enjoyed by sellers.[128] But, as we saw in Chapter 3, monopsony—the ability to withhold purchases (to squeeze suppliers)—and bargaining power *sensu*

---

[122] Lawrence Sullivan and Warren Grimes, *The Law of Antitrust: An Integrated Handbook* (2nd edn, Thomson West 2006) 3.

[123] Margrethe Vestager, 'Digital Power at the Service of Humanity' (Speech delivered at the Conference on Competition and Digitisation, 29 November 2019) <http://bit.ly/3aKiehT> accessed 18 November 2022.

[124] Robert Dahl, 'The Concept of Power' [1957] Behavioral Science 201, 201.

[125] See eg Richard Posner and William Landes, 'Market Power in Antitrust Cases' [1980] Harvard Law Review 937, 939; Hovenkamp (n 23) 95.

[126] See eg Jeffrey Perloff, *Microeconomics* (6th edn, Addison-Wesley 2012) 364.

[127] See, similarly and for an insightful study, Ioannis Lianos and Bruno Carballa-Smichowski, 'A Coat of Many Colours—New Concepts and Metrics of Economic Power in Competition Law and Economics' [2022] Journal of Competition Law & Economics 795.

[128] Sullivan and Grimes (n 122) 75.

stricto—the ability to extract favourable conditions from sellers (without being able to withhold purchases)—are both well established, although under-scrutinized, in mainstream economics and antitrust practice,[129] and relevant. Amazon's highly publicized tussles with book publishers are cases in point.

These forms of market power, moreover, can be wielded by labour platforms like Uber. The challenge here is more acute. Labour market power—the employer's ability to suppress wages[130]—may well be the mirror image of buyer-side product market power.[131] But antitrust has to a significant extent forfeited its protective function to labour law.[132] This means we currently do not even have the tools to measure it.

Still, insofar as they can be shown to exist, refocusing antitrust towards these more marginalized forms of market power is noncontroversial. Beyond the platform context, it appears to have already gained considerable traction with decision-makers.[133] The same is not true for all remaining forms of platform power.

3.1.2 Relational/relative market power and its outgrowths

One of them is quintessentially *relational* or *relative* and, unlike market power, not structural or enjoyed *erga omnes*. It is the power a platform may wield over a particular provider resulting, in extreme cases, from fortuitous circumstances surrounding their interactions. This is not the non-transitory power a platform may hold against all providers within a precisely defined relevant market—*market* power, proper—which is exogenous to, and precedes the specific conditions of, the interplay between the platform and any given supplier.[134] Instead, we are talking about a purely vertical and situational form of superior bargaining power. It flows from a platform provider's economic dependence on the platform which, prosaically speaking, enables the latter to get what it wants from the former. This situation is reportedly quite pervasive in the platform economy.[135] Nonetheless, its supervision, particularly through antitrust, is likely to remain contentious. As is well known, bargaining power asymmetries have historically been a rather marginal, deeply divisive, and mostly unpopular topic.[136]

---

[129] Think of powerful retailers in grocery industries.

[130] i.e. the ability to lower wages below the marginal revenue product (which is extra revenue the employer gets from hiring an additional worker).

[131] Eric Posner, Glen Weyl and Suresh Naidu, 'Antitrust Remedies for Labor Market Power' [2018] Harvard Law Review 536, 538.

[132] Indeed, employees typically fall outside the personal scope of antitrust as they do not have the autonomy required to qualify as economic undertakings.

[133] Eduardo Frade and Vinicius Marques de Carvalho, 'New Approaches to Cartel Enforcement and Spillover Effects in Brazil: Exchange of Information, Hub and Spoke Agreements, Algorithms, and Anti-Poaching Agreements' (*Competition Policy International*, 26 November 2019) <https://perma.cc/6DNW-HKBC> accessed 18 November 2022.

[134] I borrow the conceptually useful distinction between 'situational' and 'structural' monopolies made by Michael Trebilcock, *The Limits of Freedom of Contract* (Harvard UP 1993) 93–95.

[135] See Appendix D.

[136] Liyang Hou, 'Superior Bargaining Power: The Good, the Bad and the Ugly' [2019] Asia Pacific Law Review 39, 47.

Moving on, our next two types of platform power are outgrowths of superior bargaining power.

First, there is 'gatekeeper' (or gateway or bottleneck) power.[137] We came across it in Chapter 3, which remarked that platforms will frequently have the ability and incentive to milk their dependent providers even when they are not monopolists. As economists have shown, where a multi-sided platform deals with single-homing consumers on one side and multi-homing suppliers on the other side, the platform has little incentive to prioritize the latter's interests.[138] In such a scenario, providers are stuck with that particular platform if they want to access its consumers.

Bottleneck power, however, is specific neither to *digital* platforms,[139] nor to *multi-sided* ones.[140] It is not even novel to antitrust decision-makers for that matter.[141] To date, though, it usually has not been explicitly tackled without market power and outside the merger policy context.[142]

The second offshoot is a variation of gatekeeper/gateway/bottleneck power, which is no different in substance. It may be dubbed 'infomediation' power to reflect the fact that some information platforms can effectively be gatekeepers without being legally bound to suppliers in a way recognized under private law. This is notably the case of search engines like Google Search whose relationship with content providers may be commercial in a factual and economic sense despite the absence of a binding contract.[143] Given their functional equivalence, it might be simpler to conflate gatekeeping and infomediation power into a single concept of 'intermediary' power.[144]

3.1.3 Ecosystem power

Relational market power and its outgrowth are essentially about relationships of dependency. In the platform context, these may be further exacerbated when the platform enjoys what is denoted here as 'ecosystem' power. This is the power

---

[137] Not to be confused with the 'gatekeepers' targeted by the EU's Digital Markets Act, which seems to address a broader form of power I denote as 'systemic' power.

[138] See Chapter 3 (n 32). See also Mark Armstrong, 'Competition in Two-Sided Markets' [2006] RAND Journal of Economics 668, 677ff.

[139] Think of newspapers or a shopping mall.

[140] Think of supermarkets.

[141] Gatekeeping/bottleneck power is frequently at the heart of refusal-to-deal cases. Moreover, it has been a concern in retailing industries (see eg FTC, 'Report on the Federal Trade Commission Workshop on Slotting Allowances and Other Marketing Practices in the Grocery Industry' (February 2001) 58 <https://bityl.co/FjFY> accessed 18 November 2022; BKA, 'Summary of the Final Report of the Sector Inquiry into the Food Retail Sector' (2014) 12 <https://bit.ly/3TR2UG4> accessed 19 November 2022).

[142] See eg *Kesko/Tuko* (Case IV/M784) EC Decision 97/277/EC [1997] OJ L110/53, [133]–[135].

[143] This point was noted (somewhat sceptically) by the BKA when it invoked a rarely—though, in the USA, more frequently—used procedure to make a dispositive finding of absence of infringement regarding the scrapping of news publications. See *Google/VG Media* (Case B6-126/14) BKA Decision 8 September 2015, [135]–[139].

[144] Heike Schweitzer and others, 'Modernisierung der Missbrauchsaufsicht für Marktmächtige Unternehmen' (29 August 2018) Report No 66/17, 73–75 <https://bityl.co/FjGH> accessed 18 November 2022.

a platform obtains when it manages to steer and ultimately lock-in consumers and/or providers into an array of (complementary) services that are connected to, and anchored by, a core platform infrastructure. Ironically, ecosystem power will regularly result from, or be reinforced by, an upstream platform power play. The cautionary tale of Sonos offers a good illustration of this pernicious dynamic.

In 2020, the firm accused Amazon and Alphabet/Google of coercing it to access its (allegedly) patented speaker technology with a view to making copycat speakers.[145] The move by the platforms naturally enhanced their respective ecosystem of products centred around core platform infrastructures—Amazon's online marketplace and Alphabet/Google's general search engine. The problem for Sonos? It relies on Alphabet/Google's search advertising services to market its speakers; depends on Amazon's marketplace to sell them; and has integrated both of their respective music services and digital butlers directly into its own products. To make matters worse for Sonos, its employees correspond via Alphabet/Google's emailing service, and it runs its business off Amazon's cloud-computing system.[146]

Now, despite being under-researched,[147] ecosystem power is simply a form of digital conglomeracy. It can probably be explained by supply and demand side factors (i.e. economies of scope enabled by a core platform infrastructure designed with modular and sharable inputs,[148] combined with consumers' desire for consumption synergies arising from the linkage of the platform's various products).[149] But, again, this is not something completely alien to antitrust decision-makers. In the merger policy context, many of them have toyed with it, not without considerable backlash, under the moniker of 'portfolio' power.[150] Some still do,[151] although most jurisdictions have seemingly abandoned the concept.

3.1.4 Regulatory power

Comparably to relational market power, its outgrowths (to a certain extent), and ecosystem power, there is another form of platform power that is not (solely) structural in nature. Regulatory power—the ability to set and fiddle with the rules of the within-platform game—is at the heart of some of the despotic and game-mastering tactics explored in Part II. It is something any platform enjoys, which is why there

---

[145] Jack Nicas and Daisuke Wakabayashi, 'Sonos, Squeezed by the Tech Giants, Sues Google' *New York Times* (7 January 2020) <https://nyti.ms/3atQFJC> accessed 18 November 2022.

[146] ibid.

[147] Jacques Crémer, Yves-Alexandre de Montjoye and Heike Schweitzer, 'Competition Policy for the Digital Era' (2019) 34 <https://bit.ly/3hQynLn> accessed 19 November 2022.

[148] Marc Bourreau and Alexandre de Streel, 'Digital Conglomerates and EU Competition Policy' (March 2019) 7–10 <https://ssrn.com/abstract=3350512> accessed 18 November 2022.

[149] ibid 10–11.

[150] The idea being that power deriving from a portfolio of brands could exceed the sum of its parts. OECD, 'Portfolio Effects in Conglomerate Mergers' (24 January 2002) DAFFE/COMP(2002)5, 5 <https://bit.ly/3XfuLmi> accessed 19 November 2022.

[151] For instance, Brazil (CADE, 'Guide for Horizontal Merger Review' (July 2016) 38–39 <https://bit.ly/3V9U2MV> accessed 19 November 2022).

is nothing inherently problematic about it unless one is steadfastly suspicious of private governance.[152] Remember, regulatory power is pervasive in society. What's more, economists and antitrust decision-makers have, respectively, theorized it (albeit insufficiently) and dealt with it for years. To stress this latter point, recall that sports association and leagues are effectively private regulators. Their restrictions on matters like player movement and eligibility have sometimes attracted the scrutiny of antitrust decision-makers. This is especially so in the EU where they are likened either to public restraints to be grappled with under the free movement rules,[153] or to private governance falling within the scope of antitrust.[154]

3.1.5 Informational power

Another pervasive form of platform power is 'informational'.[155] There are two components to it. One finds its source in a well-known kind of market failure. The other is more platform-specific.

3.1.5.1 Insider's power

The first will be dubbed 'insider's' power. This is essentially the ability to exploit information asymmetries. Self-preferencing and king-making strategies explored in Chapter 4 illustrate how platform providers may be affected by it. Here, the source of informational power lies in a demand and supply market failure on the consumer side of the platform infrastructure. That is, consumers' inability, in many circumstances, to discern whether they are receiving high- or low-quality information;[156] and—assuming even they know better—rival platforms' lack of incentives to provide superior information.[157]

Granted, the market failure is exacerbated by the opacity inherent to how platform infrastructures work. We cannot know for sure whether Google Search or Booking.com, for example, are really ranking providers according to our

---

[152] See eg Zephyr Teachout and Lina Khan, 'Market Structure and Political Law: A Taxonomy of Power' [2014] Duke Journal of Constitutional Law & Public Policy 37, 41ff; Thomas Nachbar, 'The Antitrust Constitution' [2013] Iowa Law Review 57.

[153] See eg Case C-415/93 *Bosman* ECLI:EU:C:1995:463 [1995] ECR I-4921 (rules enabling teams to demand a transfer fee for players on an expiring contract).

[154] See eg Case C-519/04 P *Meca-Medina and Majcen* ECLI:EU:C:2006:492 [2006] ECR I-6991 (anti-doping rules whose breach entailed a four-year ban); Case T-93/18 *ISU* ECLI:EU:T:2020:610 [2020] not yet published (rules hindering athletes from participating in unofficial events). In the USA, such cases have been rarer because these types of rules are collectively bargained and exempted from antitrust scrutiny under the non-statutory labour exemption. One recent example, though, is *National Collegiate Athletic Association v Alston* 141 SCt 2141 (2021) (rules capping student-athlete compensation). For a brief comparative analysis of competition concerns in sports governance, see Ryan Gauthier, 'Competition Law, Free Movement of Players, and Nationality Restrictions' in Michael McCann (ed), *The Oxford Handbook of American Sports Law* (OUP 2018).

[155] Mark Patterson, *Antitrust Law in the New Economy: Google, Yelp, LIBOR, and the Control of Information* (Harvard UP 2017) 69ff.

[156] ibid 80–83; Maurice Stucke and Ariel Ezrachi, 'When Competition Fails to Optimize Quality: A Look at Search Engines' [2017] Yale Journal of Law & Technology 70, 90ff.

[157] Patterson (n 155) 71–80.

preferences as search engine results are determined by algorithms whose workings are beyond us.

This, again, is nevertheless not a platform-exclusive issue. As Frank Pasquale explains, '[b]lack boxes embody a paradox of the so-called information age: [d]ata is becoming staggering in its breadth and depth, yet often the information most important to us is out of our reach, available only to insiders'.[158]

The matter is likewise not new, even for antitrust. Think of the credit rating agencies (CRAs) that still hold sway over our financial markets.[159] Their rating models have little to envy platform infrastructures when it comes to opacity.[160] Notably, CRAs, themselves multi-sided *non-digital* platforms,[161] have long been (allegedly) breaching competition laws by exploiting information asymmetries in strikingly similar ways to our game-mastering platforms. In the mid-1990s, for instance, a school district claimed before the US courts that Moody's—one head of the global CRA duopoly[162]—had unlawfully published a deliberately negative unsolicited rating of the district's bonds issue to punish it for having chosen smaller raters.[163] Plus, we now know that king-making by CRAs was endemic during the 2000s.[164]

Of course, regulation is how societies responded to CRAs' insider's power.[165] But in the early 2010s, some commentators would have had antitrust tame it instead,[166] just as others would recommend using the policy to tackle it today when wielded by platforms.

3.1.5.2 Panoptic power

The second manifestation of informational power ought to be called 'panoptic' power. Unlike other forms of platform power, the latter is *terra incognita* for antitrust. Data-twinking is its most salient manifestation as panoptic power reflects the

---

[158] Frank Pasquale, *The Black Box Society: The Secret Algorithms That Control Money and Information* (Harvard UP 2015) 191.

[159] Incidentally, many have also described them as 'regulators' (Dieter Kerwer, 'Holding Global Regulators Accountable: The Case of Credit Rating Agencies' [2005] Governance 453) or 'gatekeepers' (Deryn Darcy, 'Credit Rating Agencies and the Credit Crisis: How the Issuer Pays Conflict Contributed and What Regulators Might Do about It' [2009] Columbia Business Law Review 605, 608–09).

[160] Andrew Carroll, 'Don't Be Evil—Unless it Increases Revenue: What the Operation of Credit Rating Agencies Can Teach Us about Google' [2012] Temple Journal of Science, Technology and Environmental Law 93, 112–13.

[161] ESMA, 'ESMA's Supervision of Credit Rating Agencies and Trade Repositories: 2015 Annual Report and 2016 Work Plan' (5 February 2015) [163] <https://bit.ly/3UP5z4p> accessed 19 November 2022.

[162] Daniel Cash, *Regulation and the Credit Rating Agencies: Restraining Ancillary Services* (Routledge 2018) 89.

[163] *Jefferson County School District No R-1 v Moody's Investor's Services Inc*, 988 FSupp 1341 (DColo 1997), aff'd, 175 F3d 848 (10th Cir 1999) (complaint dismissed on First Amendment immunity).

[164] Caroll (n 160) 103.

[165] See Cash (n 162) 20–23, chs 4–6.

[166] Nicolas Petit, 'Credit Rating Agencies, the Sovereign Debt Crisis and Competition Law' [2011] European Competition Journal 587, 609–12 (discussing the superiority of antitrust), 612ff (discussing EU antitrust enforcement options).

platform's ability to leverage to its advantage the information it invariably gathers from everyone who uses the platform infrastructure it controls. Identically to regulatory power, its source is positional. It flows from the position of the platform in the exchange space where the latter is, by definition, almost omniscient.[167] Still, there is arguably something more to panoptic power than a merely informational component. We came across it in Chapter 3, which rationalized the consumer-supremacy-oriented governance implemented by platforms like Uber as a form of economic oppression. The theory behind panoptic power might thus be further bolstered by appealing to philosopher-sociologist Michel Foucault.[168] For he defined it as 'continuous individual supervision, in the form of control, punishment, and compensation, and in the form of correction, that is, the moulding and transformation of individuals in terms of certain norms'.[169]

3.1.6 Systemic power

The final form of platform power is one we once more do know of, yet generally ignore. Let us call it 'systemic' power since several platform products have been described as 'socio-economically more or less essential'[170] and 'a key structuring element of today's digital economy'.[171] Upon reflection, Google Search, Facebook, Amazon's marketplace platform, to name a few, arguably do provide services to both consumers and suppliers that are so essential that one might view them as basic infrastructures of our modern societies.[172] Why? Because their underlying economics of production are characterized by scale effects and require a certain degree of economic concentration; because they act as critical enablers of a wide range of economic but also social uses; and because many of us perceive them as basic necessities.[173] Systemic power, therefore, is the ability a platform has to behave relatively unencumbered because the platform infrastructure it offers is so crucial to the well-functioning of our social and economic orders that its failure would create a systemic shock that might undermine them.[174]

---

[167] Platforms do not necessarily enjoy 'perfect information'. Indeed, their view can be gamed or spoofed by those who use its platform infrastructure.

[168] For theoretical insights, see also Lianos and Carballa-Smichowski (n 127).

[169] Michel Foucault, *Power: Essential Works of Foucault, 1954–1984* (James Faubion (ed), The New Press 2001) 70.

[170] Study Group, 'Improvement of Trading Environment Surrounding Digital Platforms' (12 December 2018) Interim Discussion Paper, 3 <https://perma.cc/9CZ4-6ACX> accessed 18 November 2022.

[171] EC, 'Impact Assessment Report Accompanying the Proposal for a Regulation of the European Parliament and of the Council on Contestable and Fair Markets in the Digital Sector (Digital Markets Act)' SWD/2020/363 final, [14].

[172] K Sabeel Rahman, 'The New Utilities: Private Power, Social Infrastructure, and the Revival of the Public Utility Concept' [2018] Cardozo Law Review 1621.

[173] ibid 1641–44.

[174] See, similarly, Marie-Anne Frison-Roche, 'L'Apport de la Notion d'"Entreprise Cruciale" à la Régulation des Plateformes' [2015] Concurrences 1, 5. See also Carl Öhman and Nikita Aggarwal, 'What if Facebook Goes Down? Ethical and Legal Considerations for the Demise of Big Tech' [2020] Internet Policy Review <https://doi.org/10.14763/2020.3.1488> accessed 18 November 2022 (discussing the potentially 'catastrophic social and economic consequences' if Facebook were to disappear).

This form of power can easily be slotted into the antitrust thesaurus of those who share with early twentieth-century progressives the fear of bigness.[175] To be clear, though, it is not premised on corporate size.[176] Indeed, the idea of systemic power borrows from the notion of 'systemic importance', which is now commonplace in banking law. It too became tied to antitrust amidst the Great Recession when so-called too-big-to-fail institutions were marked by some for increased scrutiny.[177]

So, to recap (also in Table 6.1): platform power is protean in nature, but not completely mysterious. Our antitrust decision-makers and their advisers are attuned to this reality.[178] To varying degrees, many of them would give *antitrust* a larger role in policing the different forms it may take.[179] The question, then, is whether the policy can and/or should widen its radar's spectrum and, if so, to what degree. The answer, as argued below, is again a matter of enforcement philosophy.

3.2 Optimal, Reasonable, or Resolute Power Radar?

3.2.1 Optimal radar

Those favouring the optimal approach would readily recognize that platforms make the modern antitrust radar go haywire. Following this approach, however, the solution is not to increase the radar's range. It rather involves tweaking the *market* power antennas currently being short-circuited.

Most would surely agree that structural buyer power signals need to show up, including, and with a growing sense of urgency, in labour markets.[180] Regarding product markets, we have some tools, which are both rarely used and, by some accounts, defective.[181] With regard to labour markets, the circuits are not even in place, notwithstanding promising developments on this front.[182]

Be that as it may, optimality proponents would probably prioritize another issue: properly registering the *seller* market power of *multi-sided* platforms. For

---

[175] See eg Tim Wu, *The Curse of Bigness: Antitrust in the New Gilded Age* (Columbia Global Reports 2018); Adi Ayal, 'The Market for Bigness: Economic Power and Competition Agencies Duty to Curtail it' [2013] Journal of Antitrust Enforcement 221.

[176] For instance, Rahman (n 172) 1670ff would argue that platforms like Uber and Airbnb enjoy systemic power just as Alphabet/Google, Facebook, or Amazon would.

[177] See references in Barak Orbach and Grace Campbell Rebling, 'The Antitrust Curse of Bigness' [2012] Southern California Law Review 605, 653 (n 274).

[178] See Appendix D.

[179] ibid.

[180] See, notably, Eric Posner, *How Antitrust Failed Workers* (OUP 2021) chs 4, 7. See also OECD, 'Competition Concerns in Labour Markets—Background Note' (2019) DAF/COMP(2019)2 <https://bit.ly/3GvhDnm> accessed 19 November 2022.

[181] For instance, Peter Carstensen, *Competition Policy and the Control of Buyer Power: A Global Issue* (Edward Elgar 2017) ch 3. Arguing, by contrast, that current tools are defective because they do not consider both the upstream and downstream markets, see Ignacio Herrera Anchustegui, *Buyer Power in EU Competition Law* (Concurrences 2017) chs 4–5.

[182] See Naidu, Posner and Weyl (n 131) 549ff.

Table 6.1 Platform power

Type of platform power	Source	Expression	Scope of exertion	State of the art
Market power	Market structure	Control over market price/output	Horizontal and vertical	Known
Relative / relational market power	Bargaining power asymmetry	Control over dependent partner	Vertical	Known
Gatekeeper / gateway / bottleneck / infomediary / intermediary power	Market structure + bargaining power asymmetry	Control over dependent partners	Vertical (*erga omnes*)	Known
Ecosystem power	Synergetic linkage between products	Mutually reinforced control over dependent consumers and partners using core platform product and connected products	Horizontal and vertical	Known
Regulatory power	Position in the exchange process + business model	Control over platform infrastructure usage	Vertical	Known
Systemic power	Market structure + capital structure + societal importance	Control over economy/society	Horizontal and vertical	Known
Insider's power	Market failure + opacity	Exploitation of information asymmetries	Horizontal and vertical	Known
Panoptic power	Position in the exchange process + platform infrastructure	'God' view of the platform infrastructure	Horizontal and vertical	Novel

Informational power

Source: author's own creation.

multi-sidedness (alongside data and the zero price point so prevalent on the consumer side) does seem to render the classical 'control over market prices/output' conception of market power somewhat outdated. So much so that some economists have been working hard to make the power radar more responsive to these new dynamics.[183]

The endeavour assuredly has merit.[184] Regrettably, it has mired itself in a set of controversies that have already boiled over in courtrooms.[185] The problem is that these debates are as intractable and reputationally damaging[186] as they are symptomatic of a broader implication of the approach: its obliviousness to (or unwillingness to consider) the potential antitrust relevance of other dimensions of economic power.

Bearing this in mind, what would our other two enforcement options entail?

3.2.2 Reasonable radar

The reasonable approach is not impervious to recommendations of optimality proponents. Yet, it does take issue with the uncritical assumption implicit in them that antitrust cannot do more than inhibit exertions of market power in the technical economic sense. Adhering to such a postulate 'is not only to miss much in the history and development of the law, but to ignore much of its potential'.[187] At the same time, the reasonable power radar is one that is calibrated so as to neither overstate nor misconstrue antitrust's abilities. Briefly looking at the issue of relational/relative market power illustrates this nicely.

As previously noted, superior bargaining power is an unpopular topic, especially in antitrust circles where it is widely perceived as the policy's bastard child. The prevailing animosity towards it was perhaps best captured by Antonin Scalia (the late SCOTUS Justice) when he opined that its inclusion 'transforms [antitrust] from a specialized mechanism for responding to ... economic power to an all-purpose remedy against run-of-the-mill business torts'.[188] This objection does have teeth; antitrust decision-makers are not to be given carte blanche to satisfy their paternalistic or redistributive impulses. Even so, superior bargaining power clearly ought to flash on the policy's power radar, albeit at varying levels of intensity. Consumer

---

[183] See eg Jens-Uwe Franck and Martin Peitz, 'Market Definition and Market Power in the Platform Economy' (May 2019) Centre on Regulation in Europe report <https://bityl.co/FjHx> accessed 18 November 2022. See also Viktoria Robertson, *Competition Law's Innovation Factor: The Relevant Market in Dynamic Contexts in the EU and the US* (Hart 2020) chs 8, 10.

[184] Germany, for instance, amended its competition law to explicitly clarify the relevance of 'zero-price' markets, data, and network effects for antitrust purposes (see Act against Restraints of Competition (ARC), ss 18(2a), (3a)).

[185] For a comprehensive discussion, see Robertson (n 183) ch 8.

[186] Herbert Hovenkamp, 'Platforms and the Rule of Reason: The *American Express* Case' [2019] Columbia Business Law Review 101, 155 (comparing multi-sided market theory to contestable markets theory and predicting a similar fate).

[187] Sullivan (n 46) 1222–23.

[188] *Eastman Kodak Co v Image Technical Services Inc* 504 US 451, 503 (1992) (Scalia dissenting).

welfare, we have seen, can sometimes be harmed.[189] And given that protecting the competitive process (as articulated herein) means safeguarding the economic freedom and EOp of all those who participate in the production of economic value, it would be odd if antitrust did not regularly register superior bargaining power under this paradigm as well.[190] In other words, both sets of goals can be jeopardized at lower levels of economic power than market power proper.

Three difficulties emerge. The first—interfacing antitrust with other policies—is examined in the next chapter. The second is the potential introduction of provider-oriented outcome fairness considerations through the backdoor,[191] a risk which, to my mind, well-designed enforcement standards can mitigate. The third is the absence of robust metrics for identifying superior bargaining power.[192] Fortunately, this challenge has to a certain extent been taken up by competition agencies whose antitrust laws include provisions on superior bargaining power;[193] economists are invited to further bolster their efforts.[194]

More fundamentally, the reasonable approach would take seriously the fact that competition is not simply a horizontal game between substitutable players; it likewise has a vertical dimension on full display in the platform-to-provider context.[195] Beyond recognition, we admittedly need an analytical framework. Here, the value chain tool—essentially a mapping out of different industries and inter-firm relations running through a chain to identify the power dynamics within it[196]—looks

---

[189] See Chapter 3, Section 3.1.2. See, more generally, Patrice Bougette, Oliver Budzinski and Frédéric Marty, 'Exploitative Abuse and Abuse of Economic Dependence: What Can We Learn from an Industrial Organization Approach' [2019] Revue d'économie politique 261, 272–79 (reviewing the IO literature); Lucio Tome Féteira, *The Interplay between European and National Competition Law after Regulation 1/2003: 'United (Should) We Stand?'* (Kluwer Law International 2015) 264–66 (reviewing the evolutionary economics literature).

[190] See, similarly, Bougette, Budzinski and Marty (n 189); Mor Bakhoum, 'Abuse without Dominance in Competition Law: Abuse of Economic Dependence and Its Interface with Abuse of Dominance' in Fabiana Di Porto and Rupprecht Podszun (eds), *Abusive Practices in Competition Law* (Edward Elgar 2018); Albert Foer, 'Abuse of Superior Bargaining Position (ABSP): What Can We Learn from Our Trading Partners' (29 September 2016) AAI Working Paper No 16-02 <https://bityl.co/Fjrd> accessed 19 November 2022.

[191] This is arguably the case in Germany and Japan whose antitrust laws include specific superior bargaining power provisions, which—while ostensibly about protecting competition as such—also display a concern for outcome fairness (see, similarly, Florian Wagner-von Papp, 'Unilateral Conduct by Non-Dominant Firms: A Comparative Reappraisal' in Di Porto and Podszun (n 190)).

[192] Also recognizing this as a challenge, see BRICS Competition Law and Policy Centre, 'Digital Era Competition: A BRICS View' (2019) 333 <https://bit.ly/3EIglnE> accessed 19 November 2022.

[193] For a useful overview, see ibid 333–37.

[194] See Bougette, Budzinski and Marty (n 189) 272ff.

[195] See Chapter 2, Section 2, p 50. See also Case T-604/18 *Google and Alphabet (Google Android)* ECLI:EU:T:2022:541 [2022] not yet published, [116]–[117] ('in a digital "ecosystem", which brings together several categories of supplier, customer and consumer and causes them to interact within a platform, the products or services which form part of the relevant markets that make up that ecosystem may overlap or be connected to each other on the basis of their horizontal or vertical complementarity.... Identifying the conditions of competition relevant to the assessment ... may therefore require multilevel or multi-directional examination').

[196] Kevin Sobel-Read, 'Global Value Chains: A Framework for Analysis' [2014] Transnational Legal Theory 364.

like a worthy candidate. It could at least complement traditional antitrust analysis, which does not look beyond markets comprised of substitutes.[197] Notably, it already has gained significant endorsements.[198]

A reasonable power radar, therefore, is a coherent one. It is both in tune with the (goal(s), principles, and requirements of the) antitrust system of which it is an integral part of, and calibrated with the assistance of formal instruments.

What of our other forms of platform power? Given their positional nature, regulatory and panoptic power should not, as such, trigger antitrust alarm bells. The contrary would render the radar useless—any platform enjoys them—and undermine the idea that the policy is (or should be) business-model agnostic.[199] Where societies display a particular distrust of these forms of power, specific regulation is the solution.[200] Ditto for insider's and systemic power, albeit for slightly different reasons. The former because it flows from a *market failure*;[201] the latter since it is not purely economic in nature.[202] Finally, ecosystem power creates a relatively tricky situation. As explained earlier, its vertical aspects might warrant detection. But if one accepts the very idea of product ecosystems, it would be incoherent to discard *horizontal* competition between different ecosystems from the analysis.[203]

Hence, while attuned to antitrust's potential, the reasonable approach clearly does inhibit frictionless enforcement as it requires a profound, maybe lengthy, certainly controversial, and ultimately uncertain introspection. Stated differently, it deals poorly with urgency, which a more resolute mindset is better equipped to deal with, as illustrated now.

3.2.3 Resolute radar

Resoluteness, one will recall from our discussion on enforcement standards, is about upending the status quo. Policymakers, it bears repeating, are generally aware of platform power's protean nature and some of them have suggested broadening the spectrum of antitrust's radar.[204] (Un)surprisingly (depending on where

---

[197] The endeavour could only be complementary since 'market definition is, at least for now, too big to fail' (Robertson (n 183) 317).

[198] See BRICS Competition Law and Policy Centre (n 192) 343ff; Jason Furman and others, 'Unlocking Digital Competition: Report of the Digital Competition Expert Panel' (March 2019) 114 <https://bityl.co/FjIy> accessed 18 November 2022. See also Bougette, Budzinski and Marty (n 189) 275.

[199] Alfonso Lamadrid de Pablo, 'The Double Duality of Two-Sided Markets' [2015] Competition Law 5, 16.

[200] See further Chapter 7 of this book.

[201] Similarly, see Lina Khan, 'Sources of Tech Platform Power' [2018] Georgetown Law Technology Review 325, 329–31, 333.

[202] See Rahman (n 172); UNCTAD, 'Digital Economy Report 2019: Value Creation and Capture: Implications for Developing Countries' (2019) 140 <https://bityl.co/FjJ6> accessed 18 November 2022.

[203] Daniel Crane, 'Ecosystem Competition and the Antitrust Laws' [2019] Nebraska Law Review 412. For a more general theory, see also Nicolas Petit, *Big Tech and the Digital Economy: The Moligopoly Scenario* (OUP 2020) ch 5.

[204] See Appendix D.

one stands), most seem to deem superfluous any serious conceptual or methodological debate regarding what these adjustments would entail.

For example, whereas many would have antitrust sensitized to superior bargaining power, its offshoots, and/or ecosystem power,[205] rare are those who appreciate that these are inherently vertical, usually non-structural forms of economic power.[206] Yet, we just saw that our current toolbox cannot fully capture the latter and that a conversation on vertical competition is consequently needed.

In Europe, Commissioner Vestager has similarly stated that the competition authority she oversees is in the business of '[c]ontrolling the regulatory power of platforms'.[207] Unbeknown to her, apparently, is the aforementioned paradox such supervision entails.

And in the merits case of *Gibmedia*, the ADLC—much like the first instance judges in *Google Shopping*—even held that quasi-monopoly status, when combined with unrelenting attractiveness in the eyes of consumers and regulatory power, creates a '*very* special responsibility'[208] platforms must be wary of. This is as close as one can get to opening the door, against the letter and spirit of EU antitrust law, to no-fault liability.

Crucially, there is little in the way of hardwiring resoluteness into the antitrust radar. One option is to 'gerrymander the relevant market'[209] by artificially narrowing it down so as to cross whatever power threshold is legally mandated for intervention. This is an old trick enforcers have probably sometimes used to register superior bargaining power.[210] It could similarly be deployed with ecosystem power in mind (which is what some have effectively suggested).[211] In fact, the EU *Google Android* decision arguably foreshadows this.[212] For once a market for *licensable* smart mobile OS was deemed to exist, it almost inevitably followed that Alphabet/Google would be found to be a (quasi-) monopolist for any product directly tied to the core Android 'ecosystem' product, such as app stores.[213]

---

[205] ibid.

[206] For an exception, see BRICS Competition Law and Policy Centre (n 192) ch 4.

[207] Margrethe Vestager 'Building a Positive Digital World' (Speech delivered at the Digital Summit, 29 October 2019) <http://bit.ly/2IvI7pG> accessed 18 November 2022.

[208] *Gibmedia (merits)* (n 106) [342] together with [324]–[331] (emphasis added).

[209] *Little Rock Cardiology Clinic PA v Baptist Health* 591 F3d 591, 599 (8th Cir 2009).

[210] See eg Case C-22/78 *Hugin* ECLI:EU:C:1979:138 [1979] ECR 1869, [5]–[10] (supplier of cash registers found dominant on a market for spare parts of its own products on which independent repairers depended on). For a similar reading, see Louis Vogel, 'Competition Law and Buying Power: The Case for a New Approach in Europe' [1998] European Competition Law Review 4, 5.

[211] See eg Crémer, de Montjoye and Schweitzer (n 147) 48.

[212] *Google Android* (Case AT.40,099) EC Decision 18 July 2018, [218]–[322], upheld in *Google and Alphabet (Google Android)* (n 195) [138]–[254].

[213] For the economist, who sees market definition as an agnostic analytical tool, the EC's reasoning is flawed because it ignores the horizontal competition exerted by Apple (Frédéric Marty and Julien Pillot, 'With Uncertain Damage Theory Come Unpredictable Effects of Remedies: "Libres Propos" on the Android Case' (*CPI Antitrust Chronicle*, December 2018) <https://bit.ly/2Xw2N8I> accessed 18 November 2022).

Granted, jurisdictions are not all equally receptive to this enforcement tactic. Epic Games found out the hard way when it tried to convince a US judge that Apple's App Store was a distinct market where Apple would, by definition, enjoy monopoly power.[214]

That said, another effective avenue is to forego market definition altogether, a practice common in certain jurisdictions.[215] Advocated by some scholars for years,[216] this approach has gained increased salience in the platform context where experts,[217] policymakers,[218] and judges[219] have put their weight behind it. Naturally, if combined with resolute enforcement standards, there would be very little in the way of intervention.

In sum, striving for optimality means updating the power radar by merely tweaking its antennas to make it more responsive to *market* power. Being reasonable, by contrast, counsels a possibly lengthy and uncertain redesign of the radar's transmitter to enable the reflection of *other* power signals. When urgency strikes, some may nevertheless favour a more resolute approach which skips the process. This can be done if one accepts the idea of placing policy (*sensu stricto*) before law. That choice, though, is profoundly ideological and political.[220]

4. What (Sort of) Remedies?

Calibrating antitrust enforcement standards and its power radar to address upstream platform power plays raises difficult questions which are far from trivial. All the same, victims (and, to a certain extent, their abusers) will probably have their eyes on a prima facie more practical matter: remedies.

Decision-makers are routinely criticized for under-appreciating this aspect of the antitrust machinery.[221] The landmark *Google Shopping* saga in Europe definitely makes for a particularly relevant cautionary tale. In 2019—that is, ten years

---

[214] *Epic Games Inc v Apple Inc* 559 FSupp 3d 898, 955–68, 1021–27 (NDCal 2021). Note that based on US antitrust jurisprudence, Epic Games actually does have a case. The first instance judge was dismissive primarily because she confusingly misconstrued Epic Games' claim regarding the core 'ecosystem' product, i.e. the OS (cf ibid 955 with 1015–16). This mistake was noted on appeal but deemed 'harmless' to the conclusion, meaning that Epic Games ultimately failed (*Epic Games Inc v Apple Inc* No 21-16695 (9th Cir 2023)).

[215] The USA is a prime example (provided there is evidence of reduced output) (ibid 1031).

[216] See, notably, Louis Kaplow, 'Why (Ever) Define Markets?' [2010] Harvard Law Review 438.

[217] See eg Crémer, de Montjoye and Schweitzer (n 147) 46.

[218] See eg OECD, 'Rethinking Antitrust Tools for Multi-Sided Platforms' (2018) 13 <https://bit.ly/3Encif3> accessed 19 November 2022.

[219] See eg *Streetmap* (n 61) [42].

[220] See, similarly, José van Dijck, David Nieborg and Thomas Poell, 'Reframing Platform Power' [2019] Internet Policy Review, 2 <https://bit.ly/30vWVhM> accessed 18 November 2022.

[221] See eg William Kovacic, 'Designing Antitrust Remedies for Dominant Firm Misconduct' [1999] Connecticut Law Review 1285, 1286.

after proceedings were initiated; five years on from a mooted settlement which would have entailed far-reaching remedies deemed satisfactory at the time to all but private complainants; and two years after a final decision was adopted— the EC recognized that the solution it ultimately chose was proving ineffective at achieving the desired outcome.[222] Three years later, victims were still up and arms.[223]

The challenge here is to reconcile the imperative of responsible prosecutorial practice—having a clear and convincing remedial strategy before making a final decision[224]—with the realities of the platform economy. As the EU's antitrust enforcer-in-chief observed, 'digital markets change quickly. So by the time we step in, we may find that it's not easy to fix the damage that's been done.'[225] Let us look further.

4.1 The Remedial Toolkit

At a general level, suggesting that our upstream worries may leave antitrust im-potent seems disingenuous. From the simple cease-and-desist obligation (pos-sibly reinforced by fencing in and/or flanking measures) aimed at terminating and/or preventing unlawful behaviour, to (exemplary) damage or disgorgement orders geared towards compensating victims and sanctioning offenders, to more far-reaching, presumably forward-looking, behavioural, and structural meas-ures tailored for restoring competition: decision-makers have at their disposal a highly versatile remedial toolkit which can be implemented through a variety of (adjudicatory and non-adjudicatory) instruments.[226] In a state of emergency, one could therefore envision throwing the proverbial 'kitchen sink' at the identi-fied competition problem.[227] This is certainly what some policymakers and their advisers seem to have had in mind when it comes to platforms (generally) and

---

[222] Greg Sterling, 'European Antitrust Chief Says Google's Auction-Based Shopping Remedy not Working' (*Search Engine Land*, 8 November 2019) <http://bit.ly/38AQRVZ> accessed 18 November 2022.

[223] 'Google Should Remove Shopping Units to End Antitrust Concerns, Rivals Tell EU Commission' *mlex* (17 October 2022) <https://bityl.co/FMoE> accessed 18 November 2022.

[224] Kovacic (n 221) 1310.

[225] Margrethe Vestager, 'Defending Competition in a Digitised World' (Speech delivered at the European Consumer and Competition Day, 4 April 2019) <http://bit.ly/2VXAksl> accessed 18 November 2022.

[226] See, generally, Ioannis Lianos, 'Competition Law Remedies in Europe' in Ioannis Lianos and Damien Geradin (eds), *Handbook on European Competition Law: Enforcement and Procedure* (Edward Elgar 2013) 376ff; A Douglas Melamed, 'Afterword: The Purposes of Antitrust Remedies' [2009] Antitrust Law Journal 359. See also Cyril Ritter, 'Remedies for Breaches of EU Antitrust Law' (17 May 2016) <https://ssrn.com/abstract=2781441> accessed 18 November 2022.

[227] For an exploration of truly radical remedies, see Michal Gal and Nicolas Petit, 'Radical Restorative Remedies for Digital Markets' [2021] Berkeley Technology Law Journal 617.

their upstream exertions (in particular). Sweeping proactive remedies are currently being enacted or under serious consideration.[228] To borrow again from Commissioner Vestager, a (burgeoning) consensus appears to be that:

> Because in today's digital markets, competition can be fragile ... we need to look for imaginative solutions. We need to accept that just fining someone, or ordering them to stop what they're doing, may not be enough to restore competition. And we need to be willing to tell companies, not just to stop breaking the law, but to take positive action to recreate a competitive market.[229]

Such talk comes with its share of practical difficulties. Take data-twinking, for instance. One avenue suggested by some would be to give providers (say, sellers on Amazon's marketplace) access to sensitive data on interactions taking place on the platform infrastructure.[230] Yet, beyond the question of whether this would amount to rubber-stamping the orchestration of an otherwise illegal cartel,[231] implementing such a remedy might be hindered by data protection rules.[232] Another, much more drastic, route would be to require the platform's unbundling.[233] Assuming it was even politically palatable,[234] here the platform context compounds well-known acute upfront practical obstacles.[235] History, moreover, suggests that successful structural separation is predicated on prescriptive and difficult-to-administer behavioural measures, making this path all the more challenging.[236] Hence, a milder remedy like firewalling could be conjured whereby the platform would be prohibited from using data it gleans from its platform infrastructure to inform its strategic

---

[228] See Appendix E; OECD, 'G7 Inventory of New Rules for Digital Markets—OECD Submission to the G7 Joint Competition Policy Makers and Enforcers Summit' (October 2022) <https://bityl.co/FjJi> accessed 18 November 2022.

[229] Vestager (n 123). See also Madero Villarejo (n 22).

[230] See eg Inge Graef, 'Differentiated Treatment in Platform-to-Business Relations: EU Competition Law and Economic Dependence' [2019] Yearbook of European Law 448, 485.

[231] For this argument, see Schweitzer and others (n 144) 115. On the potential incoherence of an antitrust duty to share information under unilateral conduct rules and the resulting invitation to collude prohibited by coordinated conduct rules, see Fabiana Di Porto, 'Abuses of Information and Informational Remedies: Rethinking Exchange of Information Under Competition Law' in Josef Drexl and Fabiana Di Porto (eds), *Competition Law as Regulation* (Edward Elgar 2015) 325ff.

[232] Vikas Kathuria and Jure Globocnik, 'Exclusionary Conduct in Data-Driven Markets: Limitations of Data Sharing Remedy' [2020] Journal of Antitrust Enforcement 511.

[233] Lina Khan, 'The Separation of Platforms and Commerce' [2019] Columbia Law Review 973 (though she views antitrust as inferior to regulation).

[234] On whether platforms like Amazon might be 'too powerful to break up', see David Lynch, 'Big Tech and Amazon: Too Powerful to Break Up?' *Financial Times* (30 October 2017) <https://on.ft.com/39EU5sP> accessed 18 November 2022.

[235] See eg CMA, 'Online Platforms and Digital Advertising: Market Study Final Report' (1 July 2020) Appendix ZA [97ff] <https://bit.ly/3Avd1tA> accessed 19 November 2022 (discussing separation options to address Alphabet/Google's control in adtech markets).

[236] Howard Shelanski and J Gregory Sidak, 'Antitrust Divestiture in Network Industries' [2001] University of Chicago Law Review 1, 36, 80–82.

decisions as a player.[237] Again, pitfalls abound.[238] Depending on which enforcer one asks, some will even reply: 'firewalls are virtually impossible to monitor'.[239]

Trusting that decision-makers will always be creative enough to find practical workarounds, something else ought to intrigue us, though. Indeed, what the emerging consensus entails is a functional inversion within the standard antitrust enforcement model itself: the displacement of competition law as a regulat*ive* instrument, by competition law as regulat*ion*.

Proactive intervention, to be sure, has always been a (touchy) reality,[240] especially in some jurisdictions.[241] But how far can, and should, we go in our attempts to redress competition problems? Differently put, can—and, if so, should—our antitrust decision-makers copy central bankers in declaring that they are 'ready to do whatever it takes'?[242] The answer depends once more on how one chooses to approach the question.

4.2 Optimal, Reasonable, or Resolute Remedies?

4.2.1 Optimal remedies

Remedies are an under-theorized component of the antitrust apparatus.[243] Decision-makers thereby enjoy considerable discretion to fashion them. Those questing for optimal solutions would probably borrow again from decision theory.[244] Accordingly, they would have to be convinced that:

---

[237] See eg Andrei Hagiu, Tat-How The and Julian Wright, 'Should Platforms Be Allowed to Sell on Their Own Marketplaces?' [2022] RAND Journal of Economics 297, 320. See also EC, 'Antitrust: Commission Seeks Feedback on Commitments Offered by Amazon Concerning Marketplace Seller Data and Access to Buy Box and Prime' (14 July 2022) <https://bityl.co/FjK4> accessed 18 November 2022.

[238] A firewall's effectiveness depends on whether the firm (and its staff) behave(s), which in turn depends on whether enforcers can identify and plug loopholes.

[239] EC, 'Remedies in Merger Cases' (2011) DAF/COMP/WP3/WD(2011)59 6 <https://bit.ly/3ghz H9R> accessed 19 November 2022. Similarly, see BKA, 'Guidance on Remedies in Merger Control' (May 2017) [87] <https://bit.ly/3hYodIR> accessed 19 November 2022. cf CMA, 'Merger Remedies' (13 December 2018) [7.24]–[7.26], but see [3.52] <https://bityl.co/FjKC> accessed 18 November 2022.

[240] For categorical rejections, see Lianos (n 226) 435; Gregory Werden, 'Remedies for Exclusionary Conduct Should Protect and Preserve the Competitive Process' [2009] Antitrust Law Journal 65, 75–78. For more nuanced accounts, see Mariateresa Maggiolino, 'The Regulatory Breakthrough of Competition Law: Definitions and Worries' in Drexl and Di Porto (n 231); Adi Ayal, 'Anti-Anti Regulation: The Supplanting of Industry Regulators with Competition Agencies and How Antitrust Suffers as a Result' ibid.

[241] In the USA, the SCOTUS has denounced it (see *Verizon Communications Inc v Law Offices of Curtis V Trinko LLP* 540 US 398, 415 (2004)). In the EU, proactive antitrust has been much more prevalent, especially in regulated industries (see Colomo (n 71) 261).

[242] Mario Draghi, 'Verbatim of the Remarks Made by Mario Draghi' (Speech delivered at the Global Investment Conference, 26 July 2012) <https://bityl.co/FjKO> accessed 18 November 2022.

[243] Spencer Weber Waller, 'The Past, Present, and Future of Monopolization Remedies' [2009] Antitrust Law Journal 11, 11. For an insightful attempt at a theory, see Lianos (n 226).

[244] See eg *Fleet Wholesale Supply Co v Remington Arms Co* 846 F2d 1095, 1097 (7th Cir 1988) ('The court should try to minimize the error costs, the sum of the costs of erroneously granting an injunction (should it turn out that none is warranted) and of denying an injunction (should the plaintiff prevail in the end)').

[T]he expected [benefits of the contemplated remedy] will offset any production cost increases or losses in consumer-side network externalities; that the net gain from such [benefits] will not entail offsetting costs in the form of inefficiently reduced innovation incentives; and that the remaining net gains can then not be achieved at a lower cost through an alternative remedial plan.[245]

Yet, this cannot be done with any sense of accuracy[246] and simply invites antitrust decision-makers to 'resort to their own tried and tested version of peering into a crystal ball'.[247] Striving for optimality thus paves the way for a kind of conservative 'discretionary remedialism'[248] that contrasts sharply with our other two enforcement routes explored below.

4.2.2 Reasonable remedies

The reasonable approach, we have seen, is not oblivious to cost concerns animating those favouring optimal solutions. But its operation is guided primarily by the fact that antitrust is a system of law, which, itself, is part of a broader legal order whose overall coherence is deemed paramount. What does this mean in practice for our inquiry on upstream platform power plays?

- Reasonable remedial discretion is invariably bounded

The ethos of the reasonable approach is aptly captured by an oft-cited US ruling where the presiding judge opined that, having entrusted antitrust decision-makers with powers they have in no other branch of law, society expects such authority will not be ruthlessly exercised to achieve what is sometimes beyond the policy's reach.[249]

Reasonable remedial discretion *ipso facto* hits a conceptual boundary, one defined by the nature of the antitrust proceedings.[250] On the one hand, relief for private claimants ought to be correlatively connected to the wrong(s) they have suffered, reflecting the demand for corrective justice.[251] On the other hand, public enforcers need to be granted whatever remedy follows from the trade-off device used by the decision-maker—in many jurisdictions, this will be (some version of) the

---

[245] Shelanski and Sidak (n 236) 39.
[246] *Fleet Wholesale* (n 244) 1097 ('That inquiry requires the court to consider many factors that cannot be measured precisely').
[247] *Deutsche Telekom AG* (n 7) 187.
[248] i.e. 'discretion to award the "appropriate" or optimal remedy in the circumstances of each individual case rather than being limited to specific (perhaps historically determined) remedies for each category of causative events' (Lianos (n 226) 380).
[249] *United States v United Shoe Mach Corp* 110 FSupp 295, 348 (DMass 1953).
[250] On the 'normative impossibility of discretionary remedialism' in antitrust, see Lianos (n 226) 380ff.
[251] ibid 382–98. See also Areeda and Hovenkamp (n 99) [657a].

proportionality principle. Why? Because their action is guided by the greater good and invariably affects an assortment of (sometimes legally protected) interests.

These precepts are well established in numerous antitrust systems[252] and, under this approach, are not to be waived because of urgency, perceived or proven.[253]

- • Reasonable remedies fit the liability theory

From the above-outlined precepts, it also follows that a reasonable remedy has to map onto the theory of harm giving rise to liability.[254] This is equally well recognized in several jurisdictions[255] where, in the context of public enforcement, it reflects the imperative for legal certainty.[256] The constraint has key implications for our discussion.

Consider the *Navx* decision examined previously, which dealt with the issue of king-making. There, the ADLC did not just order the re-establishment of Navx's suspended account.[257] So too did it enjoin Alphabet/Google to treat all advertisers using its general search platform infrastructure (via the formerly named AdWords service) in an objective, transparent, and non-discriminatory manner. Crucially, the authority recognized this would require:

- ⊳ defining unambiguous terms of service;
- ⊳ clearly informing advertisers (with sufficient notice where appropriate) of the existence of these rules and of their subsequent modifications;
- ⊳ establishing an objective and transparent control and suspension procedure;
- ⊳ ensuring the non-discriminatory application of these rules and procedures.[258]

The question is: does the remedy 'fit' the liability theory? For one, it dispels any lingering doubts on whether consumer welfare (however understood) was ever at stake—such a scheme doesn't make sense unless one intends to restore EOp between advertisers. For another, this is a highly proactive remedy the type of which (under EU competition law at least) is seldom administered for products

---

[252] See Lianos (n 226); Erling Hjelmeng, 'Competition Law Remedies: Striving for Coherence or Finding New Ways?' [2013] Common Market Law Review 1007, 1027.

[253] cf BRICS Competition Law and Policy Centre (n 192) 425–26.

[254] See Lianos (n 226) 433ff; Colomo (n 71) 261, 277; Thomas Barnett, 'Section 2 Remedies: What to Do after Catching the Tiger by the Tail' [2009] Antitrust Law Journal 31, 36; Phillip Areeda, 'Antitrust Violations without Damage Recoveries' [1976] Harvard Law Review 1127, 1127.

[255] See Joined cases C-6 and 7/73 *ICI and Commercial Solvents* ECLI:EU:C:1974:18 [1974] ECR 223, [45] (remedies 'must be applied in relation to the infringement which has been established'); *United States v Microsoft Corp*, 253 F3d 34, 107 (DC Cir 2001) ('we note again that [relief] should be tailored to fit the wrong creating the occasion for the remedy').

[256] See Case C-279/95 P *Langnese-Iglo* ECLI:EU:C:1998:447 [1998] ECR I-5609, [74], [78] (upholding the first instance quashing of an EC remedy that had not been 'applied according to the nature of the infringement found' and connecting this constraint to the principle of legal certainty).

[257] *Navx* (n 105) art 4.

[258] ibid [248] and arts 1–3.

not considered essential facilities.[259] But the agency never meant to demonstrate that Alphabet/Google's platform was 'indispensable' to advertisers. Ergo, one may doubt the reasonableness of such a scheme.[260]

- Reasonable remedies are business model agnostic

A second corollary of bounded remedial discretion, which finds anchorage in multiple jurisdictions as well, is the principle that antitrust 'does not give [decision-makers] *carte blanche* to insist that a monopolist alter its way of doing business whenever some other approach might yield greater competition.'[261] For the public enforcer, this reflects consideration for the defendant's legally protected interests, in particular its economic freedoms and property rights, which 'must remain the rule.'[262] Again, the limitation has considerable ramifications for our upstream platform power plays.

Recall the issue of 'Sherlocking' analysed in Chapter 5. Victims (say, app developers) who fear the 'expropriation' of their ideas by app store operators (like Apple or Alphabet/Google) would probably lobby decision-makers for some form of separation regime and/or line-of-business restrictions. However, this would effectively entail a targeted ban on an otherwise usually legal business move: organic vertical integration.[263]

As the BKA found in its *VG Media* decision, redressing news 'scraping' presents a similar challenge. Unless publishers have an (IP) entitlement to claim compensation for their content, it is hard to describe as reasonable the *antitrust* remedy that forces decision-makers into creating (a mangled) one.[264] Reasonableness, here, would probably mean capping the amount a powerful platform is allowed to scrape.[265]

---

[259] Colomo (n 100) 532.

[260] cf Marie-Anne Frison-Roche, 'Faute de Régulation Efficace, l'Autorité Française de la Concurrence se Substitue à un Régulateur pour Contrôler Google: L'Exemple d'Adwords' (*Journal of Regulation & Compliance*, 2015) <https://bityl.co/FjKY> accessed 18 November 2022 (favouring regulation).

[261] *Trinko* (n 241) 415–16. See also *Google/VG Media* (n 143) [197].

[262] Case T-24/90 *Automec II* ECLI:EU:T:1992:97 [1992] ECR II-2223, [51].

[263] *Google and Alphabet (Google Shopping)* (n 51), [162] (vertical integration is not in itself unlawful). See also *Filtrona v Tabacalera* (Case IV/32,426) EC Decision 26 April 1989. The press release of this unpublished decision states that 'a company's production of its own requirements is not in itself an abnormal act of competition' (EC, 'Commission Decides not to Oppose the Production by Tabacalera of its Own Cigarette Filters' (8 May 1989) <https://bityl.co/FjKe> accessed 18 November 2022).

[264] See *Google/VG Media* (n 143), [195]–[200], [211] ('[A]n obligation to pay a fee or to display a snippet length subject to a fee would only be conceivable under antitrust law if Google were subject to an obligation to enter into a contract which obliged the company to acquire a licence') (free translation). Similarly, see ACCC (n 8) 253 (rejecting the creation of a 'new bespoke access regime' though mainly for practical reasons).

[265] See CMA (n 235) Appendix S, [51]; ACCC (n 8) 231 (implicitly). cf *Google/VG Media* (n 143) [207] (rejecting this remedy).

This is not a task many competition agencies will relish.[266] It may be impossible anyway,[267] which brings me to the next point.

- Reasonable proactive remedies account for unintended consequences

Given the aforementioned constraints, proactive yet reasonable antitrust remedies to remediate upstream platform power plays will not always be available. Take the 'App Store tax' Apple levies on app developers but not on itself when it offers competing apps (say, Apple Music). If the liability theory is framed as an EOp issue under the competitive process approach to antitrust, regulating the tax (i.e. setting the commission level) becomes a difficult proposition, given the risks of misusing antitrust to achieve an objective—stakes fairness—that cannot coherently be pursued under this policy paradigm. However, the most intuitive solution here—a non-discrimination obligation[268]—would either be pointless or disproportionate. Pointless because requiring the platform to tax its own apps amounts to mandating an internal transfer; disproportionate because prohibiting the levy undermines a legitimate business model.[269] Breaking up the platform, then, would arguably be the most effective and befitting course of action in the context of public enforcement.[270] Doing so would restore EOp and serve as a prophylactic on like-effect practices. At the same time, it would imperil much of the firm's social and economic value.[271] This consequence cannot be ignored, which leads us to a final observation.

- Status quo-altering reasonable remedies should be legitimate

Far-reaching behavioural and structural solutions will often establish a new status quo, affecting a variety of interests other than those of the parties to a dispute and those immediately adjacent to it. When ordered by the antitrust decision-maker, competition law stretches beyond its core regulative function to take on a regulatory role. Cost considerations notwithstanding, an issue of input legitimacy thereby arises.[272]

---

[266] One example is the ADLC whose president publicly stated that he 'do[es] not want the authority to become a press supervisor' (Nicholas Hirst, 'Google Copyright Spat with Publishers Shouldn't Lead to Permanent Supervision, France's Coeuré Says' *mlex* (4 May 2022) <https://bityl.co/EDE4> accessed 18 November 2022).

[267] See ACCC (n 8) 231 ('It is not clear … that an optimum or fair snippet length can necessarily be determined').

[268] See for this suggestion JFTC (n 121) 68.

[269] Similarly, see *Epic Games* (n 214) 1009–11, 1039, 1042 (finding that although a specific 30 per cent rate has no basis, Apple is still entitled to *some* compensation).

[270] As noted by Areeda and Hovenkamp (n 99) [653h], it would generally be unwise for compelled breakups to be ordered at the behest of private enforcers because such remedies will generally affect interests extending beyond those immediately involved in the dispute.

[271] See, similarly, Rahman (n 172) 1682.

[272] 'Input' (or 'normative' or 'process') legitimacy relates to how decisions are made and is about whether decisions reflect the 'authentic preferences' of those they affect (Fritz Scharpf, 'Economic Integration, Democracy and the Welfare State' [1997] Journal of European Public Policy 18, 19).

Unlike regulators who, in their rule-making (and sometimes adjudicative) duties, routinely deal with diverse and frequently conflicting sector-wide interests, antitrust decision-makers usually see themselves as adjudicators of disputes whose resolution will produce confined effects. Where the envisioned remedy is proactive and liable to establish a new equilibrium, reasonable antitrust should, accordingly, borrow from regulation the legitimacy-building mechanisms the latter ought to be deploying to ensure all potentially affected interests are properly accounted for.[273]

Hence, what is the takeaway from the foregoing points? It is, again, that reasonableness undeniably does impede—significantly in some respects—our antitrust decision-makers' ability to tackle upstream effects of platform power plays. This reality does not mean intervention is not to even be contemplated.[274] As Douglas Melamed puts it, '[t]he law wisely does not refrain from prosecuting murder cases just because it cannot resurrect the corpse'.[275] Enforcement cannot always restore competition, but it may have a hand in preventing and deterring bad behaviour while enabling (some) follow-on compensation for victims. Nevertheless, there is no denying that antitrust's immediate potency will sometimes be quite limited as a result, in particular where interim relief is sought.[276] Faith in the policy's output legitimacy might ultimately be threatened.[277] When the stakes are high, can and should we ramp up our resolve?

4.2.3 Resolute remedies

A recurring theme in our inquiry so far has been that when a sense of urgency prevails, a resolute approach to enforcement may be warranted. Now, as it concerns upstream platform power plays, some decision-makers (and their advisers) would resort to other policy levers rather than push antitrust down the path of remedial resoluteness.[278] Yet, those who favour the latter option, even as a fallback or as a complement, can find solace in the fact that it can be implemented, sometimes with surprising ease.

The earlier-mentioned *Navx* decision and its progeny are cases in point, although a favourable institutional background maybe contributed to the ADLC's

---

[273] Ioannis Lianos, 'The Principle of Effectiveness, Competition Law Remedies and the Limits of Adjudication' in Philip Lowe, Mel Marquis and Giorgio Monti (eds), *European Competition Law Annual 2013* (Hart 2016). The 'ought' phraseology is appropriate because regulators apparently do not always put their best efforts into engaging with stakeholders (see CMA, 'Regulation and Competition: A Review of the Evidence' (January 2020) [1.33], [7.11] <https://bityl.co/FjKn> accessed 18 November 2022).

[274] cf Barnett (n 254) 31, 33; Shelanski and Sidak (n 236) 1, 1–2.

[275] Melamed (n 226) 366.

[276] See eg Case T-184/01 R *IMS Health* ECLI:EU:T:2001:200 [2001] ECR II-2349, [25] (suggesting that proactive interim remedies which would alter the status quo are likely inappropriate).

[277] Unlike input legitimacy mentioned at (n 272), 'output' (or 'outcome') legitimacy pertains to the consequences of decisions and is about whether the latter are subjectively perceived as achieving their objectives (JHH Weiler, 'In the Face of Crisis: Input Legitimacy, Output Legitimacy and the Political Messianism of European Integration' [2012] Journal of European Integration 825, 826–28).

[278] See Appendices A, E.

success there. It does seem plausible that jurisdictions more reliant on private enforcement will be more wary of preserving antitrust's coherence than of achieving a desired policy outcome.[279] A pattern of curial deference could, likewise, feed into remedial resoluteness. In other words, had *Navx* and co. been litigated elsewhere, remedies might not have been as far-reaching. Chances are they wouldn't have been across the Atlantic if the landmark *Microsoft* precedent is anything to go by.[280]

Even so, remedial resoluteness can also be subtly deployed. Consider the EC's handling of Alphabet/Google in *Google Shopping*. Having found the platform's self-preferencing to be unlawful, the authority ordered it to cease and desist and thereby restore EOp within Google Search between the firm's own comparison-shopping service and those of rivals. Why is this a marker of resolve?—cease and desist, after all, epitomizes conventional, reactive antitrust. The answer lies in what the order implies. To comply, Alphabet/Google *necessarily* has to tinker with the platform infrastructure by changing how search results are ranked or how they are displayed. If this is technically infeasible or deemed ineffective, divestiture and the behavioural prescriptions that will inevitably chaperone it are the lone, coherent way forward. So, while formally reactive in nature, the imposed remedy invariably entails (unspecified) proactive duties. More subtly still, the EC appears to have relied on the formally reactive nature of the envisioned solution to partly justify the resolute legal test against which Alphabet/Google's behaviour was assessed. How so? Well, if one accepts the premise that, under current EU law, proactive enforcement against a monopolist implies that the latter holds an 'essential facility' of sorts,[281] then the enforcer should have established this. It did not. Actually, the EC explicitly refuted the requirement in part because the remedy it was considering merely involved a cease-and-desist obligation.[282]

In brief, resolute decision-makers can sometimes 'kill two birds with one stone'. That is, evade the critique of discretionary remedialism while altering the expected standards of intervention by formally covering proactive enforcement in its more traditional reactive attire.[283]

Remedial resoluteness, though, is not limited to deploying substantive antitrust principles creatively and/or strategically. Another one of its markers involves leveraging procedural traits of the antitrust system that enable its 'hybridization'.[284]

More specifically, public enforcers in many jurisdictions can double down on non-adjudicatory instruments to potentially achieve more than they otherwise could. Recall the EU *Google Shopping* case again. Initially, proceedings were

---

[279] See, similarly, Colomo (n 15) 337.
[280] *United States v Microsoft Corp* 253 F3d 34, 101–103 (DC Cir 2001) (lambasting the District Court's laconic reasoning and procedural shortcutting).
[281] See (n 101).
[282] *Google Search (Shopping)* (n 51) [651].
[283] See, similarly, Colomo (n 100) 532.
[284] Niamh Dunne, *Competition Law and Economic Regulation: Making and Managing Markets* (CUP 2015) chs 2, 5, discusses the full scope of hybridization.

engaged through a negotiated route. And, at the time, some observers opined that the concessions the EC had obtained from Alphabet/Google exceeded what it would have been able to achieve in a traditional adjudicatory setting.[285] That the EU executive chose to run a similar script with its Amazon data-twinking probe therefore makes sense. Indeed, in 2022, it bargained with the platform on a commitments package—essentially a fast-tracking of some regulatory duties enshrined in the freshly adopted Digital Markets Act (DMA)[286]—whilst candidly acknowledging that its ambition here was to 'transform Amazon's business model as a marketplace and retailer'.[287] The future will tell how things ultimately pan out.

In the meantime, enforcers around the globe will presumably monitor closely developments in the UK where the CMA has been using a different, more expansive, procedural device—market investigations—to deal with platform provider grievances like those levelled by advertisers and publishers, as well as app providers against Meta/Facebook, Alphabet/Google, and Apple.[288] A feature of only a handful of jurisdictions, market investigations are particularly appealing since they allow redress where unlawful behaviour cannot be established but the market is found to be failing nonetheless.[289] Although the CMA has voiced a preference for regulation, the door on antitrust enforcement has been kept open, paving the way for far-reaching proactive remedies.[290] To witness competition agencies elsewhere lobbying for such a tool in the future would hence not be surprising.[291] In fact, the EC had envisioned doing just that before pushing for a regulatory agenda instead.[292]

Alternatively (or in combination), resolute jurisdictions can choose to reform their existing competition rules to facilitate remediation by easing the enforcer's burden regarding the establishment of liability. Think of the Tenth Amendment to the German competition statute enacted in 2021: it empowers the BKA to

---

[285] See eg Alfonso Lamadrid de Pablo, 'Preliminary Thoughts on Google's Proposed Commitments' (*Chillin'Competition*, 13 June 2013) <https://bit.ly/3gOGPpe> accessed 18 November 2022; Robert O'Donoghue and Jorge Padilla, *The Law and Economics of Article 102 TFEU* (2nd edn, Hart 2013) 898.

[286] Alba Ribera Martínez, 'An Inverse Analysis of the DMA: Amazon's Proposed Commitments to the European Commission' (*Kluwer Competition Law Blog*, 27 July 2022) <https://bityl.co/ExSt> accessed 18 November 2022. On the DMA, see also Chapter 7 of this book.

[287] Margrethe Vestager, 'Speech by EVP Vestager at the Fordham's 49th Annual Conference on International Antitrust Law and Policy "Antitrust for the Digital Age"' (16 September 2022) <https://bityl.co/FjL2> accessed 18 November 2022. An amended commitment package was made legally binding in December 2022 (see *Amazon Marketplace* (Case AT.40,462) and *Amazon Buy Box* (Case AT.40,703) EC Decision 20 December 2022).

[288] CMA (n 235) ch 5; CMA, 'Mobile Ecosystems: Market Study Final Report' (10 June 2022) ch 6 <https://bityl.co/Exy1> accessed 18 November 2022.

[289] Enterprise Act 2002, s 131(2)(a).

[290] CMA (n 235) chs 9–10; CMA (n 288) chs 8–10.

[291] In September 2022, the German Ministry for Economic Affairs and Climate Change (BMWK) announced a draft bill openly inspired by the UK model (BMWK, 'Bundeswirtschaftsministerium legt Entwurf zur Verschärfung des Wettbewerbsrechts vor' (20 September 2022) <https://bit.ly/3OsDgXh> accessed 19 November 2022).

[292] EC, 'Antitrust: Commission Consults Stakeholders on a Possible New Competition Tool' (2 June 2020) <https://bityl.co/FjLG> accessed 18 November 2022.

designate platforms as holding a uniquely powerful position across several markets and, subsequently, target seven broadly defined practices these firms may have deployed, which are presumed unlawful (barring objective justifications or a successful appeal under an abridged judicial review procedure).[293] Having zeroed in on Alphabet/Google, Meta/Facebook and Amazon within eighteen months of the reform entering into force, the German watchdog definitely wasted no time putting its new powers to use.[294]

Beyond all this, public enforcers can always play the bluffing game, i.e. launch proceedings against powerful platforms and waive the threat of maximum remedies. Success is admittedly far from guaranteed. Still, to discount this enforcement strategy outright is to fumble. Amazon's brief stint in the doghouse of the German and Austrian agencies is a case in point.[295] In 2019, the two authorities teamed up to investigate allegations that the platform's business terms towards Austrian and German merchants were abusive.[296] Within eight months, both probes were closed without the adoption of formal commitment or infringement decisions after Amazon volunteered to modify the contentious terms. Notably, concessions were obtained sans clear liability theory[297] or detailed appraisal of facts.[298] More practically significant: their scope is global (rather than national).

In short, the optimal approach to remedies will generally underwhelm because it is conservative by design. Being reasonable, by contrast, *can* translate into far-reaching intervention, but never more than permitted by the rule of law, which limits decision-makers' remedial discretion by requiring them to be business-model-agnostic and mindful of antitrust's adjudicative setting, its systemic coherence, as well as the unintended consequences of its unthrottled deployment. Relaxing (some of) these constraints enables swifter and, sometimes, more effective remediation. All the same, this resolute attitude treads a thin line between creating a reasonable 'policeman at the elbow effect'[299] and illegitimately

---

[293] For an analysis, see Jens-Uwe Franck and Martin Peitz, 'Digital Platforms and the New 19a Tool in the German Competition Act' [2021] Journal of European Competition Law & Practice 513.

[294] See *Google* (Case B7-61/21) BKA Decision 30 December 2021; *Meta* (Case B6-27/21) BKA Decision 2 May 2022; *Amazon* (Case B2-55/21) BKA Decision 5 July 2022.

[295] See *Amazon* (Case B2-88/18) BKA Decision17 July 2019; *Amazon* BWB Case summary 17 July 2019 <https://perma.cc/FVL2-VWKG> accessed 18 November 2022.

[296] Technically, this was not a 'joint' investigation. Rather, both agencies cooperated closely to investigate what can only be described as claims of oppressive and discriminatory terms.

[297] For instance, the BWB took issue with Amazon's consumer-centric refund policy that only left merchants three days to contest a consumer's potentially abusive refund claim. However, while acknowledging that Amazon's pro-consumer policy should be welcomed, the authority does not substantiate why the platform has an *antitrust* duty to give merchants thirty days to appeal beyond stating the obvious: merchants might otherwise be liable for potentially unjustified costs (see *Amazon* BWB Case summary (n 295) [70]–[78]).

[298] The case summaries in both cases refer to merchant complaints and Amazon's responses to them. They do not contain any findings of facts.

[299] The expression is from Tim Wu, 'Tech Dominance and the Policeman at the Elbow' (26 February 2019) Columbia Public Law Research Paper No 14-623 <https://ssrn.com/abstract=3342598> accessed 18 November 2022.

reshaping market outcomes. The issue will morph into something more conten-tious if countries begin bolstering their antitrust apparatuses with public an-nouncement mechanisms entitling enforcers to effectively name-and-shame firms without demanding formal work beforehand,[300] as is already the case in Japan.[301]

Of course, that tightening our resolve is a viable option to redress upstream con-cerns is probably not so noteworthy. Some antitrust decision-makers can presumably be shown to have consistently displayed resoluteness when faced with exceptional market circumstances or to support other policy levers.[302] Similarly, non-adjudicatory instruments have a proven track record of success, despite being routinely criticized for bypassing reasonable enforcement constraints.[303] What *is* striking, though, is the emerging consensus that remedial resoluteness must become the norm for digital markets. If this is the way forward, we again need to accept that antitrust is to be more policy (*sensu stricto*) than law.

5. Concluding Reflections

Upstream platform power plays present a particularly knotty conundrum for antitrust decision-makers. On the one hand, consensus has it that enforcement is urgently re-quired; on the other hand, operating the antitrust machinery has always involved a series of difficult choices—what (kind of) standards to use? What (form(s) of) power to tame? What (sort of) remedies to impose? All of which are now exacerbated by the problems unfolding today.

Ultimately, these questions really boil down to whether antitrust agencies and courts should be taking a page from the powerful platforms' playbook, which would have them 'move fast and break things'; or whether they ought to be adopting a less disruptive, but also less effective approach. This, we have seen, is a practical, yet pro-foundly cultural, political, and ideological quandary, which, at bottom, reflects the very dilemma of liberal democracy. That is, how do we prevent the bounds of illegit-imate private power from being trespassed without exceeding the limits of legitimate public power?[304]

---

[300] See CMA (n 59) 17–18 (suggesting this and explicitly recognizing it would need protection from defamation liability). Similarly, see French Senate, 'Rapport Fait au Nom de la Commission d'Enquête sur la Souveraineté Numérique—Tome I: Rapport' (1 October 2019) 30 <https://bit.ly/3GuABKF> ac-cessed 19 November 2022 (enjoining the state to 'target the stock price' of super-platforms).

[301] Sachiko Sakamaki, 'Japanese Companies Refusing to Accept Higher Costs from Smaller Trading Partners to Be Named by JFTC' *mlex* (5 October 2022) <https://bityl.co/EwRU> accessed 18 November 2022.

[302] For this, see Colomo (n 15).

[303] See ibid 287–99; Dunne (n 284) 97–119, 279–94.

[304] Giuliano Amato, *Antitrust and the Bounds of Power: The Dilemma of Liberal Democracy in the History of the Market* (Hart 1997) 3.

Antitrust is not, as some would have it, merely 'a tool in the arsenal of economic regulation rather than a law'.[305] And societies that established such provisions will have probably 'made sure that impartiality and the rule of law were deeply ingrained in the way [they] work'.[306] This is what fundamentally drives a reasonable approach to antitrust enforcement, which, accordingly, does 'not allow itself to be influenced so much by current thinking ("Zeitgeist") or ephemeral trends'.[307] Here, the practical relevance of choosing between available antitrust paradigms— 'consumer welfare' or 'competitive process'—becomes apparent. From Part II, we understand that upstream worries can be rationalized as potential competition problems under either approach. With this chapter, we now see how, when directed towards the protection of competition as such, antitrust can do more: adopting rule-based liability tests is more readily justifiable; broadening antitrust's power radar can more easily be defended; and mandating proactive remedies may be more rigorously vindicated. Nevertheless, reasonableness does impose significant limits on antitrust decision-makers. These inevitably affect the policy's ability to deal swiftly with competition problems, especially those that generate concerns (mainly) unrelated to competition.

Alternative enforcement approaches do exist. The practical feasibility and desirability of one of them—optimal enforcement—appears somewhat doubtful, though. The other—resolute enforcement—is possible, perhaps (more) likely in systems heavily reliant on public enforcers and/or where decision-makers concurrently hold antitrust and regulatory duties.[308] Compellingly, this approach does make competition law more potent in alleviating our upstream anxieties. But there is a price: antitrust, partly severed of its legal essence.

This, mind you, isn't *necessarily* a bad thing. Indeed, '[a]t its best, policy represents thoughtful judgement, an exercise in high politics drawing upon both sentiment and analysis and seeking politically balanced methods of dealing with consequential issues'.[309] That being said, judging which enforcement approach to (dis)favour might also be informed by one's understanding of how market supervision ought to be executed. Let us therefore entertain this topic from here on out.

---

[305] Giovanna Massarotto, *Antitrust Settlements: How a Simple Agreement Can Drive the Economy* (Wolters Kluwer 2019) 210.

[306] Margrethe Vestager, 'Competition and the Rule of Law' (Speech delivered at the European Association of Judges, 10 May 2019) <https://bit.ly/2xo55MQ> accessed 18 November 2022.

[307] Case C-23/14 *Post Danmark II* ECLI:EU:C:2015:343 [2015] electronic Reports of Cases, Opinion of AG Kokott, [4].

[308] See Dunne (n 284) 86, 266ff. Interestingly, both competition and digital policy portfolios have been entrusted to the same commissioner in the EU for the 2019–24 term.

[309] Lawrence Sullivan, 'Monopolization: Corporate Strategy, the IBM Cases, and the Transformation of the Law' [1982] Texas Law Review 587, 589.

7

Antitrust's Interplays

1. Introduction

Antitrust, we just saw, is a powerful and flexible tool whose ability to effectively deal with upstream platform power plays will vary according to the chosen enforcement approach. So far, our focus has been squarely on the policy's internal machinery. In this chapter, the blinders are off as antitrust is but one of several potentially relevant levers of public action.[1]

Naturally, despite mounting evidence of upstream-oriented misconduct, questions about whether intervention is at all needed will always be raised. For one, the state might be an inferior problem-solver to the market. For another, maybe all things digital enhance the curative virtues of markets.[2] Although powerful arguments can be levelled against this pro-market/anti-state narrative,[3] this is not the place for such a debate. For present purposes, a bias in favour of intervention is adopted simply because momentum has shifted decisively in this direction over the past few years.

The more interesting question, ergo, is: what role for antitrust? In response, a simple argument will be offered: enforcing antitrust to redress our upstream worries is not necessarily an apt prescription, especially if reasonable constraints on decision-makers are bypassed or weakened; yet, that does not mean antitrust has no role to play whatsoever.

To this end, starting with a brief mapping exercise is apropos. Existing laws effectuating market supervision have obvious complementarities, sometimes overlaps, and specificities which must be properly interfaced (Section 2). It is then shown that deference in antitrust decision-making need not be equated to abdication. Rather, it may constitute a marker of respect and, occasionally, boldness (Section 3). Finally, in some instances, neither antitrust enforcement nor deference are becoming. At that point, the course of action does not have to be either

---

[1] See, similarly, Jason Furman and others, 'Unlocking Digital Competition: Report of the Digital Competition Expert Panel' (March 2019) [1.164] <https://bityl.co/FjIy> accessed 18 November 2022.
[2] On the potential role of blockchain technology for instance, see Christian Catalini and Catherine Tucker, 'Antitrust and Costless Verification: An Optimistic and a Pessimistic View of the Implications of Blockchain Technology' [2019] Antitrust Law Journal 861.
[3] For a discussion, see Jonathan Baker, *The Antitrust Paradigm: Restoring a Competitive Economy* (Harvard UP 2019) 82–95.

Antitrust and Upstream Platform Power Plays. A. K. von Moltke, Oxford University Press. © A. K. von Moltke 2023.
DOI: 10.1093/oso/9780192873057.003.0008

exclusively market-driven or skippered solely by the state, nor should antitrust decision-makers necessarily stay mum (Section 4).

2. Market Supervision and the Interfacing Question

Law is about values and is thus 'deeply and thoroughly political',[4] albeit not in an idiosyncratically personal or partisan way. With this premise, it becomes apparent that market supervision laws can display a certain degree of complementarity and even overlap.

Take self-preferencing and king-making, examined in Chapter 4. As we saw there, these practices may be of concern to antitrust because they can affect consumer welfare, either:

- o *directly* (if one assumes the policy aims to protect *strong* consumer surplus or consumer sovereignty) as consumers may end up with less choice or because their ability to make effective decisions might be compromised; or
- o *indirectly* (if the alternative competitive process paradigm is endorsed) since, having had their right to equality of opportunity (EOp) compromised, (some) suppliers may be foreclosed or have lower incentives to innovate.

But self-preferencing and king-making could equally unnerve the consumer protection law decision-maker whose primary mission is to secure consumer welfare by ensuring that consumers' subjective ability to choose remains unimpaired. Potential complementarity and even overlap resultingly arise if consumer sovereignty is taken as antitrust's lodestar.

Similarly, think of 'coercive' contractual practices (as theorized in Chapter 3) that may be expressions of superior bargaining power. These might trouble antitrust decision-makers, especially those guided by the protection of competition as such (and hence the economic freedom of providers). However, they could likewise unsettle the contract law judge as orthodoxy in the latter's field has it that these are 'the laws of freedom'.[5] There is again scope for overlap.

Accordingly: how do we interface antitrust with other market supervision levers? Dealing with this question is necessary since some would argue that self-preferencing and king-making are matters of consumer protection law, which specifically targets misleading behaviour.[6] Plus, others would direct our coercion fears

---

[4] Ronald Dworkin, *A Matter of Principle* (Harvard UP 1985) 146.
[5] Charles Fried, *Contract as Promise: A Theory of Contractual Obligation* (Harvard UP 1981) 132.
[6] Heike Schweitzer, Thomas Fetzer and Martin Peitz, 'Digitale Plattformen: Bausteine für einen künftigen Ordnungsrahmen' (29 May 2016) ZEW Discussion Paper No 16-042, 10–12, 32 <https://bityl.co/FjLg> accessed 18 November 2022.

to contract law doctrines of economic duress known to many civil and common law jurisdictions.[7]

One option, in this regard, is to effectively deny the existence of an interfacing issue. If these policy levers are all about market supervision, why not leave it at that, conceptually conflate them within this broader category, and cumulate them in practice where appropriate.[8] Aside from probably making the legally non-trivial matter of double jeopardy more prevalent, such a move could lead to solipsistic antitrust enforcement. To wit, intervention without consideration for, and, therefore, to the potential detriment of, trade-offs achieved within other fields of law. News scraping, we shall see shortly, is a case in point.

The problem of antitrust solipsism (or 'imperialism')[9] becomes acute if, while accepting the interfacing conundrum, one views competition law as 'the "repair service" for sectors in need'.[10] The reason is that this position paves the way for the misuse of antitrust to achieve objectives (that should be) alien to the policy, something which is (or ought to be) legally curbed in most liberal democracies.[11]

At the other extreme, a third stance effectively immunizes from antitrust conduct already covered by another legal area of supervision whose goal(s) may not even necessarily overlap. Yet, this approach—based on the assumption that antitrust enforcement will be often too costly, inconsistent, mistaken, otiose,[12] and/or of little added value[13]—appears more reflective of laissez-faire ideology than empirically grounded analysis.

A more reasonable mindset, then, would be to accept a residual, gap-filling role for antitrust insofar as intervention can be properly rationalized.[14] Put differently,

---

[7] On this, see Pinar Akman 'The Relationship between Economic Duress and Abuse of a Dominant Position' [2014] Lloyd's Maritime and Commercial Law Quarterly 99.

[8] See eg Reto Hilty, *Law Against Unfair Competition: Towards a New Paradigm in Europe* (Springer 2007) 50 (arguing that doing so 'helps circumnavigating futile delimitation attempts').

[9] David Bailey, 'The New Frontiers of Article 102 TFEU: Antitrust Imperialism or Judicious Intervention' [2018] Journal of Antitrust Enforcement 25.

[10] Rupprecht Podszun, 'Can Competition Law Repair Patent Law and Administrative Procedures? *AstraZeneca*' [2014] Common Market Law Review 281, 294.

[11] In the EU, for instance, misuse of power is a specific ground for annulling EC decisions (see TFEU, art 263). Annulment follows when 'it appears, on the basis of objective, relevant and consistent evidence, to have been taken with the exclusive or main purpose of achieving an end other than that stated' (Case C-225/17 P *Islamic Republic of Iran Shipping Lines a.o.* ECLI:EU:C:2019:82 [2019] electronic Reports of Cases, [115]). In my view, there is also misuse of power if an EC antitrust decision properly rationalizes the competition problem but then imposes a remedy serving a different end (see, similarly, Case C-477/10 P *Agrofert Holding* ECLI:EU:C:2011:817 [2011] electronic Reports of Cases, Opinion of AG Cruz Villalón, fn 16).

[12] See *Credit Suisse Securities (USA) LLC v Billing* 551 US 264, 265–66 (2007) (interpreting US securities regulation as precluding antitrust enforcement against efforts by investment banks underwriting an IPO to collect potentially excessive commissions).

[13] See *Verizon Communications Inc v Law Offices of Curtis V Trinko LLP* 540 US 398, 399–400 (2004) (rejecting antitrust enforcement against an incumbent local exchange carrier accused of denying interconnection services to rivals).

[14] See, similarly, Jacques Crémer, Yves-Alexandre de Montjoye and Heike Schweitzer, 'Competition Policy for the Digital Era' (2019) 5, 63–65 <https://bit.ly/3hQynLn> accessed 19 November 2022); Mark Patterson, *Antitrust Law in the New Economy: Google, Yelp, LIBOR, and the Control of Information* (Harvard UP 2017) ch 1.

problematic practices that cannot be effectively redressed by other policy levers can be handled through competition law *provided* they are genuine competition problems which can be enforced. And to ward off misuse concerns, the better view would be to countenance such policy excursions only where, in addition, they do not *actively* pursue non-antitrust objectives and/or undermine (or conflict with) those other areas of law.

3. Deferential Antitrust: Between Respect and Boldness

In dealing with upstream platform power plays, proper interfacing will inevitably sometimes require deference from antitrust decision-makers to the choices made by those responsible for other policy levers. In some instances, this may just be a necessary marker of respect (Section 3.1). In others, deference can actually signal boldness (Section 3.2).

3.1 Deference as Respect

Consider the specific matter of news scraping which, as explained in Chapter 5, is particularly difficult to rigorously rationalize as a competition problem. From a consumer welfare perspective, there is an intuitive innovation theory of harm that is not (and probably cannot currently be) formalized. Under the competitive process paradigm, by contrast, we can make a rigorous EOp case. Enforcement, though, would come close to accepting the empirically refutable (and plausibly undesirable) idea that economic competition is (or ought to be) a *desert*-based process. To repeat, the *main* (if not lone) issue with news scraping is that it offends our sense of *outcome* (in particular, stakes) *fairness* towards *publishers*. This is something antitrust cannot reasonably (be misused to) achieve directly.

So, assuming that the plight of publishers is socially troubling, how do we address it?

If a free-riding problem does exist, the most obvious solution is property.[15] One option would hence be to trust IP law's ability to incrementally correct its own perceived defects. Recall that news scraping is virtually inseparable from the act of hyperlinking; copyright courts could thereby try to refine their case law on the right to communicate protected works to the public to strike a better balance between preserving the internet as a vector of free speech and the interests of publishers.[16]

---

[15] See eg Jonathan Barnett, 'The Costs of Free: Commoditization, Bundling and Concentration' [2018] Journal of Institutional Economics 1097.

[16] For a useful US–EU comparative analysis on hyperlinking and copyright law, see Jane Ginsburg and Alain Strowel, 'Copyright Liability for Hyperlinking' in Tanya Aplin (ed), *Research Handbook on Intellectual Property and Digital Technologies* (Edward Elgar 2020).

We have the possibility for democratic reform as well where existing copyright laws reach their limits. In this regard, by endowing press publishers with new (neighbouring) rights covering their press publications on explicitly redistributive grounds, the EU has laid the groundwork other societies may choose to follow or, better still, improve upon if they share similar anxieties over outcome fairness.[17]

Granted, antitrust enforcement will always be opportune for some.[18] Copyright, it has already been argued, is simply not redistributive enough since 'the issue is not whether Google and Facebook should compensate news publishers for displaying parts of their content on the platform (they should), but whether they should also compensate them for the enormous indirect value they bring to these platforms'.[19]

Such advocacy is undeniably laudable. It likewise underscores a concern which is no longer about scraping but pertains to the perceived unfairness of the platforms' business models as such. More fundamentally, the claim displays precisely the type of solipsistic attitude copyright lawyers have long railed against.[20]

To me, societal choices are paramount. IP is not simply property. In liberal democracies it represents democratic regulation *for* economic competition through the establishment of entitlements that determine both its objects and organization.[21] Crucially, outcome fairness can and is woven into the very fabric of IP, whether IP lawyers like it or not.[22] Competition, in turn, is the process that diffuses value generated by market players across the economy.[23] And antitrust serves to ensure its

---

[17] Directive (EU) 2019/790 of the European Parliament and of the Council of 17 April 2019 on Copyright and Related Rights in the Digital Single Market and Amending Directives 96/9/EC and 2001/29/EC [2019] OJ L130/92. In effect, platforms—not just the most powerful ones—have to take out licences whenever they display press publications within their respective platform infrastructures, including snippets of a certain length. For a comprehensive analysis, see Maria-Daphne Papadopoulou and Evanthia-Maria Moustaka, 'Copyright and the Press Publishers Right on the Internet: Evolutions and Perspectives' in Tatiana-Eleni Synodinou and others (eds), *EU Internet Law in the Digital Era: Regulation and Enforcement* (Springer 2020).

[18] See eg Damien Geradin, 'Complements and/or Substitutes? The Competitive Dynamics Between News Publishers and Digital Platforms and What It Means for Competition Policy' (2019) TILEC Discussion Paper No 2019-003 <https://ssrn.com/abstract=3338941> accessed 18 November 2022.

[19] ibid.

[20] See eg Robin Jacob, *IP and Other Things: A Collection of Essays and Speeches* (Hart 2005) ch 19. Tangentially, note that a rare consensus among IP lawyers holds that (i) digitization—not free-riding platforms—is the driver behind declining press publisher revenues, and that (ii) publishers shouldn't be endowed with additional property rights because they already are sufficiently protected (see, inter alia, 'Academics against Press Publishers' Right: 169 European Academics warn against it' (2018) <https://bit.ly/3hWXvjK> accessed 19 November 2022).

[21] Hanns Ullrich, 'Intellectual Property, Access to Information and Antitrust: Harmony, Disharmony, and International Harmonization' in Rochelle Dreyfuss, Diane Zimmerman and Harry First (eds), *Expanding the Boundaries of Intellectual Property: Innovation Policy for the Knowledge Society* (OUP 2001) 372–74.

[22] Under most accounts, property and fairness are incompatible. However, Robert Merges, *Justifying Intellectual Property* (Harvard UP 2011), makes the powerful argument that 'fairness considerations not only surround or transcend individual property rights; they are also built into the structure of individual property rights'. As he explains, distributional nuggets—for instance, limitations and the 'fair use' doctrine in EU and US copyright law, respectively—can be found at all levels of an IP regime and 'go a long way toward justifying IP institutions as a whole'.

[23] Similarly, see Ullrich (n 21) 378 ('Competition is to determine the economic yield of the system').

proper operation. Therein lies the policy's sole function. Competition law is not 'a device to fine-tune markets via top-down planning',[24] nor is it there to correct perceived defects in the political process.[25]

In short, news scraping requires antitrust deference because, as Justice Brandeis would have said:

[T]aking and gainful use of a product of another which, for reasons of public policy, the law has refused to endow with the attributes of property, does not become unlawful because the product happens to have been taken from a [vertical or horizontal] rival and is used in competition with him.[26]

Deferential antitrust is likewise desirable as other options for redress do exist. Unfair competition law looks particularly apt where doctrines of misappropriation still have some bite.[27] Continental Europe, for instance, seems especially apropos since investment, *as such*, 'is in certain national legal systems or, at any rate, in terms of case law, regarded as a subject matter worthy of protection'.[28] Take France, where the Paris Commercial Tribunal condemned an OTA for scraping the website of a well-known budget airline of its flights-related data to sell tickets at a markup.[29] Why? Because the practice (apparently) deprived the latter of its opportunity to recoup its investments by selling complementary products (like hotel and rental car booking services) on its own website.[30]

Another avenue worth considering is one several antitrust authorities have endorsed. It involves legislatively requiring certain platforms to implement a code of conduct governing their relations with providers, including press publishers.[31] More on this shortly.

Finally, if societies value things like quality journalism, they could choose to assist publishers either through public grants, and/or tax breaks, and/or fiscally incentivized philanthropy.[32]

---

[24] Pablo Ibáñez Colomo, 'Restrictions on Innovation in EU Competition Law' [2016] European Law Review 201, 217.

[25] Herbert Hovenkamp, *The Antitrust Enterprise: Principle and Execution* (Harvard UP 2005) 254.

[26] *INS* 248 US 215, 258 (1918) (Brandeis dissenting).

[27] Admittedly, there is little judicial appetite in the USA (Adam Tragone, 'Defining the Press Clause: The End of Hot News and the Attempt to Save Traditional Media' [2016] Chicago-Kent Journal of Intellectual Property 237).

[28] Hilty (n 8) 20. See also Ansgar Ohly, 'The Freedom of Imitation and Its Limits—A European Perspective' [2010] International Review of Intellectual Property and Competition Law 506 (exploring the European legal landscape).

[29] *Voyages sur Mesures and LMnext FR v Ryanair* (RG 2013031969) Paris Commercial Court Judgement 20 March 2018, upheld in *Voyages sur Mesures and LMnext FR v Ryanair* (Case No 18/07621) Paris Court of Appeal Judgement 11 May 2022.

[30] ibid 9–10.

[31] See CMA, 'Online Platforms and Digital Advertising: Market Study Final Report' (1 July 2020) [7.76] and app S <https://bit.ly/3Avd1tA> accessed 19 November 2022; ACCC, 'Digital Platforms Inquiry: Final Report' (June 2019) 255–57 <http://bit.ly/3TKrNmY> accessed 19 November 2022.

[32] See ACCC (n 31) ch 6.9. See also Maurice Stucke and Allen Grunes, 'Why More Antitrust Immunity for the Media Is a Bad Idea' [2011] Northwestern University Law Review 1399, 1416.

Do the preceding arguments entail foreclosing antitrust decision-makers from the discussion altogether? Certainly not. With regard to the news sector in particular, public enforcers can promote joint ventures for testing new approaches to monetizing content by applying more relaxed enforcement standards.[33] Ironically for publishers, the powerful platforms they routinely vilify probably are part of the solution.[34] Furthermore, where new regulatory ventures are considered, competition issues—and hence antitrust decision-makers—have to be included in debates.[35] Lastly, when confronted with upstream platform power plays that chiefly offend non-antitrust values, antitrust agencies and courts can evaluate the merits of being boldly deferential, which is what I now turn to.

3.2 Deference as Boldness

Deference on the part of the antitrust decision-maker can be a marker of boldness when non-enforcement simultaneously fits within the selected antitrust paradigm and indirectly furthers the aim(s) of another policy lever. To understand this, one needs to appreciate again the practical relevance of choosing between available antitrust paradigms. Otherwise, deference (or non-enforcement) would often rightly be construed as the grant of an unwarranted immunity, which, for public enforcers, can be just as sinful as erroneous intervention.[36]

Recall that bargaining power imbalances favouring platforms appear to be a key driver of alleged upstream abuses. Distributive effects of these power plays might be mitigated if suppliers somehow managed to coalesce. Press publishers, for example, clearly think so as they routinely lobby to have agreements between them exempted from antitrust liability, sometimes successfully.[37] Bargaining power asymmetries, of course, ought to flash on the radar of reasonable consumer welfare-minded antitrust decision-makers.[38] Yet, even where market power is at play, the latter may not see the problem; battle-tested static models surely are better than speculative intuitions on innovation. Moreover, complicated game-theoretic studies might mislead them when available. Under the consumer welfare paradigm,

---

[33] See Stucke and Grunes (n 32) 1415.

[34] Patricia Nilsson, 'Google to Invest Millions in UK News Group' *Financial Times* (19 September 2019) <https://on.ft.com/2PEdGkJ> accessed 18 November 2022.

[35] See Section 4 of this chapter.

[36] See eg TFEU, art 265.

[37] In 2017, Germany amended its competition law to his effect (see ARC, s 30). At EU level, the EC notified its intention to exempt a resale-price-maintenance agreement covering newspapers sold in Belgium in *Agence et Messageries de la Presse* (Case IV/31,609) EC Notice [1987] OJ C164/2. In the USA, the Newspaper Preservation Act of 1970 provided a partial antitrust exemption which press publishers would have society expand in the platform age (OECD, 'News Media and Digital Platforms—Note by the United States' (3 December 2021) DAF/COMP/WD(2021)72 <https://bit.ly/3V3EI4I> accessed 19 November 2022).

[38] See Chapter 6, Section 3.2.2.

there is thus little cause for permitting what would otherwise be frowned upon—a cartel—to remedy a competition problem reasonable decision-makers will have troubles formally rationalizing and/or enforcing.

The (in)famous *e-books* conspiracy mentioned in Chapter 3 is a particularly apt illustration of the point. Publishers assuredly did have an Amazon-size counter-vailing bargaining power reason for enlisting the support of Apple to raise the re-tail price of e-books. For US trustbusters, though, pressing forward would have been akin to making a rod for their own backs. As one commentator puts it:

> While Amazon's substantial market share and relentless demands for concessions made it impossible to rule out future effects, their likelihood was not great enough to warrant a conspiracy that imposed immediate and substantial price increases on consumers. In the e-books case, in short, Amazon's buyer power did not justify collusion.[39]

Still, does adopting the competitive process paradigm, which is sensitive to wor-ries over providers' economic freedom, mean endorsing a bonfire of antitrust ex-emptions? The answer has to be negative for two reasons.

One: although jurisdictions known to have historically embraced this alterna-tive approach (such as the EU) do absolve (*ex ante* or *ex post*) some anticompetitive agreements, these immunities are really quite limited in number and may owe more to political capture and/or genuine social fears than to any serious pledge to competi-tion as such.[40] Besides, a comparative analysis with countries long committed to con-sumer welfare (such as the USA and Australia) would probably reveal that deferential antitrust is both more prevalent[41] and just as unrelated to competition.[42]

Two: protecting competition as such, to repeat, should not imply disregarding en-tirely its outcomes. The competitive process paradigm *assumes* that, by preserving an adequate balance between economic power and freedom on the market, desir-able results will ensue, notably by way of lower prices, greater output, higher quality, more diversity, and increased innovation. But if a cartel—itself a restriction of the

---

[39] John Kirkwood, 'Collusion to Control a Powerful Customer: Amazon, E-Books, and Antitrust Policy' [2014] University of Miami Law Review 1, 51.

[40] See eg TFEU, arts 39–42 for the agricultural sector, discussed by KJ Cseres, ' "Acceptable" Cartels at the Crossroads of EU Competition Law and the Common Agricultural Policy: A Legal Inquiry into the Political, Economic, and Social Dimensions of (Strengthening Farmers') Bargaining Power' [2020] Antitrust Bulletin 401.

[41] The USA contains a long list of federal immunities (i) granted by government or courts under the *Noerr–Pennington* doctrine, or (ii) explicitly or implicitly provided in federal regulation. Added to this are the numerous exemptions granted by states under the *Parker* doctrine (see, generally, ABA Section of Antitrust Law, *Federal Statutory Exemptions from Antitrust Law* (American Bar Association 2007)). In Australia, a 'class exemption' to be granted by the ACCC has been available since 3 June 2021 and provides cover for many agreements (ACCC, 'Collective Bargaining Class Exemption' (2021) <https://bityl.co/E11x> accessed 18 November 2022).

[42] The consensus among US commentators is that most antitrust immunities are the result of polit-ical capture (see Stucke and Grunes (n 32) 1402).

cartelists' freedom—created to offset the superior bargaining power of a platform is shown to (likely) do nothing more than shift rents, then there is no reason for antitrust decision-makers to defer. If an immunity is truly justified in such a case, society should establish it through a political decision that reflects a conscious and deliberate sacrifice of competition on the altar of outcome fairness.

So, in practice, would the reasonable antitrust decision-maker, guided by the competitive process imperative, have deferred in the above-mentioned *e-books* case? Not if, as some have convincingly argued, the conspiracy could not deliver credible benefits.[43] Situations where deferential antitrust will constitute a warranted act of boldness do exist, however.

Consider the plight of labour platform 'partners'. In Chapter 3, it was contended that a theory of oppression could explain the potential competition problem in powerful platforms hardwiring within their respective infrastructures various institutional constraints on providers/workers that systematically 'sovereignize' the interests of consumers/employers. Unfortunately, pursuant to what was argued in Chapter 6, reasonable antitrust *enforcement* will be stymied by difficulties in establishing a structured legal test, which, it bears repeating, wards off arbitrariness. What's more, devising a suitable remedy would prove devilishly complex. To stick with the liability theory, one would have to compel the labour platform to return to labourers part of their autonomy regarding, for instance, price-setting or job selection. Such a solution would put the reasonable antitrust decision-maker in uncomfortable regulatory shoes.[44] This is where deference comes into play.

Now, why would turning a blind eye to unions of labour platform providers/workers reflect boldness and not capture? The answer flows from what this section suggested at the outset.

First, there is a (potential) competition problem—oppression—to which deferential, competitive process-minded, antitrust provides a fix (i.e. the 'fit' condition). Importantly, collective bargaining by these individuals would probably not create the same sure-fire negative effects, as would that of, say, independent physicians. Unionization by the latter is not to be blithely waved through as some have argued.[45] Why? Because it can demonstrably be predicted to impede economic efficiency and inflate healthcare costs without necessarily improving (and perhaps even diminishing) its quality and access to it.[46] By contrast, immunizing collective action by labour platform providers/workers is more likely to make labour markets

---

[43] Christopher Sagers, *United States v. Apple: Competition in America* (Harvard UP 2019); Kirkwood (n 39).

[44] Interestingly, Uber tested these solutions in California where it suffered several legal setbacks on the labour law front. It stopped soon after when consumers started cancelling en masse (see Rachel Sandler, 'Uber Won't Let California Drivers Set Their Own Prices Anymore After Rider Cancellations Increased 117%' (*Forbes*, 8 April 2021) <https://bit.ly/3SzZyHE> accessed 18 November 2022).

[45] See eg Sandeep Vaheesan, 'Accommodating Capital and Policing Labor: Antitrust in the Two Gilded Ages' [2019] Maryland Law Review 766, 809ff.

[46] William Brewbaker III, 'Will Physician Unions Improve Health System Performance?' [2002] Journal of Health Politics, Policy and Law 575.

more efficient[47] and 'help companies respond to demographic and technological change.'[48] Doing so definitely would generate some upward pricing pressure and/or output reductions on the product market. Nevertheless, that impact would likely be no greater than what antitrust laws around the world already condone today when functionally equivalent employees are concerned.[49]

Second, there is a regulatory failure here: labour lawyers recognize that platforms have disrupted their field. As one judge put it, determining whether labour platform providers are independent/self-employed contractors unprotected by labour laws, or instead employees falling within their protective scope, is often like being 'handed a square peg and asked to choose between two round holes'.[50] In a striking parallel to antitrust, some scholars have even been debating whether labour law's normative foundations need to be reconceptualized as a result.[51] The dilemma is that the right response under this policy lever remains unclear.[52]

Without compromising its internal coherence, antitrust can therefore (temporarily and imperfectly) fill the regulatory vacuum by being boldly deferential when confronted with a coalition of labour platform providers/workers. In truth, this is a necessary step since labour and competition laws are currently set up as antagonistic, rather than complementary, policy levers.[53] Several options could accordingly be contemplated.

One involves narrowing antitrust's personal scope that today catches all economic undertakings. How? Maybe by relying on a functional approach, which leverages the idea of false self-employment and/or economic dependence;[54] or by devising a new antitrust concept of 'worker' decoupled from labour law.[55]

---

[47] OECD, *OECD Employment Outlook 2019: The Future of Work* (OECD Publishing 2019) 206–07.

[48] ibid 194.

[49] See, similarly, Marina Lao, 'Workers in the "Gig" Economy: The Case for Extending the Antitrust Labor Exemption' [2018] University of California Davis Law Review 1543, 1572.

[50] *Cotter v Lyft Inc* 60 FSupp 3d 1067, 1081 (NDCal 2015).

[51] See the special edition of the *International Journal of Comparative Labour Law and Industrial Relations* [2017] 331.

[52] Some argue that a new category of workers with more limited rights than employees should be recognized under labour law (see eg Matthew Taylor and others, 'Good Work: The Taylor Review of Modern Working Practices' (2017) 35 <https://bit.ly/3GvGmYD> accessed 19 November 2022). Others claim the legal tests for employment relations needs to be updated, either by tweaking the employee-centric tests (see eg Miriam Cherry, 'Beyond Misclassification: The Digital Transformation of Work' [2016] Comparative Labor Law & Policy Journal 577) or by shifting to an employer-focused perspective (see Jeremias Prassl and Martin Risak, 'Uber, Taskrabbit and Co: Platforms as Employers? Rethinking the Legal Analysis of Crowdwork' [2016] Comparative Labor Law & Policy Journal 619). A minority would rely on market-based solutions (see eg Martin Malin, 'Protecting Platform Workers in the Gig Economy: Look to the FTC [2018] Indiana Law Review 377).

[53] Ioannis Lianos, Nicola Countouris and Valerio De Stefano, 'Re-thinking the Competition Law/Labour Law Interaction: Promoting a Fairer Labour Market' [2019] European Labour Law Journal 291, 307, 331.

[54] In Europe, this is already positive law. At EU level, the ECJ developed a multifactorial test to be applied on a case-by-case basis whereby a sufficiently dependent contractor has to be viewed as an employee immunized from antitrust liability (see Case C-413/13 *FNV Kunsten* ECLI:EU:C:2014:2411 [2014] electronic Reports of Cases). In Ireland, the legislator enshrined a collective bargaining antitrust exemption for a defined category of 'false self-employed workers' (see Competition (Amendment) Act 2017).

[55] See Lianos, Countouris and De Stefano (n 53) 291, 310–22. Note that their third option—using a social dumping rationale—is not about competition as such even if it does reflect a genuine social concern.

Alternatively, antitrust's material reach could be tinkered with, possibly by broadening the range of justifications for prima facie illegal activities or, indirectly, by narrowing down the scope of antitrust proscriptions. For legal certainty's sake, one could enshrine this in legislation (such as a block exemption regulation in the EU) or in a soft law instrument (such as public enforcer guidelines).

These options can even be combined. In fact, a template for such a move already exists: Europe. In 2022, the EC indeed approved guidelines meant to clarify its interpretation of the EU antitrust rules when 'solo self-employed persons' collectively try to improve their working conditions.[56] In so doing, the authority de facto narrowed the law's personal and material scope by, respectively, (i) assimilating certain independent contractors—platform labourers, in particular—to 'workers', and by (ii) signalling that collective agreements concluded by other self-employed individuals will not be prosecuted in certain cases of clear bargaining power imbalances. Importantly, the move was both circumscribed—principles and useful examples are provided—and unambiguously motivated, first, by (a 'left-leaning' vision of) competition, with unmistakeable considerations for outcome fairness lurking in the background.[57]

The foregoing notwithstanding, it bears repeating that bold deference will not always be possible. As noted earlier, those steered by consumer welfare will regularly have a justifiably hard time seeing platform provider coalitions as anything other than plain vanilla cartels, even when labour is involved. The FTC and DoJ's joint torpedoing of the city of Seattle's attempt to grant collective bargaining rights to Uber drivers in the mid-2010s is another case in point.[58] Here, this time in litigation initiated by a private enforcer, the federal antitrust agencies teamed up to argue that the move unlawfully sanctioned a per se antitrust violation.[59]

Furthermore, there will be instances where, irrespective of which paradigm the antitrust decision-maker is committed to, neither enforcement against a powerful platform, nor deference towards a countervailing collective effort of victimized providers, are reasonable prescriptions. When antitrust reaches its limits, though, the answer is not necessarily (only) the market. Sometimes, we (also) need regulation.

---

[56] EC, 'Communication from the Commission—Guidelines on the Application of EU Competition Law to Collective Agreements Regarding the Working Conditions of Solo Self-Employed Persons' [2022] OJ C374/2.

[57] See ibid [4] and the examples provided in ss 2–3 therein.

[58] Brief for the United States and the Federal Trade Commission as Amici Curiae in Support of Appellant and in Favor of Reversal, *Chamber of Commerce and Rasier v City of Seattle et al*, 2017 WL 5166667 (CA9).

[59] Marshall Steinbaum, 'The Feds Side against Alt-Labor' (Roosevelt Institute, 16 November 2017) <https://bit.ly/3djVOWN> accessed 25 August 2022. As noted earlier (Chapter 3, Section 4.3.2, p 102), the FTC has since disavowed the consumer welfare paradigm. Notably, in a footnote (!) of a policy statement released in September 2022, the FTC rebuked the position it had taken in the *City of Seattle* case, signalling that it would refrain from 'enforcement or policy efforts that might undermine the ability of gig workers to organize' (see FTC, 'FTC Policy Statement on Enforcement Related to Gig Work' (15 September 2022) n 65 <https://perma.cc/ZPR3-XN3R> accessed 18 November 2022).

4. Regulation

4.1 The Need for Regulation

Upstream platform power plays, it was shown, can prove difficult to redress effectively through antitrust, especially when reasonably enforced. Other policy levers will sometimes have to be activated. And where the latter fail, the befitting response might well be new regulation. This option should be seriously considered if the identified upstream anxieties are (mainly) about redirecting wealth towards suppliers. Ditto when they pertain to systemic, regulatory, panoptic, and/or informational power, as such. These issues, as others have explained, 'comprise the substantive, inescapable core of regulation'.[60] Two additional reasons further bolster this conclusion.

First, the type of remedies touted for effective redress. Recall that these range from far-reaching behavioural obligations (such as non-discrimination and transparency requirements, forced interoperability and data-sharing obligations, and even extensive duties of care) to platform unbundling.

Second, historical precedents where decision-makers were pitted against similarly problematic 'foes', most notably telecommunications operators. To illustrate, in the EU, a telco market may warrant regulatory intervention when it displays stubbornly high market concentration and entry barriers that antitrust alone cannot sufficiently address.[61] Across the Atlantic, regulatory ventures against telcos have likewise been premised on the fact that these operators wield 'gatekeeper' power.[62]

Granted, to speak of platform regulation was until recently somewhat taboo. Conventional wisdom, after all, has it that the regulatory enterprise is inefficient, corrupt, captured, or enacted with the best of intentions but impossible to get right in practice.[63] Regulation, however, is 'no[t] some form of chemotherapy for the body politic'.[64] It is simply another policy lever 'by which we simultaneously express the values of our society and the mechanism by which we seek to achieve real-world outcomes consistent with those values'.[65]

This does not mean objections to regulation are meritless. While difficult to test empirically, those grounded in public choice (i.e. private interest) theory (which

---

[60] Niamh Dunne, *Competition Law and Economic Regulation: Making and Managing Markets* (CUP 2015) 174. See also Stephen Weatherill, 'The Challenge of Better Regulation' in Stephen Weatherill (ed), *Better Regulation* (Hart 2007) 5 (regulation 'is not simply a matter of curing market failure [but is also] devoted to dealing with the consequences of the operation of markets—and, in particular, to curtailing what may be seen as excessive successes accruing to some participants').

[61] See Directive (EU) 2018/1972 of the European Parliament and of the Council of 11 December 2018 Establishing the European Electronic Communications Code [2018] OJ L321/36, art 67(1).

[62] See eg *Protecting and Promoting the Open Internet* 30 FCC Rcd 5601 (2015), [20].

[63] For a discussion, see Dunne (n 60) ch 3.

[64] Harold Feld, 'The Case for the Digital Platform Act: Market Structure and Regulation of Digital Platforms' (Roosevelt Institute, May 2019) 15 <https://bit.ly/30iwQ4j>accessed 19 November 2022.

[65] ibid.

claims decision-makers are unable, or have little incentive, to serve the public good) are not inherently misguided.[66] Other complaints reflecting discontent with past regulatory mishaps may be justified too.[67] Still, to elevate both gripes from caution to dogma is to replace careful analysis with plain cynicism or to draw the wrong lessons from history. What is required, then, is regulatory innovation.

4.2 What Regulation?

Time, it seems, is of the essence when it comes to platforms. If so, our traditional 'command-and-control' way of conceiving regulation has to change. Here again, decision-makers are in a bind. On the one hand, there is pressure to act fast; on the other hand, platforms are atypical regulatory targets,[68] operating in markets regulation has typically struggled with.[69] Moreover, double-information asymmetry disadvantages—adverse selection and moral hazard—that saddle any regulatory venture are exacerbated, thereby magnifying the risk of failure.[70] To top things off, conventional-style regulation generally means protracted processes resulting in rigid rules,[71] which, to make matters worse, have been found to be associated with a broadly negative impact on competition.[72]

With this in mind, what is the becoming regulatory approach for those upstream worries (reasonable) antitrust cannot (sufficiently) remediate by itself?

Self-regulation—for years, the default—hardly seems appropriate anymore, although some jurisdictions may maintain their faith in it. For instance, South Korea surprisingly pivoted in this direction in the summer of 2022 when the government announced that it would favour resolving upstream concerns in the platform economy through dispute mediation, voluntary guidelines, and/or contract templates.[73] Similarly, in India, the CCI concluded its 2020 study into e-commerce

---

[66] CMA, 'Regulation and Competition: A Review of the Evidence' (January 2020) [3.10] <https://bityl.co/FjKn> accessed 18 November 2022, finds that there is 'some evidence in the available literature to support the private interest theories of regulation to a greater extent than public interest theories'.

[67] Christine Wilson and Keith Klovers, 'The Growing Nostalgia for Past Regulatory Misadventures and the Risk of Repeating These Mistakes with Big Tech' [2020] Journal of Antitrust Enforcement 10 (discussing the failures of twentieth-century US railroad and airline regulations).

[68] Indeed, typical regulation is either sector-specific or issue-specific. Platforms are business models that cut across sectors and touch upon a variety of issues.

[69] For instance, telco markets—which are both similarly fast-moving and exhibit 'natural monopoly-like' features (including network effects)—have notoriously bedevilled regulatory ventures on both sides of the Atlantic.

[70] Jean Tirole, *Economics for the Common Good* (Steven Rendall tr, Princeton UP 2017) 457 ('The company has better knowledge of the environment in which it is operating: its technology, its supply costs, the demand for its products, and its services (adverse selection). Its actions also affect cost and demand through the management of human resources, strategic decisions about production capacities, R&D, brand image, quality control, and risk management (moral hazard)') (footnote omitted).

[71] See, similarly, CMA (n 31) [7.67].

[72] See CMA (n 66) [4.61] ('greater regulation is—on average—associated with lower competition').

[73] Jenny Lee, 'Comment: The Uncertainty at the Heart of South Korea's Bold Platform Self-Regulation Experiment' *mlex* (1 July 2022) <https://bityl.co/F7PN> accessed 19 November 2022.

marketplace platforms by throwing its weight behind self-regulatory measures geared towards promoting transparency in search rankings, data practices, review/rating mechanisms, revision of contractual terms, and discount policies.[74] This, the agency argued, would better solve the bargaining power imbalances and information asymmetries identified as the crux of the issue.[75]

That said, the EU's landmark DMA[76]—with its vaguely termed ambitions and unclear nature[77] infused in a quite rigid set of asymmetrically applicable positive duties and negative proscriptions, informed by (recent, limited, and controversial) antitrust enforcement practice,[78] crafted so as to leave little room for regulatory variation or experimentation,[79] and without any meaningful escape route for socially desirable conduct[80]—appears to veer too much in the opposite direction despite its good intentions.[81]

To me, given the twin imperatives of speed and effectiveness, the right approach would be less permissive than self-regulation but more incentivizing and flexible than its command-and-control variant. The method—somewhat vaguely

---

[74] CCI, 'Market Study on E-Commerce in India: Key Findings and Observations' (8 January 2020) [113] <https://bityl.co/Fjpq> accessed 19 November 2022.

[75] ibid [112].

[76] Regulation (EU) 2022/1925 of the European Parliament and of the Council of 14 September 2022 on Contestable and Fair Markets in the Digital Sector and Amending Directives (EU) 2019/1937 and (EU) 2020/1828 (Digital Markets Act) [2022] OJ L265/1.

[77] To borrow from Larouche and de Streel, the DMA 'sits in a difficult and perhaps ominous epistemological position [lacking both] . . . reasonably well-articulated policy goals from which concrete implementation measures can be deduced . . . [and the] benefit from experience and practice in individual cases' (Pierre Larouche and Alexandre de Streel, 'The European Digital Markets Act: A Revolution Grounded on Traditions' [2021] Journal of European Competition Law & Practice 542, 548).

[78] In a nutshell, the DMA lays down myriad core obligations to address unfair (data) practices, leveraging behaviours, multi-homing, and switching restrictions, as well opaqueness in digital advertising. Some of these obligations are supposed to be self-executing and are contained in article 5, which can be seen as a 'blacklist'. The others are 'grey-listed' in articles 6 and 7 with the EC being empowered to further specify them. There is also a duty to inform the EC of acquisitions (art 14) and a requirement to submit independently audited descriptions of consumer profiling techniques (art 15). Importantly, all these obligations are 'asymmetric': they are only meant to apply to 'gatekeepers' of 'core platform services' (CPS), i.e. firms that possess (or can be foreseen to enjoy in the near future) an entrenched and durable position in (for now) either online intermediation services, online search, social networking, video-sharing, number-independent interpersonal communications services, operating systems, web browsers, virtual assistants, cloud computing, or online advertising.

[79] Article 8 is admittedly billed as enshrining a regulatory dialogue of sorts. But the provision's drafting seems to envision a very one-sided affair, the outcome of which—should the EC actually choose to engage—will apparently stand insofar as the enforcer does not change its mind down the road.

[80] An exemption from core obligations is only envisaged (in article 10) for public health or public security reasons and at the EC's discretion. There is a suspension clause (laid down in article 9). But it is an extremely narrow one as the gatekeeper must convincingly demonstrate that complying with a specific obligation 'would endanger, due to exceptional circumstances beyond [its] control, the economic viability of its operation in the [EU]'. Again, the EC has full discretion on this. Moreover, gatekeepers will not be able to use compliance with data protection rules to water down their DMA obligations or 'segment, divide, fragment or split' their CPS to evade gatekeeper status altogether (as per the 'anti-circumvention' clause in article 13).

[81] For detailed commentary, see Oliver Budzinski and Juliane Mendelsohn, 'Regulating Big Tech: From Competition Policy to Sector Regulation?' [2023] ORDO (forthcoming).

dubbed by Tirole as 'participative antitrust'[82] but to be understood as referring to regulation—must thus be more collaborative, adaptive, anticipative, and reflexive.

If fair and sustainable *outcomes* for suppliers is something societies want, regulation is needed; regulation, however, that catalyses collective innovation from the market to conduce these desired results, while remaining attuned to its effects on competition. At a high level, participative regulation tries to achieve this by combining two ingredients. One is traditional regulatory 'Lamarckism' with a spin, i.e. prescribing market behaviours to realize defined outcomes but via first-order principles. The other is a hint of 'Darwinism'. In the first instance, platforms and providers are thereby entrusted to negotiate solutions, possibly through a code of conduct. Crucially, though, the setting is overseen by the antitrust decision-maker whose role is twofold: neutralize bargaining power asymmetries among stakeholders; and ensure negotiated correctives stay within limits delineated by the legislature and do not compromise competition.[83]

The result? It cannot be set in stone. Participative regulation might birth something of the likes initially envisioned by the EU to create a fair, transparent, and predictable platform-to-business environment.[84] Therein an attempt was made at taming upstream-facing regulatory, informational, and relative market power through an instrument that combines two sets of restrictions: transparency obligations (similar to, but more extensive than, those recommended by the CCI under a self-regulatory approach) and light-touch duties of care.[85] What is notable is the collaborative backdrop: platforms and suppliers are given the lead, although negotiations are to be monitored and periodically reviewed by the EC.[86]

Of course, this experiment to address upstream concerns that overstretch reasonable antitrust could prove (or be deemed) insufficient. Japan, which has been testing it as well since 2021, will probably find out that goodwill does have its limits.[87] Yet, societies can always choose to push further while remaining within

---

[82] Jean Tirole quote by Allison Schrager, 'A Nobel-Winning Economist's Guide to Taming Tech Monopolies' *Quartz* (27 June 2018) <https://bityl.co/Fjq9> accessed 19 November 2022.
[83] Nicolas Curien, 'Innovation and Regulation Serving the Digital Revolution' (*The Journal of Regulation & Compliance*, 2011) 3–6 <https://bityl.co/FjqL> accessed 19 November 2022; Winston Maxwell, *Smart(er) Internet Regulation through Cost–Benefit Analysis: Measuring Harms to Privacy, Freedom of Expression, and the Internet Ecosystem* (Presses des Mines 2017) 174. See also OECD, 'OECD Principles for Making Internet Policy' (2014) 8–9 <https://bityl.co/FjqT> accessed 19 November 2022.
[84] Regulation (EU) 2019/1150 of the European Parliament and of the Council of 20 June 2019 on Promoting Fairness and Transparency for Business Users of Online Intermediation Services [2019] OJ L186/57 (hereinafter 'P2B Regulation').
[85] For instance, P2B Regulation, art 8 includes obligations geared towards ensuring that P2B contracts are 'conducted in good faith and based on fair dealing'.
[86] See P2B Regulation, arts 16–18.
[87] The Japanese Act on Improvement of Transparency and Fairness in Trading on Specified Digital Platforms is moulded on the aforementioned EU P2B Regulation. At the time of writing, evaluation reports are being drafted with first indications pointing to a bag of mixed results. For details, see Sachiko Sakamaki, 'Digital Platforms in Malls, App Stores to Be Urged by Japanese Minister to Improve Transparency' *mlex* (14 November 2022) <https://bityl.co/Fe8K> accessed 19 November 2022.

this broad regulatory *modus operandi*. This is precisely what some of our anti-trust decision-makers and their advisers seemingly recommended when they advanced regulation as a solution to broader matters of systemic power and outcome fairness-related practices, such as news scraping.[88]

The UK, in this regard, may eventually be the first to concretize such an approach on a large scale. Indeed, a noteworthy feature of its proposed regulatory regime for digital markets is the ability for a specialized institution (the 'Digital Markets Unit') to design and enforce bespoke statutory codes of conduct tailored to specific platforms (namely, those found to possess 'strategic market status').[89] Importantly, requirements under the codes would apparently (i) be principles-based, (ii) involve considerable guidance from the enforcer, (iii) provide exemptions for infringing practices that generate wider countervailing benefits,[90] and, most significantly, (iv) be enforced through a participative approach whereby the regulator is meant to 'engage constructively with all affected parties, resolving issues through advice and informal engagement.'[91]

Critics favouring a more heavy-handed approach will doubtless argue that it plays into powerful platforms' hands.[92] And, to be sure, shortcomings do exist. Even so, doesn't this stance border on empty cynicism? There are only 'imperfect alternatives.'[93] Among them, participative regulation seems particularly fit for purpose. For example, it appears to have proven effective in the UK to address similar outcome fairness considerations in the groceries industry.[94] Plus, if we are to learn something from telco regulation, it is that this more 'maieutic' method can succeed where a command-and-control strategy will struggle. The EU is a case in point. There, national regulatory authorities can saddle powerful telcos with obligations

---

[88] See eg CMA (n 31) ch 7 (esp [7.35]–[7.39]), [8.15]–[8.18]) and apps P, S, U; ACCC (n 31) 253–56. See also Furman and others (n 1) [2.45]; Stigler Center, 'Stigler Committee on Digital Platforms: Final Report' (September 2019) 115–16 <https://bityl.co/Fjqi> accessed 19 November 2022; BRICS Competition Law and Policy Centre, 'Digital Era Competition: A BRICS View' (2019) 456 <https://bit.ly/3EIglnE> accessed 19 November 2022; Study Group, 'Improvement of Trading Environment Surrounding Digital Platforms' (12 December 2018) Interim Discussion Paper, 8 <https://perma.cc/9CZ4-6ACX> accessed 18 November 2022.

[89] See, generally and providing a useful comparison with EU and US initiatives, Thomas Tombal, 'Ensuring Contestability and Fairness in Digital Markets through Regulation: A Comparative Analysis of the EU, UK and US Approaches' [2022] European Competition Journal 468.

[90] The CMA and Ofcom have provided advice on how such a code might work to assist news publishers (CMA and Ofcom, 'Platforms and Content Providers, Including News Publishers—Advice to DCMS on the Application of a Code of Conduct' (November 2021) <https://bityl.co/FjrQ> accessed 19 November 2022).

[91] UK Secretary of State for Digital, Culture, Media & Sport and the Secretary of State for Business, Energy and Industrial Strategy, 'A New Pro-Competition Regime for Digital Markets' (July 2021) [125] <https://bityl.co/FjrV> accessed 19 November 2022.

[92] Alphabet/Google representatives, writing in their personal capacity, have publicly endorsed the approach while trying to poke holes at it to make it more permissive (Oliver Bethell, Gavin Baird and Alexander Waksman, 'Ensuring Innovation through Participative Antitrust' [2020] Journal of Antitrust Enforcement 30, 50ff).

[93] Neil Komesar, *Imperfect Alternatives: Choosing Institutions in Law, Economics, and Public Policy* (University of Chicago Press 1994).

[94] See CMA (n 66) [6.9].

relating to access and interconnection. In France, the regulator—ARCEP—created an interconnection committee where details of the incumbent's interconnection products and reference interconnection offer were debated. Because the committee comprised representatives from the involved stakeholders, ARCEP managed to nudge market players towards a consensus on complex issues like local loop unbundling, something it would have struggled to achieve on its own due to information asymmetries.[95]

5. Concluding Reflections

Powerful platforms seem brazenly settled. Consumers and suppliers, though, appear somewhat content and often dishearteningly short-changed respectively. Upstream platform power plays should therefore prompt private and public antitrust enforcers into action when intervention can be rigorously rationalized. At the end of the day, effective competition is supposed to be unpredictable. So, it has to be out of kilter if powerful platforms always win. Just the same, where decision-makers end up mangling antitrust to achieve (moderately) effective redress, this is perhaps a sign that we need to look elsewhere. Not necessarily to the market, but to other policy levers (as well).

Competition law is not a Swiss Army knife for fixing all problems. 'Bigness', while a catalyst for its development (especially in the USA), is not the central target.[96] Moreover, despite it being undeniably vital to ensuring a sustainable platform economy, outcome fairness for suppliers cannot justifiably be engineered directly through antitrust. If these dogmas no longer reflect reality, we should stop referring to the policy as having anything to do with competition and societies ought to seriously contemplate amending and renaming their respective competition laws.

As observed by Commissioner Vestager, antitrust:

[C]an't deliver all the sustainable results that our society demands. And that's OK. It means we won't build a sustainable world just on the foundation of companies' voluntary actions. But we don't have to—because we also have the power, as a society, to put regulations in place that can make our economy more sustainable. We've done that for many years, of course, when we've found that competition isn't enough to make sure our markets respect our society's values. And this is the way a society should work.[97]

---

[95] Maxwell (n 83) 175.

[96] Barak Orbach and Grace Campbell Rebling, 'The Antitrust Curse of Bigness' [2012] Southern California Law Review 605.

[97] Margrethe Vestager, 'Competition and Sustainability' (Speech delivered at the GCLC Conference on Sustainability and Competition Policy, 24 October 2019) <https://bit.ly/2QIUUJB> accessed 18 November 2022.

Nonetheless, when looking at past regulatory ventures for inspiration, the right lessons must be drawn. One is that some of those regulations that have attracted near-universal scorn—say, the US Interstate Commerce Act—sometimes cannot be seen (only) as costly and/or captured policy mistakes; they probably are (likewise) politically efficient responses to (prevent) 'backlash' in an unfair society.[98] Another insight is that, if these types of traditional regulation—legitimate and well intentioned as they may have been—ultimately failed to deliver and even harmed competition, innovating our regulatory ways by infusing more flexibility is more likely to yield the desired results.[99]

---

[98] Mark Roe, 'Backlash' [1998] Columbia Law Review 217, 229.

[99] CMA (n 66) [4.65] (finding that 'in dynamic markets more flexible forms of regulation can reduce the risk of deterring innovation, and therefore harming competition').

Conclusion

At the outset, this book was billed as an introspection into antitrust. Not just by reason of wayward curiosity, but because developments on the policymaking front impel it. Policymakers and antitrust decision-makers seem to have indeed assumed that upstream platform power plays are competition concerns, concerns for antitrust at that. Yet, anything powerful platforms do triggers 'footballized' debates among antitrust academics nowadays.[1] The full breadth of the issue of 'upstream' effects in the platform economy is, furthermore, something we do not have a clear handle on. More paradoxically, the same fears have been all but written off the policy agenda for the brick-and-mortar economy and the long-standing consensus tenet in the antitrust community that supplier welfare cannot be a lodestar apparently still holds today.

So, what comes out of the exercise? Let us first briefly recap what was uncovered before turning to some final reflections.

1. Taking Stock

The nutshell message is that platform practices which harm platform suppliers (who may themselves be platform operators) are potential competition problems, but antitrust enforcement, far-reaching as it can be, should not be oversold. To rephrase: while antitrust is obviously relevant in the sense that decision-makers have to be unnerved when they see platform providers being victimized, relevance is a question of degree. Prodding the argument further leads to three general claims.

- The battle for antitrust's soul should be waged, but not for conventional reasons

Contrary to what some would have us believe, 'consumer welfare'—antitrust's dominant paradigm for the last few decades—is not *inherently* conducive to upgaze paresis. That contemporary theorists and practitioners have tended to only 'look down' because of their focus on a specific variation of the lodestar—consumer

---

[1] Pablo Ibáñez Colomo, 'Against the Footballisation of Competition Policy: How to Advance the General Interest and Avoid Polarisation' (*Chillin'Competition*, 18 September 2019) <https://bit.ly/33RS IH8> accessed 19 November 2022.

Antitrust and Upstream Platform Power Plays. A. K. von Moltke, Oxford University Press. © A. K. von Moltke 2023.
DOI: 10.1093/oso/9780192873057.003.0009

surplus, reflected in short-run pricing effects—is a reality few would deny today. This, however, is a methodological weakness, not a foundational one. In other words, the critique would be moot if economists were to develop analytical tools decision-makers could use to consistently and robustly predict the long-term consequences of business practices on things like supplier incentives to innovate; or, failing that, if we were to agree that indulging in more speculation is justified.

Nevertheless, those who favour a paradigm shift do have legs to stand on. For one, consumer welfare is a rather beguiling ideal whose different avatars rest on potentially shaky foundations. That antitrust should be guided by 'welfare' (which is to say Pareto or Kaldor–Hicks efficiency) or be grounded in a theory of (distributive or corrective) justice to consumers/customers, is a *normative* issue the community has buried under aspirations of scientific rigour. That economics has given us the means to articulate claims with analytical precision is not a good enough reason to have antitrust aimed at a goal many reasonable minds might find undesirable. Our platform provider anxieties, therefore, exacerbate the evident: we need to openly and thoroughly (re)discuss the normative fulcrums of what we have been doing for the past few decades. All the more so since, for another, the lone other credible lodestar can be seen as a worthy replacement when time is taken to unpack it.

Antitrust, most of us would agree, has to be about 'competition' and cannot pander to suppliers for their own sake. Properly construed, then, the alternative paradigm must (or at least ought to) mean safeguarding the constitutive values of the competitive process: economic freedom and *ex ante* fairness. By design, (platform) providers would have an immediate right to antitrust protection, which is only indirectly forthcoming under the consumer welfare lodestar.

Ultimately, the battle for antitrust's soul is not a fight for the inclusion of upstream considerations per se. It is rather an ethical struggle over why economic competition is worth protecting in liberal societies.

- Upstream platform power plays are potential competition problems, but, as usual, the devil is in the detail

Regardless of the antitrust paradigm one favours, victimized providers do have a case for antitrust enforcement against the powerful platforms they depend on in a variety of situations. In fact, if (informed) intuition is the accepted reasoning benchmark, it will almost always be possible to theorize some form of relevant harm.

Consider each of the three scenarios examined in this book. When can we not argue innovation and/or diversity in the marketplace *might* diminish to the detriment of consumers where powerful platforms exploit providers through their despotic, game-mastering, or free-riding practices? The latter actions aside, can we not always contend that the same behaviours *could* undermine the economic freedom of suppliers or equality of opportunity (EOp) without which the sustainability of competition would be jeopardized?

There is, nonetheless, a consensus imperative for rigour when it comes to rationalizing potential competition problems. Naturally, this complicates things.

From a consumer welfare perspective, difficulties track the technocratic nature of the antitrust enterprise it entails, one almost exclusively driven by economic analysis. What competition lawyers sometimes forget is that '[i]t is unimportant that "there are models" showing anticompetitive effects, the key is whether such models need assumptions that tightly map into the market circumstances of the case'.[2] When it comes to upstream platform power plays (especially those explored in this book), the difficulty is that predictions on consumer welfare implications are not merely ambiguous; they are based on assumptions which:

○ are not always spelled out in ways non-economists can understand (recall our discussion of Alphabet/Google's self-preferencing tactics);
○ often cannot be generalized (as in the case of king-making);
○ are sometimes so finely grained that when competing models exist for a particular situation it becomes virtually impossible to choose the 'correct' one (as illustrated by the tussle between Amazon and book publishers); and
○ can ultimately be denied by empirical findings which may themselves paint an ambiguous picture depending on the setting, as well as the data and methodology used (like our analysis of Sherlocking showed).

Naturally, such complexity is not new.[3] The well-known problems it generates, however, are exacerbated in the context of platforms since research is still playing catch-up. Some less equipped decision-makers—generalist courts and inexperienced and/or under-funded competition agencies—will therefore be more likely than they already are to shun sophisticated, yet potentially more accurate models, in favour of simpler, but inaccurate ones;[4] others may simply follow their (informed) intuition. And those who (think they) are better armed to deal with higher levels of complexity might shift even more attention to making resource-draining, and ultimately value-laden, decisions on the suitability of each model instead of focusing on the legality of impugned practices.[5]

A particularly penetrating example of this point is the SCOTUS' controversial *AmEx* judgment over the despotic behaviour of an autocratic, multi-sided,

---

[2] OECD, 'Rethinking Antitrust Tools for Multi-Sided Platforms' (2018) 27 <https://bit.ly/3Encif3> accessed 19 November 2022.
[3] See, generally, Frédéric Marty, 'La Révolution n'a-t-elle pas eu lieu? De la place de l'analyse économique dans le contentieux concurrentiel de l'UE' in Valérie Giacobbo-Peyronnel and Christophe Verdure (eds), *Contentieux du Droit de la Concurrence de l'Union Européenne: Questions d'Actualité et Perspectives* (Larcier 2017).
[4] ibid 69.
[5] ibid.

non-digital platform.[6] At issue, more specifically, were the rules a payment card operator—American Express—imposed on merchants using its infrastructure. These prevented them from encouraging consumers to use rival credit cards with lower merchant fees (like Visa). Now, economists have explained how such 'anti-steering' rules can generate positive consumer welfare effects when certain assumptions are made.[7] But the facts of *AmEx* did not map onto them. Furthermore, the most probable counterfactual—the 'but-for' world absent those rules—suggested that consumer welfare (however understood) would have improved.[8] The likely effects of the impugned practice, in sum, were negative. The SCOTUS majority overlooked this. Worse, it completely ignored the extensive trial record, which clearly showed that AmEx's behaviour had led to price hikes. Not only for AmEx merchants, but also for those using rival platforms like Discover, as well as for consumers to whom merchants passed on higher fees via inflated product prices.[9] The sole winners from the restrictive scheme were AmEx and the subset of AmEx cardholders whose subjective valuation of AmEx perks would have prevented them from choosing other payment methods absent the steering restrictions.

So why did the SCOTUS majority support such an outcome? The answer is that it relied on multi-sided markets economics without fully untangling its implications. Indeed, the Court properly took the theory to mean that all sides of the platform had to be accounted for, yet failed to engage in any such examination.[10] The majority likewise confused multi-sided market economists' insistence on balancing the effects borne by each side of the platform with the idea that *market*-wide consequences are trivial. Steering, the Court stated, 'endangers the viability of the entire Amex network'.[11] This is a truism no economist would seriously describe as a problem—not without evidence showing that AmEx's anti-steering was vital to the entire two-sided credit card *market* (it wasn't); or proof that the damage to consumers or society resulting from AmEx's ensuing failure would have exceeded the verified costs of the platform's restrictive rules (in all likelihood, it wouldn't). In short, complex economics led an overconfident decision-maker to disregard facts and effectively immunize from competition a practice that curbed merchants' freedom, consequently harming everyone to the benefit of one platform—AmEx—and a potentially small subset of its consumers.

The rigour test, mind you, would similarly bedevil the competitive process paradigm as there is nothing simple about economic freedom and EOp. Relevant harm

---

[6] *Ohio v American Express Co* 138 SCt 2274 (2018).

[7] For a good discussion, see Erik Hovenkamp, 'Platform Antitrust' [2019] Journal of Corporation Law 713, 734ff.

[8] ibid.

[9] Justice Breyer highlighted this in his dissent (see *AmEx* (n 6) 2293–94 (Breyer dissenting)).

[10] See *AmEx* (n 6) 2287–88.

[11] ibid 2289.

definitely can be formalized in a way that does not take these values as if they were self-evident. Platform providers could further stake a prima facie claim for relief in a wider array of situations than when consumer welfare is used as a lodestar. Nevertheless, seriously embracing the idea of protecting competition, as such, has implications one has to fully appreciate.

First, antitrust turns into an overtly moralizing enterprise. History shows that decision-makers have been either (a) unwilling to engage in the sort of analysis this paradigm requires were it to be implemented rigorously, or (b) convinced by the superiority of the exclusively economic approach. Besides, although political philosophical theories can help us pass the rigour test, they are not devoid of the complexity that similarly hampers the application of the consumer welfare lodestar. Philosophers, like economists, have their own language, which an untrained audience, myself included, can easily misunderstand. This, in turn, exacerbates the dangers inherent to moralizing antitrust. Decision-makers in liberal democracies cannot simply pick whichever theory is convenient for their case; they must act coherently with the underlying vision of the market system established by the peoples they serve. To illustrate: powerful free-riding platforms may restrict the competitive process envisioned by societies wanting to structure competition according to desert; but for those living by the idea that competition should be won by the best players and not those who try the hardest, antitrust enforcement would be inapposite.

The second implication is that the competitive process paradigm is potentially more costly to operate. For it does (or at least, should) not render economic analysis of business practices redundant, in particular where the platform-to-provider dynamic is at stake. In other words, whereas this alternative approach to antitrust focuses primarily on what makes competition sustainable, it cannot disregard the process's predictable benefits when they can be proven to a requisite standard set by the competent authority acting within the bounds of reason. Returning to platforms: (almost) everyone recognizes that their mischiefs (proven or alleged) will frequently generate positive effects. On balance, these may be found to outweigh their restrictive impact on the competitive process. Consequently, in cases where the legal burden is on antitrust enforcers to establish the benefits of the impugned behaviour, protecting competition as such will encounter the added difficulties which beset them when consumer welfare is the lodestar.

- Antitrust is *a* solution, but not necessarily the right one, nor should the price of resolute enforcement be always paid

Antitrust is a notoriously unwieldy instrument. This creates a mismatch when, as in the case of platforms, consensus has it that competition problems are not just endemic, but demand urgent redress as well. As we have seen, though, there is flexibility built into the antitrust apparatus.

At the extreme, the bar for liability can be set at a very low standard; the power radar can be fiddled with to register more than market power in the economic sense; and sweeping proactive remedies can quite swiftly be prescribed. The prospect is appealing, especially in jurisdictions like the USA and (maybe) the EU, where (public and private) enforcers have (increasingly) been kept on a tight leash over the last few decades. *AmEx* is a case in point. Enforcement standards set by the SCOTUS there are so exacting that one can only sympathize with those who argue that they are 'tantamount to saying that [antitrust] does not apply at all'.[12] Epic Games would certainly concur.[13] While the odds clearly are stacked (sometimes overwhelmingly) against enforcers nowadays, does this mean the pendulum has to swing full circle to make enforcement as frictionless as possible?

Doing so surely signals resolve on the part of our decision-makers to get the job done. The move has political upsides as well, given that popular support for antitrust intervention against powerful platforms seems to be on the rise (although this too could be debated).[14] As history's most resolute trustbuster once bemoaned, output legitimacy is something the policy cannot do without.[15] Still, treading this path comes with a considerable cost: antitrust amputated of many of its rule-of-law checks.

The antitrust enforcer's commitment is to the law. Ergo, while (s)he undoubtedly 'owes this allegiance to an evolving legal system',[16] there is a serious case for favouring a more reasonable approach when genuine willingness to reconcile policy-driven enforcement with a sense of balance cannot be mustered. This entails:

---

[12] ibid 2302 (Breyer dissenting). Briefly, the majority required evidence of *actual* increases in the 'net price' of credit card transactions (i.e. the joint price paid by merchants *and* consumers) or of *actual* decreases in the number of credit card transactions (i.e. 'net output', which accounts for demand by merchants *and* consumers of credit card services). But, for one, assuming the District Court's unchallenged findings could indeed be ignored, how then can increases in the 'net price' be objectively established? After all, the price on the consumer side is negative—consumers receive perks for using credit cards—which means its valuation is a matter of subjective preferences. For another, as Justice Breyer noted in his dissent, 'because the relevant question is a comparison between reality and a hypothetical state of affairs, to require actual proof of reduced output is often to require the impossible'.

[13] Epic Games failed *AmEx* despite showing that Apple had been behaving anticompetitively (see *Epic Games Inc v Apple Inc* 559 FSupp 3d 898, 1033–44 (NDCal 2021), affirmed in part, No 21-16695 (9th Cir 2023)).

[14] cf Brian Schaffner, 'Public Demand for Regulating Big Tech' (6 June 2022) Tech Oversight Project <https://bityl.co/Fjro> accessed 19 November 2022; with US Chamber of Commerce, 'New National Poll: Voters Oppose Proposed Antitrust Regulations for Technology Companies' (21 July 2022) <https://bityl.co/Fjrr> accessed 19 November 2022.

[15] See Thurman Arnold in Dexter Keezer, 'The Effectiveness of the Federal Antitrust Laws: A Symposium' [1949] American Economic Review 689, 690 ('Unfortunately, all antitrust law enforcement under any plan depends on the public attitude').

[16] C Wilfred Jenks, 'Craftsmanship in International Law' [1956] American Journal of International Law 32, 51.

- setting enforcement standards in line with the chosen policy lodestar;
- seriously discussing the forms of economic power antitrust can, and must, deal with; and
- abiding by antitrust's essential role in a market economy, given its proscriptive nature, which is that of a (chiefly) regulat*ive* (not regulat*ory*) institution.

Let us not forget, moreover, that resolute enforcement does not guarantee effective redress. It can even deflect attention from what may be the crux of many platform-to-provider cases: *outcome* fairness.

Consider the idea of firewalling Amazon to remedy its data-twinking tendencies. When it released its Echo Show device in 2017, Amazon was accused of having data-twinked the product developed by Nucleus, a start-up it had poured money into through its investment arm, Alexa Fund. Following the incident, it was reported that 'Alexa Fund representatives called a handful of its portfolio companies to say a clear "firewall" exists between the Alexa Fund and Amazon's product development teams.'[17] While the platform vowed compliance, it allegedly conditioned investments in these start-ups on close cooperation with its own product teams.[18] Hardly an effective remedy, then. Worse, what if the real issue is not data-twinking, but free-riding? Unlike the former, the latter, as we have seen, has little to do with 'competition'. It rather relates to a perceived unfairness in *providers' outcomes*. Whether or not this situation warrants remediation, however, is something societies ought to decide for themselves.

So, upstream platform power plays create a Procrustean dilemma for antitrust. The intended meaning of the metaphor becomes more apparent once the myth of Procrustes is recounted. Procrustes (according to Apollodorus of Athens) was the cruel owner of a small estate located on the hills of Attica. There, he would cater to footsore wayfarers with his particular brand of hospitality: force travellers into one of two beds; hammer out shorter individuals until they fit the longer bed; lop the taller to match the shorter one. Faced with our upstream concerns, though, Procrustes would probably lose the plot. Indeed, do platform power plays against providers overextend antitrust or do they instead reveal the need for a policy stretch? Either way, by how much? As we have seen, the answer to these questions turns on beliefs regarding both the nature of the antitrust apparatus and the lodestars which guide its application.

With this in mind, three final reflections are in order.

---

[17] Eugene Kim, 'Amazon Wants to Invest in Start-Ups, but Some are Nervous about Taking the Money' *CNBC* (13 September 2017) <https://cnb.cx/2VZsKNW> accessed 19 November 2022.
[18] ibid.

2. Final Reflections

- Antitrust and change

According to one eminent scholar, the ongoing platformization and, more generally, digitization of our world, have pushed antitrust into a ' "liminal" moment, a period of transition during which the normal limits to thought, self-understanding and behaviour are relaxed, opening the way to novelty and imagination, construction and destruction'.[19] Reality is slightly more nuanced.

Many are undeniably striving to further our economic understanding of how these businesses work so as to refine the analytical frameworks we currently rely upon. There is likewise considerable advocacy pressing for paradigmatic change. Yet, what is fundamentally new and constructive? Most observers still look at platforms with the assumption that competition is a purely horizontal phenomenon; this is the lone reason they take interest in some upstream-facing power plays—the ones involving suppliers with whom powerful platforms also compete horizontally within the digital infrastructures they run. Similarly, those who claim antitrust cannot be insensitive to the misfortune of, say, Uber drivers and Amazon merchants, are more forthcoming with objections to the current approach than they are regarding their alternative.

The truth, then, is that antitrust is maybe not traversing an authentic liminal moment. For how can the 'normal limits to thought, self-understanding and behaviour' be relaxed when there is so much partisanship and suspicion running through the antitrust community? It is as if debates over powerful platforms have to be binary: with or against them. To borrow again from Keynes, what discussions over platforms really reveal is rather that '[t]he difficulty lies, not in the new ideas, but in escaping from the old ones, which ramify, for those brought up as most of us have been, into every corner of our minds'.[20]

- Antitrust, complexity, and problem-solving

The theories and arguments advanced in this book are sometimes complex. They will doubtless have irked staunch platform advocates and critics alike.

The former would probably not take issue with complexity as such. Rather, they would likely reject the alternative approach articulated herein by portraying the lengthy excursions into political philosophy it requires as metaphysical

---

[19] Ioannis Lianos, 'Competition Law for a Complex Economy' [2019] International Review of Intellectual Property and Competition Law 643, 643.

[20] John Maynard Keynes, *The General Theory of Employment, Interest, and Money* (first published 1936, Palgrave Macmillan 2018) vii.

gibberish. The reason? Presumably, a desire for scientific 'hardness' in antitrust's methodology.

Scientific disciplines, we are often told, are to be fitted within a 'hard–soft' hierarchy continuum, with physics at the top and fields like philosophy or sociology at the bottom.[21] When it comes to the social sciences, economics reigns supreme— at least, many economists see it that way.[22] Unsurprisingly so, since the hard–soft dichotomy is a matter of disciplinary precision, which economics assuredly does possess due to its powerful analytical tools.

This is not to say economists are a bane to the antitrust enterprise; on the contrary. The riposte is instead to stress that foreclosing insights from other, 'softer', intellectual disciplines in the name of scientific hardness is a misguided approach to problem-solving. The supremacy claim of economics is itself quite shaky anyway: dollar calculations of economic welfare definitely are value-free but, as we have seen, they only acquire significance when one makes normative judgements regarding what welfare means, whose welfare counts, and for what reasons. Furthermore, sealing antitrust to all but lawyers and the *mainstream* economists advising them is costly as well. Take it from Nobel economist George Akerlof who has bemoaned the 'sins of omission' many in his profession commit due to their obsession with the place of economics in the scientific hierarchy.[23] Important topics, he argues, are being dismissed or under-explored. Why? Because they are harder to fit into a precise model, require the development of new analytical tools, and/ or cannot be tested according to prevailing methodologies.[24] This sounds eerily familiar. Provider harm and non-market power forms of economic power: these are issues mainstream antitrust economics has tended to ignore. They need not be, though.

Consider the competitive process paradigm. Assuming we all accepted that antitrust's methodology *must* be 'hard', there would still be no reason to dismiss it outright. The rich literature pioneered by the likes of John Roemer and Mark Fleurbaey shows us how even a value like EOp can be modelled with mathematical precision for policymaking purposes.[25] More fundamentally, given the impressive number of Nobel economists who have contributed to debates over the ethics of

---

[21] Stephen Cole, 'The Hierarchy of the Sciences?' [1983] American Journal of Sociology 111, 112ff.

[22] Marion Fourcade, Etienne Ollion and Yann Algan, 'The Superiority of Economics' [2015] Journal of Economics Perspectives 89 (analysing the dominance of economics within the US social sciences network).

[23] George Akerlof, 'Sins of Omission and the Practice of Economics' [2020] Journal of Economic Literature 405.

[24] ibid 406, 408.

[25] For a non-technical survey, see Alain Trannoy, 'Equality of Opportunity: A Progress Report' (August 2016) ECINEQ Working Paper 2016-408 <https://bityl.co/Fjrz> accessed 19 November 2022. See also Francisco Ferreira and Vitorocco Peragine, 'Individual Responsibility and Equality of Opportunity' in Matthew Adler and Marc Fleurbaey (eds), *The Oxford Handbook of Well-Being and Public Policy* (OUP 2016).

competition,[26] it is perhaps the antitrust expert who should be better versed in the techniques of ethical analysis.[27]

Now, disappointed detractors will likewise be critical of (some of) the arguments advanced in this book. Unlike platform defenders, they would probably object to all the added complexity, which does hinder swift problem-solving.

Take our discussion of free-riding. A lot was written to articulate what is effectively a basic idea. That is, fears borne from scraping and Sherlocking are, in most jurisdictions, not for antitrust to quench because they are not really (or at least not primarily) competition problems, although one can make them out to be. Some will no doubt read stubborn rigidity into the complex arguments supporting this claim. Why? Presumably because, for them, '[w]hether the juridical basis of an action for misappropriation be a proprietary right or a matter of conscience, little turns on the underlying theory. Whatever its theoretical basis the business values it should protect are clear.'[28]

This argument is surely attractive as it supports an appealing idea: if there is a 'problem' antitrust can attend to more swiftly and with more bang for buck than existing alternatives, one must pull the trigger without hesitation. The argument likewise does have the benefit of simplicity. And everyone can agree that '[i]n an area of the law that has become increasingly more complex and difficult for nonexperts to understand without spending hundreds of thousands of dollars on attorneys and economists, simplicity deserves more respect.'[29] There is, after all, a widely shared assumption, regularly expressed by reference to the well-known 'razor of Occam', that simplicity is a virtue.[30] However, Occam's razor comes in many shapes. To me, the one commonly attributed to Albert Einstein strikes the right balance: everything ought to be made as simple as possible, but not simpler.[31] So when a problem and its solution are not self-evident, it is wrong to depict them as if they were, which is precisely what the aforementioned argument does.

---

[26] Among others, think of Arrow, Buchanan, Coase, Harsanyi, Hayek, Kahneman, Friedman, Samuelson, Sen, or Stiglitz.

[27] Lionel Robbins (the famed economist who invented the 'positive–normative' distinction in economics while rejecting the idea that economists should study the latter) acknowledged that '[positive] economics alone is a very imperfect education' (Lionel Robbins, *An Essay on the Nature and Significance of Economic Science* (3rd edn, Macmillan 1984) xxxvi).

[28] Andrew Terry, 'Unfair Competition and the Misappropriation of a Competitor's Trade Values' [1988] Modern Law Review 296, 312 (albeit in the context of a discussion on unfair competition law).

[29] Timothy Brennan, 'Is Complexity in Antitrust a Virtue? The Accuracy–Simplicity Tradeoff' [2014] Antitrust Bulletin 827, 852.

[30] See, generally, Alan Baker, 'Simplicity' in Edward Zalta (ed), *The Stanford Encyclopedia of Philosophy* (rev edn, Stanford University 2022) <https://stanford.io/31tTR6r> accessed 19 November 2022.

[31] Albert Einstein, 'On the Method of Theoretical Physics' [1934] Philosophy of Science 163, 165 ('It can scarcely be denied that the supreme goal of all theory is to make the irreducible basic elements as simple and as few as possible without having to surrender the adequate representation of a single datum of experience').

Cynics, of course, might accuse me of finessing into complexity a particular brand of conservative ideology. Problem-solving is unquestionably stymied when antitrust enforcement is required to be coherent or when participative regulation is touted over unreasonably swift trustbusting. Yet, these impediments, we have seen, inhere the rule of law itself. Its defence, to my mind, is not a prerogative of conservatives. For antitrust is *law*, first and foremost. As Commissioner Vestager once stated, this means 'there are some corners that we just can't cut'.[32]

- Sustainable platform capitalism

Capitalism, according to historian Donald Sassoon, has no real alternative;[33] survival is actually its *raison d'être*.[34] At the same time, capitalism's triumph was never preordained, nor is its continued existence. To function properly, the system requires 'a supportive infrastructure and a wide consensus around itself that the capitalists themselves, often forced to think for the short term, could not possibly achieve on their own'.[35] The market economy, in other words, only thrives when everyone has a stake in its development, which in turn has to deliver on the ideological promise underlying it: progress.[36]

Platform capitalism is no different. Its advent—a response to anxieties triggered by the 1970s downturn and compounded by both the dotcom bubble explosion and the Great Recession[37]—is just another step in the system's perpetual mutation. Like its predecessors, platform capitalism came with a promise of progress, which has undeniably been met for many, including platform providers—yes, *independent* studies do support the claim that, on the whole, platformization has been more a boon than a bane so far.[38] On the other hand, many suppliers have become disillusioned. This was predictable. As one observer puts it, 'it's not hard to understand the resentment towards a [platform] that delivers you a bunch of business, but also takes a big chunk of your money, sets rules that can seem arbitrary and

---

[32] Margrethe Vestager, 'Competition in a Digital Age: Changing Enforcement for Changing Times' (Speech delivered at the ASCOLA Annual Conference, 26 June 2020) <https://bityl.co/Fjs8> accessed 19 November 2022.

[33] Donald Sassoon, *The Anxious Triumph: A Global History of Capitalism 1860–1914* (Allen Lane 2019).

[34] ibid 506 ('Capitalism's only criterion of success is its own survival').

[35] ibid xxxi.

[36] ibid xxxviii.

[37] Nick Srnicek, *Platform Capitalism* (Polity Press 2017) ch 1.

[38] Alberto Bailin Rivares and others, 'Like It or Not? The Impact of Online Platforms on the Productivity of Incumbent Service Providers' (21 May 2019) OECD Economics Department Working Papers No 1548 <https://doi.org/10.1787/080a17ce-en> accessed 19 November 2022 (finding that platform developments tend to have positive or neutral effects on providers' productivity); Cyrille Schwellnus and others, 'Gig Economy Platforms: Boon or Bane?' (21 May 2019) OECD Economics Department Working Papers No 1550 <https://doi.org/10.1787/fdb0570b-en> accessed 19 November 2022 (finding that, overall, labour platforms have positive employment effects and insignificant consequences on dependent employment and wages).

grows more powerful because of your work.'[39] What was evidently unfair to Karl Marx apparently still rings true today: 'in all spheres of social life the lion's share falls to the middleman.'[40]

For sure, many of platform capitalism's discontents are themselves platforms and first-order intermediaries, not actual producers. Disintermediated middlemen will always cry foul, so caution is warranted. Yelp, for instance, has put a lot of effort into blaming Alphabet/Google for its woes to coax antitrust agencies into action—it once purchased a US$3,000 toy elephant at a charity auction simply because Commissioner Vestager had knitted it![41] Yelp's own investors, though, tend to point the finger at management for its travails.[42]

Nonetheless, the answer to the losers of the platformized market economy is not to say 'society doesn't look a gift horse in the mouth'; 'all intermediaries are evil anyway'; or, 'the consumer is the arbiter of the entire system'.

Capitalism (as noted a few paragraphs above) only triumphed when it became a collective project. We need not ascertain its promise of progress solely by reference to the quantifiable prosperity generated. Progress is also delivered through human flourishing, which seems to be currently best approximated by the notion of well-being.[43] On this front, platform capitalism is evidently failing. Far from the sense of belonging and esteem one would expect to see in flourishing capitalist societies, there is considerable isolation and humiliation on the supplier side.[44] How could it be otherwise when the system, as presently structured, is based upon a coalition—among platform founders, their patient investors, and many unwitting consumers—which leaves out the producers and workers without whom there would be no value proposition to begin with?[45] Plainly stated, platform capitalism is on an unsustainable path because it is morally bankrupt. Unfortunately, the solution is multi-pronged, complex, and beyond the scope of this book. Yet, to my mind, any blueprint would have to involve the market, the state, and civil society itself.

The market because, as economist Paul Collier argues, '[t]he starting point for a new approach is to recognize that the role of the large corporation in society has never properly been thought through.'[46] Big business's decades-long adherence to

---

[39] Shira Ovide, 'Sorry, eBay and Uber. You're Hated. Why the Middlemen Are the Internet's Villains' *New York Times* (24 June 2020) <https://nyti.ms/2Bu8hZJ> accessed 19 November 2022.

[40] Karl Marx, *Capital: A Critique of Political Economy*, vol 1 (tr Ben Fowkes, 2nd edn, Penguin 1990) 907 (n 3).

[41] Tom Braithwaite, 'Is Yelp a Business or a Howl of Pain?' *Financial Times* (15 February 2019) <https://on.ft.com/2D4U6uB> accessed 19 November 2022.

[42] ibid.

[43] Tyler VanderWeele, 'On the Promotion of Human Flourishing' [2017] Proceedings of the National Academy of Sciences of the United States of America 8148.

[44] See also Paul Collier, *The Future of Capitalism: Facing the New Anxieties* (HarperCollins 2018) ch 2.

[45] See, similarly, K Sabeel Rahman and Kathleen Thelen, 'The Rise of the Platform Business Model and the Transformation of Twenty-First-Century Capitalism' [2019] Politics & Society 177.

[46] Collier (n 44) ch 4.

the shareholder primacy principle has no doubt contributed to the unethical platform capitalism we have today.[47] Alternatives do exist, though.

Progressives like Trebor Scholz, but pragmatists such as Collier as well, have supported the idea of vesting ownership and control of firms with those who participate in the company and have direct interests in its performance, i.e. workers.[48] In fact, platform co-ops can already be found in a variety of forms. Think of:

- ○ Fairmondo (the German co-op alternative to Amazon and eBay, which has a multi-stakeholder approach to distributing profits);[49]
- ○ Resonate (the music streaming co-op challenger to Spotify and Apple Music that shares 45 per cent of its profits with artists);[50]
- ○ Stocksy (the co-op equivalent to Google Images or Getty Images, which gives photographers 50 per cent to 75 per cent of every licence sold);[51] or
- ○ Braintrust (the community-governed labour platform which is rivalling incumbents like Upwork or TaskRabbit by combining low fees and blockchain technology).[52]

Platform cooperativism, therefore, is one worthy option. So much so, *en passant*, that during the first wave of the COVID-19 pandemic the French government announced plans to develop a booking platform in cooperation with the tourism industry to compete with the likes of Airbnb and Booking Holdings.[53]

Beyond corporate governance, the market has to update its business ethos. Platforms, as any undertaking, require a sense of purpose. The latter doesn't have to be exclusively bent on profit maximization nor does it have to be strictly about servicing the disadvantaged or producing products that deliver large positive externalities. Take it from philosopher Elizabeth Anderson, who argues that we can theorize the ethical business as 'a "nexus of reciprocal relationships" with internal and external stakeholders'.[54] Under this model, the for-profit corporation defines

---

[47] Sujeep Indap, 'Revisiting the Principle of "Shareholder Primacy"' *Financial Times* (24 September 2018) <https://on.ft.com/2XfTREn> accessed 19 November 2022.

[48] Trebor Scholz, *Uberworked and Underpaid: How Workers Are Disrupting the Digital Economy* (Polity Press 2017) ch 7; Collier (n 44) ch 4.

[49] Chelsea Rustrum, 'Q&A with Felix Weth of Fairmondo, the Platform Co-op that's Taking on eBay' (*Shareable*, 14 March 2016) <https://bityl.co/FjsL> accessed 19 November 2022.

[50] Isabelle Morrison, 'Bye, Spotify: Can This New Streaming Service Help Listeners Play Fair?' *The Guardian* (25 May 2018) <https://bit.ly/2YRWltJ> accessed 19 November 2022.

[51] Ruby Irene Pratka, 'With a Focus on Artists, the Platform Cooperative Stocksy Is Redefining Stock Photography' (*Shareable*, 10 October 2018) <https://bityl.co/FjsT> accessed 19 November 2022.

[52] Jeff John Robert, 'Why Companies Like Porsche and Nestle Are Turning to Worker-Owned Talent Site Braintrust for New Hires' (*Fortune*, 24 June 2020) <https://bit.ly/2NLFfHG> accessed 19 November 2022.

[53] François De Beaupuy, 'France to Build Online Platform to Rival Airbnb, Booking.com' *Bloomberg* (14 May 2020) <https://bloom.bg/3eTmgqD> accessed 19 November 2022.

[54] Elizabeth Anderson, 'The Business Enterprise as an Ethical Agent' in Subramanian Rangan (ed), *Performance and Progress: Essays on Capitalism, Business, and Society* (OUP 2015) 191.

its mission 'in a way that incorporates the positive good of all stakeholders, and focus primarily on achieving that mission by following through on the teamwork and contractual and extracontractual commitments that make that achievement sustainable over time'.[55] Platforms, accordingly, have to re-embrace what platform capitalism was meant to be: a competitive partnership.

In September 2019, some of the world's largest firms, including platforms like Amazon, acknowledged this reality by publicly reneging on the long-held view that maximizing shareholder benefits must be the singular corporate objective. In signalling what is a potential paradigm shift in corporate culture, these firms vowed, among other things, to deal 'fairly and ethically with ... suppliers'.[56] But, of course, the state has to be there to hold them to their word.

Antitrust, then, is one important lever through which the public sector can do its part. This book has nevertheless suggested that adopting a reasonable stance is usually the way to go even if doing so limits the reach and effectiveness of the instrument. Not that antitrust enforcement mustn't be envisaged at all; quite the reverse. Reasonable interventions can still be significant, just constrained by rule-of-law safeguards. Furthermore, antitrust's insuperable limits may serve as an impetus for reform in the areas of action which really ought to take centre stage when it comes to dealing with some platform provider issues. IP and labour laws were mentioned, but other obvious examples are merger control and taxation. Major obstacles no doubt abound. Still, these are not necessarily insurmountable even when geopolitical shenanigans are accounted for.[57]

Despite this, as Commissioner Vestager rightly pointed out, 'there's only so much these existing powers can do. We also need new ways to tackle the problems that digitisation causes. And one part of the answer could be new regulatory rules'.[58]

The regulatory enterprise has admittedly been widely loathed in recent times. While justified in some respects, such disdain is nonetheless paradoxical: even the Gilded Age 'robber barons' *welcomed* it for railways.[59] All the same, history is useful insofar as the proper insights are drawn from it. And, to me, these are that platform capitalism requires both the market, 'but harnessed by a sense of purpose securely grounded in ethics',[60] *and* an active yet less paternalistic state.

Civil society, finally, has an important role to play here. Maybe capitalism truly 'has no purpose except to keep the show going'.[61] However, the institutions that

---

[55] ibid 200–01.

[56] Business Roundtable, 'Statement on the Purpose of a Corporation' (September 2019) <https://perma.cc/87PU-E695> accessed 19 November 2022.

[57] Mary McDougall, 'OECD Tax Chief Warns of Trade Wars if Global Deal Is not Implemented' *Financial Times* (31 October 2022) <https://bityl.co/FNoL> accessed 19 November 2022.

[58] Vestager (n 32).

[59] Sassoon (n 33) 232–33.

[60] Collier (n 44) ch 1.

[61] Joan Robinson, *Economic Heresies: Some Old-Fashioned Questions in Economic Theory* (Palgrave Macmillan 1971) 143.

together mould and support capitalism can be, and (in most liberal democracies) probably are, individually *ordered*, i.e. shaped by intentional societal decisions. Hence, to borrow from Maurice Stucke and Ariel Ezrachi, 'while we think we are powerless to stop the toxic [platform capitalism], that's not true. We can take a stand.'[62]

Antitrust laws, for example, can be reformed to reflect a new collective vision on how to structure competitive outcomes. If we genuinely do want a marketplace where success is more tied to effort than it is today or one which accords more importance to diversity per se, then we have 'to tell our elected officials ... and vote for those who want to enact change'.[63]

Change, moreover, is not merely a matter of civil society exercising its citizenry rights. It is a question of conscience. Ethical alternatives to some of the most powerful platforms, we have seen, already exist. Together, the citizen-voter and the citizen-consumer can thus make the choice a more credible reality because even the Googles of the world are probably *not* natural monopolies.[64] So, there is room for more than one platform per niche in the long run. More fundamentally, societies as consumers will have to change *how* they consume. For if a platform like Amazon should be called out for some of the certainly unreasonable demands it places on its workers and merchants, there is a paradox that arises when we, consumers, double down on the platform during a pandemic only to throw an unprecedented tantrum when deliveries are delayed or not up to usual standards.[65] The cruel irony with platform capitalism is perhaps that its sustainability is also threatened by what makes it so appealing to us as consumers: the great enabler of hyper-consumption[66] imperilled by hyper-consumption; or, as Shakespeare would have said, platform capitalism '[c]onsumed with that which it was nourished by'.[67]

---

[62] Maurice Stucke and Ariel Ezrachi, *Competition Overdose: How Free Market Mythology Transformed Us from Citizen Kings to Market Servants* (HarperCollins 2020) ch 10.

[63] ibid.

[64] See CMA, 'Online Platforms and Digital Advertising: Market Study Final Report' (1 July 2020) app D, [76ff] <https://bit.ly/3Avd1tA> accessed 19 November 2022. See also Francesco Ducci, *Natural Monopolies in Digital Platform Markets* (CUP 2020) (finding that e-commerce marketplace and, to a certain extent, ride-hailing platforms are not natural monopolies, though the opposite conclusion is reached for general search).

[65] Jay Greene, 'Amazon Shoppers Complaining at Record Levels' *Washington Post* (22 May 2020) <https://wapo.st/2VNLBdZ> accessed 19 November 2022.

[66] George Ritzer and Steven Miles, 'The Changing Nature of Consumption and the Intensification of McDonaldization in the Digital Age' [2019] Journal of Consumer Culture 3 (arguing that platforms 'further enshrine and supercharge the process of "hyperconsumption"').

[67] William Shakespeare, *The Oxford Shakespeare: Complete Sonnets and Poems* (Colin Burrow (ed), OUP 2002) 527.

Platform Economy Diagnosis in Policy Reports

Note to reader: Due to formatting constraints, it was not possible to fit all columns of the following table onto the same page. Column headers were therefore split over side-by-side consecutive pages. For ease of understanding, the table and each of its entries should be read horizontally, from left to right, over consecutive pages.

Table A.1　Platform economy diagnosis in policy reports

	Report	Inquiry scope*	Industry concentration	Causes of industry concentration		
				Online intermediation trend	Network effects	Data-driven competitive advantages
EU	EC SWD (2020) [DMA IA]	Online search / marketplace / app stores / social media / OSs / video sharing / cloud / online advertising	✓ §§31ff	✓ (§274)	✓ (§§73, 77–79)	✓ (§83)
	EC SWD (2018) [P2B regulation IA]	Online search / marketplace / app stores/ social media	✓ Generic (pp 23–24)	✓ (pp 21–23)	✓ (pp 23–24)	✓ (p 24)
	EC SWD (2016) [Copyright Directive IA]	Creative / press publishing industries	△	△	△	△
	Crémer et al (2019) [Report for EC]	Generic	✓ Generic (pp 19, 23) △		✓ (pp 20–23, 31)	✓ (pp 24, 31)
UK	CMA (2022) [Mobile ecosystems market study final report]	Mobile ecosystems	✓ Mobile OSs (§§3.18, 3.24, 3.176); app stores (§§4.32–4.35); mobile browsers (§§5.24–5.32, 5.121, 5.125)	△	✓ Mobile OSs (§§3.132–3.137; app stores (§4.78); mobile browsers (§§5.78– 5.79)	✓ Mobile OSs (§§3.97–3.102, 3.155); mobile apps (§§6.102ff)
	CMA (2020) [Online advertising market study final report]	Online search / advertising, social media	✓ Generic (§2.10 + box 2.2); online search/ advertising, social media (§§3.17–3.23, 3.165–3.173, 5.46, 5.131–5.132, 5.215, 5.218, 5.222, 5.227)	△ ($2.10 + box 2.2, §§3.59ff, 3.158ff, 5.154)	✓ ($2.10 + box 2.2, §§3.64ff, 3.236ff, 5.60– 5.62, 5.127, 5.145, 5.162– 5.168, 5.268)	✓
	CMA (2017) [DCT market study report]	DCTs in car / home insurance, energy, broadband, flights, credit cards	✓ Some DCT sectors (pp 20–21)	△	△	△
	HoL (2019) [Regulating in a Digital World report]	Generic	✓ Generic (§160); online advertising (§129)	△	✓ (§§130–138, juncto 139)	✓ (§131)
	HoL (2016) [Platforms & the DSM report]	Generic	✓ Generic (§100)	△	✓ (§§73, 100)	✓ (§§68–69)
	Furman et al (2019) [Report for UK Gov]	Generic	✓ Generic (p 4, §§1.30–1.31); online search/advertising, marketplaces, social media, mobile OSs, app stores (§§1.42– 1.61, 1.100–1.117)	△	✓ (p 4, §§1.80–1.88)	✓ (p 4, §§1.37– 1.41, 1.71–179)
DE	BMWi (2019) [Competition 4.0 report]	Generic	✓ Generic (pp 17, 22, 49)	✓ (p 23)	✓ (pp 16–17, 22, 49)	✓ (pp 18, 49)
	BMWi (2019) [Draft ARC amendment]	Generic	✓ Generic (p 73)	✓ (p 69)	✓ (p 73)	✓ (p 73)
	Schweitzer et al (2018) [Report for BMWi]	Generic	✓ Generic (p 12)	✓ (pp 7–10, 66)	✓ (p 12)	✓ (p 12)

Economies / advantages of scale and/or scope	Other	Urgent need for intervention	Type of intervention	
			Antitrust	Regulation (existing, amended, and/or new) (including 'co-regulation')
✓ (§74)	✓ (§§75, 80–83)	✓ Generic (§51)	✓ Secondary tool (§§119, 153 + recital (11) DMA)	✓ New (asymmetric) regulation
✓ (pp 23–24)	✓ (p 26)	✓ Generic (pp10, 30)	✓ Secondary tool (p 3)	✓ Co-regulation (p 76ff)
△	△	✓ Generic (pp 143–144, 10–161)	✓ Secondary tool (p 161)	✓ Bolstered copyright regulation (pp 155, 173, 192)
✓ (pp 20, 33)	✓ (pp 29, 33–34)	✓ Generic (pp 42, 51)	✓ Primary tool (pp 14, 53)	✓ New regulation (pp 52–53, 70–72)
✓ Mobile OSs (§3.131) ; app stores (§4.78)	✓ Mobile OSs (§§3.69ff); app stores (§§4.54ff); mobile browsers (§§5.43ff)	✓ (§8.224 + §§9.12, 9.14–9.15)	✓ Secondary tool (§§8.215, 8.224 + §10.6)	✓ New (co-) regulation (§§8.208–8.214, 8.224–8.226)
✓ (§2.10 + box 2.2, §§3.57ff, 5.46ff)	✓ (§2.10 + box, chs 3, 5)	✓ Online search/ advertising, social media (p 322, §§8.4, 8.260, 9.16)	✓ Secondary tool (§§7.35ff)	✓ New (co-) regulation (§§7.14ff)
△	✓ Paper E (§§2.42–2.58)	✗ Not generally for antitrust (§5.29)	✓ Default (§§5.2, 5.28–5.30)	✓ Bolstered sector regulations + clarified CP law (§§5.2, 5.3–5.20) + Paper C)
△	✓ (§§132, 143–144)	✓ Generic (§§232, 240)	✓ Secondary tool (§§232–233)	✓ New coordinated cross-sectoral regulation (§§172, 233, 2.38–2.39)
✓ (§89)	✓ (§101)	✓ OTA sector (§123)	△ Default (?)	✓ Co-regulation (§133); sceptical about new top-down regulation (§§103, 276)
✓ (p 4, §§1.68–1.170)	✓ (§§1.87–1.190)	✓ Generic (§§2.131, 3.111, 3.118) online advertising (§3.197)	✓ Secondary tool (§§2.8, 2.12, 2.18–2.23, 2.131, 3.115)	✓ New/existing regulation (incl. targeted co-regulatory elements) (Ch 2, §3.152)
✓ (pp 17–18, 22)	✓ (pp 17–20)	✓ Generic (p 24)	✓ Secondary tool (p 51)	✓ New regulation (pp 25–26, 51–52)
✓ (p73)	✓ (p 74)	✓ Generic (p 1)	✓ Bolstered (pp 8–9, 70–72) + special regime (pp 4, 8–9, 74–78)	✓ Bolstered SBP law (pp 9, 78–84)
✓ (p 12)	✓ (pp 11–14)	✓ Generic (pp 166–167)	✓ Default (p 165)	✓ Existing UC/SBP/CP/contract laws (pp 106–107,118, 165)

(continued)

Table A.1 Continued

	Report	Inquiry scope*	Industry concentration	Causes of industry concentration		
				Online intermediation trend	Network effects	Data-driven competitive advantages
FR	ADLC (2020) [Antitrust & digital issues paper]	Generic	△	△	△	△
	ADLC (2018) [Online advertising opinion]	Online search / advertising, social media	✓ Online search/ mapping, social media, email, app stores, browsers, video sharing (§§203–212)	△	✓ (§§114, 228)	✓ (§§137–138)
	Senate (2019) [Digital sovereignty report]	Generic	✓ Generic (p 29) online search/ advertising, social media, mobile OSs, browsers, ecommerce, cloud (pp 32–33)	△	✓ (pp 30–31)	✓ (p 29)
	ESEC (2019) [Digital sovereignty report]	Generic	✓ Mobile OSs, browsers, online search (p 5)	△	△	△
	IGF & CGE (2019) [Report for FR Gov]	Generic	✓ Generic (p 18)	△	✓ (p 18)	✓ (p 18)
	Parliament (2015) [Freedoms in the digital age]	Generic	✓ Generic (p 200)	△	✓ (p 200)	✓ (p 200)
	Council of the State (2014) [Fundamental rights in the digital age]	Generic	✓ Generic (p 106)	△	✓ (p 106)	✓ (p 106)
	CNNum (2015) [Digital Ambition report]	Generic	✓ Generic (p 7)	△	✓ (p 7)	✓ (pp 8–9)
	CNNum (2014) [Platform Neutrality report]	Generic	✓ Generic (pp 42, 90)	✓ (p 69)	✓ (pp 43, 64)	✓ (pp 77–82)
NL	ACM (2019) [Mobile app store market study]	App stores	✓ App stores (p 15)	✓ (p 15)	✓ (p 34)	△
PT	AdC (2019) [Digital issues report]	Generic	✓ Generic (§20)	✓ (§§1–9)	✓ (§§20, 74, 79–82)	✓ (§§21, 96)
US	HoR (2020) [Competition in digital markets report]	Online Search / advertising, e-commerce marketplaces, social media, app stores, mobile OSs, digital mapping, cloud computing, voice assistance, web browsing	✓ Generic (pp 11, 38); online search / advertising (pp 77–78 /132); e-commerce (p 86); social media (pp 91–92); app stores (p 95); mobile OSs (pp 101–103); digital mapping (pp 108–109; cloud computing (p 114); voice assistance (p 123); web browsers (p 128)	△	✓ (pp 13, 40–42, 77, 87, 96, 105–106, 115, 124, 141–145)	✓ (pp 42–44, 80–81, 109, 125, 132, 148)

Economies / advantages of scale and/or scope		Other		Urgent need for intervention		Type of intervention			
						Antitrust		Regulation (existing, amended, and/or new) (including 'co-regulation')	
△		△		✓	Generic (p 2)	△	Unclear if proposed preventive system would be part of reformed antitrust or new (co-) regulation (pp 7–9)	✓	If proposed preventive system is established through new (co-) regulation (pp 7–9)
✓	(§227)	✓	(§§115, 119–124, 139–148)	△		△	Default (?)	✓	Bolstered regulation (§§262, 305)
✓	(pp 30–31, 33)	✓	(p 33)	✓	Generic (pp 8, 30, 38)	△	Default (?)	✓	New regulation (p 46)
△		△		△		✓	Secondary (p 24)	✓	Bolstered regulation (pp 25–27, 29–32) + new regulation (pp 27–28)
✓	(p 18)	✓	(p 18)	△		✓	Secondary (p 21)	✓	New regulation (p 21)
✓	(p 200)	✓	(pp 200–201)	△		✓	Default (p 225)	✓	Bolstered UC/SBP/CP laws + new regulation (pp 218, 225)
✓	(p 106)	△		△		✓	Secondary (pp 222–223)	✓	New regulation (p 223)
△		✓	(p 59)	△		✓	Default (p 59)	✓	UC/SBP laws (pp 59, 72) + new regulation (p 36)
△		✓	(p 43)	△		✓	Default (pp 28–29)	✓	UC/SBP laws (p 29) + bolstered CP law (p 30) + new co-regulation (pp 30–31)
△		✓	(pp 52–56)	✓	App stores (pp 106, 108)	✓	Default (p 17)	✓	CP law (p 17) + (co-)regulation (p 108)
✓	(§§74, 76–79, 96)	✓	(§§74, 83, 96)	△		△	Default (?)	△	
✓	(pp 45–46, 78–81, 87, 116)	✓	(pp 11–12, 14–16, 81–83, 103–105, 109–110, 115–120, 126, 129, 145–148)	✓	(p 7)	✓	Bolstered (pp 7, 20–21, 393–405)	✓	New regulation (pp 20, 379–392)

(*continued*)

Table A.1 Continued

	Report	Inquiry scope*	Industry concentration		Causes of industry concentration		
					Online intermediation trend	Network effects	Data-driven competitive advantages
AU	ACCC (2019) [Platforms inquiry final report]	Online search / advertising, social media, news referral	✓	Online search/advertising, social media (pp 65, 78, 94, 99)	✓ (pp 44–46)	✓ (pp 8–9, 44, 66–67, 79, 96, 99)	✓ (pp 8–9, 12 84–89)
JP	JFTC (2019) [P2B report]	E-commerce marketplaces / app stores	✓	E-commerce/app stores (pp 7, 22)	✓ (pp 15–16, 19)	✓ (pp 6–7, 22)	✓ (p 7)
JP	Study Group (2018) [platforms interim paper]	Generic	✓	Generic (pp 2–3)	✓ (p 1)	✓ (p 2)	✓ (p 2)
IN	CCI (2020) [e-commerce market study]	E-commerce	✓	E-commerce (goods marketplaces; OTAs: §§49–50)	✓ (§§12ff, 34)	✓ (§49)	△
BRICS	BRICS Centre (2019) [Digital competition report]	Generic	✓	Generic (p 254); online search/advertising, social media, and several others (pp 925, 968, 871, 1022–1024, 1089–1093)	✓ (pp 369, 546)	✓ (pp 254, 1267)	✓ (pp 552, 1224)
OTHER	IMF (2019) [World Economic Outlook report]	Generic	✓	Generic (p 57)	△	△ (p 57)	△ (p 57)
OTHER	UNCTAD (2019) [Competition issues paper]	Generic	✓	Online search / advertising / e-commerce (pp 3–4)	△	✓ (p 4)	✓ (p 4)
OTHER	UNCTAD (2019) [Digital economy report]	Generic	✓	Generic (pp 83–84); e-commerce marketplaces (p 40)	✓ (pp 25ff)	✓ (p 84)	✓ (p 84)
OTHER	DE, FR & PL economy ministries (2019) [Modernising EU competition policy]	Generic	✓	Generic (pp 2–3)	△	△	△
OTHER	Stigler Center (2019) [Platforms report]	Generic	✓	Generic (pp 7–8, 34)	△	✓ (pp 7, 38–39)	✓ (pp 7–8, 47–51)
OTHER	BEUC (2019) [Competition policy in digital era report]	Generic	✓	Generic (p 7)	△	✓ (pp 6–7)	✓ (p 6)

*: to the extent inquiry somehow covers upstream concerns

✓: claimed/suggested

✗: rejected

△: not discussed/claimed or unclear

Source: author's own creation.

Economies / advantages of scale and/or scope		Other		Urgent need for intervention		Type of intervention		
						Antitrust		Regulation (existing, amended, and/or new) (including 'co-regulation')
✓	(pp 8–9, 46, 73–74, 79–80)	✓	(pp 8–9, 44, 68–75, 80)	✓	Generic (pp 27, 140)	✓	Secondary (pp 139–140)	✓ Existing CP law (pp 139–140) + new ASBP, media, tax (co-)regulation (pp 141, 255ff, 199, 329ff) + the market (p 150)
△		✓	(p 7)	✓	E-commerce marketplace/app stores (p 9)	△	Default (?)	✓ UC/SBP laws (pp 12, 33, 38, 40, 44–45, 51, 53, 56, 77) + regulation (pp 11, 107)
△		✓	(p 2)	✓	Generic (p 13)	✓	Default (p 13)	✓ Co-regulation (p 8)
△		✓	(§51)	✓	E-commerce (§§84–85, 87, 92, 98, 106, 109)	△	Default (?)	✓ Self-regulation (§113)
△		✓	(pp 1268–1269, 1280–1286)	✓	Generic (p 224)	△	Default (?)	✓ New/existing (co-)regulation (pp 355–359, 456)
△		△		✓	(p 69)	✓	Default (p 69)	✓ Taxation (p 69)
△		✓	(pp 4–5)	✓	Generic (pp 5, 14–15)	△	Default (?)	✓ New regulation (pp 11–14)
△		✓	(pp 84–88)	✓	Generic (p 148)	✓	Default (p 138)	✓ New regulation (p 140)
△		△		✓	Generic (p 1)	✓	Default (p 2)	✓ New regulation (p 2)
△		✓	(pp 8, 41–42)	✓	Generic (pp 9, 81, 94)	✓	Default/secondary (pp 89–90)	✓ New regulation (pp 100–101, 188ff)
△		✓	(p 7)	✓	Generic (pp 8–9)	✓	Default (pp 15ff)	✓ New regulation (targeted where necessary (p 24)

Concern for the Upstream in Policy Reports

Note to reader: Due to formatting constraints, it was not possible to fit all columns of the following table onto the same page. Column headers were therefore split over side-by-side consecutive pages. For ease of understanding, the table and each of its entries should be read horizontally, from left to right, over consecutive pages.

Table B.1 Concern for the upstream in policy reports

	Report	Inquiry scope*		Explicit
EU	EC SWD (2020) *[DMA IA]*	Online search / marketplace / app stores / social media / OSs / video sharing / cloud / online advertising	✓	(All)
	EC SWD (2018) *[P2B regulation IA]*	Online search / marketplaces / app stores/social media	✓	(All)
	EC SWD (2016) *[Copyright Directive IA]*	Creative/press publishing industries	✓	(All)
	Crémer et al (2019) *[Report for EC]*	Generic	△	(pp 41, 61)
UK	CMA (2022) *[Mobile ecosystems market study final report]*	Mobile ecosystems	✓	(Ch 6)
	CMA (2020) *[Online advertising market study final report]*	Online search / advertising, social media	✓	(Ch 5)
	CMA (2017) *[DCT market study report]*	DCTs in car / home insurance, energy, broadband, flights, credit cards	✓	(§§4.90ff + Paper E (§§3.1ff))
	HoL (2019) *[Regulating in a Digital World report]*	Generic	✓	(§172)
	HoL (2016) *[Platforms & the DSM report]*	Generic	✓	(§§81–83, 122, 126–128, 133)
	Furman et al (2019) *[Report for UK Gov]*	Generic	✓	(§§1.134–1.152)
DE	BMWi (2019) *[Draft ARC amendment]*	Generic	✓	(pp 9, 69, 78)
	BMWi (2019) *[Competition 4.0 report]*	Generic	✓	(p 50)
	Schweitzer et al (2018) *[Report for BMWi]*	Generic	✓	(pp 66–67, 70, 103–104, 113)

Upstream focus		
Direct (ie not tied to, or conditioned by, substantiated consumer harm)	Influenced or driven by concern for fair (?) value distribution towards providers	Exclusive or predominant (ie no, or little focus on, other substantiated platform-related issues/concerns)
✓ (§§28, 41, 57, 153, 276, 303)	✓ (§§153, 276, 277)	✓
△ (cf pp 28–30 with p 29)	✓ (pp 26–28)	✓
✓ (pp 142–143, 160–161)	✓ (pp 143, 160)	✓
✓ (fn 124, pp 41–42, 60–66)	△ (pp 41, 61)	✗
✓ (Ch 6 [except §§6.140–6.162, 6.192–6.193, 6.223] + Ch 7 [except §§7.38–7.51, 7.58–7.71])	△ (but see §§7.52, 8.103, 8.105)	✗
△ (cf §§2.83–2.85, 3.143–3.144, 3.256, 5.372–5.373 + Ch 6 with absence of actual evidence of consumer harm)	✓ (§§6.28–6.29, 7.77 + Appendix S but note §§7.79–7.80)	✗
✗ (Paper E §§3.12, 3.14, 3.34ff, 3.52)	△	✗
✓ (§172)	△	✗
✓ (§133)	△ (§§126–128, 133)	✗
✗ (§§1.134–1.152)	✓ (§§1.137, 1.141–1.147)	✗
✓ (pp 69–71, 76, 78)	△	✗
✓ (p 50)	△	✗
✓ (pp 103–104, 113)	△	✗

(*continued*)

Table B.1 Continued

	Report	Inquiry scope*		Explicit
FR	ADLC (2020) *[Antitrust & digital issues paper]*	Generic	△	
	ADLC (2018) *[Online advertising opinion]*	Online search / advertising, social media	✓	(§§248–257)
	Senate (2019) *[Digital sovereignty report]*	Generic	✓	(pp 34–35)
	ESEC (2019) *[Digital sovereignty report]*	Generic	✓	(pp 9–11)
	IGF & CGE (2019) *[Report for FR Gov]*	Generic	△	
	Parliament (2015) *[Freedoms in the digital age]*	Generic	✓	(p 201)
	Council of the State (2014) *[Fundamental rights in the digital age]*	Generic	✓	(pp 35–36)
	CNNum (2015) *[Digital Ambition report]*	Generic	✓	(pp 58ff)
	CNNum (2014) *[Platform Neutrality report]*	Generic	✓	(pp 66, 83–89, 104–106)
NL	ACM (2019) *[Mobile app store market study]*	App stores	✓	(chs 4–6)
PT	AdC (2019) *[Digital issues report]*	Generic	✓	(§111)
US	HoR (2020) *[Competition in digital markets report]*	Online Search / advertising, e-commerce marketplaces, social media, app stores, mobile OSs, digital mapping, cloud computing, web browsing	✓	(All)
AU	ACCC (2019) *[Platforms inquiry final report]*	Online search / advertising, social media, news referral	✓	(chs 3, 5–6)
JP	JFTC (2019) *[P2B report]*	E-commerce marketplaces / app stores	✓	(All)
	Study Group (2018) *[platforms interim paper]*	Generic	✓	(pp 9, 11)
IN	CCI (2020) *[e-commerce market study]*	E-commerce	✓	(All)

Upstream focus		
Direct (ie not tied to, or conditioned by, substantiated consumer harm)	**Influenced or driven by concern for fair (?) value distribution towards providers**	**Exclusive or predominant (ie no, or little focus on, other substantiated platform-related issues/ concerns)**
△	△	✗
△	✓ (§82)	✗
✓ (pp 34–35)	✓ (p 40)	✗
✓ (pp 9–11)	✓ (pp 9–11, 17–18)	✗
△	△	✗
✓ (p 201)	✓ (p 201)	✗
✓ (pp 35–36)	✓ (p 268)	✗
✓ (pp 59ff)	✓ (pp 8, 72)	✗
✓ (pp 66, 83–89, 104–106)	✓ (pp 38, 83)	✗
✓ (pp 102–104, 106–107)	△	✗
✗ (§§111–112)	△ (§§97, 111–112)	✗
✓ All (except, pp 51–53, 197–207, 347, 353)	✓ (pp 6, 14–17, 20, 40, 50–51, 59, 64–69, 162–165, 185–186, 220–221, 241, 275–284, 316, 327–328, 340–353, 363–366)	✓
△ (cf pp 12–13, 16, 134–138, 529–530 with 138–140)	✓ (pp 16, 163, 225, 232, 235, 245)	✗
✓ (All)	△	✓
✓ (pp 9, 11)	△	✗
✓ (All)	✓ (pp 13, 33, 38, 40–41, 44, 51, 56, 68, 71, 77)	✗

(*continued*)

Table B.1 Continued

	Report	Inquiry scope*		Explicit
BRICS	BRICS Centre (2019) *[Digital competition report]*	Generic	✓	(pp 141, 194, 255, 260, 317, 359ff, 534–538, 549)
OTHER	IMF (2019) *[World Economic Outlook report]*	Generic	✓	(p 57 [not platform conduct-specific])
	UNCTAD (2019) *[Competition issues paper]*	Generic	✓	(p 7)
	UNCTAD (2019) *[Digital economy report]*	Generic	✓	(pp 38–40, 94, 97–99)
	DE, FR & PL economy ministries (2019) *[Modernising EU competition policy]*	Generic	△	
	Stigler Center (2019) *[Platforms report]*	Generic	✓	(p 61)
	BEUC (2019) *[Competition policy in digital era report]*	Generic	✓	(p 9)

*: to the extent inquiry somehow covers upstream concerns

✓: claimed/suggested

✗: rejected

△: not discussed/claimed or unclear

Source: author's own creation.

Upstream focus		
Direct (ie not tied to, or conditioned by, substantiated consumer harm)	Influenced or driven by concern for fair (?) value distribution towards providers	Exclusive or predominant (ie no, or little focus on, other substantiated platform-related issues/ concerns)
✓ (pp 141, 174, 255, 260, 317, 359ff, 549)	✓ (pp 51, 58, 97, 141, 174, 255, 260, 317)	✗
△	△	✗
✓ (p 7)	✓ (p 7)	✗
✓ (pp 38–40, 94, 97–99)	✓ (pp 38–40, 94, 97–100)	✗
△	△	✗
✓ (p 61)	✓ (pp 36, 61, 68, 89, 115)	✗
✓ (p 9)	✓ (pp 9, 13)	✗

Enforcement Standards in Policy Reports

Note to reader: Due to formatting constraints, it was not possible to fit all columns of the following table onto the same page. Column headers were therefore split over side-by-side consecutive pages. For ease of understanding, the table and each of its entries should be read horizontally, from left to right, over consecutive pages.

Table C.1 Enforcement standards in policy reports

	Report	Inquiry scope*
EU	EC SWD (2020) *[DMA IA]*	Online search / marketplace / app stores / social media / OSs / video sharing / cloud / online advertising
	EC SWD (2018) *[P2B regulation IA]*	Online search / marketplaces / app stores/ social media
	EC SWD (2016) *[Copyright Directive IA]*	Creative/press publishing industries
	Crémer et al (2019) *[Report for EC]*	Generic
UK	CMA (2022) *[Mobile ecosystems market study final report]*	Mobile ecosystems
	CMA (2020) *[Online advertising market study final report]*	Online search / advertising, social media
	CMA (2017) *[DCT market study report]*	DCTs in car / home insurance, energy, broadband, flights, credit cards
	HoL (2019) *[Regulating in a Digital World report]*	Generic
	HoL (2016) *[Platforms & the DSM report]*	Generic
	Furman et al (2019) *[Report for UK Gov]*	Generic
DE	BMWi (2019*) [Competition 4.0 report]*	Generic
	BMWi (2019) *[Draft ARC amendment]*	Generic
	Schweitzer et al (2018) *[Report for BMWi]*	Generic

Type of liability test		Standard of proof
Rules (illegality by-object or per se)	Standards (illegality by likely or actual effects)	Lower than current standard
✓ Regulation (§§184ff + arts 5–6 DMA)	✗ Regulation (§§184ff + arts 5–6 DMA)	✓ Regulation (§§184ff + arts 5–6 DMA)
✓ Co-regulation (specific: pp 76ff + arts 3–11 P2B Regulation)	△	△
✓ Regulation (specific: pp 155, 173, 192 + arts 15, 17 of the Directive)	△	△
✓ Antitrust (generic: pp 51, 71) (specific: pp 51, 57–58, 66–67)	✓ Antitrust (MFN: p 57; multi-homing restrictions: pp 57–58)	✓ Antitrust (pp 42, 51)
△	△	△
✓ (Co-)regulation (§7.83)	△	△ (Co-)regulation (Appendix U, §§176–182)
✓ Antitrust (wide MFN: §5.28 + Paper E §§3.6–3.28)	✓ Antitrust (narrow MFN clauses: §5.29 + Paper C §§3.29–3.88)	△
△	△	△
△	✓ Antitrust (generic: §102; MFN clauses: §122; vertical integration-related conduct: §155)	△
✓ Regulation (generic and specific: §§2.34–2.42, 2.46)	△	✗ Antitrust (§3.114)
✓ Antitrust (but sceptical) and/or regulation (generic and specific) (pp 25, 51, 53–54, 73)	✗ Antitrust and/or regulation (generic: p 25)	△
✓ Antitrust (specific: pp 8–9, 75–78)	△	△
✗ Antitrust (pp 127–128, 166–167); specific (p 111)	✓ Antitrust (pp 127–128, 166–167); specific (p 111)	△

(continued)

Table C.1 Continued

	Report	Inquiry scope*
FR	ADLC (2020) *[Antitrust & digital issues paper]*	Generic
	ADLC (2018) *[Online advertising opinion]*	Online search / advertising, social media
	Senate (2019) *[Digital sovereignty report]*	Generic
	ESEC (2019) *[Digital sovereignty report]*	Generic
	IGF & CGE (2019) *[Report for FR Gov]*	Generic
	Parliament (2015) *[Freedoms in the digital age]*	Generic
	Council of the State (2014) *[Fundamental rights in the digital age]*	Generic
	CNNum (2015) *[Digital Ambition report]*	Generic
	CNNum (2014) *[Platform Neutrality report]*	Generic
NL	ACM (2019) *[Mobile app store market study]*	App stores
PT	AdC (2019) *[Digital issues report]*	Generic
US	HoR (2020) *[Competition in digital markets report]*	Online Search / advertising, e-commerce marketplaces, social media, app stores, mobile OSs, digital mapping, cloud computing, web browsing
AU	ACCC (2019) *[Platforms inquiry final report]*	Online search / advertising, social media, news referral
JP	JFTC (2019) *[P2B report]*	E-commerce marketplaces / app stores
	Study Group (2018) *[platforms interim paper]*	Generic
IN	CCI (2020) *[e-commerce market study]*	E-commerce
BRICS	BRICS Centre (2019) *[Digital competition report]*	Generic

Type of liability test		Standard of proof
Rules (illegality by-object or per se)	Standards (illegality by likely or actual effects)	Lower than current standard
✓ Antitrust (?) or (co-)regulation (p 8)	△	△
✓ Antitrust (generic: p 8)	△	△
△	△	△
△	△	△
✓ Regulation (p 22)	△	△
✓ UC/SBP laws (specific: pp 215–216)	△	△
△	△	△
✓ Antitrust (generic: p 69)	△	△
✓ Antitrust (generic and specific: pp 28–29)	△	△
△	△	△
△	△	△
✓ Regulation (pp 382–385, 389, 392); antitrust (pp 399–400)	△	✓ Antitrust (pp 404–405)
△	△	△
△	△	△
✓ Antitrust (?) (generic: p 13) and/ or regulation (generic: p 12)	△	△
△	△	△
✓ Antitrust (specific: pp 581, 594, 599)	✓ Antitrust (generic: pp 136–137)	△

(*continued*)

Table C.1 Continued

	Report	Inquiry scope*
OTHERS	IMF (2019) *[World Economic Outlook report]*	Generic
	UNCTAD (2019) *[Competition issues paper]*	Generic
	UNCTAD (2019) *[Digital economy report]*	Generic
	DE, FR & PL economy ministries (2019) *[Modernising EU competition policy]*	Generic
	Stigler Center (2019) *[Platforms report]*	Generic
	BEUC (2019) *[Competition policy in digital era report]*	Generic

*: to the extent inquiry somehow covers upstream concerns

✓: claimed/suggested

✗: rejected

△: not discussed/claimed or unclear

Source: author's own creation.

Type of liability test		Standard of proof
Rules (illegality by-object or per se)	Standards (illegality by likely or actual effects)	Lower than current standard
△	△	△
✓ Antitrust (?) and/or regulation (generic: p 139)	△	△
✓ Regulation (specific: pp 11–13)	△	△
✓ Antitrust (?) and/or regulation (p 2)	△	△
✓ Antitrust (pp 95, 98) and/or regulation (pp 115–116)	✓ Antitrust (relaxed: pp 96–98)	✓ Antitrust (pp 95, 98–99)
△	△	✓ Antitrust (p 17)

Platform Power in Policy Reports

Note to reader: Due to formatting constraints, it was not possible to fit all columns of the following table onto the same page. Column headers were therefore split over side-by-side consecutive pages. For ease of understanding, the table and each of its entries should be read horizontally, from left to right, over consecutive pages.

Table D.1 Platform power in policy reports

	Report	Inquiry scope*	Systemic (strategic, structuring, critical, societal) power		Significant market power (dominant, preponderant, influential position)		Intermediary power	
			Existence	Relevance	Existence	Relevance	Existence	Relevance
EU	EC SWD (2020) [DMA IA]	Online search / marketplace / app stores / social media / OSs / video sharing / cloud / online advertising	✓ (§§14, 128ff)	✓ Regulation (via 'gatekeeper' test [§§128ff + recitals (1)–(6) + arts 2(1), 3 DMA])	✓ (fn 16)	✓ Antitrust (§§119, 153)	✓ (§14, p 57)	✓ Regulation (via 'gatekeeper' test [§151 + recital (26) DMA])
	EC SWD (2018) [P2B regulation IA]	Online search / marketplaces / app stores / social media	△	△	✗ (p 3)	✓ Antitrust (p 3)	✓ (pp 24–30)	△
	EC SWD (2016) [Copyright Directive IA]	Creative / press publishing industries	△	△	△	△	△	△
	Crémer et al (2019) [Report for EC]	Generic	△	△	✓ (pp 48–49)	✓ Antitrust (pp 46–50, 69–70)	✓ (pp 13, 48, 64, 69–70)	✓ Antitrust (pp 49, 69–70)
UK	CMA (2022) [Mobile ecosystems market study final report]	Mobile ecosystems	✓ (§8.120 + Appendix L)	✓ (Co)-regulation (8.211 + Table 8.1 + Appendix L)	△	△ Antitrust (default)	✓ Appendix L (§§27, 103, 120)	✓ (Co-)regulation (Appendix L [via SMS test])
	CMA (2020) [Online advertising market study final report]	Online search / advertising, social media	✓ (§§7.58-7.64)	✓ (Co-)regulation (§§7.55ff)	✓ (chs 3, 5)	△ Antitrust (default)	✓ (§§3.47, 5.315)	✓ (Co-)regulation (via SMS test [§7.56])
	CMA (2017) [DCT market study report]	DCTs in car / home insurance, energy, broadband, flights, credit cards	△	△	△	△ Antitrust (default)	✓ (§5.21)	△
	HoL (2019) [Regulating in a Digital World report]	Generic	✓ (§171)	✓ Regulation (§§171–172)	✓ (§§4, 121+ §129)	✓ Antitrust (§161)	✓ (§§161, 171, 180)	✓ Antitrust (§161)
	HoL (2016) [Platforms & the DSM report]	Generic	△	△	△ Seemingly assumes dominance (§§153–154)	✓ Antitrust (§179)	✓ (§100)	△
	Furman et al (2019) [Report for UK Gov]	Generic	✓ (§1.117)	✓ Regulation (§§2.10, 2.117)	✓ (§1.30 + §§1.42-1.61, 1.100-1.117)	✓ Antitrust (§3.114)	✓ (§§1.117, 1.148, 1.161 + §§1.55, 1.58)	✓ Regulation (§§2.10, 2.117) (antitrust's role: §§3.114-3.115)

Platform power									
Relational power (SBP/ economic dependence)		Ecosystem power		Regulatory power		Informational power			
						Insider's power		Panoptic power	
Existence	Relevance	Existence	Relevance	Existence	Relevance	Existence	Relevance	Existence	Relevance
✓ (§§14, 28)	✓ Regulation (via 'gatekeeper' test [recitals (20), (40), (43) DMA])	✓ (§§37, 50)	✓ Regulation (via 'gatekeeper' test [implicit in arts 5–6, 12 DMA])	✓ (§§37, 60, 91)	✓ Regulation (via 'gatekeeper' test [implicit in parts of arts 5–6 DMA])	✓ (§109)	✓ Regulation (via 'gatekeeper' test [implicit in parts of 5–6 DMA])	△	✓ Regulation (via 'gatekeeper' test [implicit in parts of 5–6 DMA])
✓ (pp 23–24)	✓ Co-regulation (pp 3, 10)	△	△	✓ Implicit in duty of care solutions	✓ Co-regulation (pp 3, 33, 77, 79)	✓ Implicit in transparency solutions	✓ Co-regulation (pp 3, 33, 77–78)	△	✗
✓ (pp 142, 160)	✓ Regulation (pp 142, 160)	△	△	△	△	△	△	△	△
△	✓ Antitrust (if intermediary power)	△	✓ Antitrust (implicitly: p 48)	✓ (pp 16, 60)	✓ Potentially antitrust (if dominance: pp 12, 62–63)	✓ (pp 5–6)	✓ Antitrust (if dominance: pp 64–65)	△	△
△ Probably implied by SMS finding (Appendix L)	✓ (Co-)regulation (Appendix L [via SMS test])	✓ Appendix L (§§27, 29, 46, 61, 82, 85, 105, 122)	✓ (Co-)regulation (Appendix L [via SMS test])	✓ (§6.44–6.46 + Appendix L [§§28, 45, 60, 84, 104, 121])	✓ (Co-)regulation (Appendix L [via SMS test])	✓ (Implicitly: §6.11)	✓ (Co-)regulation (Appendix L [via SMS test])	✓ (Implicitly: §§6.11, 6.102–6.106, 7.29)	✓ (Co-)regulation (Appendix L [via SMS test])
✓ (§5.362, Appendices P & S)	✓ (Co-)regulation (via SMS test [Appendices P & S])	✓ (§59)	△ (Co-)regulation (§§7.65–7.66)	✓ (§§52, 7.36)	✗ (Co-)regulation (§§7.35–7.36)	✓ (§§102, 5.331ff)	✓ (Co-)regulation (§§7.74ff)	△	△
✓ (§ 4.80 + Paper E §§2.39–2.65)	△	△	△	△	△	△	△	△	△
△	✓ Antitrust (if intermediation power)	△	△	△	△	△	△	△	△
✓ (§§83, 126– 128, 133 + §82 + §122)	✓ Co-regulation (§§126–128, 133)	△	△	△	△	△	△	△	△
✓ (§1.135)	✓ Regulation (§§2.10, 2.117)	△	✗ Antitrust (§3.114)	✓ Implicitly: §1.117	✓ (Co-)regulation (if strategic power) (§117) (?)	✓ (Implicitly: §1.117)	✓ (Co-)regulation (if strategic power (?)) (§117)	△	△

(continued)

Table D.1 Continued

	Report	Inquiry scope*	Systemic (strategic, structuring, critical, societal) power		Significant market power (dominant, preponderant, influential position)		Intermediary power	
			Existence	Relevance	Existence	Relevance	Existence	Relevance
DE	BMWi (2019) *[Competition 4.0 report]*	Generic	△	✓ Regulation (pp 52–53)	△	✓ Antitrust (pp 28–31); regulation (pp 52–53)	✓ (pp 16, 49–50)	✓ Antitrust (pp 31–32)
	BMWi (2019) *[Draft ARC amendment]*	Generic	✓ (pp 4, 8–9, 74)	✓ Antitrust (special rules: pp 8, 74–75)	✓ (p 73)	✓ Antitrust (pp 8, 69)	✓ (p 69)	✓ Antitrust (pp 8, 69)
	Schweitzer et al (2018) *[Report for BMWi]*	Generic	△	△	△	✓ Antitrust (pp 66–75, 77–78, 158)	✓ (pp 8, 66, 70)	✓ Antitrust (pp 66–75, 77–78, 158)
FR	ADLC (2020) *[Antitrust & digital issues paper]*	Generic	△	✓ Antitrust (p 5) or (co-)regulation (p 8)	△	△ Antitrust (default)	△	✓ Antitrust (p 5) or (co-)regulation (p 8)
	ADLC (2018) *[Online advertising opinion]*	Online search / advertising, social media	△	✗ Antitrust (§190)	✓ (§§2, 96, 111, 113, 203–212, 215, 229–230 + p 101)	✓ Antitrust (§190)	△	✗ Antitrust (§190)
	Senate (2019) *[Digital sovereignty report]*	Generic	✓ (p 29 + Annex 1)	✓ Regulation (pp 46–47)	✓ (pp 19, 30 + pp 32–33)	△ Antitrust (default)	△	△
	ESEC (2019) *[Digital sovereignty report]*	Generic	✓ (p 6)	△	✓ (p 5)	△ Antitrust (default)	✓ (pp 9–10)	△
	IGF & CGE (2019) *[Report for FR Gov]*	Generic	✓ (p 19)	✓ Regulation (p 21)	✓ (p 18 + p 19)	△ Antitrust (default)	△	△
	Parliament (2015) *[Freedoms in the digital age]*	Generic	✓ (p 197)	✓ Regulation (pp 222–223); not antitrust (pp 211–212)	✓ (p 200)	△ Antitrust (default)	✓ (pp 201–203)	✓ UC/SBP laws (p 215)
	Council of the State (2014) *[Fundamental rights in the digital age]*	Generic	△	△	✓ (p 106)	△ Antitrust (default)	✓ (p 216)	△
	CNNum (2015) *[Digital Ambition report]*	Generic	✓ (pp 8–9)	✓ Regulation (pp 60–61, 72)	✓ (p 36)	✓ Antitrust (pp 60–61 *juncto* pp 72, 74)	✓ (pp 36, 58, 72)	△

Platform power									
Relational power (SBP/economic dependence)		Ecosystem power		Regulatory power		Informational power			
						Insider's power		Panoptic power	
Existence	Relevance	Existence	Relevance	Existence	Relevance	Existence	Relevance	Existence	Relevance
△	✓	✓	✓	✓	✗	✓	△	△	△
	Antitrust (implicitly: pp 28–31)	(pp 28–31)	Antitrust (implicitly: pp 28–31)	(p 50)	(Not a problem as such: p 50)	(p 23)			
✓	✓	△	△	△	△	✓	✓	△	△
(pp 69, 73)	SBP law (pp 9, 78–80)					(pp 71, 77)	Antitrust (if dominance (?) [p 71] or paramount power (?)) [p 77]		Antitrust (if dominance (?) [p 71] or paramount power (?)) [p 76]
✓	✓	✓	✗	✓	✓	✓		△	△
(pp 56, 70, 73)	SBP law (pp 9, 78–80)	(pp 15–19)	Antitrust (pp 84–89)	(pp 8, 70)	Antitrust (pp 70–71)	(pp 42–43)	Antitrust (if SBP (?), intermediary power, dominance [pp 78, 110])		Antitrust (if dominance) (?) (p 114)
△	△	△	△	△	✓	△			
					Antitrust (?) or (co-)regulation (p 8)				
✓	✗	△	✗	△	△	△	✓	△	△
(§§242–244)	Antitrust (§190)	(§114)	Antitrust (§190)			(§262)	Regulation (§262)		
△	△	△	△	△	△	✓	✓	△	△
						(pp 48–49)	(Co-)regulation (pp 48–49)		
✓	△	△	△	△	△	△	△	△	△
(pp 9–10)									
△	△	△	△	△	△	△	△	△	△
						(Implicitly (?) [p 19])			
✓	✓	△	△	✓	✓	✓	✓	△	△
(p 201)	UC/SBP laws (p 215)			(pp 201–202)	Antitrust (if dominance); UC/SBP laws (if SBP) (pp 208ff)	Implicit in suggested transparency solution	CP law (p 216); regulation (p 224)		
✓	△	△	△	✓	✓	✓	✓	△	△
(p 55)				(pp 21, 216)	Regulation (pp 39, 216–217ff)	(p 107)	Regulation (pp 39, 216–217ff)		
✓	✓	✓	△	✓	✓	✓	✓	△	△
(pp 36, 58, 72)	UC/SBP laws (p 72)	(p 59)		(p 58)	Antitrust (?) and/or regulation (pp 60–66)	(p 58)	Antitrust (?) and/or regulation (pp 60–66)		

(continued)

Table D.1 Continued

	Report	Inquiry scope*	Systemic (strategic, structuring, critical, societal) power		Significant market power (dominant, preponderant, influential position)		Intermediary power	
			Existence	Relevance	Existence	Relevance	Existence	Relevance
	CNNum (2014) [Platform Neutrality report]	Generic	✓ (pp 8, 10, 67)	△	✓ (pp 9, 69–89 + p 67)	✓ Antitrust (p 28)	✓ (pp 8–9, 15)	△ Antitrust (?) (p 15)
NL	ACM (2019) [Mobile app store market study]	App stores	△	△	✗ (p 18)	△ Antitrust (default)	✓ (ch 3)	△ Antitrust (?) ch 3
PT	AdC (2019) [Digital issues report]	Generic	△	△	✓ (§105)	△ Antitrust (§§125ff)	△	△
US	HoR (2020) [Competition in digital markets report]	Online Search / advertising, e-commerce marketplaces, social media, app stores, mobile OSs, digital mapping, cloud computing, web browsing	✓ (p 10)	✓ Regulation (pp 379–383)	✓ (pp 11–12, 14–16, 77–78, 86, 90, 95, 101, 108, 114, 134, 171, 177, 197, 207–208, 212, 220, 225, 231, 235, 255–256, 320, 336)	✓ Antitrust (default)	✓ (pp 6, 15–17, 39, 57, 98, 100, 149, 181, 203, 214, 220, 226, 257–258, 271, 336)	✓ Regulation (pp 379–392); antitrust (pp 397, 400)
AU	ACCC (2019) [Platforms inquiry final report]	Online search / advertising, social media, news referral	✓ (p 13)	✓ (Co-)regulation (p 255)	✓ (ch 2, p 212)	△ Antitrust (default)	✓ (pp 1, 6, 8–9)	△
JP	JFTC (2019) [P2B report]	E-commerce marketplaces / app stores	△	△	△ (pp 7, 22)	△ Antitrust (default)	△	△
JP	Study Group (2018) [platforms interim paper]	Generic	✓ (p 3)	✓ Antitrust (?) (p 13)	✓ (pp 2–3)	△ Antitrust (default)	✓ (p 4)	△
IN	CCI (2020) [e-commerce market study]	E-commerce	△	△	△	△ Antitrust (default)	△	△
BRICS	BRICS Centre (2019) [Digital competition report]	Generic	✓ (p 51)	△	✓ (p 254)	△ Antitrust (default)	✓ (pp 204, 254, 332)	✓ Antitrust (pp 322–326)

Platform power									
Relational power (SBP/economic dependence)		Ecosystem power		Regulatory power		Informational power			
						Insider's power		Panoptic power	
Existence	Relevance	Existence	Relevance	Existence	Relevance	Existence	Relevance	Existence	Relevance
✓	✓	✓	✓	✓	✓	✓	✓	✓	△
(pp 92, 104)	UC/SBP laws (p 29)	(pp 9, 64–67)	Antitrust (?) (p 43)	(p 9)	Antitrust (?) (pp 28, 43–44)	(p 8)	Antitrust (?) (pp 43–44)	(p 8)	
✓	✓	△	△	△	△	△	△	△	△
(p 71)	Antitrust (?) (pp 68–71)	(?) (§105)							
△	△	△	△	△	△	△	△	△	△
✓	✓	△	△	△	△	△	△	△	△
(pp 14–15, 17, 62, 64, 181, 203, 214, 220, 226, 235–236, 257–258, 271, 336)	Regulation (pp 20, 392)	(p 15)	Regulation (pp 379–382)	(pp 7, 98, 230)	Regulation (pp 383–385, 392)	(p 15)	(Implicitly: p 380?)	(pp 218–219, 284, 315–316, 364–365)	Regulation (pp 380–382)
✓	✓	△	△	△	△	△	△	△	△
(pp 8–9, 15–16, 99–105, 163–164, 206ff)	(Co-)regulation (pp 164, 255–256, 509)					(Implicitly: p 139?)			
✓	✓	△	△	✓	✓	✓	✓	✓	✓
(p 23)	UC/SBP laws (default)			(Indirectly: p 55)	UC/SBP laws (if SBP)	Implicit in guidance and suggested transparency solution	Antitrust (if dominance?); UC/SBP laws (if SBP) (ch 1, §4); regulation (p 105)	(Implicitly: p 63)	Antitrust (if dominance?); UC/SBP laws (if SBP [p 63])
△	✓	△	△	✓	✓	✓	✓	△	△
	UC/SBP laws (default)			(p 5)	(Co-)regulation (p 12)	(p 6)	(Co-)regulation (p 12)		
✓	✗	△	△	✓	△	✓	△	✓	△
(§§51, 64, 90)	Self-regulation (§§112–113)			(§91)		(§88)		(§59)	
✓	✓	✓	✓	✓	✓	△	△	✓	✓
(pp 196, 255 + implicitly chs 3–4)	Antitrust (pp 330–331)	(p 552)	Antitrust (pp 300, 552)	(p 358)	Antitrust (p 549)			(pp 337–338)	Antitrust (pp 337–338)

(continued)

Table D.1 Continued

Report	Inquiry scope*	Systemic (strategic, structuring, critical, societal) power		Significant market power (dominant, preponderant, influential position)		Intermediary power	
		Existence	Relevance	Existence	Relevance	Existence	Relevance
IMF (2019) [World Economic Outlook report]	Generic	△	△	✓ (pp 57–61)	△ Antitrust (default)	△	△
UNCTAD (2019) [Competition issues paper]	Generic	△ (p 11)	△ (p 11)	✓ (pp 3–4)	✓ Antitrust (p 7)	✓ (p 7)	✓ Antitrust (?) (p 7) and/or regulation (pp 11ff)
UNCTAD (2019) [Digital economy report]	Generic	△ (p 83)	✓ Regulation (p 140)	✓ (pp 83–84 + p 40)	✓ Antitrust (p 139)	△	△
DE, FR & PL economy ministries (2019) [Modernising EU competition policy]	Generic	✓ (pp 2–3)	✓ Antitrust and/or regulation (p 2)	✓ (pp 2–3)	△ Antitrust (default)	△	△
Stigler Center (2019) [Platforms report]	Generic	△	△	✓ (pp 7–8, 34 + p 9)	△ Antitrust (default)	✓ (pp 143, 150 + p 61)	✓ Regulation (p 106)
BEUC (2019) [Competition policy in digital era report]	Generic	△	△	△	△ Antitrust (default)	△	✓ Regulation (p 24)

(left margin: OTHER)

*: to the extent inquiry somehow covers upstream concerns

✓: claimed/suggested

✗: rejected

△: not discussed/claimed or unclear

Source: author's own creation.

Platform power									
Relational power (SBP/ economic dependence)		Ecosystem power		Regulatory power		Informational power			
						Insider's power		Panoptic power	
Existence	Relevance	Existence	Relevance	Existence	Relevance	Existence	Relevance	Existence	Relevance
△	△	△	△	△	△	△	△	△	△
✓ (p 7)	✓ Antitrust (?) (p 7) and/ or regulation (pp 11ff)	△	△	△	△	△	△	△	△
△	△	△	△	△	△	✓ (p 88)	△	✓ (p 27)	△
△	△	△	△	△	△	△	△	△	△
✓ (p 173)	△	△	△	△	△	△	△	△	△
△	△	△	△	△	△	△	△	△	△

Remedies in Policy Reports

Note to reader: Due to formatting constraints, it was not possible to fit all columns of the following table onto the same page. Column headers were therefore split over side-by-side consecutive pages. For ease of understanding, the table and each of its entries should be read horizontally, from left to right, over consecutive pages.

Table E.1 Remedies in policy reports

	Report	Inquiry scope*	Transparency duties		Non-discrimination duties
EU	EC SWD (2020) [DMA IA]	Online search / marketplace / app stores / social media / OSs / video sharing / cloud / online advertising	✓	Regulation (pp 55–56 + arts 5–6 DMA)	✓ Regulation (p 57 + arts 5–6 DMA)
	EC SWD (2018) [P2B regulation IA]	Online search / marketplaces / app stores / social media	✓	Co-regulation (pp 77–78 + arts 3–10 P2B regulation)	✓ Co-regulation (recital 48 P2B regulation)
	EC SWD (2016) [Copyright Directive IA]	Creative / press publishing industries	△		△
	Crémer et al (2019) [Report for EC]	Generic	✓	Antitrust and regulation (pp 61, 63–65)	✓ Antitrust (p 61)
UK	CMA (2022) [Mobile ecosystems market study final report]	Mobile ecosystems	✓	(Co-)regulation (§§8.153ff) and antitrust (?) (§§8.224, 10.6)	✓ (Co-)regulation (§§8.162ff) and antitrust (?) (§§8.224, 10.6)
	CMA (2020) [Online advertising market study final report]	Online search / advertising, social media	✓	(Co-)regulation (§§7.85ff + ch 8) and antitrust (?) (§§10.28–10.29)	△ (Co-)regulation (§7.77 + ch 8) and antitrust (?) (§§10.28–10.29)
	CMA (2017) [DCT market study report]	DCTs in car/home insurance, energy, broadband, flights, credit cards	✓	Regulation (§§5.6–5.19)	△
	HoL (2019) [Regulating in a Digital World report]	Generic	✓	Regulation (§172)	✓ Regulation (§§167, 172)

Type of remedies			
Good faith (duty of care, loyalty, fiduciary duties, including special duties toward providers on labour platforms)	Data-sharing duties	Interoperability duties	Unbundling
✓ Regulation (pp 53–56, 60 + arts 5–6 DMA)	✓ Regulation (pp 59–60 + arts 5–6 DMA)	✓ Regulation (p 58 + arts 5–6 DMA)	✓ Regulation (§168 + recital (75), art 18 DMA)
✓ Co-regulation (pp 77, 79 + arts 11, 17 P2B Regulation)	✗ (pp 38–42, 73)	△	△
✓ Regulation (pp 155, 192 + art 17 of the Directive)	△	△	△
△	✓ Regulation (antitrust as fallback: pp 68, 91, 109)	✓ Antitrust and/or regulation (pp 58–60, 70–71, 82)	✓ Antitrust (pp 67–68)
✓ (Co-)regulation (§§8.153ff) and antitrust (?) (§§8.224, 10.6)	✓ ✗ (Co-)regulation (via access to APIs [§§8.38, 8.128, 8.169 but see §§8.44–8.49]) and antitrust (?) [§§8.224, 10.6])	✓ (Co-)regulation (§§8.24ff) and antitrust (?) (§§8.224, 10.6)	✗ (§§8.60–8.62, 8.66, 8.197–8.207)
✓ (Co-)regulation (§7.77 + ch 8) and antitrust (?) (§§10.28–10.29)	✓ (Co-)regulation (§§7.83, 7.111ff + ch 8) and antitrust (?) (§§10.28–10.29)	✓ (Co-)regulation (§§7.83, 7.111ff + ch 8) and antitrust (?) (§§10.28–10.29)	✓ (Co-)regulation (§§7.116ff + ch 8) and antitrust (?) (§§10.28–10.29)
✓ Regulation (§§5.6–5.19)	△	△	△
✓ Regulation (§172)	△	△	△

(*continued*)

Table E.1 Continued

	Report	Inquiry scope*		Transparency duties		Non-discrimination duties
DE	HoL (2016) [Platforms & the DSM report]	Generic	✓	CP law (§§285–286)	✓	Co-regulation (§133)
	Furman et al (2019) [Report for UK Gov]	Generic	✓	(Co-)regulation (§§2.31ff)	✓	(Co-)regulation (§§2.36ff)
	BMWi (2019) [Competition 4.0 report]	Generic	✓	Co-regulation (p 52)	✗	(p 54)
	BMWi (2019) [Draft ARC amendment]	Generic	✓	Antitrust (pp 9, 77)	✓	Antitrust (pp 8, 75)
	Schweitzer et al (2018) [Report for BMWi]	Generic	✓	UC/CP/ contract laws + new regulation (pp 118–119)	✓	Antitrust (p 115)
FR	ADLC (2020) [Antitrust & digital issues paper]	Generic	△		△	
	ADLC (2018) [Online advertising opinion]	Online search / advertising, social media	✓	Regulation (§§262–276)	△	Antitrust (?) (§§252ff)
	Senate (2019) [Digital sovereignty report]	Generic	✓	(Co-?) regulation (pp 47–49)	✓	Regulation (pp 44–45)
	ESEC (2019) [Digital sovereignty report]	Generic	✓	Regulation (pp 16, 32–33)	✓	Regulation (pp 16–18, 33)
	IGF & CGE (2019) [Report for FR Gov]	Generic	✓	Regulation (p 22)	△	
	Parliament (2015) [Freedoms in the digital age]	Generic	✓	CP law (p 216); regulation (p 224)	✓	Antitrust (pp 211–212); regulation (pp 223–225)

Type of remedies			
Good faith (duty of care, loyalty, fiduciary duties, including special duties toward providers on labour platforms)	Data-sharing duties	Interoperability duties	Unbundling
✓ Co-regulation (§133)	△	△	△
△	✓ Regulation (§§2.87–2.94)	✓ Regulation (§§2.68–2.78)	✗ (§5.13)
△	✓ Regulation (antitrust as fallback: pp 36–38)	△	✓ Antitrust (p 78)
△	✓ Antitrust (pp 8, 72)	✓ Antitrust (pp 9, 76–77)	△
✓ UC/CP/contract laws + new regulation (pp 118–119)	✓ Antitrust (pp 159–160, but see also p 115)	△	✗ (p 121)
△	△	△	△
△	△	△	△
✓ Regulation (p 47)	✓ Regulation (p 47)	△	✗ (pp 38–39)
✓ Labour law (p 27)	△	△	△
✓ Regulation (p 22)	✓ Regulation (p 22)	✓ Regulation (p 22)	△
✓ UC/SBP laws (p 215); regulation (pp 223–225)	△	△	△

(*continued*)

Table E.1 Continued

	Report	Inquiry scope*	Transparency duties		Non-discrimination duties	
	Council of the State (2014) [Fundamental rights in the digital age]	Generic	✓	(Co-) regulation (pp 278–279)	✓	Antitrust (but no search neutrality) (p 223)
	CNNum (2015) [Digital Ambition report]	Generic	✓	Antitrust (?), UC/SBP laws, and/or regulation (pp 59–66, 72, 74	✓	Antitrust (?), UC/SBP laws, and/or regulation (pp 59–60, 62, 69)
	CNNum (2014) [Platform Neutrality report]	Generic	✓	Antitrust (?), UC/SBP laws, and regulation (pp 12, 44–45)	✓	Antitrust (?), UC/SBP laws, and regulation (pp 11, 28–29, 31)
NL	ACM (2019) [Mobile app store market study]	App stores	✓	Antitrust (pp 107–108) and/or regulation (p 108)	✓	Antitrust (pp 106–107) and/or regulation (p 108)
PT	AdC (2019) [Digital issues report]	Generic	✓	Co-regulation (§306)	△	Antitrust (?) (§§301–304)
US	HoR (2020) [Competition in digital markets report]	Online Search / advertising, e-commerce marketplaces, social media, app stores, mobile OSs, digital mapping, cloud computing, web browsing	△	Antitrust (?)	✓	Regulation (pp 20, 393–395); antitrust as fallback (?)
AU	ACCC (2019) [Platforms inquiry final report]	Online search / advertising, social media, news referral	✓	(Co-) regulation (p 256)	✓	(Co-)regulation (p 256); antitrust (p 531)
JP	JFTC (2019) [P2B report]	E-commerce marketplaces / app stores	✓	Antitrust (?) + UC/SBP laws (?) (pp 33, 38, 44, 51, 53, 56, 63, 68, 71, 78, 94, 99); regulation (p 105)	✓	Antitrust (?) + UC/SBP laws (?) (p 68); regulation (p 105)

Type of remedies			
Good faith (duty of care, loyalty, fiduciary duties, including special duties toward providers on labour platforms)	**Data-sharing duties**	**Interoperability duties**	**Unbundling**
✓ New/bolstered (Co-)regulation (pp 224, 278–281)	△	△	△
✓ UC/SBP laws and/or regulation (p 72)	△	✓ Antitrust and/or regulation (pp 70–71)	△
✓ UC/SBP laws (p 29)	✓ Regulation (?) (pp 39, 41)	△	✓ Antitrust (?) (p 28)
△	△	△	△
△	△	△	△
✓ Regulation (pp 20, 392); antitrust as fallback (?)	△	✓ Regulation (pp 20, 385–387); antitrust as fallback (?)	✓ Regulation (pp 20, 379–382); antitrust as fallback (?)
✓ (Co-)regulation (pp 164, 249, 256–257, 274ff)	✓ (Co-)regulation (pp 249, 256–257)	△	✗ (p 117)
✓ UC/SBP laws (?) (pp 33, 47, 51, 56, 68, 71, 83, 99, 103)	✓ Antitrust (?) + UC/SBP laws (pp 11–12)	△ Yes, if this is included in the unexplained 'data openness' remedy (pp 12–13)	△

Table E.1 Continued

	Report	Inquiry scope*		Transparency duties		Non-discrimination duties
	Study Group (2018) *[platforms interim paper]*	Generic	✓	Antitrust (?) (p 13) and/or co-regulation (p 12)	✓	Antitrust (?) (p 13) and/or co-regulation (p 12)
IN	CCI (2020) *[e-commerce market study]*	E-commerce	△		△	
BRICS	BRICS Centre (2019) *[Digital competition report]*	Generic	✓	Co-regulation (pp 455–456)	✓	Antitrust (p 566)
OTHER	IMF (2019) *[World Economic Outlook report]*	Generic	△		△	
	UNCTAD (2019) *[Competition issues paper]*	Generic	✓	Regulation (p 12)	✓	Antitrust and/or regulation (pp 11–13)
	UNCTAD (2019) *[Digital economy report]*	Generic	△		✓	Regulation (p 140)
	DE, FR & PL economy ministries (2019) *[Modernising EU competition policy]*	Generic	△		△	Antitrust (?) and/or regulation (p 2)
	Stigler Center (2019) *[Platforms report]*	Generic	✓	Regulation (pp 187–189)	✓	Regulation (p 118)
	BEUC (2019) *[Competition policy in digital era report]*	Generic	△		△	

*: to the extent inquiry somehow covers upstream concerns

✓: claimed/suggested

✗: rejected

△: not discussed/claimed or unclear

Source: author's own creation.

Type of remedies			
Good faith (duty of care, loyalty, fiduciary duties, including special duties toward providers on labour platforms)	Data-sharing duties	Interoperability duties	Unbundling
✓ Antitrust (?) (p 13) and/or co-regulation (p 12)	△	△	△
△	△	△	△
✓ Antitrust and/or bolstered labour law (pp 384–395); UC/SBP laws (p 610)	✓ Antitrust (p 600)	✓ Antitrust and/or regulation (p 450)	✓ Antitrust or regulation (pp 430, 435–436)
△	△	△	✓ Antitrust (p 69)
✓ Antitrust (?) and/or regulation (pp 11–13)	△	△	△ (pp 13–14)
✓ Regulation (p 140)	✓ Regulation (p 140)	△	△ (p 141)
✓ Antitrust (?) and/or regulation (p 2)	✓ Antitrust (?) and/or regulation (p 2)	✓ Antitrust (?) and/or regulation (p 2)	△
✓ Regulation (pp 194–195)	✓ Antitrust and/or regulation (p 117)	✓ Regulation (pp 117–118)	✓ Regulation (pp 100, 144)
△	△	△	✓ Antitrust (p 21)

Bibliography

Books and Chapters

ABA Section of Antitrust Law, *Federal Statutory Exemptions From Antitrust Law* (American Bar Association 2007).

Akman P, *The Concept of Abuse in EU Competition Law: Law and Economic Approaches* (Hart 2015).

Amato G, *Antitrust and the Bounds of Power: The Dilemma of Liberal Democracy in the History of the Market* (Hart 1997).

Anchustegui IH, *Buyer Power in EU Competition Law* (Concurrences 2017).

Anderson E, 'The Business Enterprise as an Ethical Agent' in S Rangan (ed), *Performance and Progress: Essays on Capitalism, Business, and Society* (OUP 2015).

Andriychuk O, 'Thinking Inside the Box: Why Competition as a Process Is a Sui Generis Right—A Methodological Observation' in D Zimmer (ed), *The Goals of Competition Law* (Edward Elgar 2012).

Andriychuk O, *The Normative Foundations of European Competition Law: Assessing the Goals of Antitrust through the Lens of Legal Philosophy* (Edward Elgar 2017).

Areeda P and H Hovenkamp, *Antitrust Law: An Analysis of Antitrust Principles and Their Application* (Supplement 8/2019, rev edn, Wolters Kluwer 1978).

Arendt H, *On Revolution* (Penguin 1990).

Arneson R, 'Equality of Opportunity' in E Zalta (ed), *The Stanford Encyclopedia of Philosophy* (rev edn, Stanford University 2015) <https://stanford.io/2XBJ3SB> accessed 18 November 2022.

Attas D, 'Lockean Justification of Intellectual Property' in A Grosseries, A Marciano and A Strowel (eds), *Intellectual Property and Theories of Justice* (Palgrave Macmillan 2008).

Ayal A, 'Anti-Anti Regulation: The Supplanting of Industry Regulators with Competition Agencies and How Antitrust Suffers as a Result' in J Drexl and F Di Porto (eds), *Competition Law as Regulation* (Edward Elgar 2015).

Ayal A, *Fairness in Antitrust: Protecting the Strong from the Weak* (Hart 2016).

Baker A, 'Simplicity' in E Zalta (ed), *The Stanford Encyclopedia of Philosophy* (rev edn, Stanford University 2022) <https://stanford.io/31tTR6r> accessed 19 November 2022.

Baker J, *The Antitrust Paradigm: Restoring a Competitive Economy* (Harvard UP 2019).

Bakhoum M, 'Abuse without Dominance in Competition Law: Abuse of Economic Dependence and Its Interface with Abuse of Dominance' in F Di Porto and R Podszun (eds), *Abusive Practices in Competition Law* (Edward Elgar 2018).

Barrère C, 'Defining Economic Democracy: A Challenge. An Institutionalist Framework' in A Marciano and J-M Josselin (eds), *Democracy, Freedom and Coercion: A Law and Economics Approach* (Edward Elgar 2007).

Behrens P, 'The Ordoliberal Concept of "Abuse" of a Dominant Position and Its Impact on Article 102 TFEU' in F Di Porto and R Podszun (eds), *Abusive Practices in Competition Law* (Edward Elgar 2018).

Belleflamme P and M Peitz, *Industrial Organization: Markets and Strategies* (2nd edn, CUP 2015).

Belleflamme P and M Peitz, 'Platforms and Network Effects' in L Corchón and M Marini (eds), *Handbook of Game Theory and Industrial Organization, Volume II: Applications* (Edward Elgar 2018).

Belleflamme P and M Peitz, *The Economics of Platforms: Concepts and Strategy* (CUP 2021).

Berlin I, *Freedom and Its Betrayal: Six Enemies of Human Liberty* (H Hardy ed, 2nd edn, Princeton UP 2014).

Böhm F, 'Democracy and Economic Power' in Institut für ausländisches und internationals Wirtschaftsrecht an der Johann-Wolfgang-Goethe Universität (ed), *Cartel and Monopoly in Modern Law*, vol 1 (CF Müller 1961).

Böhm F, W Eucken and H Großmann-Doerth, 'The Ordo Manifesto of 1936' in A Peacock and M Willgerodt (eds), *Germany's Social Market Economy: Origins and Evolution* (Palgrave Macmillan 1989).

Bork R, *The Antitrust Paradox: A Policy at War with Itself* (Basic Books 1978).

Boudreau K and A Hagiu, 'Platform Rules: Multi-Sided Platforms as Regulators' in A Gawer (ed), *Platforms, Markets and Innovation* (Edward Elgar 2009).

Boyer S, 'German Contemporary Analyses of Economic Order: Standard Ordnungstheorie, Ordoliberalism and Ordnungsökonomik in Perspective' in A Labrousse and J-D Weisz (eds), *Institutional Economics in France and Germany: German Ordoliberalism versus the French Regulation School* (Springer 2001).

Boyle J, *The Public Domain: Enclosing the Commons of the Mind* (Yale UP 2008).

Brennan G and J Buchanan, *The Reason of Rules: Constitutional Political Economy* (CUP 1985).

Buchanan J, 'Fairness, Hope, and Justice' in R Skurski (ed), *New Directions in Economic Justice* (University of Notre Dame Press 1983).

Budzinski O, 'Modern Industrial Economics: Open Problems and Possible Limits' in J Drexl, W Kerber and R Podszun (eds), *Competition Policy and the Economic Approach: Foundations and Limitations* (Edward Elgar 2011).

Carstensen P, *Competition Policy and the Control of Buyer Power: A Global Issue* (Edward Elgar 2017).

Carter I, *A Measure of Freedom* (OUP 1999).

Carter I, 'Positive and Negative Liberty' in E Zalta (ed), *The Stanford Encyclopedia of Philosophy* (rev edn, Stanford University 2022) <https://stanford.io/2LExXnc> accessed 18 November 2022.

Cash D, *Regulation and the Credit Rating Agencies: Restraining Ancillary Services* (Routledge 2018).

Cavanagh M, *Against Equality of Opportunity* (OUP 2002).

Chen MK, 'Dynamic Pricing in a Labor Market: Surge Pricing and Flexible Work on the Uber Platform' in *Proceedings of the 2016 ACM Conference on Economics and Computation* (Association for Computing Machinery 2016) <https://doi.org/10.1145/2940716.2940 798> accessed 18 November 2022.

Cheng T and M Gal, 'Superior Bargaining Power: Dealing with Aggregate Concentration Concerns' in F Di Porto and R Podszun (eds), *Abusive Practices in Competition Law* (Edward Elgar 2018).

Christiano T, *The Rule of the Many: Fundamental Issues in Democratic Theory* (Routledge 2018).

Christiano T, 'Democracy' in C McKinnon, R Jubb and P Tomlin (eds), *Issues in Political Theory* (4th edn, OUP 2019).

Cohen GA, *Why Not Socialism?* (Princeton UP 2009).

Cohen J, 'Between Truth and Power' in M Hildebrandt and B van den Berg (eds), *Information, Freedom and Property: The Philosophy of Law Meets the Philosophy of Technology* (Routledge 2016).

Cohen R and T Wang, *Android Application Development for Intel® Platform* (Apress 2014).

Collier P, *The Future of Capitalism: Facing the New Anxieties* (HarperCollins 2018).

Colomo PI, *The Shaping of EU Competition Law* (CUP 2018).

Colquitt J and J Rodell, 'Measuring Justice and Fairness' in R Cropanzano and M Ambrose (eds), *The Oxford Handbook of Justice in the Workplace* (OUP 2015).

Cortada J, *IBM: The Rise and Fall and Reinvention of a Global Icon* (MIT Press 2019).

Cudd A, *Analyzing Oppression* (OUP 2006).

Cusumano M, A Gawer and D Yoffie, *The Business of Platforms: Strategy in the Age of Digital Competition, Innovation, and Power* (HarperBusiness 2019).

Davies W, *The Limits of Neoliberalism: Authority, Sovereignty and the Logic of Competition* (revised edn, SAGE 2017).

De Tocqueville A, *Democracy in America: Historical–Critical Edition of* De la Démocratie en Amérique (E Nolla ed, JT Schleifer tr, Liberty Fund 2010).

DeFillippi R and others, 'Crowd-Sourcing and the Evolution of the Microstock Photography Industry: The Case of iStockphoto and Getty Images' in R DeFillippi and P Wikström (eds), *International Perspectives on Business Innovation and Disruption in the Creative Industries: Film, Video and Photography* (Edward Elgar 2014).

Di Porto F, 'Abuses of Information and Informational Remedies: Rethinking Exchange of Information under Competition Law' in J Drexl and F Di Porto (eds), *Competition Law as Regulation* (Edward Elgar 2015).

Drexl J, 'On the (A)political Character of the Economic Approach to Competition Law' in J Drexl, W Kerber and R Podszun (eds), *Competition Policy and the Economic Approach: Foundations and Limitations* (Edward Elgar 2011).

Drexl J, 'Déséquilibres Économiques et Droit de la Concurrence' in L Boy (ed), *Les Déséquilibres Économiques et le Droit Économique* (Larcier 2014).

Drexl J, 'Consumer Welfare and Consumer Harm: Adjusting Competition Law and Policies to the Needs of Developing Jurisdictions' in M Gal and others (eds) *The Economic Characteristics of Developing Jurisdictions: Their Implications for Competition Law* (Edward Elgar 2015).

Ducci F, *Natural Monopolies in Digital Platform Markets* (CUP 2020).

Dunne N, *Competition Law and Economic Regulation: Making and Managing Markets* (CUP 2015).

Dworkin G, *The Theory and Practice of Autonomy* (CUP 1988).

Dworkin R, *A Matter of Principle* (Harvard UP 1985).

Dworkin R, *Sovereign Virtue: The Theory and Practice of Equality* (Harvard UP 2000).

Economides N, 'Competition, Compatibility, and Vertical Integration in the Computing Industry' in J Eisenach and T Lenard (eds), *Competition, Innovation and the Microsoft Monopoly: Antitrust in the Digital Marketplace* (Springer Science+Business Media 1999).

Evans D and R Schmalensee, *Matchmakers: The New Economics of Multisided Platforms* (Harvard Business Review Press 2016).

Ezrachi A and M Stucke, *Virtual Competition: The Promise and Perils of the Algorithm-Driven Economy* (Harvard UP 2016).

Feldman A, 'Welfare Economics' in S Durlauf and L Blume (eds), *The New Palgrave Dictionary of Economics* (rev edn, Palgrave Macmillan 2008).

Ferreira F and V Peragine, 'Individual Responsibility and Equality of Opportunity' in M Adler and M Fleurbaey (eds), *The Oxford Handbook of Well-Being and Public Policy* (OUP 2016).

Féteira LT, *The Interplay between European and National Competition Law after Regulation 1/2003: 'United (Should) We Stand?'* (Kluwer Law International 2015).

Fikentscher W, P Hacker and R Podszun, *FairEconomy: Crises, Culture, Competition and the Role of Law* (Springer 2013).

Fishkin J, *Bottlenecks: A New Theory of Equal Opportunity* (OUP 2014).

Flew A, *The Politics of Procrustes: Contradictions of Enforced Equality* (Prometheus Books 1981).

Foster K, 'Is There a Global Sports Law?' in R Siekmann and J Soek (eds), *Lex Sportiva: What Is Sports Law?* (TMC Asser Press 2012).

Foucault M, *Power: Essential Works of Foucault, 1954–1984* (J Faubion ed, New Press 2001).

Frankfurt H, 'Coercion and Moral Responsibility' in T Honderich (ed), *Essays on Freedom of Action* (Routledge 2015).

Fried B, *The Progressive Assault on Laissez-Faire: Robert Hale and the First Law and Economics Movement* (Harvard UP 2001).

Fried C, *Contract as Promise: A Theory of Contractual Obligation* (Harvard UP 1981).

Fuller L, *The Morality of Law* (2nd edn, Yale UP 1969).

Galbraith JK, *American Capitalism: The Concept of Countervailing Power* (Hamish Hamilton 1952).

Galbraith JK, *American Capitalism: The Concept of Countervailing Power* (2nd edn, Blackwell 1980).

Galston W, 'A Liberal Defense of Equality of Opportunity' in L Pojman and R Westmoreland (eds), *Equality: Selected Readings* (OUP 1997).

Gates B, *The Road Ahead* (Viking 1995).

Gauthier R, 'Competition Law, Free Movement of Players, and Nationality Restrictions' in M McCann (ed), *The Oxford Handbook of American Sports Law* (OUP 2018).

Gawer A and M Cusumano, *Platform Leadership: How Intel, Microsoft, and Cisco Drive Industry Innovation* (Harvard Business School Press 2002).

Gawer A and M Cusumano, 'Platforms and Innovation' in M Dodgson, D Gann and N Phillips (eds), *The Oxford Handbook of Innovation Management* (OUP 2014).

Gerber D, 'The Future of Article 82: Dissecting the Conflict' in C-D Ehlermann and M Marquis (eds), *European Competition Law Annual: 2007* (Hart 2008).

Gilbert R, *Innovation Matters: Competition Policy for the High-Technology Economy* (MIT Press 2020).

Ginsburg J and A Strowel, 'Copyright Liability for Hyperlinking' in T Aplin (ed), *Research Handbook on Intellectual Property and Digital Technologies* (Edward Elgar 2020).

Glas R, *Battlefields of Negotiation: Control, Agency, and Ownership in World of Warcraft* (Amsterdam UP 2012).

Gomberg P, *How to Make Opportunity Equal: Race and Contributive Justice* (Blackwell 2007).

Graef I, *EU Competition Law, Data Protection and Online Platforms: Data as Essential Facility* (Wolters Kluwer 2016).

Greenstein S, 'Internet Infrastructure' in M Peitz and J Waldfogel (eds), *The Oxford Handbook of the Digital Economic* (OUP 2012).

Grimes W, 'The Sylvania Free Rider Justification for Downstream-Power Vertical Restraints: Truth or Invitation for Pretext?' in R Pitofsky (ed), *How the Chicago School Overshot the Mark: The Effect of Conservative Economic Analysis on U.S. Antitrust* (OUP 2008).

Grimm D, *Sovereignty: The Origin and Future of a Political and Legal Concept* (Columbia UP 2015).

Großmann-Doerth H, 'Selbstgeschaffenes Recht der Wirtschaft und staatliches Recht' in N Goldschmidt and M Wohlgemuth (eds), *Grundtexte zur Freiburger Tradition der Ordnungsökonomik* (Mohr Siebeck 2008).

Harvard Business Review, *Monopolies and Tech Giants: The Insights You Need from Harvard Business Review* (Harvard Business School Publishing 2020).

Hayashi S, 'The Goals of Japanese Competition Law' in J Drexl, L Idot and J Monéger (eds), *Economic Theory and Competition Law* (Edward Elgar 2009).

Hayek FA, *Individualism and Economic Order* (first published 1948, University of Chicago Press 1980).

Hayek FA, *The Constitution of Liberty: The Definitive Edition* (R Hamowy ed, University of Chicago Press 2011).

Hayek FA, *Law, Legislation and Liberty: A New Statement of the Liberal Principles of Justice and Political Economy* (first published 1976, first published in one volume, 1982, Routledge 2013).

Hilty R, *Law Against Unfair Competition: Towards a New Paradigm in Europe* (Springer 2007).

Holmes W and M Mangiaracina, *Antitrust Law Handbook: 2018–2019 Edition* (Thomson Reuters 2018).

Hovenkamp H, *The Antitrust Enterprise: Principle and Execution* (Harvard UP 2005).

Jacob R, *IP and Other Things: A Collection of Essays and Speeches* (Hart 2005).

Jacobs L, *Pursuing Equal Opportunities: The Theory and Practice of Egalitarian Justice* (CUP 2004).

Just R, D Hueth and A Schmitz, *The Welfare Economics of Public Policy: A Practical Approach to Project and Policy Evaluation* (Edward Elgar 2004).

Kalintiri A, *Evidence Standards in EU Competition Enforcement: The EU Approach* (Hart 2019).

Kaplow L, 'On the Choice of Welfare Standard in Competition Law' in D Zimmer (ed), *The Goals of Competition Law* (Edward Elgar 2012).

Kaplow L and C Shapiro, 'Antitrust' in AM Polinsky and S Shavell (eds), *Handbook of Law and Economics*, vol 2 (Elsevier 2007).

Kelly K, *New Rules for the New Economy* (Viking 1998).

Kerber W, 'Competition, Innovation, and Competition Law: Dissecting the Interplay' in D Gerard, B Meyring and E Morgan de Rivery (eds), *Dynamic Markets, Dynamic Competition and Dynamic Enforcement* (Bruylant 2018).

Keynes JM, *The General Theory of Employment, Interest, and Money* (first published 1936, Palgrave Macmillan 2018).

Kirkpatrick D, *The Facebook Effect: The Inside Story of the Company That Is Connecting the World* (Simon & Schuster 2010).

Kirkwood J and R Lande, 'The Chicago School's Foundation Is Flawed: Antitrust Protects Consumers, Not Efficiency' in R Pitofsky (ed) *How the Chicago School Overshot the Mark: The Effect of Conservative Economic Analysis on U.S. Antitrust* (OUP 2008).

Komesar N, *Imperfect Alternatives: Choosing Institutions in Law, Economics, and Public Policy* (University of Chicago Press 1994).

Kuhn T, *The Structure of Scientific Revolutions* (University of Chicago Press 1962).

Labrousse A and J-D Weisz (eds), *Institutional Economics in France and Germany: German Ordoliberalism versus the French Regulation School* (Springer 2001).

Lakatos I, 'History of Science and Its Rational Reconstructions' in J Worrall and G Currie (eds), *The Methodology of Scientific Research Programmes* (CUP 1978).

Lamond G, 'Coercion' in H LaFollette (ed), *International Encyclopedia of Ethics* (Blackwell 2013).

Lao M, 'Free Riding: An Overstated, and Unconvincing, Explanation for Resale Price Maintenance' in R Pitofsky (ed), *How the Chicago School Overshot the Mark: The Effect of Conservative Economic Analysis on U.S. Antitrust* (OUP 2008).

Levine R, *Free Ride: How Digital Parasites Are Destroying the Culture Business, and How the Culture Business Can Fight Back* (Doubleday 2011).

Lianos I, 'The Vertical/Horizontal Dichotomy in Competition Law: Some Reflections with Regard to Dual Distribution and Private Labels' in A Ezrachi and U Bernitz (eds), *Private Labels, Brands and Competition Policy: The Changing Landscape of Retail Competition* (OUP 2009).

Lianos I, 'Some Reflections on the Question of the Goals of EU Competition Law' in I Lianos and D Geradin (eds), *Handbook on European Competition Law: Substantive Aspects* (Edward Elgar 2013).

Lianos I, 'Competition Law Remedies in Europe' in I Lianos and D Geradin (eds), *Handbook on European Competition Law: Enforcement and Procedure* (Edward Elgar 2013).

Lianos I, 'The Principle of Effectiveness, Competition Law Remedies and the Limits of Adjudication' in P Lowe, M Marquis and G Monti (eds), *European Competition Law Annual 2013* (Hart 2016).

Lianos I, 'The Poverty of Competition Law' in D Gerard and I Lianos (eds), *Reconciling Efficiency and Equity: A Global Challenge for Competition Policy* (CUP 2019).

Lindblom C, *Politics and Markets: The World's Political–Economic Systems* (Basic Books 1977).

Lippert-Rasmussen K, *Luck Egalitarianism* (Bloomsbury 2016).

Locke J, *Two Treatises of Government* (McMaster University Archive of the History of Economic Thought 1999).

Lovett F, *A General Theory of Domination and Justice* (OUP 2010).

Lütge C, *The Ethics of Competition: How a Competitive Society Is Good for All* (Edward Elgar 2019).

Lynskey O, 'The Power of Providence: The Role of Platforms in Leveraging the Legibility of Users to Accentuate Inequality' in M Moore and D Tambini (eds), *Digital Dominance: The Power of Google, Amazon, Facebook, and Apple* (OUP 2018).

MacCormick N, *Rhetoric and the Rule of Law: A Theory of Legal Reasoning* (OUP 2005).

Maggiolino M, 'The Regulatory Breakthrough of Competition Law: Definitions and Worries' in J Drexl and F Di Porto (eds), *Competition Law as Regulation* (Edward Elgar 2015).

Maillé P and B Tuffin, *Telecommunication Network Economics: From Theory to Applications* (CUP 2014).

Marty F, 'La Révolution n'a-t-elle Pas Eu Lieu? De la Place de l'Analyse Économique Dans le Contentieux Concurrentiel de l'UE' in V Giacobbo-Peyronnel and C Verdure (eds), *Contentieux du Droit de la Concurrence de l'Union Européenne: Questions d'Actualité et Perspectives* (Larcier 2017).

Marx K, *Capital: A Critique of Political Economy*, vol 1 (tr Ben Fowkes, 2nd edn, Penguin 1990).

Mason A, *Levelling the Playing Field: The Idea of Equal Opportunity and Its Place in Egalitarian Thought* (OUP 2006).

Massarotto G, *Antitrust Settlements: How a Simple Agreement Can Drive the Economy* (Wolters Kluwer 2019).

Maxwell W, *Smart(er) Internet Regulation through Cost–Benefit Analysis: Measuring Harms to Privacy, Freedom of Expression, and the Internet Ecosystem* (Presses des Mines 2017).

McAfee A and E Brynjolfsson, *Machine, Platform, Crowd: Harnessing Our Digital Future* (Norton 2017).

McQuarrie E, *The New Consumer Online: A Sociology of Taste, Audience, and Publics* (Edward Elgar 2015).

Merges R, *Justifying Intellectual Property* (Harvard UP 2011).

Mestmäcker E-J, 'The Development of German and European Competition Law with Special Reference to the EU Commission's Article 82 Guidance of 2008' in LF Pace (ed), *European Competition Law: The Impact of the Commission's Guidance on Article 102* (Edward Elgar 2011).

Miller D, *Principles of Social Justice* (Harvard UP 1999).

Miller D, 'Liberalism, Equal Opportunities and Cultural Commitments' in P Kelly (ed), *Multiculturalism Reconsidered Culture and Equality and Its Critics* (Polity Press 2002).

Miller D, 'Introduction' in David Miller (ed), *The Liberty Reader* (first published 2006, Routledge 2016).

Mokyr J, *A Culture of Growth: The Origins of the Modern Economy* (Princeton UP 2016).

Möller K, *The Global Model of Constitutional Rights* (OUP 2012).

Motta M, *Competition Policy: Theory and Practice* (CUP 2004).

Nazzini R, *The Foundations of European Union Competition Law: The Objective and Principles of Article 102* (OUP 2011).

Nihoul P and P Van Cleynenbreugel (eds), *The Roles of Innovation in Competition Law Analysis* (Edward Elgar 2018).

Nozick R, 'Coercion' in S Morgenbesser, P Suppes and M White (eds), *Philosophy, Science, and Method: Essays in Honor of Ernest Nagel* (St Martin's Press 1969).

Nozick R, *Anarchy, State, and Utopia* (first published 1974, Basic Books 2013).

O'Donoghue R and J Padilla, *The Law and Economics of Article 102 TFEU* (2nd edn, Hart 2013).

O'Donoghue R and J Padilla, *The Law and Economics of Article 102 TFEU* (3rd edn, Hart 2020).

Op Den Kamp C and Hunter D, 'Introduction: Of People, Places, and Parlance' in C Op Den Kamp and D Hunter (eds), *A History of Intellectual Property in 50 Objects* (CUP 2019).

Papadopoulou M-D and E-M Moustaka, 'Copyright and the Press Publishers Right on the Internet: Evolutions and Perspectives' in T-E Synodinou and others (eds), *EU Internet Law in the Digital Era: Regulation and Enforcement* (Springer 2020).

Parker G, M Van Alstyne and S Choudary, *Platform Revolution: How Networked Markets Are Transforming the Economy and How to Make Them Work for You* (Norton 2016).

Pasquale F, *The Black Box Society: The Secret Algorithms That Control Money and Information* (Harvard UP 2015).

Patterson M, *Antitrust Law in the New Economy: Google, Yelp, LIBOR, and the Control of Information* (Harvard UP 2017).

Peritz R, *Competition Policy in America: History, Rhetoric, Law* (rev edn, OUP 2000).

Perloff J, *Microeconomics* (6th edn, Addison-Wesley 2012).

Petit N, *Big Tech and the Digital Economy: The Moligopoly Scenario* (OUP 2020).

Pettit P, *Republicanism: A Theory of Freedom and Government* (Clarendon Press 1997).

Piketty T, *Capital et Idéologie* (Seuil 2019).

Pitofsky R, 'Introduction: Setting the Stage' in R Pitofsky (ed), *How the Chicago School Overshot the Mark: The Effect of Conservative Economic Analysis on U.S. Antitrust* (OUP 2008).

Posner E, *How Antitrust Failed Workers* (OUP 2021).

Posner R, *The Economics of Justice* (Harvard UP 1981).

Posner R, *The Problems of Jurisprudence* (Harvard UP 1990).

Posner R, *Antitrust Law* (2nd edn, University of Chicago Press 2001).

Posner R, *Economic Analysis of Law* (9th edn, Wolter Kluwer Law & Business 2014).

Raustiala K and C Sprigman, *The Knockoff Economy: How Imitation Sparks Innovation* (OUP 2012).

Rawls J, *A Theory of Justice* (Harvard UP 1971).

Rawls J, *A Theory of Justice: Revised Edition* (Harvard UP 1999).

Robbins L, *An Essay on the Nature and Significance of Economic Science* (3rd edn, Macmillan 1984).

Robertson V, *Competition Law's Innovation Factor: The Relevant Market in Dynamic Contexts in the EU and the US* (Hart 2020).

Robinson J, *Economic Heresies: Some Old-Fashioned Questions in Economic Theory* (Palgrave Macmillan 1971).

Roemer J, *Theories of Distributive Justice* (Harvard UP 1996).

Roemer J, *Equality of Opportunity* (Harvard UP 1998).

Roemer J and A Trannoy, 'Equality of Opportunity' in A Atkinson and F Bourguignon (eds), *Handbook of Income Distribution*, vol 2A (Elsevier 2015).

Sagers C, *United States v. Apple: Competition in America* (Harvard UP 2019).

Samuels W, 'The Concept of "Coercion" in Economics' in W Samuels, S Medema and AA Schmid (eds), *The Economy as a Process of Valuation* (Edward Elgar 1997).

Samuelson P, *The Collected Scientific Papers of Paul A. Samuelson*, vol 2 (JE Stiglitz ed, Oxford/IBH Publishing 1966).

Sandel M, *What Money Can't Buy: The Moral Limits of the Market* (Allen Lane 2012).

Sandel M, *The Tyranny of Merit: What's Become of the Common Good?* (Allen Lane 2020).

Sassoon D, *The Anxious Triumph: A Global History of Capitalism 1860–1914* (Allen Lane 2019).

Sauter W, *Coherence in EU Competition Law* (OUP 2016).

Scanlon T, *Why Does Inequality Matter?* (OUP 2018).

Schaar J, 'Equality of Opportunity, and Beyond' in L Pojman and R Westmoreland (eds), *Equality: Selected Readings* (OUP 1997).

Schmidt E and J Cohen, *The New Digital Age: Reshaping the Future of People, Nations and Business* (Alfred A Knopf 2013).

Scholz T, *Uberworked and Underpaid: How Workers Are Disrupting the Digital Economy* (Polity Press 2017).

Schweitzer H, 'The Role of Consumer Welfare in EU Competition Law' in J Drexl and others (eds), *Technology and Competition: Contributions in Honour of Hanns Ullrich* (Larcier 2010).

Schweitzer H and KK Patel, 'EU Competition Law in Historical Context' in KK Patel and H Schweitzer (eds), *The Historical Foundations of EU Competition Law* (OUP 2013).

Segall S, *Equality and Opportunity* (OUP 2013).

Sen A, 'Moral Codes and Economic Success' in S Brittan and A Hamlin (eds), *Market Capitalism and Moral Values* (Edward Elgar 1995).

Shakespeare W, *The Oxford Shakespeare: Complete Sonnets and Poems* (C Burrow (ed), OUP 2002).

Sinnott-Armstrong W, 'Consequentialism' in E Zalta (ed), *The Stanford Encyclopedia of Philosophy* (rev edn, Stanford University 2021) <https://goo.gl/sp4sbP> accessed 18 November 2022.

Sokol DD, 'Antitrust, Industrial Policy, and Economic Populism' in D Gerard and I Lianos (eds), *Reconciling Efficiency and Equity: A Global Challenge for Competition Policy* (CUP 2019).

Spulber D, *Market Microstructure: Intermediaries and the Theory of the Firm* (CUP 1999).

Srnicek N, *Platform Capitalism* (Polity Press 2017).

Stewart J, *Public Policy Values* (Palgrave Macmillan 2009).

Stiglitz J, *People, Power, and Profits: Progressive Capitalism for an Age of Discontent* (Norton 2019).

Stucke M, *Breaking Away: How to Regain Control over Our Data, Privacy, and Autonomy* (OUP 2021).

Stucke M and A Ezrachi, *Competition Overdose: How Free Market Mythology Transformed Us from Citizen Kings to Market Servants* (HarperCollins 2020).

Sullivan L and W Grimes, *The Law of Antitrust: An Integrated Handbook* (2nd edn, Thomson West 2006).

Suzumura K, 'Competition, Welfare, and Competition Policy' in U Schmidt and S Traub (eds), *Advances in Public Economics: Utility, Choice and Welfare* (Springer 2005).

Tetlock P and E Henik, 'Theory- versus Imagination-Driven Thinking about Historical Counterfactuals: Are We Prisoners of Our Preconceptions?' in D Mandel, D Hilton and P Catellani (eds), *The Psychology of Counterfactual Thinking* (Routledge 2005).

Thomas S, '*Ex Ante* and *Ex Post* Control of Buyer Power' in F Di Porto and R Podszun (eds), *Abusive Practices in Competition Law* (Edward Elgar 2018).

Tirole J, *Economics for the Common Good* (S Rendall tr, Princeton UP 2017).

Townley C, *A Framework for European Competition Law: Co-ordinated Diversity* (Hart 2018).

Trebilcock M, *The Limits of Freedom of Contract* (Harvard UP 1993).

Tychsen A and others, 'The Game Master' in Y Pisan (ed), *Proceedings of the Second Australasian Conference on Interactive Entertainment* (Creativity & Cognition Studios Press 2005).

Ullrich H, 'Intellectual Property, Access to Information and Antitrust: Harmony, Disharmony, and International Harmonization' in R Dreyfuss, D Zimmerman and H First (eds), *Expanding the Boundaries of Intellectual Property: Innovation Policy for the Knowledge Society* (OUP 2001).

Van den Bergh R, *Comparative Competition Law and Economics* (Edward Elgar 2017).

Van Rompuy B, *Economic Efficiency: The Sole Concern of Modern Antitrust Policy? Non-Efficiency Considerations within Article 101 TFEU* (Kluwer Law International 2012).

Vanberg V, 'Consumer Welfare, Total Welfare and Economic Freedom—On the Normative Foundations of Competition Policy' in J Drexl, W Kerber and R Podszun (eds), *Competition Policy and the Economic Approach: Foundations and Limitations* (Edward Elgar 2011).

Viehoff D, 'Power and Equality' in D Sobel, P Vallentyne and S Wall (eds), *Oxford Studies in Political Philosophy*, vol 5 (OUP 2019).

Wadlow C, 'Unfair Competition by Misappropriation: The Reception of *International News* in the Common Law World' in CW-N Ng, L Bently and G D'Agostino (eds), *The Common Law of Intellectual Property: Essays in Honour of Professor David Waver* (Hart 2010).

Wagner-von Papp F, 'Unilateral Conduct by Non-Dominant Firms: A Comparative Reappraisal' in F Di Porto and R Podszun (eds), *Abusive Practices in Competition Law* (Edward Elgar 2018).

Waldfogel J, *Digital Renaissance: What Data and Economics Tell Us about the Future of Popular Culture* (Princeton UP 2018).

Walker D, 'Early General Equilibrium Economics: Walras, Pareto, and Cassel' in W Samuels, J Biddle and J Davis (eds), *A Companion to the History of Economic Thought* (Blackwell 2003).

Walzer M, *Spheres of Justice: A Defense of Pluralism and Equality* (Basic Books 1983).

Weatherill S, 'The Challenge of Better Regulation' in S Weatherill (ed), *Better Regulation* (Hart 2007).

Weil D, *The Fissured Workplace: Why Work Became So Bad for So Many and What Can Be Done to Improve It* (Harvard UP 2014).

Werden G, 'Consumer Welfare and Competition Policy' in J Drexl, W Kerber and R Podszun (eds), *Competition Policy and the Economic Approach: Foundations and Limitations* (Edward Elgar 2011).

Wertheimer A, *Coercion* (Princeton UP 1987).

Williams B, 'The Idea of Equality' in L Pojman and R Westmoreland (eds), *Equality: Selected Readings* (OUP 1997).

Willis J, *The Mind of a Journalist: How Reporters View Themselves, Their World, and Their Craft* (SAGE 2010).

Wu T, *The Curse of Bigness: Antitrust in the New Gilded Age* (Columbia Global Reports 2018).

Zimmer D, 'Consumer Welfare, Economic Freedom and the Moral Quality of Competition Law—Comments on Gregory Werden and Victor Vanberg' in J Drexl, W Kerber and R Podszun (eds), *Competition Policy and the Economic Approach: Foundations and Limitations* (Edward Elgar 2011).

Zimmer D, 'The Basic Goal of Competition Law: To Protect the Opposite Side of the Market' in D Zimmer (ed), *The Goals of Competition Law* (Edward Elgar 2012).

Journal Articles

Abhishek V, K Jerath and ZJ Zhang, 'Agency Selling or Reselling? Channel Structures in Electronic Retailing' [2016] Management Science 2259.

Aguiar L and J Waldfogel, 'Platforms, Power, and Promotion: Evidence from Spotify Playlists' [2021] Journal of Industrial Economics 653.

Ahdar R, 'Consumers, Redistribution of Income and the Purpose of Competition Law' [2002] European Competition Law Review 341.

Akerlof G, 'Sins of Omission and the Practice of Economics' [2020] Journal of Economic Literature 405.

Akman P, '"Consumer" versus "Customer": The Devil in the Detail' [2010] Journal of Law and Society 315.

Akman P, 'The Relationship Between Economic Duress and Abuse of a Dominant Position' [2014] Lloyd's Maritime and Commercial Law Quarterly 99.

Alexander L, 'Zimmerman on Coercive Wage Offers' [1983] Philosophy & Public Affairs 160.

Aloisi A, 'Commoditized Workers: Case Study Research on Labor Law Issues Arising from a Set of On-Demand/Gig Economy Platforms' [2016] Comparative Labor Law & Policy Journal 653.

Amelio A and others, 'Recent Developments at DG Competition: 2017/2018' [2018] Review of Industrial Organization 653.

Anderson E, 'What Is the Point of Equality?' [1999] Ethics 287.

Andriychuk O, 'Rediscovering the Spirit of Competition: On the Normative Value of the Competitive Process' [2010] European Competition Journal 575.

Areeda P, 'Antitrust Violations without Damage Recoveries' [1976] Harvard Law Review 1127.

Armstrong M, 'Competition in Two-Sided Markets' [2006] RAND Journal of Economics 668.

Arneson R, 'Equality and Equal Opportunity for Welfare' [1989] Philosophical Studies 77.

Arneson R, 'Equality of Opportunity: Derivative Not Fundamental' [2013] Journal of Social Philosophy 316.

Auer D and Petit N, 'Two-Sided Markets and the Challenge of Turning Economic Theory into Antitrust Policy' [2015] Antitrust Bulletin 426.

Auer D and N Petit, 'Two Systems of Belief about Monopoly: The Press vs. Antitrust' [2019] Cato Journal 99.

Averitt N and R Lande, 'Consumer Sovereignty: A Unified Theory of Antitrust and Consumer Protection Law' [1997] Antitrust Law Journal 713.

Averitt N and R Lande, 'Using the Consumer Choice Approach to Antitrust Law' [2007] Antitrust Law Journal 175.

Ayal A, 'The Market for Bigness: Economic Power and Competition Agencies Duty to Curtail It' [2013] Journal of Antitrust Enforcement 221.

Baarsma B, 'Rewriting European Competition Law from an Economics Perspective' [2011] European Competition Journal 559.

Bailey D, 'The New Frontiers of Article 102 TFEU: Antitrust Imperialism or Judicious Intervention' [2018] Journal of Antitrust Enforcement 25.

Baird D, 'Common Law Intellectual Property and the Legacy of International News Service v. Associated Press' [1983] University of Chicago Law Review 411.

Balganesh S, ' "Hot News": The Enduring Myth of Property in News' [2011] Columbia Law Review 419.

Barnett J, 'The Costs of Free: Commoditization, Bundling and Concentration' [2018] Journal of Institutional Economics 1097.

Barnett T, 'Section 2 Remedies: What to Do after Catching the Tiger by the Tail' [2009] Antitrust Law Journal 31.

Basu K, 'Coercion, Contract and the Limits of the Market' [2007] Social Choice and Welfare 559.

Beales III JH, 'The Federal Trade Commission's Use of Unfairness Authority: Its Rise, Fall, and Resurrection' [2003] Journal of Public Policy & Marketing 192.

Belhadj N, D Laussel and J Resende, 'Marketplace or Reselling? A Signalling Model' [2020] Information Economics and Policy 100834.

Benkler Y, 'Degrees of Freedom, Dimensions of Power' [2016] Dædalus 18.

Benson P, 'Analyzing Oppression by Ann E. Cudd' [2009] Hypatia 178.

Bernhard R, 'Competition in Law and in Economics' [1967] Antitrust Bulletin 1099.

Berta N, L Julien and F Tricou, 'On Perfect Competition: Definitions, Usages and Foundations' [2012] Papers in Political Economy 7.

Besanko D and D Spulber, 'Contested Mergers and Equilibrium Antitrust Policy' [1993] Journal of Law, Economics & Organization 1.

Bethell O, G Baird and A Waksman, 'Ensuring Innovation through Participative Antitrust' [2020] Journal of Antitrust Enforcement 30.

Biggar D and A Heimler, 'Digital Platforms and the Transactions Cost Approach to Competition Law' [2021] Industrial and Corporate Change 1230.

Biglaiser G, E Calvano and J Crémer, 'Incumbency Advantage and Its Value' [2019] Journal of Economic & Management Strategy 41.

Blair R and DD Sokol, 'Welfare Standards in U.S. and E.U. Antitrust Enforcement' [2013] Fordham Law Review 2497.

Blaug M, 'The Fundamental Theorems of Modern Welfare Economics, Historically Contemplated' [2007] History of Political Economy 185.

Bork R and W Bowman Jr, 'The Crisis in Antitrust' [1965] Columbia Law Review 363.

Bork R and JG Sidak, 'What Does the Chicago School Teach about Internet Search and the Antitrust Treatment of Google?' [2012] Journal of Competition Law & Economics 663.

Bostoen F, 'The ACM's Apple Decision: To Boldly Go Where No Enforcer Has Gone Before' [2022] Journal of Antitrust Enforcement 583.

Boudreau K, 'Platform Boundary Choices & Governance: Opening-Up While Still Coordinating and Orchestrating' [2017] Entrepreneurship, Innovation, and Platforms 227.

Bougette P, O Budzinski and F Marty, 'Exploitative Abuse and Abuse of Economic Dependence: What Can We Learn from an Industrial Organization Approach' [2019] Revue d'économie politique 261.

Bourreau M and G Gaudin, 'Streaming Platform and Strategic Recommendation Bias' [2022] Journal of Economics & Management Strategy 25.

Bouzoraa Y, 'Between Substance and Autonomy: Finding Legal Certainty in Google Shopping' [2022] Journal of European Competition Law & Practice 144.

Brennan T, 'Is Complexity in Antitrust a Virtue? The Accuracy–Simplicity Tradeoff' [2014] Antitrust Bulletin 827.

Brennan T, 'Should Antitrust Go Beyond "Antitrust"?' [2018] Antitrust Bulletin 49.

Brewbaker III W, 'Will Physician Unions Improve Health System Performance?' [2002] Journal of Health Politics, Policy & Law 575.

Brietzke P, 'Robert Bork, The Antitrust Paradox: A Policy at War with Itself' [1979] Valparaiso University Law Review 403.

Brietzke P, 'The Constitutionalization of Antitrust: Jefferson, Madison, Hamilton, and Thomas C. Arthur' [1988] Valparaiso University Law Review 275.

Brodley J, 'The Economic Goals of Antitrust: Efficiency, Consumer Welfare, and Technological Progress' [1987] New York University Law Review 1020.

Budzinski O and K Köhler, 'Is Amazon the Next Google?' [2015] ORDO 265.

Budzinski O and J, Mendelsohn, 'Regulating Big Tech: From Competition Policy to Sector Regulation?' [2023] ORDO (forthcoming).

Bulmash H, 'An Empirical Analysis of Secondary Line Price Discrimination Motivations' [2012] Journal of Competition Law & Economics 361.

Burns J, 'The New Role of Coercion in Antitrust' [1991] Fordham Law Review 379.

Buttà A and A Pezzoli, 'Buyer Power and Competition Policy: From Brick-and-Mortar Retailers to Digital Platforms' [2014] Economia e Politica Industriale 159.

Callmann R, 'What Is Unfair Competition' [1940] Georgetown Law Journal 585.

Callmann R, 'He Who Reaps Where He Has Not Sown: Unjust Enrichment in the Law of Unfair Competition' [1942] Harvard Law Review 595.

Calo R and A Rosenblat, 'The Taking Economy: Uber, Information, and Power' [2017] Columbia Law Review 1623.

Calvano E and M Polo, 'Market Power, Competition and Innovation in Digital Markets: A Survey' [2021] Information Economics and Policy 100853.

Calzada J and R Gil, 'What Do News Aggregators Do? Evidence from Google News in Spain and Germany' [2020] Marketing Science 134.

Carrier M, 'Only "Scraping" the Surface: The Copyright Hold in the FTC's Google Settlement' [2013] University of British Columbia Law Review 750.

Carroll A, 'Don't Be Evil—Unless It Increases Revenue: What the Operation of Credit Rating Agencies Can Teach Us about Google' [2012] Temple Journal of Science, Technology and Environmental Law 93.

Carstens D, 'Preemption of Direct Molding Statutes: Bonito Boats v. Thunder Craft Boats' [1990] Harvard Journal of Law & Technology 167.

Cass R, 'Antitrust for High-Tech and Low: Regulation, Innovation, and Risk' [2013] Journal of Law, Economics and Policy 169.

Catalini C and C Tucker, 'Antitrust and Costless Verification: An Optimistic and a Pessimistic View of the Implications of Blockchain Technology' [2019] Antitrust Law Journal 861.

Catricalà A, 'Google in Italy...' [2011] Journal of European Competition Law & Practice 293.

Caves K and H Singer, 'When the Econometrician Shrugged: Identifying and Plugging Gaps in the Consumer-Welfare Standard' [2018] George Mason Law Review 395.

Chambers C, 'Each Outcome Is Another Opportunity: Problems with the Moment of Equal Opportunity' [2009] Politics, Philosophy & Economics 374.

Chen L and others, 'Governance and Design of Digital Platforms: A Review and Future Research Directions on a Meta-Organization' [2022] Journal of Management 147.

Cherry M, 'Beyond Misclassification: The Digital Transformation of Work' [2016] Comparative Labor Law & Policy Journal 577.

Chiou L and C Tucker, 'Content Aggregation by Platforms: The Case of the News Media' [2017] Journal of Economics & Management Strategy 782.

Choi JP, G Lee and C Stefanadis, 'The Effects of Integration on R&D Incentives in Systems Markets' [2003] Netnomics 21.

Choi JP and D-S Jeon, 'A Leverage Theory of Tying in Two-Sided Markets with Nonnegative Price Constraints' [2021] American Economic Journal: Microeconomics 283.

Christiano T, 'The Uneasy Relationship between Democracy and Capital' [2010] Social Philosophy & Policy 195.

Chyi IH, S Lewis and N Zheng, 'Parasite or Partner? Coverage of Google News in an Era of News Aggregation' [2016] Journalism & Mass Communications Quarterly 789.

Cohen GA, 'On the Currency of Egalitarian Justice' [1989] Ethics 906.

Cohen J, 'Cyberspace as/and Space' [2007] Columbia Law Review 210.

Cohen J, 'Property as Institutions for Resources: Lessons from and for IP' [2015] Texas Law Review 1.

Cohen J, 'Law for the Platform Economy' [2017] University of California Davis Law Review 133.

Cole S, 'The Hierarchy of the Sciences?' [1983] American Journal of Sociology 111.

Colomo PI, 'On the Application of Competition Law as Regulation: Elements for a Theory' [2012] Yearbook of European Law 261.

Colomo PI, 'Restrictions on Innovation in EU Competition Law' [2016] European Law Review 201.

Colomo PI, 'Indispensability and Abuse of Dominance: From Commercial Solvents to Slovak Telekom and Google Shopping' [2019] Journal of European Competition Law & Practice 532.

Colomo PI and A Kalintiri, 'The Evolution of EU Antitrust Policy: 1966–2017' [2020] Modern Law Review 321.

Colomo PI, 'Will Article 106 TFEU Case Law Transform EU Competition Law?' [2022] Journal of European Competition Law & Practice 385.

Constantinides P, O Henfridsson and G Parker, 'Platforms and Infrastructures in the Digital Age' [2018] Information Systems Research 381.

Crane D, 'Ecosystem Competition and the Antitrust Laws' [2019] Nebraska Law Review 412.

Crane D, 'Antitrust Antitextualism' [2020] Notre Dame Law Review 1205.

Cseres KJ, '"Acceptable" Cartels at the Crossroads of EU Competition Law and the Common Agricultural Policy: A Legal Inquiry into the Political, Economic, and Social Dimensions of (Strengthening Farmers') Bargaining Power' [2020] Antitrust Bulletin 401.

da Cruz Vilaça JL, 'The Intensity of Judicial Review in Complex Economic Matters––Recent Competition Law Judgments of the Court of Justice of the EU' [2018] Journal of Antitrust Enforcement 173.

Dahl R, 'The Concept of Power' [1957] Behavioral Science 201.

Daniels N, 'Merit and Meritocracy' [1978] Philosophy & Public Affairs 206.

Darcy D, 'Credit Rating Agencies and the Credit Crisis: How the Issuer Pays Conflict Contributed and What Regulators Might Do about It' [2009] Columbia Business Law Review 605.

Das Acevedo D, 'Unbundling Freedom in the Sharing Economy' [2018] Southern California Law Review 793.

Daskalova V, 'Regulating the New Self-Employed in the Uber Economy: What Role for EU Competition Law?' [2018] German Law Journal 461.

Datta H, G Knox and B Bronnenberg, 'Changing Their Tune: How Consumers' Adoption of Online Streaming Affects Music Consumption and Discovery' [2017] Marketing Science 5.

de Cornière A and G Taylor, 'A Model of Biased Intermediation' [2019] RAND Journal of Economics 854.

de Reuver M, C Sørensen and R Basole, 'The Digital Platform: A Research Agenda' [2017] Journal of Information Technology 124.

Decker C and others, 'Competition Law Enforcement and Household Inequality in the United Kingdom' [2022] Journal of Competition Law & Economics 905.

Dehdashti SA, 'B2B Unfair Trade Practices and EU Competition Law' [2018] European Competition Journal 305.

Dellarocas C, Z Katona and W Rand, 'Media, Aggregators, and the Link Economy: Strategic Hyperlink Formation in Content Networks' [2013] Management Science 2360.

Dellarocas C and others, 'Attention Allocation in Information-Rich Environments: The Case of News Aggregators' [2016] Management Science 2457.

Deutscher E and S Makris, 'Exploring the Ordoliberal Paradigm: The Competition Democracy Nexus' [2016] Competition Law Review 181.

Devlin M and B Peixoto, 'Reformulating Antitrust Rules to Safeguard Societal Wealth' [2008] Stanford Journal of Law, Business & Finance 225.

Dube A and others, 'Monopsony in Online Labor Markets' [2020] American Economic Review: Insights 33.

Ducci F, 'Procedural Implications of Market Definition in Platform Cases' [2019] Journal of Antitrust Enforcement 419.

Duhamel M and P Townley, 'An Effective and Enforceable Alternative to the Consumer Surplus Standard' [2003] World Competition 3.

Dunne N, 'Fairness and the Challenge of Making Markets Work Better' [2021] Modern Law Review 230.

Dworkin R, 'What Is Equality? Part 2: Equality of Resources' [1981] Philosophy & Public Affairs 283.

Dworkin R, 'In Praise of Theory' [1997] Arizona State Law Journal 353.

Eaton B, and others, 'Distributed Tuning of Boundary Resources: The Case of Apple's iOS Service System' [2015] Management Information Systems Quarterly 217.

Edelman B, 'Using Internet Data for Economic Research' [2012] Journal of Economic Perspectives 189.

Einav L, C Farronato and J Levin, 'Peer-to-Peer Markets' [2016] Annual Review of Economics 615.

Einstein A, 'On the Method of Theoretical Physics' [1934] Philosophy of Science 163.

Eisenmann T, G Parker and M Van Alstyne, 'Platform Envelopment' [2011] Strategic Management Journal 1270.

Etro F, 'Product Selection in Online Marketplaces' [2021] Journal of Economics Management and Strategy 614.

Evans D, 'Governing Bad Behavior by Users of Multi-Sided Platforms' [2012] Berkeley Technology Law Journal 1201.

Ezrachi A, 'Sponge' [2017] Journal of Antitrust Enforcement 49.

Ezrachi A and M Stucke, 'The Fight over Antitrust's Soul' [2018] Journal of European Competition Law & Practice 1.

Farrell J and M Katz, 'Innovation, Rent Extraction, and Integration in Systems Markets' [2000] Journal of Industrial Economics 413.

Farrell J and M Katz, 'The Economics of Welfare Standards in Antitrust' [2006] Competition Policy International Journal 3.

Fengler S and S Russ-Mohl, 'The Crumbling Hidden Wall: Towards an Economic Theory of Journalism' [2008] Kyklos 520.

Filippas A, J Horton and J Golden, 'Reputation Inflation' [2022] Marketing Science 305.

Fleurbaey M, 'Equal Opportunity or Equal Social Outcome?' [1995] Economics and Philosophy 25.

Fleurbaey M, 'The Facets of Exploitation' [2014] Journal of Theoretical Politics 653.

Foer A, 'Civil Liberties and Competition Policy: A Personal Essay Dedicated to John J. Flynn' [2011] Antitrust Bulletin 731.

Foerderer J and others, 'Does Platform Owner's Entry Crowd Out Innovation? Evidence from Google Photos' [2018] Information Systems Research 444.

Fontaine P, 'Free Riding' [2014] Journal of the History of Economic Thought 359.

Foros Ø, HJ Kind and G Shaffer, 'Apple's Agency Model and the Role of Most-Favored-Nation Clauses' [2017] RAND Journal of Economics 673.

Fourcade M, E Ollion and Y Algan, 'The Superiority of Economics' [2015] Journal of Economics Perspectives 89.

Fox E, 'Modernization of Antitrust: A New Equilibrium' [1981] Cornell Law Review 1140.

Fox E, 'Against Goals' [2013] Fordham Law Review 2157.

Franck J-U and M Peitz, 'Digital Platforms and the New 19a Tool in the German Competition Act' [2021] Journal of European Competition Law & Practice 513.

Frankel C, 'Equality of Opportunity' [1971] Ethics 191.

Frison-Roche M-A, 'L'Apport de la Notion d'"Entreprise Cruciale" à la Régulation des Plateformes' [2015] Concurrences 1.

Gal M and N Petit, 'Radical Restorative Remedies for Digital Markets' [2021] Berkeley Technology Law Journal 617.

Gaudin G, 'Vertical Bargaining and Retail Competition: What Drives Countervailing Power?' [2017] The Economic Journal 2380.

Gaudin G and A White, 'Vertical Agreements and User Access' [2021] American Economic Journal: Microeconomics 328.

Gavil A, 'Moving Beyond Caricature and Characterization: The Modern Rule of Reason in Practice' [2012] Southern California Law Review 733.

Gawer A and R Henderson, 'Platform Owner Entry and Innovation in Complementary Markets: Evidence from Intel' [2007] Journal of Economics & Management Strategy 1.

Gerber D, 'Constitutionalizing the Economy: German Neo-Liberalism, Competition Law and the "New" Europe' [1994] American Journal of Comparative Law 25.

Gerbrandy A, 'Rethinking Competition Law within the European Economic Constitution' [2019] Journal of Common Market Studies 127.

Gilbert R, 'E-books: A Tale of Digital Disruption' [2015] Journal of Economic Perspectives 165.

Giocoli N, 'Competition versus Property Rights: American Antitrust Law, the Freiburg School, and the Early Years of European Competition Policy' [2009] Journal of Competition Law & Economics 747.

Goldman B and R Cropanzano, '"Justice" and "Fairness" are Not the Same Thing' [2015] Journal of Organizational Behavior 313.

Graef I, 'Differentiated Treatment in Platform-to-Business Relations: EU Competition Law and Economic Dependence' [2019] Yearbook of European Law 448.

Graef I, 'What the Dutch Apple Case Can Teach Us about Future Challenges for Competition Enforcement' [2022] Journal of Antitrust Enforcement 570.

Graham M, I Hjorth and V Lehdonvirta, 'Digital Labour and Development: Impacts of Global Digital Labour Platforms and the Gig Economy on Worker Livelihoods' [2017] Transfer 135.

Grimes W, 'Antitrust Law as a Response to Economic Oppression: The United States' Experience' [1997] Nihon University Comparative Law 113.

Groot Kormelink, 'Why People Don't Pay for News: A Qualitative Study' [2022] Journalism <https://doi.org/10.1177/14648849221099325> accessed 18 November 2022.

Guildea B, 'App Stores: A Digital No Man's Land or Innovation's Bane?' [2016] Journal of Intellectual Property Law & Practice 445.

Hafiz H, 'Beyond Liberty: Toward a History and Theory of Economic Coercion' [2016] Tennessee Law Review 1071.

Hagiu A and D Spulber, 'First-Party Content and Coordination in Two-Sided Markets' [2013] Management Science 933.

Hagiu A and J Wright, 'Marketplace or Reseller' [2015] Management Science 184.

Hagiu A, T-H The and J Wright, 'Should Platforms Be Allowed to Sell on Their Own Marketplaces?' [2022] RAND Journal of Economics 297.

Hahnel R, 'Why the Market Subverts Democracy' [2009] American Behavioral Scientist 1006.

Hale R, 'Coercion and Distribution in a Supposedly Non-Coercive State' [1923] Political Science Quarterly 470.

Hammer P, 'Antitrust Beyond Competition: Market Failures, Total Welfare, and the Challenge of Intramarket Second-Best Tradeoffs' [2000] Michigan Law Review 849.

Herzog B, 'Valuation of Digital Platforms: Experimental Evidence for Google and Facebook' [2018] International Journal of Financial Studies 87.

Hicks J, 'Annual Survey of Economic Theory: The Theory of Monopoly' [1935] Econometrica 1.

Hicks J, 'The Foundations of Welfare Economics' [1939] Economic Journal 696.

Hirschey J, 'Symbiotic Relationships: Pragmatic Acceptance of Data Scraping' [2014] Berkeley Technology Law Journal 897.

Hjelmeng E, 'Competition Law Remedies: Striving for Coherence or Finding New Ways?' [2013] Common Market Law Review 1007.

Höppner T, 'Google: Friend or Foe of Ad-Financed Content Providers?' [2013] Journal of Media Law 14.

Hornuf L and D Vrankar, 'Hourly Wages in Crowdworking: A Meta-Analysis' [2022] Business & Information Systems Engineering 553.

Horton T, 'Fairness and Antitrust Reconsidered: An Evolutionary Perspective' [2013] McGeorge Law Review 823.

Hou L, 'Superior Bargaining Power: The Good, the Bad and the Ugly' [2019] Asia Pacific Law Review 39.

Hovenkamp E, 'Platform Antitrust' [2019] Journal of Corporation Law 713.

Hovenkamp H, 'Legislation, Well-Being, and Public Choice' [1990] University of Chicago Law Review 63.

Hovenkamp H, 'Exclusive Joint Ventures and Antitrust Policy' [1995] Columbia Business Law Review 1.

Hovenkamp H, 'Progressive Antitrust' [2018] University of Illinois Law Review 71.

Hovenkamp H, 'Platforms and the Rule of Reason: The *American Express* Case' [2019] Columbia Business Law Review 101.

Hunold M, R Kesler and U Laitenberger, 'Rankings of Online Travel Agents, Channel Pricing, and Consumer Protection' [2020] Marketing Science 92.

Hunold M and others, 'Evaluation of Best Price Clauses in Online Hotel Bookings' [2018] International Journal of Industrial Organization 542.

Iacobucci E and F Ducci, 'The Google Search Case in Europe: Tying and the Single Monopoly Profit Theorem in Two-Sided Markets' [2019] European Journal of Law and Economics 15.

Irani L, 'Difference and Dependence among Digital Workers: The Case of Amazon Mechanical Turk' [2015] South Atlantic Quarterly 225.

Jenks CW, 'Craftsmanship in International Law' [1956] American Journal of International Law 32.

Jeon D-S and J-C Rochet, 'The Pricing of Academic Journals: A Two-Sided Market Perspective' [2010] American Economic Journal: Microeconomics 222.

Jeon D-S and N Nasr, 'News Aggregators and Competition among Newspapers on the Internet' [2016] American Economic Journal: Microeconomics 91.

Jiang B, K Jerath and K Srinivasan, 'Firm Strategies in the "Mid Tail" of Platform-Based Retailing' [2011] Marketing Science 757.

Johnson E, 'The Economics and Sociality of Sharing Intellectual Property Rights' [2014] Boston University Law Review 1935.

Johnson J, 'The Agency Model and MFN Clauses' [2017] Review of Economic Studies 115.

Johnson J, 'The Agency and Wholesale Models in Electronic Content Markets' [2020] International Journal of Industrial Organization 1.

Jullien B and W Sand-Zantman, 'The Economics of Platforms: A Theory Guide for Competition Policy' [2021] Information Economics and Policy 100880.

Kang HY, 'Intra-Platform Envelopment: The Coopetitive Dynamics Between the Platform Owner and Complementors' [2017] Academy of Management Proceedings 11205.

Kaplow L, 'Rules versus Standards: An Economic Analysis' [1992] Duke Law Journal 557.

Kaplow L, 'Why (Ever) Define Markets?' [2010] Harvard Law Review 438.

Kaplow L and S Shavell, 'Fairness versus Welfare' [2001] Harvard Law Review 961.

Kathuria V and J Globocnik, 'Exclusionary Conduct in Data-Driven Markets: Limitations of Data Sharing Remedy' [2020] Journal of Antitrust Enforcement 511.

Katsoulacos Y, 'On the Concepts of Legal Standards and Substantive Standards (and How the Latter Influences the Choices of the Former)' [2019] Journal of Antitrust Enforcement 365.

Katsoulacos Y, 'On the Choice of Legal Standards: A Positive Theory for Comparative Analysis' [2019] European Journal of Law and Economics 125.

Katsoulacos Y, S Avdashevab and S Golovan, 'Legal Standards and the Role of Economics in Competition Law Enforcement' [2016] European Competition Journal 277.

Katz L and A Krueger, 'The Rise and Nature of Alternative Work Arrangements in the United States, 1995–2015' [2019] Industrial & Labor Relations Review 382.

Katz M and C Shapiro, 'Network Externalities, Competition, and Compatibility' [1985] American Economic Review 424.

Keezer D, 'The Effectiveness of the Federal Antitrust Laws: A Symposium' [1949] The American Economic Review 689.

Kenney M and J Zysman, 'Unicorns, Cheshire Cats, and the New Dilemmas of Entrepreneurial Finance' [2019] Venture Capital 35.

Kerwer D, 'Holding Global Regulators Accountable: The Case of Credit Rating Agencies' [2005] Governance 453.

Keynes JM, 'National Self-Sufficiency' [1933] Studies: An Irish Quarterly Review 177.

Khan L, 'Amazon's Antitrust Paradox' [2017] Yale Law Journal 712.

Khan L, 'Sources of Tech Platform Power' [2018] Georgetown Law Technology Review 325.

Khan L, 'The Separation of Platforms and Commerce' [2019] Columbia Law Review 973.

Khan L and S Vaheesan, 'Market Power and Inequality: The Antitrust Counterrevolution and Its Discontents' [2017] Harvard Law & Policy Review 235.

Kim H and M Luca, 'Product Quality and Entering through Tying: Experimental Evidence' [2019] Management Science 596.

Kim K, C Baek and J-D Lee, 'Creative Destruction of the Sharing Economy in Action: The Case of Uber' [2018] Transportation Research 118.

Kirkwood J, 'The Fundamental Goal of Antitrust: Protecting Consumers, Not Increasing Efficiency' [2008] Notre Dame Law Review 191.

Kirkwood J, 'Collusion to Control a Powerful Customer: Amazon, E-Books, and Antitrust Policy' [2014] University of Miami Law Review 1.

Kirkwood J, 'Reforming the Robinson-Patman Act to Serve Consumers and Control Powerful Buyers' [2015] Antitrust Bulletin 358.

Kovacic W, 'Designing Antitrust Remedies for Dominant Firm Misconduct' [1999] Connecticut Law Review 1285.

Krämer J and D Schnurr, 'Is There a Need for Platform Neutrality Regulation in the EU?' [2018] Telecommunications Policy 514.

Kreis AM and R Christensen, 'Law and Public Policy' [2013] Policy Studies Journal 38.

Kronman A, 'Contract Law and Distributive Justice' [1980] Yale Law Journal 472.

Lam CT and M Liu, 'The Geography of Ridesharing: A Case Study of New York City' [2021] Information Economics and Policy 100941.

Lamadrid de Pablo A, 'The Double Duality of Two-Sided Markets' [2015] Competition Law 5.

Lamadrid de Pablo A, 'Competition Law as Fairness' [2017] Journal of European Competition Law & Practice 147.

Lan S, K Liu and Y Dong, 'Dancing with Wolves: How Value Creation and Value Capture Dynamics Affect Complementor Participation in Industry Platforms' [2019] Industry and Innovation 943.

Lande R, 'Consumer Choice as the Ultimate Goal of Antitrust' [2001] University of Pittsburgh Law Review 503.

Lao M, 'Ideology Matters in the Antitrust Debate' [2014] Antitrust Law Journal 649.

Lao M, 'Workers in the "Gig" Economy: The Case for Extending the Antitrust Labor Exemption' [2018] University of California Davis Law Review 1543.

Larmore C, 'Liberal and Republican Conceptions of Freedom' [2003] Critical Review of International Social and Political Philosophy 96.

Larouche P and A de Streel, 'The European Digital Markets Act: A Revolution Grounded on Traditions' [2021] Journal of European Competition Law & Practice 542.

Lemley M, 'Property, Intellectual Property and Free Riding' [2005] Texas Law Review 1031.

Lerner AP, 'The Concept of Monopoly and the Measurement of Monopoly Power' [1934] Review of Economic Studies 157.

Lettl T, 'Missbräuchliche Ausnutzung einer Marktbeherrschenden Stellung nach Art. 102 AEUV, § 19 GWB und Rechtsbruch' [2016] Wirtschaft und Wettbewerb 214.

Li Z and A Agarwal, 'Platform Integration and Demand Spillovers in Complementary Markets: Evidence from Facebook's Integration of Instagram' [2017] Management Science 3438.

Lianos I, 'Competition Law for a Complex Economy' [2019] International Review of Intellectual Property and Competition Law 643.

Lianos I, N Countouris and V De Stefano, 'Re-thinking the Competition Law/Labour Law Interaction: Promoting a Fairer Labour Market' [2019] European Labour Law Journal 291.

Lianos I and B Carballa-Smichowski, 'A Coat of Many Colours—New Concepts and Metrics of Economic Power in Competition Law and Economics' [2022] Journal of Competition Law & Economics 795.

Liebeler W, 'Resale Price Maintenance and Consumer Welfare: Business Electronics Corp. v. Sharp Electronics Corp' [1989] University of California Los Angeles Law Review 889.

Lindeboom J, 'Rules, Discretion, and Reasoning According to Law: A Dynamic-Positivist Perspective on *Google Shopping*' [2022] Journal of European Competition Law & Practice 63.

Liu M, E Brynjolfsson and J Dowlatabadi, 'Do Digital Platforms Reduce Moral Hazard? The Case of Uber and Taxis' [2021] Management Science 4665.

Liu X, 'Vertical Integration and Innovation' [2016] International Journal of Industrial Organization 88.

Lukes S, 'The Singular and the Plural: On the Distinctive Liberalism of Isaiah Berlin' [1994] Social Research 687.

Makris S, 'Applying Normative Theories in EU Competition Law: Exploring Article 102 TFEU' [2014] University College London Journal of Law & Jurisprudence 30.

Malin B and C Chandler, 'Free to Work Anxiously: Splintering Precarity among Drivers for Uber and Lyft' [2017] Communication, Culture & Critique 382.

Malin M, 'Protecting Platform Workers in the Gig Economy: Look to the FTC' [2018] Indiana Law Review 377.

Manne G and J Wright, 'Google and the Limits of Antitrust: The Case Against the Case Against Google' [2011] Harvard Journal of Law & Public Policy 171.

Manne G and D Auer, 'Antitrust Dystopia and Antitrust Nostalgia: Alarmist Theories of Harm in Digital Markets and Their Origins' [2021] George Mason Law Review 1279.

Mantovani A, C Piga and C Reggiani, 'Online Platform Price Parity Clauses: Evidence from the EU Booking.com Case' [2021] European Economic Review 103625.

May J, 'Antitrust in the Formative Era: Political and Economic Theory in Constitutional and Antitrust Analysis, 1880–1918' [1989] Ohio State Law Journal 257.

McNulty P, 'Economic Theory and the Meaning of Competition' [1968] Quarterly Journal of Economics 639.

Melamed D, 'Afterword: The Purposes of Antitrust Remedies' [2009] Antitrust Law Journal 359.

Melamed D and N Petit, 'The Misguided Assault on the Consumer Welfare Standard in the Age of Platform Markets' [2019] Review of Industrial Organization 741.

Mérel P and R Sexton, 'Buyer Power with Atomistic Upstream Entry: Can Downstream Consolidation Increase Production and Welfare?' [2017] International Journal of Industrial Organization 259.

Miller D, 'Invention under Uncertainty and the Threat of Ex Post Entry' [2008] European Economic Review 387.

Moglia M and others, 'Evaluation of Smartphone Menstrual Cycle Tracking Applications Using an Adapted APPLICATIONS Scoring System' [2016] Obstetrics & Gynecology 1153.

Möller K, 'Proportionality: Challenging the Critics' [2012] International Journal of Constitutional Law 709.

Mosquera R and others, 'The Economic Effects of Facebook' [2020] Experimental Economics 575.

Muldoon J and P Raekstad, 'Algorithmic Domination in the Gig Economy' [2022] European Journal of Political Theory <https://doi.org/10.1177/14748851221082078> accessed 18 November 2022.

Mungan M and J Wright, 'Optimal Standards of Proof in Antitrust' [2022] International Review of Law and Economics 106083.

Nachbar T, 'The Antitrust Constitution' [2013] Iowa Law Review 57.

Naidu S and E Posner, 'Labor Monopsony and the Limits of the Law' [2022] Journal of Human Resources 284.

Nazzini R, 'Google and the (Ever-Stretching) Boundaries of Article 102 TFUE' [2015] Journal of European Competition Law & Practice 301.

Neven D and L-H Röller, 'Consumer Surplus vs. Welfare Standard in a Political Economy Model of Merger Control' [2005] International Journal of Industrial Organization 829.

Newman J, 'Procompetitive Justifications in Antitrust Law' [2019] Indiana Law Journal 501.

Nihoul P, '"Freedom of Choice": The Emergence of a Powerful Concept in European Competition Law' [2012] Concurrences 55.

Oh J, B Koh and R Raghunathan, 'Value Appropriation Between the Platform Provider and App Developers in Mobile Platform Mediated Networks' [2015] Journal of Information Technology 245.

Ohly A, 'The Freedom of Imitation and Its Limits—A European Perspective' [2010] International Review of Intellectual Property and Competition Law 506.

Öhman C and N Aggarwal, 'What if Facebook Goes Down? Ethical and Legal Considerations for the Demise of Big Tech' [2020] Internet Policy Review <https://doi.org/10.14763/2020.3.1488> accessed 18 November 2022.

Omori H, 'Liberty and the Rule of Law in Two Strands of Republicanism' [2019] Okayama Law Journal 926.

Orbach B, 'The Antitrust Consumer Welfare Paradox' [2010] Journal of Competition Law & Economics 133.

Orbach B and Campbell Rebling, 'The Antitrust Curse of Bigness' [2012] Southern California Law Review 605.

Osti C, 'Antitrust: A Heimlich Manoeuvre' [2015] European Competition Journal 221.

Page W, 'Legal Realism and the Shaping of Modern Antitrust' [1995] Emory Law Journal 1.

Paul S, 'Uber as For-Profit Hiring Hall: A Price-Fixing Paradox and Its Implications' [2017] Berkeley Journal of Employment and Labor Law 233.

Peeperkorn L, 'Conditional Pricing: Why the General Court Is Wrong in *Intel* and What the Court of Justice Can Do to Rebalance the Assessment of Rebates' [2015] Concurrences 43.

Peticca-Harris A, N de Gama and MN Ravishankar, 'Postcapitalist Precarious Work and Those in the "Drivers" Seat: Exploring the Motivations and Lived Experiences of Uber Drivers in Canada' [2018] Organization 36.

Petit N, 'Credit Rating Agencies, the Sovereign Debt Crisis and Competition Law' [2011] European Competition Journal 587.

Petit N, 'Intel, Leveraging Rebates and the Goals of Article 102 TFEU' [2015] European Competition Journal 26.

Petit N, 'Analysis and Reflections: Intel and the Rule of Reason in Abuse of Dominance Cases' [2018] European Law Review 728.

Pettit P, 'Freedom in the Market' [2006] Politics, Philosophy & Economics 131.

Pignataro G, 'Equality of Opportunity: Policy and Measurement Paradigms' [2012] Journal of Economic Surveys 800.

Pitofsky R, 'The Political Content of Antitrust' [1979] University of Pennsylvania Law Review 1051.

Pittman R, 'Consumer Surplus as the Appropriate Standard for Enforcement' [2007] Competition Policy International Journal 205.

Podszun R, 'Can Competition Law Repair Patent Law and Administrative Procedures? *AstraZeneca*' [2014] Common Market Law Review 281.

Porter M, 'The Five Competitive Forces That Shape Strategy' [2008] Harvard Business Review 78.

Posner R, 'An Economic Approach to Legal Procedure and Judicial Administration' [1973] Journal of Legal Studies 399.

Posner R, 'Misappropriation: A Dirge' [2003] Houston Law Review 621.

Posner R and W Landes, 'Market Power in Antitrust Cases' [1980] Harvard Law Review 937.

Posner E, G Weyl and S Naidu, 'Antitrust Remedies for Labor Market Power' [2018] Harvard Law Review 536.

Prassl J and M Risak, 'Uber, Taskrabbit and Co: Platforms as Employers? Rethinking the Legal Analysis of Crowdwork' [2016] Comparative Labor Law & Policy Journal 619.

Prendergast R, 'The Concept of Freedom and Its Relation to Economic Development—A Critical Appreciation of the Work of Amartya Sen' [2005] Cambridge Journal of Economics 1145.

Prüfer J and C Schottmuller, 'Competing with Big Data' [2021] Journal of Industrial Economics 967.

Rahman KS, 'Domination, Democracy, and Constitutional Political Economy in the New Gilded Age: Towards a Fourth Wave of Legal Realism' [2016] Texas Law Review 1329.

Rahman KS, 'The New Utilities: Private Power, Social Infrastructure, and the Revival of the Public Utility Concept' [2018] Cardozo Law Review 1621.

Rahman KS and K Thelen, 'The Rise of the Platform Business Model and the Transformation of Twenty-First-Century Capitalism' [2019] Politics & Society 177.

Rapp G, 'Monopoly's Hidden Justice: How Lax Antitrust Enforcement May Stimulate Charitable Giving and Overcome the Political Economy Barriers to Redistributive Taxation' [2001] University of Missouri-Kansas City Law Review 303.

Richards J, 'Equality of Opportunity' [1997] Ratio 253.

Ritzer G and S Miles, 'The Changing Nature of Consumption and the Intensification of McDonaldization in The Digital Age' [2019] Journal of Consumer Culture 3.

Roe M, 'Backlash' [1998] Columbia Law Review 217.

Roemer J, 'Defending Equality of Opportunity' [2003] The Monist 261.

Rosas C, 'The Future Is Femtech: Privacy and Data Security Issues Surrounding Femtech Applications' [2019] Hastings Business Law Journal 319.

Rosenblat A and L Stark, 'Algorithmic Labor and Information Asymmetries: A Case Study of Uber's Drivers' [2016] International Journal of Communication 3759.

Rostbøll C, 'Non-Domination and Democratic Legitimacy' [2015] Critical Review of International Social and Political Philosophy 424.

Rule C and D Meyer, 'An Antitrust Enforcement Policy to Maximize the Economic Wealth of All Consumers' [1988] Antitrust Bulletin 677.

Saffon M and N Urbinati, 'Procedural Democracy, the Bulwark of Equal Liberty' [2013] Political Theory 441.

Salop S, 'Question: What Is the Real and Proper Antitrust Welfare Standard? Answer: The True Consumer Welfare Standard' [2010] Loyola Consumer Law Review 336.

Sarkar MB, B Butler and C Steinfield, 'Intermediaries and Cybermediaries: Sarkar, Butler and Steinfield' [1995] Journal of Computer-Mediated Communication <https://bit.ly/2PsVWs6> accessed 18 November 2022.

Scharpf F, 'Economic Integration, Democracy and the Welfare State' [1997] Journal of European Public Policy 18.

Schmidt H, 'Competition Law and IP Rights: Not So Complementary: Time for Re-alignment of the Goals?' [2019] World Competition 451.

Schmitz S, 'The Effects of Electronic Commerce on the Structure of Intermediation' [2000] Journal of Computer-Mediated Communication <https://bit.ly/33wXDgD> accessed 18 November 2022.

Schrepel T, 'New Structured Rule of Reason Approach for High-Tech Markets' [2017] Suffolk University Law Review 103.

Schrepel T, 'Antitrust Without Romance' [2020] New York University Journal Law & Liberty 326.

Schwarz J, 'Platform Logic: An Interdisciplinary Approach to the Platform-Based Economy' [2017] Policy & Internet 374.

Sen A, 'The Impossibility of a Paretian Liberal' [1970] Journal of Political Economy 152.

Shafiei Gol E, M-K Stein and M Avital, 'Crowdwork Platform Governance Toward Organizational Value Creation' [2019] Journal of Strategic Information Systems 175.

Shapiro C, 'Antitrust in a Time of Populism' [2018] International Journal of Industrial Organization 714.

Shapiro I, 'On Non-Domination' [2012] University of Toronto Law Journal 293.

Shelanski H, 'Information, Innovation, and Competition Policy for the Internet' [2013] University of Pennsylvania Law Review 1663.

Shelanski H and JG Sidak, 'Antitrust Divestiture in Network Industries' [2001] University of Chicago Law Review 1.

Sobel-Read K, 'Global Value Chains: A Framework for Analysis' [2014] Transnational Legal Theory 364.

Sokol DD, 'Tensions Between Antitrust and Industrial Policy' [2015] George Mason Law Review 1247.

Sokol DD, 'Antitrust's "Curse of Bigness" Problem' [2020] Michigan Law Review 1259.

Spulber D, 'The Economics of Markets and Platforms' [2019] Journal of Economics & Management Strategy 159.

Stangl B, A Inversini and R Schegg, 'Hotels' Dependency on Online Intermediaries and Their Chosen Distribution Channel Portfolios: Three Country Insights' [2016] International Journal of Hospitality Management 87.

Steinbaum M, 'Antitrust, the Gig Economy, and Labor Market Power' [2019] Law and Contemporary Problems 45.

Steinbaum M, 'Establishing Market and Monopoly Power in Tech Platform Antitrust Cases' [2022] Antitrust Bulletin 130.

Steinbaum M and M Stucke, 'The Effective Competition Standard: A New Standard for Antitrust' [2019] University of Chicago Law Review 595.

Steiner R, 'Vertical Competition, Horizontal Competition, and Market Power' [2008] Antitrust Bulletin 251.

Stephany F and others, 'Distancing Bonus or Downscaling Loss? The Changing Livelihood of Us Online Workers in Times of COVID-19' [2020] Tijdschrift voor Economische en Sociale Geografie 561.

Stewart H, 'A Formal Approach to Contractual Duress' [1997] University of Toronto Law Journal 175.

Stucke M, 'Behavioral Economists at the Gate: Antitrust in the Twenty-First Century' [2007] Loyola University Chicago Law Journal 513.

Stucke M, 'Should Competition Policy Promote Happiness' [2013] Fordham Law Review 2576.

Stucke M and AP Grunes, 'Why More Antitrust Immunity for the Media Is a Bad Idea' [2011] Northwestern University Law Review 1399.

Stucke M and A Ezrachi, 'When Competition Fails to Optimize Quality: A Look at Search Engines' [2017] Yale Journal of Law & Technology 70.

Sullivan K, 'Unconstitutional Conditions' [1989] Harvard Law Review 1413.

Sullivan L, 'Trade Regulation, Cases and Materials' [1974] Columbia Law Review 1214.

Sullivan L, 'Economics and More Humanistic Disciplines: What Are the Sources of Wisdom for Antitrust?' [1977] University of Pennsylvania Law Review 1214.

Sullivan L, 'Monopolization: Corporate Strategy, the IBM Cases, and the Transformation of the Law' [1982] Texas Law Review 582.

Tarantino E, 'A Simple Model of Vertical Search Engines Foreclosure' [2013] Telecommunications Policy 1.

Taylor R, 'Market Freedom as Antipower' [2013] American Political Science Review 593.

Teachout Z and L Khan, 'Market Structure and Political Law: A Taxonomy of Power' [2014] Duke Journal of Constitutional Law & Public Policy 37.

Teh T-H, 'Platform Governance' [2022] American Economic Journal: Microeconomics 213.

Terry A, 'Unfair Competition and the Misappropriation of a Competitor's Trade Values' [1988] Modern Law Review 296.

Tombal T, 'Ensuring Contestability and Fairness in Digital Markets through Regulation: A Comparative Analysis of the EU, UK and US Approaches' [2022] European Competition Journal 468.

Torfing J, 'Rethinking Path Dependence in Public Policy Research' [2009] Critical Policy Studies 70.

Tragone A, 'Defining the Press Clause: The End of Hot News and the Attempt to Save Traditional Media' [2016] Chicago-Kent Journal of Intellectual Property 237.

Ursu R, 'The Power of Rankings: Quantifying the Effect of Rankings on Online Consumer Search and Purchase Decisions' [2018] Marketing Science 530.

Vacklavik M and L Pithan, 'The Agency Search: The Meaning of Work for App Drivers' [2018] Revista de Administração Mackenzie 1.

Vaheesan S, 'Accommodating Capital and Policing Labor: Antitrust in the Two Gilded Ages' [2019] Maryland Law Review 766.

van der Woude M, 'Judicial Control in Complex Economic Matters' [2019] Journal of European Competition Law & Practice 415.

van Dijck J, D Nieborg and T Poell, 'Reframing Platform Power' [2019] Internet Policy Review <https://bit.ly/30vWVhM> accessed 18 November 2022.

Van Doorn N, 'Platform Labor: On the Gendered and Racialized Exploitation of Low-Income Service Work in the "On-Demand" Economy' [2017] Information, Communication & Society 898.

Van Loo R, 'The Corporation as Courthouse' [2016] Yale Journal on Regulation 547.

Van Loo R, 'Rise of the Digital Regulator' [2017] Duke Law Journal 1267.

VanderWeele T, 'On the Promotion of Human Flourishing' [2017] Proceedings of the National Academy of Sciences of the United States of America 8148.

Varian H, 'Seven Deadly Sins of Tech?' [2021] Information Economics & Policy 100893.

Veen A, T Barratt and C Goods, 'Platform-Capital's "App-etite" for Control: A Labour Process Analysis for Food-Delivery Work in Australia' [2020] Work, Employment and Society 388.

Veljanovski C, 'Wealth Maximization, Law and Ethics—On the Limits of Economic Efficiency' [1981] International Review of Law & Economics 5.

Vogel L, 'Competition Law and Buying Power: The Case for a New Approach in Europe' [1998] European Competition Law Review 4.

Wadlow C, 'A Riddle Whose Answer Is "Tort": A Reassessment of International News Service v Associated Press' [2013] Modern Law Review 649.

Wang Q, B Li and PV Singh, 'Copycats vs. Original Mobile Apps: A Machine Learning Copycat-Detection Method and Empirical Analysis' [2018] Information Systems Research 273.

Weber Waller S, 'The Past, Present, and Future of Monopolization Remedies' [2009] Antitrust Law Journal 11.

Weiler JHH, 'In the Face of Crisis: Input Legitimacy, Output Legitimacy and the Political Messianism of European Integration' [2012] Journal of European Integration 825.

Weitz B and Q Wang, 'Vertical Relationships in Distribution Channels: A Marketing Perspective' [2004] Antitrust Bulletin 859.

Wen W and F Zhu, 'Threat of Platform-Owner Entry and Complementor Responses: Evidence from the Mobile App Market' [2019] Strategic Management Journal 1336.

Werden G, 'Remedies for Exclusionary Conduct Should Protect and Preserve the Competitive Process' [2009] Antitrust Law Journal 6.

Werden G, 'Antitrust's Rule of Reason: Only Competition Matters' [2014] Antitrust Law Journal 713.

Werron T, 'Why Do We Believe in Competition? A Historical-Sociological View of Competition as an Institutionalized Modern Imaginary' [2015] Journal of Social Theory 186.

Whinston M, 'Tying, Foreclosure and Exclusion' [1990] American Economic Review 837.

White M, 'On the Justification of Antitrust: A Matter of Rights and Wrongs' [2016] Antitrust Bulletin 323.

Wight J, 'The Ethics Behind Efficiency' [2017] Journal of Economic Education 15.

Williamson O, 'Economies as an Antitrust Defense Revisited' [1977] University of Pennsylvania Law Review 699.

Wilson C and K Klovers, 'The Growing Nostalgia for Past Regulatory Misadventures and the Risk of Repeating These Mistakes with Big Tech' [2020] Journal of Antitrust Enforcement 10.

Wood A and others, 'Good Gig, Bad Gig: Autonomy and Algorithmic Control in the Global Gig Economy' [2019] Work, Employment and Society 56.

Woodcock J and M Johnson, 'Gamification: What It Is, and How to Fight It' [2018] Sociological Review 542.

Wright J, 'One-sided Logic in Two-sided Markets' [2004] Review of Network Economics 44.

Wright J and A Portuese, 'Antitrust Populism: Towards a Taxonomy' [2020] Stanford Journal of Law, Business & Finance 131.

Wright J and J Yun, 'Use and Abuse of Bargaining Models in Antitrust' [2020] University of Kansas Law Review 1055.

Zabriskie J, 'Bots, Scrapers, and Other Unwanted Visitors to Your Web Site: Can You Keep Them Out?' [2009] Computer & Internet Lawyer 5.

Zäch R and A Künzler, 'Efficiency or Freedom to Compete? Towards an Axiomatic Theory of Competition Law' [2009] Zeitschrift für Wettbewerbsrecht 269.

Zennyo Y, 'Platform Encroachment and Own-Content Bias' [2022] Journal of Industrial Economics 684.

Zimmerman D, 'Coercive Wage Offers' [1981] Philosophy & Public Affairs 121.

Zhu F and Q Liu, 'Competing with Complementors: An Empirical Look at Amazon.com' [2018] Strategic Management Journal 2618.

Theses

Callaci B, 'The Historical and Legal Creation of a Fissured Workplace: The Case of Franchising' (PhD thesis, University of Massachusetts Amherst 2019).

Chung JH, 'Estimation of Sequential Search Models' (PhD thesis, University of Chicago Booth School of Business 2019).

Denny M, 'Star Wars Galaxies: Control and Resistance in Online Gaming' (MA thesis, Carleton University 2010).

Larrieu T, 'Topics in Industrial Organization Applied to Competition Policy' (PhD thesis, University of Paris-Saclay 2019).

Qiu Y, 'Strategizing for E-Commerce: Science and Art in Communication and Pricing' (PhD thesis, University of Texas 2018).

Working Papers

Athey S, M Mobius and J Pal, 'The Impact of Aggregators on Internet News Consumption' (January 2017) (April 2021) NBER Working paper No 28746 <https://bityl.co/FjtY> accessed 19 November 2022.

Belleflamme P and M Peitz, 'Inside the Engine Room of Digital Platforms: Reviews, Ratings, and Recommendations' (22 February 2018) Aix-Marseille School of Economics WP 2018 No 06 <http://dx.doi.org/10.2139/ssrn.3128141> accessed 18 November 2022.

Boik A, 'Prediction and Identification in Two-Sided Markets' (March 2018) Working Paper <https://dx.doi.org/10.2139/ssrn.3104846> accessed 18 November 2022.

Bourreau M and A de Streel, 'Digital Conglomerates and EU Competition Policy' (March 2019) <https://ssrn.com/abstract=3350512> accessed 18 November 2022.

Castillo JC, 'Who Benefits from Surge Pricing?' (8 August 2022) <https://ssrn.com/abstract=3245533> accessed 18 November 2022.

Cohen P and others, 'Using Big Data to Estimate Consumer Surplus: The Case of Uber' (2016) NBER Working Paper No 22627 <https://www.nber.org/papers/w22627> accessed 18 November 2022.

De los Santos B, DP O'Brien and MR Wildenbeest, 'Agency Pricing and Bargaining: Evidence from the E-Book Market' (October 2021) <https://bityl.co/Fjtk> accessed 19 November 2022.

Deng Y and others, 'Can Third-Party Sellers Benefit from a Platform's Entry to the Market?' (11 October 2022) <https://ssrn.com/abstract=4254034> accessed 18 November 2022.

Edelman B, 'Impact of OTA Bias and Consolidation on Consumers' (12 July 2017) <https://perma.cc/4K47-QFT2> accessed 18 November 2022.

Evans D, 'Why the Dynamics of Competition for Online Platforms Leads to Sleepless Nights, but not Sleepy Monopolies' (25 July 2017) <https://ssrn.com/abstract=3009438> accessed 18 November 2022.

Ezrachi A, 'EU Competition Law Goals and the Digital Economy' (6 June 2018) Oxford Legal Studies Research Paper No 17/2018 <https://ssrn.com/abstract=3191766> accessed 18 November 2022.

Foer A, 'Abuse of Superior Bargaining Position (ABSP): What Can We Learn from Our Trading Partners' (29 September 2016) AAI Working Paper No 16-02 <https://bityl.co/Fjrd> accessed 19 November 2022.

Gaudin G and A White, 'On the Antitrust Economics of the Electronic Books Industry' (24 September 2014) <https://ssrn.com/abstract=2352495> accessed 18 November 2022.

Geradin D, 'Complements and/or Substitutes? The Competitive Dynamics between News Publishers and Digital Platforms and What It Means for Competition Policy' (2019) TILEC Discussion Paper No 2019-003 <https://ssrn.com/abstract=3338941> accessed 18 November 2022.

Jakhu G, 'Bundling in Platform Markets in the Presence of Data Advantage' (18 September 2018) <https://bit.ly/3tYGF6E> accessed 19 November 2022.

Kamepalli SK, RG Rajan and L Zingales, 'Kill Zone' (15 February 2021) <https://dx.doi.org/10.2139/ssrn.3555915> accessed 18 November 2022.

Lam CT and M Liu, 'Demand and Consumer Surplus in the On-demand Economy: The Case of Ride Sharing' (11 October 2017) <https://bityl.co/FjuA> accessed 19 November 2022.

Lam WMW and X Liu, 'Data Usage and Strategic Pricing: Does Platform Entry Benefit Independent Traders?' (2021) Toulouse School of Economics <https://bityl.co/FjuG> accessed 19 November 2022.

Lyons B, 'Could Politicians Be More Right Than Economists? A Theory of Merger Standards' (2003) EUI Working Papers <https://bit.ly/3EBXqcP> accessed 25 November 2022.

Newlands G, C Lutz and C Fieseler, 'Power in the Sharing Economy' (30 April 2017) <https://ssrn.com/abstract=2960938> accessed 18 November 2022.

Newlands G, C Lutz and C Fieseler, 'European Perspective on Power in the Sharing Economy' (3 January 2018) <https://ssrn.com/abstract=3046473> accessed 18 November 2022.

Padilla J, 'Neoclassical Competition Policy without Apology' (2 November 2022) <https://bit.ly/3VhQJDI> accessed 21 November 2022.

Ritter C, 'Remedies for Breaches of EU Antitrust Law' (17 May 2016) <https://ssrn.com/abstract=2781441> accessed 18 November 2022.

Rivares AB and others, 'Like It or Not? The Impact of Online Platforms on the Productivity of Incumbent Service Providers' (21 May 2019) OECD Economics Department Working Papers No 1548 <https://doi.org/10.1787/080a17ce-en> accessed 19 November 2022.

Schweitzer H, Fetzer T and Peitz P, 'Digitale Plattformen: Bausteine für einen künftigen Ordnungsrahmen' (29 May 2016) ZEW Discussion Paper No 16-042 <https://bityl.co/FjLg> accessed 18 November 2022.

Schwellnus C and others, 'Gig Economy Platforms: Boon or Bane?' (21 May 2019) OECD Economics Department Working Papers No 1550 <https://doi.org/10.1787/fdb0570b-en> accessed 19 November 2022.

Scott Morton F and D Dinielli, 'Roadmap for an Antitrust Case Against Facebook' (June 2020) <https://bityl.co/Fjsw> accessed 19 November 2022.

Stutz R, 'The Evolving Antitrust Treatment of Labor-Market Restraints: From Theory to Practice' (31 July 2018) <https://ssrn.com/abstract=3332642> accessed 20 August 2022.

Tirole J, 'Competition and the Industrial Challenge for the Digital Age' (3 April 2020) Working Paper <https://perma.cc/Y6VK-ZCZA> accessed 18 November 2022.

Trannoy A, 'Equality of Opportunity: A Progress Report' (August 2016) ECINEQ Working Paper 2016-408 <https://bityl.co/Fjrz> accessed 19 November 2022.

Wu T, 'Tech Dominance and the Policeman at the Elbow' (26 February 2019) Columbia Public Law Research Paper No 14-623 <https://ssrn.com/abstract=3342598> accessed 18 November 2022.

Press Articles

Bond S, 'Uber and Lyft to Offer Shares to Drivers as Part of IPOs' *Financial Times* (28 February 2019) <https://on.ft.com/2H5AaYu> accessed 18 November 2022.

Bond S and H Mance, 'Book Wars: Amazon's Page Turner' *Financial Times* (15 August 2014) <https://on.ft.com/2xMEjhS> accessed 18 November 2022.

Bowles N, 'For Cities Wooing Amazon's New Headquarters, Nothing Is too Strange' *New York Times* (25 September 2017) <https://nyti.ms/2xDgKFD> accessed 18 November 2022.

Braithwaite T, 'Is Yelp a Business or a Howl of Pain?' *Financial Times* (15 February 2019) <https://on.ft.com/2D4U6uB> accessed 19 November 2022.

Carr D, 'Giving Viewers What They Want' *New York Times* (25 February 2013) <https://nyti.ms/3fdbkVd> accessed 18 November 2022.

Cookson R, 'Spotify Bans "Payola" on Playlists' *Financial Times* (20 August 2015) <https://on.ft.com/2KTk1qG> accessed 18 November 2022.

Crofts L, 'Pursuit of "Fairness" Alone Can't Underpin Antitrust Probes, UK's Marsden Says' *mlex* (25 October 2017) <https://bityl.co/EDEA> accessed 18 November 2022.

De Beaupuy F, 'France to Build Online Platform to Rival Airbnb, Booking.com' *Bloomberg* (14 May 2020) <https://bloom.bg/3eTmgqD> accessed 19 November 2022.

Dredge S, 'Should Apple Take More Action Against March of the iOS Clones?' *The Guardian* (3 February 2012) <https://bit.ly/2FtFUNd> accessed 18 November 2022.

Dwoskin E, 'Facebook's Imitation Not Quite Flattery' *Washington Post* (11 August 2017) <https://bit.ly/2zrpl1d> accessed 18 November 2022.

Dwoskin E, 'Tech Giants Are Profiting--and Getting more Powerful--Even as the Global Economy Tanks' *Washington Post* (29 April 2020) <https://wapo.st/2DA8pYt> accessed 18 November 2022.

The Economist, 'How to Tame the Tech Titans' *The Economist* (18 January 2018) <https://econ.st/2BnIK4c> accessed 18 November 2022.Emont J, L Stevens and R McMillan, 'Amazon Investigates Employees Leaking Data for Bribes' *Wall Street Journal* (16 September 2018) <https://on.wsj.com/2MBY511> accessed 18 November 2022.

'Google Should Remove Shopping Units to End Antitrust Concerns, Rivals Tell EU Commission' *mlex* (17 October 2022) <https://bityl.co/FMoE> accessed 18 November 2022.

Greene J, 'Aggressive Amazon Tactic Pushes You to Consider Its Own Brand before You Click "Buy"' *Washington Post* (28 August 2019) <https://wapo.st/349hj85> accessed 18 November 2022.

Greene J, 'Amazon Shoppers Complaining at Record Levels' *Washington Post* (22 May 2020) <https://wapo.st/2VNLBdZ> accessed 19 November 2022.

Hale T, 'Tech Companies Become the State, Phase One' *Financial Times* (5 November 2019) <https://on.ft.com/2VFOsFd> accessed 18 November 2022.

Harwell D, 'Is Your Pregnancy App Sharing Your Intimate Data with Your Boss?' *Washington Post* (10 April 2019) <https://wapo.st/2EZCD83> accessed 18 November 2022.

Hirst N, 'Google Copyright Spat With Publishers Shouldn't Lead to Permanent Supervision, France's Coeuré Says' *mlex* (4 May 2022) <https://bityl.co/EDE4> accessed 18 November 2022.

Hirst N, 'Intel, Google Shopping Rulings Don't Conflict, Top EU Judge Says' *mlex* (31 March 2022) <https://bityl.co/EpC0> accessed 18 November 2022.

Indap S, 'Revisiting the Principle of "Shareholder Primacy"' *Financial Times* (24 September 2018) <https://on.ft.com/2XfTREn> accessed 19 November 2022.

Iqbal N, 'Forget the DJs: Spotify Playlists Are the New Musical Starmakers' *The Guardian* (28 April 2019) <http://bit.ly/2PfBu0E> accessed 18 November 2022.

Keegan V, 'Will MySpace Ever Lose Its Monopoly?' *The Guardian* (8 February 2007) <https://bit.ly/3gFr9Vs> accessed 18 November 2022.

Kim E, 'Amazon Wants to Invest in Start-Ups, but Some Are Nervous about Taking the Money' *CNBC* (13 September 2017) <https://cnb.cx/2VZsKNW> accessed 18 November 2022.

Klonick K, 'Inside the Making of Facebook's Supreme Court' *New Yorker* (12 February 2021) <https://bityl.co/FEWG> accessed 18 November 2022.

Krugman P, 'Amazon's Monopsony Is Not OK' *New York Times* (19 October 2014) <https://nyti.ms/2Cs48pR> accessed 18 November 2022.

Laurent O, 'Why We Do It: Photographers and Photo Editors on the Passion That Drives Their Work' (30 June 2017) *Time Magazine* <https://perma.cc/86N2-Z8YC> accessed 18 November 2022.

Lee D, 'Uber Announces Further 3,000 Job Cuts' *Financial Times* (18 May 2020) <https://on.ft.com/3ftGkQn> accessed 18 November 2022.

Lee J, 'South Korea's Coupang Target of Fresh Antitrust Probe for Allegedly Manipulating Search Algorithms' *mlex* (6 July 2021) <https://bityl.co/F7O8> accessed 18 November 2022.

Lee J, 'Comment: The Uncertainty at the Heart of South Korea's Bold Platform Self-Regulation Experiment' *mlex* (1 July 2022) <https://bityl.co/F7PN> accessed 19 November 2022.

Lombardi P and G Leali, 'Italy Fines Amazon €1.13B for Abusing Market Dominance' *Politico* (9 December 2021) <https://bityl.co/Dw6Y> accessed 18 November 2022.

Lynch D, 'Big Tech and Amazon: Too Powerful to Break Up?' *Financial Times* (30 October 2017) <https://on.ft.com/39EU5sP> accessed 18 November 2022.

Mattioli D, 'Amazon Changed Search Algorithm in Ways That Boost Its Own Products' *Wall Street Journal* (16 September 2019) <https://on.wsj.com/2J8QyYq> accessed 18 November 2022.

McDougall M, 'OECD Tax Chief Warns of Trade Wars if Global Deal Is not Implemented' *Financial Times* (31 October 2022) <https:// bityl.co/ FNoL> accessed 19 November 2022.

McMillan R, 'Lyrics Site Accuses Google of Lifting Its Content' *Wall Street Journal* (16 June 2019) <https:// on.wsj.com/ 35Of 23q> accessed 18 November 2022. 'Major Luxury Shopping Platforms Scrutinized by South Korean Regulator for Possible Unfair Terms' *mlex* (31 August 2022) <https:// cont ent.mlex.com/ #/ cont ent/ 1405 322> accessed 18 November 2022.

Mickle T, 'Big Tech Is Proving Resilient as the Economy Cools' *New York Times* (28 July 2022) <https://bityl.co/FL1A> accessed 18 November 2022.

Morrison I, 'Bye, Spotify: Can This New Streaming Service Help Listeners Play Fair?' *The Guardian* (25 May 2018) <https://bit.ly/2YRWltJ> accessed 19 November 2022.

Mundy S, 'India's Ecommerce Crackdown Upends Big Foreign Players' *Financial Times* (14 January 2019) <https://on.ft.com/2Hi6pFK> accessed 18 November 2022.

Nicas J and D Wakabayashi, 'Sonos, Squeezed by the Tech Giants, Sues Google' *New York Times* (7 January 2020) <https://nyti.ms/3atQFJC> accessed 18 November 2022.

Nilsson P, 'Google to Invest Millions in UK News Group' *Financial Times* (19 September 2019) <https://on.ft.com/2PEdGkJ> accessed 18 November 2022.

Oliver C, 'FT Explainer: What Is Getty's Complaint Against Google?' *Financial Times* (27 April 2016) <https://on.ft.com/2Sho4Cr> accessed 18 November 2022.

Ovide S, 'Sorry, eBay and Uber. You're Hated. Why the Middlemen Are the Internet's Villains' *New York Times* (24 June 2020) <https://nyti.ms/2Bu8hZJ> accessed 19 November 2022.

Romm T and J Greene, 'House Lawmakers Demand Amazon CEO Jeff Bezos Testify in Antitrust Probe, Threatening Potential Subpoena' *Washington Post* (1 May 2020) <https://wapo.st/2Wnc2a0> accessed 18 November 2022.

Rose C, 'Amazon's Jeff Bezos Looks to the Future' *CBS News* (1 December 2013) <https://cbsn.ws/2WkjF1X> accessed 18 November 2022.

Sainato M, '"They Treat Us Like Crap": Uber Drivers Feel Poor and Powerless on Eve of IPO' *The Guardian* (7 May 2019) <https://bit.ly/3f52ibU> accessed 18 November 2022.

Sakamaki S, 'Japanese Companies Refusing to Accept Higher Costs from Smaller Trading Partners to Be Named by JFTC' *mlex* (5 October 2022) <https://bityl.co/EwRU> accessed 18 November 2022.

Sakamaki S, 'Digital Platforms in Malls, App Stores to Be Urged by Japanese Minister to Improve Transparency' *mlex* (14 November 2022) <https://bityl.co/Fe8K> accessed 19 November 2022.

Salkowski J, 'AOL May Also Have Monopoly' *Chicago Tribune* (19 June 2000) <https://bit.ly/2ZZdKl8> accessed 18 November 2022.

Sanger D, 'Tech Firms Sign "Digital Geneva Accord" Not to Aid Governments in Cyberwar' *New York Times* (17 April 2018) <https://nyti.ms/2ETvMqU> accessed 18 November 2022.

Schechner S, 'You Give Apps Sensitive Personal Information. Then They Tell Facebook' *Wall Street Journal* (22 February 2019) <https://on.wsj.com/2WRhlyL> accessed 18 November 2022.

Scheiber N, 'How Uber Uses Psychological Tricks to Push Its Drivers' Buttons' *New York Times* (4 April 2017) <https://nyti.ms/2VWm3xi> accessed 18 November 2022.

Schrager A, 'A Nobel-Winning Economist's Guide to Taming Tech Monopolies' *Quartz* (27 June 2018) <https://bityl.co/Fjq9> accessed 19 November 2022.

Shubber K, 'US Antitrust Chief Signals Comfort with Tech Deals' *Financial Times* (12 July 2018) <https://on.ft.com/2JhF8Pr> accessed 18 November 2022.

Streitfeld D, 'Writers Feel an Amazon-Hachette Spat' *New York Times* (9 May 2014) <https://nyti.ms/35bNo24> accessed 18 November 2022.

Thiel P, 'Competition Is for Losers' *Wall Street Journal* (12 September 2014) <https://on.wsj.com/2JRRGQm> accessed 18 November 2022.

Toplensky R and A Nicolaou, 'Spotify Files EU Antitrust Complaint Against Apple' *Financial Times* (13 March 2019) <https://on.ft.com/2ktVJJF> accessed 18 November 2022.

Trachtenberg JA, 'Authors Guild Met with DoJ to Seek Investigation into Amazon's Practices' *Wall Street Journal* (1 October 2014) <https://on.wsj.com/2yzk87h> accessed 18 November 2022.

Tracy R, 'Tech Giants Draw Fire in Congress; Lawmakers Suggest Internet Companies Need More Oversight to Ensure Competition' *Wall Street Journal* (16 July 2019) <https://on.wsj.com/2WhzyFg> accessed 18 November 2022.

Van Dorpe S, 'EC Official Flags Theory of Harm to Innovation through Scraping' *PaRR* (8 September 2017) <https:// perma.cc/ T6EB- UFJB> accessed 18 November 2022.

Wigglesworth R, 'How Big Tech Got Even Bigger in the Covid-19 Era' *Financial Times* (1 May 2020) <https://on.ft.com/3hvX76T> accessed 18 November 2022.

Specialized Blogs and Magazines

Beilinson J, 'Glow Pregnancy App Exposed Women to Privacy Threats, Consumer Reports Finds' (*Consumer Reports*, 28 July 2016) <https://bit.ly/3cv47OK> accessed 18 November 2022.

Colomo PI, 'Against the Footballisation of Competition Policy: How to Advance the General Interest and Avoid Polarisation' (*Chillin'Competition*, 18 September 2019) <https://bit.ly/33RSIH8> accessed 18 November 2022.

Curien N, 'Innovation and Regulation Serving the Digital Revolution' (*Journal of Regulation & Compliance*, 2011) <https://bityl.co/FjqL> accessed 19 November 2022.

Denissen N, 'Survey Says: Small Businesses Find Success with Amazon' (*Amazon blog*, 16 January 2020) <https://bityl.co/Fjv6> accessed 19 November 2022.

Edelman G, 'The Big Tech Hearing Proved Congress Isn't Messing Around' (*Wired*, 29 July 2020) <https://bit.ly/3id6LuT> accessed 18 November 2022.

Ek D, 'Consumers and Innovators Win on a Level Playing Field' (*Spotify*, 13 March 2019) <https://bityl.co/FjvH> accessed 19 November 2022.

Evans D and R Schmalensee, 'Ignoring Two-Sided Business Reality Can Also Hurt Plaintiffs' (*CPI Antitrust Chronicle*, April 2018) 47 <https://bit.ly/3kmyc7c accessed 18 November 2022.

Farber D, 'What Steve Jobs Really Meant When He Said "Good Artists Copy; Great Artists Steal"' (*CNET*, 28 January 2014) <https://bityl.co/FjvM> accessed 19 November 2022.

Finley K, '"Scraper" Bots and the Secret Internet Arms Race' (*Wired*, 23 July 2018) <https://perma.cc/X8R5-TXLQ> accessed 18 November 2022.

Frade E and V Marques de Carvalho, 'New Approaches to Cartel Enforcement and Spillover Effects in Brazil: Exchange of Information, Hub and Spoke Agreements, Algorithms, and Anti-Poaching Agreements' (*Competition Policy International*, 26 November 2019) <https://perma.cc/6DNW-HKBC> accessed 18 November 2022.

Frison-Roche M-A, 'Faute de Régulation Efficace, l'Autorité Française de la Concurrence se Substitue à un Régulateur pour Contrôler Google: L'Exemple d'Adwords' (*Journal of Regulation & Compliance*, 2015) <https://bityl.co/FjKY> accessed 18 November 2022.

Gans J, '"Information Wants to Be Free": The History of That Quote' (25 October 2015) *Digitopoly* <https://perma.cc/DB5K-HNYY> accessed 18 November 2022.

Guadamuz A, 'Avatars Behaving Badly' (*TechnoLlama*, 3 June 2009) <https://perma.cc/RS7W-G2L5> accessed 18 November 2022.

Hayhurst L, 'Coronavirus: Expedia and Booking among the Big Losers as Billions Wiped Off Valuations' (*Travolution*, 27 March 2020) <https://bityl.co/FjtJ> accessed 19 November 2022.

Kanter J and B Kressin, 'Online Platforms and the Commoditization of News Content' (*CPI Antitrust Chronicle*, December 2017) <https://bit.ly/36hEoc3> accessed 18 November 2022.

Kelly K, 'A Brief History of American Payola' (*Vice*,14 February 2016) <https://bit.ly/35It l9R> accessed 18 November 2022.

Kumar VD, 'How Does Amazon Put a Customer on the "Path of Least Resistance"?' (*Hackernoon*, 20 November 2018) <https://bit.ly/2VDZqgd> accessed 18 November 2022.

Lamadrid de Pablo A, 'Preliminary Thoughts on Google's Proposed Commitments' (*Chillin'Competition*, 13 June 2013) <https://bit.ly/3gOGPpe> accessed 18 November 2022.

Lomas N, 'Online Travel Giant Booking.com Faces Antitrust Probe in Spain' (*TechCrunch*, 17 October 2022) <https://bityl.co/FCyA> accessed 18 November 2022.

Lyons K, 'Google Wins Court Battle with Genius over Song Lyrics' (*The Verge*, 11 March 2022) <https://bityl.co/EJrr> accessed 18 November 2022.

Martínez AR, 'An Inverse Analysis of the DMA: Amazon's Proposed Commitments to the European Commission' (*Kluwer Competition Law Blog*, 27 July 2022) <https://bityl.co/ExSt> accessed 18 November 2022.

Marty F and J Pillot, 'With Uncertain Damage Theory Come Unpredictable Effects of Remedies: "Libres Propos" on The Android Case' (*CPI Antitrust Chronicle*, December 2018) 38 <https://bit.ly/2Xw2N8I> accessed 18 November 2022.

Maschewski F and A-V Nosthoff, 'Res Publica ex Machina: On Neocybernetic Governance and the End of Politics' (*Institute of Network Cultures*, 18 October 2018) <https://bit.ly/2VtsqDb> accessed 18 November 2022.

Masters K, '89% of Consumers Are More Likely to Buy Products from Amazon than other E-Commerce Sites: Study' (*Forbes*, 20 March 2019) <https://bit.ly/2Y057p7> accessed 18 November 2022.

Moorman C, 'Why Apple Is Still a Great Marketer and What You Can Learn' (*Forbes*, 12 January 2018) <https://bit.ly/3cA1ivT> accessed 18 November 2022.

Neely A, 'Hands on with Cycle, Apple's New Menstrual Cycle Tracker in iOS 13' (*appleinsider*, 19 June 2019) <https://bit.ly/2xXWHEw> accessed 18 November 2022.

Panettieri J, 'Big Tech Antitrust Investigations: Amazon, Apple, Facebook and Google Updates' (*ChannelE2E*, 8 November 2022) <https://bit.ly/3cFO4hJ> accessed 18 November 2022.

Patel N, 'Apple's App Store Fees Are "Highway Robbery", Says House Antitrust Committee Chair' (*The Verge*, 18 June 2020) <https://bit.ly/3cLv6bo> accessed 18 November 2022.

Podszun R, 'Conference Debriefing (21/22): Sustainability, Platforms' (*D'Kart*, 3 October 2020) <https://bit.ly/3oOA2Qm> accessed 18 November 2022.

Pot J, 'What Does It Mean When Apple "Sherlocks" an App?' (*How-To Geek*, 14 March 2017) <https://bityl.co/Fjvj> accessed 19 November 2022.

Pratka RI, 'With a Focus on Artists, the Platform Cooperative Stocksy Is Redefining Stock Photography' (*Shareable*, 10 October 2018) <https://bityl.co/FjsT> accessed 19 November 2022.

Quoteresearch, 'Your Margin Is My Opportunity: Jeff Bezos? Adam Lashinsky? Om Malik? Apocryphal?' (*Quote Investigator*, 13 January 2019) <https://perma.cc/Y69Q-F23P> accessed 19 November 2022.

Remaly B, 'Vestager Hints at Amazon Concerns' (*Global Competition Review*, 28 September 2018) <https://bit.ly/2LMHbjA> accessed 18 November 2022.

Risch C, 'Too Big to Sue: Why Getty Images Isn't Pursuing a Copyright Case against Google in the U.S' (*Photo District News*, 17 May 2016) <https://perma.cc/D2LN-HQ8C> accessed 18 November 2022.

Robert J, 'Why Companies Like Porsche and Nestle Are Turning to Worker-Owned Talent Site Braintrust for New Hires' (*Fortune*, 24 June 2020) <https://bit.ly/2NLFfHG> accessed 18 November 2022.

Rubin B and C Reichert, 'Google, Facebook and Amazon Face Tough Questioning over Potential Monopolies' (16 July 2019) *CNET* <https://bityl.co/Fjve> accessed 19 November 2022.

Rustrum C, 'Q&A with Felix Weth of Fairmondo, the Platform Co-op that's Taking on eBay' (*Shareable*, 14 March 2016) <https://bityl.co/FjsL> accessed 19 November 2022.

Sandler R, 'Uber Won't Let California Drivers Set Their Own Prices Anymore after Rider Cancellations Increased 117%' (*Forbes*, 8 April 2021) <https://bit.ly/3SzZyHE> accessed 18 November 2022.

Shermer M, 'The Mind of the Market: Evolutionary Economics Explains Why Irrational Financial Choices Were Once Rational' (*Scientific American*, 2008) <https://bit.ly/2LvUNg0> accessed 18 November 2022.

Steinbaum M, 'The Feds Side against Alt-Labor' (*Roosevelt Institute*, 16 November 2017) <https://bit.ly/3djVOWN> accessed 18 November 2022.

Sterling G, 'European Antitrust Chief Says Google's Auction-Based Shopping Remedy not Working' (*Search Engine Land*, 8 November 2019) <http://bit.ly/38AQRVZ> accessed 18 November 2022.

Stross R, 'How Yahoo! Won the Search Wars' (*Fortune*, 2 March 1998) <https://bityl.co/Fjsl> accessed 19 November 2022.

Stucke M and A Ezrachi, 'Looking up in the Data-Driven Economy' (*CPI Antitrust Chronicle*, May 2017) <https://perma.cc/BSN3-NH6H> accessed 18 November 2022.

Sullivan D, 'Wall Street Journal's Google Traffic Drops 44% after Pulling Out of First Click Free' (*Search Engine Land*, 5 June 2017) <https://bit.ly/2xU1VkU> accessed 18 November 2022.

Thompson B, 'Ends, Means, and Antitrust' (*Stratechery*, 28 June 2017) <https://perma.cc/D6P4-G9WN> accessed 18 November 2022.

Uber, 'We're Committed to our Driver-Partners' (*Uber Blog*, 3 November 2017) <https://perma.cc/R6RD-7ET7> accessed 18 November 2022.

Vergé T, 'Are Price Parity Clauses Necessarily Anticompetitive?' (*CPI Antitrust Chronicle*, January 2018) <https://bit.ly/31oCYsh> accessed 18 November 2022.

Welch C, 'Apple HealthKit Announced: A Hub for All Your iOS Fitness Tracking Needs' (*The Verge*, 2 June 2014) <https://bit.ly/3bUYF6r> accessed 18 November 2022.

Wood A, 'The UK Government's Consultation on Employment Classification and Control: A Response' (*The Digital Inequality Group*, 15 May 2018) <https://bit.ly/2W3q KEJ> accessed 18 November 2022.

Other Documents

Competition Authority Press Releases, Statements, and (Internal) Memoranda

BWB, 'Austrian Federal Competition Authority Initiates Investigation Proceedings Against Amazon' (14 February 2019) <https://bityl.co/Fjvn> accessed 19 November 2022.

CMA, 'Hotel Booking Sites to Make Major Changes after CMA Probe' (6 February 2019) <http://bit.ly/31xnznw> accessed 18 November 2022.

EC, 'Commission Decides not to Oppose the Production by Tabacalera of Its Own Cigarette Filters' (8 May 1989) <https://bityl.co/FjKe> accessed 18 November 2022.

EC, 'Commission Seeks Feedback on Commitments Offered by Google to Address Competition Concerns—Questions and Answers' (25 April 2013) <https://bit.ly/3Gvw 5M8> accessed 19 November 2022.

EC, 'Antitrust: Commission Fines Google €2.42 Billion for Abusing Dominance as Search Engine by Giving Illegal Advantage to Own Comparison Shopping Service' (27 June 2017) <https://bit.ly/2shvEeB> accessed 18 November 2022.

EC, 'Antitrust: Commission Opens Investigation Into Possible Anti-Competitive Conduct of Amazon' (17 July 2019) <https://bit.ly/2JC4JWU> accessed 18 November 2022.

EC, 'Antitrust: Commission Consults Stakeholders on a Possible New Competition Tool' (2 June 2020) <https://bityl.co/FjLG> accessed 18 November 2022.

EC, 'Antitrust: Commission Seeks Feedback on Commitments Offered by Amazon Concerning Marketplace Seller Data and Access to Buy Box and Prime' (14 July 2022) <https://bityl.co/FjK4> accessed 18 November 2022.

FTC, 'Statement of the Federal Trade Commission Regarding Google's Search Practices *In the Matter of Google Inc.* FTC File Number 111-0163' (3 January 2013) <https://bityl.co/Fjvs> accessed 19 November 2022.

FTC, 'Concurring and Dissenting Statement of Commissioner J. Thomas Rosch Regarding Google's Search Practices *In the Matter of Google Inc.*, FTC File no 111-0163' (3 January 2013) <https://bityl.co/Fjvu> accessed 19 November 2022.

FTC, 'Separate Statement of Commissioner Maureen Ohlhausen *In the Matter of Google Inc*' (3 January 2013) <https://bityl.co/Fjvv> accessed 19 November 2022.

FTC, 'FTC Rescinds 2015 Policy that Limited Its Enforcement Ability under the FTC Act' (1 July 2021) <https://bityl.co/Fjw0> accessed 19 November 2022.

FTC, 'FTC to Crack Down on Companies Taking Advantage of Gig Workers: Agency Policy Statement Outlines Areas Where FTC Will Act to Protect Gig Workers from Unfair, Deceptive, and Anticompetitive Practices' (15 September 2022) <https://bit.ly/3tUV1VG> accessed 23 November 2022.

FTC, 'FTC Policy Statement on Enforcement Related to Gig Work' (15 September 2022) <https://perma.cc/ZPR3-XN3R> accessed 18 November 2022).

FTC, 'FTC Restores Rigorous Enforcement of Law Banning Unfair Methods of Competition' (10 November 2022) <https://bityl.co/FjEY> accessed 18 November 2022.

FTC, 'Policy Statement Regarding the Scope of Unfair Methods of Competition under Section 5 of the Federal Trade Commission Act' (10 November 2022) <https://bityl.co/FjEq> accessed 18 November 2022.

FTC, 'Dissenting Statement of Commissioner Christine S. Wilson Regarding the "Policy Statement Regarding the Scope of Unfair Methods of Competition under Section 5 of the Federal Trade Commission Act"' (10 November 2022) 6, 13 <https://bityl.co/FjF2> accessed 18 November 2022.

FTC Bureau of Competition, 'Internal Memorandum re Google Inc. File No 111-0163' (8 August 2012) <https://bityl.co/Fjy0> accessed 19 November 2022.

Khan L, 'Memo from Chair Lina M. Khan to Commission Staff and Commissioners Regarding the Vision and Priorities for the FTC' (22 September 2021) 2 <https://perma.cc/X2QR-XT7M> accessed 18 November 2022.

State of California DoJ, 'Attorney General Bonta Announces Lawsuit Against Amazon for Blocking Price Competition' (14 September 2022) <https://bityl.co/FjyB> accessed 19 November 2022.

Competition Authority Policy Documents and Reports

ACCC, 'DigitalPlatforms Inquiry: Final Report' (June 2019) <http://bit.ly/3TKrNmY> accessed 19 November 2022.

ACCC, 'Collective Bargaining Class Exemption' (2021) <https://bityl.co/E11x> accessed 18 November 2022.

ACM, 'Market Study Into Mobile App Stores' (11 April 2019) <https://bityl.co/Fjys> accessed 19 November 2022.

AdC, 'Digital Ecosystems, Big Data and Algorithms' (July 2019) Issues Paper <https://bit.ly/3VfoLbH> accessed 19 November 2022.

ADLC, 'Avis no 18-A-03 du 6 mars 2018 portant sur l'exploitation des données dans le secteur de la publicité sur internet' (6 March 2018) <https://bit.ly/3u1zSJz> accessed 19 November 2022.

BKA, 'Summary of the Final Report of the Sector Inquiry into the Food Retail Sector' (2014) <https://bit.ly/3TR2UG4> accessed 19 November 2022.

BKA, 'Guidance on Remedies in Merger Control' (May 2017) <https://bit.ly/3hYodIR> accessed 19 November 2022.

CADE, 'Guide for Horizontal Merger Review' (July 2016) 38 <https://bit.ly/3V9U2MV> accessed 19 November 2022.

CCI, 'Market Study on E-Commerce in India: Key Findings and Observations' (8 January 2020) <https://bityl.co/Fjpq> accessed 19 November 2022.

CMA, 'Digital Comparison Tools Market Study: Final Report' (2017) <https://bit.ly/3Xkx T0f> accessed 19 November 2022.

CMA, 'Merger Remedies' (13 December 2018) <https://bityl.co/FjKC> accessed 18 November 2022.

CMA, 'Letter to the Secretary of State for Business, Energy and Industry Strategy' (21 February 2019) <https://bit.ly/3USe9zp> accessed 19 November 2022.

CMA, 'Regulation and Competition: A Review of the Evidence' (January 2020) <https://bityl.co/FjKn> accessed 18 November 2022.

CMA, 'Online Platforms and Digital Advertising: Market Study Final Report' (1 July 2020) <https://bit.ly/3Avd1tA> accessed 19 November 2022.

CMA and Ofcom, 'Platforms and Content Providers, Including News Publishers—Advice to DCMS on the Application of a Code of Conduct' (November 2021) <https://bityl.co/FjrQ> accessed 19 November 2022.

CMA, 'Mobile Ecosystems: Market Study Final Report' (10 June 2022) <https://bityl.co/Exy1> accessed 18 November 2022.

CMA, 'Music and Streaming: Final Report ' (29 November 2022) <https://bityl.co/JsZ6> accessed 29 November 2022.

EC, 'First Evaluation of Directive 96/9/EC on the Legal Protection of Databases' (12 December 2005) <https://bit.ly/3tHniyO> accessed 19 November 2022.

EC, 'Guidance on the Commission's Enforcement Priorities in Applying Article 82 of the EC Treaty to Abusive Exclusionary Conduct by Dominant Undertakings' [2009] OJ C45/7.

EC, 'Remedies in Merger Cases' (2011) DAF/COMP/WP3/WD(2011)59 <https://bit.ly/3ghzH9R> accessed 19 November 2022.

EC, 'Report on Competition Policy 2017' COM(2018) 482 final <https://bit.ly/3OjUOVo> accessed 19 November 2022.

EC, 'Communication From the Commission—Guidelines on the Application of EU Competition Law to Collective Agreements Regarding the Working Conditions of Solo Self-Employed Persons' [2022] OJ C374/2.

ECN, 'Report on the Monitoring Exercise Carried Out in the Online Hotel Booking Sector by EU Competition Authorities in 2016' (2017) <https://bityl.co/FjrD> accessed 19 November 2022.

FTC, 'Report on the Federal Trade Commission Workshop on Slotting Allowances and Other Marketing Practices in the Grocery Industry' (February 2001) <https://bityl.co/FjFY> accessed 18 November 2022.

FTC, 'Hearings on Competition and Consumer Protection in the 21st Century' (15 October 2018) <https://bit.ly/3Em90J4> accessed 19 November 2022.

FTC, 'Hearings on Competition and Consumer Protection in the 21st Century' (16 October 2018) <https://bit.ly/3tK6Mhz> accessed 19 November 2022.

ICN, 'Unilateral Conduct Workbook—Chapter 1: The Objectives and Principles of Unilateral Conduct Laws' (April 2012) 11th Annual ICN Conference <https://bit.ly/3u24 M4J> accessed 19 November 2022.

JFTC, 'Report Regarding Trade Practices on Digital Platforms (Business-to-Business Transactions on Online Retail Platform and App Store)' (31 October 2019) <https://perma.cc/KLL7-XXZB> accessed 18 November 2022.

OECD Documents

OECD, 'Portfolio Effects in Conglomerate Mergers' (2002) DAFFE/COMP(2002)5 <https://bit.ly/3XfuLmi> accessed 19 November 2022.

OECD, 'Competition on the Merits' (2005) DAF/COMP(2005)27 <https://bit.ly/3ghZ4Z7> accessed 19 November 2022.

OECD, 'OECD Principles for Making Internet Policy' (2014) <https://bityl.co/FjqT> accessed 19 November 2022.

OECD, 'Rethinking Antitrust Tools for Multi-Sided Platforms' (2018) <https://bit.ly/3Encif3> accessed 19 November 2022.

OECD, *OECD Employment Outlook 2019: The Future of Work* (OECD Publishing 2019).

OECD, 'Competition Concerns in Labour Markets—Background Note' (2019) DAF/COMP(2019)2 <https://bit.ly/3GvhDnm> accessed 19 November 2022.

OECD, 'Global Forum on Competition Discusses Competition under Fire' (2019)<https://bit.ly/3GpGfxM> accessed 19 November 2022.

OECD, 'Lines of Business Restrictions—Background Note' (2020) DAF/COMP/WP2(2020)1 <https://bit.ly/3Grnb2d> accessed 19 November 2022.

OECD, 'News Media and Digital Platforms—Note by the United States' (3 December 2021) DAF/COMP/WD(2021)72 <https://bit.ly/3V3EI4I> accessed 19 November 2022.

OECD, 'G7 Inventory of New Rules for Digital Markets—OECD Submission to the G7 Joint Competition Policy Makers and Enforcers Summit' (October 2022) <https://bityl.co/FjJi> accessed 18 November 2022.

UNCTAD Documents

UNCTAD, 'Competition Issues in the Digital Economy' (1 May 2019) <https://bit.ly/3ghZsXz> accessed 19 November 2022.

UNCTAD, 'Digital Economy Report 2019: Value Creation and Capture: Implications for Developing Countries' (2019) <https://bityl.co/FjJ6> accessed 18 November 2022.

Other Reports and Studies

Abbas, 'How Google's Image Search Update Killed Image SEO' (15 April 2013) Define Media Group report <https://perma.cc/E78C-YYDN> accessed 18 November 2022.

Allen J and N Flores, 'The Role of Government in the Internet' (18 April 2013) Final report for the Dutch Ministry of Economic Affairs <https://perma.cc/3YA8-E4G6> accessed 18 November 2022.

Antitrust Modernization Commission, 'Report and Recommendation' (2007) <https://bit.ly/3USu6FT> accessed 19 November 2022.

BEUC, 'The Role of Competition Policy in Protecting Consumers' Well-being in the Digital Era' (October 2019) <https://bit.ly/3USSvv9> accessed 19 November 2022.

BMWi, 'White Paper on Digital Platforms: Digital Regulatory Policy for Growth, Innovation, Competition and Participation' (March 2017) <https://perma.cc/AH32-GHZN> accessed 18 November 2022.

BMWi, 'Bundesministeriums für Wirtschaft und Energie, 'Entwurf eines Zehnten Gesetzes zur Änderung des Gesetzes gegen Wettbewerbsbeschränkungen für ein fokussiertes, proaktives und digitales Wettbewerbsrecht 4.0 (GWB-Digitalisierungsgesetz)' (7 October 2019) <https://bit.ly/3EmF67p> accessed 19 November 2022.

BRICS Competition Law and Policy Centre, 'Digital Era Competition: A BRICS View' (2019) <https://bit.ly/3EIglnE> accessed 19 November 2022.

CNNum, 'Neutralité des Plateformes: Réunir les Conditions d'un Environnement Numérique Ouvert et Soutenable' (May 2014) <https://bit.ly/3URhr6a> accessed 19 November 2022.

CNNUm, 'Ambition Numérique: Pour une Politique Française et Européenne de la Transition Numérique' (June 2015) <https://bit.ly/3EL28q5> accessed 19 November 2022.

Crémer J, Y-A de Montjoye and H Schweitzer, 'Competition Policy for the Digital Era' (2019) Report prepared for the European Commission <https://bit.ly/3hQynLn> accessed 19 November 2022.

DCMSC, 'Disinformation and "Fake News": Final Report' (18 February 2019) <http://bit.ly/31jVgc5> accessed 19 November 2022.

EC (DG GROW), 'Business-to-Business Relations in the Online Platform Environment: Final Report' (2017) <https://data.europa.eu/doi/10.2873/713211> accessed 18 November 2022.

EC (Joint Research Center), 'What Makes a Fair Society? Insights and Evidence' (2017) <https://data.europa.eu/doi/10.2760/861535> accessed 18 November 2022.

ESEC, 'Towards a European Digital Sovereignty Policy' (March 2019) <https://bit.ly/3Ef8 Any> accessed 19 November 2022.

ESMA, 'ESMA's Supervision of Credit Rating Agencies and Trade Repositories: 2015 Annual Report and 2016 Work Plan' (5 February 2015) <https://bit.ly/3UP5z4p> accessed 19 November 2022.

Feld H, 'The Case for the Digital Platform Act: Market Structure and Regulation of Digital Platforms (May 2019) Roosevelt Institute <https://bit.ly/30iwQ4j> accessed 18 November 2022.

Field F and A Forsey, 'Delivering Justice? A Report on the Pay and Working Conditions of Deliveroo Riders' (July 2018) <https://perma.cc/V2PJ-MQUL> accessed 18 November 2022.

Fina D and others, 'Market Study on the Distribution of Hotel Accommodation in the EU' (2022) COMP/2020/OP/002 <https://perma.cc/RGH9-KDQM> accessed 18 November 2022.

Karanikolova K and others, 'Study in Support of the Evaluation of the Database Directive' (2018) <https://data.europa.eu/doi/10.2759/04895> accessed 19 November 2022.

Franck J-U and M Peitz, 'Market Definition and Market Power in the Platform Economy' (May 2019) Centre on Regulation in Europe report <https://bityl.co/FjHx> accessed 18 November 2022.

French Council of the State, 'Le Numérique et les Droits Fondamentaux' (2014) <https://bit.ly/3hYmfIs> accessed 19 November 2022.

French Parliament (Commission for reflections and proposals on the law and freedoms in the digital age), 'Numérique et Libertés: Un Nouvel Âge Démocratique' (October 2015) Report n°3119 <https://bit.ly/3AtYBtv> accessed 19 November 2022.

French Senate, 'Rapport Fait au Nom de la Commission d'Enquête sur la Souveraineté Numérique—Tome I: Rapport' (1 October 2019) <https://bit.ly/3GuABKF> accessed 19 November 2022.

Furman J and others, 'Unlocking Digital Competition: Report of the Digital Competition Expert Panel' (March 2019) <https://bityl.co/FjIy> accessed 18 November 2022.

German, French and Polish Economic Ministries, 'Modernising EU Competition Policy' (4 July 2019) <https://bit.ly/3VdSgu7> accessed 19 November 2022.

House of Lords (Select Committee on Communications), 'Online Platforms and the Digital Single Market', 10th Report of Session 2015–16, 20 April 2016 <https://bit.ly/3gzGGWv> accessed 19 November 2022.

House of Lords (Select Committee on Communications), 'Regulating in a Digital World' (9 March 2019) 2nd Report of Session 2017–19 <http://bit.ly/2NtVmsM> accessed 19 November 2022.

House of Representatives (Judiciary Subcommittee on Antitrust, Commercial and Administrative Law), 'Investigation of Competition in Digital Markets: Majority Staff Report and Recommendations' (2 October 2020) <https://bit.ly/3EMRD5m> accessed 19 November 2022.

IGF and CGE, 'La Politique de la Concurrence et les Intérêts Stratégiques de l'UE' (4 April 2019) Report for the French Ministry of Economy and Finance <https://bit.ly/3hVQ WxU> accessed 19 November 2022.

IMF, 'World Economic Outlook: Growth Slowdown, Precarious Recovery' (April 2019) <https://bit.ly/3acayG8> accessed 19 November 2022.

Monopolkommission, 'Competition policy: The Challenge of Digital Markets' (2015) Special Report No 68 <https://perma.cc/6B3V-55QT> accessed 18 November 2022.

Newman N and others, 'Reuters Institute Digital News Report 2022' (2022) <https://bit.ly/3TPB6SH> accessed 19 November 2022.

Paes de Barros R and others, *Measuring Inequality of Opportunities in Latin America and the Caribbean* (World Bank and Palgrave Macmillan 2009).

Schweitzer H and others, 'Modernisierung der Missbrauchsaufsicht für Marktmächtige Unternehmen' (29 August 2018) Report No 66/17 <https://bityl.co/FjGH> accessed 18 November 2022.

Stigler Center, 'Stigler Committee on Digital Platforms: Final Report' (September 2019) <https://bityl.co/Fjqi> accessed 19 November 2022.

Study Group on Improvement of Trading Environment surrounding Digital Platforms, 'Improvement of Trading Environment surrounding Digital Platforms' (12 December 2018) Interim Discussion Paper <https://perma.cc/9CZ4-6ACX> accessed 18 November 2022.

Taylor M and others, 'Good Work: The Taylor Review of Modern Working Practices' (Report to the UK Government, 2017) <https://bit.ly/3GvGmYD> accessed 19 November 2022.

UK Secretary of State for Digital, Culture, Media & Sport and the Secretary of State for Business, Energy and Industrial Strategy, 'A New Pro-Competition Regime for Digital Markets' (July 2021) <https://bityl.co/FjrV> accessed 19 November 2022.

van Gorp N and P de Bijl, 'Digital Gatekeepers. Addressing Exclusionary Conduct' (7 October 2019) <http://dx.doi.org/10.13140/RG.2.2.10666.95689> accessed 18 November 2022.

World Bank, *World Development Report 2019: The Changing Nature of Work* (World Bank 2019) <https://bit.ly/3EMOdQr> accessed 19 November 2022.

Speeches and Lectures

Almunia J, 'Statement on the Google Investigation' (5 February 2014) <https://bit.ly/3TLE cqF> accessed 19 November 2022.

Delrahim M, '"… And Justice for All": Antitrust Enforcement and Digital Gatekeepers' (Remarks for the Antitrust New Frontiers Conference, 11 June 2019) <https://bit.ly/3gr4 XD8> accessed 19 November 2022.

Draghi M, 'Verbatim of the Remarks Made by Mario Draghi' (Speech delivered at the Global Investment Conference, 26 July 2012) <https://bityl.co/FjKO> accessed 18 November 2022.

Finch A, 'Principal Deputy Assistant Attorney General Andrew Finch Delivers Introductory Remarks at the 2018 Antitrust Writing Award Ceremony' (12 April 2018) <https://bit.ly/3OjlvcS> accessed 19 November 2022.

Juncker J-C, 'State of the Union 2016' (14 September 2016) <https://data.europa.eu/doi/10.2775/968989> accessed 19 November 2022.

Kanter J, 'Solving the Global Problem of Platform Monopolization' (Speech delivered at the Fordham Competition Law Institute's 49th Annual Conference on International Antitrust Law and Policy, 16 September 2022) <https://bityl.co/Fjsq> accessed 19 November 2022.

Lawrence D, 'Antitrust Division Policy Director David Lawrence Delivers Keynote at Brigham Young University Law Conference "Tech Platforms in a New Age of Competition Law"' (21 October 2022) <https://bit.ly/3EjWeL7> accessed 19 November 2022.

Leary TB, 'Freedom as the Core Value of Antitrust in the New Millennium' (Speech delivered at the ABA Antitrust Section 48th Annual Spring Meeting, Chair's Showcase Program, Antitrust at the Millennium: Looking Back and Moving Forward, 6 April 2000) <https://perma.cc/T7BU-2A59> accessed 18 November 2022.

Lowe P, 'Consumer Welfare and Efficiency—New Guiding Principles of Competition Policy?' (27 March 2007) 13th International Conference on Competition and 14th European Competition Day <https://bityl.co/Fk2h> accessed 19 November 2022.

Madero Villarejo C, 'Antitrust in Times of Upheaval' (10 December 2019) Speech delivered at the 2019 CRA Conference <https://bityl.co/FjJq> accessed 18 November 2022.

Vestager M, 'Setting Priorities in Antitrust' (Speech delivered at the GCLC, 1 February 2016) <https://bit.ly/3gx4Bpw> accessed 18 November 2022.

Vestager M, 'Competition Is a Consumer Issue' (Speech delivered at the BEUC General Assembly, 13 May 2016) <https://bit.ly/2w3uVpi> accessed 18 November 2022.

Vestager M, 'Competition and the Digital Single Market' (Speech delivered at the Forum for EU–US Legal–Economic Affairs, 15 September 2016) <https://bit.ly/3axnJRd> accessed 18 November 2022.

Vestager M, 'Competition and a Fair Deal for Consumers Online' (Speech delivered at the Netherlands Authority for Consumers and Markets Fifth Anniversary Conference, 26 April 2018) <https://bit.ly/2VjYwn2> accessed 18 November 2022.

Vestager M, 'Dealing with Power in a Brave New World: Economy, Technology and Human Rights' (Speech delivered at the Anna Lindh Lecture, 18 March 2019) <https://bit.ly/2XjSLbx> accessed 18 November 2022.

Vestager M, 'Defending Competition in a Digitised World' (Speech delivered at the European Consumer and Competition Day, 4 April 2019)' <http://bit.ly/2VXAksl> accessed 18 November 2022.

Vestager M, 'Competition and the Rule of Law' (Speech delivered at the European Association of Judges, 10 May 2019) <https://bit.ly/2xo55MQ> accessed 18 November 2022.

Vestager M, 'Competition and Sustainability' (Speech delivered at the GCLC Conference on Sustainability and Competition Policy, 24 October 2019) <https://bit.ly/2QIUUJB> accessed 18 November 2022.

Vestager M, 'Building a Positive Digital World' (Speech delivered at the Digital Summit, 29 October 2019) <http://bit.ly/2IvI7pG> accessed 18 November 2022.

Vestager M, 'Digital Power at the Service of Humanity' (Speech delivered at the Conference on Competition and Digitisation, 29 November 2019) <http://bit.ly/3aKiehT> accessed 18 November 2022.

Vestager M, 'Competition in a Digital Age: Changing Enforcement for Changing Times' (Speech delivered at the ASCOLA Annual Conference, 26 June 2020) <https://bityl.co/Fjs8> accessed 19 November 2022.

Vestager M, 'Defending Competition in a Digital Age' (Speech delivered at the Florence Competition Summer Conference, 24 June 2021) <https://bit.ly/3ELh9bh> accessed 19 November 2022.

Vestager M, 'Merger Control: The Goals and Limits of Competition Policy in a Changing World' (Speech delivered at the International Bar Association 26th Annual Competition Conference, 9 September 2022) <https://bit.ly/3EKDcif> accessed 19 November 2022.

Vestager M, 'Speech by EVP Vestager at the Fordham's 49th Annual Conference on International Antitrust Law and Policy "Antitrust for the Digital Age"' (16 September 2022) <https://bityl.co/FjL2> accessed 18 November 2022.

Vestager M, 'EVP Vestager Remarks at the Schwarzkopf Foundation Virtual Event: "Competition: the Rules of the Game"' (13 October 2022) <https://bit.ly/3tOe yXW> accessed 21 November 2022.

Vestager M, 'Keynote of EVP Vestager at the European Competition Law Tuesdays: A Principles Based Approach to Competition Policy' (25 October 2022) <https://bit.ly/3Eqc JFw> accessed 21 November 2022.

Other

'Academics against Press Publishers' Right:169 European Academics Warn Against It' (2018) <https://bit.ly/3hWXvjK> accessed 19 November 2022.

Alphabet, 'Annual Report (Form 10-K) (2 February 2022) <https://bityl.co/Dx24> accessed 18 November 2022.

Barlow JP, 'A Declaration of the Independence of Cyberspace' (1996) <https://bit.ly/3gok ALB> accessed 19 November 2022.

Barnett J and others, 'Joint Submission of Antitrust Economists, Legal Scholars, and Practitioners to the House Judiciary Committee on the State of Antitrust Law and Implications for Protecting Competition in Digital Markets' (18 May 2020) <https://ssrn. com/abstract=3604374> accessed 18 November 2022.

BDZV and VDZ, 'Press Publishers' Response to Google's Third Commitments Proposal. European Commission's Competition Investigation of Google—AT.39.740' (4 September 2014) <https://perma.cc/Y59C-6ZXJ> accessed 18 November 2022.

BMWK, 'Bundeswirtschaftsministerium legt Entwurf zur Verschärfung des Wettbewerbsrechts vor' (20 September 2022) <https://bit.ly/3OsDgXh> accessed 19 November 2022.

Booking Holding, 'Annual Report (Form 10-K)' (23 February 2022) <https://bit.ly/30Gj 4KI> accessed 18 November 2022.

Business Roundtable, 'Statement on the Purpose of a Corporation' (September 2019) <https://perma.cc/87PU-E695> accessed 19 November 2022.

Capital Forum, 'Amazon: EC Investigation to Focus on Whether Amazon Uses Data to Develop and Favor Private Label Products; Former Employees Say Data Key to Private Label Strategy' (5 November 2018) <https://perma.cc/4XRW-TGTC> accessed 18 November 2022.

Council of the EU, 'DMA: Council Gives Final Approval to New Rules for Fair Competition Online' <https://bityl.co/E3BF> accessed 18 November 2022.

Dow Jones, 'Comment of Dow Jones & Company to the Federal Trade Commission' (20 August 2018) Hearings on Competition and Consumer Protection in the 21st Century <https://perma.cc/82HK-L4YY> accessed 18 November 2022.

European Commission for Democracy through Law (Venice Commission), 'Report on the Timeline and Inventory of Political Criteria for Assessing an Election' (21 October 2010) Study No. 558/2009 <https://bit.ly/3UR6fXf> accessed 19 August 2022.

European External Action Service, 'US/Digital: EU opens new Office in San Francisco to Reinforce Its Digital Diplomacy' (1 September 2022) accessed <https://bityl.co/EBkQ> accessed 18 November 2022.

European Publishers Council, 'Public Comments of the European Publishers Council submitted in the context of the FTC "Hearings on Competition and Consumer Protection in the 21st Century"' (20 August 2018) <https://perma.cc/AG2M-2UBA> accessed 18 November 2022.

FairSearch, 'Google's Transformation From Gateway to Gatekeeper: How Google's Exclusionary and Anticompetitive Conduct Restricts Innovation and Deceives Consumers' (2011) <https://perma.cc/S9HM-DZW9> accessed 18 November 2022.

GCR, 'Rating Enforcement 2022' (7 September 2022) <https://bityl.co/EwHe> accessed 18 November 2022.

Getty Images, 'Letter to Commissioner Vestager' (2016) <https://perma.cc/6LGW-KCAE> accessed 18 November 2022.

Getty Images, 'Submission to the ACCC Digital Platforms Inquiry Issues Paper' (10 April 2018) <https://perma.cc/U9AJ-YGLS> accessed 18 November 2022.

Google, 'Annual Report (Form 10-K) (28 March 2005) <https://bit.ly/3fHz4jD> accessed 18 November 2022.

Google, 'Information Quality and Content Moderation' (2020) <https://perma.cc/HCX7-Y7H2> accessed 18 November 2022.

News Corp Australia, 'Submission to the ACCC's Digital Platform Inquiry' (20 April 2018) <https://perma.cc/6MQL-DRCS> accessed 18 November 2022.

Raff A and S Raff, 'Penalties, Self-Preferencing, and Panda: Why Google's Behavior Makes Antitrust Sanctions Inevitable' (31 August 2011) *Foundem* <https://bityl.co/Fjqu> accessed 19 November 2022.

Schaffner B, 'Public Demand for Regulating Big Tech' (6 June 2022) The Tech Oversight Project <https://bityl.co/Fjro> accessed 19 November 2022.

Warren E, 'Warren on Amazon' (*Twitter*, 24 April 2019) <https://bit.ly/2SayDoC> accessed 18 November 2022.

Yelp, 'Letter to FTC Chairman Maureen Ohlhausen' (11 September 2017) <https://perma.cc/FW8C-E5QP> accessed 18 November 2022.

US Chamber of Commerce, 'New National Poll: Voters Oppose Proposed Antitrust Regulations for Technology Companies' (21 July 2022) <https://bityl.co/Fjrr> accessed 19 November 2022.

Index